Time Out Guides Limited
Universal House
251 Tottenham Court Road
London W1T 7AB
Tel + 44 (0)20 7813 3000
Fax + 44 (0)20 7813 6001
Email guides@timeout.com
www.timeout.com

Editorial
Editors Steve Korver, Kim Renfrew
Deputy Editor Cyrus Shahrad
Listings Editor Petra Timmerman
Proofreader Gill Harvey
Indexer James Mitchell

Managing Director Peter Fiennes
Financial Director Gareth Garner
Editorial Director Ruth Jarvis
Deputy Series Editor Dominic Earle
Editorial Manager Holly Pick
Assistant Management Accountant Ija Krasnikova

Design
Art Director Scott Moore
Art Editor Pinelope Kourmouzoglou
Senior Designer Henry Elphick
Graphic Designer Gemma Doyle
Junior Graphic Designer Kei Ishimaru
Digital Imaging Simon Foster
Ad Make-up Jodi Sher

Picture Desk
Picture Editor Jael Marschner
Deputy Picture Editor Tracey Kerrigan
Picture Researcher Helen McFarland
Picture Desk Assistant Troy Bailey

Advertising
Sales Director Mark Phillips
International Advertising Manager Kasimir Berger
International Sales Consultant Ross Canadé
International Sales Executive Charlie Sokol
Advertising Sales (Amsterdam) Boom Chicago
Advertising Assistant Kate Staddon

Marketing
Group Marketing Director John Luck
Marketing Manager Yvonne Poon
Sales and Marketing Director North America Lisa Levinson

Production
Group Production Director Mark Lamond
Production Manager Brendan McKeown
Production Coordinator Caroline Bradford
Production Controller Susan Whittaker

Time Out Group
Chairman Tony Elliott
Financial Director Richard Waterlow
Group General Manager/Director Nichola Coulthard
Time Out Magazine Ltd MD Richard Waterlow
Time Out Communications Ltd MD David Pepper
Time Out International MD Cathy Runciman
Group Art Director John Oakey
Group IT Director Simon Chappell

Contributors
Introduction Kim Renfrew. **History** Steve Korver, Kim Renfrew, Floris Dogterom. **Amsterdam Today** Willem de Blaauw, Steve Korver. **Architecture** Steve Korver. **Art** Steve Korver. **Sex & Drugs** Petra Timmerman, Steve Korver. **Creative City** Steve Korver. **Sightseeing** Steve Korver, Mark Wedin, Kim Renfrew, Willem de Blaauw, Floris Dogterom. **Where to Stay** Kim Renfrew. **Restaurants** Steve Korver, Cecily Layzell. **Bars** Kim Renfrew. **Coffeeshops** Mark Wedin. **Shops & Services** Kate Holder, Steve Korver, Karina Hof, Kim Renfrew. **Festivals & Events** Willem de Blaauw, Steve Korver. **Children** Georgina Bean. **Film** Luuk van Huët. **Galleries** Steve Korver, Anneloes van Gaalen. **Gay & Lesbian** Willem de Blaauw, Kim Renfrew, Dara Colwell. **Music** Steve McCarron, Steve Korver, Mark Wedin. **Nightclubs** Joost Baaij, Mark Wedin. **Sport & Fitness** Steve McCarron. **Theatre, Comedy & Dance** Shyama Daryanani, Monique Gruter, Steve Korver. **Trips Out of Town** Steve Korver, Marinus de Ruiter, Steven McCarron, Kim Renfrew. **Directory** Steve Korver, Petra Timmerman, Willem de Blaauw.

Maps john@jsgraphics.co.uk. **Amsterdam transport map** Studio Olykan.

Photography by Michelle Grant, except pages 20, 31, 86, 91 Olivia Rutherford; page 46 Bijbels Museum; pages 48 World History Archive/ TopFoto; page 49 Art Media/ HIP/ TopFoto; page 102 Stadsarchief Amsterdam; page 159 Joost Dijk; page 219 Dewi Pinatih; page 253 (top) Spyker F1/ Peter van Egmond; page 253 (bottom) Spyker F1/ Peter J. Fox/ Crash.net; pages 260, 261 Frederik Menning.

The following images were provided by the featured establishments/ artists: pages 25, 45, 125, 126, 198, 201.

The Editor would like to thank
Amsterdam Weekly, Nel & Klaas, Claire Cavanagh-Willis, Will Fulford-Jones, Petra Timmerman, Simon Cropper, Jaro Renout, Pip@underwateramsterdam.com, Ken Wilkie, Todd Savage, Rene Nuijens, Nepco, Mr & Mrs Cameron, Mike Belitsky, and all the contributors from previous editions, whose work formed the basis for parts of this book.

Contents

Introduction

'My experience of Amsterdam,' the writer Terry Pratchett once said, 'is that cyclists ride where the hell they like and aim in a state of rage at all pedestrians while ringing their bells loudly, the concept of avoiding people being foreign to them.'

Like those cyclists, Amsterdam assails you from all angles, managing to be all things to all people, depending where you go. It's a druggie paradise for stoner backpackers. It's a bottomless well of live (and interactive) sex and no-holds-barred pornography for stag parties. It's a sleazy, subterranean warren of darkrooms for S&M gay men. It's a living, breathing museum for international art and architecture connoisseurs.

While all of these different faces of the city are true, Amsterdam is also in a process of change. Certainly, those same things that Amsterdam is most notorious for abroad are gradually being clamped down on: smoking cannabis is no longer a ubiquitous freedom (though unlike many other cities, you can still spark up that other evil weed, tobacco, almost anywhere you like); sex in the Red Light District is facing stricter new laws; and the city's tolerance has taken a battering, first with the murder of Pim Fortuyn, then with the murder of Theo van Gogh and later, to a lesser degree, with the attack upon a gay American journalist in the city centre, events that led to plenty of soul searching, hand wringing and, unfortunately, mud slinging.

Things have settled down now, at least spiritually, because one look around town reveals that this place is quite literally rebuilding itself in a massive regeneration programme that has turned the centre into a huge building site. The main locus of this is the docklands, the new cultural quarter and the reason that, a few hundred years ago, Amsterdam originally sparkled in the Golden Age. In among the plate-glass high-rises you'll still see old barques and spice warehouses, the building blocks on which the nation's wealth was first founded.

In fact, it's this same ability to find balance that makes this Janus-faced city so unique. Squalor sits alongside gentility in the Red Light District, the part of town that symbolises modern Amsterdam, for good or bad, to many, but which is also its historical heart. It was near here that the river was dammed in the 13th century; then came man-made canals, imprinting the city with a shape still seen in Cornelis Anthonisz's 15th-century map, now in the Amsterdams Historisch Museum. Then came wealth, and with it expansion, including the addition of the Jordaan and the Pijp, residential areas lacking in major attractions but irresistibly attractive in their own funky ways. Less explored but up-and-coming suburbs include Noord, on the far bank of the IJ, and even the Bijlmermeer, a concrete '60s experiment that houses immigrant factories, which comes alive with summer's Kwakoe festival and is now getting some groovy galleries exploring the area's unique heritage.

One thing's for certain: whatever happens in the future, Amsterdam will continue to grow, as it has done since 1200, whether literally or metaphorically. Like those pesky cyclists, this city will fling off every which way – and no one will ever put the brakes on.

ABOUT TIME OUT CITY GUIDES

This is the tenth edition of *Time Out Amsterdam*, one of an expanding series of Time Out guides produced by the people behind the successful listings magazines in London, New York and Chicago. Our guides are all written by resident experts who have striven to provide you with all the most up-to-date information you'll need to explore the city, regardless of whether you're a local or a first-time visitor.

THE LIE OF THE LAND

Central Amsterdam divides fairly neatly into distinct neighbourhoods. The Old Centre is split down the middle into the Old Side and the New Side, bordered by a ring of man-made canals called the *grachtengordel*.

Outside these canals lie a number of smaller, primarily residential neighbourhoods, such as the Pijp, the Museum Quarter and the Jordaan. Each of these areas has its own section within the Sightseeing chapter and these geographical divisions are used consistently throughout the guide. Maps of all the areas start on page 321.

ESSENTIAL INFORMATION

For all the practical information you might need when visiting Amsterdam – on such topics as visas, facilities and access for the disabled, emergency telephone numbers

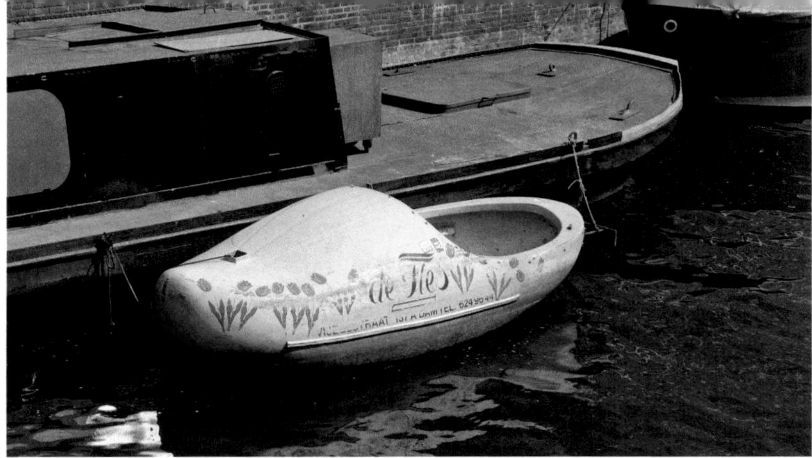

and the local transport system – turn to the Directory chapter at the back of the guide. It starts on page 295.

THE LOWDOWN ON THE LISTINGS

Above all, we've tried to make this book as useful as possible. Addresses, telephone numbers, websites, transport information, opening times, admission prices and credit card details have all been included in the listings. And, as far as possible, we've given details of facilities, services and events, all checked and correct as we went to press. However, Amsterdam is a famously laid-back and fluid city; owners and managers can change their arrangements at any time, and they often do. Before you go out of your way, we'd advise you to telephone and check opening times, ticket prices and other particulars.

While every effort has been made to ensure the accuracy of the information contained in this guide, the publishers cannot accept responsibility for any errors it may contain.

PRICES AND PAYMENT

We have noted where venues such as shops, hotels, restaurants, museums, attractions and the like accept the following credit cards: American Express (AmEx), Diners Club (DC), MasterCard (MC) and Visa (V). Many will also accept travellers' cheques, along with other, less widely held credit cards.

Advertisers

We would like to stress that no establishment has been included in this guide because it has advertised in any of our publications and no payment of any kind has influenced any review. The opinions given in this book are those of Time Out writers and entirely independent.

After some wild fluctuations following the introduction of the euro as the national currency, costs have generally settled down in the Netherlands, but the prices we've supplied should be treated as guidelines, not gospel. However, if they vary greatly from those we've quoted, please write and let us know, and do tell us if you've been badly treated or overcharged somewhere.

TELEPHONE NUMBERS

The area code for Amsterdam is 020. All the phone numbers in this guide, when dialled from outside the city, take this code unless otherwise stated. Dialling from abroad you'll need to preface them with the country code for the Netherlands, 31, and then the 020 city code (but first dropping the initial zero). We have stipulated where phone numbers are charged at non-standard rates – such as 0800 numbers (free) and 0900 (premium rate). For more details on telephone codes and charges, *see p311.*

MAPS

The map section at the back of this book includes street maps of central Amsterdam, an overview map of the city and of the Netherlands, and a map of Amsterdam's tram network. The maps start on p295, and now pinpoint specific locations of hotels (❶), restaurants (❶), and bars and cafés (❶).

LET US KNOW WHAT YOU THINK

We hope you enjoy *Time Out Amsterdam* and we'd like to know what you think of it. We welcome tips for places you think we should include in future editions and take note of your criticisms. Email us at guides@timeout.com.

There is an online version of this book, along with guides to over 100 international cities, at **www.timeout.com**.

Miami
Milan
Mumbai & Goa
Naples
New Orleans
New York
Paris
Patagonia
Prague
Budapest
San Francisco
Seville & Andalucía
Shanghai
Singapore
South of France
Stockholm
Sydney
Tokyo 東京
Turin
Venice
Vienna
Washington, DC
Amsterdam
Athens
Bangkok
Barcelona
Beijing
Boston
Brussels
Budapest
Buenos Aires
California
Cape Town
Chicago
Copenhagen
Croatia
Dublin
Edinburgh
Florence
Havana
Hong Kong
Istanbul
Las Vegas
Lisbon
London
Madrid
Mallorca
Marrakech
Miami
Milan
Mumbai & Goa
Naples
New Orleans
New York
Patagonia
Prague
Rio de Janeiro
Rome
San Francisco
Seville & Andalucía
Shanghai
Singapore
Sydney
Tokyo 東京
Toronto
Turin
Venice
Vienna
Washington, DC
Amsterdam
Athens
Barcelona
Beijing
Berlin
Boston
Brussels
Budapest
Buenos Aires
California
Cape Town
Copenhagen
Croatia
Dubai
Dublin
Edinburgh
Florence
Havana
Hong Kong
Istanbul

In Context

Features

History

The forces that shaped both a city and a state of mind.

According to legend, Amsterdam was founded by two lost fishermen who vowed to build a town where they made landfall. They reached terra firma, and their seasick dog anointed the chosen patch with his vomit.

The reality is much more mundane. Although the Romans occupied other parts of Holland, they didn't reach the north. Soggy bog was not the stuff on which empires were built, so the legions moved on. Archaeologists have found no evidence of settlement before AD 1000, though there are prehistoric remains further east in Drenthe. Amsterdam's site, in fact, was partially under water for years, and the River Amstel had no fixed course until enterprising farmers from around Utrecht built dykes during the 11th century. Once the peasants had done the work, the nobility took over.

During the 13th century the most important place in the newly reclaimed area was the tiny hamlet of Oudekerk aan de Amstel. In 1204 the Lord of Amstel built a castle nearby on what is now the outskirts of Amsterdam. After the Amstel was dammed in about 1270, a village grew up on the site of what is now Dam Square, acquiring the name Aemstelledamme.

The Lord of Amstel back at this time was Gijsbrecht, a pugnacious man often in trouble with his liege lord, the Bishop of Utrecht, and with his nearest neighbour, Count Floris V of Holland. Tension increased when Floris bestowed toll rights – and some independence – on the young town in 1275. (Medieval gossip also whispers of cuckolding amongst the counts.) Events culminated with Gijsbrecht murdering Floris at Muiden (where Floris's castle, Muiderslot, can still be seen to this day). Gijsbrecht's estates, meanwhile, were eventually confiscated by the Bishop of Utrecht and given over in their entirety to the Counts of Holland, and Amsterdam has remained part of the province of North Holland ever since.

In 1323 the Count of Holland, Floris VI, made Amsterdam one of only two toll points in the province for the import of brews. This was no trivial matter at a time when most people drank beer; drinking the local water, in fact, was practically suicidal. Hamburg had the largest brewing capacity in northern Europe and within 50 years a third of that city's production was flowing through Amsterdam. Thanks to its position between the Atlantic and Hanseatic ports, and by pouring its beer profits into other ventures, the city increased its trade in an assortment of essential goods.

Yet Amsterdam still remained small. As late as 1425 the 'city' consisted of a few blocks of houses with kitchen gardens and two churches, arranged along the final 1,000-metre (0.62-mile) stretch of the River Amstel and bordered by what are now known as Geldersekade, Singel and Kloveniersburgwal. Virtually all these

Pondering polder multiculturalism

Historically, the Netherlands has always been a haven for minorities and refugees who were persecuted in their own countries, from Spanish and Portuguese Jews in the 16th century and the Huguenots in the 1700s to the Belgians during World War I and Hungarians after the 1956 revolution. Freedom of religion was widely accepted and set in the constitution of 1848; there was never very much tension between the Dutch and the communities of newcomers, which were always relatively small.

The situation changed, however, during the second half of the 20th century. After the Netherlands was forced to surrender its colonies in the Dutch East Indies, 300,000 Indonesians came to the former motherland, followed, in the 1960s, by tens of thousands of labour migrants from Turkey and Morocco. The next wave of 300,000 foreigners came in the 1970s, when another colony, Surinam in South America, gained its independence. Dutch passport-holders from the Netherlands Antilles and refugees from all over the world have also contributed to a serious shake-up of the Dutch demographic landscape, which had been white for many centuries but was finally starting to change colour.

Initially, very little happened. Predominantly Christian Surinamese and Indonesians spoke Dutch, something the Muslim migrant workers from the Mediterranean countries did not. Starting in the 1960s, Turks and Moroccans were hired to help the post-war reconstruction of the Netherlands, most of them in low-paid, industrial jobs. Not much attention was given to their language skills, because the idea was that they would go home after a couple of years. But they didn't. They decided to stay here, brought their families over, and now, in 2007, this secularising nation of 16.4 million is faced with a million Muslims that it finds rather difficult to deal with.

Until the 1990s, the Netherlands had a great reputation for being a free and tolerant country, where each and everybody, regardless of faith, gender, political beliefs or sexual orientation, could do whatever he or she wanted. At the same time, an ever-growing number of non-Western immigrants and their offspring, badly educated and with very low incomes, often living on social welfare, were occupying dilapidated apartment buildings in and around neighbourhoods like the Bijlmer, where the crime rates were high and the future looked bleak. From a mixture of indifference and the belief that stigmatising ethnic groups was wrong and would lead to racism, society chose to ignore the problem. Until Pim Fortuyn – a genuine populist politician, who made no secret of his anti-Islam feelings – stood up and made his voice heard. His death in 2002 – the first political assassination since the murder of the father of the fatherland, William of Orange, in 1584 – shocked the nation. It wasn't a Muslim extremist, however, who pulled the trigger, but a left-wing one. And yet the next bullet did come from an Islamic extremist. In November 2004, Mohammed Bouyeri murdered the provocative film-maker Theo van Gogh, a big Fortuyn supporter.

For a short while, everything seemed to change. Fortuyn's allies took the parliament by storm, and even made it into the coalition government. Listening to the common man became the new credo. But pretty soon the Fortuynist party crumbled, through internal conflicts and empty-headedness, and the old political parties picked up where they left off. The Christian Democrats are at the centre of power once again, ruling the country as they do in varying coalition parties.

Sadly, no one seems to have the solution for the problems of a still growing underclass of second- and third-generation immigrants. But then again, would Fortuyn?

old buildings – such as the Houtenhuis, still standing in the Begijnhof – were wooden, and so fire was a perpetual threat; in the great fire of May 1452, three-quarters of the town was razed. One of the few examples of medieval architecture left is the Munttoren (Mint Tower; *photo p20*) at Muntplein. Those structures built after the fire had to be faced with stone and roofed with tile or slate. These developments also coincided with a rush of urban expansion, as – most notably – new foreign commerce led to improvements in shipbuilding.

RADICALISM AND REACTION

None of the wealth and glory of Amsterdam's Golden Age would have been possible without the turbulence that preceded it. During the 16th century, Amsterdam's population increased from 10,000 (low even by medieval standards) to 50,000 by 1600. The city's first big expansion accommodated this growth, but people coming to the city found poverty, disease and squalor in the workers' quarters. Local merchants, however, weren't complaining: during the 1500s, the city started to emerge as one of the world's major trading powers.

'In 1566 this religious discontent erupted into what became known as the Iconoclastic Fury.'

Amsterdam may have been almost entirely autonomous as a chartered city, but on paper it was still under the thumbs of absentee rulers. Through the intricate marriage bureau and shallow genetic pool known as the European aristocracy, the Low Countries (the Netherlands and Belgium) had passed into the hands of the Catholic Austro-Spanish House of Habsburg. The Habsburgs were the mightiest monarchs in Europe; Amsterdam was still a comparative backwater among their European possessions, but events soon brought the city to prominence among its near neighbours.

Amsterdam's new status as a trade centre attracted all kinds of radical religious ideas that were flourishing across northern Europe, encouraged by Martin Luther's condemnation of Catholicism in 1517. When they first arrived from Germany in about 1530, the Catholic city fathers tolerated the Anabaptists. But when they started to run around naked and even seized the Town Hall in 1534 during an attempt to establish a 'New Jerusalem' upon the River Amstel, the leaders were arrested, forced to dress, and then executed, signalling an unparalleled period of religious repression: 'heretics' were burned at the stake on the Dam.

After the Anabaptists were culled, Calvinist preachers arrived from Geneva, where the movement had started, and via France. Their coming caused a transformation. In 1566 this religious discontent erupted into what became known as the Iconoclastic Fury. Churches and monasteries were sacked and Philip II of Spain sent an army to suppress the heresy.

THE EMERGENCE OF ORANGE

The Eighty Years' War (1568-1648) between the Habsburgs and the Dutch is often seen as a struggle for religious freedom, but there was more to it than that. The Dutch were, after all, looking for political autonomy from an absentee king who represented a continual drain on their coffers. By the last quarter of the 16th century Philip II of Spain was fighting wars against England and France, in the east against the Ottoman Turks, and also in the New World for control of his colonies. The last thing he needed was a revolt in the Low Countries.

Amsterdam toed the Catholic line during the revolt, supporting Philip II until it became clear he was losing. Only in 1578 did the city patricians side with the Calvinist rebels, led by the first William of Orange. The city and William then combined to expel the Catholics and dismantle their institutions in what came to be called the Alteration. A year later, the Protestant states of the Low Countries united in opposition to Philip when the first modern-day European Republic was first born at the Union of Utrecht. The Republic of Seven United Provinces was made up of Friesland, Gelderland, Groningen, Overijssel, Utrecht, Zeeland and Holland. Though initially lauded as the forerunner of the modern Netherlands, it wasn't the unitary state that William of Orange wanted, but rather a loose federation with an impotent States General assembly.

Each province appointed a Stadhouder (or viceroy), who commanded the Republic's armed forces and had the right to appoint some of the cities' regents or governors. The Stadhouder of each province sent delegates to the assembly, held at the Binnenhof in the Hague. While fitted with clauses set to hinder Catholicism from ever suppressing the Reformed religion again, the Union of Utrecht also enshrined freedom of conscience and religion (at least until the Republic's demise in 1795), thus providing the blueprint that made Amsterdam a safe haven for future political and religious refugees.

A SOCIAL CONSCIENCE WITH CLAWS

From its earliest beginnings, Amsterdam had been governed by four Burgomasters – mayors, basically – and a council representing citizens' interests. By 1500, though, city government

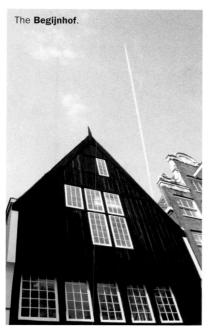

The **Begijnhof**.

had become an incestuous business: the city council's 36 members were appointed for life, 'electing' the mayors from their own ranks. Selective intermarriage meant that the city was, in effect, governed by a handful of families. When Amsterdam joined the rebels in 1578, the only change in civic administration was that the Catholic elite were replaced by a Calvinist faction of equally wealthy families. The city, now home to 225,000, remained the third city of Europe, after London and Paris.

However, social welfare was transformed. Welfare under the Calvinists was incorporated into government. The Regents, as the Calvinist elite became known, took over the convents and monasteries (one such convent is now home to the Amsterdams Historisch Museum; *photos p16*), starting charitable organisations such as orphanages. But the Regents would not tolerate any kind of excess: crime, drunkenness and immorality were all punishable offences.

During the two centuries before the Eighty Years' War, Amsterdam had developed its own powerful maritime force. Even so, it remained overshadowed by Antwerp until 1589, when that city fell to those darned Spaniards. In Belgium, the Habsburg Spanish had adopted siege tactics, leaving Amsterdam unaffected by the hostilities and free to benefit from the blockades suffered by rival ports. Thousands of refugees fled north, among them some of Antwerp's most prosperous merchants, who were mostly Protestant and Jewish (specifically Sephardic Jews who had earlier fled their original homes in Spain and Portugal to escape the Inquisition). These refugees brought the skills, the gold and, famously, the diamond industry that would soon help make the city one of the greatest trading centres in the world.

TRADE WINDS OF CHANGE

European history seems to be littered with Golden Ages, but in Amsterdam's case the first six decades of the 17th century genuinely deserve the label. It's truly remarkable that such a small and isolated city on the Amstel could come to dominate world trade and set up major colonies, resulting in a local population explosion and a frenzy of urban expansion. Its girdle of canals was one of the great engineering feats of the time. This all happened while the country was at war with Spain and presided over not by kings, but businessmen.

The East India Company doesn't have much of a ring to it, but Verenigde Oost Indische Compagnie (VOC), the world's first transnational, loses something in translation. The VOC was

Amsterdams Historisch Museum. *See p15.*

created by a States General charter in 1602 to finance the wildly expensive and hellishly dangerous voyages to the East. Drawn by the potential fortunes to be made out of trade in spices and silk, the shrewd Dutch saw sense in sending out merchant fleets, but they also knew that one disaster could leave an individual investor penniless. As a result, the main cities set up trading 'chambers', which evaluated the feasibility (and profitability) of ventures, then sent ships eastwards. The power of the VOC was far-reaching: it had the capacity to found colonies, establish its own army, declare war and sign treaties. With 1,450 ships, the VOC made over 4,700 profitable journeys.

'New Amsterdam became New York and came under British control. The Dutch got Surinam in consolation.'

While the VOC concentrated on the spice trade, a new company received its charter from the Dutch Republic in 1621. The Dutch West India Company (West Indische Compagnie), while not as successful as its sister, dominated trade with Spanish and Portuguese territories in Africa and America, and in 1623 began to colonise Manhattan Island. The settlement was laid out on a grid similar to Amsterdam's, and adopted the Dutch city's name. But although it flourished to begin with, New Amsterdam didn't last. After the Duke of York's invasion in 1664, the peace treaty between England and the Netherlands determined that New Amsterdam would change its name to New York and come under British control. The Dutch got Surinam as a feeble consolation prize.

Though commerce with the Indies became extensive, it never surpassed Amsterdam's European business: the city had become the major European centre for distribution and trade. Grain from Russia, Poland and Prussia, salt and wine from France, cloth from Leiden and tiles from Delft all passed through the port. Whales were hunted by Amsterdam's fleets, generating a flourishing soap trade, and sugar and spices from Dutch colonies were distributed throughout Scandinavia and the north of Europe. All this activity was financed by the Bank of Amsterdam, which had been set up in the cellars of the City Hall by the municipal council as early as 1609. It was a unique initiative in an age characterised by widespread financial ineptitude, and one that led to the city being considered the single most powerful money vault in all Europe, its notes exchangeable throughout the trading world.

A BATTLE OF WILLS

The political structure of the young Dutch Republic was complex. When the Union of Utrecht was signed in 1579, no suitable monarch or head of state was found, so the existing system was adapted to fit new needs. The seven provinces were represented by a 'national' council, the States General. In addition, provinces appointed a Stadhouder. The obvious choice for Stadhouder after the union was William of Orange, the wealthy Dutchman who had led the rebellion against Philip II of Spain. William was then succeeded by his son, Maurits of Nassau, who was as successful against the Spanish as his father had been, eventually securing the Twelve Years' Truce (1609-21). While each province could, in theory, elect a different Stadhouder, in practice they usually chose the same person. After William's popular tenure, it became a tradition to elect an Orange as Stadhouder. By 1641 the family had become sufficiently powerful for William II to marry a British princess, Mary Stuart. It was their son, William III, who set sail in 1688 to accept the throne of England in the so-called Glorious Revolution.

But the Oranges were not so popular with everyone. The provinces' representatives at the States General were known as regents, and Holland's – and so Amsterdam's – regent was in a powerful enough position to challenge the authority and decisions of the Stadhouder. This power was exercised in 1650, in a crisis caused by Holland's decision to disband its militia after the Eighty Years' War against Spain. Stadhouder William II wanted the militia to be maintained – and, importantly, paid for – by Holland, and in response to the disbandment, he had kinsman William Frederick launch an attack on the city.

When William II died three months later, the leaders of the States of Holland called a Great Assembly of the provinces. Even though there was no outward resistance to the Williams' earlier attack on the city, the provinces – with the exception of Friesland and Groningen, which remained loyal to William Frederick – decided that there should be no Stadhouders, and Johan de Witt, Holland's powerful regent, swore no prince of Orange would ever become Stadhouder again. This subsequently became law in the Act of Seclusion of 1653.

During this era, Amsterdam's ruling assembly, the Heren XLVIII (a sheriff, four mayors, a 36-member council and seven jurists), kept a firm grip on all that went on both within and without the city walls. The system was self-perpetuating and pioneered by prominent families, but these people were merchants, not aristocrats, and anyone who made enough money could, in theory, become a member.

The less elevated city folk – the craftsmen, artisans and shopkeepers – were equally active in maintaining their position. A guild system had developed in earlier centuries, linked to the Catholic Church, but under the new order, guilds were independent organisations run by their members. The original Amsterdammers – known as *poorters* from the Dutch for 'gate', as they originally lived within the gated walls of the city – began to see their livelihoods being threatened by an influx of newcomers who were prepared to work for lower wages.

Things came to a head when the shipwrights began to lose their trade to competitors in the nearby Zaan region and protested. The shipwrights' lobby was so strong that the city regents decreed Amsterdam ships had to be repaired in Amsterdam yards. This kind of protectionism extended to almost all industrial sectors in the city and effectively meant most crafts became closed shops. Only *poorters*, or those who had married *poorters*' daughters, were allowed to join a guild, thereby protecting Amsterdammers' livelihoods and, essentially, barring outsiders from joining their trades.

THE PRICE OF PROGRESS

Though Amsterdam's population had grown to 50,000 by 1600, this was nothing compared with the next 50 years, when it ballooned fourfold. Naturally, the city was thus obliged to expand. The most elegant of the major canals circling the city centre was Herengracht (Lords' Canal): begun in 1613, this was where many of the Heren XLVIII had their homes. So there would be no misunderstanding about status, Herengracht was followed further out by Keizersgracht (Emperors' Canal) and Prinsengracht (Princes' Canal). Immigrants were housed in the Jordaan.

'Soon, the idealistic houses of correction became little more than prisons.'

For all its wealth, famine hit Amsterdam with dreary regularity in the 17th century. Guilds had benevolent funds set aside for their members in times of need, but social welfare was primarily in the hands of the ruling merchant class. Amsterdam's elite was noted for its philanthropy, but only *poorters* were eligible for assistance; even they had to fall into a specific category, known as 'deserving poor'. Those seen as undeserving were sent to houses of correction. The initial philosophy behind these had been idealistic: hard work would produce useful citizens. But soon, the institutions became little more than prisons for those condemned to work there.

Religious freedom was still not what it might have been, either. As a result of the Alteration of 1578, open Catholic worship was banned in the city during the 17th century, and Catholics were forced to practise in secret. Some Catholics started attic churches, which are exactly what their name suggests: of those set up during the 1600s, the Museum Amstelkring has preserved Amsterdam's only surviving example – Our Lord in the Attic – in its entirety (*see p93*).

THE HARDER THEY FALL

Though Amsterdam remained one of the single wealthiest cities in Europe until the early 19th century, its dominant trading position was lost to England and France after 1660. The United Provinces then spent a couple of centuries bickering about trade and politics with Britain and the other main powers. Wars were frequent: major sea conflicts included battles against the Swedes and no fewer than four Anglo-Dutch wars, from which the Dutch came off worse. It wasn't that they didn't win any battles; more that they ran out of men and money.

Despite – or perhaps because of – its history with the Orange family, Amsterdam became the most vocal opponent of the family's attempt to acquire kingdoms, though it supported William III when he crossed the sea to become King of England in 1688. The city fathers believed a Dutchman on their rival's throne could only be an advantage, and for a while they were proved right. However, William was soon back in Amsterdam looking for more money to fight more battles, this time against France.

The naval officers who led the wars against Britain are Dutch heroes, and the Nieuwe Kerk has monuments to admirals Van Kinsbergen (1735-1819), Bentinck (1745-1831) and, most celebrated of all, Michiel de Ruyter (1607-76). The most famous incident, although not most prominent in British history books, occurred during the Second English War (1664-67), when de Ruyter sailed up the rivers Thames and Medway to Chatham, stormed the dockyards and burnt the *Royal Charles*, the British flagship, as it lay at anchor. *The Royal Charles*'s coat of arms was stolen, and is now displayed in the Rijksmuseum (*photo p25*). The Dutch put fear in the English, as reflected in the propaganda of the time: from one-liners like 'a Dutchman is a lusty, fat, two-legged cheese worm' and the still-common 'Dutch courage', to pamphlets like *The Dutch-men's Pedigree as a Relation, Showing how They Were First Bred and Descended from a Horse-Turd which Was Enclosed in a Butter-Box*.

Despite its diminished maritime prowess, Amsterdam had the highest living standard in Europe until the 18th century, something reflected in the foundation of the Plantage.

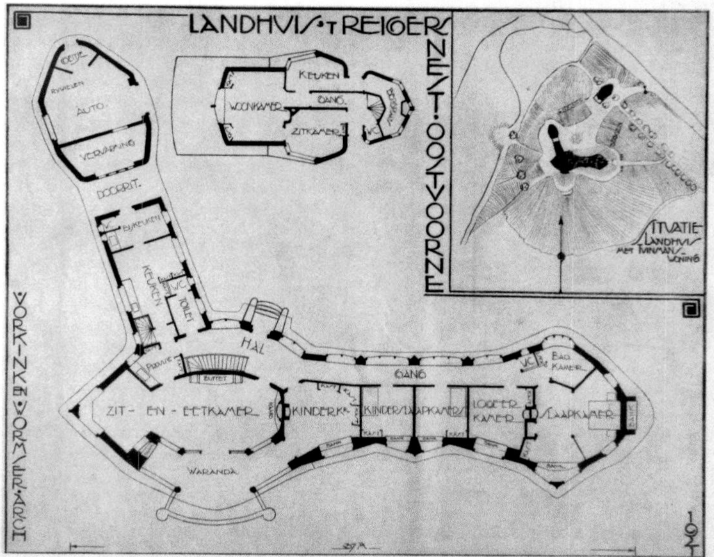

Back to the drawing board: unconventional blueprints of the **Amsterdam School**. *See p21.*

And yet, despite all this, change came when the Dutch Republic began to lag behind the major European powers in the 18th century. The Agricultural and Industrial Revolutions didn't get off the ground in the Netherlands until later: Amsterdam was nudged out of the shipbuilding market by England, and its lucrative textile industry was lost to other provinces. However, the city managed to exploit its position as the financial centre of the world until the final, devastating Anglo-Dutch War (1780-84). The British hammered the Dutch merchant and naval fleets with unremitting aggression, crippling profitable trade with their Far Eastern colonies in the process.

The closest the Dutch came to the Republican movements of France and the United States was with the Patriots. During the 1780s, the Patriots managed to shake off the influence of the Stadhouders in many smaller towns, but in 1787 they were foiled in Amsterdam by the intervention of the Prince of Orange and his brother-in-law, Frederick William II, King of Prussia. Hundreds of Patriots then fled to exile in France, where their welcome convinced them that Napoleon's intentions towards the Dutch Republic were benign. In 1795, they returned, backed by a French army of 'advisers'. With massive support from Amsterdam, they thus celebrated the new Batavian Republic.

It sounded too good to be true, and it was. According to one contemporary, 'the French moved over the land like locusts'. Over *f*100 million (about €50 million today) was extracted from the Dutch, and the French also sent an army, 25,000 of whom had to be fed, equipped and housed by their Dutch 'hosts'. Republican ideals seemed hollow when Napoleon installed his brother, Louis, as King of the Netherlands in 1806, and so the symbol of Amsterdam's mercantile ascendancy and civic pride, the City Hall of the Dam, was requisitioned as the royal palace. Even Louis was disturbed by the impoverishment of a nation that had been Europe's most prosperous. However, after Louis had allowed Dutch smugglers to break Napoleon's blockade of Britain, he was forced to abdicate in 1810 and the Low Countries were absorbed into the French Empire.

Even so, government by the French wasn't an unmitigated disaster for the Dutch. The foundations of the modern state were laid in the Napoleonic period, and a civil code introduced – not to mention a huge broadening of culinary possibilities. However, trade with Britain ceased, and the cost of Napoleon's wars prompted the Dutch to join the revolt against France. After Napoleon's defeat, Amsterdam became the capital of a constitutional monarchy, including what is now Belgium; William VI of Orange was crowned King William I in 1815. But while the Oranges still reigned across the north, the United Kingdom of the Netherlands, as it then existed, lasted only until 1830.

A RETURN TO FORM

When the French were finally defeated and left Dutch soil in 1813, Amsterdam emerged as the capital of the new kingdom of the Netherlands but very little else. With its coffers depleted and its colonies occupied by the British, Amsterdam faced a hard fight for recovery.

The fight was made tougher by two huge obstacles. For a start, Dutch colonial assets had been reduced to present-day Indonesia, Surinam and the odd island in the Caribbean. Just as important, though, was the fact that the Dutch were slow to join the Industrial Revolution. The Netherlands had few natural resources to exploit, and business preferred sail power to steam. Add to this the fact that Amsterdam's opening to the sea, the Zuider Zee, was too shallow for the new steamships, and it's easy to see why the Dutch were forced to struggle.

Prosperity, though, returned to Amsterdam after the 1860s. The city adjusted its economy, and its trading position was improved by the building of two canals. The opening of the Suez Canal in 1869 sped up the passage to the Orient and led to an increase in commerce, while the first discovery of diamonds in South Africa revitalised the diamond industry. But what the city needed most was easy access to the major shipping lanes of northern Europe. When it was opened in 1876, the Noordzee Kanaal (North Sea Canal) let Amsterdam take advantage of German industrial trade and it became the Netherlands' greatest shipbuilding port again, at least for a while. Industrial machinery was introduced late to Amsterdam. However, by the late 19th century, the city had begun to modernise production of the luxury goods for which it would eventually become so internationally famous: beer, chocolates, cigars and diamonds.

Of course, not all of Amsterdam's trade was conducted on water, and the city finally got a major rail link in 1889. Centraal Station was designed by PJH Cuypers in 1876 and worked counterproductively to a degree by separating the city from the vital lifeblood of its seafront. Meanwhile Cuyper's Rijksmuseum on the other fringe of the city became, like Centraal Station, uniquely eclectic and was even widely derided as a 'cathedral of the arts'. Still, Amsterdam consolidated its position at the forefront of Europe with the building of a number of other landmarks such as the Stadsschouwburg (in 1894), the Stedelijk Museum (1895) and the Tropen Institute (1926). The city's international standing had soon improved to such a point that, in 1928, it hosted the Olympics.

MISERY OF THE MASSES

Amsterdam's population had stagnated at 250,000 for two centuries after the Golden Age, but between 1850 and 1900 it more than doubled. Extra labour was needed to meet the demands of a revitalised economy, but the major problem was how to house the new workers. Today the old inner-city quarters are

Money for nothing: a stone relief on the mint-making **Munttoren**. *See p14.*

desirable addresses, but they used to be the homes of Amsterdam's poor. The picturesque Jordaan, where regular riots broke out at the turn of the century, was occupied primarily by the lowest-paid workers, its canals were used as cesspits and the mortality rate was high. Around the centre, new developments – the Pijp, Dapper and Staatslieden quarters – were built: they weren't luxurious, but at least they enjoyed simple lavatory facilities, while the Amsterdam School of architects (*photo p19*), inspired by socialist beliefs, designed now classic housing for the poor. Wealthier city-dwellers, meanwhile, found elegance in homes constructed near Vondelpark and further south.

The city didn't fare badly during the first two decades of the 20th century, but Dutch neutrality throughout World War I brought problems to parts of the population. While the elite lined their pockets selling arms, the poor were confronted with food shortages. In 1917, with food riots erupting, the city had to open soup kitchens and introduce rationing. The army was called in to suppress another outbreak of civil unrest in the Jordaan in 1934. This time the cause was unemployment, endemic throughout the industrialised world following the Wall Street Crash of 1929.

Unfortunately, the humiliation of means testing for unemployment benefit meant that many families suffered in hungry silence. Many Dutch workers moved to Germany, where National Socialism was creating jobs. The city was just emerging from the Depression when the Nazis invaded in May 1940.

THE RAVAGES OF WAR

Amsterdam endured World War II without being flattened by bombs, but nonetheless its buildings, infrastructure, inhabitants and morale were reduced to a terrible state by the occupying Nazi forces. The Holocaust also left an indelible scar on a city whose population in 1940 was ten per cent Jewish.

Early in the morning of 10 May 1940, German bombers mounted a surprise attack on Dutch airfields and barracks. The government and people had hoped that the Netherlands could remain neutral, as it had in World War I, so the armed forces were unprepared for war. Though the Dutch aimed to hold off the Germans until the British and French could come to their assistance, their plan failed. Queen Wilhelmina fled to London to form a government in exile, leaving Supreme Commander Winkelman in charge. After Rotterdam was destroyed by bombing and the Germans threatened other cities with the same treatment, Winkelman surrendered on 14 May. The Dutch colonies of Indonesia and New Guinea were invaded by the Japanese in January 1942. After their capitulation on 8 March, Dutch colonials were imprisoned in Japanese concentration camps.

During the war, Hitler appointed Austrian Nazi Arthur Seyss-Inquart as Rijkskommissaris (State Commissioner) of the Netherlands, and asked him to tie the Dutch economy to the German one and help to Nazify Dutch society. Though it gained less than five per cent of the votes in the 1939 elections, the National Socialist Movement (NSB) was the largest fascist political party in the Netherlands, and was the only Dutch party not prohibited during the occupation. Its doctrine resembled German Nazism, but the NSB wanted to maintain Dutch autonomy under the direction of Germany.

'The Dutch police dragged Jews out of their houses for deportation.'

During the first years of the war, the Nazis let most people live relatively unmolested. Rationing, however, made the Dutch vulnerable to the black market, while cinemas and theatres eventually closed because of curfews and censorship. Later, the Nazis adopted more aggressive measures: Dutch men were forced to work in German industry, and economic exploitation assumed appalling forms. In April 1943, all Dutch soldiers, who had been captured during the invasion and then released in the summer of 1940, were ordered to give themselves up as prisoners of war. Within an atmosphere of deep shock and outrage, strikes broke out, but were violently suppressed.

To begin with, ordinary citizens, as well as the political and economic elite, had no real reason to make a choice between collaboration and resistance. But as Nazi policies became more virulent, opposition to them swelled, and thus a growing minority of people were confronted with the difficult choice of whether to obey German measures or to resist. There were several patterns of collaboration. Some people joined the NSB, while others intimidated Jews, got involved in economic collaboration or betrayed people in hiding or members of the Resistance. Amazingly, a small number even signed up for German military service. But in general there was a small resistance, a small group of collaborators, and a very large majority of 'grey' in between.

The most shocking institutional collaboration involved Dutch police, who dragged Jews out of their houses for deportation, and Dutch Railways, which was paid for transporting Jews to their deaths. When the war was over, 450,000 people were arrested for collaborating – although most

Set in stone

Paris has Père Lachaise and Montmartre. London has Highgate and Kensal Green. Amsterdam, though it may lack celebrity cemeteries boasting big buried names, nevertheless has plenty of history just waiting to be disinterred, helping dedicated and casual necrophiliacs alike piece together the city's intriguing narrative.

The most scenically located of Amsterdam's burial grounds is **Zorgvlied** (Amsteldijk 273, 644 5236; *pictured*). Beside the Amstel, this departure lounge for sybarites is perfectly located for nautical funeral processions. One bon vivant who got the full works was gay scene and nightlife impresario Manfred Langer; his likeness, complete with priapic peaked cap and a cluster of drained vodka bottles scattered around the base, stands by the railings near the road. His 1994 send-off included a waterborne pink coffin accompanied by pumping house music and gyrating go-go boys. Other residents include suicidal rock 'n' roll junkie Herman Brood and kid's writer Annie MG Schmidt, whose Jip and Janneke characters adorn almost all the children's goods at HEMA. Her homely grave is covered in multicoloured mosaics, and many visitors have left behind miniature jenever bottles and little figurines in fond tribute to the storyteller. Wandering around these beautifully landscaped surrounds (designed by Jan David Zocher in 1870), you'll stumble on familiar names from the cityscape – a Carré here, a Krasnapolsky there – in amongst the grand mausoleums. Worth looking out for, too, are the crazy gravestones: Amsterdammetjes, stainless steel, glass; anything goes. There are sober reminders here – and in all of the city's burial places – of Amsterdam's most terrible period: occupation. Here and there are dotted graves which read 'born Amsterdam, died Auschwitz' – or many of the other death camps.

A similarly sombre memorial denotes the entrance of **Rustoord** (Weesperstraat 84, 690 2439) in Diemen. It says: 'To the memory of those who fell in the years 1940-45 at the hands of the occupier and who rest in this graveyard.' This place is also notable for its Hell's Angels vault – containing no less than seven brothers – which is generally strewn with empty Jack Daniels bottles. At the centre of it all is a pet cemetery.

Also on the eastern side of the city is the great sprawling graveyard the **Nieuwe Ooster** (Kruislaan 126, 608 0608, www.denieuwe ooster.nl), which contains poets, politicians and painters aplenty – most famous (and most recent) among them is Theo van Gogh. It also contains a brand new and genuinely unique visitor attraction: the **Dutch Funeral Museum** (www.uitvaartmuseum.nl), which explores deathly Dutch traditions, and whose collection includes everything from horse-drawn hearses to uniforms, paintings, prints and documents.

The least showy but most restful city cemetery is modest **Huis te Vraag** (Rijnburgstraat) in the South, not far from the Olympic Stadium. No longer in use for burials – now a nature reserve – it's an atmospheric delight of gnarled tree trunks, creeping ivy and sinking stones. There are no grand names or big mausoleums here, just ordinary people who led ordinary lives and did ordinary jobs, but who nonetheless made Amsterdam into the city it is. And just like life itself, Huis te Vraag's pleasures are fleeting. Under Dutch law, a graveyard that has been out of use for 50 years can be cleared and the land sold on; the last burial here was in 1962, and thus the date for clearance (2012) creeps ever nearer. It's also on a prime slice of real estate, so grab the chance to look while it's still there.

were quickly released. Mitigating circumstances – NSB members who helped the Resistance, for example – made judgments complicated. Of 14,500 sentenced, only 39 were executed.

The Resistance was made up chiefly of Communists and, to a lesser extent, Calvinists. Anti-Nazi activities took several forms, with illegal newspapers keeping the population informed and urging them to resist the Nazi dictators. Underground groups took many shapes and sizes. Some spied for the Allies, others fought an armed struggle against the Germans through assassination and sabotage, and others falsified identity cards and food vouchers. A national organisation took care of people who wanted to hide, and aided the railway strikers, Dutch soldiers and illegal workers being sought by the Germans, with other groups helping Jews into hiding. By 1945, more than 300,000 people had gone underground in the Netherlands.

'By the end of the winter, 20,000 people had died of starvation and disease.'

Worse was to follow towards the close of the war. In 1944, the Netherlands plunged into Hongerwinter – the Hunger Winter. Supplies of coal vanished after the liberation of the south and a railway strike, called by the Dutch government in exile in order to hasten German defeat, was disastrous for the supply of food. In retaliation, the Germans damaged Schiphol Airport and the harbours of Rotterdam and Amsterdam – foiling any attempts to bring in supplies – and grabbed everything they could. Walking became the only means of transport, domestic refuse was no longer collected, sewers overflowed and the population fell to disease.

To survive, people stole fuel: more than 20,000 trees were cut down and 4,600 buildings were demolished. Floors, staircases, joists and rafters were plundered, causing the collapse of many houses, particularly those ones left by deported Jews. Supplies were scarce and many couldn't afford to buy their rationing allowance, let alone the expensive produce on the black market. By the end of the winter, 20,000 people had died of starvation and disease, and much of the city was seriously damaged.

But hope was around the corner. The Allies liberated the south of the Netherlands on 5 September 1944, Dolle Dinsdag (Mad Tuesday), and complete liberation came on 5 May 1945, when it became apparent that the Netherlands was the worst-hit country in western Europe.

In spite of the destruction and the loss of so many lives, there were effusive celebrations. But more blood was shed on 7 May, when German soldiers opened fire on a crowd who had gathered in Dam Square to welcome their Canadian liberators: 22 people were killed.

THE HOLOCAUST

'I see how the world is slowly becoming a desert, I hear more and more clearly the approaching thunder that will kill us,' wrote Anne Frank in her diary on 15 July 1944. Though her words obviously applied to the Jews, they were relevant to all those who were persecuted during the war. Granted, anti-Semitism in Holland had not been as virulent as in Germany, France or Austria. But even so, most – though not all – of the Dutch population ignored the persecution, and there's still a sense of national guilt as a result.

The Holocaust happened in three stages. First came measures to enforce the isolation of the Jews: the ritual slaughter of animals was prohibited, Jewish government employees were dismissed, Jews were banned from public places and, eventually, all Jews were forced to wear a yellow Star of David. (Some non-Jews wore the badge as a mark of solidarity.) Concentration was the second stage. From early 1942, all Dutch Jews were obliged to move to three areas in Amsterdam, isolated by signs, drawbridges and barbed wire. The final stage was deportation. Between July 1942 and September 1943, most of the 140,000 Dutch Jews were deported, via Kamp Westerbork. Public outrage at deportations was foreshadowed by the one and only protest, organised by dock workers, against the anti-Semitic terror, the February Strike of 1941.

The Nazis also wanted to eliminate Gypsies: more than 200,000 European Gypsies, including many Dutch, were exterminated. Homosexuals, too, were threatened with extermination, but their persecution was less systematic: public morality acts prohibited homosexual behaviour, and gay pressure groups ceased their activities. Amsterdam has the world's first memorial to persecuted gays – the Homomonument – which incorporates pink triangles, turning the Nazi badge of persecution into a symbol of pride.

THE DUST SETTLES

The country was scarred by the occupation, losing ten per cent of its housing, 30 per cent of its industry and 40 per cent of its production capacity. Though Amsterdam escaped the bombing raids that devastated Rotterdam, it bore the brunt of deportations: only 5,000 Jews, out of a pre-war Jewish population of 80,000, remained. Despite intense poverty and drastic shortages of food, fuel and building materials, the Dutch tackled the task of post-war recovery with a strong sense of optimism. In 1948, people threw street parties, firstly to celebrate the inauguration of Queen Juliana and, later, the four gold medals won by Amsterdam athlete Fanny Blankers-Koen at the London Olympics. Some Dutch flirted briefly with communism after the war, but in 1948 a compromise was agreed between the Catholic KVP and the newly created Labour party PvdA, and the two proceeded to govern in successive coalitions until 1958. Led by Prime Minister Willem Drees, the government resuscitated social programmes and laid the basis for a welfare state. The Dutch now reverted to the virtues of a conservative society: decency, hard work and thrift.

The country's first priority, however, was economic recovery. The city council concentrated on reviving the two motors of its economy: Schiphol Airport and the Port of Amsterdam, the latter of which was boosted by the opening of the Amsterdam-Rhine Canal in 1952. Joining Belgium and Luxembourg in the Benelux also brought the country trade benefits, and the Netherlands was the first European nation to repay its Marshall Plan loans. The authorities dusted off their pre-war development plans and embarked on a rapid phase of urban expansion. But as people moved into the new suburbs, businesses flowed into the centre, worsening congestion on the already cramped roads.

After the war, the Dutch colonies of New Guinea and Indonesia were liberated from the Japanese and pushed for independence. With Indonesia accounting for 20 per cent of their pre-war economy, the Dutch launched military interventions in 1947 and 1948. But these did not prevent the transfer of sovereignty to Indonesia on 27 December 1949, while the dispute with New Guinea dragged on until 1962 and did much to damage the Netherlands' reputation abroad. Colonial immigrants to the Netherlands – including the later arrival of Surinamese (fully half the population of that country) – and Turkish and Moroccan 'guest workers' now comprise 16 per cent of the population. Though poorer jobs and housing have been their lot, racial tensions were notable for being low until the mid 1990s.

Although the economy and welfare state revived in the 1950s, there was still civil unrest. Strikes flared at the port and council workers defied a ban on industrial action. In 1951 the protesters clashed with the police outside the Concertgebouw, angered by the appointment of a pro-Nazi conductor, and in 1956 demonstrators besieged the Dutch Communist Party, outraged by the Soviet invasion of Hungary.

In the late '40s and '50s most Amsterdammers returned to their pre-war pursuits: fashion and celebrity interviews filled the newspapers and cultural events mushroomed. In 1947 the city launched the prestigious Holland Festival, while the elite held the Boekenbal, an annual event where writers met royalty and other dignitaries. New avant-garde movements emerged, notable among them the CoBrA art group, whose 1949 exhibition at the Stedelijk Museum of Modern Art caused an uproar, and the Vijftigers, a group of experimental poets led by Lucebert. Many of these artists met in brown cafés around Leidseplein.

THE WINTER OF DISCONTENT

The '60s proved to be one of the most colourful decades in Amsterdam's history. There were genuine official attempts to improve society. The IJ Tunnel eased communications to north Amsterdam just as the national economy took off. There were high hopes for new rehousing developments such as the Bijlmermeer, and influential new architecture from the likes of Aldo van Eyck and Herman Herzberger.

'The royal wedding turned nasty after Provos let off a smoke bomb on the carriage.'

Yet the generous hand of the welfare state was being bitten. Discontent began on a variety of issues, among them the nuclear threat, urban expansion and industrialisation, the consumer society and state authority in general. Popular movements very similar to those in other west European cities were formed, but with a unique zaniness all their own. Protest and dissent have always been a vital part of the Netherlands' democratic process, yet the Dutch have a habit of keeping things in proportion; so, popular demonstrations took a playful form.

Discontent gained focus in 1964, when pranks around 't Lieverdje statue, highlighting political or social problems, kick-started a new radical subculture. Founded by anarchist philosophy student Roel van Duyn and 'anti-smoke magician' Robert Jasper Grootveld, the Provos – their name inspired by their game plan: to provoke – numbered only about two dozen, but were enormously influential. Their style influenced the major anti-Vietnam demos in the US and the Situationist antics in 1969 Paris, and set the tone for Amsterdam's love of liberal politics and absurdist theatre. Their finest hour came in March 1966, when protests about Princess Beatrix's controversial wedding to the German Claus van Amsberg turned nasty after the Provos let off a smoke bomb on the carriage route, and a riot ensued. Some Provos, such as Van Duyn, went on to fight the system from within: five won city seats under the surrreal banner of the Kabouter (a mythical race of forest-dwelling dwarves) in 1970.

The **Rijksmuseum**. *See p18.*

Perhaps the single most significant catalyst for discontent in the '70s – which exploded into civil conflict by the '80s – was the issue of housing. Amsterdam's small size and historic city centre had always been a nightmare for its urban planners. The city's population increased in the '60s, reaching its peak (nearly 870,000) by 1964. Swelling the numbers further were immigrants from the Netherlands' last major colony, Surinam, many of whom were dumped in the Bijlmermeer. It degenerated into a ghetto and, when a 747 crashed there in October 1992, the final number of fatalities was impossible to ascertain: many victims were unregistered.

The Metro link to Bijlmermeer is in itself a landmark to some of Amsterdam's most violent protests. Passionate opposition erupted against the proposed clearance in February 1975 of the Jewish quarter of Nieuwmarkt. Civil unrest culminated in 'Blue Monday', 24 March 1975, when police sparked clashes with residents and supporters. Police fired tear gas into the homes of those who refused to move out, and battered down doors. Despite further violence, the first Metro line opened in 1977, with the Centraal Station link following in 1980, though only one of the four planned lines was completed.

City planners were shocked by the fervent opposition to their schemes for large, airy suburbs. It was not what people wanted: they cherished the narrow streets, the small squares and the cosy cafés. The public felt the council was selling out to big business, complaining that the centre was becoming unaffordable. In 1978, the council decided to renovate street by street. But with roughly 90,000 people still on the housing list in 1980, public concern grew.

Speculators who left property empty caused acute resentment, which soon turned into direct action: vacant buildings were occupied illegally by squatters. In March 1980 police turned against them for the first time and used tanks to evict the squatters from a former office building in Vondelstraat. Riots ensued, but the squatters were victorious. In 1982, as Amsterdam's squatting movement reached its peak, clashes with police escalated: a state of emergency was called after one eviction battle. Soon, though, the city – led by new mayor Ed van Thijn – had gained the upper hand over the movement, and one of the last of the city's big squats, Wyers, fell amid tear gas in February 1984 to make way for a Holiday Inn. Squatters were no longer a force to be reckoned with, though their ideas of small-scale regeneration have since been absorbed into official planning.

THE SHAPE OF THINGS TO COME

Born and bred in Amsterdam, Ed van Thijn embodied a new strand in Dutch politics. Though a socialist, he took tough action against 'unsavoury elements' – petty criminals, squatters, dealers in hard drugs – and upgraded facilities to attract new businesses and tourists. A new national political era also emerged, where the welfare system and government subsidies were trimmed to ease the country's large budget deficit, and aimed to revitalise the economy with more businesslike policies. The price of Amsterdam's new affluence (among most groups, except the very poorest) has been a swing towards commercialism, with the squatters largely supplanted by well-groomed yuppies. Flashy cafés, galleries and nouvelle cuisine restaurants replaced the alternative scene and a mood of calm settled on the city. Still, a classic example of Dutch free expression was provoked by the city's mid-'80s campaign to host the 1992 Olympics. Amsterdam became the first city ever to send its own (ultimately successful) official anti-Olympics delegation.

The current mayor Job Cohen stills holds to a course that hopes to see Amsterdam reinvented as a 'Business Gateway to Europe', where future visitors will be more prone to point their cameras towards the arising eastern docklands than towards the ever-photogenic Red Light District. But with the current economic decline, the main advantages of nurturing Amsterdam's long-held reputation as a hotbed for edgy creativity become more apparent – both for business and the general atmosphere. So worry not: the city isn't ready to relinquish its rebel status just yet.

Key events

EARLY HISTORY
1204 Gijsbrecht van Amstel builds a castle in the settlement that will eventually become the city of Amsterdam.
1270 The Amstel is dammed at Dam Square.
1300 Amsterdam is granted city rights by the Bishop of Utrecht.
1306 Work begins on the Oude Kerk.
1313 The Bishop of Utrecht grants Aemstelledamme full municipal rights and leaves it to William III of Holland.
1342 The city walls (*burgwallen*) are built.
1421 The St Elizabeth's Day Flood occurs, as does Amsterdam's first great fire.
1452 Fire destroys most wooden houses.
1489 Maximilian grants Amsterdam the right to add the imperial crown to its coat of arms.

WAR AND REFORMATION
1534 Anabaptists try to seize City Hall but fail. A sustained and brutal period of anti-Protestant repression begins.
1565 William the Silent organises a Protestant revolt against Spanish rule.
1566 The Beeldenstorm (Iconoclastic Fury) is unleashed. Protestant worship is made legal.
1568 The Eighty Years' War with Spain begins.
1577 The Prince of Orange annexes the city.
1578 Catholic Burgomasters are replaced by Protestants in the Alteration.
1579 The Union of Utrecht is signed, allowing freedom of religious belief but not of worship.
1589 Antwerp falls to Spain; there is a mass exodus to the north.

THE GOLDEN AGE
1602 The Verenigde Oost Indische Compagnie (VOC) is founded.
1606 Rembrandt van Rijn is born.
1611 The Zuiderkerk is completed.
1613 Work starts on the western stretches of Herengracht, Keizersgracht and Prinsengracht.
1623 WIC colonises Manhattan Island; Peter Stuyvesant founds New Amsterdam in 1625.
1642 Rembrandt completes the *Night Watch*.
1648 The Treaty of Munster is signed, ending the Eighty Years War with Spain.
1654 England begins a bloody and drawn-out war against the United Provinces.
1667 England and the Netherlands sign the Peace of Breda.

DECLINE AND FALL
1672 England and the Netherlands go to war; Louis XIV of France invades.
1675 The Portuguese Synagogue is built.
1685 French Protestants take refuge after the revocation of the Edict of Nantes.
1689 William of Orange becomes King William III of England.
1696 Undertakers riot against funeral tax.
1787 Frederick William II, King of Prussia, occupies Amsterdam.
1795 French Revolutionaries are welcomed to Amsterdam by the Patriots. The Batavian Republic is set up and run from Amsterdam.
1806 Napoleon's brother is made king.
1810 King Louis is removed from the throne.
1813 Unification of the Netherlands. Amsterdam is no longer a self-governing city.
1815 Amsterdam becomes capital of Holland.

BETWEEN THE OCCUPATIONS
1848 The city's ramparts are pulled down.
1876 Noordzee Kanaal links Amsterdam with the North Sea.
1880s Oil is discovered in Sumatra. The Royal Dutch Company (Shell Oil) is founded.
1883 Amsterdam holds the World Exhibition.
1887 The Rijksmuseum is completed.
1889 Centraal Station opens.
1922 Women are granted the vote.
1928 The Olympics are held in Amsterdam.
1934 Amsterdam's population is 800,000.

WORLD WAR II
1940 German troops invade Amsterdam.
1941 The February Strike, in protest against the deportation of Jews.
1944-5 20,000 die in the Hunger Winter.
1945 Canadian soldiers free Amsterdam.
1947 Anne Frank's diary is published.

THE POST-WAR ERA
1966 The wedding of Princess Beatrix and Prince Claus ends in riots.
1968 The IJ Tunnel opens.
1976 Cannabis is decriminalised.
1977 First Metrolijn (underground) opens.
1980 Queen Beatrix's coronation (30 April).
1986 The controversial 'Stopera' civic headquarters-cum-opera house is built.
1997 The euro is approved as a European currency in the Treaty of Amsterdam.
1999 Prostitution is made legal after years of decriminalisation.
2002 The guilder is dead; long live the euro. Pim Fortuyn murdered.
2004 Film-maker/columnist Theo Van Gogh murdered by an Islamic fundamentalist.

Amsterdam Today

Keeping it together amid cultural and commercial uncertainty.

'The most relaxed city in Europe.' 'It really has everything, from the best art and new design to the old sex, drugs and rock 'n' roll.' 'The people are so friendly.' 'It's compact and beautiful, you can bike and walk everywhere and everybody speaks perfect English.'

These are just a few reasons why tourists flock en masse to the Dutch capital. 'Amsterdam has it' was the city's slogan in the mid '70s. After 30-odd years – and despite the rather cryptic 'Iamsterdam' slogan (*see p55*) – this still rings true, though a lot has changed in recent years. Compared to London or Paris, Amsterdam used to be like a kid brother who didn't want to grow up; it was a playground where all involved had a jolly good time, bar a few superficial bumps.

In recent years, however, the city has been forced to grow up rather quickly due to cultural tensions that seem to be perpetually testing that famously relaxed attitude.

A MELTING POT AT BOILING POINT

After the murder of film director, writer and big mouth Theo van Gogh, shot and knifed in broad daylight in November 2004 by a young Dutch-Moroccan man wildly incensed by Van Gogh's constant moaning about Islam – notably in his controversial movie *Submission* – the city shook to its foundations. Racial tension was in the air. Mayor Job Cohen's speech at the impromptu 'noise' demonstration immediately following the brutal event included the now-famous line '*we moeten de boel bij elkaar houden*' ('we have to try to keep things together'), and that's exactly what he did. Many Amsterdammers praised his swift and balanced moves, focusing more on dialogue than action to keep the peace in the multicultural city that Amsterdam has become over the years. Others, however, feel he's not being tough enough and have dubbed him 'Mr Pickwick' (after a Dutch tea brand), claiming

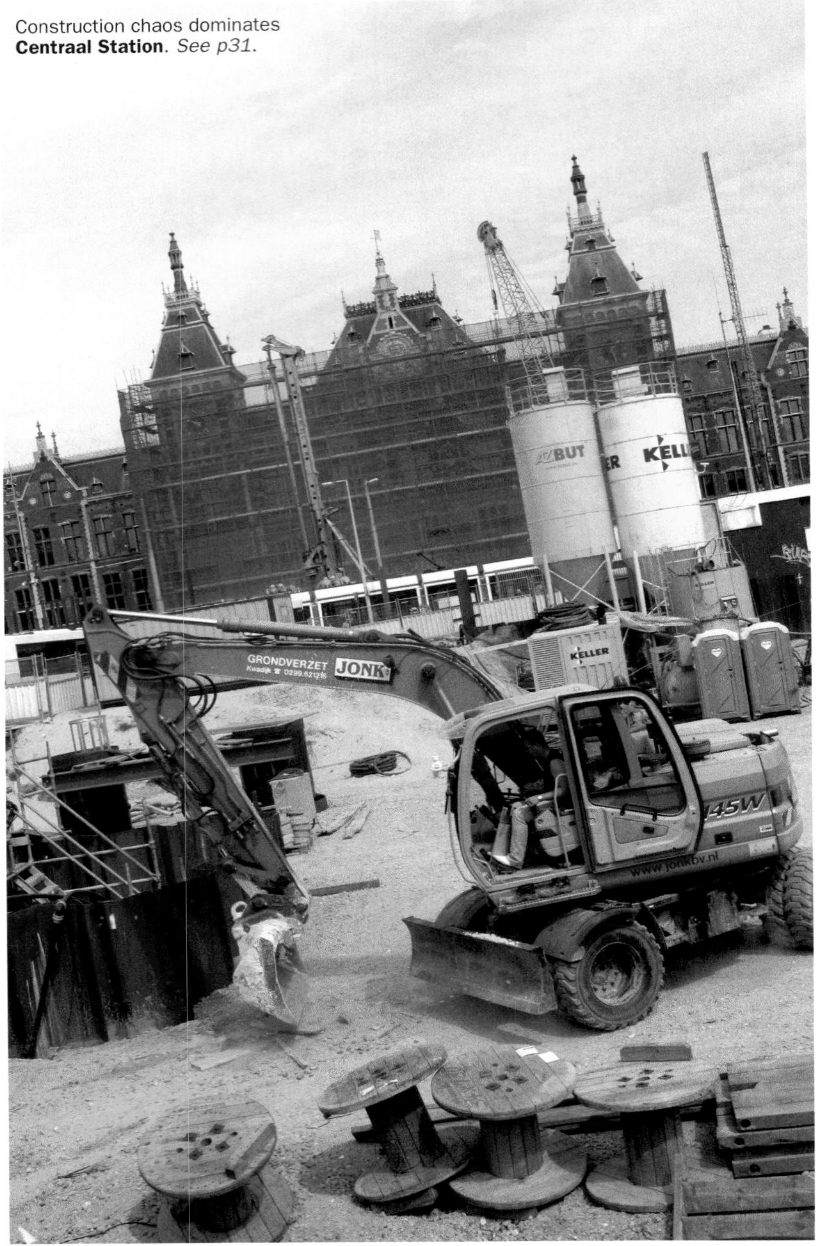

Construction chaos dominates **Centraal Station**. *See p31.*

he spends too much time drinking mint tea in mosques with Muslim delegates instead of setting an example by taking firm measures.

The murder put Amsterdam in international headlines, and Cohen was named one of *Time* magazine's 'Heroes of 2005' because he ensured emotion didn't get the upper hand and turn into rioting, as in France; he was also voted number two in the 2006 World Mayor Awards.

One of the city's most recent initiatives for bringing back unity, cohesion and solidarity between the different nationalities that make up Amsterdam was the much-debated Amsterdam Day, created in 2006. It is part of the touted 'We Amsterdammers' campaign introduced shortly after the murder of Van Gogh, which finances initiatives from volunteers, organisations and local residents to stop polarisation, anti-social behaviour and extremism. However, the event – a daytime concert with local acts and bands on Dam Square at a cost of 250,000 euros – failed miserably, as only a handful of locals and tourists turned up. This was all in glaring contrast to the Kwakoe festival (*see p199* **Kwak addict**), an annual non-political, multicultural festival in the south of Amsterdam, set up by locals, costing next to nothing and attracting the desired cultural crowd. Some things just can't be forced. Still, not giving up easily, the council will continue organising Amsterdam Day annually, though after the initial failure it isn't clear in what form.

LEGALISING LICENTIOUSNESS

Now comfortably in his second term of office, Cohen is stricter and more outspoken when it comes to cleaning up the seedy Red Light District. According to the council, about 30 buildings – and therefore 'windows' – are in the hands of criminals who bought the premises with illicit money that was either laundered or gained from selling drugs. Keeping them open means the council is facilitating criminals in their illegal activities, so a new law (the 'Bibob') has been passed to make it easier to withdraw permits in cases of questionable activities.

The prostitutes' union isn't pleased, however, since closing windows means that women start working the streets again, with the undesirable effects of invisibility and danger. Though the council would indeed like to see the Red Light District minimised and cleaned up to lessen its magnetic reputation abroad, it did give permission to the prostitutes' union to erect a statue of a prostitute in the area, honouring the sex workers of the district.

Due Noord

There was a time when Amsterdam Noord was right off the map. Even in centuries past, the land on the other side of that big, watery body called the IJ was known as little more than the spot where the remains of freshly executed criminals were hung on display. Once that practise stopped, there was really very little of interest to pull short-term visitors northwards – except perhaps the lure of cycling routes towards such scenic fishing villages as Volendam and Marken, or the trip on the free ferry from the back of Centraal Station, the latter always good for 20 minutes of seafaring fun. But with the impending **Noord-Zuidlijn metro link** (*see also p31*) aiming to unite this once isolated area with the city, plus the various accompanying (and suitably ambitious) redevelopment plans, things are set to change very quickly.

Already the cultural breeding ground of **Kinetic Noord**, located in the former shipping yard NDSM (*see p262*), is by far the largest in the country, with over a hundred artists' studios, a skate hall and a whole slew of singular spaces. It sports a wonderful and totally unique post-apocalyptic vibe that's ideal for parties, concerts and wacky theatre festivals such as **Over het IJ** and **Robodock** (for both, *see p265*). It's also home to a surrounding neighbourhood of arty student container dwellings, a 'clean energy' exhibition, a great restaurant and café (www.noorderlicht cafe.nl) and boasts regular visits from the highly alternative party boat **Stubnitz** (www.stubnitz.com), an inspired floating zone that books bands, DJs, art and general weirdness for parties that bob as much as they bounce.

And now this new ground zero for Dutch subculture is also a home to the Benelux headquarters of MTV networks, which moved into a wildly revamped former woodwork factory in 2007. It's the hope of the powers-that-be to reinvigorate Amsterdam as a culturally-connected 'creative capital' for the 21st century – that MTV and the other similarly commercially-oriented creative industries currently setting up shop will cross-fertilise with the more squat-edged original artistic denizens. They also hope that a great deal of inspiration and money will be made by all concerned, and that the creative cycle will be self-perpetuating. Only time will tell.

The controversial **Noord-Zuidlijn** aims to link north and south – but at what cost?

Another much-debated issue is that of dope laws. In 2006, a ban on al fresco toking in De Baarsjes (*see p166* **Anti-smoke signals**), a rather neglected residential area in the west, was introduced because youths were causing too much trouble and noise. In true Amsterdam style, the red pictograms were nicked as soon as they were hung up. The council – in another Dutch 'we can make money out of everything' move – started selling them to collectors as far afield as the US. Despite this, there are now plans to extend the ban to other areas, and there are also talks about banning coffeeshops within 250 metres (820 feet) of schools – extremely difficult in a city as small as this one.

A METRO LINE RUNS THROUGH IT

The most visible manifestation of change – and one that visitors can't miss – is the work on the Noord-Zuidlijn, the new metro that will connect north Amsterdam to south. Work on the 9.5-kilometre (six-mile) line started in 2003 and will continue until 2013, if not longer; many locals think the new link is unnecessary and far too expensive (*see p29* **Due Noord**). Most of the aldermen responsible for initiating this highly unpopular project are now working in other parts of the country, leaving the city with a legacy that's at best merely too expensive, and at worst out of control and irreversible. The Noord-Zuidlijn is way over its original budget – a staggering €1.8 billion – paid for by the council and the government. The whole thing will in fact cost the council well over €600 million, and not the estimated €314 million. Part of the problem lies in the technical difficulties of digging under a city built on poles; new, time-consuming processes had to be invented to construct tunnels. The area designated for the station in the Pijp, for example, is so small that there's no room for adjacent north- and southbound platforms, so one has to be plopped on top of the other. With the new metro line on its way, Centraal Station is also undergoing a change (*photo p28*). The building needed much renovation anyway, but now even more so, just to be able to welcome the extra commuters who will – on top of the extant 250,000 a day – use the station once the new Noord-Zuidlijn is in operation. Also, all tram and bus terminals will be removed to a new section, creating a whole new, more user-friendly transport area.

It's hoped that the new metro line will give the city an economic boost, especially around the

Two wheels good

Bicycles may be largely taken for granted these days, but as 'iron horses that need no feeding', they are still majestic beasts whose invention transformed life as much as the car and commercial flight. The *fiets* – as the Dutch call it – democratised movement by being both functionally and financially accessible. As an efficient agent of mobility, freeing up time for more noble pursuits, bikes also participated in the emancipation of women and found one of their biggest local cheerleaders in pioneering feminist Alleta Jacobs (1854-1929), herself the Netherlands' first female doctor and famous inventor of the family-planning 'Dutch cap'. And thanks to a bicycle's mechanical nudity – the artist Saul Steinberg called it an 'X-ray of itself' – bikes are easy to maintain as well.

Don't mention it to the Dutch (more on this later), but it was in fact a German, Karl van Drais (1785-1851), who envisioned two in-line wheels being steered by handlebars at the front. But this was only a 'walking bike', and it was not until 1861 that Ernest Michaux, the son of a Parisian wagon-maker, put pedals on the front wheel and created the *vélocipède*.

Then, in 1871, Englishman James Starley first made the discovery that a huge front wheel made things more efficient – only to be outdone in 1885 by his own nephew, John Kemp Starley, who made his 'Rover' with two equal-sized wheels being back-propelled with a chain. Although later appended with inflatable rubber tyres to cure riders of their headaches, this design had already managed to achieved near-perfection. And it's this standard old 'bone-shaker', called an *oma fiets* ('granny bike'), that you still see most around town. This horizontal land – where only the wind offers any real challenges – has no need for those light frames that enable overachievers like Lance Armstrong to pedal like lightning. Bikes, in their simplest forms, are intrinsic to Dutch identity: sensible, sober and befitting the Calvinist doctrine, 'no pain, no gain'.

The Dutch also show their respect by buying 1.5 million bikes annually and then, across Amsterdam alone, stealing 150,000 of them. (Professional thieves steal 40 per cent, junkies 30 per cent, and 'occasion stealers' – read: broke students – account for the other 30 per cent.) It has been calculated that if the city's 540,000 bikes were all put together, they would fill Vondelpark twice over.

The term *fiets* has entered the language in many ways. 'Bicycle bread' refers to raisin bread so sadly skimpy on the raisins that a bike could ride between them. And if you see someone with gapped teeth, feel free to point, laugh and call them 'bike rack'. But the most widely used cycling phrase is 'Okay, first return the bike', which means 'first things first'. This commemorates the requisition by retreating Germans of the nation's bikes at the end of World War II, and provides part of the reason why spiteful locals will direct German tourists to the Anne Frank Huis when asked about the location of the nearest coffeeshop.

Bicycles played a particularly heady role for the Provos in the 1960s. This left-wing group combined anti-capitalist politics with a sense of the absurd, and their 'happenings' – which were to later become blueprints for both the Yippies in America and the Situationists in France – were actually orchestrated mind games meant to provoke the authorities into embarrassing actions like drug busts of hay stacks. Their infamous 1965 'White Bicycle Plan' donated a single white-painted bicycle to the many citizens of Amsterdam for their free use in the hope that the city would follow through with thousands more, but it only provoked the police to impound it. While there were many other 'White Plans' – such as the 'White Constable Plan' that envisioned white-clad cops boasting lighters for joint-smokers, chickens for the hungry and oranges for the thirsty – only the 'White Bicycle Plan' managed to enter the realm of the nearly-real. The idea was originally formulated by Luud Schimmelpenninck, who, as a newly-elected councillor in 1967, wanted to eradicate cars across the city, and saw this as the first step. A designer, Schimmelpenninck had clung to his bicycle vision for 30 years. He managed to deal with the logistics of finding sponsorship, weaving through the required bureaucracy, inventing an 'asshole-proof' bicycle and developing a computerised distribution system that would minimise theft. But after test runs in 1998 and millions of guilders of investment, the plan proved unworkable – though versions are being implemented in Copenhagen and Barcelona.

But there are also many other local bike visionaries. VMX Architects' temporary shed for 2,500 bicycles, currently pile-drived in a canal just west of Centraal Station to keep the bike clutter at bay while the Noord-Zuid metro line is being constructed, won first prize at the 2002 Venice International Architecture Biennial. There's also a whole team of squatters who weld together 'tall bikes' for **jousting contests** (http://squat.net/hogefiets). You can even hire a **fietscafe** (www.fietscafe.nl) to pedal on while drinking with a group of friends. Meanwhile, the obsessive bicycle fanatics over at **Workcycles** (Veemarkt 150, 689 7879, www.workcycles.com) can build or rent you any type of work bike, and the year 2007 will have seen the debut of alternative art bike fest **Me Bike – The Dream Bike Project** (www.mebike.org), taking place in Westerpark.

But Amsterdam-based American artist **Eric Staller** (www.ericstaller.com), famed for his *Lightmobile* (1985), a Volkswagen Beetle covered with 1659 computerised lights, has truly embraced the bicycle as long-term muse. Inspired by Dutch socialism and bike culture, he invented the ConferenceBike, where seven people sit in a circle elbow to elbow. One person steers while all seven pedal to propel the bike forward. In 2003, Staller reinvented his ConferenceBike as a PeaceTank with the hopes of getting seven world leaders to pedal towards peace. None have yet dared to take the plunge but 1,000 have been sold to those charmed by the idea around the world.

For those who want to get on a bike and ride, here are some tips. Firstly, ignore traffic lights (unless the police are around, of course). Amsterdam cyclists hate to queue behind people waiting for a red light and in general regard traffic lights as inconsequential pop-art town-decorations. And if you do get into an accident, it's usually the car drivers who lose in court and hence are the ones who will pay for your shiny new wheelchair. Also, remember to stick to your right and to watch out for the tram tracks and deer-like tourists reading maps on the bike path (*see p86* **Theme park Amsterdam**). It may also help to read a few books on chaos theory before setting out. And for the love of God do not regard Amsterdam as some sort of Disney-esque pedal world. Only bike if you know how!

In general, cycling locally – or even simply gracefully side-saddling on the back of one – will help link you to the city and its singular vibe. It's not easy to do, but just imagine, if you can, if everyone drove a car here; the city would be unliveable. And the fact that this city is so very liveable may help account for why Amsterdam's cyclists are rightfully proud – or psychotically smug, depending on your view – about their rights to the road. And with a third of all gasoline pumped in the developed world being used for trips of five kilometres (three miles) or less (with the majority of these rides for a single passenger), the bike can still play a much larger role in the long-term future of our sweet little planet. So happy pedalling!

south area, which will be more easily accessible once the line is finally up and running. In eager anticipation of the new line – and its hoped-for draw to new companies – many new office blocks were built over the last few years in the south. Sadly, most of them stood empty for ages, and there was even a plan to halt the construction work altogether. Luckily, there's been a late blossoming in business, and most blocks have now been rented out to big names like Mitsubishi. The city council is not only actively lobbying in Asia, it has also started a campaign to make the city more interesting for foreign businesses and their employees, such as creating a bureau for all aspects of being an expat in the city and offering training to help civil servants and those working in the hotel and catering industries to be more polite and flexible.

Apart from big hopes for the south, the city has also been developing the east, especially around Centraal Station. Along with the noted Post CS building and the new Muziekcentrum Amsterdam, it's also home to the Netherlands' newest, biggest and highest library (*see p307*). The 11-storey, €88 million tower is part of an ambitious plan to link all the small old 'island' neighbourhoods, such as Kattenburg and Wittenburg, with the newly developed areas that were once part of the harbour but have now become trendy residential zones, like Java and KNSM-eiland. The idea is to create a lively mix of shops, houses, entertainment and hotels. The British City Inn chain is building itself a five-star hotel, home to three restaurants and congress facilities, set to open in 2010.

SMOOTH CRIMINALS

Amsterdam is clearly growing up hard and fast, and like any big city, it has its fair share of crime and violence. But that said, crime rates have been steadily decreasing for the last seven years. And despite some run-down areas like Ganzenpoort in Bijlmermeer – not exactly a tourist hangout anyway – there aren't any real no-go areas. Numbers for robbery, as well as shoplifting, pickpocketing and theft of cars and bikes, are all shifting downwards, and even the number of road accidents in the city decreased by 15 per cent in 2006. Cynics claim that this is because Amsterdammers are too jaded to report the crimes any more. Others suggest that potential perpetrators are deterred by an increased police presence and the introduction of CCTV in many city areas. The increasing aggression on public transport has also been addressed, with more frequent inspectors, CCTV installed on some trams and police patrolling high-risk stations like Lelylaan. Slightly less comforting were the self-defence courses given to tram drivers. In an effort to target the habitual criminals responsible for the vast majority of crime, the police were also

issued with a set of cards depicting the men most wanted by the law. Then, to make sure the police really took notice, wanted posters were put up in police canteens. Sure enough, many of the thugs and thieves were caught. However, the police were less successful in solving the dozens of gangland killings that have taken place in the last five years. Most were drug related and occured in residential areas in broad daylight; one of them even occurred in Dam Square on a busy Saturday afternoon.

Late 2006 saw a new wave of pickpocketing in Amsterdam's city centre by organised groups of children as young as nine. In a modern version of *Oliver Twist,* an international gang of adults trained the children in Romania and then shipped them over to Amsterdam to 'work'. Though all were arrested and put into homes, it's of course still advisable to be on your guard, as there'll always be pickpockets around, most notably in tourist areas and on crowded trams and buses.

SQUATS OF YEARS GONE BY

The squat scene, always a great incubator of more interesting and edgier art, ideas and initiatives, has disintegrated over the past few years due to the demolition of many of the squatted buildings that had been transformed into venues. To invest in Amsterdam's creative scene, the same council that decided to knock these squats down came up with the new idea of 'breeding spaces' – appointed living and working spaces for artists who were only just starting out. While it's true that some things can't be steered from above, particularly not art, at the same time it's better than nothing at all, and shows that the powers-that-be realise that Amsterdam needs creative souls if it wants to compete with other European cities.

Though the council has introduced a 'zero tolerance' campaign and the police often patrol and hand out fines for minor offences like cycling without lights (not to mention the spoilsport mayor Cohen being firmly against heated terraces in winter), Amsterdam hasn't turned into a no-fun zone. There are plans to appoint a special events coordinator to stream the many events held regularly. The year 2007 passed under the motto 'Amsterdam Feel The Rhythm' to promote the city through modern and classical dance and music-related shows and events. In the pipeline for 2008 and 2009 is 'Amsterdam Art City', with lots of events tuning in, and the extension or reopening of museums like the Hermitage and Rijksmuseum, currently causing chaos across the entire city. There's also a brand new, volunteer-driven 'Amsterdam Initiatief', which is exactly that: a platform for initiatives to promote creative cooperation between locals and politicians alike, to make Amsterdam an even more interesting city to live, work and party in.

Post CS.

Architecture

A skyline less ordinary.

'The colours are strong and sad, the forms symmetric, the façades kept new,' wrote Eugène Fromentin, the noted 19th-century art critic, of Amsterdam. 'We feel that it belongs to a people eager to take possession of the conquered mud.'

The treacherous, blubbery soil on which the merchants' town of Amsterdam is built meant that most attempts at monumental display were destined soon to return to their original element. It's this unforgiving land, combined with the Protestant restraint that characterised the city's early developments and the fact that there were no royals out to project monstrous egos, that ensures Amsterdam's architectural highlights are often practical places like warehouses, homes, the stock exchange and former city hall, rather than overblown palaces and castles.

Amsterdam's architectural epochs have followed the pulse of the city's prosperity. The highly decorative façades of wealthy 17th- and 18th-century merchant houses still line canals. A splurge of public spending in the affluent 1880s gave the city two of its most notable landmarks – Centraal Station and the Rijksmuseum. Rather conversely, social housing projects in the early 20th century stimulated the innovative work of the Amsterdam School, while Amsterdam's late-'80s resurgence as a financial centre and transport hub led to an economic upturn and to thickets of ambitious modern architecture on the outskirts of town and along the eastern docks.

Prime view time for Amsterdam architecture is late on a summer's afternoon, when the sun gently picks out the varying colours and the patterns of the brickwork. Then, as twilight falls, the canal houses – most of them more window than wall – light up like strings of lanterns, and you get a glimpse of the beautifully preserved, frequently opulent interiors that lie hidden behind the façades.

UNDERNEATH THE PAVING STONES

Amsterdam is built on reclaimed marshland, with a thick, soft layer of clay and peat beneath the topsoil. About 12 metres (39 feet) down is a hard band of sand, deposited 10,000 years ago during the Little Ice Age, and below that, after about five metres (16 feet) of fine sand, there is another firm layer, this one left by melting ice after the Great Ice Age. A further 25 metres (82 feet) down, through shell-filled clay and past the bones of mammoths, is a third hard layer, deposited by glaciers over 180,000 years ago.

The first Amsterdammers built their homes on muddy mounds, making the foundations from tightly packed peat. Later on, they dug trenches, filled them with fascines (thin, upright alder trunks) and built on those. And yet still the fruits of their labours sank slowly into the swamp. By the 17th century builders were using longer underground posts and were rewarded with more stable structures, but it wasn't until around 1700 that piles were driven deep enough to hit the first hard sand layer.

'Amsterdam is full of old buildings that prop each other up in higgledy-piggledy rows.'

The method of constructing foundations that subsequently developed has remained more or less the same ever since, though nowadays most piles reach the second sand level and some make the full 50-metre (164-foot) journey to the third hard layer. To begin, a double row of piles is sunk along the line of a proposed wall (since World War II, concrete has been used instead of wood). Then, a crossbeam is laid across each pair of posts, planks are fastened longitudinally on to the beams, and the wall is built on top. Occasionally piles break or rot, which is why Amsterdam is full of old buildings that teeter precariously over the street, tilt lopsidedly or prop each other up in higgledy-piggledy rows.

TRIALS BY FIRE

Early constructions in Amsterdam were timber-framed, built mainly from oak with roofs of rushes or straw. Wooden houses were relatively light and less likely to sink into the mire, but after two devastating fires (in 1421 and 1452), the authorities began stipulating that outer walls be built of brick, though wooden front gables were still permitted. In a bid to blend in, the first brick gables were shaped in imitation of their spout-shaped wooden predecessors.

But regulations were hardly necessary, for Amsterdammers took to their brick with relish. Granted, some grander 17th-century buildings were built of sandstone, while plastered façades were first seen a century later and reinforced concrete made its inevitable inroads in the 20th century. But Amsterdam is still essentially a city of brick: red brick from Leiden, yellow from Utrecht and grey from Gouda, all laid in curious formations and arranged in complicated patterns. Local architects' attachment to – and flair with – brick reached a zenith in the highly fantastical, billowing façades designed by the Amsterdam School early in the 20th century.

FORCE AND REINFORCEMENT

Only two wooden buildings remain in central Amsterdam: one (built in 1460) in the quiet courty of the **Begijnhof** (No.34, known as the Houtenhuis; *see p97*), and the other on Zeedijk. The latterof the two, **In't Aepjen** (Zeedijk 1; *see p87*), was built in the 16th century as a lodging house, getting its name from the monkeys that impecunious sailors used to leave behind as payment. Though the ground floor dates from the 19th century, the upper floors provide a clear example of how, in medieval times, each wooden storey protruded a little beyond the one below it, allowing rainwater to drip on to the street rather than run back into the body of the building. Early brick gables had to be built at an angle over the street for the same reason, though it also allowed objects to be winched to the top floors without crashing against the windows of the lower ones.

Amsterdam's oldest building, however, is the **Oude Kerk** (Old Church, Oude Kerksplein 23; *see p93*). It was begun in 1300, though only the base of the tower dates from then: over the ensuing 300 years the church, once boasting the simplest of forms, developed a barnacle crust of additional buildings, mostly in a Renaissance style with a few Gothic additions. The Gothic building in town is the **Nieuwe Kerk** (at Dam and Nieuwezijds Voorburgwal; *see p85*), still called the 'New Church' even though work on it began at the end of the 14th century.

When gunpowder first arrived in Europe in the 15th century, Amsterdammers realised that the wooden palisade that surrounded their settlement would offer scant defence, and so set about building a new stone wall. Watchtowers and gates left over from it make up a significant proportion of the city's surviving pre-17th-century architecture, though most have been altered over the years. The **Schreierstoren** (Prins Hendrikkade 94-95; *see p87*) of 1480, however, has kept its original shape, with the addition of doors, windows and a pixie-hat roof. The base of the **Munttoren** (Muntplein; *see p98*) originally formed part of the Regulierspoort, a city gate built in 1490. Another city gate from the previous decade, the St Antoniespoort

School of rock

Amsterdam's monuments are not the bland products of imperial imaginations imposing their stone wills on an unwilling populace, but rather the homes of merchants, and working men and women. And it was for the workers that the **Amsterdam School** largely built its gentler versions of Gaudí, working with a strong socialist vision during the early part of the 20th century.

While due credit can and should be given to the stonemasons who perforce had to practise non-geometrical brickwork when repairing houses slowly sinking into the mud, it was Hendrik Berlage who formed the nexus of the movement. Not only did his work strip things down, rejecting all the neo-styles that defined most 19th-century Dutch architecture, but he also provided the opportunity to experiment with new forms by coming up with **Plan Zuid**, an urban development meant to provide housing for the working classes.

Although the Amsterdam School was short-lived – it was forced to simplify within a decade when the money ran out, the Functionalism-obsessed De Stijl started to diss its more self-indulgent tendencies, and its greatest proponent, Michel de Klerk, died – examples of its work remain on view in Rivierenbuurt, Spaarndammerbuurt and Concertgebouwbuurt, plus the area around Mercantorplein. What follows, though, are some of the highlights.

Located along the waterfront, the eerie, epic **Scheepsvaarthuis** (Prins Hendrikkade 108-114) is generally considered to be the school's first work and still one of its most popular. Completed in 1916, it was the work of three major names: JM van der Mey, Piet Kramer and de Klerk. Among the hallmarks on show are obsessively complex brickwork, allegorical decorations (reflecting its use as offices for shipping companies), sculptures and wrought-iron railings seamlessly fused. It's now a hotel (*see p66* **A room with a view**).

Behind Westerpark lies the Spaarndammer neighbourhood, which sports the school's most frolicsome work and remains a huge draw for more dedicated architectural tourists. **The Ship** *(pictured)*, as the locals call it, takes up a whole block, its boundaries Zaanstraat, Hembrugstraat and Oostzaanstraat. Completed in 1919, it was originally commissioned by the Eigen Haard housing association and includes 102 homes and a school. Be sure to pop your head through the grand archway at Oostzaan 1-21, where you can view the courtyard and its central meeting hall, before visiting the **Museum Het Schip** next door. This former post office runs Amsterdam School boat and walking tours and is an exhibition space devoted to the school. You can also visit an apartment that has been returned to a state envisioned by de Klerk.

However, the school's real playground is Plan Zuid, at the border of the Pijp and Rivierenbuurt. Josef Israelkade, between 2e Van der Helststraat and Van Woustraat, is a pleasant stretch along the Amstelkanaal; enter PL Takstraat and then slowly encircle Burg Tellegenstraat, without forgetting to peek into the courtyard of **Cooperatiehof**. Socialist housing association de Dageraad (the Dawn) allowed de Klerk and Kramer to do their hallucinatory best, while employing their favourite sculptor, Hildo Krop. Kramer, incidentally, went on to design more than 200 bridges; after visiting the Plan, you shouldn't have any problem recognising his constantly unique work around the city.

It's a different story elsewhere, however. Backtrack and cross the Amstelkanaal, and then walk down Waalstraat; here you'll find later examples of the school's work, where tightening purse-strings resulted in more restraint. Nearby, on Vrijheidslaan and its side-streets, are some more classic buildings, scrubbed and renovated. End your tour at Roelof Hartplein, where a window seat at Wildschut (Roelof Hartplein 1-3, 676 8220) offers rather spectacular views of a whole range of architectural goodies. Look out for **House Lydia** (across the street at No.2), which first served as a home to Catholic girls; finished in 1927, it stands as one of the very last buildings in which wacky window shapes and odd forms were allowed.

Museum Het Schip

Spaarndammerplantsoen 140 (418 2885/ www.hetschip.nl). Bus 22. **Open** 1-5pm Wed-Sun. **Admission** €5; €2.75 over-65s; €2 students; free MK. **No credit cards.** **Map** p325 A1.

(Nieuwmarkt 4), was converted into a public weighhouse (**De Waag**) in 1617, then further refashioned to become a Guild House and finally a café-restaurant. It remains one of the city's most menacing monuments (*see p88*).

CALL OF THE CLASSICAL

A favourite 16th-century amendment to these somewhat stolid defence towers was the later addition of a sprightly steeple. Hendrick de Keyser (1565-1621) delighted in designing such spires, and it is largely his work that gives Amsterdam's present skyline a faintly oriental appearance. He added a lantern-shaped tower with an openwork orb to the Munttoren, and a spire that resembled the Oude Kerk steeple to the Montelbaanstoren (Oudeschans 2), a sea-defence tower that had been built outside the city wall. His **Zuiderkerk** (Zuiderkerkhof 72; *see p109*), built in 1603, sports a spire said to have been much admired by Christopher Wren. The appointment of De Keyser as city mason and sculptor in 1595 had given him free rein, and his buildings represent the pinnacle of the Dutch Renaissance style (also known as Dutch Mannerist) – the greatest perhaps being the **Westerkerk** (Prinsengracht 279; *see p103*), completed in 1631 as the single biggest Protestant church in the world.

Since the very beginning of the 17th century, Dutch architects had been gleaning inspiration from translations of Italian pattern books, adding lavish ornament to the classical system of proportion they found there. Brick façades were decorated with stone strapwork (scrolls and curls derived from picture frames and leatherwork). Walls were built with alternating layers of red brick and white sandstone, a style that came to be called 'bacon coursing'. The old spout-shaped gables were also replaced with cascading step-gables, often embellished with vases, escutcheons and masks (before house numbers were introduced in Amsterdam in the 18th century, ornate gables and wall plaques were a means of identifying addresses).

The façade of the Vergulde Dolphijn (Singel 140-142), designed by De Keyser in 1600 for Captain Banning Cocq (the commander of Rembrandt's *Night Watch*), is a lively mix of red brick and sandstone, while the Gecroonde Raep (Oudezijds Voorburgwal 57) has a neat step-gable, with riotous decoration featuring busts, escutcheons, shells, scrolls and volutes. De Keyser's magnificent 1617 construction that hugged the canal, the Huis Bartolotti (Herengracht 170-72, now a part of the Theater Instituut; *see p101*), is the finest example of the style.

This decorative step-gabled style was to last well into the 17th century. But gradually a stricter use of classical elements came into play;

the façade of the Bartolotti house features rows of Ionic pilasters, and it wasn't long before others followed where De Keyser had led. The Italian pattern books that had inspired the Dutch Renaissance were full of the less-ornamented designs of Greek and Roman antiquity. This appealed to many young architects who followed De Keyser, and who were to develop a more restrained, classical style. Many, such as Jacob van Campen (1595-1657), went on study tours of Italy, and returned fired with enthusiasm for the symmetric designs, simple proportions and austerity of Roman architecture. The buildings they constructed during the Golden Age are among the finest Amsterdam has to offer.

THE GOLDEN AGE

The 1600s were a boom time for builders as well as for businessmen. There was no way it could have been otherwise, as Amsterdam's population more than quadrupled during the first half of the century. Grand new canals were constructed, and wealthy merchants lined them with mansions and warehouses. Van Campen, along with fellow architects Philips Vingboons (1607-78) and his younger brother Justus (1620-98), were given the freedom to try out their ideas on a flood of new commissions.

Stately façades constructed of sandstone began to appear around Amsterdam, but brick still remained the most popular material. Philips Vingboons's Witte Huis (Herengracht 168, now part of the Theatre Instituut) has a white sandstone façade with virtually no decoration: the regular rhythm of the windows is the governing principle of the design. The house he built in 1648 at Oude Turfmarkt 145 has a brick façade adorned with three tiers of classical pilasters – Tuscan, Ionic and Doric – and festoons that were characteristic of the style. However, the crowning achievement of the period was Amsterdam's boast to the world of its mercantile supremacy and civic might: namely, the Stadhuis (City Hall) on the Dam, designed by Van Campen in 1648 and now known as the **Koninklijk Paleis** (*see p85*).

There was, however, one fundamental point of conflict between classical architecture and the requirements of northern Europe. For more practical reasons, wet northern climes required steep roofs, yet low Roman pediments and flat cornices looked odd with a steep, pointed roof behind them. The architects solved the problem by adapting the Renaissance gable, with its multiple steps, into a tall, central gable with just two steps. Later, neck-gables were built with just a tall central oblong and no steps. The right angles formed at the base of neck-gables were often filled in with decorative sandstone carvings called claw-pieces.

On very wide houses, it was possible to build a roof parallel to the street rather than end-on, making an attractive backdrop for a classical straight cornice. The giant **Trippenhuis** (Kloveniersburgwal 29; *see p89*), built by Justus Vingboons in 1662, has such a design, with a classical pediment, a frieze of cherubs and arabesques, and eight enormous Corinthian pilasters. It wasn't until the 19th century, when zinc cladding became cheaper, that flat and really low-pitched roofs became feasible.

Waterfront new media mecca **Pakhuis de Zwijger**. *See p116.*

Classic canalside architecture.

RESTRAINT VS REFURBISHMENT

Working towards the end of the 17th century, Adriaan Dortsman (1625-82) had been a strong proponent of the straight cornice. His stark designs – such as for the Van Loon house at Keizersgracht 672-674 – ushered in a style that came to be known as Restrained Dutch Classicism (or the 'Tight Style' as it would translate directly from the Dutch description: *Strakke Stijl*). It was a timely entrance. Ornament was costly and, by the beginning of the 18th century, the economic boom was over.

The merchant families were prosperous, but little new building went on. Instead, the families gave their old mansions a facelift or revamped the interiors. A number of 17th-century houses got new sandstone façades (or plastered brick ones, which were cheaper), and French taste – said to have been introduced by Daniel Marot, a French architect based in Amsterdam – became hip. As the century wore on, ornamentation regained popularity. Gables were festooned with scrolls and acanthus leaves (Louis XIV), embellished with asymmetrical rococo fripperies (Louis XV) or strung with disciplined lines of garlands (Louis XVI). The baroque grandeur of Keizersgracht 444-446, for example, is hardly Dutch at all. Straight cornices appeared even on narrow buildings, and became extraordinarily ornate: a distinct advantage, this, as it hid the steep roof that lay behind, with decorative balustrades adding to the deception. The lavish cornice at Oudezijds Voorburgwal 215-217 stands as a prime example of such construction.

REMIXING MASONRY

Fortunes slumped after 1800, and during the first part of the century more buildings were demolished than constructed. When things picked up after 1860, architects raided past eras for inspiration. Neoclassical, neo-Gothic and neo-Renaissance features were sometimes lumped together in mix-and-match style. The Krijtberg Church (Singel 446) from 1881 has a soaring neo-Gothic façade and a high, vaulted basilica, while the interior of AL van Gendt's **Hollandsche Manege** (Vondelstraat 140; *see p126*), also 1881, combines the classicism of the Spanish Riding School in Vienna with a state-of-the-art iron and glass roof.

In stark contrast, the **Concertgebouw** (Van Baerlestraat 98; *see p238*), a Van Gendt construction from 1888, borrows from the late Renaissance, with 1892's **City Archive** (Amsteldijk 67) as De Keyser revisited. But the period's most adventurous building is the Adventskerk (Keizersgracht 676), which has a classical base, Romanesque arches, Lombardian moulding and fake 17th-century lanterns.

The star architect of the period was PJH Cuypers (1827-1921), who landed commissions for both the **Rijksmuseum** (Stadhouderskade 41; *see p123*) of 1877-85 and what would become its near mirrored twin on the other side of town, Centraal Station (Stationsplein), built from 1882 to 1889. Both are in traditional red brick, adorned with Renaissance-style decoration in sandstone and gold leaf. Responding to those who thought his tastes too catholic, Cuypers – while still slipping in some of his excesses later during the construction – decided to organise each building according to a single coherent principle. This became the basis for modern Dutch architecture.

A NEW AGE DAWNS

Brick and wood – good, honest, indigenous materials – appealed to Hendrik Petrus Berlage (1856-1934), as did the possibilities offered by industrial developments in the use of steel and glass. A rationalist, he took Cuypers' ideas a step further in his belief that a building should openly express its basic structure, with a modest amount of ornament in a supportive role. Notable also was the way he collaborated with sculptors, painters and even poets throughout construction. His **Beurs van Berlage** (Beursplein; *see p84*), built between 1898 and 1903 – a mix of clean lines and functional shapes, with the mildest patterning in the brickwork – was startling at the time, and earned him the reputation of being the father of modern Dutch architecture.

'The Amsterdam School reacted against Berlage's sobriety by producing its uniquely whimsical buildings.'

Apart from the odd shop front and some well-designed café interiors, the art nouveau and art deco movements had little direct impact on Amsterdam, though they did draw a few wild flourishes: HL de Jong's **Tuschinski** cinema (Reguliersbreestraat 26; *see p210*) of 1918-21, for example, is a delightful and seductive piece of high-camp fantasy. Instead, Amsterdam architects developed a style of their own, an idiosyncratic mix of art nouveau and Old Dutch using their favourite materials: wood and brick.

This movement, known as the **Amsterdam School** (*see p38* **School of rock**), reacted against Berlage's sobriety by producing its uniquely whimsical buildings with waving, almost sculptural brickwork. Built over a reinforced concrete frame, the brick outer walls go through a complex series of pleats, bulges, folds and curls that earned them the nickname *Schortjesarchitectuur* ('Apron Architecture'). Windows can be trapezoid or parabolic; doors are carved in strong, angular shapes; brickwork is highly decorative and often polychromatic; and sculptures are abundant.

The driving force behind the school came from two young architects, Michel de Klerk (1884-1923) and Piet Kramer (1881-1961). Two commissions for social housing projects – one for Dageraad (constructed around PL Takstraat, 1921-23), one for Eigen Haard (located in the Spaarndammerbuurt, 1913-20) – allowed them to treat entire blocks as single units. Just as importantly, the pair's adventurous clients gave them freedom to express their ideas. The school also produced more rural variants suggestive of village life, such as the rather charming BT Boeyinga-designed 'garden village' Tuindorp Nieuwendam (Purmerplein, Purmerweg).

In the early 1920s a new movement emerged that was the very antithesis of the Amsterdam School – although certain crossover aspects can be observed in JF Staal's 1930-completed Wolkenkrabber (Victorieplein), the first ever residential high-rise in the country, whose name appropriately translates as 'cloudscraper'. Developing rather than reacting wildly against Berlage's ideas, the **Functionalists** believed that new building materials such as concrete and steel should not be concealed, but that the basic structure of a building should be visible. Function was supreme, ornament anathema. Their hard-edged concrete and glass boxes have much in common with the work of Frank Lloyd Wright in the USA, Le Corbusier in France and the Bauhaus in Germany. Perhaps unsurprisingly, such radical views were not shared by everyone, and the period was a turbulent one in Amsterdam's architectural history. Early Functionalist work, such as the 1930's Openluchtschool (Open-air School, Cliostraat 40), 1934's striking Cineac Cinema (Reguliersbreestraat 31) and the **Het Blauwe Theehuis** (in Vondelpark; *see p126*), has a clean-cut elegance, and the Functionalist garden suburb of Betondorp (literally, 'Concrete Village'), built between 1921 and 1926, is much more attractive than the name might suggest. But after World War II, Functionalist ideology became an excuse for more dreary, derivative, prefabricated eyesores. The urgent need for housing, coupled with town-planning theories that favoured residential satellite suburbs, led to the appearance of soulless, high-rise horrors on the edge of town, much the same as those put up elsewhere in Europe.

A change of heart during the 1970s refocused attention on making the city centre a pleasant jumble of residences, shops and offices. At the same time, a quirkier, more imaginative trend began to show itself in building design. The ING Bank (Bijlmerplein 888), inspired by anthroposophy and built in 1987 of brick, has hardly a right angle in sight. A use of bright colour, and a return to a human-sized scale, is splendidly evident in Aldo van Eyck's Hubertushuis (Plantage Middenlaan 33-35) from 1979, which seems to personify the architect's famed quotation: 'my favourite colour is the rainbow'. New façades – daringly modern, yet built to scale – began to appear between the old houses along the canals. The 1980s also saw, amid an enormous amount of controversy, the construction of what soon became known as the Stopera, a combined City Hall (Stadhuis) and opera house on Waterlooplein. The eye-catching brick and marble of the **Muziektheater** (*see p240*) is more successful than the dull oblongs that make up the City Hall.

Housing projects of the 1980s and 1990s have provided Amsterdam with some imaginative modern architecture – especially on the islands of the once derelict eastern docklands (*see p116* **Architectural reflections**). You can get a good view of some it from the roof of Renzo Piano's recognisable **Nemo** building (*see p115*).

EYES FORWARD

At the municipal information centre for planning and housing in **Zuiderkerk** (*see p109*), visitors can admire scale models of current and future developments set to transform the city within the near future. Those interested should pay a visit to NEMO's neighbour, mighty **ARCAM** – the Architectuurcentrum Amsterdam (*see p218*) – or pick up a copy of their excellent publication *25 Buildings You Should Have Seen, Amsterdam*. Bureau Monumentenzorg Amsterdam, meanwhile, provides an overview of the city's architecture from its origins to 1940 at www.bmz.amsterdam.nl. Another excellent resource is www.amsterdamarchitecture.nl.

Architectural travesties of the past have politicised the populace and referendums are held prior to many developments. Although 130,000 local votes against the construction of **IJburg** (*see p159* **United we sand**) – a new residential community being built on a series of man-made islands in the IJ-meer, just east of Amsterdam – was not enough to arrest development around this ecologically sensitive area, they did inspire the promise that *f*15 million (now around €7 million) would be invested in 'nature development'. Parts of the area will also be a showcase for the recently hyped Dutch concept of *wilde wonen* – 'wild living' – where residents get to design and build their own houses, a radical concept in this space-constrained country.

Similarly, the referendum result against the the new **Noord-Zuidlijn** (*see p29* **Due Noord**) on the Metro network didn't halt the project, but it did establish that the city needed to be considerably more diligent in its thinking. The powers that be apparently overlooked such significant details as financing, loss of revenue for shopkeepers and the potential for all this digging to bring about the speedier sinking of historical buildings above when planning the line, none of which endeared them to voters.

Now that the facelift of **Museumplein** (*see p123*) has long been completed save for the extension of the Stedelijk Museum, due to be finished in 2010, all eyes are on the eastern docks (*see p116* **Architectural reflections**). It's hoped redevelopments will turn it into a harbourfront like that of Sydney. Similarly, construction around the ArenA stadium will hopefully pump some life into the nearby architectural prison known as Bijlmermeer. This should become home to many businesses and – thanks to the recent leaps and bounds made in building vertically on bog – the single largest residential tower in the country. In 2004 a building called Living Tomorrow (www.livingtomorrow.com) also opened as a joint project of companies out to pedal their 'visionary' designs in this 'house and office of the future'.

Another hotspot currently roping in a who's who of architects is Zuidas (www.zuidas.nl) in the south. Zuidas is grouped around the World Trade Center, close to the wacky ING House (Amstelveenseweg 500); no doubt it caught your eye on the ride in from Schiphol airport.

Dutch architecture – thanks in part to notable exponents like Rem Koolhaas (who coincidentally has his rather embarrassingly ugly 1991 work, Byzantium, viewable at the north entrance to Vondelpark on Stadhouderskade) – is currently very much in vogue. Brad Pitt's own favourite architecture firm, MVRDV, who renovated the **Lloyd Hotel** (*see p72*), also helped put Dutch architecture back on the map at Hanover World Expo 2000 with their 'Dutch Big Mac', featuring such delicious ingredients as water- and windmills for electricity on the roof, a theatre on the fourth floor, an oak forest on the third floor, flowers on the second floor, and cafés, shops and a few dunes on the first floor. Yes, dunes. And in 2007 they began developing the idea of an entirely floating neighbourhood of 35,000 houses called Almere-Pampus.

International periodicals, no longer casting LA and Hong Kong as the primary visionaries, now see the 'Dutch Model' – where boundaries between building, city and landscape planning have blurred beyond recognition – as both pragmatic and futuristic. After all, ecological degradation is now a worldwide phenomenon, and the space-constrained Netherlands has long seen nature as a construct that needs to be nurtured. Expect this principle to define some of the Dutch architecture of the future – although knowing what's gone before, it'll likely be implemented in unexpected fashion. For instance, in 2004, hundreds of old steel containers were reinvented as living spaces for students at both **NDSM** (*see p262*) in the north and Houthavens in the west (where they were joined by a cruise ship to house an additional 200 penny-saving students).

Now how's that for pragmatic?

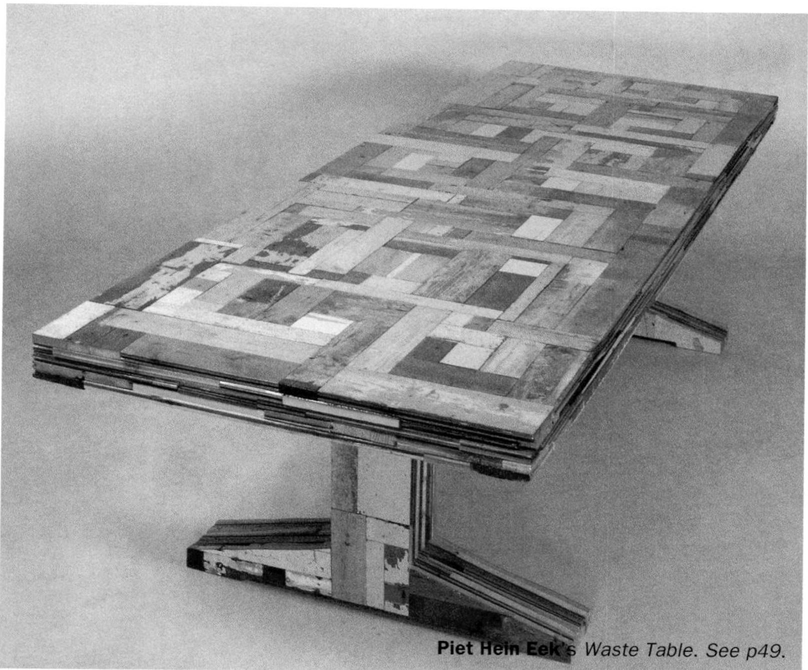
Piet Hein Eek's *Waste Table. See p49.*

Art

Rocking the cradle of modern creativity.

Ah, the Golden Age. The living was certainly sweet during those first six decades of the 17th century, starting with the founding of the East India Company (VOC) and ending when the Brits changed New Amsterdam to New York. Not only did the economic benefits of being the world's leading trading power result in the building of Amsterdam's image-defining ring of canals, but it also led to a flourishing of the arts that continues to this day. That's why it's easy to get lost in the sheer number of viewable works in Amsterdam. Sometimes it's better to simply focus on a few key works – to stop and smell the tulips, as it were.

The groundwork for this vital efflorescence was laid by a rich medieval artistic tradition under the sponsorship of the Church. Later artists, not content to labour solely *ad majorem dei gloriam*, found more 'individual' masters in the Flemings Bosch and Brueghel. Foremost among the early artists was **Jacob Cornelisz van Oostsanen** (c.1470-1533). Also known as Jacob van Amsterdam, he represents the beginning of the city's artistic tradition, and his sharpness of observation went on to become a trademark for all Dutch art that was to follow. The one painting of his that survived the Iconic Fury, *Saul and the Witch of Endor* (on display at the **Rijksmuseum**; *see p124*) tells the whole biblical story in one panoramic, almost comic book-like swoop; beginning on the left where Saul seeks advice from a strange witch about his impending battle with the Philistines, and ending in the far distance, behind the central witches' sabbath, with his 'poetic justice' of a suicide in the face of certain defeat. And all this, needless to say, at a time when witches could have used some more favourable PR.

Jacob de Wit at the Bijbels Museum.

The Baker of Eeklo (displayed at **Muiderslot**; *see p280*), another example that seemingly comes from a very much pre-modern time, hangs in the castle built for Count Floris V. Painted in the second half of the 16th century by two rather obscure painters, **Cornelis van Dalem** and **Jan van Wechelen**, the depicted tableaux – of people whose heads have been replaced by cabbages while they await the re-baking of their actual heads – will only make sense to a people weaned on medieval stories of magic windmills that could grind old people up and then churn them out young again. In this related story, bakers are slicing the heads off clients to re-bake them to specification; a cabbage – a symbol for the empty and idle head – was used to keep the spewing of blood to a minimum, although sometimes people's heads came out 'half-baked' or 'misfired'.

In contrast, painters had no problems with PR once the Golden Age proper arrived and the aspirant middle classes became hungry for art. **Rembrandt van Rijn** (1606-69) is, of course, the best known of all those who made art while the money shone. However, *The Company of Captain Frans Banning Cocq and Lieutenant Willem van Ruytenburch* (1642) didn't prove the snappiest title for a painting. *Night Watch* (on display at the Rijksmuseum), though, is far more memorable, and it's by this name that the most famous work of Rembrandt's is now known. Amsterdam's Civic Guard commissioned this group portrait to decorate their building, but rather than conjure up a neat, unexciting portrait, Rembrandt went for spontaneity, capturing a moment of lively chaos: the captain issuing an order as his men jostle to his rear. It's now the city's most popular work in what is easily its most popular museum.

Rembrandt couldn't decorate Amsterdam on his own, however, and the likes of Jan Vermeer, Frans Hals, Ferdinand Bol, Jan Steen and Jacob van Ruisdael thrived creatively and economically at this time. Delft-born **Jan Vermeer** (1632-75) painted pictures, like *The Kitchen Maid* (at the Rijksmuseum; *picture p49*), that radiate an extraordinary serenity. In his essential essay, *Vermeer in Bosnia*, Lawrence Weschler suggests that the artist's works are not depictions of actual peace, but rather hopeful invocations of a peace yet to come. For Vermeer was painting at a time when Europe was slowly emerging from the ravages of the Thirty Years' War (1618-48), and at the time peace still remained a hope rather than an expectation for the exhausted, war-weary people of Europe.

Leiden's **Jan Steen** (c.1625-79) dealt with the chaos of the times in another way – a way that got him a bad rep as a rowdy. While he did run a tavern in his own home, his patchy reputation is more likely based on the drunken folk that inhabit his paintings of everyday life. In fact, if one looks carefully at, for example, *The Merry Family* (at the Rijksmuseum; *picture p48*), Steen comes across as highly moralistic. With the inscription over the mantelpiece ('As the Old Sing, So Pipe the Young') putting literally what the painting reflects figuratively (through a plethora of symbols that help to represent the emptiness of a life spent smoking, drinking and talking about nothing), this painting offers a lesson as valid today as the day it was painted. The Alfred Hitchcock of his era, Steen himself cameos as the puffy-cheeked bagpiper.

Defying the downturn, art continued to develop after the Golden Age began to tarnish. The Jordaan-born **Jacob de Wit** (1695-1754), long before the invention of sticky glow-in-the-dark stars, brightened up many a local ceiling with cloud-dappled skies, gods and flocks of cherubs. Initially influenced by Rubens' altar work in Antwerp, De Wit developed a much more delicate and sympathetic touch that he used to great rococo effect in a number of Amsterdam buildings, among them the **Theater Instituut** (*see p101*), the attic church at the **Museum Amstelkring** (*see p93*), the Rijksmuseum, the **Pintohuis** (now a library; *see p109*) and **Huis Marseille** (*see p101*). However, his mastery of trompe l'oeil illusion, later named *witjes* after him, is probably best seen at the **Bijbels Museum** (*see p100*). One ceiling was painted for local merchant Jacob Cromhout, while the other, entitled *Apollo and the Four Seasons*, was salvaged in the 1950s from a nearby property on Herengracht. Both paintings have recently been restored to stylish and seriously lively effect (*picture p46*).

The 18th century produced Monet's inspirer, Johan Jongkind, while the 19th century offered George Breitner and Van Gogh – two artists out to reinvent the very relevance of painting in a post-photography world. The career of everyone's favourite earless genius, **Vincent Van Gogh** (1853-90), is on full display in Amsterdam, most notably at the popular **Van Gogh Museum** (*see p125*). Here you can marvel at the fact that the creator of the dark shadows of *Skull with Smoking Cigarette* went on to paint, a mere two years later in 1888, the almost kinetic *Bedroom*. By then he had settled in France's clearer light and abandoned the Vermeer-inspired subdued colouring of his earlier work to embrace the Expressionist style that would make him famous. While the self-portrait clearly reflects his restless nature, *Bedroom* depicts the very bed he would have perhaps been better off sleeping in. Just two months later he had the first of the nervous breakdowns that led finally to his suicide.

The Merry Family by **Jan Steen** (*see p47*), on display at the Rijksmuseum.

Like Van Gogh, **Isaac Israëls** (1865-1934) sought to reinvent the relevance of painting in a post-photographic age. But unlike his buddy GH Breitner, who chose to embrace this new technology by using photographs as the basis for his paintings, Israëls chose a more athletic path and achieved the 'snapshot' feel of his paintings by running around like a ninny and painting very fast. And *Two Girls by a Canal* (on display at the **Amsterdam Historisch Museum**; *see p98*) does successfully reflect an essentially Impressionist view of the city.

There's a fair case to be made that the 20th century belonged to **Piet Mondrian** (1872-1944), whose career can also be used as a one-man weathervane of modern art. He moved through Realism, Impressionism and Cubism, before embracing the purely abstract and becoming one of the true founders of **De Stijl** (*see p214*). His use of only lines and primary colour blocks inspired accusations of sterility, but actually represented a very personal and subjective quest for essence and harmony. He was also something of a wit, tilting his ultra-minimal canvas, *Composition with Two Lines* (on display at the **Stedelijk Museum**; *see p125*) – the title essentially describes it as well as any reproduction could ever hope to – by 45 degrees.

Karel Appel (1920-2001) once confounded his critics by describing his style as: 'I just mess around.' Most agree when confronted with his childish forms, bright colours and heavy strokes. But art that chose instinct over intellect is just what was needed after World War II, when **CoBrA** (*see p214*) exploded on to the scene. Today, the late New York resident is arguably the best-known modern Dutch artist. His rate of production was so huge that the Amsterdam ex-forger Geert Jan Jansen claims that Appel had verified several of Jansen's works as his own.

As we move deeper into the 21st century, the focus shifts away from painting and over towards design. **Marcel Wanders**' 1997-produced *Knotted Chair* could not be more different from that other iconic Dutch chair of the 20th century: the highly geometric *Red-Blue Chair* (1918-23) by De Stijl guy **Gerrit Rietveld**. But *Knotted Chair* – which reinvents the frumpy hippy art of macramé with the aid of hi-tech epoxy – came to represent the work of a new vanguard of local designers (*see p189*

The Kitchen Maid by **Jan Vermeer** (*see p47*), also at the Rijksmuseum.

Design driven), who seek to encapsulate a uniquely Dutch aesthetic with a fusion of wit, hipness and function – also to be witnessed in **Piet Hein Eek**'s *Waste Table* (*photo p45*).

Since the Dutch are as well famed for their business acumen as their dykes, this no doubt leads the less scrupulous to a somewhat free and easy attitude towards a work's provenance. An estimated 30 per cent of the world art market consists of forgeries, and even the most famous institutions can be caught out. Back in 1938 the Rijksmuseum, to its eventual relief, lost a bidding war for a Vermeer to Rotterdam's Boijmans Van Beuningen (*see p290*), who bought it for a then astronomical *f*550,000 (€224,000). Proof, if it were needed, that desire has the ability to blind – for how on earth else could Hans van Meegeren's heavy-handed *De Emmaüsgangers* be mistaken for a Vermeer? It was only in 1945, when the forger was facing a traitor's death penalty for selling the Nazis another 'Vermeer', that Van Meegeren admitted both were forgeries, painted to avenge himself on a critic's poor reviews. That self-same critic had fallen for the forgeries, although it's highly unlikely that the satisfaction of making his arch nemesis face his own incompetence was sufficient compensation for Van Meegeren's subsequent jail term: the forger actually died in 1947 while serving out his sentence.

But despite this lapse you can generally trust the provenance of the art in Amsterdam's museums. And to miss out on the heritage on show would be a sin comparable to anything you might contemplate doing over in the Red Light District. To pass up on Amsterdam's art offerings is like skipping the Guinness on a visit to Dublin. So open your eyes to sensual bliss. With so many 'names' coming from such a tiny country, one cannot help wonder if the Netherlands' battle with the sea is really all about creating wall-space for the pictures. And in Amsterdam, the best of five centuries is here waiting for you to absorb: from the more traditional artistic treasures on display at the Rijksmuseum, **Museum van Loon** (*see p107*) and Museum Amstelkring through to the zanily modern, as best experienced at the Stedelijk or **Droog Design** (*see p189* **Design driven**), or by simply keeping your eyes open when walking around town. After all, Amsterdam's art is on display on more than just its walls.

Sex & Drugs

What happens in Amsterdam stays in Amsterdam.

It's pragmatism at its finest: what better way to stamp out crime than by legalising it? Granted, the story of Amsterdam's very liberal attitudes isn't quite so straightforward, but here's a fact known the world over: this city does sex and drugs with fewer hang-ups than anywhere else on the planet. It's little wonder that the visitors keep sliding in like iron filings to a magnet.

Some elements among local authorities would prefer to reinvent Amsterdam as a business capital and attract a higher-minded breed of tourist (read: people with money). However, if you ask most non-residents the first words that come to mind when they hear 'Amsterdam', their answers will usually be 'Red Light District' or 'coffeeshops'. And since the city has such forward-thinking policies on sex and drugs, who can really blame them?

Of course, we wouldn't want you to forget the other 95 per cent of the guide to this most multi-faceted city – but we'd be shirking our duty if we didn't tell you the history behind the hundreds of naked ladies in their neon-framed windows, or the easy availability of joints the size of Oklahoma. The fun starts here.

Sex

What is it about travel that makes people so frisky? Even if you've never had a one-night stand with a hotel bartender, nor applied for membership of the Mile High Club, you can't deny that strange places inspire a sense of adventure. However, the legal consequences of, say, hiring a prostitute vary from country to country: most national governments prohibit prostitution but then selectively police the more public levels of the sex industry, or hand out licences to escort agencies and dance clubs, or create 'special zones' where men can let off steam without getting arrested. But the Netherlands has chosen a more open approach.

The city's history of prostitution dates from its 13th-century roots. Amsterdam has always resisted efforts to banish sex as an industry, and eventually the Dutch came to accept the advantages of a more pragmatic approach. Although working as a prostitute has been completely legal here since 1911, it was not until 2000 that the ban on brothels was lifted, thus formally permitting window and brothel sex-work. But with the legalisation of brothels came bureaucratisation: now all sex workers must have an EU passport, and a 200-page rule book was introduced to govern the business of selling sexual services, covering everything from fire escapes to the appropriate length of a prostitute's fingernails.

By the 15th century, the city was a major port attracting money, merchants and sailors – or, more specifically, merchants and sailors with money – which in turn increased the amount of sex for sale. Yet it wasn't only randy men who influenced the industry's growth, but also the fact that many local women, separated from their seafaring husbands for months on end, were left with little or no other means to sustain themselves or their children. Prostitution was one of the few money-making options available.

In the Middle Ages, prostitutes were permitted to work in one of the brothels located on what is now Damstraat. Keeping a whorehouse was then the exclusive privilege of the city's sheriff, and women found working elsewhere in the city were forcibly marched back to said sheriff to the 'sound of drums and flutes'. But in the 15th century prostitutes began working the area around Zeedijk, and by the 17th century some were walking through the Old Side with red lanterns to advertise their profession. Soon after, enterprising women turned to advertising themselves in the windows of their own homes, or from front-facing rooms rented from other homeowners; it's from this practice that today's rather more garish window trade is descended.

More 'traditional' methods of conducting the business still apply, but it's the red-lit windows that have earned Amsterdam its notoriety as a major sex capital. And no matter how prepared you think you are, you'll be taken aback the first time you see street after street of huge picture windows, each decorated with red velvet-effect soft furnishings, each sparingly lit, and each dominated by a nearly-naked woman. The women are in your face, obliging you to notice them. They come in all shapes, sizes, skin tones and ages. Not all of them look terribly excited to be there, but neither would you if your job involved standing up for hours and answering a string of stupid questions. Many of the women pass the time between clients by gossiping with colleagues, dancing and cavorting or teasing

The **Red Light District**.

Questionable behaviour

Founded in 1994 by ex-prostitute Mariska Majoor, the **Prostitution Information Centre** (**PIC**, *pic* also being slang for 'dick') is right by the Oude Kerk and open to absolutely everyone out to expand their understanding of prostitutes and prostitution. PIC supports its efforts through the sale of print information and books relating to prostitution, PIC and Red Light District souvenirs, and donations. Groups can also arrange for a lecture session or private walking tour. Staff will do their very best to answer all your questions – although check first that they're not covered below.

PIC

Enge Kerk Steeg 3 (420 7328/www.pic-amsterdam.com). Tram 4, 9, 16, 24, 25, 26. **Open** noon-7pm Tue-Sat. **Map** p326 D2.

PIC Quiz

1. How do I negotiate a date with a prostitute?
2. How much will it cost?
3. Are all the prostitutes legally required to have medical checks for STDs?
4. Who controls the girls?
5. Has legalisation made working conditions better for prostitutes?

Answers

1. Be polite and make clear arrangements about your desires, the duration and fee.
2. Expect to pay in the region of €35 to €50 for around 20 minutes.
3. While medical checks are not required by law, prostitutes do visit local clinics and will insist upon condom use.
4. Window workers are self-employed; they decide for themselves who they will see and what they will do with clients.
5. Legalisation sees prostitution as work and thereby allows prostitutes to demand better working conditions, healthcare and benefits for their efforts.

passers-by. If you see someone who takes your fancy, talk to her politely and you'll be inside before you can say 'I love Amsterdam'.

Amsterdam's best-known Red Light District spreads out around Oudezijds Voorburgwal and Oudezijds Achterburgwal canals, and the famous windows alternate with the butcher, the baker and the candlestick maker. Two smaller, less heralded Red Light areas sit on the New Side (between Kattengat and Lijnbaanssteeg) and in the Pijp (Ruysdaelkade, from Albert Cuypstraat to 1e Jan Steenstraat).

What you see is not all you get; there are loads of other options to choose from. A quick scan of the internet or *Gouden Gids* (Yellow Pages) will lead you to escort services, professional S&M services, sex clubs, striptease clubs, swingers' clubs, brothels, live sex shows, sex services for gay men, peep shows, sex cinemas and more. The only thing that is not permitted is street prostitution. Although a *tippelzone* (tolerated 'walking zone') was set up on Theemsweg – complete with private parking stalls, police security and prostitute support services – the city elected to close it in December 2003, since the prostitutes it was intended for were using it less. Some street prostitution still occurs, most notoriously behind Centraal Station.

In the game of commercial sex, the big losers are female customers. Sorry, gals: your options are limited. There are a few escort services that will supply male or female prostitutes for you, and you may find a window prostitute who is happy to get busy with a woman – though this is more likely to happen if you visit her with your male partner in tow. Another option for the adventurous is to visit a swingers' club; they generally have an overabundance of single men looking for a free frolic. You could also make a point of visiting the most female-friendly sex shop in Amsterdam, **Female & Partners** (*see p193*), to pick up a little consolation gift for yourself (though remember, batteries are rarely included). For visitors who want to look but not touch, a visit to a live sex show, at **Casa Rosso** (*see p91*) for instance, might inspire an evening of more private and personal fun elsewhere.

The most unique quality about the Red Light District is its integration into the Old Centre neighbourhood (for more, *see p87*). Police patrol the area with just enough visibility to dissuade most troublemakers. CCTV cameras keep a close eye on street activity and every window is equipped with an emergency alarm system that the woman behind it can activate if necessary. While the majority of clients, almost half of whom are locals, have no interest at all in harming a prostitute, these safeguards give workers a much-neeeded feeling of reassurance. One misdemeanour that's guaranteed to cause trouble is taking a photo of a window prostitute. They're not zoo animals: if you really need a picture of an Amsterdam window gal, some of the tourist shops sell suitable postcards.

The subject of prostitution always raises concerns about STDs. Sex workers take their healthcare seriously and will insist on using a condom – and clients should do likewise. There are no laws requiring prostitutes to have check-ups but there's an STD clinic in the Old Side's Red Light District where sex workers can go anonymously for free check-ups. There's also a prostitute rights organisation, De Rode Draad (the Red Thread), and a sex workers' union, Vakwerk. You can find out about both over at the **Prostitution Information Centre** (*see p52* **Questionable behaviour**).

That said, the situation is by no means perfect. 2000's reforms were largely aimed at reducing the number of illegal immigrants in prostitution, but this isn't the main problem: only a minority of prostitutes have no legal status. There are still exploitative situations involving coercion, parasitic and controlling 'boyfriends', and problems related to substance abuse. The most positive effect of the legal changes has been to legitimise prostitution as a profession, which means that sex workers have access to social services and can legitimately band together to improve their working conditions. However, the stigma still remains. Even in the most ideal circumstances it's still difficult for prostitutes to balance work and private lives. Furthermore, prostitutes have problems when trying to get bank accounts, mortgages and insurance, despite being liable for taxes and generating an estimated €450 million a year.

The locals' liberal, grown-up attitudes certainly merit applause, and the methods they've employed to deal with the inevitability of a sex industry have arguably resulted in a better deal for both customer and sex worker. Visit with an open mind, but don't be surprised if Amsterdam's fabled Red Light District falls short of at least some of the hype.

Drugs

It's a uniquely surreal experience from the first. You strut right in through the front door of the coffeeshop, engage in a simple transaction and then smoke the sweet smoke. You soon strut out through the front door, giggly, wasted and – most importantly, for you have done no wrong – paranoia-free. Welcome to the Netherlands.

A large part of the country's image has been defined by its apparently lax attitude towards drugs. But this is misleading: soft drugs are still only semi-legal. Simply put, the famously pragmatic Dutch began to put drug laws into perspective back in the early 1970s. Swamped with heroin and repeatedly reminded by the ex-Provos and hippies then entering mainstream politics of the relatively benign nature of pot, the fight against wimpy drugs came to be seen as a ludicrous waste of time and money.

And so, in 1976, a vaguely worded law was passed to make a distinction between hard and soft drugs, effectively separating their markets from each other's influence and allowing the use and sale of small amounts of soft drugs under 30 grams (one ounce). The 'front door' of the then embryonic 'coffeeshop' was now legal, although the 'back door', where produce arrived by the kilo, looked out on an illegal distribution system. While the coffeeshop owner now deals on the condoned side of this economy and can redirect his profits into other legal ventures (as many do, investing in hotels and nightclubs), and while suppliers experience the profitability of being illegal, the couriers who provide the link and run the risks without high returns remain in a legal limbo where such clichés as 'Kafkaesque' or 'Catch 22' are very real.

And yet the wobbly system has worked. Time passed without the increase in soft drug use that doomsayers expected. The coffeeshop became a part of the Amsterdam streetscape. And the concerted efforts against hard-drug use – less through law enforcement and more via education, methadone programmes, needle exchanges, drop-in shoot-up centres and also counselling – have resulted in one of the lowest junkie populations in the world. Junkies may have more street visibility here than in other European cities, but that's more to do with an openness that lets junkies dare to be seen.

Moves towards a total legalisation of soft drugs have always been thwarted by a variety of factors: pressure from fellow EU members (France – which, funnily enough, is Holland's pipeline for heroin – and more recently Germany); tension between the government and coffeeshop owners (who have come to enjoy testing the boundaries of the vague laws); and the lack of a local supply. This last factor, though, was weakened by the 'green wave' of the early '90s, when the US-designed skunk blew over and was found to grow very nicely under artificial light; its descendants are the basis for the near-infinite variety of Nederweeds. Technology has even produced viable hash from the harvest; foreign suppliers need no longer be involved.

After years of derision, many countries are now waking up to the advantages of Dutch policies. Vancouver is now cited as the 'New Amsterdam', especially since British Columbian buds have started to become winners at the annual Cannabis Cup. So you might think it would be a good time for the Netherlands to fully legalise the growth, distribution and use of soft drugs. But as it turns out, the opposite seems to be happening. A conservative stream in government began to crack down on home-growing, allowing only the cultivation of four plants at a time and banning the use of artificial light. Tighter restrictions also caused a decline in the number of coffeeshops: from 1,200 in 1997 to 729 in 2005. Amsterdam, home to about 20 per cent of these, now won't let any new coffeeshops open, and in 2007 a new law forced coffeeshops that also sold alcohol to choose between dope and booze.

There's an obvious difference between the locals' blasé attitude and how visitors behave. The majority of Amsterdammers treat soft drugs as just something else to do. Dope tourists, though, hit the coffeeshops with wide-eyed, giggling greed, then face truly maddening trips and subsequently painful comedowns when they belatedly realise that Dutch drugs are far stronger and sneakier than those they're used to at home.

The easy availability of soft drugs has produced its own brand of tourist: those who come to the city merely to get so stoned they can't remember a thing about it. A full six per cent of visitors cite coffeeshops as the reason they come here (with 25 per cent of all visitors finding time to at least visit one of them). And it's this six per cent that has led the authorities to look upon their city's most famous law with ambivalence. On the one hand, the coffeeshops attract many visitors to the city. On the other, the kind of visitors the law attracts are, not to put too fine a point on it, hardly the kind of tourists the authorities welcome with open arms. Two-thirds of ambulances called for drug problems are for tourists.

Although many of Amsterdam's weekend funseekers only blight the Red Light District, the authorities' displeasure is less a matter of principle than a question of economics. Such visitors show up on Friday, spend three days getting wasted on big spliffs, spacecake and Amstel, then go home on Monday having made a negligible contribution to the Dutch GNP.

Then there's the issue of organised crime, something no one is in a position to ignore. Every country has it in some form, of course, but the gangs in the Netherlands are able to go about their drug-running businesses with more ease than the government would like. Worse still, many Dutch gangs are believed to be freely trafficking drugs both hard and soft all over Europe, a fact that hasn't exactly endeared the Netherlands to its neighbours.

Yet, at the same time, the policy works. And before the world has caught up, the Dutch have moved on: in fact, since 1998 the pleasure-seeking public has become less hedonistic, smoking fewer joints (from 28 per cent to 19 per cent), dropping less ecstasy (from 27 per cent to eight per cent) and snorting less coke (ten per cent to three per cent). So you might want to put a bit of that in your pipe and smoke it.

NDSM. *See p56.*

The Creative City

There must be something in the water.

It was all much simpler in the '70s. To entice people to visit Amsterdam all you had to do was what KLM did: put out some posters cajoling its long-haired American targets to come 'Sleep in Hippie Park'. Word of mouth did the rest. And before that there was the tourist board's 'Get In Touch With The Dutch' campaign during the 1960s – surely a slogan from a more innocent period. Compared to that halcyon era, the boom years of the 1990s were surely the most boring of times, if you take their yawn-inducing slogans ('Capital of Inspiration' and 'Business Gateway to Europe') as typical of the mindset.

IN SEARCH OF A SLOGAN

But now it's the 21st century, and every city needs its own marketing campaign to establish its advantages over every other city on the planet. 'City marketing' is the rather dubious science that might never have been called into existence save for the stratospheric success of the ubiquitous 'I ♥ NY' logo. Now it seems we are all doomed to adopt our own versions of the slogan, whatever we think of our place of residence. So in 2004, the city of Amsterdam paid the usually inspired advertising bureau KesselsKramer to work their glamorous magic and come up with a slogan that would reflect Amsterdam as a 'creative city' – and they came up with 'I amsterdam'.

Unfortunately, a year earlier, the designer Vanessa van Dam had already invented an 'I amsterdammer' logo with a similar accent on 'I am'. This logo even graced 120,000 postcards – it was sort of hard to miss. It thus seemed only fair that Van Dam was awarded a €20,000 settlement from the city. So almost before it got off the mark, the city's 'I amsterdam' campaign made a big creative oopsie. (Let's hope Van Dam will not get sued in turn by the estate of that other local boy René Descartes, who is widely known to have remarked: 'I think, therefore I amsterdam'. But at least no one is accusing anyone of a crime. Like those other inspired plays on the city's name, 'Amsterdamned' and the even better 'Amsterdamaged', 'I amsterdam' is so obvious that we can assume that the slogan has occurred independently in many different minds on many different occasions. The only really annoying thing about the campaign is that it's trying to peddle the idea that the logo will not only attract outside business but also work to unify regular Amsterdammers. This is solidly contradicted whenever an actual Dutchie tries to say 'I amsterdam' out loud. Their accent makes them stutter out something that sounds far more like 'I hamster am', as though they were arrogant rodents rather than a legion of proud Amsterdammers.

Okay, so it's easy to mock. We admit that marketing a city can't be easy. There must be more to it than producing a catchy T-shirt slogan. But just what other choices were there? Well, it could be argued that 'Amsterdamned' and 'Amsterdamaged' are in fact much better ambassadors for the city. After all, today's visiting army of dopeheads may hold the city's economic future in their rather shaky hands.

It's happened before: sentimental (and rich) ex-hippies, looking for somewhere to recover their lost youths and salve their consciences, were the ones who invested in the place during the booming 1990s. They figured it would be a good excuse to come and visit a few times a year in the hopes of recreating those perfect relaxed coffeeshop moments from decades past.

Thinking of which, isn't being relaxed one of the things that Amsterdam has always been famous for? And neither the campaign nor the brouhaha surrounding it have contributed to this obvious brand benefit. Shame on them.

HOW CREATIVE IS AMSTERDAM?

This town has a lot of nostalgists weeping for those '80s and '90s salad days when cultural squats like Silo and Vrieshuis Amerika were the coolest, edgiest and most frolicsome things around. But while no one likes a whiner, when the powers-that-be closed these cultural beehives in order to make Amsterdam the 'Business Gateway to Europe', it was soon seen to be a monumental blunder in a city defined by its artistic traditions. So the city bureaucrats, in an effort to claw back lost prestige and emigrating artists, did what all such functionaries do and threw money at the problem, creating non-squat squats called *broedplaatsen* (breeding grounds).

Don't worry if it all gets confusing: the world of Amstersquats is nothing if not divided into umpteen different categories. In addition to the *broedplaatsen* are proper squats (reappropriated buildings that had been left empty for more than a year); 'anti-squats' (those buildings with temporary residents paying no rent at all so that squatters can't squat in them); and 'bought squats' (old squats that were then sold cheaply by the city to their inhabitants – like **Vrankrijk** (Spuistraat 216, www.vrankrijk.org), which is still a hotbed of cheap beer and radical politics.

It seems those places that began as bona fide squats are the ones making the crossover most efficiently. The former film academy **OT301** (*see p213*) is totally happening, as is former shipping yard art complex **NDSM** (*see p114* and *p262*). And although not actually itself a *broedplaats*, **Westergasfabriek** (*see p263*) is street-smart due to its reclaimed industrial cred.

Meanwhile, the city's cultural players continue to pump up the image of Amsterdam as ground zero for creative industries. Not only are there excellent schools and a range of innovative design firms (*see p214*), but its local creative advertising agencies like **KesselsKramer**, **180** and **Strawberryfrog** are kicking ass on a global level with some seriously stunning work. Meanwhile, the awesome **Pakhuis de Zwijger** (Piet Heinkade 179, 788 4444, www.zwijger.nl) opened in 2006 as a hub bringing together a range of cutting-edge institutions complete with an inspiring programme of discussions and exhibitions. That very same year saw the arrival of the 'cross media week' **PICNIC** (www.picnicnetwork.org), an annual congress in September of shows, meetings, readings, seminars and conferences around the latest developments in media, technology, art, science and entertainment. It was an immediate success with over 5,000 visitors, and the 2007 edition will feature the esteemed likes of David Silverman, director of *The Simpsons Movie*, and Neil Gershenfeld from MIT's Centre for Atoms & Bits. So it's safe to say that Amsterdam as 'creative city' is no mere empty hype.

ONE BIG GALLERY

There's certainly a case to be made that this fine city is one huge gallery. With a long tradition of all-new construction projects having to dedicate a percentage of their costs to public art, one can hardly walk a metre without bumping into some kind of creative endeavour. And while not all attempts are successful (please someone start a petition to remove the garishly coloured geometric stacks acting as lighting poles that line the Damrak), one cannot deny the beauty of things like Hans van Houwelingen's bronze iguanas frolicking in the grass around Kleine Gartmanplantsoen; Atelier Van Lieshout's breast-appended houseboat floating in the Langer Vonder in Amsterdam Noord; the stained glass of cartoonist Joost Swarte in the buildings on the east of Marnixstraat's northern end; and Rombout & Droste's insane walking bridges on Java-eiland (*see p116* **Architectural reflections**). All work together to make the urban landscape of Amsterdam a much richer place indeed.

Where to Stay

Features

Where to Stay

With options from cosy to colossal, Amsterdam is a truly accommodating city.

Three words sum up the latest developments on the Amsterdam accommodation front: big, big, big. The key hotel opening of the decade – if not century – is the **Grand Hôtel Amrâth Amsterdam** in the Scheepvaarthuis (*see p66* **Jewel in the chain**), a landmark rivalling the **Krasnapolsky** (*see p59*) and **Amstel** (*see p67*) in the swish stakes. Another newcomer is the modern, multi-storey **Mövenpick** (*see p72*), which recently opened in the increasingly fashionable eastern docklands. In that same area, work has also begun on what will be the biggest hotel in the country: a part of the groovy British City Inn chain, it will have no fewer than 550 rooms and is due to open in 2010.

For the visitor, this translates into oodles of choice at the top end of the market. For those on smaller budgets, it's the same old same old story: Amsterdam is not the place to come for a bargain break. Because of limited space in the city, hotel rooms tend to be small, and you don't get that much bang for your buck. The more canny hoteliers generally capitalise on rooms with canal views, charging (sometimes hefty) supplements just for a look at the very thing that makes Amsterdam unique. Also, you will often find that there is little price difference between a hotel in the thick of things and one in the sticks; the good news is that in a city this compact, nowhere is really that far flung.

Unless you are staying in a hotel on the very top (or bottom) rung – where you'll inevitably have to fork out extra – breakfast is usually included in the room price and, wherever you stay, it will be a filling, help-yourself affair based around cheese, meat, eggs and bread. Another hidden cost to look out for is city tax, charged at a rate of five per cent: there is no obligation to include it in the advertised price, so it may be lumped on top of your final bill.

It's advisable to book way in advance: good early deals can be had at www.bookings.nl. If you don't book independently, the Dutch Reservations Centre will do so for you by phone (0299 689144, 8.30am-5.30pm, message service out of hours) or online (www.hotelres.nl). If you turn up without arranging accommodation, the Amsterdam Tourist Board (VVV) will find a room for a small fee; *see p312* for branches.

The best Hotels

For classical music and food lovers
Hotel Pulitzer. *See p63.*

For late getaways or early arrivals
Ibis Amsterdam Centre. *See p62.*

For eastern docklands exploration
Mövenpick Amsterdam City Centre. *See p72.*

For a boutique break
Bilderberg Jan Luyken. *See p73.*

For super-stylish bed and breakfast
Kamer01. *See p77.*

For getting stoned and staggering into bed
Greenhouse Effect. *See p62.*

For sightings of Brangelina
Inter-Continental Amstel Amsterdam. *See p67.*

Hotels

The Old Centre

Deluxe

The Grand

Oudezijds Voorburgwal 197, 1012 EX (555 3111/ www.thegrand.nl). Tram 4, 9, 14, 16, 24, 25. **Rates** €400-€560 single/double; €590-€1,895 suite. **Credit** AmEx, DC, MC, V. **Map** p326 D3 ❶

Steeped in centuries of history, this hotel began life as a staging post for royals in the Golden Age, and has also been Amsterdam's town hall. Near the epicentre of the Red Light District, guests nevertheless

❶ Green numbers given in this chapter correspond to the locations of individual hotels as marked on the street maps. *See pp325-332.*

feel like they've been whisked a million miles away from the risqué surroundings the moment they step into the luxurious courtyard. Rooms are spacious and airy thanks to huge windows; bathrooms are art deco-style and embellished with Roger & Gallet smellies, and the suites range from junior to royal. On-site facilities include a spa, pool and an Albert Roux restaurant. No bargain breaks here; there are nevertheless luxury deals like the Dream Package, which includes champagne, dinner and use of the spa. Sunday brunch (€45) in the Council Chamber is an indulgent treat for guests and non-guests alike.
Bar. Business centre. Gym. Internet (wireless €14.95/ 3hr, €19.95/24hr; high-speed €12.50/hr, €25/24hr; business centre free). No-smoking rooms. Parking (€6/hr; €35/night). Restaurant. Spa. Pool (1 indoor). Room service.

Grand Hotel Krasnapolsky

Dam 9, 1012 JS (554 9111/www.nh-hotels.com). Tram 1, 2, 4, 5, 9, 13, 14, 16, 17, 24, 25. **Rates** €250-€320 single/double; €450-€850 suite; €60 extra bed. **Credit** AmEx, DC, MC, V. **Map** p326 D3 ❷
Amsterdam's best-known hotel is slam-dunk in the middle of the action, directly opposite the Royal Palace, which it challenges in terms of looks, grace and glamour. Facilities here, unsurprisingly, are excellent: there are several restaurants and bars, a ballroom, a beauty salon, and the spectacular glass Winter Garden (a listed monument) is open to non-guests for weekend brunch. Accommodation ranges from the untrammelled indulgence of the Tower Suite to cheaper, compact rooms at the rear, which is what you'll end up with if you book one of the many bargain deals. The least expensive rooms come without baths, but are equipped with super-invigorating multi-head showers.
Bars (2). Business centre. Concierge. Disabled-adapted room. Gym. Internet (wireless, prices vary between suppliers; business centre €10/30min). Lift. No-smoking floors. Parking (€3.75/hr, €45/ 24hr). Restaurant. Room service. TV: pay movies.

Hotel de l'Europe

Nieuwe Doelenstraat 2-8, 1012 CP (531 1777/ www.leurope.nl). Tram 4, 9, 14, 16, 24, 25. **Rates** €325 single; €400 double; €510-€995 suite. **Credit** AmEx, DC, MC, V. **Map** p330 D4 ❸
A luxury landmark with fabulous views across the Amstel, this is the place to head for an indulgent splurge or a honeymoon hideaway. As should be expected at these prices, every detail is taken care of – bathrooms are made of marble, toiletries are by Bulgari, and all rooms are supplied with fruit and mineral water. The bridal suite has a four-poster bed and an in-room Jacuzzi big enough for two. The hotel is one of the few in Amsterdam to boast a pool, and restaurant Excelsior is highly rated.
Bar. Business centre. Concierge. Gym. Internet (wireless, €27/24hr). No-smoking rooms. Parking (€5.50/hr, €84/24hr). Restaurants (3). Room service. Pool (1 indoor). TV: pay movies.

Design dining in the Winter Garden of the **Grand Hotel Krasnapolsky**.

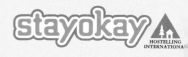

Expensive

Barbizon Palace

Prins Hendrikkade 59-72, 1012 AD (556 4564/www.nh-hotels.com). Tram 1, 2, 4, 5, 9, 13, 14, 16, 17, 24, 25. **Rates** €179 single; €234-€259 double; €450-€875 suite. **Credit** AmEx, DC, MC, V. **Map** p326 D2 ❹

A flash branch of the reliable, homegrown NH chain, the Barbizon is right opposite Centraal Station, so ideal if you want to hop off the train laden with luggage. The public parts of the hotel are all decked out in nice, sleek monochrome, which makes the rooms themselves (decorated in upmarket hotel bland and beige) a bit disappointing. The on-site facilities, however, could never be accused of being run-of-the-mill. They include a meeting room in the 15th-century St Olof Chapel and the superb Michelin-starred restaurant Vermeer for the financially limber diner.

Bar. Business centre. Gym. Internet (wireless, €10/hr, €17/2hr; high-speed, €10/hr, €17/2hr). No-smoking rooms. Parking (€45/24hr). Restaurant. Room service.

Renaissance Amsterdam

Kattengat 1, 1012 SZ (621 2223/www.marriott.com). Tram 1, 2, 4, 5, 9, 13, 14, 16, 17, 24, 25. **Rates** €159 single; €159-€269 double. **Credit** AmEx, DC, MC, V. **Map** p326 C2 ❺

An smart option for exploring the Bohemian charms of nearby Harlemmerstraat and Jordaan areas, this 400-roomed place compensates for its flowery décor with top-end hotel luxuries like in-house films, interactive videos and even Playstations, making it a good bet for flush families with recalcitrant kids. There's also a babysitting service.

Bar. Business centre. Gym. Internet (wireless, €19.95/24hr). Parking (€36/24hr). Restaurant. Room service. TV: pay movies.

Swissotel

Damrak 96, 1012 LP (522 3000/www.amsterdam.swissotel.com). Tram 1, 2, 4, 5, 9, 13, 14, 16, 17, 24, 25. **Rates** €185-€290 double; €315-€390 suite. **Credit** AmEx, DC, MC, V. **Map** p326 D3 ❻

One of the best looking of the international chains, this hotel is geared firmly towards the business market – some rooms come with LAN and Wi-Fi internet and multiple phonelines – but it's still a good destination for holidaymakers. First of all, it's right next to Dam Square and opposite department store De Bijenkorf (*see p173*). Secondly, all rooms come with big beds, on-demand film and music and are soundproofed against the hullabaloo outside. Fork out for pricier rooms and you get espresso machines and some swish design; suites overlook the square.

Bar. Business centre. Disabled-adapted rooms. Gym. Internet (wireless, €22/24hr; high-speed, €15/24hr). Restaurant. Room service. TV: pay movies.

Victoria

Damrak 1-5, 1012 LG (623 4255/www.parkplaza.com/amsterdamnl_victoria). Tram 1, 2, 4, 5, 9, 13, 14, 16, 17, 24, 25. **Rates** €150-€199 double; €250-€290 suite. **Credit** AmEx, DC, MC, V. **Map** p326 D2 ❼

A stalwart of the city hotel scene, the Victoria has recently been spruced up; the public areas (including lobby and bar) of this 300-roomed hotel opposite Centraal Station now look very dapper indeed, decked out in browns, creams and reds. Rooms themselves are of a good size, and come with all the expected trappings. A big plus is the excellent health club and pool, both open to non-guests for a fee.

Bars (2). Business centre. Concierge. Gym. Disabled-adapted rooms. Internet (€5.25/15min, 15c/min thereafter, €10/hr, €17/24hr). No-smoking floors. Restaurants (2). Spa. Pool (1 indoor). Room service.

Moderate

Hotel des Arts

Rokin 154-156, 1012 LE (620 1558/www.hoteldesarts.nl). Tram 4, 9, 14, 16, 24, 25. **Rates** €89-€108 single; €98-€158 double; €148-€177 triple; €176-€188 quad; €180-€215 quintuple. **Credit** AmEx, DC, MC, V. **Map** p330 D4 ❽

A cosy hotel that exudes a touch of faded glamour. Rooms – though a touch dark – are nicely decorated with clunky, polished period furniture and chandeliers; most of them are spacious and are geared towards use by groups and families, though there are also a couple of smaller ones if needed. It's well positioned near the main shopping street and most sights are within walking distance.

Internet (wireless, €5/hr).

Nova

Nieuwezijds Voorburgwal 276, 1012 RD (623 0066/www.novahotel.nl). Tram 1, 2, 5. **Rates** €83-€113 single; €102-€155 double; €185-€192 triple; €220-€225 quad. **Credit** AmEx, DC, MC, V. **Map** p326 D3 ❾

A reliable presence among the city's hotels, the rooms here – arranged across five town houses – are comfortable, plainly furnished yet good looking in an Ikea kind of way, and smell fresh as daisies since the place went totally non-smoking in February 2007. Bathrooms, though, can be a bit of a tight squeeze. Nova is also handily located for the Nieuwezijds nightlife, as well as all of the cultural sights. For longer stays, they rent apartments on Nicolaas Maesstraat 72, near Museumplein.

No smoking throughout. Internet (wireless, €5.95/hr).

Residence le Coin

Nieuwe Doelenstraat 5, 1012 CP (524 6800/www.lecoin.nl). Tram 4, 9, 14, 16, 24, 25. **Rates** €112 single; €132-€147 double; €220 quad; €35 extra bed. **Credit** AmEx, DC, MC, V. **Map** p326 D3 ❿

On a quiet, café-lined street between the Old Centre and the main shopping district, this medium-sized hotel arranged across seven buildings has spacious, very stylish rooms in muted colours with minimal fussy extras. They are drenched in light thanks to big windows. Furniture is a classy mix of old and new, with designer chairs and lots of shiny wood; attic rooms are particularly full of character. Many rooms come equipped with kitchenettes.

Internet (wireless, €5/hr).

Flying Pig Downtown.

RHO Hotel

Nes 5-23, 1012 KC (620 7371/www.rhohotel.nl). Tram 1, 2, 4, 5, 9, 13, 14, 16, 17, 24, 25. **Rates** €80-€110 single; €99-€165 double; €130-€195 triple. **Credit** AmEx, MC, V. **Map** p326 D3 11

If the budget doesn't stretch as far as the swankier hotels on and around Dam Square, this one is the match for them on location, if not on style itself. Nestling on an interesting backstreet bustling with lovely bars, restaurants and theatres, the hotel lobby is pure 1930s art deco glam – reflecting the building's past as a gold merchant's offices – though rooms are plain and tidy. Single rooms, it has to be said, are really rather miniscule.

Bar. Concierge. Internet (wireless, free). No-smoking rooms. Parking (€25/night).

Ibis Amsterdam Centre

Stationsplein 49, 1012 AB (638 9999/www.ibis hotel.com). Tram 1, 2, 5, 9, 13, 17, 24, 25. **Rates** €95-€138 single/double. **Credit** AmEx, DC, MC, V. **Map** p326 C1 12

If you're arriving in town late or leaving first thing, this place is ideal, not only because it's as close to the railway station as it's physically possible to be without actually being in it, but also because the bar is open 24 hours and breakfast begins at an eyelid-drooping 4am. There's no fancy business here – just the reliable Ibis formula of basic but comfortable rooms and reasonable facilities, plus their 'Fifteen Minute Satisfaction' promise: if a problem isn't sorted out in a quarter of an hour, your stay is free. Other branches of the Ibis hotel chain in Amsterdam are located at Valkenburgerstraat 68 (531 9135) near the Stopera, on Transformatorweg 36 (581 1111), and also at Schipholweg 181 (502 5100) in Badhoevedorp.

Bar. Disabled-adapted rooms. Internet (wireless, €6/hr, €14/3hr, €24/24hr; high-speed, €5/15min, €12.50/90min). No smoking throughout. Restaurant.

Budget

Greenhouse Effect

Warmoesstraat 55, 1012 HW (624 4974/www. greenhouse-effect.nl). Tram 4, 9, 17, 24, 25. **Rates** €65 (shared facilities) single; €95 (shared facilities) double/twin; €110-€130 (private facilities) double; €130 triple; €160 quad; €195 quintuple; €230 sextuple; €120-€180 apartments. **Credit** AmEx, MC, V. **Map** p326 D2 13

Planning on immersing yourself in cannabis culture? Then this is just the place to rest your addled head. Perched above the coffeeshop of the same name (*see p165*) on the fringes of the Red Light District, there are plenty of druggie draws in the area. Some rooms have shared facilities; several are kitted out in suitably trippy style with appropriate crazy names, like Mary Jane, Outer Space and Red Man, while others are just plain, old-fashioned nice, and overlook a canal. To take the edge off sore heads, breakfast is served until midday, and the attached bar has an all-day happy hour and arranges drum 'n' bass, reggae and also rare groove nights. Good if you're young and into smoking weed.

Bar.

Winston Hotel

Warmoestraat 129, 1012 JA (623 1380 www. winston.nl). Tram 4, 9, 14, 16, 24, 25. **Rates** €50-€105 single; €60-€105 double; €84-€129 triple; €105-€165 quad; €20-€28 dorm. **Credit** AmEx, DC, MC, V. **Map** p326 D2 14

Now part of St Christopher's Inns, a UK-based hostel chain, the legendary Winston still manages to maintain its youthful, party-loving atmosphere and arty rooms. These are decorated in eccentric, eclectic style by local businesses and artists, and range from monochrome illustrations from the Chiellerie gallery (*see p216*), to the crazed teenage bedroom explosions of Gsus Heavens Playground, to the kinky sub-dom den provided by Absolute Danny (*see p193*). Dormitory places are available in six- or eight-bed rooms, which are much cheaper – but also much less fun. There's a late-opening bar on site, and a good club to boot (*see p243*).
Bar. Disabled-adapted room. Internet (wireless, free; high-speed, €1/15min). No-smoking rooms.

Hostels

Flying Pig Hostels

Flying Pig Downtown *Nieuwendijk 100, 1012 MR (420 6822/group bookings 421 0583/www.flyingpig.nl). Tram 1, 2, 3, 5, 13, 17.* **Rates** €13.30 dorm; €36.90 bed in twin/double; €71.60-€78.40 single/twin. **Map** p326 D2 ⓯
Flying Pig Uptown *Vossiusstraat 46-47, 1071 AJ (400 4187/group reservations 421 0583/www.flyingpig.nl). Tram 2, 5, 20.* **Rates** €13.30 dorm; €29.90 bed in twin/double.
Flying Pig Beach *Parallel Boulevard 208, 2202 HT Noordwijk (071 362 2533/www.flyingpig.nl). Train to Leiden Centraal, then bus 40.* **Rates** €12.75 dorm; €21.25 bed in twin/double. **Credit** (all) MC, V.
Not so much a hostel, more a way of life, and a stalwart of the Interrailing scene. Young (they don't accept guests over 40 – or under 16) backpackers flock here from around the world, as much for the social life as the accommodation. You can see why: the hostel organises walking tours and in-line skating for free, and there are regular parties and cheap beer. There are branches near the Vondelpark and on the beach at Noordwijk-aan-Zee; the latter is open all year but comes in to its own in the summer, when water sports, beach activities and barbecues are the order of the day. A free shuttle bus ferries guests between the beach and uptown hostels for free.
Bar. Internet (wireless, free).

Western Canal Belt

Deluxe

Amsterdam Marriott Hotel

Stadhouderskade 12, 1054 ES (607 5555/www.marriott.com). Tram 1, 2, 5, 6, 7, 10. **Rates** €143-€278 room (for 1-4 people); €478-€525 suite (for 1-4 people). **Credit** AmEx, DC, MC, V. **Map** p330 C5 ⓰
Right next to the green lungs of Amsterdam – the Vondelpark – the Marriott has just been given an overhaul, so it's goodbye to the dowdy green and brown gentleman's club styling and hello to soothing yellows and modern furnishings. All 392 rooms now come equipped with Revive beds, six pillows plus luxurious linen and duvets. Bathrooms have gone similarly upmarket too, with cherry wood and granite surfaces and cascade showerheads.
Bar. Business centre. Concierge. Disabled-adapted rooms. Gym. Internet (wireless, €19.95/24hr; business centre €7.50/15min, €15/45min, €19/90min). No-smoking floors. Parking (€2.50/hr). Restaurants (2). Room service. TV: pay movies.

The Dylan

Keizersgracht 384, 1016 GB (530 2010/www.dylanamsterdam.com). Tram 1, 2, 5. **Rates** €270-€325 single; €435-€540 double; €735-€1,200 duplex; €1,500-€1,600 suite. **Credit** AmEx, MC, V. **Map** p330 C4 ⓱
Outrageous elegance are the key words here. Guests are made to feel like superstars – even the odd bona fide star drops in from time to time too – and lodge in colour-coded chromatherapy rooms designed to enhance the mood, like zingy raspberry, Zen-like black or toasty turmeric. Every detail, from chef Dennis Kuipers' North African-inspired menu to the careful alignment of the cushions in the public areas, is well thought through by the owners.
Bar. Concierge. Gym. Internet (wireless, free). Restaurant. Room service.

Hotel Pulitzer

Prinsengracht 315-331, 1016 GZ (523 5235/www.pulitzer.nl). Tram 13, 14, 17. **Rates** €300-€305 double deluxe; €375-€380 double; €485-€550 double exec; €680 exec suite. **Credit** AmEx, DC, MC, V. **Map** p326 C3 ⓲
Sprawling, though ever so elegantly, across a staggering 25 canal houses, the Pulitzer is an ideal destination for indulgent getaways. Guests can arrive by boat, rooms are big and stylish, and there are top-notch facilities, including a Gordon Ramsay restaurant due to open in late 2007. And everywhere in the hotel there are antiques galore and glistening marble. There is a lovely garden at the back and, in August, the hotel is home to the Grachtenfestival of classical music, which occurs in and around the premises. The final concert, which takes place on a pontoon outside and is attended by hundreds of bobbing boats, is a delight to hear and see.
Bar. Concierge. Gym. Internet (wireless, €5/hr, €19/24hr). No-smoking rooms. Restaurant. Room service. TV: pay movies.

Expensive

Ambassade Hotel

Herengracht 341, 1016 AZ (555 0222/www.ambassade-hotel.nl). Tram 1, 2, 5. **Rates** €185 single; €185-€225 double; €225-€255 triple; €265-€335 suite; €295-€335 apartment; €30 extra bed. **Credit** AmEx, DC, MC, V. **Map** p330 C4 ⓳
This literary hotel arranged across ten canal houses is the place to bump in to your favourite author. Staff are discreet and attentive, and rooms – which stretch from single to suite to apartment – are decorated in Louis Quatorze style. Naturally there's a library, only begun in 1987, whose countless shelves

are stuffed with signed tomes by illustrious previous guests, which residents are free to peruse.
Business centre. Concierge. Internet (wireless, free; high-speed, free). No-smoking rooms. Room service. TV: DVD.

Estherea

Singel 303-309, 1012 WJ (624 5146/www.estherea.nl). Tram 1, 2, 5. **Rates** €171-€236 single; €182-€299 double; €256-€340 triple; €290-€368 quad. **Credit** AmEx, DC, MC, V. **Map** p326 C3 ⑳
Spread over several charming canal houses at the epicentre of the elegant canal district, this private hotel has been run by the same family for decades. The emphasis in this place is on understated, simple luxury: rooms are swathed in Fortuny-style fabrics and come equipped with DVDs and marble bathrooms, ensuring that once you're in, you won't want to stray from your front door. As well as the more usual bar, there's a guests' library.
Bar. Concierge. Internet (wireless, €10/24hr). No-smoking rooms. Room service.

Toren

Keizersgracht 164, 1015 CZ (622 6352/www.hotel toren.nl). Tram 13, 14, 17. **Rates** €70-€310 single; €80-€350 double; €125-€310 triple; €180-€460 suites. **Credit** AmEx, DC, MC, V. **Map** p326 C3 ㉑
A hotel oozing an extraordinary history: over the years it's been a Golden Age merchant's mansion, a prime minister's home, a university, and even a hiding place for underground Jews in World War II. Now it's a family-run hotel, and comes with all the usual upmarket trappings: opulent fabrics, grand public rooms, attentive staff. Standard rooms are a bit of a cramp, but deluxe ones come with jacuzzi – and the three separate bridal suites have double bubble baths to boost the atmosphere.
Bar. Internet (wireless, €25/week, high-speed, €8/24hr). Restaurant. TV: pay movies.

Moderate

Amsterdam Wiechmann

Prinsengracht 328-332, 1016 HX (626 3321/www. hotelwiechmann.nl). Tram 1, 2, 5, 7, 17. **Rates** €80-€100 single; €130-€150 double; €180-€200 triple/quad; €245 suite. **Credit** MC, V. **Map** p330 C4 ㉒
Retro touches from every era, from a suit of armour in the reception to 1950s teapots and toasters in the breakfast room, adorn this rather eccentric, long-established hotel that's an ideal base for getting to know the Jordaan. Room decoration errs towards the chintzy – and those prized canal views cost extra – but things are brought bang up to date with free Wi-Fi. It's no smoking throughout.
Bar. No smoking throughout. Internet (wireless, free).

Belga

Hartenstraat 8, 1016 CB (624 9080/www.hotel belga.nl). Tram 1, 2, 5. **Rates** €47-€61 single; €67-€130 double/€109-€225 triple/quad/quintuple. **Credit** AmEx, MC, DC, V. **Map** p326 C3 ㉓
Accommodation that is at once family-friendly and cost-conscious is a rare beast in Amsterdam, so thank heavens for cosy Belga. A complete contrast to the stealth wealth of the surrounding Nine Streets, rooms here are functional but clean and tidy, and the downstairs breakfast-lunchroom is a kitsch, hugely colourful delight for all-comers.

't Hotel

Leliegracht 18, 1015 DE (422 2741/www.thotel.nl). Tram 1, 2, 5, 13, 14, 17. **Rates** €145 double; €165 quintuple. **Credit** AmEx, MC, V. **Map** p326 C3 ㉔

Amsterdam Wiechmann.

Jewel in the chain

The 15th hotel in the Amrâth chain owned by Giovanni van Eijl has been a long time coming, but then if you're going to convert one of the landmark buildings of Dutch architecture into five-star accommodation, it's never going to be a rush job.

The **Grand Hotel Amrâth Amsterdam** (*pictured*) occupies the fabulous structure on Prins Hendrikkade known locally as the Scheepvaarthuis or 'Maritime House'. It was on this building that many of the greatest names in Dutch modernism cut their teeth, and from which the signature flowing lines of the architectural style gained a named: the Amsterdam School (*see p38* **School of rock**).

On the very spot where Cornelis Houtman and Peter de Keyser set off for the East Indies on 10 March 1595 (opening the chapter on Dutch maritime dominance), construction work began, in 1913, on grand headquarters for a number of major shipping lines, designed by Johan van der Mey – a complete unknown who would, in fact, turn out to be a bit of a one-hit wonder. The same can't be said for those who worked with him: Piet Kramer would later design more than 400 of the city's bridges and Michel de Klerk would come up with Het Schip in Westerpark. The extraordinary carvings on the façade of nautical motifs and Dutch explorers were the second commission for Hildo Krop, soon to make his mark as official city sculptor.

Completed in 1916, the building is a mad confection of brick, granite, marble, porphyry and slate, with mahogany, ebony and even coromandel wood within. For nearly 70 years, the shipping lines were based here: the last of the old tenants, the KNSM, finally set sail from the building in 1981, whereupon the council purchased it for around *f*14 million (roughly €6.4 million), and public transport and parking companies moved in.

In the mid-1990s, Amrâth stepped in, but delays with the GVB moving out meant that conversion of the monument has taken ten years to complete; add to that the difficulty of working with many listed features that had to be preserved intact, and the enormous scale of the work becomes clear.

Due to have finally opened by mid-2007, the hotel consists of 137 rooms and 26 suites, the most prestigious being a three-storey-high one in the front tower. There's a swimming pool (an addition to the select band of Amsterdam hotels offering such a facility), and although it offers the usual roster of deluxe hotel frills and fripperies (plus the welcome addition of free mini-bars), style-wise, its unique feeling of timelessness remains defiantly anti-boutique.

Grand Hotel Amrâth Amsterdam

Prins Hendrikkade 108-114 (552 0000/ www.amrathamsterdam.nl). **Map** p326 D2.

A stylish bolt hole on a beautiful Jordaan canal near some very nice restaurants and bars, and ideally placed for scenic strolls. This prosaically named place is fitted throughout in 1920s-inspired style: Bauhaus prints adorn the walls, the colour scheme is muted, and the armchairs are design classics. All rooms have great views, whether on to the canal in front or the garden behind, and are rather spacious. Split-level room eight, in the eaves, sleeps up to five.
Internet (wireless, free).

Budget

Hotel Brouwer

Singel 83, 1012 VE (624 6358/www.hotelbrouwer.nl). Tram 1, 2, 5. **Rates** €55 single; €75 single use of double; €90 double. **No credit cards. Map** p326 C2 ㉕
The eight neat, en-suite rooms here are named after Dutch painters and all of them look onto the Singel canal. This is not the hotel to come to if you expect rafts of extra touches: it's just honest, reasonably priced accommodation in a long-standing family-run hotel (they've been running the place since 1917, though the building dates back to 1652).
No smoking throughout.

Singel Hotel

Singel 13-17, 1012 VC (626 3108/www.singel hotel.nl). Tram 1, 2, 5. **Rates** €69-€119 single; €89-€169 double; €119-€209 triple. **Credit** AmEx, MC, V. **Map** p326 C2 ㉖
This medium-sized, 32-roomed building is ideally located for canal and Jordaan strolls and for arrival and departure by train – it's a five-minute walk from the station, and right next door to the beautiful, domed Koepel church. Inside its 17th-century walls, rooms are plain and furnished in a modern, basic style; they are generally clean and tidy, and all are en-suite. Front-facing rooms have been known to get noisy due to their proximity to the nightlife.
Bar. Internet (wireless, free). No-smoking rooms. TV: pay movies.

Southern Canal Belt

Deluxe

American Hotel

Leidsekade 97, 1017 PN (556 3000/www.amsterdam american.com). Tram 1, 2, 5, 6, 7, 10. **Rates** €150-€320/€320-€373 single, double (low/high season); €35 extra bed. **Credit** AmEx, DC, MC, V. **Map** p330 C5 ㉗
A dazzling art nouveau monument that's looking extra spruce now that a fountain has been added to its terrace, the public areas here – like the magnificently buttressed Café Americain – are all eye-pleasers. Rooms, though – even the deluxe ones – are pretty cramped, though they've all got good views, either on to the canal or the bustling square below. Some have their own balcony. Suites are spacious, and all the accommodation is decorated in smart-but-bland standard hotel fittings.
Bar. Concierge. Disabled-adapted room. Gym. Internet (wireless, €22/24hr; high-speed, 35c/min, €10/hr, €22/24hr). No-smoking floors. Restaurant. Room service. TV: pay movies.

Inter-Continental Amstel Amsterdam

Professor Tulpplein 1, 1018 GX (622 6060/www. interconti.com). Tram 6, 7, 10. **Rates** €550-€600 single/double; €700-€3,500 suites. **Credit** AmEx, DC, MC, V. **Map** p315 F4 ㉘
They don't come much posher than this grand hotel standing imperiously over the river it takes its name from. If movie stars or royalty are in town, they lay their heads on a super-soft pillow in one of the huge, soundproofed rooms or even bigger suites here. Everything here is superlative: arrival by the hotel's own boat is possible; staff are both liveried and top-hatted; the restaurant is Michelin-starred; the swimming pool looks out on the river; even the galleried lobby as you walk in is breathtaking. If money is no object or you're after a once-in-a-lifetime splurge, then this is the place to do it.
Bar. Concierge. Gym. Internet (wireless, €7.50/15min, €10/hr, €15/2hr, €20/8hr, €25/24hr; business centre, €5/15min, €10/40min, €12.50/90min). No-smoking rooms. Parking (€45/24hr). Restaurant. Spa. Pool (1 indoor). Room service. TV: pay movies/DVD.

Hotel 717

Prinsengracht 717, 1017 JW (427 0717/www.717 hotel.nl). Tram 1, 2, 5. **Rates** €415-€670 suites; €50 extra bed; small dogs €25. **Credit** AmEx, DC, MC, V. **Map** p330 D4 ㉙
This rather well-kept secret of a hotel is the opposite of the grand gestures of the Amstel hotel, and the epitome of understated glamour. It's a small, flower-filled building that places emphasis on searching the globe for the best accoutrements – linens from the USA, bespoke blankets from Wales, box-spring mattresses from London. There is afternoon tea every day, and a garden for summer breakfasts or general lounging. Guests are the type that shed their euros on antiques in the Spiegelkwartier.
Internet (wireless, free). No-smoking rooms. Room service. TV: pay movies.

Expensive

Banks Mansion

Herengracht 519-525, 1017 BV (420 0055/www.banks mansion.nl). Tram 16, 24, 25. **Rates** €254-€309 double. **Credit** AmEx, DC, MC, V. **Map** p330 D4 ㉚
Once you check in to this grand hotel in a former bank building, everything is yours to choose. Drinks and snacks in the lounge, films and mini-bar in your room: everything is free, because the owners want to create a homey feel. This all-inclusive holiday also involves a pillow menu, rain showerheads, plasma TVs and DVD players in every room.
Bar. Business centre. Internet (wireless, first 50min free, €10/100min; business centre, free). No smoking rooms. TV: DVD.

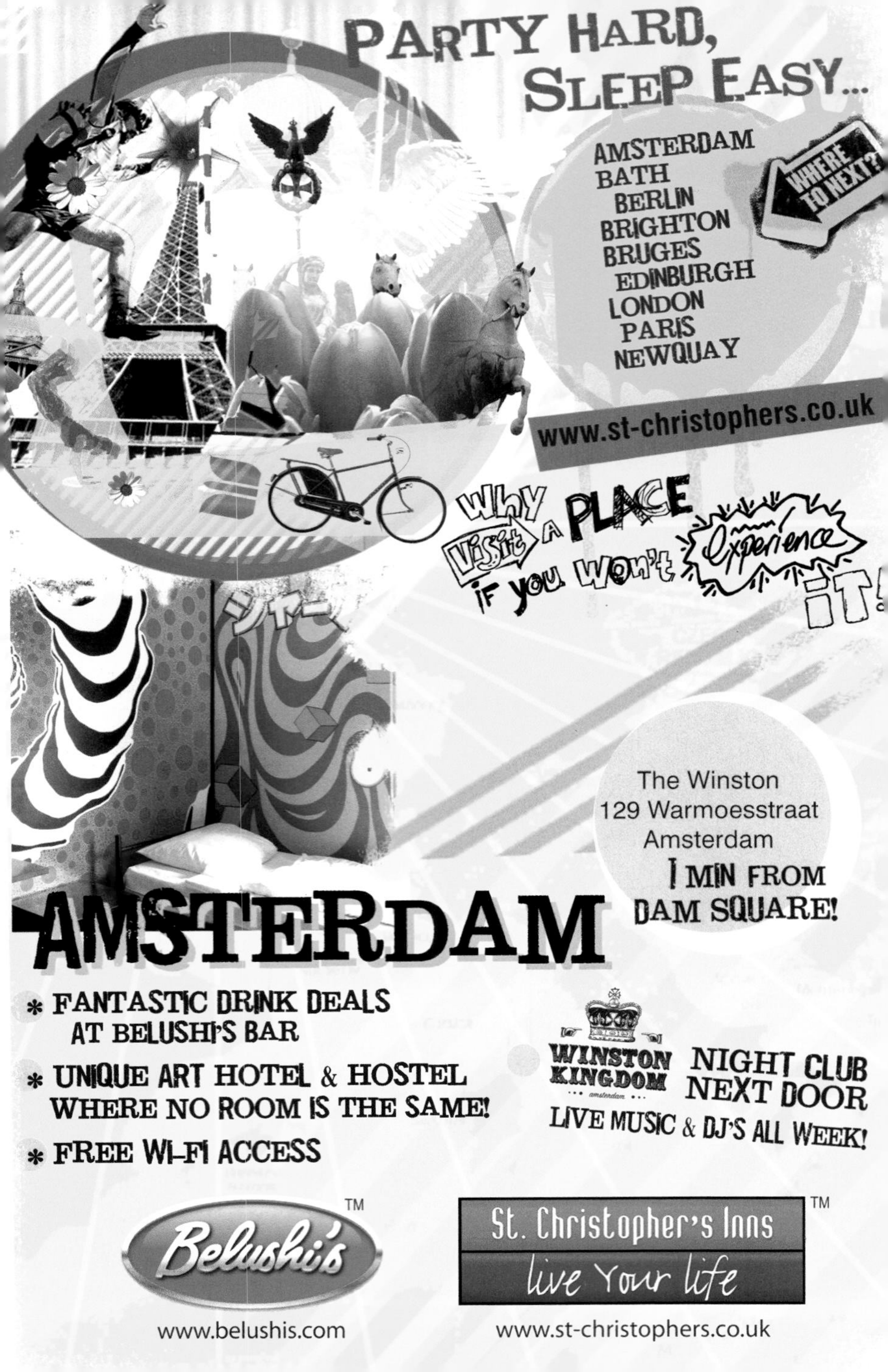
PARTY HARD, SLEEP EASY...
AMSTERDAM
BATH
BERLIN
BRIGHTON
BRUGES
EDINBURGH
LONDON
PARIS
NEWQUAY
WHERE TO NEXT?
www.st-christophers.co.uk
Why visit a PLACE if you won't experience IT!
The Winston
129 Warmoesstraat
Amsterdam
1 MIN FROM DAM SQUARE!
AMSTERDAM
* FANTASTIC DRINK DEALS AT BELUSHI'S BAR
* UNIQUE ART HOTEL & HOSTEL WHERE NO ROOM IS THE SAME!
* FREE WI-FI ACCESS
WINSTON KINGDOM amsterdam
NIGHT CLUB NEXT DOOR
LIVE MUSIC & DJ'S ALL WEEK!
Belushi's TM
St. Christopher's Inns TM
live Your life
www.belushis.com
www.st-christophers.co.uk

Dikker & Thijs Fenice Hotel

Prinsengracht 444, 1017 KE (620 1212/www.dtfh.nl). Tram 1, 2, 5, 6, 7, 10. **Rates** €80-€195 single; €115-€245 double; €195-€345 penthouse. **Credit** AmEx, DC, MC, V. **Map** p330 C5 31

A long-established name on Amsterdam's hotel scene, this upmarket place is owned by a publisher, so authors often drop in to stay. In an 18th-century warehouse building near Leidseplein, rooms are plain but smart; the glamorous penthouse has a wall made of glass for unsurpassed views over the city rooftops. At breakfast time, guests are bathed in jewel-coloured light from the stained-glass windows.
Bar. Internet (wireless, €5.95/hr).

Eden Hotel

Amstel 144, 1017 AE (530 7878/www.edenhotelgroup.com). Tram 4, 9, 14. **Rates** €115-€145 single; €135-€190 twin/double; €180-€215 triple; €205-€240 quad; €140-€220 apartments. **Credit** AmEx, MC, V. **Map** p327 E3 32

This chain hotel standard has great views over the Amstel river to the front and is well placed to crash after indulging in the fleshpots of Rembrandtplein behind, but it's beginning to look a bit tired and stuck in the 1980s. It's suited to work and long stays, though – there's a business floor, apartments and studios – and disabled travellers are well served with adapted rooms. Café Flo, the on-site restaurant, is highly rated among local gastros.
Bar. Concierge. Disabled-adapted room. Internet (wireless, free). No-smoking rooms. Restaurant. TV: pay movies.

Mercure Hotel Arthur Frommer

Noorderstraat 46, 1017 TV (622 0328/ www.mercure.com). Tram 4. **Rates** €140 single; €160 double. **Credit** AmEx, DC, MC, V. **Map** p331 E5 33

On a charming residential street within walking distance of the sights and the nightlife, this hotel, arranged around a courtyard, is an oasis of relaxation. A minute or two's stroll from the Amstelkerk, it's also in one of the nicest locations in town. Rooms, which occupy a series of attractive townhouses, are spacious and smart, though not overburdened with fancy extras. There's a cosy bar and attractive, black-and-white tiled public areas.
Bar. Internet (wireless €7/hr; high-speed, €7/hr). Parking (free).

Moderate

Bridge Hotel

Amstel 107-111, 1018 EM (623 7068/www.thebridgehotel.nl). Tram 4, 6, 7, 9, 10. **Rates** €105-€110 single; €105-€160 double; €165-€175 triple; €215-€225 studio; €250-€295 apartments. **Credit** AmEx, DC, MC, V. **Map** p331 F3 34

Feeling gloriously isolated on the eastern banks of the Amstel, this private hotel in a former stonemason's workshop is actually just a few minutes' stroll from the bright lights of Rembrandtplein and the rest of the city centre, and it's also well situated for exploring the Plantage and Jodenbuurt. Rooms are simple and bright; ones that command a river view cost more. For stays of three days or more there are two self-catering apartments and a studio sleeping four, which work out at a pretty good price. Both Amstel Gold and Amstel Light apartments have river views; the former has two bathrooms.
Bar. Internet (wireless, €1.50/hr, €5/half stay, €10/whole stay; high-speed €2/hr).

Hotel Agora

Singel 462, 1017 AW (627 2200/www.hotelagora.nl). Tram 1, 2, 5. **Rates** €108-€126 single; €126-€140 double; €165 triple; €193 quad. **Credit** AmEx, DC, MC, V. **Map** p330 D4 35

Ideal for flower power freaks who want to stock up on bulbs, this homey little place in an 18th-century house on a canal is right in the thick of it, very near the floating flower market. What the Agora lacks in extras it makes up for with nice touches like a conservatory for breakfast and a garden. Rooms are plain but neat and all have canal or garden views.
Internet (high-speed, €3.50/15min, €5/30min). Room service.

Hotel de Munck

Achtergracht 3, 1017 WL (623 6283/www.hoteldemunck.com). Tram 4. **Rates** €65-€95 single; €105-€140 double; €145-€170 triple; €190-€230 quad; €250-€290 apartment. **Credit** AmEx, DC, MC, V. **Map** p331 F4 36

This higgledy-piggledy place in an old Dutch East India Company sea captain's house is perched on a secluded little canal near the river. The rooms here are plain and basic, and some are looking a little tired, though they are clean and neat. The breakfast room is lovely, though, with a working jukebox and walls plastered with old album covers.
Bar. Internet (wireless, free; high-speed €1/15min).

Nicolaas Witsen

Nicolaas Witsenstraat 4, 1017 ZH (623 6143/www.hotelnicolaaswitsen.nl). Tram 4. **Rates** €90-€105 single; €115-€125 double; €150-€160 triple; €180 quad. **Credit** AmEx MC, V. **Map** p331 E5 37

One of the few hotels to fill the gap between the museums and the Pijp, this place, though plain, functional and a tad overpriced, is well placed for culture and fun-seekers. Ground-floor rooms can get noisy but pluses include free Wi-Fi. There's also an excellent delicatessen on the corner of the street that encourages in-room midnight feasting.
Bar. Internet (wireless, free).

Seven Bridges

Reguliersgracht 31, 1017 LK (623 1329/www.sevenbridgeshotel.nl). Tram 16, 24, 25. **Rates** €90-€220 single; €110-€260 double. **Credit** AmEx, MC, V. **Map** p315 E4 38

This is the ideal destination for hermits who want a luxury hidey-hole far from the madding crowd that's also conveniently located for the museums and city centre. There are no public spaces here, apart from the lobby and garden, just eight lovely and largely

antique-stuffed rooms. The consequence of this lack of shared space is that all guests must suffer the privation of compulsory breakfast in bed, served on Villeroy and Boch crockery. One of Amsterdam's best-kept secrets, although we have a feeling it won't remain one for much longer.
Internet (wireless, free). No-smoking rooms.

Budget

Hotel Leydsche Hof

Leidsegracht 14, 1016 CK (638 2327/www.freewebs.com/leydschehof). Tram 1, 2, 5, 6, 7, 10. **Rates** €95-€105 double. **No credit cards. Map** p330 C4 39

On twinkling Leidsegracht – a genteel canal that's just minutes from the nightlife of Leidseplein – the Piller family take good care of the seven bright, simply decorated rooms in their 17th-century house. Though basic, all the rooms are nicely turned out in dark wood, and come well equipped with fridges and hot drink-making facilities (a rarity in Amsterdam hotels of any class), and face a garden.
Internet (wireless, free). Room service.

Hotel Prinsenhof

Prinsengracht 810, 1017 JL (623 1772/www.hotelprinsenhof.com). Tram 4. **Rates** €49-€84 single; €69-€89 double; €99-€119 triple; €119-€149 quad. **Credit** AmEx, MC, V. **Map** p331 E4 40

A good option for budget travellers who just want a place to kip down at night, this dinky, ten-roomed hotel is right near the city's nightlife and foodie Utrechtsestraat, and has helpful and friendly staff. The physically less able should note that the stairs are positively vertiginous – luggage is hauled up on a pully. Rooms themselves are simple, and some have shared facilities, but they're all clean and tidy. Some of the rooms also have canal views – and they don't attract a premium, either.

Jodenbuurt, the Plantage and the Oost

Moderate

Arena

's Gravesandestraat 51, 1092 AA (850 2400/www.hotelarena.nl). Tram 3, 6, 9, 10, 14. **Rates** €99-€189 double; €180-€320 suite. **Credit** AmEx, DC, MC, V. **Map** p332 G3 41

A holy trinity of hotel, restaurant and nightclub in a former Catholic orphanage, Arena's only downside is that it's a bit out of the way – though trams whizz you in to the centre in ten minutes and it's a nice walk in to town through an utterly untouristy area. It's the ideal hotel for lazy young scenesters who are after a one-stop-shop of food, booze and boogie. However, standard and large rooms are a bit boring from an aesthetic point of view. The extra-large ones and suites, kitted out by leading local designers, look great but come with matching price tags.
Bar. Concierge. Disabled-adapted rooms. Internet (wireless, €2/hr, €10/24hr). Restaurant. TV: DVD.

Eden Lancaster

Plantage Middelaan 48, 1018 DH (535 6888/www.edenhotelgroup.com). Tram 6, 9, 14. **Rates** €59-€120 single; €65-€180 double. **Credit** AmEx, DC, MC, V. **Map** p332 G3 42

If you're planning on taking kids to Artis zoo then this hotel is just across the road, and their triple and quad rooms are very much aimed at families. Even though it's a bit out of the way of the other sights, Centraal Station is a short tram ride away or a 20-minute walk, and there are several nice cafés also nearby. Not really a place for a romantic or indulgent getaway, it's quite basic (and bathrooms are cramped), but the rooms, painted warm colours, are good for business travellers, equipped as they are with Wi-Fi and desks for those with work to do.
Internet (wireless, free; high-speed, €5/15min, €10/45min, €12.50/90min). No-smoking rooms. TV: pay movies.

Budget

Hotel Adolesce

Nieuwe Keizersgracht 26, 1018 DR (626 3959/www.adolesce.nl). Trams 4, 6, 7, 10/Metro Weesperplein. **Rates** €60-€65 single; €90-€100 double; €120 triple. **Credit** MC, V. **Map** p327 F3 43

You won't get any breakfast at this unfussy place on a canal near the Skinny Bridge, but guests are free to help themselves all day to drinks, fruit and chocs in the lounge, making it a good bet for those with children. The ten rooms are all plain – the attic room has the most character – but there's a small roof-terrace and it's close to the zoo Artis (*see p111*), Hortus Botanicus (*see p112*) and is just a few doors away from the Hermitage museum (*see p110*). Both the river and the Waterlooplein flea market (*see p192*) are just a few minutes' walk away.

Hostels

Stayokay Amsterdam Zeeburg

Timorplein 21, 1094 CC (551 3190/www.stayokay.com). Tram 7, 10. **Rates** €28-€40 twin; €23-€33 quad; €21-€30 sextuple. **Credit** MC, V.

This spanking new branch of the reliable hostel chain opened its doors in July 2007 in a grand old school building. Aimed very much at families and the more discerning hosteller – HI members get a discount – they offer City Break packages (from €79), which include a welcome drink, dinners, bike rental and museum entry – just like a proper hotel, in fact. There are a whopping 490 beds in bedrooms sleeping two to eight, and no dorms. This branch is part of Stayokay's new designer concept from Edward van Vliet, done out in warm reds, with mosaic floors, sleek but simple furniture and huge photos on the walls.
Bar. Internet (high-speed, €5/hr). Restaurant.

Mövenpick Hotel Amsterdam City Centre. *See p72.*

The Waterfront

Expensive

Mövenpick Hotel Amsterdam City Centre
Piet Heinkade 11, 1019 BR (519 1200/www.moevenpick-hotels.com). Tram 25, 26. **Rates** €150-€245 double; €295-€560 suite. **Credit** AmEx, DC, MC, V. **Map** p327 F1 44
Big, tall and glamorous, this stripy, stone-coloured hotel is brand spanking new and a great base for exploring the Waterfront and Noord on the banks opposite. Rooms are decorated in soothing greys and woods; pricier ones grant access to an executive lounge – free cocktails included – and have great views over the cruise liners ploughing through the waters, or over the city's rooftops. *Photos p71.*
Bar. Business centre. Gym. Internet (wireless, free). No smoking throughout. Restaurant. TV: pay movies.

Moderate

Lloyd Hotel
Oostelijke Handelskade 34 (561 3604/www.lloydhotel.com). Tram 10, 26. **Rates** €95-€295 double. **Credit** AmEx, DC, MC, V. **Map** p116.
Started by scene leaders of an impeccable cultural pedigree, this big hotel defies categorisation: rooms run the gamut from one to five star, there's a unique in-house 'cultural embassy' alongside the usual bar and restaurants, and the building was a borstal (among many other fascinating uses) until the late 1980s. There's usually something arty going on that guests are welcome to join in, be it an artist's party or happenings like 2006's Full Llove Inn: an extra room in a converted Opel Kadett perched on top of a four-metre-high pole. Expect the unexpected – in the nicest possible way, of course.
Bar. Business centre. Internet (wireless, free). Restaurant. Room service.

The Jordaan

Moderate

Truelove Antiek and Guesthouse
Prinsenstraat 4, 1015 DC (320 2500/06 248 056 72 mobile after 6pm/www.truelove.be). Tram 1, 2, 5. **Rates** €90-€110 double; €120 suite; €130 apartments. **Credit** MC, V. **Map** p326 C2 45
Sitting atop an antique shop (which also serves as the hotel reception), this dinky place is nicely decorated with the odd piece from downstairs here and there. The attic room is the nicest, but all rooms come with a CD player and kettle – handy, as there's no breakfast, but that does mean that the price for what you get isn't quite as friendly as it initially looks. They also have an apartment on Langestraat.
No smoking throughout.

Lloyd Hotel.

The Museum Quarter, Vondelpark & the South

Expensive

The College Hotel

Roelof Hartstraat 1, 1071 VE (571 1511/www.thecollegehotel.com). Tram 3, 12, 25. **Credit** AmEx, MC, V. **Rates** €205 single; €235-€285 double; €365-€670 suite. **Credit** AmEx, MC ,V. **Map** p331 E6 46

A practical outpost of the city's hotel and catering college, all the staff here are students who are training in situ. The boutique styling and glamorous touches (bathrooms are a strong point) ensure that prices are far from pocket money, however. The rooms look great, with flat-screen TVs, though some are small. If you're prepared to pay top dollar you get oodles of space: the TCH suite is bigger than most Amsterdam flats. There's also a bar and ambitious modern Dutch restaurant. The downside is that service is unpredictable.

Bar. Business centre. Internet (wireless, free). Restaurant. TV: pay movies.

Moderate

Bilderberg Jan Luyken

Jan Luykenstraat 58, 1071 CS (573 0730/www.bilderberg.nl). Tram 2, 5, 6, 7, 10. **Rates** €139-€179 double. **Credit** AmEx, MC, V. **Map** p330 D6 47

One of the city's most stylish secrets, this place – complete with spa and a wine bar – is just a kitten-heeled skip away from the designer shops of PC Hooftstraat. Rooms are slickly done out in chocolate and caramel tones, with designer touches and wall-mounted CD players, and are something of a bargain for a place boasting these looks and facilities. Check for special packages: the Amsterdam Beauty Arrangement, for example, gets you a cocktail, bed and breakfast, and an hour and a half at liberty in the spa for under €110 per person.

Bar. Internet (wireless, €10/6min, €17/24hr; high-speed, €22/24hr). Restaurant. Spa.

Hotel V

Victorieplein 42, 1078 PH (662 3233/www.hotelv.nl). Tram 4, 12, 25. **Rates** €80-€90 single; €120-€145 double; €170 triple. **Credit** AmEx, DC, MC, V.

A bit of a hike from the sights and the centre, but trams stop right outside to whisk you in to town in ten minutes, and the Pijp is a 15-minute walk away. This boutique B&B-style hotel is ideal for business travellers sick of corporate sterility: it's very near the RAI and business areas of Zuid. In an unassuming residential block, the bright purple doors are the only clue to the funky hotel behind. There's new age, sleek décor in all rooms, but there aren't many extras. The lounge, with pebbly fireplace and furry pouffes, looks lovely.

Bar. Internet (wireless, free).

Vondel

Vondelstraat 28-30, 1054 GE (612 0120/www.hotelvondel.nl). Tram 2, 5, 6, 7, 10. **Rates** €170-€205 double; €275 suite. **Credit** AmEx, DC, MC, V. **Map** p330 C5 48

Another hidden gem near museums and upmarket shopping opportunities, this thoroughly chic place is covered with art and boasts a lovely decked garden. Rooms, ranging from small to huge along with a junior and family suite, are thoroughly designer driven, with Burberry-checked blankets, chandeliers and swanky bathrooms. Unusually for such a trendy hotel, families are positively encouraged, which marks it out from snootier establishments.

Bar. Internet (wireless, €17/24hr; high-speed, prices vary). Restaurant. Room service.

Hostels

For Flying Pig Hostels, *see p63.*

The Pijp

Deluxe

Hotel Okura Amsterdam

Ferdinand Bolstraat 333, 1072 LH (678 7111/www.okura.nl). Tram 12, 25. **Rates** €170-€330 single; €240-€380 double; €275-€2,100 suites; €73 extra bed. **Credit** AmEx, DC, MC, V.

This multi-storey, multi-tasking and very smart business-class stopover (the choice of Japan Airlines) has everything captains of industry need: a top-floor, top-of-the-range French restaurant, Le Ciel Bleu; a full-size pool and health club (open to non-guests); state-of-the-art conference facilities; and sushi bars. Rooms offer no surprises in terms of facilities – they've got the lot – or looks. They're done up in suitably masculine style and range from small standards to the huge (and, as such, hugely expensive) Presidential Suite on the 21st floor.

Bars (2). Business centre. Concierge. Disabled-adapted rooms. Gym. Internet (wireless, €12/hr, €25/24hr; high-speed, €15/24hr). No-smoking rooms. Parking (€4/hr). Pool (1 indoor). Restaurants (4). Room service. TV: pay movies.

Expensive

Hotel Savoy

Ferdinand Bolstraat 194, 1072 LW (644 7445/www.savoyhotel.nl). Tram 3, 12, 16, 24, 25. **Rates** €150 single; €175 double; €190 twin superior. **Credit** AmEx, DC, MC, V.

One of very few accommodation options in the area, this hotel in an imposing red-brick Amsterdam School building came under new ownership in autumn 2006, and has been restyled as a 'concept' hotel, which should suit the gentrified Pijp and its evolution as a style centre down to the ground.

Bar. Business centre. Internet (wireless, free).

Budget

Van Ostade Bicycle Hotel

Van Ostadestraat 123, 1072 SV (679 3452/www.bicyclehotel.com). Tram 3, 12, 16, 24, 25. **Rates** €40-€65 single; €50-€110 double; €80-€140 triple; €100-€160 quad. **Credit** AmEx, MC, V. **Map** p315 F6 49

Much beloved of visitors to Amsterdam for many years, this cheap 'n' cheerful staging post for pedal-pushers was one of the first (and is still one of the few) places to stay in the Pijp. With good bicycle access to popular out-of-town routes (along the Amstel, off to Utrecht), the friendly staff can suggest routes and rent out bikes – and if you bring your own, you can park it securely for free. The breakfast room is cute, rooms are comfy and there are loads of excellent places nearby to refuel for the energetic day ahead, or wind down after a long ride.

Internet (wireless, free; high-speed, free). No-smoking rooms. Parking (€20/24hr).

Other Options

Floating accommodation

With water, water everywhere, it's only natural to want to float in Amsterdam. Unfortunately, there are surprisingly few options for a city literally awash with boat hotel potential. The places listed below are best of the bunch.

The Old Centre

Amstel Botel

Oosterdokskade 2-4, 1011 AE (626 4247/www.amstelbotel.nl). Tram 1, 2, 5, 9, 13, 17, 24, 25. **Rates** €78-€89 (rear side) €83-€94 (water side) single/double/twin; €119-€124 triple. **Credit** AmEx, DC, MC, V. **Map** p327 E1 50

Convenient for Centraal Station, the docklands and hops across to Noord, this a good bet if you're looking for good, clean accommodation with the odd frill, like free in-house movies. Unless you are fooled by their 'luxury' rooms boast and come expecting the QEII, you'll be perfectly satisfied. The bar has long opening hours (from 9am to after midnight) and games like pinball and pool, plus a jukebox – ideal for pacifying youngsters on rainy days. Be warned that major renovations in the area mean that views aren't quite as watery or relaxing as they have been.

Bar. Internet (wireless, €6/hr, €15/3hr). TV: pay movies.

The Waterfront

Ideaal II

Opposite No.51 Levantkade, 1019 MJ (419 7255/www.houseboats.nl). Tram 10, 26. **Rates** €150-€190 per person per night. **Credit** V. **Map** p116.

An indulgent floating option, this converted cargo boat near the up-and-coming cultural quarter sleeps up to five sybarites, and comes with two bathrooms, jacuzzi, state-of-the-art stainless steel kitchen, and decks dedicated to sunbathing and swimming. At night, sleep on (what else?) a waterbed. Overnight stays are possible, but longer ones are more economical. Check the website for last-minute deals.

Bar. Internet. TV: cable

The Jordaan

Frederic Rentabike

Brouwersgracht 78, 1013 GZ (624 5509/www.frederic.nl). Bus 18, 22. **Rates** €50-€90 per person per night (double occupancy). **No credit cards. Map** p326 C2 51

This bike shop also does a nice little sideline in renting out nine houseboats all around town, ranging from the sleek to the homey. Houseboat No.5 on the Prinsengracht is big, stylish and comes with internet.

Apartment rentals

If you like the city so much that a short holiday won't suffice, there are several options for finding longer-term accommodation, though with housing stock at a premium even for residents, the range isn't exactly enormous. Quite a few hotels have apartments that are specifically designed for lengthier stays, and they often have special rates. We have listed them in the hotel section wherever appropriate, but also try the places below. If you're thinking of moving to the city, *see p303* **Please leave.**

Apartment Services AS

Waalstraat 58, 1078 BX South (672 1840/www.apartmentservices.nl). Tram 4, 12, 25. **Open** 9.30am-5pm Mon-Fri. **No credit cards.**

Around 20 fully furnished, central apartments are available for lets of one week or more. They're stylish, but suitably pricey to boot.

stayAmsterdam

(353 1 8747791/www.stayamsterdam.com).

A Dutch offshoot of the Dublin company that specialises in providing high-quality accommodation at reasonable rates. They've got quite a range of flats in the centre, and if you book wisely, six people sharing for a week could go as low as €30 each per night.

Bed and breakfast

While B&B may be a byword for a cheap and cheerful place to stay in most other countries, in Amsterdam you'll find that it's seldom cheap – but it is usually fabulously stylish or unique. Logie en Ontbijt or L&O options are limited in the Netherlands because of restrictions on the number of people (four) allowed to stay in a house at any one time.

Twee is the magic number at **Between Art and Kitsch**.

City Mundo

Schinkelkade 30, 1075 VK (470 5705/www.citymundo.com). Tram p2/bus 15, 62. **Open** 10am-6pm Mon-Fri; 11am-6pm Sat. **Credit** AmEx, MC, V.

An agency to match visitors to accommodation, which could be anything from a room in a flat to a traditional Dutch windmill. The website gives a good overview of what's available, but be warned that the minimum stay is three nights.

Southern Canal Belt

Kamer01

3e Weteringdwarsstraat 44, 1017 TC (625 6627/www.kamer01.nl). Tram 7, 10, 16, 24, 25. **Rates** €168 Mon-Thur, Sun; €178 Fri, Sat. **No credit cards. Map** p331 E5 52

A very stylish, gay-friendly place designed by Atelier Hertogh. The Red Room is sexily scarlet and comes with a huge shower, big enough for an entire football team. The Blue Room currently comes with a sexy circular bed and private roof terrace – and exciting design plans are in place for 2007. Both are equipped with an iMac, flat-screen TV and DVD player. The downstairs kitchen area is equipped with help-yourself 'maxi bar' and tidbits from nearby bakery Holtkamp. Minimum stay is two nights, with a 25 per cent discount for more than three.

Marcel van Woerkom

Leidsestraat 87, 1017 NX (622 9834/www.marcelamsterdam.com). Tram 1, 2, 5. **Rates** €60-€110 per person per night. **Credit** V. **Map** p330 C5 53

Artist Marcel has been letting rooms in his stylish 'creative exchange' since 1970. Chances are you'll run in to other artists or designers admiring the art on the walls. No breakfast, but plenty of good choices nearby. Book well in advance.

The Museum Quarter, Vondelpark & the South

Between Art and Kitsch

Ruysdaelkade 75, 1072 AL (679 0485/www.between-art-and-kitsch.com). Tram 16, 24, 25. **Rates** €80-€90 single/double. **No credit cards. Map** p331 E6 54

Well, between the museums and the Pijp, actually. This B&B has just two rooms: one is decorated in mock deco with authentic period knick-knacks, the other in faux baroque – and yes, rooms do live up to the name's promise. On a nice canal, it's great for culture and nightlife.

Xaviera Hollander Bed & Breakfast

Stadionweg 17, 1077 RV (673 3934/www.xavierahollander.com). Tram 5, 24. **Rates** €125-€150 double. **No credit cards.**

Prudes: avert your eyes sharpish, since you won't be wanting to stay in the home of the original Happy Hooker. Rooms, upstairs in Xaviera's own banker-belt villa or in a hut at the bottom of her garden, are nice, but guests come here mainly for an outrageous anecdote (or several) from the lady herself. Only in Amsterdam, as they say.

Camping

Although none of the four campsites is what you'd call close to the centre, all are well served by good transport links. Zeeburg is a young people's site – not ideal if you plan on turning in early; Gaasper and Amsterdamse Bos are family campsites (with designated youth fields), while everyone is mixed happily together at Vliegenbos (which, incidentally, doesn't allow pets). Camping is a national pastime for the Dutch, so all the sites have good facilities and are extremely well maintained.

Gaasper Camping Amsterdam

Loosdrechtdreef 7, 1108 AZ (696 7326/www.gaaspercamping.nl). Metro 53 Gaasperplas/nightbus 75. **Open** *mid Mar-June, Sept-Nov* 9am-8pm daily. *July-Aug* 9am-10pm daily. Closed 2 Nov-14 Mar. **Rates** €4.75 per person per night. *Tent* from €5.50. *Vehicles* €4.25-€8.50. *Dog* €2.50. **No credit cards.**

Half an hour away on the metro, but feeling like it's in the depths of the countryside, this well-run site has a café, laundry and loads of water-sporting opportunities on the nearby lake.

Het Amsterdamse Bos

Kleine Noorddijk 1, 1187 NZ (641 6868/www.campingamsterdamsebos.nl). Bus 171, 172, 199. **Open** *1 Apr-15 Oct* 9am-12.30pm, 1.20-9pm daily. **Rates** €5 per person per night. *Tent* from €3. *Vehicles* €3.50-€7. **Credit** AmEx, MC, V.

The most scenically situated site of those around the city, this is easily reached by bus – though the best way to arrive is after a cycle through the woods. There are cottages, cabins and huts for the tentless, plus a café, laundry and supermarket, and watery Aalsmeer and the flower auction are nearby.

Vliegenbos

Meeuwenlaan 138, 1022 AM (636 8855/www.vliegenbos.com). Bus 32, 36/nightbus 73. **Open** *1 Apr-30 Sept* 9am-9pm daily. **Rates** €8 per person per night. *Tent* €2. *Vehicles* €8-€28. **Credit** MC, V.

More expensive than its rivals and teeming with facilities – restaurant, café, huts, lockers, laundry – this one is pitched in Noord, halfway between the city and the Waterland's lovely villages. No pets are allowed and hot showers are free.

Zeeburg

Zuider IJdijk 20, 1095 KN (694 4430/www.campingzeeburg.nl). Tram 14/bus 22, 37. **Open** year round. **Rates** €3-€5 per person per night. *Tents* €2.50-€5. *Vehicles* €3-€26.50. **Credit** AmEx, MC, V.

The nearest to the city centre and not far from IJburg, there's a tram stop right outside this campsite perched on the water's edge. A young crowd get the best out of the (good) facilities. In summer there's a bar with parties, DJs and films.

Sightseeing

Features

GASSAN
diamonds

The
Amsterdam
Diamond
Group

Introduction

From high to low culture, this is a city to open the mind and stagger the senses.

If you're looking for sex, drugs and/or rock 'n' roll, you'll find all you need for a lost weekend in Amsterdam without much preparation. But this town is also dense with plenty of higher pursuits. And while packing the cultural punch of a metropolis, Amsterdam is a remarkably convenient size. Most things are within half an hour's walk and the trams provide back-up for those low on energy. You can also slipstream the locals and saddle up on a bike (though you should beware of trams and cycle thieves).

In the centre are Amsterdam's old port, its medieval buildings, the red lights that denote a hotspot of the world's oldest trade, the grand 17th-century merchants' houses, the spires of ancient religious institutions, the earliest and prettiest canals, and many of its most famous sights. Except to stroll Museumplein and its three major art museums, very few visitors go beyond the *grachtengordel*, the calming belt of Golden Age canals – likened in Albert Camus' *The Fall* to the circles of hell – that ring the fascinating and historic Old Centre. Don't make the same mistake. While primarily residential, the Jordaan and the Pijp are hugely attractive places. Further out, too, there's much to enjoy, on the Waterfront to the north and north-east, or south around the idyllic Amsterdamse Bos. For more on Amsterdam's various areas, *see p82* **Neighbourhood watch**.

Sightseeing

TICKETS AND INFORMATION

While most Amsterdam museums charge for admission, prices are reasonable: rarely more than €7. However, if you're thinking of taking in a few, the **Museumkaart** (Museum Card) is a steal: €37.50 for adults and €17.50 for under-25s (plus a €4.95 administration fee for first-timers). The card offers free or discounted

The best Things to do in Amsterdam

For entering the past
A morning in **Amsterdams Historisch Museum** (*see p98*), an afternoon spent in the **Museum Amstelkring** (*see p93*) and an evening at the **Concertgebouw** (*see p238*).

For going back to the future
A morning in **Nemo** (*see p115*), an afternoon walk around the eastern docklands (*see p116* **Architectural reflections**), a concert at the **Muziekgebouw** (*see p239*) and a night spent in **Sugar Factory** (*see p243*).

For art both ancient and modern
Rijksmuseum (*see p124*) or the galleries in the **Jordaan** (*see p119* **Art of the matter**).

For a religious experience
The **Oude Kerk** (*see p93*), the **Joods Historisch Museum** (*see p110*) or the utterly unique **Chinese Fo Guang Shan Buddhist Temple** (*see p88*).

For a trinity of Dutch clichés
A drink at the Brouwerij 't IJ, next to a **windmill** (*see p160*), shopping at **cheese** emporium Wegewijs (*see p183*), and a wander around the floating **flower market** Bloemenmarkt (*see p183*).

For the party to end all parties
The canals on **Queen's Day** (*see p198*) or **New Year's Eve** on Nieuwmarkt (*see p202*).

For the desperate, the horny or the just plain curious
A walk around the **Red Light District** (*see p87*), a visit to the **Sexmuseum** (*see p87*) or an evening in the **Casa Rosso** (*see p91*).

For the longest queues in town
Anne Frank Huis (*see p103*), the **Van Gogh Museum** (*see p125*) or **boat tours** from near Centraal Station (*see p84*).

For getting away from it all
Vondelpark (*see p125*), **Artis** (*see p111*), **Hortus Botanicus** (*see p128*), **Begijnhof** (*see p97*) or the **Amsterdamse Bos** (*see p128*).

For sitting, drinking and thinking
The cafés that surround the **Nieuwmarkt** (*see p88*) and the **Spui** (*see p96*). Or for something slightly more surrreal, you can always take a trip to a **coffeeshop** (*see p164*).

admission to over 400 great attractions in the Netherlands and is valid for a year from date of purchase; discounted or free entry offered to holders of the Museumkaart is denoted in our listings by the letters 'MK'. You can buy the card at most participating museums. The **Amsterdam Tourist Board** (*see p312*) also sells a savings pass, the **I amsterdam Card**, that gives free entry to major museums, free public transport and a free canal trip, along with a 25 per cent discount at participating tourist attractions and restaurants. It costs €33 for 24 hours, €43 for 48 and €53 for 72 hours, and pays for itself if you use it enough.

Neighbourhood watch

THE OLD CENTRE

Amsterdam's ground zero of consumerism, vice, entertainment and history, the Old Centre is bounded by Prins Hendrikkade to the north, Oudeschans and Zwanenburgwal to the east, the Amstel to the south and Singel to the west. Within these borders, the Old Centre is split into the New Side (west of Damrak and Rokin) and the Old Side (east of Damrak and Rokin). Within the Old Side, roughly in the triangle formed by Centraal Station, the Nieuwmarkt and the Dam, is the famed Red Light District.

THE CANALS

The *grachtengordel* (girdle of canals) that guards the Old Centre is idyllic, pleasant and quintessentially Amsterdam. In the listings for shops, restaurants and the like in this guide, we've split the canals in half. Western Canal Belt denotes the stretch of canals to the west and north of Leidsegracht, while Southern Canal Belt covers the area east of here, taking in Leidseplein and Rembrandtplein.

JODENBUURT, THE PLANTAGE AND THE OOST

The area around Waterlooplein was settled by Jews two centuries ago and took its name – Jodenbuurt – from them. The Plantage, which lies east and south-east of Waterlooplein, holds many delights, among them the Hortus Botanicus and Artis. Further east – or Oost – lies the Tropenmuseum, before the city opens up and stretches outwards and onwards.

THE WATERFRONT

Once the gateway to the city's prosperity, Amsterdam's waterfront is now the setting for one of Europe's most exciting new architectural developments and an increasing number of nightlife options.

THE JORDAAN

Bordered by Brouwersgracht, Prinsengracht, Leidsegracht and Lijnbaansgracht, the Jordaan is arguably Amsterdam's most charming neighbourhood. Working-class stalwarts rub shoulders with affluent newcomers in an area that, while lacking the grandiose architecture of the canals, wants for nothing in character.

THE MUSEUM QUARTER, VONDELPARK AND THE SOUTH

With its world-class museums and stupendously posh fashion emporia, Amsterdam's Museum Quarter is a mix of culture and couture. South of Singelgracht, with approximate borders at Overtoom (west) and Hobbemakade (east), it's also home to many pleasant hotels and, at its northernmost tip, is within a stone's throw of both Leidseplein and Vondelpark.

THE PIJP

Against all the gentrification odds, the Pijp has managed to remain a wonderful melting pot of many cultures and nationalities.

Two final tips. Call ahead if you plan to visit a museum on a public holiday, as many shut for the day. And don't fret about language issues: in Amsterdam, almost all of the big museums (and many of the smaller ones) do have either captions and/or guidebooks in English, as well as English-speaking staff on hand.

Tours

Bicycle tours

For bicycle hire, *see p300.*

Yellow Bike

Nieuwezijds Kolk 29, Old Centre: New Side (620 6940/www.yellowbike.nl). Tram 1, 2, 5, 13, 17. **Open** *Mar-Nov* 8.30am-5.30pm daily. **No credit cards. Map** p326 C2.

Of the many options, there's a three-hour City Tour (€19.50) that departs daily at 9.30am and 1pm; the six-hour Waterland Tour (€27.50), leaving daily at 11am, includes a visit to a pancake house.

Boat tours

There's not an awful lot of difference between the various boat tours that rove Amsterdam's waterways for an hour at a time. For long tours, though, choose more carefully. As well as day cruises, all the firms listed run night cruises at 9pm daily in summer (less often in winter), costing from €20 to €25. **Lovers** and **Holland International** (for both, see below) do dinner cruises for €65 to €75. Booking is vital. There's also **Het Varend Restaurant** (428 8996, www.varendrestaurant.nl), which, for €75, tours the canals while serving a meal prepared by a changing roster of highly regarded local chefs. They depart from the dock in front of the café **'t Smalle** (*see p162*).

There's also a **water taxi** (535 6363, www.water-taxi.nl) for groups of one to 44, but their relatively small size means that you have access to the smaller, more charming canals; and a **canal bus** (626 5574, www.canalbus.nl), where a €16 day card, bought at the Amsterdam Tourist Board and various kiosks around town, allows you unlimited use of 14 stops until noon the next day. For information on **St Nicolaas Boat Club**, a non-profit outfit that gives toke-friendly cruises on small open-topped boats, ask **Boom Chicago** (*see p253*) or surf to www.boatclub.nl. For boat hire, *see p300.*

Best of Holland

Departure point at Damrak 34, by Centraal Station, Old Centre: New Side (420 4000/www.thebestofholland.nl). Tram 4, 9, 16, 24, 25. **Cruises** every 30min, 10am-5pm daily. **Tickets** €8.50; €5.50 under-13s. **Credit** AmEx, DC, MC, V. **Map** p325 D2.

Holland International

Departure point at Prins Hendrikkade 33A, by Centraal Station, Old Centre: New Side (622 7788). Tram 4, 9, 16, 24, 25. **Cruises** *Summer* every 15min, 9am-10pm daily. *Winter* every 30min, 10am-6pm daily. **Tickets** €9; €5 under-13s or free for two children when accompanied by two paying adults. **Credit** AmEx, MC, V. **Map** p325 D2.

Lovers

Prins Hendrikkade, opposite 25-7, by Centraal Station, Old Centre: New Side (530 1090/www.lovers.nl). Tram 4, 9, 16, 24, 25. **Cruises** *Summer* every 30min, 9am-6pm daily. *Winter* every 30min, 10am-5pm daily. **Tickets** €9; €6 under-13s. **Credit** AmEx, MC, V. **Map** p325 D2.

Rondvaarten Rederij Kooij

Corner of Rokin and Spui, Old Centre: New Side (623 3810/www.rederijkooij.nl). Tram 4, 9, 16, 24, 25. **Cruises** *Summer* every 30min, 10am-10pm daily. *Winter* every 30min, 10am-5pm daily. **Tickets** €7.50; €4 under-13s. **No credit cards. Map** p326 D3.

Walking tours

The Amsterdam Tourist Board publishes brochures in English that suggest easy routes.

Archivisie

Postbus 14603, 1001 LC (625 9123).

Tailor-made architectural tours and regular theme tours. Phone for appointments and prices.

Mee in Mokum

(625 1390). **Tours** 11am Tue-Sun. **Tickets** €4; free under-12s. **No credit cards. Map** p326 C3.

Locals, all over 55, give two-hour tours (in English and Dutch) of the Old Centre, the Jordaan and Jewish Amsterdam. Tours leave from the Amsterdams Historisch Museum (*see p98*). Booking is required; when you call, tell them if you plan to bring children.

Urban Home & Garden Tours

(688 1243/www.uhgt.nl). **Tours** *Apr-Sept 30* 10.15am Mon, Fri; 11.15am Sat. **Tickets** €25 (includes lunch). **No credit cards. Map** p331 E4.

Professional garden designers and art historians give tours in English of the 17th-, 18th- and 19th-century canal houses. Tours leave from the Museum Willet-Holthuysen (*see p108*); booking is essential.

Van Aemstel Produkties

(683 2592/www.amsterdamexcursies.nl).

Various times and prices. **No credit cards.**

Generally only available for groups of ten or more, these inspired folk have long branched out from offering tours of the Old Centre led by medieval guardsmen types. Now you can learn about the world of edible flowers from a homeless man, drink tea with a transvestite, get the inside scoop on Amsterdam's most special toilets, or learn to use a hand bow in an ancient monastery. With prices starting at €10/hour, they are even competitive on cost with their less visionary and exciting peers.

The Old Centre

History meets hedonism in a tale of two cities.

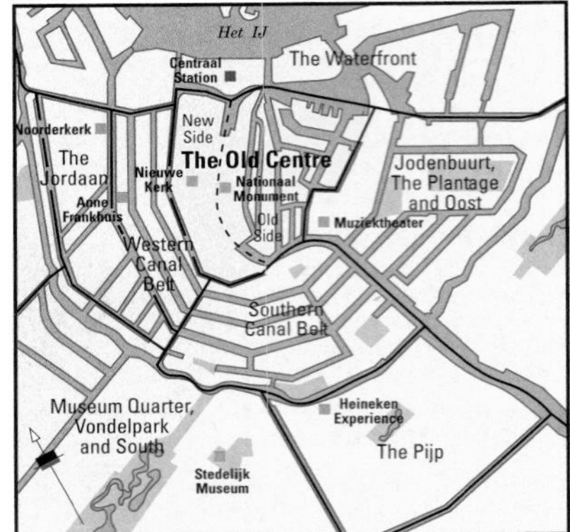

Sightseeing

One side embraces shopping and pursuits of the mind, while the other – with the Red Light District as its red neon centrepiece – is more about sex and religion. Common feature? They both drip with history. In short: Amsterdam's compelling Old Centre (aka Oud Centrum) surfs on a wave of contradiction.

Marked off by Centraal Station, Singel and Zwanenburgwal, the area is roughly bisected by Damrak, which turns into Rokin south of Dam Square. Within the Old Centre, the saucier area to the east is the ancient Old Side (Oude Zijde), while the gentler area over to the west – whose most notable landmark is Spui Square – is the far-from-new New Side (Nieuwe Zijde).

The Old Side

Around the Dam

Map p326

Straight up from **Centraal Station**, just beyond the once-watery but now-paved and touristy strip named Damrak, lies **Dam Square** (*photo p89*), the heart of the city since the first dam was built here in 1270. Today it's a convenient meeting point for many tourists, the majority of whom convene underneath its mildly phallic centrepiece, the **Nationaal Monument**. The 22-metre (70-foot) white obelisk is dedicated to the Dutch servicemen who died in World War II. Designed by JJP Oud, with sculptures from John Raedecker, it has 12 urns, 11 filled with earth collected from the (back then) 11 Dutch provinces and the 12th containing soil from war cemeteries in long-time Dutch colony Indonesia.

Both the monument and the square recently had much-needed facelifts: the roughness of the new cobblestones now deters errant bikers (and wheelchairs), and their lighter colour disguises the Jackson Pollock splodges of pigeon droppings. If you can, see it in the quiet of dawn, when the square reflects an elusive sense of the epic, which is appropriate, since the Dam has seen many singular social and political activities: nude running through the square (by Anabaptists, testing the boundaries of religious freedom in 1535), chilling in the name of peace (by hippies in the 1960s) and a catalogue of highly dramatic protests, coronations and executions.

The west side of Dam Square is flanked by the **Koninklijk Paleis** (Royal Palace; *see below*); next to it is the 600-year-old **Nieuwe Kerk** (New Church, so named as it was built a century after the Oude Kerk, or Old Church, in the Red Light District; *see p87*). In kitsch contrast, over on the south side, is **Madame Tussaud's Scenerama** (*see p85*).

Beurs van Berlage

Damrak 277, entrance at Beursplein 1 (530 4141/ Artiflex tours 620 8112/www.beursvanberlage.nl). Tram 4, 9, 14, 16, 24, 25. **Open** during exhibitions 10am-10pm daily. **Admission** varies; discount with MK. **No credit cards**. **Map** p326 D2.

Designed in 1896 by Hendrik Berlage as the city's stock exchange, the palatial Beurs, while incorporating a broad range of traditional building styles, represents a break with 19th-century architecture and prepared the way for the Amsterdam School (*see p38* **School of rock**). Although critics thought it 'a big block with a cigar box on top', it's now considered the country's most important piece of 20th-century architecture. By exposing the basic structures and fusing them with stunning decorations, it celebrates the workers and artisans who built it (as opposed to the stockbrokers who were to inhabit it). In fact, it's a socialist statement: much of the artwork warns against capitalism, and each of the nine million bricks was intended to represent the individual; the resulting monolith stands for society.

Having long driven out the moneychangers, the Beurs is now all things to all other people: a conference centre, concert halls (*see p238*), a mosaiced café/restaurant, and an exhibition space for shows that range from plastinated human bodies to organic

Centraal Station.

architecture to beer festivals. In addition, 90-minute tours of the building are conducted by art historians from Artiflex, though booking is compulsory; call the number above to do so in advance.

Koninklijk Paleis (Royal Palace)

Dam (information 620 4060/tours 624 8698/www.koninklijkhuis.nl). Tram 1, 2, 4, 5, 9, 13, 14, 16, 17, 24, 25. **Open** *July, Aug* 11am-5pm daily. *Sept-June* times vary. **Admission** €4.50; €3.60 5s-16s, over-65s; free under-6s. **No credit cards. Map** p326 C3.

Seemingly following a citywide trend, the Royal Palace will be closed for renovations until at least summer 2008. And it's a damn shame. Designed along classical lines by Jacob van Campen in the 17th century, built on 13,659 wooden piles that were rammed deep into the sand, the Royal Palace was originally built and used as the city hall. The poet Constantijn Huygens hyped it as 'the world's Eighth Wonder', a monument to the cockiness Amsterdam felt at the dawn of its Golden Age. It was intended as a smugly epic 'screw you' gesture to visiting monarchs, a species that the people of Amsterdam had thus far happily done without.

The exterior is only really impressive when viewed from the rear, where Atlas holds his 1,000-kilogram (2,205-pound) copper load at a great height. It's even grander inside than out: the Citizen's Hall, with its baroque decoration in grand marble and bronze that depicts a miniature universe (with Amsterdam as its obvious centre), is meant to make you feel about as worthy as the rats seen carved in stone over the Bankruptcy Chamber's door.

Though much of the art on display reflects the typically jaded humour of a people who have seen it all, the overall impression is one of deadly seriousness: one screw-up and you could end up among the grotesque carvings of the Tribunal and sentenced to die in some uniquely torturous and public way. Kinder, gentler displays of creativity, though, can be seen in the chimney pieces, painted by artists such as Ferdinand Bol and Govert Flinck, both pupils of Rembrandt (who, oddly enough, had his own sketches rejected). The city hall was transformed into a royal palace in 1808, shortly after Napoleon had made his brother, Louis, King of the Netherlands, and a fine collection of furniture from this period can be viewed on a guided tour. The Palace became state property in 1936 and is still used occasionally by the royal family.

Madame Tussaud's Scenerama

Peek & Cloppenburg, Dam 20 (523 0623/www.madame-tussauds.nl). Tram 4, 9, 14, 16, 24, 25. **Open** 10am-5.30pm daily. **Admission** €19.95; €14.95 5s-15s; free under-5s. **Credit** AmEx, DC, MC, V. **Map** p326 D3.

Craving some queasy kitsch factor? Waxy cheese-textured representations from Holland's own Golden Age of commerce are depicted alongside the Dutch royal family, local celebs and global superstars. Some of the models look like their subjects, some don't. But while there's much campy fun to be had, it comes at a price, and it's hard not to leave without a renewed respect for candles.

Nieuwe Kerk (New Church)

Dam (626 8168/recorded information 638 6909/www.nieuwekerk.nl). Tram 1, 2, 4, 5, 9, 13, 14, 16, 17, 24, 25. **Open** 10am-6pm daily but hours may vary. **Admission** varies with exhibition. **No credit cards. Map** p326 C3.

While the 'old' Oude Kerk in the Red Light District was built in the 1300s, the sprightly 'new' Nieuwe Kerk dates from 1408. It is not known how much damage was caused by the fires of 1421 and 1452, or even how much rebuilding took place, but most of the pillars and walls were erected after that time. Iconoclasm in 1566 left the church intact, though statues and altars were removed in the Reformation. The sundial on its tower was used to set the time on all of the city's clocks until 1890.

In 1645, the Nieuwe Kerk was gutted by the Great Fire; the ornate oak pulpit and great organ (the latter designed by Jacob van Campen) are thought to have been constructed shortly after the blaze. Also of interest here is the tomb of naval hero Admiral de Ruyter (1607-76), who initiated the ending of the Second Anglo-Dutch war – wounding British pride in the process – when he sailed up the Medway in 1667, inspiring a witness, Sir William Batten, to observe: 'I think the Devil shits Dutchmen.' Poets and Amsterdam natives PC Hooft and Joost van den Vondel are also buried here. These days, the Nieuwe Kerk hosts organ recitals, state occasions and consistently excellent exhibitions. *Photos p92.*

Theme park Amsterdam

Ain't Amsterdam sweet? It's certainly hard not to be charmed by the city's cutesy dollhouse proportions. Even the radical hippie party that arose from the ashes of Provo (*see p24*) and ended up winning five seats in city government in 1970 called themselves the Kabouters, after the happy-go-lucky forest-dwelling dwarves who feature in local folk tales. It also makes sense that the Dutch have a reputation for high quality theme parks: **Efteling** (*see p206*) is a favourite among connoisseurs who like a dash of the surreal in their rollercoaster experiences, plus there's the 'world's largest miniature village', **Madurodam** (*see p206*).

But in many ways, Amsterdam itself can be seen as a theme park – or may at least eventually become one. This process is best seen in, of all places, the Red Light District. What were once furtive pleasures have been sanitised to the point that the district has got as close to being 'fun for the whole family' as it's possible to imagine in an area that makes its living from spreading its legs. Long gone are the days when you would walk around and see – as you still could in the 1960s – condoms hanging out to dry until their next go. Yes sir, things have certainly been cleaned up over the years.

Disturbed by this trend, plenty of city locals – call them cynics or call them soothsayers – warn of the 'Disneyfication' of Amsterdam. They fear that the residents will be pushed out of the inner city in favour of hotels and restaurants, turning Amsterdam into one big water-girdled tourist attraction. Already this scenario seems to be backed up by the fact that most visitors, whether stoners or businesspersons, rarely bother to look both ways when crossing a road, tramline or bike path. Do the city's very intimate dimensions inspire a false sense of security? Be sure you don't make the same mistake. Amsterdam is a city where one can be rendered into road pizza in milliseconds. You have been warned.

Sexmuseum Venustempel

Damrak 18 (622 8376/www.sexmuseumamsterdam.nl). Tram 4, 9, 14, 16, 24, 25. **Open** 10am-11pm daily. **Admission** €2.50. **No credit cards. Map** p326 D2.

The Sexmuseum is one of two museums devoted to doing the dirty in Amsterdam, and a tawdry little operation it is too. The Damrak location, just by Centraal Station, is designed to lure in masses of passing tourists, and on this count it succeeds. But with the exception of a splendid and often hilarious collection of pornographic Victorian photographs, the presentation is largely botched. There's a fascinating exhibition on the history of porn movies to be staged, but the one here ain't it. Ivory dildos, filthy porcelain, joyless cartoons, peeling pin-ups, 'happy breastday cakes' and ugly art are all shaved of eroticism by the context and the leering gangs of gigglers that make up the majority of the punters. At least admission is appropriately cheap.

The Red Light District

Maps p326 & p327

The Red Light District, sited in an approximate triangle formed by Centraal Station, Nieuwmarkt and the Dam, is at the very root of Amsterdam's international notoriety. While more overheated imaginations the world over construct images of wild sexual abandon framed in red neon-lit windows, the reality depicted in the postcards on sale locally is a sort of small, cutesy version of Las Vegas. If truth be told, the cheesy joke shop has here been supplanted by the cheesy sex shop: instead of electric palm buzzers and comedy nose glasses, you get multi-orifice inflatables and huge dildos.

Most of the historical significance of the Red Light District – of which there is plenty, this being the oldest part of Amsterdam – has been veneered by another old and very greasy trade: marketing. Although sex is the hook upon which the whole area hangs its reputation, it's actually secondary to window-shopping. People do buy – it's estimated to be a €500-million-per-year trade – but mostly they simply wander around, gawping at the live exhibits.

Most of the window girls are self-employed and, even though prostitution was only defined as a legal and taxable profession in 1988 and bordellos have only been officially legitimate since October 2000 (a tactic intended to make taxation easier), the women have had their own union, De Rode Draad (*see p53*), since 1984. Prostitutes are mostly women: despite regular attempts to launch both male and transsexual prostitution, men have so far found it difficult to get their dicks into this particular door of opportunity. With legality has come a plethora of new rules, governing anything from the temperature at which lingerie is washed to the cleansers used to clear the adjoining showers of 'liquid-loving insects'. (For more on the sex trade and its history, *see pp50-54*.)

As at more traditional markets like **Albert Cuypmarkt** (*see p190*), where the cheese merchants line up alongside cheese merchants and fishmongers group with fishmongers, women with specialities also tend to clump together. Sultry Latinos gather along the Molensteeg and the beginning of Oudezijds Achterburgwal; ambiguously sexed Thais on Stoofstraat; amply girthed Africans around Oude Kerk; and the model-ish and skinny on Trompettersteeg, Amsterdam's smallest street. But there is much else to absorb in this most iconoclastic of neighbourhoods. Prostitutes, clerics, school kids, junkies, carpenters and cops all interact with a strange brand of social cosiness, and the tourists are mere voyeurs. It's all good fun and pretty harmless, just so long as you remember that window girls do not like having their photographs taken and that drug dealers react to eye contact like dogs to bones.

And why all the red lights? Quite simple: it's most flattering to the skin.

Zeedijk

Facing away from Centraal Station to the left are two churches, **St Nicolaaskerk** (whose interior of funky darkness can be viewed from Easter to mid October, and where one can hear Gregorian vespers every Sunday at 5pm from September to June) and the dome and odd skull-adorned exterior of **St Olafkerk** (also known locally as the 'Cheese Church', having housed the cheese exchange for many years). Between the two, you can enter **Zeedijk** (*photos p97*), a street with a rich and tattered history.

Before this dyke was built, some time near 1300, Amsterdam was a fishing village with barely enough bog to stand on. But by the 15th and 16th centuries, with the East India Company raking in the imperialist spoils, Zeedijk was where sailors came to catch up on their boozing, brawling and also bonking – or 'doing the St Nicolaas', as it was fondly termed in those days (a tribute to their patron saint, an extremely busy chap who watches over children, thieves, prostitutes and the city of Amsterdam).

Sailors who had lost all their money could trade in their pet monkey for a flea-infested bed at Zeedijk 1, which still retains its original name – **In't Aepjen**, meaning 'In the Monkeys' – and is today one of the oldest and most charming wooden houses in the city centre. Just off the street down Oudezijds Kolk, you can spot the **Schreierstoren**, aka the 'Weeping Tower' (*see p37*). It is said that wives would cry there, perhaps with relief, when husbands set off on a voyage, then cry again if the ship returned with news that said spouse was lost at sea. If the latter happened, then it was but a short walk to Zeedijk, where the bereaved lady would often continue life as a 'merry widow'. Prostitution was often the female equivalent of joining the navy: the last economic option.

During the 20th century, Zeedijk has been sparked by cultural diversity. In the 1930s, the first openly gay establishments appeared, and at the now-closed – though a replica remains on display in the **Amsterdams Historisch Museum** (*see p98*) – **Het Mandje** (Zeedijk 65), there's a window shrine to flamboyant owner Bet van Beeren (1902-67), who has gone down in local mythology as the original lesbian biker chick. In the '50s, jazz greats Chet Baker and Gerry Mulligan came to jam and hang out in the many after-hours clubs here, among them the still-functioning-as-a-shadow-of-what-it-was **Casablanca** (Zeedijk 26).

Unfortunately, this subculture rather marked Zeedijk as a place where heroin could be scored with comparative ease. By the 1970s the street had become crowded with dealers, junkies and indifferent cops, with most of the restaurants and cafés renting their tables to dealers. It was one big druggie convention. The junkies' magic number was 27: *f*25 for the drugs and *f*2 for the drink that owners insisted all the junkies purchase to maintain the façade of legality.

Amsterdam's reputation became littered with needles and foil, and never more so than when a wasted Chet Baker took his final curtain call in 1988 – on to a cement parking pole – from a window (second floor on the left) of the Prins Hendrik Hotel at the entrance of Zeedijk. A brass plaque commemorating the crooning trumpeter has been put up to the left of the hotel's entrance. Although there was a time when a German tour operator's 'criminal safari' was not even allowed on Zeedijk and street cleaners needed armed escorts, police claim to have cleaned the street up in recent years (but only after long and sustained pressure from residents); indeed, the scene is today infinitely less intimidating and packed with newish businesses and restaurants. The famed dance and ambient label **Outland Records** has its store at No.22; **Demask** offers its posh line of leathers and latexes at No.64 (*see p229*); and excellent cheap Chinese food can be found in **Nam Kee** at Zeedijk 111-13 (*see p137*). Across the street from Nam Kee, the still relatively new **Chinese Fo Guang Shan He Hua Buddhist Temple** (420 2357, www.ibps.nl, open noon-5pm Tue-Sat, 10am-5pm Sun), where monks and nuns provide a library, internet café and vegetarian restaurant, says a lot for this street's progress in terms of cultural enlightenment.

Nieuwmarkt

At the bottom of Zeedijk, your eyes will be drawn to the huge and castle-like **De Waag** (*photo p98*), or 'the Weigh House'. The Waag, previously called St Antoniespoort, stands in the centre of Nieuwmarkt and dates from 1488, when it was built as a gatehouse for the city defences. If you have a yen for mankind's darker traits, try to imagine the body parts that used to garnish the Waag's south-east side. The majority of Amsterdam's many public executions took place here, providing a steady supply of fresh corpses for the medical guild to dissect in the Waag's Anatomical Theatre (and for Rembrandt to study and paint – as in his *Anatomy Lesson of Dr Nicolaes Tulp*). In the black days of the Nazi occupation the square was surrounded by barbed wire and used as one of the collection points to hold captives from the Jewish quarter, who were shipped off to concentration camps via the **Hollandse Schouwburg** (*see p112*). More recently, in 1980, Nieuwmarkt was the site of riots when the city demolished housing to make way for the Metro. In 1991, it was saved by a citizens' committee from being irrevocably revamped by designer Phillippe Starck. Today, the Waag is home to the Society for Old and New Media (557 9898, www.waag.org, also now housed in Pakhuis de Zwijger, *see p116* **Architectural relections**), which surfs the interface between technology and culture and organises events in the Anatomical Theatre.

Pausing for breath in bustling **Dam Square**. *See p84.*

The streets leading to the north-east from Nieuwmarkt contain Amsterdam's small Chinatown, while the colourfully named side streets – among them Monnikkenstraat (Monk Street), Bloedstraat (Blood Street) and Koestraat (Cow Street) – on the south-west lead into the reddest part of the Red Light District.

At Kloveniersburgwal 29 is **Trippenhuis**, now home to the Dutch Academy of Sciences, who formerly shared it in the 18th century with the original Rijksmuseum collection. During the Golden Age the building was owned and equally shared (witness the bisecting wall in the middle window) by the two Trip brothers and their respective families. Their fortune was made by serious arms dealing (witness the mortar-shaped chimneys and the cannons engraved on the gable), and they could easily afford the imposing gunpowder grey exterior. They even – or so the story goes – built the **House of Mr Trip's Coachman**, at No.26, in response to a one-liner the coachman reputedly made about being happy with a house as wide as the Trips' front door. He got his wish. The house, capped with golden sphinxes, is now home to a clothing store and appropriately anorexic display figures.

'De Wallen'

The two canals Oudezijds Voorburgwal and Oudezijds Achterburgwal, with their quaint interconnecting streets, are where carnal sin screams loudest. So it's ironic that, right in the middle of Sin City, you'll stumble across a pair of old churches. The **Oude Kerk** (*see p93*), Amsterdam's oldest building, is literally in the centre of the sleazy action, with hookers in windows ringing the mammoth church like bullies taunting the class geek. Keep your eyes peeled for the small brass bosom inlaid by a mystery artist into the pavement by the front entrance. The **Museum Amstelkring** (*see p93*), meanwhile, is tucked away a distance from the red-lit action, but still shouldn't be overlooked on your journey around the area.

The Oudezijds Voorburgwal was known as the 'Velvet Canal' in the 16th century due to the obscene wealth of its residents. Now, though, at least along its northern stretch, the velvet has been replaced by red velour, illuminated by scarlet fluorescent lighting and complemented by bored-looking girls sat in the windows of the lovely canal houses. It's perhaps incongruous, then, that this canal should also be so densely populated with churches, chapels and orders. Representatives from the Salvation Army lurk on many a corner, although more so around the aforementioned Oude Kerk and Museum Amstelkring to the north and less so near the **Agnietenkapel** (Oudezijds Voorburgwal 231, 525 3339). Of Amsterdam's 17 medieval convents, this Gothic chapel is one of a few remnants to have survived intact. Built in the 1470s and part of the University of Amsterdam since its foundation in 1632, the chapel has an austere, Calvinistic beauty highlighted by its

Night and the city

For years, small bands of locals and tourists alike have been led through the town on **Full Moon Walks** beneath the light of a silvery orb. And they're always being led by the same enigmatic Amsterdammer: none other than Miss Moon herself. Blessed with the name Josephine Moons, it seemed pure destiny that she would combine her passion for that bright bulb of the evening sky with her knowledge of all things Amsterdam, and so she began organising full moon walks in a style that differs wildly from your more garden variety see-everything-in-a-day city tours.

For one, Miss Moon's presence – and, of course, that of the full moon above – are the only elements of the tour that remain constant; the meeting point, route and setting change. One night she'll lead you through the Jordaan (*see pp118-122*) on the trail of Amsterdam photographer Frits Weeda; another night may include a boat ride along the IJ, or a walk through Chinatown (*see p89*) to celebrate the first full moon of the Chinese New Year. A warmer evening could mean riding bikes through the polders, those large flat fields reclaimed from the sea over to the north of Amsterdam, with plenty of cows and sheep to gander at. At the end of winter, when a few stubborn snowflakes still linger in the cold air, she might take you on a brisk walk through the Pijp (*see pp129-130*), ending up at a snug café for a couple of warming drinks.

Miss Moon has run diamond tours through the old Jewish area, beer walks (stumbles?) through the old brewers' district and, in early December, a stroll with Sinterklaas, sharing the history and legends surrounding the Dutch holiday while ambling through the harbour where he arrives on his steamboat. Every walk comes with a story and usually photos of what that particular piece of Amsterdam looked like in the distant past. Depending on plans for the evening, prices range from €15 to €35. And bear in mind that spots fill up fast, so it's best to reserve early. Visit www.fullmoonwalk.nl for more info.

stained-glass windows, wooden beams and benches, not to mention a collection of portraits of humanist thinkers. The Grote Gehoorzaal (Large Auditorium), the country's oldest lecture hall, is where 17th-century scholars Vossius and Barlaeus first taught; its wooden ceiling is painted with soberly ornamental Renaissance motifs including angels and flowers. Rolling exhibitions are only occasional; since 2007 it is used mostly for readings and congresses.

The parallel Oudezijds Achterburgwal offers some of the more 'tasteful' choices for the eroto-clubber. The **Casa Rosso** nightclub (Oudezijds Achterburgwal 106-108, 627 8954) is certainly worth a look, even though its famed and peculiar marble cock-and-rotary-ball water fountain at its entrance has been removed. A short walk away at No.37 is the **Bananenbar** (622 4670), where improbably dextrous female genitalia can be seen performing night after night – and, as the central part of their belief-buggering act, spitting out an average of 15 kilograms (33 pounds) of fruit every evening. A former owner of the Bananenbar once tried to stave off taxmen – and get round the fact that his drinking licence had lapsed – by picking Satan as a deity and registering the Bananenbar as a church. It was a scam that worked for years – until 1988, when the 'Church of Satan' claimed a membership of 40,000 overseen by a council of nine anonymous persons. The tax police were called in to bust the joint, but the bar was tipped off and the 'church' disbanded. Now under the same ownership as the Erotic Museum, the Bananenbar has kept its name and returned to its roots as a purveyor of sleaze.

Nieuwe Kerk. *See p85.*

If your urges are more academic, you can conduct some, ahem, research at the **Erotic Museum** (*see below*), following it in semi-traditional fashion with a smoke at the **Hash Marihuana Hemp Museum** (which doesn't actually sell dope, but you get the picture; *see below*). Other than that, sleaze and stag parties dominate this strip, with it now particularly unpleasant and busy on weekends.

It's a far cry from the **Spinhuis**, a former convent tucked away at the southern end of the canal (on Spinhuissteeg) that used to set 'wayward women' to work spinning wool. The male equivalent was over on the New Side at Heiligeweg 9 – now an entrance to the Kalvertoren shopping complex – where audiences used to watch the prisoners being branded and beaten with a bull's penis. In a rather curious foreshadowing of Amsterdam's contemporary S&M scene, the entrance gate sports a statue bearing a striking resemblance to a scolding dominatrix.

Erotic Museum

Oudezijds Achterburgwal 54 (624 7303). Tram 4, 9, 16, 24, 25/Metro Nieuwmarkt. **Open** 11am-1am Mon-Thur, Sun; 11am-2am Fri, Sat. **Admission** €5. **No credit cards**. **Map** p326 D2.

While the Sexmuseum (*see p87*) benefits from its Damrak location in terms of passing trade, the Erotic Museum is in the more appropriate location: slap bang in the Red Light District. That's not to say, though, that it's any more authentic or interesting. Its prize exhibits are a bicycle-powered dildo and a few of John Lennon's erotic drawings, while lovers of Bettie Page (and there are many) will enjoy the original photos of the S&M muse on display. In general, however, the museum's name is somewhat inaccurate: despite its best intentions and desperate desire to shock, it's as unsexy as can be. All in all, you're probably best off going to one of the many nearby sex shops for your kicks.

Hash Marihuana Hemp Museum

Oudezijds Achterburgwal 130 (623 5961/www.hashmuseum.com). Tram 4, 9, 14, 16, 24, 25/Metro Nieuwmarkt. **Open** 10am-10pm daily. **Admission** €5.70. **No credit cards**. **Map** p326 D3.

Given the decriminalised nature of dope here, it figures that the city should have a museum entirely devoted to hash. It's just a pity that this ridiculously named operation, which tries to be all things to all people and ends up being nothing to anyone, aside from a pricey way for a backpacker to waste around half an hour in the Red Light District. There's some interesting information here, sure: the display on the medical benefits of the drug is enlightening, as are a few nuggets on the history of hemp and the smell of growing plants. But the small exhibition lacks cohesion and entertainment value, and comes across alternately as hippyish and – surprisingly – rather po-faced. Definitely a missed opportunity.

Museum Amstelkring

Oudezijds Voorburgwal 40 (624 6604/www.museumamstelkring.nl). Tram 4, 9, 14, 16, 24, 25. **Open** 10am-5pm Mon-Sat; 1-5pm Sun. **Admission** €7; €5 students, over-65s; €1 5s-18s; free under-5s, MK. **No credit cards**. **Map** p326 D2.

The Amstelkring takes its name from the group of historians who succeeded in saving it from demolition in the late 1800s. Good job they did save it, too, for what remains is one of Amsterdam's most unique spots, and one of its best-kept secrets. The lower floors of the house have been wonderfully preserved since the late 17th century, and offer a look at what life might have been like back then.

The main attraction is upstairs, and goes by the name of Ons' Lieve Heer op Solder, or 'Our Sweet Lord in the Attic'. Built in 1663, this attic church was used by Catholics during the 17th century when they were banned from worshipping after the Alteration. It's been beautifully preserved, too, the altarpiece featuring a painting by 18th-century artist Jacob de Wit. The church is often used for services and a wide variety of other meetings. Don't miss it.

Oude Kerk

Oudekerksplein 1 (625 8284/www.oudekerk.nl). Tram 4, 9, 16, 24, 25, 26. **Open** 11am-5pm Mon-Sat; 1-5pm Sun. **Admission** €5; €4 over-65s, students; free under-12s, MK; varies during special exhibitions. **No credit cards**. **Map** p326 D2.

Originally built in 1306 as a wooden chapel, and constantly renovated and extended between 1330 and 1571, the Oude Kerk is the city's oldest and most interesting church. One can only imagine the Sunday Mass chaos during its heyday of the mid 1500s when it had 38 altars each with its own guild-sponsored priest. Its original furnishings were removed by iconoclasts during the Reformation, but the church has retained its wooden roof, which was painted in the 15th century with figurative images. Keep your eyes peeled for the mixed Gothic and Renaissance façade above the northern portal, and the stained-glass windows, parts of which date from the 16th and 17th centuries. Rembrandt's wife Saskia, who died in 1642, is buried here. The inscription over the bridal chamber, which translates as 'Marry in haste, mourn at leisure', is in keeping with the church's location in the heart of the Red Light District, though this is more by accident than design. If you want to be semi-shocked, check out the carvings in the choir benches of men evacuating their bowels – apparently they tell a moralistic tale. The church is now as much of an exhibition centre as anything else, with shows covering everything from modern art installations to the annual World Press Photo Exhibition (*see p197*).

Warmoesstraat & Nes

It's now hard to believe that Warmoesstraat, Amsterdam's oldest street, was once the most beautiful of lanes, providing a sharp contrast

Water, water everywhere

Farmers, beer and water. An unlikely recipe for success, but they sure made Amsterdam what it is today. Not that the city's rise was universally greeted with delight. In 1652, in one of those periodic ebbs in Anglo-Dutch relations, the poet Owen Felltham described the Low Countries as 'the buttock of the world, full of veins and blood but no bones'. But it's that very boggy basis that is the essential foundation of Amsterdam's historical success.

Originating as a village that subsisted on a bit of fishing and some small-town frolicking, Amsterdam quickly fostered some of the first cheerleaders of democracy: stubborn local farmers, who built up large dykes to keep the sea and the mighty Amstel at bay. The teamwork needed for such a massive task formed the basis for today's famed but sadly fading 'polder model', where all conflicts are resolved at endless meetings fuelled by coffee and the thirst for consensus. Of course, since flexibility and compromise also made good business sense, the approach actually did turn out to be highly profitable.

Amsterdam was only properly set up as a centre of pragmatic trade and lusty sin in the 14th century, when it was granted beer tax exemption status. This opened the floodgates to a river of the stuff (flowing from Hamburg) and to lots of beer-drinking settlers. After beer profits, other profits followed – from sea travels to both the east and the west – and before long Amsterdam became the single richest and most powerful port in the world. The resulting Golden Age saw the construction of the canal girdle (*see pp99-108*), and these, along with the more ancient waterways of the Old Centre, formed a full circulatory system – as well as a sewage system – in which goods and also people from all over the world could easily flow in and out of the city.

Besides a knack for building canals, dykes, windmills and ships, the Dutch came up with a whole bevy of other water-worthy inventions during the Golden Age. The inventor Cornelis Drebbel (1572-1634) designed the very first submarine prototype (basically a rowing boat fitted with rawhide and tubes), and local genius Jan van der Heyden (1637-1712) invented the first pump-action fire hose. More curious still were the 'Tobacco-Smoke-Enema-Applicators', developed to attempt the reanimation of the drowners who were regularly pulled from the canals. This ancient technique – also applied with reversed 30-centimetre (12-inch) Gouda pipes – was standard practice and all part of the canalside scenery in Amsterdam until the 1850s, when the less dramatic but more effective mouth-to-mouth technique gained prominence. Talk about progress.

The fine-tuning of technologies at the end of the 19th century allowed the building of the North Sea Channel, thus giving Amsterdam a more direct route to the sea and triggering a second Golden Age of sorts. The 1990s can be seen in a similar light, thanks to the huge influx of corporations seeking a central location for their European HQs. The eastern docklands (*see pp114-117*) began transforming into a showcase for modern architecture that sought to blend both private and public spaces with its watery surrounds. Elsewhere, The artificial islands of IJburg further east continue this trend, as do the very ambitious

plans to build vast windmill parks in the North Sea and create a floating runway for Schiphol Airport. While acceptance of this last idea is still far off, it's not as ridiculous as it sounds: Schiphol itself used to be five metres (16ft) under water before the land won out. What's more, fuel of the future, hydrogen – the mighty H in H_2O – is finally being taken seriously, as proved by the successful deployment of hydrogen-powered buses across Amsterdam.

That water is of great national importance in a country where two-thirds of the land is reclaimed was shown recently, when Crown Prince Willem Alexander decided to slough off his image of rather doltish young manhood and embrace water as a personal crusade. 'Water is fantastically beautiful. It's essential to life. It's about health, environment and transport. There's the fight against water and the fight against too little water. You can actually do everything with it, and it's primordially Dutch.' Anything you say, Crown Prince.

Still, water does play a fundamental role in the recreational lives of more regular folk. While 'eel-pulling' (a folk game in the Jordaan that the powers-that-be tried to put a stop to, leading to the Eel Riot of 1886 and resulting in 26 dead) is no longer practised as a canal sport, boating remains the most popular of calm pastimes. (Sadly, its winter counterpart, ice-skating, has suffered greatly from climate change.) The opening of the city's very first bona fide beach in IJburg was the news story of summer 2003 (*see p116* **Architectural reflections**), which was only tarnished when the beach claimed its first drowning victim in 2004. And although the concept of making the Prinsengracht swimmable remains a ploy of fringe political parties to get headline space, the recent and more realistic plan to re-dig canals like Elandsgracht and Lindengracht, which were filled in to cope with motor traffic, was all set for the go ahead until suddenly it was quashed by residents who decided that, since the city was already one-quarter water, they didn't need any more. But regardless, Amsterdam is well aware that water remains one of its strongest tourist magnets.

As an almost mystical form of modern male communion with the elemental basis of the city there is, of course, the honoured practice of urinating into a canal. However, this form of *wildplassen* ('wild pissing') now risks a €50 fine, levied to stop that other unique form of historical loss, urine erosion. To prevent this happening, 'Wild Pissing Symposiums' have been convened, even coming up with *A Plan of Action: Wild Pissing*. But as the canal waters are essentially flushed daily, ever since a hi-tech alternating sluice system was implemented, what's the problem?

When compared to the original Venice, also known as the 'sewer of the south', the waters of the 'Venice of the north' are essentially stench-free. And now that Amsterdam even has its own gondola service (www.gondel.nl), there's really no competition. In fact, here you can meditate on the wiggly reflections in the canals from up close without fear of succumbing to fumes. Not merely trippy, they also act as a reminder that Amsterdam is a happily twisted town – somewhere you can throw your cares overboard and go with the flow. Just don't take that last part too literally.

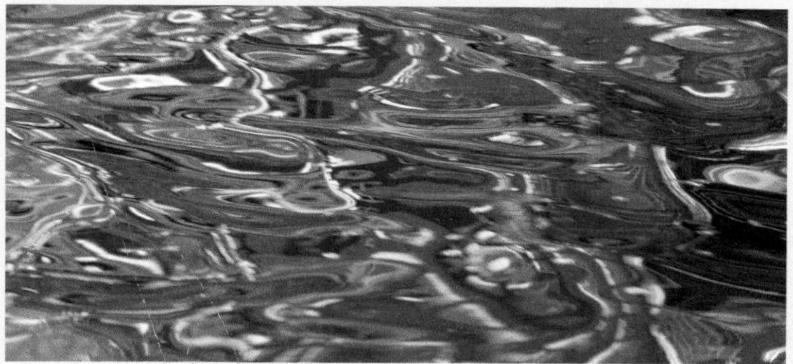

to its evil and rowdy twin, Zeedijk. The poet Joost van den Vondel ran a hosiery business at Warmoesstraat 101; Mozart's dad would try to flog tickets at the posh bars for his young son's concerts; and Marx would later come here to write in peace (or so he claimed: he was more likely to have been in town to borrow money from his cousin by marriage, the extremely wealthy Gerard Philips, founder of the globe-dominating Philips corporate machine).

But with the influx of sailors, the laws of supply and demand engineered a heavy fall from grace for Warmoesstraat. Adam and Eve in their salad days can still be seen etched in stone at Warmoesstraat 25, but for the most part, this street has fallen to accommodating only the low-end traveller. However, hipper hangouts such as gay/mixed bar **Getto** (*see p228*), excellent breakfast and lunch spot **Bakkerswinkel** (*see p135*) and the **Winston Hotel** (*see p62*), plus shops including the **Condomerie het Guiden Vlies** (*see p193*) and gallery **W139** (*see p217*) have ensured that the strip has retained some brighter and less commercial colours, while the council's serial clean-up operation reached the street quite recently and has at least had some of the desired cosmetic effect.

Just as Warmoesstraat stretches north from the Nationaal Monument into the Old Side, so Nes leaves the same spot to the south, parallel and to the west of Oudezijds Achterburgwal. Dating from the Middle Ages, this street was once home to the city's tobacco trade and the Jewish philosopher Benedict Spinoza (1623-77), who saw body and mind as the two aspects of a single substance. Appropriate, then, that you can now witness the alignment of body and mind on the stages of the many theatres that have long graced this street. You can also stop, recharge and realign your own essence at one of the many charming cafés hereabouts. At the end of Nes, either take a turn left to cross a bridge where the junkies are often out selling freshly stolen bicycles for next to nothing (be warned that buying one will have you risking jail and deportation) towards **Oudemanhuis Book Market** (where Van Gogh bought prints for his room; *see p191*) on the University of Amsterdam campus; or turn right and end up near the **Allard Pierson Museum** (*see below*).

Allard Pierson Museum

Oude Turfmarkt 127 (525 2556/www.allardpierson museum.nl). Tram 4, 9, 14, 16, 24, 25. **Open** 10am-5pm Tue-Fri; 1-5pm Sat, Sun. **Admission** €5; €2.50 4s-15s, over-65s; free under-4s, MK. **No credit cards. Map** p326 D3.

Established in Amsterdam in 1934, the Allard Pierson claims to hold one of the world's richest university collections of archaeological exhibits from ancient Egypt, Greece, Rome and the Near East. So far, so good. And, if archaeological exhibits are your thing, or your children would like their names written in hieroglyphics, then it's probably a destination that will go down well. However, if you didn't spend several years at university studying stuff like this, you'll probably be bored completely witless. Many of the exhibits (statues, sculptures, ceramics etc) are unimaginatively presented, as if they were aimed solely at scholars. English captions are minimal – though for the record, the Dutch ones are scarcely more helpful – and few staff are on hand to help explain what's what. A frustrating experience.

The New Side

Map p326

Rhyming (nearly enough) with 'cow', the Spui is the square that caps the three main arteries that start down near the west end of Centraal Station: the middle-of-the-road walking and retail street Kalverstraat (called Nieuwendijk before it crosses the Dam), plus Nieuwezijds Voorburgwal and the Spuistraat.

Coming up along Nieuwezijds Voorburgwal – translated literally as 'the New Side's Front of the Town Wall' to distinguish it from the Oudezijds Voorburgwal ('the Old Side's Front of the Town Wall'), found in near mirror image in the Red Light District, though both city walls have long since been destroyed – the effects of a tragically half-arsed urban renewal job are immediately noticeable. The Crowne Plaza hotel at Nieuwezijds Voorburgwal 5 was formerly the site of the large Wyers squat, dramatically emptied by riot police in 1985 after a widely supported campaign by squatters against the mass conversion of residential buildings into commercial spaces (such as the case of the domed Koepelkerk at Kattengat 1, a Lutheran church painted by Van Gogh, since turned into a hotel and convention centre).

The multinational, perhaps predictably, proved victorious, as did the ABN-AMRO bank further up, with its in-your-face glass plaza at the corner with Nieuwezijds Kolk. But urban renewal – not to mention the digging of new subway lines – does have its benefits, in that it affords an opportunity for city archaeologists to dig down and uncover Amsterdam's sunken history (as a general rule, every 50cm travelled downwards represents a century backwards). For instance, while the underground car park was being dug on the ABN-AMRO site, a team of researchers uncovered 13th-century wall fragments that were, for a short time, surmised to be the remains of a marsh-surrounded castle belonging to the Lords of the Amstel. While this proved to be jumping the gun, it did show that the so-called 'New Side' is not new at all.

From sex and drugs to celebrity suicide: **Zeedijk** has seen it all. *See p87.*

A quiet backwater accessible via the north side of Spui square or, when that entrance is closed, via Gedempte Begijnensloot (the alternating entrances were set up to appease residents), the **Begijnhof** is a group of houses built around a secluded courtyard and garden. Established in the 14th century, it originally provided modest homes for the Beguines, a religious and, as was the way in the Middle Ages with religious establishments for women, rather liberated sisterhood of unmarried ladies from good families who, though not nuns and thus taking no formal vows, lived together in a close community and had to take vows of chastity. Since they did not have to take vows of poverty, the Beguines were free to dispose of their property as they saw fit, further ensuring their emancipation as a community. They could, however, renounce their vows at any moment and leave, for instance if they wanted to get married. The last sister died in 1971, while one of her predecessors never left, despite dying back in 1654. She was buried in a 'grave in the gutter' under a red granite slab that remains visible – and often still adorned with flowers – on the path. Nowadays, it's part of the best-known of the city's many *hofjes* (almshouses).

Most of the neat little houses in the courtyard were modernised in the 17th and 18th centuries. In the centre stands the **Engelsekerk** (English Reformed Church), built as a church around 1400 and given over to Scottish (no, really) Presbyterians living in the city in 1607; many became pilgrims when they decided to travel further to the New World in search of religious freedom. Now one of the principal places of worship for Amsterdam's English community, the church is worth a look primarily to see the pulpit panels, designed by a young Mondrian.

Also in the courtyard is a Catholic church, secretly converted from two houses in 1665 following the complete banning of open Catholic worship after the Reformation. It once held the regurgitated Eucharist host that starred in the Miracle of Amsterdam (*see p197*), a story depicted in the church's beautiful stained-glass windows. The wooden house at Begijnhof 34, known as the **Houtenhuis**, dates from 1475

De Waag: these days mercifully free of amputated body parts. *See p88.*

and is the oldest house still standing within the city, while **Begijnhof 35** is an information centre. The Begijnhof is also very close to one of the several entrances to the **Amsterdams Historisch Museum** (*see below*), which in turn is the starting point for the highly informal **Mee in Mokum** walking tours (*see p83*).

The Spui square itself plays host to many markets – the most notable being the busy book market on Fridays – and was historically an area where the intelligentsia gathered for some serious browbeating and alcohol abuse after a day's work on the local papers. The *Lieverdje* ('Little Darling') statue in front of the **Athenaeum Nieuwscentrum** store (*see p173*), a small, spindly and guano-smeared statue of a boy in goofy knee socks, was the site for wacky Provo 'happenings' that took place in the mid 1960s (*see p24*).

You can leave Spui by going up Kalverstraat, Amsterdam's main shopping street, or Singel past Leidsestraat: both routes lead up to the **Munttoren** (Mint Tower) at Muntplein. Just across from the floating flower market (the **Bloemenmarkt**; *see p183*), this medieval tower was the western corner of Reguliersspoort, a gate in the city wall in the 1480s; in 1620, a spire was added by Hendrick de Keyser, the foremost architect of the period. The tower takes its name from when it minted coins after Amsterdam was cut off from its money supply during a war with England, Munster and France. There's a shop on the ground floor for fine Dutch porcelain (**Holland Gallery de Munt**, Muntplein 12, 623 2271), but the rest of the tower is closed to visitors. The Munttoren is prettiest when floodlit at night, though daytime visitors may hear its carillon, which often plays out for 15 minutes at noon.

From here, walk down Nieuwe Doelenstraat past the Hôtel de l'Europe (a mock-up of which featured in Hitchcock's *Foreign Correspondent*). This street connects with scenic Staalstraat – so scenic, in fact, that it's the city's most popular film location, having appeared in everything from *The Diary of Anne Frank* all the way up to *Amsterdamned*. Walk up here and you'll end up at **Waterlooplein** (*see p109* and *p192*).

Amsterdams Historisch Museum

Kalverstraat 92 (523 1822/www.ahm.nl). Tram 1, 2, 4, 5, 9, 14, 16, 24, 25. **Open** 10am-5pm Mon-Fri; 11am-5pm Sat, Sun. **Admission** €7; €5.25 65+; €3.50 6s-16s; free under-6s, MK. **No credit cards. Map** p326 D3.

A note to all those historical museums around the world that struggle to present their exhibits in an engaging fashion: head here to see how it's done. Amsterdam's Historical Museum is a gem: illuminating, interesting and entertaining. It starts with the very buildings in which it's housed: a lovely, labyrinthine collection of 17th-century constructions built on the site of a 1414 convent. You can enter it down Sint Luciensteeg, just off Kalverstraat, or off Spui, walking past the Begijnhof (*see p97*) and then through the grand Civic Guard Gallery, a small covered street hung with huge 16th- and 17th-century group portraits of wealthy burghers.

And it continues with the museum's first exhibit, a computer-generated map of the area showing how Amsterdam has grown (and shrunk) throughout the last 800 years or so. It then takes a chronological trip through Amsterdam's past, using archaeological finds (love those 700-year-old shoes), works of art and some far quirkier displays: tone-deaf masochists may care to play the carillon in the galleried room 10A, while lesbian barflies will want to pay homage to Bet van Beeren, late owner of celebrated Het Mandje. Amsterdam has a rich history, and this wonderful museum does it justice.

The Canals

God may have made the waters, but you can thank man for the *grachtengordel.*

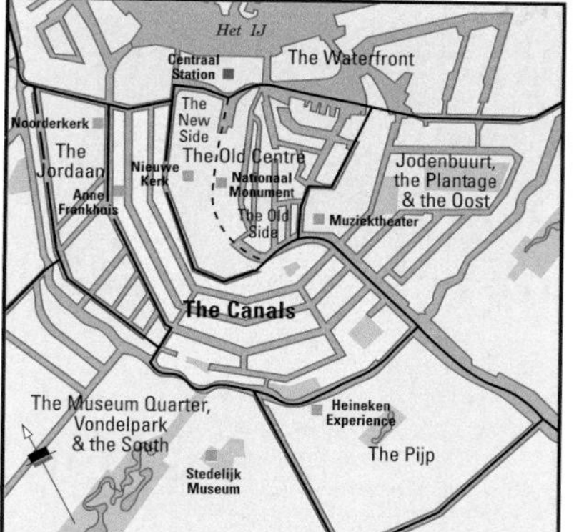

The Dutch call them *grachten*. There are 165 in Amsterdam. They stretch for 75.5 kilometres (47 miles) around the city, are crossed by 1,400 bridges and are, on average, just three metres (ten feet) deep. They keep the sea and all the surrounding bog at bay. Some 10,000 bicycles, 100 million litres (22 million gallons) of sludge and an average of 50 corpses (usually those of tramps who fell in while under the influence) are dredged from their murky depths every year.

The major canals and their radial streets are where the real Amsterdam exists. What they lack in sights, they make up for as places for scenic coffee slurping, quirky shopping, aimless walks and more meditative gable gazing. The *grachtengordel* – 'girdle of canals' – rings the centre of the town, its waterways providing a rather attractive border between the tourist-laden city centre and the gentler, artier and more 'local' locales of the Museum Quarter, the Jordaan and the Pijp.

Singel was the original medieval moat of the city, and the other three canals that follow its line outward were part of a Golden Age urban renewal scheme; by the time building finished, the city had quadrupled in size. Herengracht (named after the man who initially invested in it), Keizersgracht (named after Holy Roman Emperor Maximilian I) and Prinsengracht (named after William, Prince of Orange) are canals where the rich lived; but though parts are still residential, many properties now house offices, hotels and banks.

The connecting canals and streets, originally built for workers and artisans, have a higher density of cafés and shops, while the popular retail stretches of Rozengracht, Elandsgracht, Leidsestraat and Vijzelstraat are all former canals, filled in to deal with the traffic. Smaller canals worth seeking out include Leliegracht, Bloemgracht, Egelantiersgracht, Spiegelgracht and also historic Brouwersgracht.

In this guide, for ease of use, we've split venues on the canals into the Western Canal Belt (between Singel and Prinsengracht, south of Brouwersgracht, north and west of Leidsegracht) and the Southern Canal Belt (between Singel and Prinsengracht, from Leidsegracht south-east to the Amstel). This splitting is historically justified by the fact that the western girdle was finished before work on the eastern half began.

The Western Canal Belt

Map p326

Singel

One of the few clues to Singel's past as the protective moat surrounding the city's wall is the bridge that crosses it at Oude Leliestraat. It's called the Torensluis and did, indeed, once have a lookout tower; the space under the bridge, now ironically populated with drinkers upon its terraces, was supposedly used as a lock-up for medieval drunks. The statue of the writer on it, Multatuli, depicting his head forming as smoke from a bottle, is a reference to the way he let the genie out of the bottle by questioning Dutch imperialism in novels like *Max Havelaar* (1860), and not to the fact that he was the first recorded Dutchman to be cremated.

While you're wandering this lazy canal, you may want to join the debate on whether Singel 7 or Singel 166 is the smallest house in town. Located between them, and adored by most cat lovers, is the **Poezenboot** (Cat Boat; 625 8794, www.poezenboot.nl, open 1-3pm Mon, Tues, Thur-Sun) opposite Singel 40, home to stray and abandoned felines, though ongoing funding problems may see a demise of this institution. Slightly further down, and always good for a snort, is the **House with Noses** at Singel 116, though arty types may be more interested in Singel 140-142, once the home of Banning Cocq,

One of over 1,400 bridges spanning Amsterdam's network of canals.

the principal figure of Rembrandt's *Night Watch*, once referred to as 'the stupidest man in Amsterdam'. Further south, you may want to stake out the town's poshest old school sex club, **Yab Yum** (Singel 295, 624 9503, www.yabyum.com) to watch the country's elite enter for a good old-fashioned servicing.

Multatuli Museum

Korsjespoortsteeg 20 (638 1938/www.multatuli-museum.nl). Tram 1, 2, 5, 13, 17. **Open** 10am-5pm Tue; noon-5pm Sat, Sun; also by appointment. **Admission** free. **Map** p326 C2.

Just off Singel, this museum to the writer Eduard Douwes-Dekker (1820-87), aka Multatuli, is in the house where he was born. The various literary artefacts pay testament to his credo: 'the human calling is to be human'. There's also a small library.

Herengracht

Cross Singel at Wijde Heisteeg, and opposite you on Herengracht is the **Bijbels Museum** (Bible Museum; *see right*). A few doors further south, at the **Netherlands Institute of War Documentation** (Herengracht 380, 523 3800, www.niod.nl) – whose three kilometres (1.8 miles) of archives include Anne Frank's diary, donated by her father Otto – stonemasons knocked up a copy of a Loire mansion, complete with coy reclining figures on the gable and frolicking cherubs around its bay window.

The northern stretch of Herengracht, from here up to Brouwersgracht, is fairly sight-free; the canal also wants for cafés and decent shops. Still, it's a very pleasant walk. Also try to peek into the windows of the **Van Brienenhuis** at Herengracht 284: the excesses of bygone eras will soon become apparent. Keep walking and you'll reach a Vingboons building at No.168, dating from 1638. Along with De Keyser's Bartolotti House, this architectural gem now houses the **Theater Instituut** (*see right*). For a unique look at the history of purses, meanwhile, be sure to stop in on the **Tassenmuseum** (*see p178* **Bag habits die hard**).

Bijbels Museum

Herengracht 366 (624 2436/www.bijbelsmuseum.nl). Tram 1, 2, 5. **Open** 10am-5pm Mon-Sat; 11am-5pm Sun, public holidays. **Admission** €7.50; €3.75 13s-17s; free under-13s, MK. **No credit cards. Map** p330 C4.

Housed in two handsome Vingboons canal houses, Amsterdam's Bible Museum aims to illustrate life and worship in biblical times with archaeological finds from Egypt and the Middle East (including the remarkable mummy of an Israeli woman), models of ancient temples and a slideshow. There's also a splendid collection of Bibles from several centuries

If walls could talk: courage in every corner of the **Anne Frank Huis**. *See p103.*

(including a rhyming Bible from 1271). A little dry in places, this museum does attract folk merely looking to admire the restored houses, the splendid Jacob de Wit paintings, and the grand garden with biblical plants and a wild sculpture entitled *Apocalypse*.

Theater Instituut

Herengracht 168 (551 3300/www.tin.nl). Tram 1, 2, 5, 13, 17. **Open** 11am-5pm Mon-Fri; 1-5pm Sat, Sun. **Admission** €4.50; €2.25 students, 6s-16s, over-65s; free under-6s, MK. **Credit** AmEx, MC, V. **Map** p326 C3.

The ever-changing displays here are largely drawn from the institute's collection of costumes, props, posters, memorabilia and ephemera, much of which is digitally catalogued. Upstairs there is a massive library; call ahead for information on hours and prices. Inside is a ceiling painting by Jacob de Wit and outside there's an idyllic garden.

Keizersgracht

Walk down Keizersgracht from its northern tip (by Brouwersgracht), and you'll soon encounter the **House with the Heads** at Keizersgracht 123, a pure Dutch Renaissance classic. The official story has these finely chiselled heads representing classical gods, but according to local folklore they are the heads of burglars, chopped off by a lusty maidservant. She decapitated six and married the seventh.

Another true classic is at Keizersgracht 174, an art nouveau masterpiece by Gerrit van Arkels that, rumour has it, will become a hotel – you might want to admire it from the charming local boozer **Café Brandon** (*see p157*), whose decorations remain seemingly unchanged since the Dutch lost the 1974 World Cup Final to the Germans. Similarly difficult to ignore is the **Felix Meritis Building** at Keizersgracht 324, given that it's a neoclassical monolith with the motto 'Happiness through achievement' chiselled over its door. And achieve it did: after housing a society of arts and sciences in the 1800s, it went on to serve the Communist Party and is now the European Centre for Art and Science – complete with a high-minded and high-ceilinged café. Nearby is the equally epic home of the photography foundation, **Huis Marseille** (*see below*). This whole stretch was also the site of the legendary Slipper Parade, where the posh-footed rich strolled about every Sunday both to see and be seen. From here, take a right turn down Molenpad to Prinsengracht.

Huis Marseille

Keizersgracht 401 (531 8989/www.huismarseille.nl). Tram 1, 2, 5. **Open** 11am-5pm Tue-Sun. **Admission** €5; €3 65+, students; free under-17s, MK. **No credit cards**. **Map** p330 C4.

House of the spirits

The chequerboard **Stadsarchief** building, now home to the city's archives – the biggest municipal archive in the world – occupies a block of Vijzelstraat between Keizers- and Herengracht, and is known as 'De Bazel' in honour of its architect, KPC de Bazel. Before it became a place of study, this big chunk of real estate was an office complex for the bank ABN AMRO, and before that, the HQ of the Nederlandsche Handel-Maatschappij, or Dutch Trading Company. On the corners of the building, which was completed in 1926, carvings represent Asia and Europe, the continents the NHM's trading interests straddled; between the windows are grid-like patterns of spiralling squares. It looks the very monument of modernism, its rational lines representing a combination of commerce and design that stretches towards a brave new world.

It looks logical, but the building emerged from swirling mists of esoterica, since De Bazel himself was in fact a strict follower of Theosophy, the religion-cum-philosophy-cum-cod-science that dabbles in Eastern spirituality and new-age enlightenment. Popular with artists at the turn of the 20th century, WB Yeats, Georgia O'Keeffe and Mondrian all flirted with its crystal balls for a while. It was the brainchild of one Madame Blavatsky, a chain-smoking – tobacco and hashish both – Russian émigrée who was given religious authority by Tibetan Masters, spiritual guides who had been around for millennia. Two such guides, Morya and Koot Hoomi, accompanied her everywhere, helping promote Eastern literature, natural laws and the spiritual use of the straight line.

De Bazel discovered the movement with fellow architect JML Lauweriks; after a jaunt to London to look at the British Museum's Egyptian and Assyrian collections, they chose to join the Amsterdam Theosophical Society (now at Tolstraat 154, another Theosophically proportioned structure) and set up a practice that employed their beliefs in buildings.

Mercantile meanings apart, the design of the Vijzelstraat building is infused with its creator's religious beliefs, visible at every turn in its divine proportions. According to Blavatsky's followers, pink and yellow represent masculinity and femininity, so that chessboard pattern on the façade is as much about integrating yin and yang as it is about industrial brinkmanship. The straight line and the grid weren't just a product of the rationalist set-square: they were the *kundalini* or serpent power, prevalent both in Egyptian and Indian symbolism. This same *kundalini* is everywhere in the building, on every surface, creating what the architect referred to as the 'total environment'; that is, a cosmic entity where every detail – from the structure to the furnishings to the floor itself – works towards a spiritual whole.

The area where this is most gloriously evident is the Schatkamer. Last in use as the bank's computer room, a team of builders uncovered a Tutankhamen's tomb of embellishment: floors, ceilings, walls; every surface was decorated with the very same spiralling square pattern that adorns the façade in lustrous colours. Long neglected, the interior had to be painstakingly restored from photographs taken during the 1920s, a process that delayed the opening by several months. If all goes to plan, it should open by August 2007 – unless some fabulous new treasures are unearthed again, that is.

Stadsarchief

Vijzelstraat 32, Southern Canal Belt (251 1511/www.stadsarchief.amsterdam.nl). Tram 16, 24, 25. **Open** 10am-5pm Tue-Sat; 11am-5pm Sun. **Admission** free. **Map** p330 D4.

Located in a monumental 17th-century house, the walls of this photography foundation might host the latest from such hotshots as Hellen van Meene, David Goldblatt or Naoya Hatakeyama, classic work from perhaps contemporary photography's most influential duo, Bernd and Hilla Becher, or landscapes of Amsterdam or even the moon. Don't miss the videos and mags in the 'media kitchen'.

Prinsengracht

The most charming of the canals. Pompous façades have been mellowed with shady trees, cosy cafés and some of Amsterdam's funkier houseboats. The watery **Woonbootmuseum** (Houseboat Museum; *see p104*), not one of the funkiest, is a short stroll away. Also around here are some lovely shopping thoroughfares. Working northwards, the 'Nine Streets' linking Prinsengracht, Keizersgracht and Herengracht, between Leidsestraat and Raadhuisstraat, all offer a delightfully diverse pick of smaller, artier speciality shops that perfectly flavour a leisurely walk by the water.

On your way up Prinsengracht, the tall spire of the 375-year-old **Westerkerk** (*see right*) should loom into view. Its tower is easily the tallest structure in this part of town and if you choose to climb it, you'll be able to look down upon the expanded – but still very modestly dimensioned – **Anne Frank Huis** (*see below*). Mari Andriessen's statue of Frank (dated 1977) stands nearby, at the corner of Westermarkt and Prinsengracht. Meanwhile, any fans of René Descartes – and if you think, you therefore probably are – can pay tribute to the great savant by casting an eye on his former house around the corner at Westermarkt 6, which looks out on the pink granite triangular slabs of the understated **Homomonument** (*see p221*), the planet's first memorial to persecuted gays and lesbians throughout history.

If it's a Monday and you find yourself at the weekly **Noordermarkt** (*see p191*), then make sure you stop for coffee at the always popular **Papeneiland** (*see p162*). According to local legend, a tunnel used to run under the canal from here to a Catholic church that was located at Prinsengracht 7 at the time of the Protestant uprising. Also on this odd-numbered side of the canal, you can check to see if the doors to the courtyards of the Van Briennen *hofje* (No.85-133) or the De Zon *hofje* (No.159-171) are open, and have a quick peek inside if so.

Anne Frank Huis

Prinsengracht 267 (556 7105/www.annefrank.nl). Tram 13, 17. **Open** *Jan-Mar, Sept-Dec* 9am-7pm daily. *Apr-Aug* 9am-9pm daily. **Admission** €7.50; €3.50 10s-17s; free under-10s. **Credit** MC, V. **Map** p326 C2.

Prinsengracht 263 was the 17th-century canalside house where young Jewish girl Anne Frank and her family hid for two years during World War II. Today it's one of the most popular attractions in Amsterdam, with almost a million visitors a year.

Having fled from persecution in Germany in 1933, Anne, her sister Margot, their parents and four other Jews went into hiding on 5 July 1942. Living in an annexe behind Prinsengracht 263, they were sustained by friends who risked everything to help them; a bookcase marks the entrance to the sober, unfurnished rooms. But on 4 August 1944 the occupants were arrested and transported to concentration camps, where Anne died with Margot and their mother. Her father, Otto, survived, and decided that Anne's diary should be published. The rest, as they say, is history: tens of millions of copies of the diary have been printed in a total of 55 languages.

In the new wing, there's a good exhibition about the Jews and their persecution during the war, as well as displays charting racism, neo-Fascism and anti-Semitism, and exploring the difficulties in fighting discrimination; all have English texts. To avoid the famously long queues, arrive first thing in the morning, or (in summer) after 7pm.

Interestingly, the Amsterdam South apartment the Franks previously lived in now hosts persecuted writers from around the world. *Photos p101.*

Westerkerk

Prinsengracht 277-279 (624 7766/tower 689 2565/ www.westerkerk.nl). Tram 13, 14, 17. **Open** *Apr-Sept* 11am-3pm Mon-Fri. *Services* 10.30am Sun. **Admission** *Tower* €5. **No credit cards. Map** p326 C3.

Before noise pollution, it was said that if you could hear the bells of Westerkerk, built in 1631 by Hendrick de Keyser, you were in the Jordaan. These days, its freshly scrubbed and painted tower is just a good place from which to view its streets and canals, provided you don't suffer from vertigo: the 85m (278ft) tower sways by 3cm (1.2in) in a good wind. Although the last tour up the 186 steps is at 5pm, and tours are only scheduled in summer, groups may call to book for other times.

It's thought that Rembrandt is buried here, though no one is sure where. The artist died a pauper, and is commemorated inside with a plaque. Though his burial on 8 October 1669 was recorded in the church register, the actual spot was not; there's a good chance he shares a grave with his son, Titus.

From the street you can see that the tower is emblazoned with a gaudy red, blue and gold 'XXX' crown. Not a reference to the porn industry, it's the crown granted to the city in 1489 by Maximillian, the Holy Roman Emperor, in gratitude for treatment he received during a pilgrimage to Amsterdam. The triple-X came to be used by local traders to denote quality. It also emblazons the phallic parking poles scattered throughout the city, which incidentally can be bought for around €85 at the city's material depot (Pieter Braaijweg 10, 561 2111).

Chess set at **Max Euweplein**. *See p108.*

Woonbootmuseum

Prinsengracht, opposite No.296 (427 0750/www.houseboatmuseum.nl). Tram 13, 14, 17. **Open** *Mar-Oct* 11am-5pm Tue-Sun. *Nov-Feb* 11am-5pm Fri-Sun. Closed last 2wks of Jan. **Admission** €3.25; €2.50 children under 152cm (5ft). **No credit cards. Map** p330 C4.

The Houseboat Museum is not just a museum about houseboats: it's actually on one. In fact, it more or less is one: aside from some discreet explanatory panels, a small slide show and a ticket clerk, the Hendrika Maria is laid out as a houseboat would be, to help visitors imagine what it's like to live on the water. It's more spacious than you might expect and does a good job of selling the lifestyle afforded by its unique comforts. Until, that is, you notice the pungent scent of urine emanating from the public 'curlie' (as they are locally called), a toilet right by the boat.

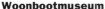

The Southern Canal Belt

Map p330

Around Rembrandtplein

In better days Rembrandtplein was called Reguliersmarkt. Then it hosted Amsterdam's butter market and in 1876 the square was renamed in honour of Rembrandt; a statue – today the oldest in the city – of the Dutch master, looking decidedly less scruffy than he does in his self-portraits, stands in the centre of the gardens, gazing in the direction of the Jewish quarter. Though there's no longer a market, it's still the centre of commercial activity, with a wild profusion of neon lights and a cacophony of music blaring out from the cafés, bars and restaurants on all sides.

The area is unashamedly, unconscionably, unbearably tacky – the façade of the **Escape** (*see p243*) now hosts Europe's largest digital screen. The square is also home to a variety of establishments, from the faded and fake elegance of the traditional striptease parlours to seedy modern peepshow joints and nondescript cafés. There are a few exceptions to the air of tawdriness – places like the zoological sample-filled grand café **De Kroon** (No.17), the art deco **Schiller** (No.26) and HL de Jong's crazily colourful dream-as-reality masterpiece, cinema **Pathé Tuschinski** on Reguliersbreestraat (*see p210*). Carry on past here and you'll end up at Muntplein, by the floating flower market at the southern tip of Singel (the **Bloemenmarkt**; *see p183*), also home to miniature art gallery the **Reflex Minituur Museum** (*see p126* **Museums for the mildly obsessed**). Over on the corner of the Amstel are some lively gay cafés and bars (*see p224*), and on the façade of

Amstel 216, the city's freakiest graffiti. This 'House with the Bloodstains' was home to former mayor Coenraad van Beuningen (1622-93), whose brilliance was eclipsed by insanity. After seeing visions of fireballs and fluorescent coffins above the Reguliersgracht, he scrawled the still visible graffiti of sailing ships, stars, strange symbols and his and his wife's name with his own blood on the grey stone walls. Subsequent attempts to scrub the stains off have all proved futile. Or, at least, so the story goes.

From Rembrandtplein, walk south along the prime mid-range shopping and eating street Utrechtsestraat, or explore Reguliersgracht and Amstelveld. Whichever you choose, you'll cross Herengracht as you wander.

The canals

As the first canal to be dug in the glory days, Herengracht attracted the richest of merchants, and this southern stretch is where you'll find the most stately and overblown houses on any of Amsterdam's canals. The **Museum Willet-Holthuysen** (*see p108*) is a classic example of such a 17th-century mansion.

However, it's on the stretch built between Leidsestraat and Vijzelstraat, known as the Golden Bend, that things really get out of hand. By then the rich saw the advantage of buying two adjoining lots so that they could build as wide as they built high. Excess defines the Louis XIV style of Herengracht 475, while tales of pre-rock 'n' roll excess are often told about Herengracht 527, whose interior was trashed by Peter the Great while he was here learning to be a ship's carpenter and picking up urban ideas for his dream city, St Petersburg. Around the corner on Vijzelstraat is the imposing building **Gebouw de Bazel**, since 2007 the brand new home of the city archives Gemeentearchief Amsterdam (*see p102* **House of the spirits**). More mischievous types may want to annoy the mayor by mooring up on his personal dock in front of the official residence at Herengracht 502. If you're caught, attempt palming off the authorities with the excuse that you're visiting the **Kattenkabinet** (Cat Cabinet; *see p107*).

It's a similarly grand story on this southern section of Keizersgracht, too. For evidence, pop into the **Museum van Loon** or photography museum **Foam** (for both, *see p107*), both of them on Keizersgracht just east of Vijzelstraat. But for an alternative view of this area, head half a block south to Kerkstraat, parallel to and located directly between Keizersgracht and Prinsengracht. The houses here are less grand, but what they lack in swank they more than make up for in funkiness, with their galleries and shops only adding to the community feel.

Cheap thrills

There's a wealth of, well, wealth on display in this fine city, but don't think you have to spend a fortune to have a fantastic time in Amsterdam. The following list of activities shows how easily cheapskates can have fun for free.

- The view from **Nemo**'s roof (*see p115*).
- Complimentary coffee at **Albert Heijn** (*see p191* **Back to basics**).
- The **ferry trips** from Centraal Station (*see p116* **Architectural reflections**).
- The gardens on the **Rijksmuseum**'s western side (*see p123*).
- Open-air concerts and the great outdoors of **Vondelpark** (*see p125*).
- The Civic Guard Gallery over at the **Amsterdams Historisch Museum** (*see p98*).
- The **Noordermarkt** flea market on Monday mornings (*see p191*).
- Tuesday lunchtime concerts at the **Muziektheater** (*see p240*).
- Wednesday lunchtime concerts at the **Concertgebouw** (*see p238*).
- Exploring the unique **hofjes** (courtyard almshouses) of the Jordaan (*see p118*).
- Watching horseriding in AL van Gendt's beautiful **Hollands Manege** (Vondelstraat 140, 618 0942).
- Tasting free food in the Saturday **farmers' market** at the Noordermarkt (*see p191*).
- Peering in Hendrick de Keyser's atmospheric **Zuiderkerk** (*see p109*).
- Smelling the flowers on sale at the floating **Bloemenmarkt** (*see p183*).
- Checking out the biggest barometer in the Netherlands. The neon light on the **Hotel Okura Amsterdam** (*see p73*) predicts tomorrow's weather: blue for good, green for bad and white for changeable.
- Taking a lift to the top of **Post CS** (*see p114*) for unsurpassed city views.
- Lounging on a deckchair and soaking up the rays at one of the city's many **urban beaches** (*see p159* **United we sand**).
- Taking in art exhibition openings every Friday night at **Chiellerie** (*see p216*).
- Going queer clubbing every first Saturday of the month at **Hot Peper**, in the fabulous De Peper café (*see p151*).
- Reading international papers at the new **Centrale Bibliotheek** (*see p307*).
- Seeing top-notch bands being recorded for TV at **Club 3voor12** (*see p232*).

Canal dreams

On a sojourn through the city of Amsterdam, Hans Christian Andersen wrote: 'The view from my window, through the elms, onto the canal outside, is like a fairy tale.' The canals are still what everyone imagines when they think about Amsterdam, and they continue to engender enchantment today. Like any city built on water, it's best seen from a boat. There are over 76 kilometres (46 miles) of waterways in the city, spread across 165 canals and spanned by 1,400 bridges (more than Venice); look at the bottom right-hand corner of a bridge to find its individual number.

The tourist boats between them provide a doughty service, but they can't get into the smaller waterways. Self-piloted hire boats were sadly banned years ago, so you may need to befriend a boat-bearing local or even charter a tour (*see p83*). If you can't get a boat, you can always do it by bike or foot – but it won't be as much fun as bobbing along the water.

The tour begins on the Amstel, in front of the Stopera. Head up the Singel, the channel built to girdle the city in 1450. Go through the tunnel under the Munt; during the summer particularly, note the hundreds of empty bottles and cans – this is the boating community's partying HQ-turned-recycling depot – and watch out for the spiders. Pass along the back of the **Bloemenmarkt** (*see p183*), taking care to avoid getting squirted by the hideous fire-gnomes' hoses just before the first bridge. A couple of hundred yards before the third bridge, hover mid-canal to try and espy high-profile visitors entering **Yab Yum** (Singel 295, 624 9503, www.yabyum.nl), a rather upmarket knocking shop, notable for its large green lantern, on your right.

Sail on for another two bridges; as you start coming closer to the second, the Torensluis – the widest bridge in Amsterdam at 42m (138ft) – note the steps leading downward to barred windows and doors. These were once used as grim prison cells for vagabonds and drunkards, and date from the 1800s – pull up and press your face to the railings for the full story. If required, duck into **Villa Zeezicht** (Torensteeg 7, 626 7433, www.villa zeezicht.com) for a drink or a toilet break, or go on to the end of Singel for an alternative stopping point: there's a very handy platform outside the 17th-century architect Adriaan Dortsman's lovely yet ill-fated Koepelkerk (it caught fire in 1822 and 1993). Good food, refreshments and a loo can be found inside the charming **Village Bagels** (Stromarkt 2, 528 9152, www.villagebagels.nl).

Take a left into Brouwersgracht (beware of the big tour boats). During the 17th and 18th centuries, this still gorgeous canal was lined with breweries. There are no proper sights to be seen these days, just a glimpse at the now converted warehouses in one of Amsterdam's most minted des res addresses. Tourist boats only go a short distance here, so persist up to the end – you'll have it all to yourself as a result. Next, veer into Prinsengracht while copping a glance up and right at cheerful café **Papeneiland** (*see p162*). Immediately below the water you're sailing on, there's a tunnel running to the opposite bank; during the long period of religious persecution in the 17th century, this was used to deliver Catholics over to a secret church on the far side.

Continue towards the scaffolded **Westerkerk** (*see p103*). Just before the second bridge, you'll see Egelantiersgracht, where **'t Smalle** (*see p162*) has by far the boat-friendliest terrace in town, perfect for a quick break and a beer. Alternatively, duck into Bloemgracht to view the Jordaan at its residential best.

Pass beneath the bridge by the Westerkerk and you'll eventually find **Hotel Pulitzer** (*see p63*). This is the place to be in mid August, when the hotel hosts the grand finale of the Grachtenfestival (www.grachtenfestival.nl), which sees hundreds of boats bob along to classical music blaring from a floating pontoon.

Hang a left into Leidsegracht, then right into Keizersgracht. Two bridges down, you can't miss the modernist masterpiece **De Bazel** (*see p102* **House of the spirits**); as you pass under Vijzelstraat, glance over your shoulder to get a sense of its scale, dwarfing the dainty houses you've seen so far on your journey.

Next, hang a sharp right into Reguliersgracht, going as far as the sign declaring *doodlopende vaart* ('dead end'). Turn and look back: these are the famous seven bridges, best viewed when illuminated at night.

Sail back now and take the third left into Herengracht. You are entering the Gouden Bocht or 'Golden Bend', the 17th century's most desirable address. It is here you'll find the great mansions that refute all those famous claims about the Dutch disinclination to flaunt wealth. No.508-510 is easily one of the most exuberantly decorated: note the frolicking sea gods rising from the sculpted foam of the gables. Cut your boat's engine outside the house with the columns a couple of doors down; you may see Job Cohen in his pyjamas, as this is the official mayoral residence. Don't even think about trying to land on its stage, though: signs reading *streng verboden* translate into 'strongly forbidden', and sadly they aren't joking around, especially after the late filmmaker Theo van Gogh's murderer threatened to exact a similar fate upon Cohen in the note that he left knifed to his victim's body.

After passing under two more bridges (and a couple of hundred metres before the third) look right into Beulingsluis. This is the only Venetian-style canal in town, with houses directly on the water. In the unlikely event that you've managed to procure a gondola or row boat, float down and puzzle how people get into their homes.

Four bridges on, turn left into Leliegracht, where there's pull-up potential at the café **Spanjer & Van Twist** (No.60, 639 0109). Before turning into Keizersgracht, look up at the beautiful Emaux de Briare mosaic of an angel and small child on the **Jugendstil building** on the corner, an old insurance office – you can still see its initials, EHLB, in the wrought iron of the tower. Continue past the **Homomonument** (don't be tempted to moor here, as it's a memorial; *see p221*), and head back down the Keizersgracht for nine bridges.

You've been along this one before (sailing in the opposite direction), but the ever-changing cityscape never gets boring or repetitive. Peer up at the gable details, or enviously across at other people's pleasure-craft. At the tenth bridge, under Utrechtsestraat, exercise caution: only low boats can get under. This short stretch before the river is a great place to ogle upmarket houseboats. On the Amstel, turn right, then another right again into Prinsengracht. Once more watching for low bridges, head back under Utrechstestraat and moor at the final point of the canal tour, charming **Café Marcella** (Amstelveld 21, 623 1900).

After all that hard work, you're well in line for a few cold beers, and this is a great place to enjoy them as the ancient water rolls on endlessly beside you.

The pleasant oasis of Amstelveld helps, too, with **Amstelkerk** – the white wooden church that once took a break from sacred duties to act as a stable for Napoleon's horses – worth a look.

Heading east along Kerkstraat will get you to the Magerebrug (Skinny Bridge), the most photographed bridge in the city and one said to have been built in the 17th century by two sisters – living on opposite sides of the Amstel – who wanted an easy way to get together for morning coffee. If you cross it and go down Nieuwe Kerkstraat, you'll get to the Plantage (*see p111*). Alternatively, turn right at Amstel and right again down Prinsengracht for yet more grand canal houses – or if you want to smoke your way through the 2,000-plus exhibits at the **Pijpenkabinet** (Pipe Cabinet; *see p126* **Museums for the mildly obsessed**).

Foam (Photography Museum Amsterdam)

Keizersgracht 609 (551 6500/www.foam.nl). Tram 16, 24, 25. **Open** 10am-5pm Mon-Wed, Sat, Sun; 10am-9pm Thur, Fri. **Admission** €7; €5 65+, students; free under 12s, MK. **No credit cards. Map** p331 E4.

This excellent photography museum, located in a renovated canal house, holds regular exhibitions of works by shutter-button maestros like August Sander as well as advertising from local agency KesselsKramer, and shows covering local themes such as Amsterdam crime scene photos (plus universal themes like Kate Moss). They also organise talks and events for the photographically obsessed.

Kattenkabinet (Cat Cabinet)

Herengracht 497 (626 5378/www.kattenkabinet.nl). Tram 1, 4, 9, 14, 16, 24, 25. **Open** 10am-2pm Tue-Fri; 1-5pm Sat, Sun. **Admission** €5; €2.50 under-12s. **No credit cards. Map** p330 D4.

Housed in a grand 17th-century canal house (and a location for the film *Ocean's 12*), the Cat Cabinet differs from Amsterdam's more notorious pussy palaces. It's a veritable temple to the feline form: in fact, it boasts that it's the world's only museum with a permanent exhibition devoted to cats, and so far no one's come forward to disagree. Paintings, statues, posters and cattish ephemera fill the vast rooms, guarded (after a fashion) by moggies who spend the time lying around, cocking a silent snook at guests.

Museum van Loon

Keizersgracht 672 (624 5255/www.museumvan loon.nl). Tram 16, 24, 25. **Open** 11am-5pm Mon, Wed-Sun. **Admission** €6; €4 6s-18s, students; free under-6s, MK. **No credit cards. Map** p331 E4.

Amsterdam's waterways are chock-a-block with grand houses. Few of their interiors have been preserved in anything approaching their original state, but the former Van Loon residence is one that has. Designed by Adriaan Dortsman, the house was originally the home of artist Ferdinand Bol. Hendrik van Loon, after whom the museum is named, bought the house in 1884; it was opened as a museum in 1973.

The posh mid-18th-century interior is terrifically grand, and admirers of Louis XIV and XV decor will find much that excites. So will art-lovers: the house holds a collection of family portraits from the 17th to the 20th centuries; perhaps more unexpectedly, it hosts a modern art show every two years. The 18th-century French-style garden contains Ram Katzir's striking sculpture of a headless man, *There*.

Museum Willet-Holthuysen

Herengracht 605 (523 1870/www.museumwillet holthuysen.nl). Tram 4, 9, 14. **Open** 10am-5pm Mon-Fri; 11am-5pm Sat, Sun. **Admission** €5; €3.75 over-65s; €2.50 6s-18s; free under-6s, MK. **Credit** MC, V. **Map** p331 E4.

Built in the 1680s, this mansion was purchased in the 1850s by the Willet-Holthuysen family. When Abraham, remembered as 'the Oscar Wilde of Amsterdam', died in 1889, his wife Sandrina Louisa, a hermaphrodite (that's right: a chick with a dick) left the house and its contents to the city on the condition it was preserved and opened as a museum – a nice gesture, were it not for the fact that cats were the main residents for many years. The family had followed the fashion of the time and decorated it in the neo-Louis XVI style: it's densely furnished, with the over-embellishment extending to the collection of rare objets d'art, glassware, silver, fine china and paintings – including a portrait of a rather shocked-looking Abraham (taken on his honeymoon, perhaps?). English texts accompany the exhibits, and there's an English-language video explaining the history of the house and the city's canal system. The view into the recently renovated 18th-century garden almost takes you back in time, but the illusion is disturbed by the adjoining modern buildings.

Torture Museum

Singel 449 (320 6642/www.torturemuseum.nl). Tram 1, 2, 4, 5, 9, 16, 24, 25. **Open** 10am-11pm daily. **Admission** €5; €3.50 under-12s. **No credit cards**. **Map** p330 D4.

The Torture Museum is just another of those Amsterdam tourist traps that should really have been more informative, engaging and – most importantly – fun. OK, torture museums don't really have to be fun, but this one's a particularly frustrating experience, riddled with tattily maintained exhibits and uninvolving, even illegible, captions. Torturous.

Around Leidseplein

Leidseplein, which from Prinsengracht is best reached via the chaotic pedestrian- and tram-packed Leidsestraat, is the tourist centre of the city. It's always crammed with merrymakers drinking at pavement cafés, listening to buskers and soaking up the atmosphere, not to mention the huge variety of booze.

Leidseplein lies on the bottom of the 'U' made by the Canal Belt, and although it's called a square, it is, in fact, L-shaped, running south from the end of Leidsestraat to the Amsterdam School-style bridge over Singelgracht and east towards the 'pop temple' **Paradiso** (*see p235*) – where you can admire brass iguanas on the grass in front of an entrance made of classical columns and a chiselled Latin profundity that translates as 'wise men don't piss into the wind' – to the Max Euweplein (a handy passage to **Vondelpark**; *see p125*) with its **Max Euwe Centrum** (*see below*) and giant chess set (*photos p104*) for those looking to engage in a little super-sized checkmating.

Leidseplein has always been a focal point. Artists and writers used to congregate here in the 1920s and '30s, when it was the scene of clashes between communists and fascists. In the war, protests were ruthlessly broken up by the Nazis: there's a commemorative plaque on nearby Kerkstraat. But Leidseplein's latter-day persona is more jockstrap than political, especially when local football team Ajax wins anything and their fans take over the square.

The area has more cinemas, theatres, clubs and restaurants than any other part of town. It's dominated by the **Stadsschouwburg** (the municipal theatre; *see p240*) and by the cafés that take over the pavements during summer; this is when fire-eaters, jugglers, musicians and small-time con-artists and pickpockets fill the square. Unfortunately, development has meant that there are now fast-food restaurants on every corner, and many locals feel that the Dutch flavour of the district has been destroyed.

The café society associated with Leidseplein began with the opening of the city's first terrace bar, the Café du Théâtre. It was sadly demolished in 1877, 20 years before the final completion of Kromhout's **American Hotel** (*see p67*) at the south-west end of the square – its café-restaurant's resplendent art deco interior is the perfect setting for a revitalizing espresso. Opposite the American is a building, dating from 1882, that reflects Leidseplein's dramatic transformation: once grand, it's now illuminated by huge, vile adverts. Just off the square, in the Leidsebos, is the more intriguing Adamant, a pyramid-like, hologram-effect sculpture that commemorated 400 years of the city's central diamond trade in 1986.

Max Euwe Centrum

Max Euweplein 30A (625 7017/www.maxeuwe.nl). Tram 1, 2, 5, 6, 7, 10. **Open** noon-4pm Tue-Fri. **Admission** free. **No credit cards**. **Map** p330 D5.

Named after the only chess world champion the Netherlands has produced and occupying the city's old House of Detention – it held Resistance leaders in World War II – the Max Euwe Centrum harbours a library of works in dozens of languages, various chess artefacts, vast archives and chess computers that visitors can use and abuse at their leisure.

Jodenbuurt, the Plantage & the Oost

Music, museums and mind-blowing gardens in the city's original Jewish jewel.

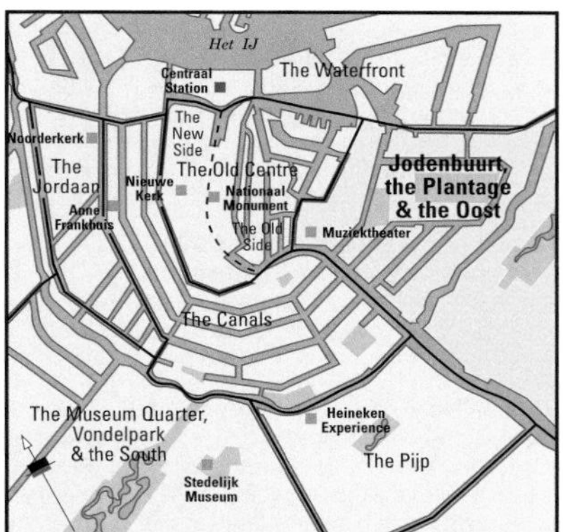

Jodenbuurt

Map p327

Located south-east of the Red Light District, Amsterdam's old Jewish neighbourhood is a peculiar mix of old and new architectural styles. If you leave the Nieuwmarkt along Sint Antoniesbreestraat, you'll pass several bars, coffeeshops, chic clothes stores and the modern yet tasteful council housing designed by local architect Theo Bosch. In contrast, there's the Italian Renaissance-style **Pintohuis** at No.69, renovated by the Jewish refugee and VOC founder, Isaac de Pinto. It still houses a public library – its continued existence as such is currently being fought for by the neighbourhood – where you can browse under Jacob de Wit's ceiling paintings. Pop through the bizarre skull-adorned entrance across the street between Sint Antoniesbreestraat 130 and 132, and enter into the former graveyard and now restful square near **Zuiderkerk** (South Church). Designed by De Keyser and built between 1603 and 1614, it was the first Protestant church to appear after the Reformation, and is now the municipal information centre for planning and housing; development plans are presented as interactive scale models. But as you wander around the neighbourhood – or view it from the church's formidable tower (689 2565, every half-hour from noon-4pm Mon-Sat, Apr-Sept, €6 adults, €3 6-12s) – it becomes obvious that shiny ideals can often create more obtuse realities.

Crossing over the bridge at the end of Sint Antoniesbreestraat, you'll arrive at the obtuse reality of a performing arts school, the Arts Academy (aka De Hogeschool voor de Kunsten), on the left and the **Rembrandthuis** (*see p111*) on the right. Immediately before this, though, a few steps will find **Waterlooplein Market** (*see p192*). Though touristy, it can be a bargain-hunter's dream if you're a patient shopper.

Nearby you'll find the 19th-century **Mozes en Äronkerk**, built on Spinoza's birthplace. This former clandestine Catholic church, where Liszt reportedly played his favourite concert in 1866, is on the corner where Waterlooplein meets Mr Visserplein – the square-cum-traffic roundabout where the obtuse reality of the copper-green Film and Television Academy meets the much chirpier underground children's playground **TunFun** (*see p207* **State of play**). Also nearby is the **Joods Historisch Museum** (Jewish Historical Museum; *see p110*) and the new **Hermitage aan de Amstel** (*see p110*).

Dominating Waterlooplein is the **Stadhuis-Muziektheater** (City Hall-Music Theatre; *see p240*). The area where it stands was once a Jewish ghetto and later, in the 1970s, the site of dozens of gorgeous 16th- and 17th-century residences turned into squats, before it was decided to replace them with a €136-million civic headquarters-cum-opera house. This decision was highly controversial, as was the 'denture'-like design by Wilhelm Holtzbauer and Cees Dam, and locals quickly showed their discontent by protesting; in 1982, a riot caused damage estimated at €450,000 to construction equipment. Such displeasure is the reason why the home to the Nederlands Opera and the Nationale Ballet is still known as the 'Stopera'.

It's rare that science and art meet on the level, but in the small passage between City Hall and the Muziektheater, the **Amsterdam Ordnance Project** includes a device showing the NAP (normal Amsterdam water level) and a cross-section of the Netherlands' geological structure.

Hermitage aan de Amstel

Gebouw Neerlandia, Nieuwe Herengracht 14 (530 8751/www.hermitage.nl). Tram 9, 14/Metro Waterlooplein. **Open** 10am-5pm daily. **Admission** €7; €5.60 65+; free under-16s, MK. **No credit cards. Map** p327 E3.

Partly opened in 2004, this outpost of the Hermitage in St Petersburg is expected to put on two exhibitions a year using objects and art taken from its prestigious Russian parent collection. The projected massive exhibition space will only be completed by the end of 2008, but meanwhile visitors can have a look around part of this 19th-century building and all of its 17th-century courtyard.

The Hermitage's riches owe much to the collecting obsession of Peter the Great (1672-1725), who came to Amsterdam to learn shipbuilding and how to build a city on a bog – the latter knowledge was applied to his pet project, St Petersburg. A giant of a man, Peter befriended the local doctor Frederik Ruysch, perhaps the greatest ever anatomist and preserver of body bits and mutants. Not content with pickling Siamese foetuses in jars, Ruysch constructed moralistic 3D collages with gall and kidney stones piled up to suggest landscapes, dried veins woven into lush shrubberies and testicles crafted into pottery, and he animated his scenes with dancing skeletal foetuses. After kissing the forehead of a preserved baby, Peter paid Ruysch a small fortune for the whole lot (much of which is still on display in St Petersburg's Kunstkammer collection). With luck, some of Peter's old souvenirs – including Rembrandts – will return for a visit, but thus far it's focused on an extensive collection of lustrous Greek jewellery, artefacts from the last Tsar and Tsarina, Nicolas and Alexandra, and Persian treasures.

Amsterdam: rock city

Amsterdam is famous for its diamond trade, something it owes largely to the Jewish population originally settling in and around the Jodenbuurt area. Indeed, it's a heritage that's still marketed heavily to this day. To be honest, the city's sparkler shops are as much tourist attractions as they are retail outlets – to experience an aspirational brush with luxury, take a tour around any one of them. But beware: falling in love with a piece of crushed carbon is the easy part; paying for it may prove to be a little more tricky.

Amsterdam Diamond Centre

Rokin 1-5, Old Centre: New Side (624 5787/www.amsterdamdiamondcenter.nl). Tram 4, 9, 14, 16, 24, 25. **Open** 10am-6pm Mon-Wed, Fri, Sat; 10am-8.30pm Thur; 10am-5pm Sun. **Credit** AmEx, DC, MC, V. **Map** p326 D2.

Diamant Museum Amsterdam

Paulus Potterstraat 8, Museum Quarter (305 5300/www.diamantmuseum amsterdam). Tram 2, 5. **Open** 9am-5pm daily. **Admission** €6; €4 students/65+; free under-12s. **Credit** AmEx, DC, MC, V. **Map** p330 D6.

Gassan Diamond BV

Nieuwe Uilenburgerstraat 173, Old Centre: Old Side (622 5333/www.gassandiamonds.com). Tram 9, 14. **Open** 9am-5pm daily. **Credit** AmEx, DC, MC, V. **Map** p327 E2.

Joods Historisch Museum (Jewish Historical Museum)

Nieuwe Amstelstraat 1 (531 0310/www.jhm.nl). Tram 9, 14/Metro Waterlooplein. **Open** 11am-5pm daily; closed Jewish New Year and Yom Kippur. **Admission** €7.50; €4.50 over-65s, students; €3 13s-17s; free under-12s, MK. **No credit cards. Map** p327 E3.

Housed since 1987 in four former synagogues in the old Jewish quarter, the Jewish Historical Museum is full of religious items, photographs and paintings detailing the rich history of Jews and Judaism in the Netherlands throughout the centuries. A recent revamping has created more warmth and a sense of the personal in its permanent displays, which concentrate on religious practice and Dutch Jewish culture; among the exhibits is the painted autobiography of artist Charlotte Salomon, killed at Auschwitz at the age of 26. An excellent children's wing crams interactive exhibits on aspects of Jewish culture (including a nice one on music) into its space. The temporary shows explore various aspects of Jewish culture, while the Jonas Daniël Meijerplein site, with its Dock Worker statue commemorating the February Strike of 1941 in protest against Jewish deportations, is right across the street, beside the Portuguese Synagogue (*see below*).

Portuguese Synagogue

Mr Visserplein 3 (624 5351/guided tours 531 0380/www.esnoga.com). Tram 4, 9, 14, 20. **Open** *Apr-Oct* 10am-4pm Mon-Fri, Sun. *Nov-Mar* 10am-4pm Mon-Thur, Sun; 10am-2pm Fri. Closed Yom Kippur. **Admission** €6.50; €5 65+; €4 10s-17s; free under-10s. **No credit cards. Map** p327 E3.

Architect Elias Bouwman's mammoth synagogue, one of the largest in all the world and reputedly inspired by the Temple of Solomon, was inaugurated in 1675. It's built on wooden piles and is surrounded by smaller annexes (offices, archives, the rabbinate and one of the oldest libraries in the world). Renovation in the late 1950s restored the synagogue to an extremely high standard and the low-key tours are informative and interesting.

A statue of the **February Strike of 1941**.

Rembrandthuis

Jodenbreestraat 4 (520 0400/www.rembrandthuis.nl). Tram 9, 14/Metro Waterlooplein. **Open** 10am-5pm Mon-Sun. **Admission** €8; €5.50 students; €1.50 6s-16s; free under-6s, MK. **Credit** AmEx, DC, MC, V. **Map** p327 E3.

Rembrandt bought this house in 1639 for ƒ13,000 (around €6,000), a massive sum at the time. Indeed, the pressure of the mortgage payments eventually got to the free-spending artist, who went bankrupt in 1656 and was forced to move to a smaller house (Rozengracht 184). When he was declared bankrupt, clerks inventoried the house room by room; it's these records that provided the renovators with clues as to what the house looked like in Rembrandt's time.

You can't help but admire the skill and effort with which craftsmen have tried to re-create the house, along with the antiquities, objets d'art (Rembrandt was a compulsive collector) and 17th-century furniture. However, the presentation is, on the whole, dry and unengaging. Nagging at you all the time is the knowledge that this isn't really Rembrandt's house, but rather a mock-up of it – which lends an unreal air that is only relieved when guest artists are allowed to use the studio. There's also a remarkable collection of Rembrandt's etchings, which show him at his most experimental, but if it's his paintings you're after, make for the Rijksmuseum (*see p123*).

The Plantage

Map p327 & p332

The largely residential area known as the Plantage lies south-east of Mr Visserplein and is reached via Muiderstraat. The attractive Plantage Middenlaan winds past the **Hortus Botanicus** (*see p112*), passes close to the **Verzetsmuseum** (Museum of the Dutch Resistance; *see p112*), runs along the edge of the zoo **Artis** (*see below*) and heads towards the **Tropenmuseum** (*see p113*).

Jews first began to settle here over 200 years ago, and the area was soon redeveloped on 19th-century diamond money. The headquarters of the diamond cutters' union, designed by Berlage as a far more outward expression of socialism than his Stock Exchange (aka **Beurs van Berlage**; *see p84*), still exists on Henri Polaklaan as the **Vakbondsmuseum** (Trade Unions Museum; *see p112*), and other extant buildings like the Gassan, the Saskiahuis and the Coster act as reminders that the town's most profitable trade was at one time based here (*see p116* **Architectural reflections**). However, the spectre of World War II reappears at the **Hollandse Schouwburg** (*see p112*) and Van Eyck's **Moedershuis** at Plantage Middenlaan 33, used as a mother and child refuge.

The Plantage is still a wealthy part of town, with graceful buildings and tree-lined streets, although its charm has somewhat faded over the years. The area has seen some extensive redevelopment, and work is continuing with mixed results: while the housing association flats and houses erected where the old army barracks and dockside warehouses once stood (just past Muiderpoort city gate) are extremely unattractive, Entrepotdok works far better: to wander down this stretch is to admire a delicate balance between the new and the old, with docked post-hippie houseboats and good views of Artis providing a charming contrast to the apartment buildings. Here you are also right by the energy centre **Energetica** (Hoogte Kadijk 400, 422 1227, www.energetica.nl) and **Werf 't Kromhout** (*see p115*).

Artis

Plantage Kerklaan 38-40 (523 3400/www.artis.nl). Tram 6, 9, 14. **Open** *Summer* 9am-6pm daily. *Winter* 9am-5pm daily. **Admission** €17.50; €16.50 over-65s; €14 4s-11s; free under-4s. **No credit cards**. **Map** p327 F3.

The first zoo on mainland Europe (and the third oldest in the world) provides a great day out for children and adults. Along with the usual animals, Artis has an indoor 'rainforest' for nocturnal creatures and a 120-year-old aquarium that includes a simulated Amsterdam canal (the main difference is that clear water improves your chances of spotting the eels).

A former Jewish warehouse, now a café: a rare reminder of the area's Hebrew heritage.

The zoo expanded a couple of years ago after a long battle for extra land, and now features a savannah that wraps around a light-infused restaurant.

The narration in the planetarium is in Dutch, but an English translation is available. Further extras include a geological museum, a zoological museum, an aquarium and, for kids, a petting zoo and playgrounds; you could easily spend all day here. And while there's no guarantee, staff will often let you hang out long after closing hours.

Hollandse Schouwburg

Plantage Middenlaan 24 (531 0340/www.hollandsche schouwburg.nl). Tram 6, 9, 14. **Open** 11am-4pm daily. **Admission** free. **Map** p327 F3.

In 1942, this grand theatre became a main point of assembly for between 60,000 and 80,000 of the city's Jews before they were taken to the transit camp at Westerbork. It's now a monument with a small but very impressive exhibition and a memorial hall displaying 6,700 surnames by way of tribute to the 104,000 Dutch Jews who were exterminated. The façade has been left intact, with most of the inner structure removed to make way for a memorial.

Hortus Botanicus

Plantage Middenlaan 2A (625 9021/www.dehortus.nl). Tram 9, 14/Metro Waterlooplein. **Open** *Feb-June, Sept-Nov* 9am-5pm Mon-Fri; 10am-5pm Sat, Sun. *July, Aug* 9am-9pm Mon-Fri; 10am-9pm Sat, Sun. *Jan, Dec* 9am-4pm Mon-Fri; 10am-4pm Sat, Sun. **Admission** €6; €3 5s-14s; free under-5s. **No credit cards. Map** p332 G3.

This beautiful garden has been here since 1682, although it was set up 50 years earlier when East India Company ships brought back tropical plants and seeds originally intended to supply doctors with medicinal herbs. Some of those specimens (which include the oldest potted plant in the world, a 300-year-old cycad) are still here in the palm greenhouse – which itself dates from 1912 – while three other greenhouses maintain desert, tropical and subtropical climates. There's also a new butterfly house.

Vakbondsmuseum (Trade Unions Museum)

Henri Polaklaan 9 (624 1166/www.deburcht-vakbonds museum.nl). Tram 6, 9, 14. **Open** 11am-5pm Tue-Fri; 1-5pm Sun. **Admission** €2.50; €1.25 12s-18s; free under-12s, MK. **No credit cards. Map** p327 F3.

The Vakbondmuseum offers a permanent exhibition showing the progress and history of unions in Dutch history. If you think that kind of thing sounds interesting, you'll enjoy it; if not, don't make a special trip – unless, perhaps, for the fascinating collection of posters. That said, for those whose interest in labour relations is even casual, the building itself is worth a peek: it was designed by Berlage, who viewed it as his favourite, to house the offices of the country's first trade union – that of the diamond workers.

Verzetsmuseum (Museum of the Dutch Resistance)

Plantage Kerklaan 61 (620 2535/www.verzets museum.org). Tram 6, 9, 14. **Open** noon-5pm Mon, Sat, Sun; 10am-5pm Tue-Fri. **Admission** €5.50; €3 7s-16s; free under-6s, MK. **No credit cards. Map** p327 F3.

The Verzetsmuseum is one of Amsterdam's most illuminating museums and quite possibly its most moving. It tells the story of the Dutch Resistance through a wealth of artefacts: false ID papers, clandestine printing presses and illegal newspapers, spy gadgets and an authentic secret door behind which Jews hid. The exhibits all help to explain the ways people in the Netherlands faced up to and dealt with the Nazi occupation. The engaging presentation is enhanced by the constant use of personal testimony; indeed, the museum's disparate exhibits are linked effectively by these stories – told, by those who lived through the war, on small panels that act as adjuncts to the main displays. Regular temporary shows explore wartime themes (like the much more predominant flipside of resistance, collaboration) and modern-day forms of oppression, and there's a small research room as well. An excellent enterprise.

The Oost

Map p332

South of Mauritskade is Amsterdam Oost (East), where the **Arena** hotel complex (*see p70*) is located along the edge of a former graveyard that was long ago transformed into **Oosterpark**. Disaster tourists take note: near the corner of Oosterpark and Linneaustraat is where film-maker Theo van Gogh was brutally murdered by an extremist in 2004 after causing outrage with polemic depictions of the Islamic faith in his movies (*see p27*); a new sculpture, *The Scream* in Oosterpark, also home to a Speaker's Corner, was erected in 2007 in his memory. While hardly Amsterdam's most beautiful sculpture (a cold depiction of a contorted face), it's not without its charms, not least because the area isn't notable for much else; the **Tropenmusem** (*see right*) and **Dappermarkt** (*see p191*) are the only notable exceptions.

It's a very similar story in the Indische Buurt (Indonesian neighbourhood) north-east of here, although the **Brouwerij 't IJ**, a brewery in a windmill (*see p160*), is a good place to sip a beer. North of here are the **eastern docklands** (*see p116* **Architectural reflections**), but as you head east from the centre of Amsterdam, you'll find little of interest save for the pleasant green expanses of **Flevopark** and the beach over in **IJburg** (*see p159* **United we sand**).

Tropenmuseum

Linnaeusstraat 2 (568 8200/www.tropenmuseum.nl). Tram 9, 14. **Open** 10am-5pm daily. **Admission** €7.50; €6 students, over-65s; €4 6s-17s; free under-6s, MK. **Credit** MC, V. **Map** p332 H3.

This is a handsome and vast building, sitting rather grandly in a slightly out-of-the-way (by the pocket handkerchief standards of Amsterdam, anyway) location. Better still: the exhibitions in the Tropical Museum are terrific. Through a series of informative and lively displays – the majority of which come with English captions – the visitor gets a vivid, interactive glimpse of daily life in the tropical and subtropical parts of the world (a strange evolution for a museum originally erected in the 1920s to glorify Dutch colonialism). Exhibits – from religious items and jewellery to washing powder and vehicles – are divided by region and broad in their catchment. A musical display allows visitors to hear a variety of different instruments at the push of a button (the Tropenmuseum is also the city's leading venue for world music); walk-through environments include simulated North African and South Asian villages and a Manilan street; and a Latin American exhibit is highlighted by a fun room complete with videos of sporting highlights and a jukebox. The new Africa exhibit is particularly inspired as it foregoes the usual history of decolonisation and merely presents beautiful objects. Temporary art and photography exhibitions fill a large central space on the ground floor, the shop has an excellent selection of books and souvenirs, and the restaurant offers fine global eats with a view-worthy terrace.

Butterfly house, **Artis**. *See p111.*

The Waterfront

From industrial to inspirational, a former wasteland on the cultural cutting edge.

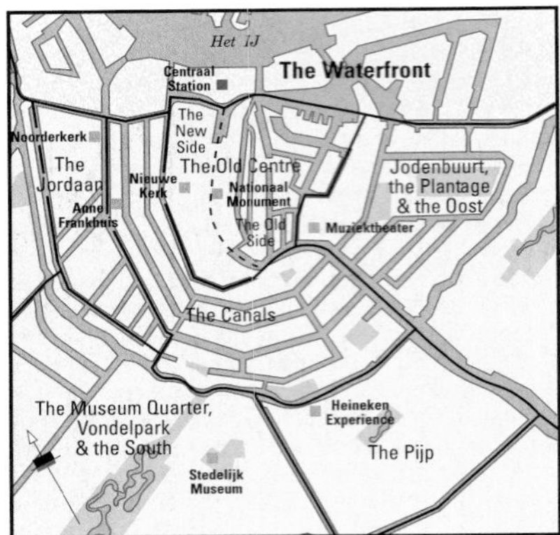

Map p116 & p327

Amsterdam's historic wealth owes a lot to the city's waterfront, for it was here that all the goods were unloaded, weighed and prepared for storage in the warehouses still found in the area. During Amsterdam's trading heyday in the 17th century, most maritime activity was centred east of Centraal Station, along Prins Hendrikkade and on the artificial islands east of Kattenburgerstraat. At the time, the harbour and its arterial canals formed a whole with the city itself. A drop in commerce unbalanced this unity, and the construction of Centraal Station late in the 19th century served as the final psychological cleavage. This neo-Gothic monument to modernity blocked both the city's view of the harbour and its own past.

North-west of Centraal Station, and just to the north of the Jordaan, the **Westelijke Eilanden** (Western Islands) are artificial islands created in the 17th century for shipping activities. While there are now warehouse flats and a yacht basin on Realeneiland, Prinseneiland and Bickerseiland, where once shipyards, tar distillers, fish-salters and smokers were located, the area remains the city's best setting for a scenic stroll that harks back to more seafaring times.

Since 1876 access to the sea has been via the North Sea Canal. Because the working docks are also to the west, there is little activity on the IJ behind Centraal Station beyond a handful of passenger ships and the free ferries that run across to Amsterdam Noord – an area of little interest except as a bicycling route towards the scenic fishing villages of **Waterland** (*see p276*) or the vast cultural breeding ground of the former shipping yard **NDSM** (*see p262*).

A big recent cultural success story was the reinvention of **Post CS** (Oosterdokskade 5), the former post office building just east of Centraal Station (CS). This late modernist classic from 1969, designed by architect Piet Elling, is the only building on Oosterdokeiland, an artificial isle, to have temporarily escaped destruction while the whole area is being transformed into a home for New China Town, the city's music conservatory, the country's largest library and a whole mess of shops and hotels, all set to open at time of press. While Post CS is due to be stripped of its walls and then encased in glass in the summer of 2008 at the very earliest, it is meanwhile serving as the temporary home to the **Stedelijk Museum of Modern Art** (*see p124*), **Mediamatic** (*see p218*), hip club-restaurant **11** (*see p145*) and a slew of other creative enterprises. People are already expressing a desire that Post CS stays exactly as it is; besides offering spectacular views of the city from 11, the building has a certain vital rawness that has been missed since the demise of such cultural fulcrums as squats Vrieshuis Amerika and the Silo.

South of Post CS, the **Schreierstoren**, or 'Weeping Tower', is one of the first things you'll notice on the right side if you walk east from Centraal Station. It's the most interesting relic of Amsterdam's medieval city wall. Built in 1487, it was successfully restored in 1966. In 1927, a bronze memorial plaque was added by the Greenwich Village Historical Society of New York; its text states that it was from this point, on 4 April 1609, that Henry Hudson departed in search of shorter trade routes to the Far East. He failed, and ended up colonising a small island in the mouth of a river in North America. The river was subsequently named after him and the colony itself was called New Amsterdam, only to have its name changed by the English to New York. (Today, some of the boroughs still have a *nederstamp* on them: in particular Harlem, after Haarlem, and Brooklyn, after Breukelen.) The next eye-opener you'll see is **Nemo** (*see p115*), a science museum whose green building dominates the horizon. It also dwarfs the bizarre **ARCAM** gallery (*see p218*).

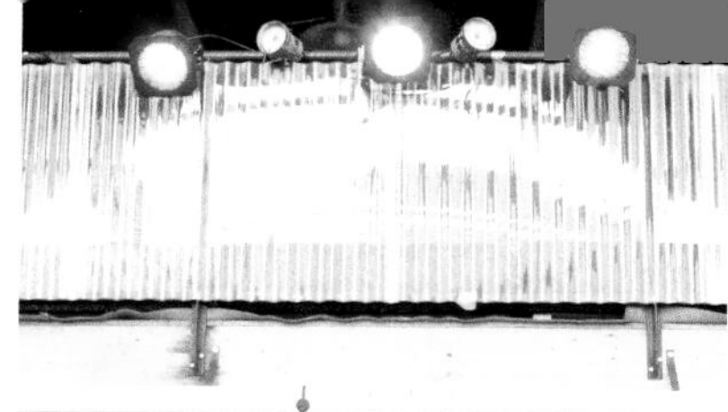

NDSM.

The **Nederlands Scheepvaartmuseum** (www.scheepvaartmuseum.nl), closed until 2009, is itself a very grand structure and major tourist draw. Dutch nautical history is rich and fascinating, and it follows that the country should boast one of the world's finest nautical museums; second only, say experts, to London's National Maritime Museum. And let's hope the current renovation only boosts the remarkable collection of models, portraits, boat parts and other naval ephemera. There can certainly be no quibbling with the wonderful original building in which it's all housed (built well over 350 years ago by Daniel Stalpaert). Meanwhile, you can visit its huge **replica VOC ship**, now temporarily docked by Nemo, which comes complete with costumed 'sailors'.

Nemo

Oosterdok 2 (531 3233/www.e-nemo.nl). Bus 22, 42. **Open** 10am-5pm Tue-Sun. *School holidays* 10am-5pm daily. **Admission** €11.50; €6.50 students; free under-3s. **Credit** AmEx, DC, MC, V. **Map** p327 F2.

Nemo opened in 1998 and has gone from strength to strength as a truly kid-friendly science museum. It eschews exhibits in favour of hands-on trickery, gadgetry and tomfoolery (in English and Dutch): you can play DNA detective games, blow mega soap bubbles or explode things in a 'wonderlab'.

Persmuseum (Press Museum)

Zeeburgerkade 10 (692 8810/www.persmuseum.nl). Bus 22, 43. **Open** 10am-5pm Tue-Fri; noon-5pm Sun. **Admission** €3.50; €2.50 6s-18s; free under-6s, MK. **No credit cards.**

This newly revamped museum covers the 400-year history of journalism, both magazine and news paper, in Amsterdam and the Netherlands. The temporary exhibitions are usually focused on graphics, cartoons, photography and particular magazines.

Werf 't Kromhout

Hoogte Kadijk 147 (627 6777/www.machinekamer.nl/museum). Bus 22. **Open** 10am-3pm Tue. **Admission** €4.50; €2.75 under-15s. **No credit cards. Map** p327 F2.

A nostalgic museum, full of old, silent ship engines and tools. The shipyard is proud of the fact that it's the oldest remaining original yard still in use, but its 18th-century heritage is no longer very apparent, nor is the yard especially active nowadays.

Walk Architectural reflections

Amsterdam's eastern docklands area is the city's up-and-coming eating and entertainment hotspot. But, perhaps more interestingly, it's also a fantastic showcase for the Netherlands' rather more out-there experiments in modern residential living. If you want to explore the future of the city, hop on a bike, grab a map and get moving on the double.

If you stay on the south side, hug the water eastward from Centraal Station before hooking up with and following Oostelijke Handelskade and its parallel boardwalk. First, you pass the **Muziekgebouw** (*see p239*). This new epicentre of modern music, also home to the **Bimhuis** (*see p235*), comes appended with studios, rehearsal spaces, exhibition galleries and a grand café and restaurant complete with a charming terrace overlooking the scenic wateriness of the IJ. Its neighbour is the glass wave-shaped **passenger terminal** for luxury cruise-ships (www.pta.nl lists docking times should you wish to admire them within their natural watery habitat).

Before heading further on to club **Panama** (*see p245*), restaurant **Odessa** (*see p147*) and the youth prison-cum-designer accommodation **Lloyd Hotel** (*see p72*), take the spacey Jan Schaeferbrug to the left that starts over at the **Pakhuis de Zwijger** (www.dezwijger.nl), an old warehouse that has been reinvented as a new media centre with an excellent in-house café.

The bridge will take you to the tip of **Java-eiland**, although the less energetic can travel on the free ferryboat, which departs every 20 minutes from directly behind Centraal Station. At first glance, Java-eiland may look quite like a rather dense designer prison, but it's hard not to be charmed while on the island's bisecting walking street, which will have you crossing canals on funkily designed bridges

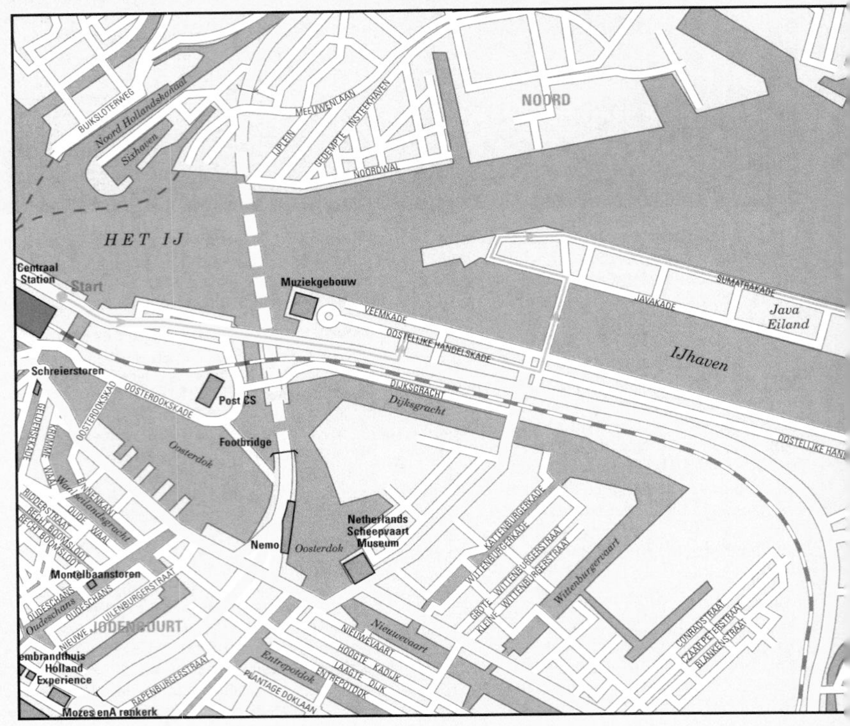

and passing beside startling architecture. At Azartplein, the island's name changes to **KNSM-eiland**, a nod to the Royal Dutch Steam Company once located here.

Veer north to follow Surinamekade, with its houseboats on one side and the visible interiors of artists' studios on the other. Pass by **Black Widow tower** – you'll know it when you see it – then loop around the island's tip and head back along KNSM-laan, hanging a sharp left into Barcelonaplein and then a right when you pass through the abstract but strangely suggestive sculpted steel archway. You may want to make some time for refreshment at one of the many waterside bars and eateries, or invest in an art coffin at the alternative burial store **De Ode** (*see p189* **Design driven**), but do check out the imposing residential Piraeus building from German architect Hans Kollhoff and its eye-twisting inner court.

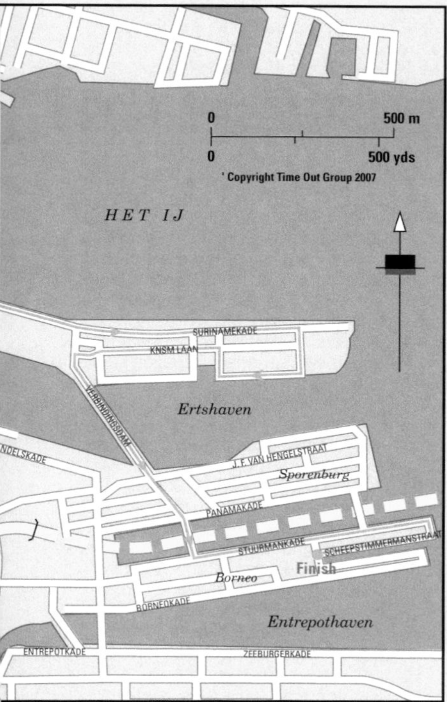

The two peninsulas to the south are **Borneo-Sporenburg**, designed by urban planners and landscape architects West 8. The plots are all sized differently in a direct attempt to inspire the many participating architects – a veritable who's who of the internationally acclaimed – to come up with creative low-rise living. Cross to Sporenburg via the Verbindingsdam to the crazed building that has probably already caught your eye: the mighty raised silver **Whale residential complex**, designed by noted architect Frits van Dongen, set over on Baron GA Tindalplein. For a far more folksy contrast, an enormous floating **Styrofoam park** from the design studio of erstwhile Provo Robert Jasper Grootveld stands opposite on Panamakade.

From here, cross to Borneo via a swooping red bridge. Turn left up Stuurmankade – past a more violently undulating pedestrian bridge – and enjoy the view at the end while imagining the even better one enjoyed by those living in the blue and green glass cubes that jut out of the buildings. Then head back to the west via Scheepstimmermanstraat, easily Amsterdam's most eccentric architectural street, where every façade manages to be significantly odder than the one that follows it.

Where Panamalaan meets Piet Heinkade, you may take the IJtram from CS to IJburg – the stop is right by the stack of giant tables with beehives underneath – although more energetic types might prefer to make the 20-minute bike ride over to IJburg, heading south via C van Eesterenlaan and Veelaan and then left down Zeeburgerdijk. This in turn connects up with Zuiderzeeweg, which then turns into a bridge that ends at a set of traffic lights. Here, follow the cycle path to the right, which takes you to **IJburg**. When completed in 2012, the seven islands will be home to 45,000; they will also be a showcase for Dutch landscape and residential architecture, with houses fusing aesthetics with environmental friendliness. That said, there's already plenty to look at, with beach **Blijburg** (*see p159* **United we sand**) the notable highlight.

On the way back to town, explore the south end of the eastern half of **Zeeburg island**, one of few 'free' places where squatters and artists are still allowed to make their funky homes from trailers and boats.

For more information on architectural tours of the area, call **ARCAM** (*see p218*).

The Jordaan

A working-class hero with Bohemian sensibilities.

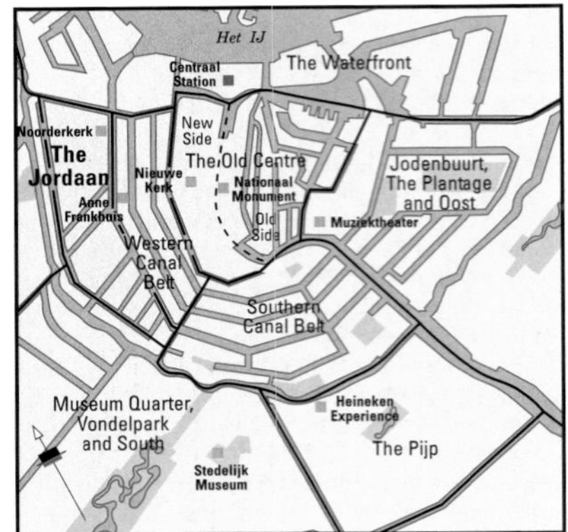

Imagine, if you will, a part of town where the hungry feed the hungrier, the broke buy beer for the more broke, money-making schemes are things to be shared and a sense of family extends to all one's neighbours. Sound like an episode of *EastEnders*? Well you're not far off, since there are many ways to see the folk of the Jordaan as a cheerful crowd of clog-wearing Cockneys, sharing working class backgrounds, cramped living spaces, a fierce sense of identity known throughout the nation and a uniquely laidback attitude embodied by drinking joints like the casual Café Nol at Westerstraat 109 (*photo p122*).

The Jordaan is roughly sock-shaped, with its borders at Brouwersgracht, Prinsengracht, Leidsegracht and Lijnbaansgracht. The area emerged when the city was extended in the 17th century and was designated for the working classes and smelly industries; it also provided a haven for victims of religious persecution, such as Jews and Huguenots. In keeping with the residents' modest financial circumstances, the houses are mostly small and densely packed, at least when compared to dwellings along the swankier canals to the east.

The area is a higgledy-piggledy mixture of old buildings, bland modern social housing and the occasional eyesore. Despite its working-class associations, properties are now highly desirable, and though the residents are mainly proud, community-spirited Jordaaners, the nouveaux riches have moved in to yuppify the 'hood: once one of the most densely populated areas in Europe, with almost 100,000 residents at the end of the 19th century, it now houses less than a fifth of that number.

There are several theories about the origin of the name 'Jordaan'. Some say it's based on the area being on the wrong side of the River Jordan, as the Prinsengracht was at one point nicknamed. Others believe it to be a corruption of *joden*, Dutch for Jews, while some linguistic dissenters think it's from *jardin*, the French word for garden. The latter certainly seems more plausible: the area was formerly a damp meadow, and many streets are named after flowers or plants. Other streets are named after animals whose pelts were used in tanning, one of the main – and stinkiest – industries here in the 17th century. Looiersgracht ('Tanner's Canal') sits near streets like Hazenstraat ('Hare Street'), Elandsgracht ('Elk Canal') and Wolvenstraat ('Wolf Street').

North of Rozengracht

Map p325

The Jordaan has no major sights; it's more of an area where you just stumble across things. It's also constantly surprising to wander through its streets and see hardly a soul. In general, the area north of the shopping-dense Rozengracht, the Jordaan's approximate mid-point, is more interesting and picturesque, with the area to the south more commercial.

Much of the area's charm comes from what's hidden from the uninformed eye. Chief among these treats are the *hofjes* or almshouses, many of which are pretty and deliciously peaceful. As long as you behave well, the residents don't mind people admiring their garden courtyards. Best known are **Venetiae** (Elandsstraat 106-136; the only one on this list south of Rozengracht), **Sint Andrieshofje** (Egelantiersgracht 107-114), **Karthuizerhof** (Karthuizerstraat 21-31), **Suyckerhofje** (Lindengracht 149-163), **Claes Claesz Hofje** (1e Egelantiersdwarsstraat 3), **Raepenhofje** (Palmgracht 28-38), and the oldest, **Lindenhofje** (Lindengracht 94-112). *Hofje*-hopping is a gamble, as entrances are sometimes locked in deference to the residents.

The area north of Rozengracht is easy to get pleasantly lost in. Little lanes and alleys link the already quiet main streets in a mazy

Art of the matter

Dipping into the Jordaan's many galleries can pleasantly punctuate an afternoon of strolling – best between Thursday and Saturday to ensure the greatest number of open galleries – with little exclamation marks of real culture. Alternatively, you could determinedly fill up an entire holiday studying the displays in each and every one of the 40-odd spaces. Since they occupy places that were once homes or shops, none are big, and most specialise in one medium – photography, for example, or modern Dutch art. Almost all of the local galleries sell works by artists they show.

Rockarchive (110 Prinsengracht, 423 0489, www.rockarchive.com) is one of just four outlets (the others are in London and Dublin) owned by photographer Jill Furmanovsky. There's always a selection of iconic pictures showing from artists of the calibre of Gered Mankowitz, Sheila Rock and even the owner herself, and everything from digital to rare silver gelatine prints is for sale.

There are more high quality photos on show at **Gallery Vassie** (1e Tuindwarsstraat 16, 489 4042), run by an ex-V&A curator. Artists from Lee Miller to Antoni & Alison have been shown here, as well as treasures from the likes of Walfred Moisio.

If you're feeling seriously flush, then head to the less well known **Arthouse Marc Chagall**, located at Bloemgracht 134 (330 7577, www.chagallkunst.com). So exclusive that it's only open for a few hours every day (noon-6pm Mon-Fri), it houses a collection of lithographs, graphic works and woodcuts by the Russian master, many of them signed.

Over at the opposite end of the spectrum is **KochxBos Gallery** (1e Anjeliersdwarsstraat 3, 681 4567, www.kochxbos.nl; *pictured*), with art from the dark and dirty side – queasy surrealist Ray Caesar, who they regularly show, could be considered their mascot.

Other Jordaanese peddlers of odd art include the **Stedelijk Museum Bureau Amsterdam** (Rozenstraat 59, 422 0471, www.smba.nl), **Torch** (Lauriergracht 94, 626 0284, www.torchgallery.com), **Galerie Diana Stigter** (Hazenstraat 17, 624 2361, www.dianastigter.nl) and **Galerie Fons Welters** (Bloemstraat 140, 423 3046, www.fonswelters.nl).

If you want to see the stuff being made rather than simply hanging from a fancy wall, then visit during **Open Ateliers** (www.openateliersjordaan.nl; *see p199*), which offers an opportunity each June to poke your nose into over 70 artists' studios.

haze, and it's no surprise that such a chilled atmosphere incorporates some of the city's best cafés: **'t Smalle** (Egelantiersgracht 12; *see p162*), for example, set on a small canal, where Peter Hoppe (of Hoppe & Jenever, the world's first makers of gin) founded his distillery in 1780. (The Japanese have built an exact replica of 't Smalle in Nagasaki's Holland Village.)

Between scenic coffees or decadent daytime beers, check out some of the specialist shops tucked away on these adorable side streets. Apart from these shops, many of the best of the outdoor markets are also found nearby: Monday morning's bargain **Noordermarkt** and Saturday's paradise of organic foodstuffs **Boerenmarkt** (for both, *see p191*) are held around the Noorderkerk, the city's original Calvinist church, built in 1623. Adjacent to the Noordermarkt is the equally bargain-packed **Westermarkt** (*see p192*), while another general market fills Lindengracht on Saturdays.

Between Brouwersgracht and the blisteringly scenic **Westelijk Eilanden** (*see p114*), more quirky shopping opportunities can be found on Haarlemmerstraat and its westerly extension, Haarlemmerdijk. Though not officially part of

Blowing minds in De Baarsjes

The first quarters of this old town that fell victim to the forces of yuppification were the former working-class neighbourhoods of Jordaan and the Pijp; Oud-West was the next target to succumb. And now, rumour has it that **De Baarsjes** is ripe for the same treatment, although many Amsterdammers might raise an eyebrow at this thought. Isn't that, they ask, the overcrowded part of town that houses big Surinamese, Turkish and Moroccan families? Er, yes it is. And while there are occasional flare-ups of racial tension resulting from the semi-ghettoisation of the area's inhabitants (still a million miles away from recent events in Paris' *banlieues*), De Baarsjes is a lively, multicultural residential and shopping area, boasting a few obscure and fascinating architectural gems.

At first sight, there's seemingly little to report. Much of De Baarsjes is made up of basic, pre-World War II housing. The great exception is the quarter between, roughly, Admiralengracht and Surinameplein. These buildings formed part of the 1920s urban expansion **Plan West**, built in Amsterdam School style (*see p38* **School of rock**). The noted architect HP Berlage was responsible for **Mercatorplein**, with its characteristic corner towers, while his pupil HT Wijdeveld designed the world record-breaking 300m (984-foot) façades along Hoofdweg.

At the edge of De Baarsjes and overlooking neighbouring Oud-West, a whopper of an Amsterdam School building truly dominates the whole area. **Het Sieraad** (Postjesweg 1, www.het-sieraad.nl) was also built in the 1920s, this time by Arend Jan Westerman. Admire it from the outside, with its wild bent façade and many sculptures; or, even better (assuming you're made of cold, hard cash), rent a helicopter and examine it from above to see the spectacular pentagonal outline in force. Once a trade college for craftsmen, the building is now home to several projects, one of which is the restaurant and bar Edel, which has a fantastic drinking terrace on the waterside. Just a minute's walk away from Het Sieraad is another hip restaurant, **Con-Fusion** (Postjesweg 7, 616 2122), which also boasts a terrace on the water – albeit a little noisier this time due to the nearby road. And there's also culture in De Baarsjes. In the area around Admiraal de Ruijterweg and Witte de Withstraat, local authorities have begun setting up a string of adventurous contemporary art galleries, one of which is the **Illuseum** (Witte de Withstraat 120, 770 5581, www.illuseum.com), where the tradition of the 17th-century 'wonder room' is kept alive. On top of all that, nightlife has reached the area: **Club 8** (Admiraal de Ruijterweg 56B, 685 1703, www.club-8.nl) has a cool and very varied programme with DJs, live bands and also video screenings, which always keep a keen eye placed firmly on the arty side of things.

De Baarsjes even made the international press for a short period in 2006 with its near-legendary Blowverbod signs (*see p166* **Anti-smoke signals**). Prohibiting the smoking of marijuana, the signs very clearly depict two fingers holding a joint, with marijuana leaves spiralling up from it. The measure was first intended to reduce loitering and petty crime. One unintended side-effect, though, was the enormous popularity of the signs, resulting in the theft of several of them within days of their being set up, thus cementing their eventual cult status among collectors.

Still, there are some left. Go there before it's too late, take a picture and tell friends back home: 'Only in De Baarsjes!'

Noordermarkt.

Café Nol sets a suitably laid-back pace for day-to-day living. *See p118.*

the Jordaan, this strip and its alleys share an ambience. Head east towards Centraal Station past **West Indische Huis** (Herenmarkt 93-97). This home to the famous West Indies Trading Company (WIC) stored the silver that Piet Hein took from the Spanish after a sea battle in 1628, and was the setting for such dubious decisions as selling all of Manhattan for 60 guilders and running the slave trade between Africa and the Caribbean. Today you can pop your head into the courtyard to say hello to the statue of Peter Stuyvesant. Heading west, Haarlemmerdijk ends at Haarlemmerplein, where you'll see the imposing Haarlemmerpoort city gate, built in 1840. Behind it is wonderful **Westerpark**, which connects to the happening arts complex **Westergasfabriek** (*see p263*).

Rozengracht & further south

Map p325, p329 and p330

As its name suggests, Rozengracht was once a canal. It's now filled in, and scythes through the heart of the Jordaan in unappealing fashion. It's unlikely it was quite so traffic-clogged when Rembrandt lived at No.184 from 1659 until his death a decade later; all that remains of his former home is a plaque on the first floor bearing an inscription that translates as 'Here stood Rembrandt's home 1410-1669'. While you're here, look up at the gable of Rozengracht 204 to spy an iron stickman wall anchor, or visit some of the many Jordaan galleries (*see p119* **Art of the matter**).

The area south of Rozengracht is notable for two antique markets: **Rommelmarkt** and **Looier** (for both, *see p191*). Elandsgracht 71-77 is where the labyrinthine Sjako's Fort was said to have once stood. Sjako is often referred to as the 'Robin Hood of Amsterdam', which glosses over the fact that while he was happy stealing from the rich, he usually neglected to give to the poor. Still, he had style: not many burglars go about their business dressed in white and accompanied by henchmen clad in black. In 1718 his 24-year-old head ended up spiked on a pole where the Shell Building now stands, but local band Sjako!, anarchist bookstore Fort van Sjako (Jodenbreestraat 24, 625 8979), and a shrine in the window of the building that replaced his fort keep his name alive – even though 2007 saw the release of a study by a local historian that proved the story of Sjako was almost completely myth.

The Museum Quarter, Vondelpark & the South

The city's main exhibit feels temporarily on loan, but it's still worth the entry fee.

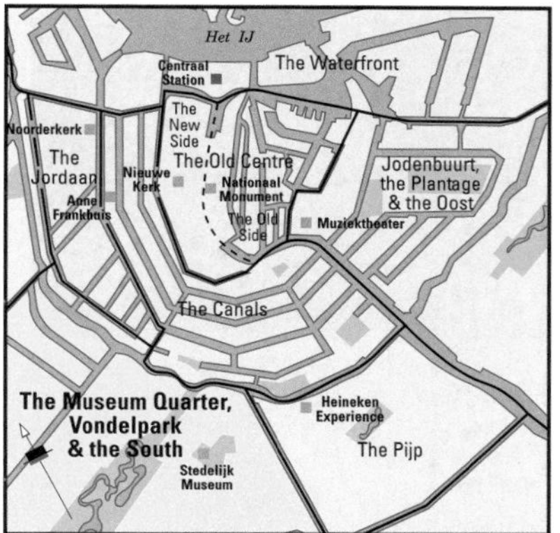

The Museum Quarter

Map p330

Just over a century ago, the area now known as the Museum Quarter was still outside the city limits. Towards the end of the 19th century, though, the city expanded rapidly and the primarily upper-class city fathers decided to erect a swanky neighbourhood between the working-class areas to the west and south. Most of the beautiful mansions, with their art deco gateways and stained-glass windows, were built in the late 1890s and early 1900s.

The heart of the area is Museumplein, the city's largest square, bordered by the **Rijksmuseum** (*see p124*), the **Stedelijk Museum of Modern Art**, the **Van Gogh Museum** (for both, *see p125*) and also the **Concertgebouw** (*see p238*). However, the heart will be beating fainter in the coming years, what with the Rijksmuseum being partially closed and the Stedelijk moving to a temporary space by Centraal Station (*see p114*). Museumplein itself is not really an authentic Amsterdam square, a new revamp accenting its more park-like – or, rather, rural – aspects. Developed in 1872, it served as a location for the World Exhibition of 1883, and was then rented out to the Amsterdam ice skating club between 1900 and 1936. During the Depression the field was put to use as a sports ground and during World War II the Germans built bunkers on it. The square was further mucked around in 1953 when the country's 'shortest motorway', Museumstraat, cut it in two. But the recent additions of grass, wading pool, skate ramp, café and wacky new extension to the Van Gogh Museum have helped.

As you might expect in such seriously highfalutin' cultural surroundings, property doesn't come cheap, and the affluence is apparent. Van Baerlestraat and, especially, PC Hooftstraat are as close as Amsterdam gets to Rodeo Drive, offering solace to ladies who would otherwise be lunching. Not surprisingly, this is where you'll find most of Amsterdam's diamond retailers (*see p110* **Amsterdam: rock city**).

Concertgebouw.

Skate of mind

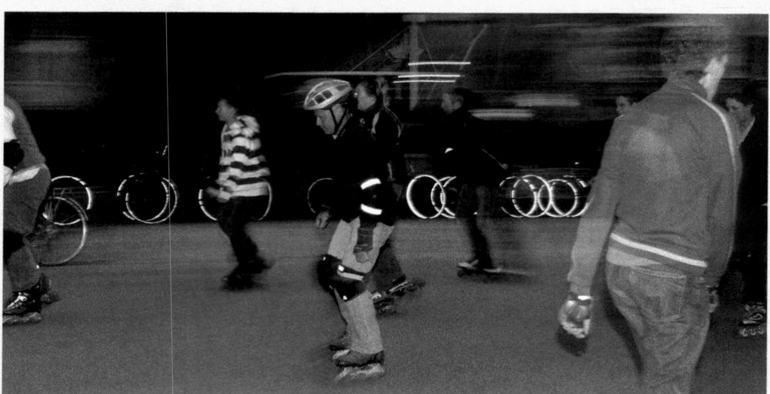

It's 9pm on a Friday night. Most people are slumped in front of the telly or drinking in a bar. But not the people currently assembling in Vondelpark. Unless it's raining, every Friday night a group of eager skate fanatics meet to snake a 20km (12.5-mile), three-hour-long skate tour through the streets of Amsterdam.

It all started back in 1997, when three friends decided to do something special to kick off the weekend. Ten years later, the group varies from a handful of die-hards in winter to hundreds in summer, but they all have one thing in common: a love of skating around the city. Forget boring parks and going round in circles – it's bridges, car parks, canals, tunnels and urban roads this lot are after. Each week there's a new route, available online from Thursday, and every other month or so a theme for dressing up.

The start and finish of the skate is always in Vondelpark, opposite the Filmmuseum. There are 'blockers' who – you've guessed it – block the roads so cars and cyclists can't get in the way, and there are 'flying nurses' who'll come straight to your rescue in case you have an unscheduled meeting with the tarmac. And then there's music too – some skaters carry a sound system on their backs to provide tunes to move to. It's free, it's fun, and before you know it you find yourself making new friends on the move.

A word of warning, though: you do need to be able to skate well and fast, and (most importantly) know how to brake in an instant. And do yourself a favour: wear the proper protective gear to avoid serious injury.

Information can be found on the website, www.fridaynightskate.com.

While you're in the area, it's worth visiting nearby Roemer Visscherstraat. This road, which leads to Vondelpark, is notable not for its labels but rather for its buildings. The houses from Nos.20 to 30 each represent a different country and are all built in the appropriate 'national' architectural style: thus Russia comes with a miniature dome, Italy has been painted pastel pink, and Spain's candy stripes have made it one of the street's favourites.

Rijksmuseum

Stadhouderskade 42 (674 7047/www.rijksmuseum.nl). Tram 2, 5, 6, 7, 10. **Open** 9am-6pm Mon-Thur, Sat, Sun; 9am-10pm Fri. **Admission** €10; free under-19s, MK. **Credit** AmEx, MC, V. **Map** p330 D5.

Designed by PJH Cuypers and opened in 1885, the Rijksmuseum holds the country's largest collection of art and artefacts, including 40 Rembrandts and four Vermeers. However, most of its million exhibits will be out of the public eye until after the summer of 2010 while the Rijksmuseum gets a €227 million facelift at the hands of Spanish architect Cruz y Ortiz (for those interested, the museum regularly organises 'Hard Hat Tours' to show the state of the renovations). The closure may turn out to be a blessing in disguise: instead of overdosing on the vastness of the place, visitors will be able to see the 400 most masterful masterpieces in the Philips Wing. Some of the collection will be used in other exhibitions organised by museums throughout the Netherlands. In addition, the Rijksmuseum Amsterdam Schiphol

(Schiphol Airport, Holland Boulevard between E and F) has a few choice pieces by the likes of Rembrandt, Steen and Ruysdael. In short: there will still be plenty of Golden Age art to look at, but you'd do well to check the museum website before you visit, just to be on the safe side.

The collection was started when William V began to acquire pieces just for the hell of it, and has been growing ever since: it includes Dutch paintings from the 15th century until 1900, as well as decorative and Asian art. The Old Masters' works that will almost certainly stay on display include such noted jewels as Rembrandt's *Night Watch* and Vermeer's *Kitchen Maid* and *Woman Reading a Letter*, plus a selection from the likes of Frans Hals, Jacob de Wit and Ferdinand Bol. There should also be a wealth of decorative arts on display, including 17th-century furniture and intricate silver and porcelain, 17th- and early 18th-century dolls' houses, plus furnishings to give a glimpse of how the interiors of canal houses looked. Eighteenth- and 19th-century paintings, art objects from Asia, statues, lacquer work, paintings, ceramics, jewellery, weaponry and the textile and costume collection will also undoubtedly be visible; the freely accessible garden, filled with Golden Age gateways and architectural fragments on the west side, will remain an oasis of rest.

Stedelijk Museum of Modern Art

Paulus Potterstraat 13 (573 2911/www.stedelijk.nl). Tram 2, 3, 5, 12. **Open** 10am-6pm daily (at Post CS). **Admission** €9; €4.50 7s-16s; free under-7s, MK. **Credit** *Shop* AmEx, MC, V. **Map** p330 D6.

It's moved. Until summer 2008, temporary modern art exhibitions organised by the Stedelijk are on display on the second and third floors of the Post CS building near Centraal Station (*see p114*). But since the Stedelijk's rebuilding will take until at least 2009, it may stay put or there may be yet another transfer before the collection finally returns to Paulus Potterstraat. But wherever it finds itself, the museum has an amazing collection to draw from. Pre-war highlights include works by Cézanne, Picasso, Matisse and Chagall, plus a collection of paintings and drawings by Malevich. Post-1945 artists represented include De Kooning, Newman, Ryman, Judd, Stella, Lichtenstein, Warhol, Nauman, Middleton, Dibbets, Kiefer, Polke, Merz and Kounellis. Displays change regularly: some exhibitions are drawn from the collection, while others are made up from works loaned to the museum, but each tends to focus on a particular trend or the work of a specific artist.

Van Gogh Museum

Paulus Potterstraat 7 (570 5200/www.vangogh museum.nl). Tram 2, 3, 5, 12. **Open** 10am-6pm Mon-Thur, Sat, Sun; 10am-10pm Fri. **Admission** €10; €2.50 13s-17s; free under-13s, MK; exhibition prices vary. **Credit** MC, V. **Map** p330 D6.

As well as the bright colours of his palette, Vincent van Gogh is known throughout the world for his productivity, and that's reflected in the 200 paintings and 500 drawings that form part of the permanent exhibition here. In addition to this collection, there are also examples of his Japanese prints and works by the likes of Toulouse-Lautrec that add perspective to Van Gogh's own artistic efforts.

After a major and impressive refurbishment, the enlarged Rietveld building remains the home base for the permanent collection, while the new wing by Japanese architect Kisho Kurokawa is usually the home to temporary exhibitions that focus on Van Gogh's contemporaries and his influence on other artists. These shows are assembled from both the museum's own extensive archives and private collections. Do yourself a favour and get there early in the morning, though: the queues in the afternoon can get frustratingly long, and the gallery unbearably busy. And it's worth noting that Friday evenings often feature lectures, concerts and films.

Vondelpark

Map p330

Amsterdam's largest green space is named after the city's best-known poet, Joost van den Vondel (1587-1679), whose controversial play *Lucifer* caused the religious powers of the time to crack down hard on those who engaged in what was termed 'notorious living'. The campaign helped bring about the end of Rembrandt and Vondel; the latter ended his days as a pawnshop doorman.

Fine art in flux at the **Rijksmuseum**.

Museums for the mildly obsessed

For planes

Aviodome *Pelikaanweg 50, Lelystad Airport (0900 284 6376/www.aviodome.nl). Lelystad NS station then bus 147.* **Open** 10am-5pm Tue-Sun. **Admission** €14.90 adults; €13.90 65+; €12.90 4s-12s; free under-4s. **No credit cards.**

Aeroplane enthusiasts will loop the loop over this aviation theme park and museum. They have a 1903 Wright Flyer, a Spider (designed by Dutch pioneer Anthony Fokker) and more recent aeronautical exhibits.

For trams

Electrische Museumtramlijn Amsterdam *Haarlemmermeerstation, Amstelveenseweg 264 (673 7538/info 618 8528/www.museumtram.nl). Tram 16.* **Open** *Apr-Oct* 11am-5pm Sun; *July, Aug* special timetable Wed. **Tickets** €4; €2 4s-11s, over-65s; free under-4s. **No credit cards.**

The pride and raison d'être of the Electrical Museumtramline, housed in a beautiful 1915 former railway station, is its rolling stock. Antique streetcars from several cities offer roughly hour-long round trips (*pictured*).

For pianos

Pianola Museum *Westerstraat 106, the Jordaan (627 9624/www.pianola.nl). Tram 3, 10.* **Open** 2pm-5pm Sun. **Admission** €5; €4 65+; €3 under-12s. **No credit cards. Map** p325 B2.

Ever wanted the full scoop on piano-playing devices? Look no further. But do call ahead: budget cuts may see the museum's demise.

For strange specimens

Museum Vrolik *Entrance on south side of AMC medical faculty, Meibergdreef 15 (info 566 9111). Metro Holendrecht.* **Open** 9.30am-5pm Mon-Fri. **Admission** free.

This museum way out south-east contains 18th- and 19th-century specimens of human embryos and malformations collected by one Professor Gerardus Vrolik and his son. It's clearly not for those with weak stomachs, and young children may find it alarming.

For mini modern art

Reflex Minituur Museum voor Hedendaagse Kunst *Singel 548, in the Fortis Bank (627 2832/www.reflex-art.nl). Tram 1, 2, 4, 5, 9, 14.* **Open** 10am-5pm Mon-Fri. **Admission** free.

Some 1,500 separate works no larger than ten centimetres (four inches) across: artists on show include Warhol, Appel, Scholte, Beuys, Kienholz, Lichtenstein, Leibovitz and LeWitt.

For pipes

Pijpenkabinet *Prinsengracht 488, Southern Canal Belt (421 1779/www.pijpenkabinet.nl). Tram 1, 2, 5.* **Open** noon-6pm Wed-Sat. **Admission** €5. **No credit cards. Map** p330 D5.

Vondelpark is the most central of the city's major parks, its construction inspired by the large development of the Plantage, which had formerly provided the green background for the leisurely walks of the rich. It was designed in the 'English style' by Zocher, with the emphasis on natural landscaping; the original ten acres opened in 1865. The park has actually sunk some two to three metres (seven to ten feet) since it was first built – some larger trees are in fact 'floating' on blocks of styrofoam or reinforced with underground poles.

There are several ponds and lakes in the park – no boating, though – plus a number of play areas and cafés; try **'t Het Blauwe Theehuis** (Round Blue Teahouse; *see p162*) and the always charming Café Vertigo at the **Nederlands Filmmuseum** (*see p213*). The NFM is less of a museum and more a cinema with a café attached and a library nearby. Keep your eye out for a huge Picasso sculpture in the middle of the park, and the wild parakeets who were mistakenly released in 1976. Around the corner – and providing a unique place for coffee – is

This national pipe museum staggers both mind and lungs with a truly vast collection: clay pipes, opium pipes and paraphernalia. Good 'Smokiana' shop for connoisseurs and souvenir hunters alike.

For lifts

Energetica *Hoogte Kadijk 400, Amsterdam East (422 1277/www.energetica.nl). Tram 9, 14/bus 22, 32.* **Open** 10am-4pm Tue-Fri; noon-4pm Sun. **Admission** €4; free under-12s, MK. **No credit cards. Map** p327 F2.
This big museum of 'energy techniques, elevators, household appliances and city gas' is a world leader among functioning lift collections; it includes the famous Pater Noster. In 2007, they began a series of renovations to turn it into the National Public Center for Energy, which may affect opening hours.

For booze

House of Bols *Paulus Potterstraat 14 (www.houseofbols.nl). Tram 2, 3, 5, 12.* **Open** noon-6pm Mon, Wed-Sun. **Admission** €10 (over-18s only, includes free cocktail). **Map** p330 D6.
The Bols were one of the first producers of fine jenever – the original gin – and began it all in 1575. Besides a 'World of Bartending', they also have a 'Hall of Taste' where you can taste with your eyes, hands and nose. Very cheesy, but good fun if you're in the right mood.

For all and sundry

For **cats** *see p107*; for **Bibles** *see p100*; for **coffee and tea** *see p187*; for **beer** see *p130*; for **torture** see *p108*; for **drugs** *see p53* and *p93*; for **condoms** *see p193*; for **sex** *see p87* and *p93.*

the epic **Hollandsche Manege** (Vondelstraat 140, 618 0942; *see p42*), a wooden version of the Spanish Riding School in Vienna.

Vondelpark gets fantastically busy on sunny days and Sundays, when bongos abound, dope is toked and football games take up any space that happens to be left over. The dicky-tickered would do well to look out for rollerbladers, who meet here weekly for the **Friday Night Skate** (*see p124* **Skate of mind**). Films, plays and concerts are also put on, with a festival of free open-air performances in summer (*see p235*).

Further south

The Museum Quarter is the northernmost tip of Amsterdam's Oud Zuid (Old South), which stretches down beyond Vondelpark. This area is defined by residential housing, with the more Bohemian streets around the park contrasting nicely with their smarter equivalents by the museums, and comparing favourably with the uglier modern buildings nearby.

Nieuw Zuid

Stretching out in a ring beneath Vondelpark is a fairly indeterminate region known as Nieuw Zuid (New South), bordered to the north by Vondelpark, to the east by the Amstel and to the west by the Olympisch Stadion (www.olympisch-stadion.net). This was built for the 1928 Olympics, now renovated to its original Amsterdam School glory and most notable for its highly popular club/restaurant **Vakzuid** (*see p127*). The New South was planned by Berlage and put into action by a variety of Amsterdam School architects, who designed both private and public housing for the area. It's the former that's given the New South what character it has, most notably around Apollolaan and Beethovenstraat (worth visiting simply for the **Oldenburg** bakery at No.17).

The few visitors tend to be here on business, especially around the **World Trade Center** and the steadily rising modern architecture neighbourhood of Zuidas. The controversial Noord-Zuidlijn Metro is set to link this district with the centre of town and Amsterdam Noord. East of here is another staple of Amsterdam business life: the ugly **RAI Exhibition and Congress Centre**, which holds numerous trade fairs, conventions and a range of public exhibitions throughout the year.

However, in between the RAI and the WTC lies one of Amsterdam's most beautiful parks. Extended and renovated in 1994, **Beatrixpark** is a wonderfully peaceful place, very handy if you want to avoid the crowds in town on a summer's day. The Victorian walled garden is worth a visit, as is the pond, complete with geese, black swans and herons. Amenities include a wading pool and play area for kids. Nearby is also the arts/design centre **Platform 21** (*see p219*) housed in a round former church.

Still further south, **Amstelpark** was created for a garden festival in 1972, and today offers recreation and respite to locals in the suburb of Buitenveldert, near the RAI. A formal rose garden and rhododendron walk are among the seasonal spectacles, and there is also a labyrinth, pony rides and a children's farm, plus tours on a miniature train. The Rosarium

Vondelpark. *See p125.*

Restaurant serves expensive meals, though its outdoor café is less pricey. Just north of Amstelpark, along the scenic banks of the Amstel, lies the city's most evocative cemetery, **Begraafplaat Zorgvlied** (Amsteldijk 273, 644 5236; *see p22* **Set in stone**), which is filled with ancient and arty headstones – good for those seeking a more introspective stroll.

Amstelveen

Of all the southern suburbs, Amstelveen is the most welcoming to the casual visitor. Though the **CoBrA Museum** (*see right*) helps, the main attraction here is the **Amsterdamse Bos**, a mammoth, artificially built wood that's treasured by locals yet neglected by visitors. And after 80-odd years of growth, it feels like an authentic forest at that. The 2,000-acre site sprawls beautifully, and comes with a great many attractions in case the tranquillity isn't enough. The man-made Bosbaan is used for boating and swimming, with canoe and pedalo rental available. Other attractions include play areas, a horticultural museum, jogging routes, a buffalo and bison reserve, a bike-hire centre (open March to October), a water sports centre, stables and a picnic area. The goat farm sells cheese, milk and ice-cream: you can even feed the goats. The wood feels a lot further away from Schiphol than it actually is: the airport is less than a mile from the wood's western edge, although you'd never know it at a glance.

Bezoekerscentrum de Molshoop

Bosbaanweg 5, near Amstelveenseweg, Amsterdamse Bos (545 6100). Bus 170, 171, 172. **Open** noon-5pm Tue-Sat; 10am-5pm Sun. **Admission** free.

The Amsterdamse Bos visitor centre recounts the history and use of the Amsterdamse Bos. Its mock woodland grotto, which can turn from day to night at the flick of a switch, is wonderful for kids.

CoBrA Museum of Modern Art

Sandbergplein 1, Amstelveen (547 5050/www.cobra-museum.nl). Tram 5/Metro 51/bus 170, 172. **Open** 11am-5pm Tue-Sun. **Admission** €7; €4 over-65s; €3 5s-16s; free under-5s, MK. **Credit** *Shop* MC, V.

Artists such as Karel Appel, Eugene Brands and Corneille were once regarded as little more than eccentric troublemakers; they've now been absorbed into the canon. This museum provides a sympathetic environment in which to trace the development of one of the most influential Dutch artistic movements of the 20th century. They've also now started having exhibitions of more modern artists to attract more visitors. *See also p48.*

Hortus Botanicus (Vrije Universiteit)

Van de Boechorststraat 8, Zuid (444 9390/www.vu.nl/hortus). Tram 5/Metro 50, 51/bus 142, 170, 171, 172. **Open** *Sept-May* 8am-4.30pm Mon-Fri; *May-Sept* 8am-4.30pm Mon-Fri; 9am-5pm Sat. **Admission** free.

This small garden doesn't have the charm of its city-centre counterpart (*see p112*), but it's a pleasant place for a stroll. The fern collection is one of the largest in the world; the Dutch garden next door shows the great variety of flora native to this country.

The Pijp

Creative, multicultural and kicking like the proverbial mule.

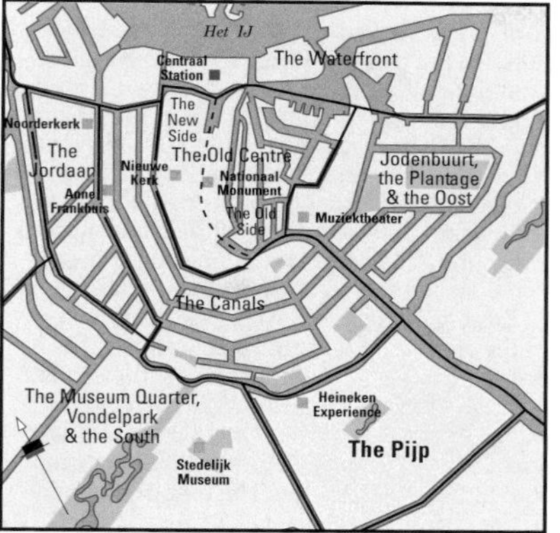

Map p331

A trip to the Pijp offers a window into one of the city's most unique communities, an oft-neglected nugget off the tourist track. While it's hardly a treasure trove of history and sights, the Pijp's time is the present, with over 150 different nationalities keeping its global village vibe alive and the recent economic upturn seeing the opening of more upmarket eateries and bars than ever before. Gentrification is in full effect.

The Pijp is the best known of the working-class quarters built in the late 19th century. Harsh economics saw the building of long, narrow streets, which probably inspired the change in name from the official, double-yawn-inducing 'Area YY' to its appropriate nickname, 'the Pipe'. Because rents were high many tenants were forced to sublet rooms to students, who then gave the area its Bohemian character.

That said, the many Dutch writers who lived here helped add to it. Among the locals were luminaries such as Heijermans, De Haan and Bordewijk, who most famously described World War I Amsterdam as a 'ramshackle bordello, a wooden shoe made of stone'. Many painters had studios here, too – people like Piet Mondrian, who once lived in the attic of Ruysdaelkade 75, where he began formulating de Stijl while enjoying a view of the decidedly old-school Rijksmuseum. It's estimated that over 250 artists currently live in the area, a very healthy crop gaining status in a district where most streets are named after their forebears. Jan Steen, Ferdinand Bol, Gerard Dou and Frans Hals (whose street, Frans Halsstraat, is very pretty, and rich with cafés and bars) are just a few of the artists honoured.

And, of course, the area was packed with brothels and drinking dens. In the basement of Quellijnstraat 64 the Dutch cabaret style – distinguished by witty songs with cutting social commentary for lyrics – was formulated by Eduard Jacobs and continues to live on through the likes of Freek de Jonge, Hans Teeuwen and Najib Amhali.

At the turn of the century, the Pijp was a radical socialist area. The place has lost much of its bite since those days and many families with children have fled to suburbia. Still, the number of cheap one- and two-bedroom places, combined with the reasonably central location, makes the area very attractive to students, young single people and couples, and the Pijp has the densest gay population in Amsterdam.

During the last 40 years, many immigrants have found their way to the Pijp, setting up shop and so inspiring the general economic upswing of the area. The Pijp now houses a mix of nationalities, providing locals with halal butchers, Surinamese, Spanish, Indian and Turkish delicatessens, and restaurants offering authentic Syrian, Moroccan, Thai, Pakistani, Chinese and Indian cuisine. Thanks to these low-priced exotic eats, the Pijp is easily the best place in town for quality snacking treats, the ingredients for which are mostly bought fresh from the single largest daily market in all the Netherlands: **Albert Cuypmarkt** (*see p190*), the hub around which the Pijp turns. This market attracts thousands of customers every day, and spills merrily into the adjoining roads: the junctions of Sweelinckstraat, Ferdinand Bolstraat and 1e Van der Helststraat, north into the lively Gerard Douplein, and south towards Sarphatipark. The chaos will be heightened over the next few years by the construction of the Metro's controversial Noord-Zuidlijn, whose route will follow a line pretty much directly underneath Ferdinand Bolstraat.

Still on Albert Cuypstraat, cross Ferdinand Bolstraat and you'll find a cluster of fine, cheap Chinese-Surinamese-Indonesian restaurants. After passing former Van Moppes & Zoon Diamond Factory, diamond turns to ruby around the corner on Ruysdaelkade, the Pijp's

Sarpharipark.

very own mini red light district. Enjoy the sight of steaming, hooter-happy motorists caught in their own traffic gridlock while you lounge casually around an otherwise restful canal.

Head back away from the water (and the red lights) a few blocks along 1e Jan Steenstraat, past splendid bric-a-brac shop **Nic Nic** (*see p188*), and you'll soon run across the Pijp's little green oasis: the grass-, pond- and duck-dappled **Sarphatipark**, designed and built as a mini Bois de Boulogne by the slightly mad genius Samuel Sarphati (1813-66). Aside from building the Amstel hotel and the Paleis voor Volksvlijt, Sarphati showed philanthropic tendencies as a baker of inexpensive bread for the masses, and as initiator of the city's rubbish collection. The centrepiece fountain comes complete with a statue of Sammy himself.

Edging along and beyond the south edge of Sarphatipark, Ceintuurbaan offers little of note for the visitor, with the exception of the buildings at Nos.251-255. Well, there aren't many other houses in the city that incorporate giant ball-playing green gnomes with red hats in their wooden façades. The unique exterior of the **Gnome House** was inspired by the owner's name: Van Ballegooien translates (clumsily) as 'of the ball-throwing'.

If you stay for a stroll in the park, wander north up 1e Van der Helststraat towards Gerard Douplein. This little square, with its cafés, coffeeshops, chip shops and authentic Italian ice-cream parlour, turns into one big terrace during the summer, and is hugely popular with the locals. Bargain second-hand knick-knacks can be bought from **Stichting Dodo** at No.21; trivia hounds should know that the Dutch – or rather their egg-eating animals – were largely responsible for this bird's extinction after they colonised Mauritius in 1598. A few streets away is the **Heineken Experience** (*see below*).

Heineken Experience

Stadhouderskade 78 (523 9666/www.heineken experience.com). Tram 6, 7, 10, 16, 24, 25.
Open 11am-7pm (no entry after 6.45pm) daily.
Admission €15. **Credit** MC, V. **Map** p331 E5.

In 1988, Heineken stopped brewing here, but kept the building open for tours: for *f*2 (less than €1 in today's money), you got an hour-long guided walk through the site, plus as much Heineken as you could neck. It's safe to say that more punters were there for the free beer than the brewing education.

Heineken cottoned on to this, and renovated the building as the Heineken Experience: flashier but less fun. Plus points: the virtual reality ride through a brewery from the perspective of a Heineken bottle is easily the most ludicrous exhibit in Amsterdam, and you still get to enjoy a free beer at the end. The Experience will close for renovation at the end of 2007 and is due to reopen in 2008.

Eat, Drink, Shop

Features

Restaurants

A city where all options remain on the table.

While many restaurants continue to drop like flies into pea soup, there has been an almost endless stream of new and often daring ventures to replace them. Gossip seems most fevered around places that combine culinary delight with deeply eccentric locations: **De Kas**, for example, in an old greenhouse; **Hotel de Goudfazant**, in a warehouse; **Dauphine** (for all three, *see p145*) in a former Renault showroom; and **Pont 13** (*see p147*) in a retired ferry. And be sure to drop in for at least a coffee and a view at **11** (*see p145*), located atop the former post office building and now temporary home to the Stedelijk Museum (*see p25*). At time of writing there was also much anticipation for the imminent opening of 'crazy' **Restaurant Freud** (Spaarndammerstraat 424, 688 5548, www.restaurantfreud.nl), which offers 'insanely tasty food' prepared and served up by former psychiatric patients. Meanwhile, **As** (Prinses Irenestraat 19, 644 0100, www.platform21.com), located in a former round church turned art gallery (Platform 21; *see p219*), has just begun to flaunt conscious eating habits by offering dishes defined by season and temperature. So yes: it's safe to say that the local eating scene is bolder and more adventurous than ever, and is just getting quirkier by the day.

All this action makes one forget that the term 'Dutch cuisine' once tended to inspire peals of laughter. But well-travelled chefs have returned home to apply their lessons to fresh local and often organic ingredients (you can source your own at Noordermarkt's Saturday organic market; *see p191*). Transcending its setting as a land best suited to spuds, cabbages, carrots and cows, the nation is now employing its greenhouses to grow an array of ingredients.

Fish, gruel and beer formed the trinity of the medieval diet. (Yes, Homer: beer! Would you want to drink the canal water?) But during the Golden Age, the rich indulged in hogs and pheasants, although apparently only after having these table-groaning meals painted for posterity – as the Rijksmuseum attests. But it was with Napoleonic rule at the dawn of the 19th century that the middle classes were seduced by innovations like herbs, spices and the radical concept that overcooking is bad. Sadly, a century later it all went utterly, terribly wrong (*see p149* **The dark past of Dutch dining**). But still, there's nothing quite like a hotchpotch of potato, crispy bacon and still-crunchy greens all swimming in gravy.

The spicy food of Indonesia re-eroticised the Dutch palate after World War II, when the colony was granted independence and the Netherlands took in Indonesian immigrants. Take your pick from the cheap Surinamese-Indonesian-Chinese snack bars or visit the purveyors of the *rijsttafel* ('rice table'), where every known variety of fish, meat and vegetable is worked into a filling extravaganza. Along with fondue – a 'national' dish shamelessly stolen from the Swiss because its shared pot appealed to the Dutch sense of the democratic – Indo is the food of choice for any celebratory meals. Other waves of immigrants helped create today's vortex of culinary diversity.

Go to the Pijp if you crave econo-ethnic; cruise Haarlemmerstraat, Utrechtsestraat, Nieuwmarkt, the 'Nine Streets' area and Reguliersdwarsstraat if you want something posher; and only surrender to Leidseplein if you don't mind being overcharged for a cardboard steak and day-old sushi (that said, we do list some notable exceptions).

The best Restaurants

Blijburg
A good place for a picnic. *See p145.*

Gartine
For the love of a slow lunch. *See p139.*

Hap Hmm
Cheap and cheerful and with real Dutch cosiness in abundance. *See p141.*

Nam Kee
Central and with killer oysters. *See p137.*

Pont 13
Best float on a boat. *See p147.*

Riaz
Where Gullit scores his helpings of hearty rice and beans. *See p151.*

La Rive
A wallet weakener for those with bank accounts to match appetites. *See p143.*

Latei. *See p135.*

Sure, check out the posh places, but quality and economic snack opportunities can be found in the form of fish – raw herring! smoked eel! – available from the ubiquitous fish stalls, rolled 'pizzas' from Turkish bakeries, Dutch *broodjes* (sandwiches) from bakers and butchers, and spicy Surinamese *broodjes* from 'Suri-Indo-Chin' snack bars. And you really should visit an Albert Heijn supermarket (*see p191* **Back to basics**) to get an insight into Dutch eating habits. After all, sometimes you can eat your best meals from the comfort of a scenic bench.

In addition to the restaurants listed below, there are many bars serving good food at fair prices; for these, *see pp153-163*. For gay-friendly restaurants and cafés, *see p228*. For places to take the children, *see p205*. And if you want to hit an urban beach, *see p159* **United we sand**.

LEISURELY DINING

Dining in Amsterdam is a laid-back affair, although those who keep nocturnal hours should note that the Dutch tend to eat early: many kitchens close by 10pm. All bills should, by law, include 19 per cent tax and a 15 per cent service charge, though it's customary to round up between five and ten per cent if the service merits it. If you have any special requirements, like high chairs or disabled access, it's always best to phone the restaurant before setting out.

Since the euro was adopted in 2002, prices have shot up; those listed here should only be used as a guideline. Local foodies weigh in at www.iens.nl and www.specialbite.nl – with the latter being a real winner that can reliably scoop you on highly anticipated late 2007 openings, such as those from local Michelin-starred top cooks Imko Binnerts (of Imko's fame) and Pascal Jalhaij (of Vermeer fame), plus international celebrity and notorious potty-mouth Gordon Ramsay.

❶ Purple numbers given in this chapter correspond to the locations of individual restaurants as marked on the street maps. *See pp325-332.*

METALLICA
YOU KNOW WHO YOU ARE.
AMSTERDAM • MAX EUWEPLEIN 57-61
+31 (0)20 523 ROCK • HARDROCK.COM
Hard Rock

The Old Centre: Old Side

Cafés & snack stops

1e Klas

Centraal Station, Line 2B (625 0131). Tram 1, 2, 4, 5, 6, 9, 13, 16, 17, 24, 25. **Open** 8.30am-11pm daily. **Main courses** €16-€22. **Credit** AmEx, DC, MC, V. **Map** p326 D1 ❶

This former brasserie for first-class commuters is now open to anyone who wants to kill some time in style – with a full meal or snack – while waiting for a train. The art nouveau interior will whisk you to the 1890s. But if you are running for the train, score a coffee, shake and bagel from Shakies (west tunnel by stairs to lines 10/11, 423 4377, www.shakies.nl).

Brasserie Harkema

Nes 67 (428 2222/www.brasserieharkema.nl). Tram 4, 9, 14, 16, 24, 25. **Open** 11am-1am daily. *Kitchen* noon-11pm. **Main courses** *Lunch* €8-€17. *Dinner* €13-€17. **Credit** MC, V. **Map** p326 D3 ❷

A new landmark, this former tobacco factory has titillated the local scene with its sense of designer space, excellent wines and a kitchen that stays open late pumping out reasonably-priced French classics.

De Bakkerswinkel

Warmoesstraat 69 (489 8000/www.bakkerswinkel.nl). Tram 1, 2, 4, 5, 9, 13, 14, 16, 17, 24, 25. **Open** 8am-4pm Tue-Sat; 10am-4pm Sun. **Main courses** €3.50-€11. **No credit cards**. **Map** p326 D2 ❸

A bakery-tearoom where you can indulge in lovingly prepared and hearty sandwiches, soups and the most divine slabs of quiche you've ever had.

Other locations Roelof Hartstraat 68 (662 3594); Polonceaukade 1 (688 0632).

Latei

Zeedijk 143 (625 7485/www.latei.net). Tram 4, 9, 14, 16, 24, 25/Metro Nieuwmarkt. **Open** 8am-6pm Mon-Wed; 8am-10pm Thur, Fri; 9am-10pm Sat; 11am-6pm Sun. **Main courses** €3-€8. **No credit cards**. **Map** p326 D2 ❹

Packed with kitsch and funky Finnish wallpaper – all of which, including wallpaper, is for sale – this little café serves up healthy juices and snacks all day long, plus vegetarian dinners based around couscous (from 6pm Thur-Sat). *Photos p133.*

Chinese & Japanese

A Fusion

Zeedijk 130 (330 4068). Tram 4, 9, 14, 16, 24, 25/Metro Nieuwmarkt. **Open** noon-11pm daily. **Main courses** €7-€14. **Credit** AmEx, DC, MC, V. **Map** p326 D2 ❺

This loungey affair obviously took notes from the hip side of NYC's Chinatown. The dark and inviting interior harbours big screens playing Hong Kong music videos, bubble teas (lychee!) and some of the tastiest confusion-free pan-Asian dishes in town.

Dolores. *See p139.*

Eat, Drink, Shop

Grease of mind

The correct local terminology for a greasy snack – *vette hap* – can be translated literally as 'fat bite', which says a lot for the honesty of the Dutch when it comes to the less healthy end of the belly-ballast spectrum. And seriously, why go to a multinational burger chain when there's such a rich local grease tradition to indulge in?

The best chips

Vleminckx
Voetboogsteeg 31, Old Centre: New Side (no phone). Tram 1, 2, 5. **Open** noon-6pm Mon, Sun; 11am-6pm Tue-Sat. **No credit cards. Map** p330 D4.
Chunky Belgian (*Vlaamse*) chips served along with your pick of toppings. Go for *oorlog* ('war') chips: mayo, spicy peanut sauce and onions.

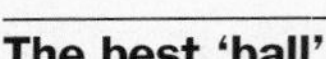

The best 'ball'

Het Koffiekeldertje
Frederiksplein 4, Southern Canal Belt (626 3424). Tram 4, 6, 7, 10. **Open** 9am-5pm Mon-Fri. **No credit cards. Map** p329 F4.
A large melts-in-your-mouth sphere of ground beef served on a bun – and with a smile – in a charming basement café. Watch your head.

The best pancake

Pancake Bakery
Prinsengracht 191, the Jordaan (625 1333/ www.pancake.nl). Tram 13, 17. **Open** noon-9.30pm daily. **Main courses** €6.25-€11.50. **Credit** AmEx, MC, V. **Map** p326 C2.
Dutch recipes stress the importance of sheer density so that the pancake can hold a large array of toppings, from sweet to hardcore savouries like bacon and cheese.

The best steak

Eetcafé Loetje Johannes
Vermeerstraat 52, Museum Quarter (662 8173/www.cafeloetje.nl). Tram 16. **Open** 11am-1am Mon-Fri; 5.30pm-1am Sat. *Kitchen* 11am-10pm Mon-Fri; 6-10pm Sat. **Main courses** €5.50-€18. **No credit cards. Map** p330 D6.
After a day's tourism there's nothing better than beef steak served with fries and mayo. A fine antidote to the rarefied air you may have inhaled while gazing at a Rembrandt, and hugely effective comfort food as a result.

The best kroket

Van Dobben
Korte Reguliersdwarsstraat 5-9, Southern Canal Belt (624 4200/www.vandobben.com). Tram 4, 9, 25. **Open** 9.30am-1am Mon-Thur; 9.30am-2am Fri, Sat; 11.30am-8pm Sun. **Main courses** €1.60-€9.80. **No credit cards. Map** p331 E4.
A *kroket* is a version of a croquette: a mélange of meat and potato with a crusty, deep-fried skin best served on a bun with hot mustard. This 1945-vintage late-nighter is the champion, but you can also find a more refined shrimp variation nearby at famous bakery Holtkamp (Vijzelgracht 15, 624 8757).

The best all-round grease merchant

Febo
Venues across town (www.febo.nl).
Grease goes space age at the Febo automats (*pictured*): you put your change into a hole in the wall and, in exchange, get a dollop of grease in the form of a hot hamburger, *kroket*, *bamibal* (a deep-fried noodle-like ball of vaguely Indonesian origin) or a *kaas soufflé* (a popular cheese treat that's tasty enough if eaten when still hot but rather uninviting when cold and congealing).

Nam Kee

Zeedijk 111-113 (624 3470/www.namkee.nl). Tram 4, 9, 14, 16, 24, 25/Metro Nieuwmarkt. **Open** noon-11pm Mon-Sat; noon-10pm Sun. **Main courses** €6.50-€19. **No credit cards. Map** p326 D2 ❻

Cheap and terrific food has earned this Chinese joint a devoted following: the oysters in black bean sauce have achieved classic status. If it's busy, try massive sister operation and dim sum maestros Nam Tin nearby (Jodenbreestraat 11-13, 428 8508) or equally stellar New King (Zeedijk 115-117, 625 2180). **Other locations** Geldersekade 117 (639 2848).

Oriental City

Oudezijds Voorburgwal 177-179 (626 8352/www.oriental-city.nl). Tram 4, 9, 14, 16, 24, 25. **Open** 11.30am-11pm daily. **Main courses** €8-€23. **Credit** AmEx, DC, MC, V. **Map** p326 D3 ❼

The views overlook Damstraat, the Royal Palace and the canals. And that's not even the best bit: they serve some of city's most authentic dim sum.

Dutch & Belgian

Café Bern

Nieuwmarkt 9 (622 0034). Tram 4, 9, 14, 16, 24, 25/Metro Nieuwmarkt. **Open** 4pm-1am daily. *Kitchen* 6-11pm. Closed mid July-mid Aug. **Main courses** €9-€15. **No credit cards. Map** p327 E2 ❽

Despite its Swiss origins, the Dutch adopted the cheese fondue as a 'national dish' long ago. Sample its culinary conviviality at this suitably cosy brown bar that was established by the rather unlikely fiat of a nuclear physicist: the menu is affordable and the bar stocked with a generous variety of grease-cutting agents. It's best to book ahead.

French & Mediterranean

Blauw aan de Wal

Oudezijds Achterburgwal 99 (330 2257). Tram 9, 16, 24. **Open** 6.30-11.30pm Mon-Sat. **Main courses** €24.50-€25.50. **Set menu** 3 courses €42.50. **Credit** AmEx, MC, V. **Map** p326 D2 ❾

The hallmarks of this culinary mainstay are tempting dishes and a wine list likely to inspire long bouts of grateful contemplation in visiting oenophiles.

Café Roux

The Grand, Oudezijds Voorburgwal 197 (555 3560/www.thegrand.nl). Tram 4, 9, 14, 16, 24, 25. **Open** *Breakfast* 6.30-10.30am. *Lunch* noon-3pm. *Tea* 3-5pm. *Dinner* 6.30-10.30pm daily. **Main courses** €17-€39. **Credit** AmEx, DC, MC, V. **Map** p326 D3 ❿

Despite Albert Roux's status among gastronomes, meals here still represent good value for money, especially at lunchtimes. *See also p58.*

Centra

Lange Niezel 29 (622 3050). Tram 4, 9, 14, 16, 24, 25. **Open** 1.30-10.30pm daily. **Main courses** €7-€17. **No credit cards. Map** p326 D2 ⓫

Good, wholesome, homely Spanish cooking with a suitably unpretentious atmosphere to match.

Indonesian & Thai

Thaise Snackbar Bird

Zeedijk 72 (snack bar 420 6289/restaurant 620 1442/www.thai-bird.nl). Tram 1, 2, 4, 5, 9, 13, 14, 16, 17, 24, 25. **Open** *Snack bar* 5-11pm daily. *Restaurant* 4-10pm daily. **Main courses** €10-€25. **Credit** (restaurant only) AmEx, DC, MC, V. **Map** p326 D2 ⓬

Home cooking like mama used to make at **Hap Hmm**. *See p141.*

The most authentic Thai place in town. No doubt because of that, it's also the most crowded, but nevertheless it's worth waiting for, whether you drop by to pick up a pot of tom yam soup or go for a full-blown meal. If you plan to linger, settle into the restaurant across the street.

The Old Centre: New Side

Cafés & snack stops

Al's Plaice

Nieuwendijk 10 (427 4192). Tram 1, 2, 4, 5, 9, 14, 16, 17, 24, 25. **Open** noon-10pm daily. **Main courses** €3-€9. **No credit cards. Map** p326 C2 ⓭

Brits will spot the pun from 50 paces: yep, it's an English fish 'n' chip gaff. Besides fish, there's a selection of pies, pasties, peas and downmarket tabloids. Hearty fare for expats hungry for the national dish.

Dolores

Nieuwezijds Voorburgwal, opposite No.289 (626 5649). Tram 1, 2, 5. **Open** noon-6pm Mon-Wed, Fri-Sun; noon-9pm Thur. **Main courses** €7-€15. **No credit cards. Map** p326 D3 ⓮

Conveniently located in the hipster bar zone, this former police post is now a snack bar. Greasy fries have been replaced with healthy snacks and meals, harsh colours forsaken for funky warmth. *Photos p135.*

Gartine

Taksteeg 7 (320 4132/www.gartine.nl). Tram 4, 9, 13, 14, 16, 17, 24, 25. **Open** 8am-6pm daily. **Main courses** €5-€20. **No credit cards. Map** p326 D3 ⓯

Open only for breakfast, lunch and a full-blown high tea, Gartine is a testament to slow food served up by a friendly couple who grow their own veg and herbs in a greenhouse. Simple but marvellous.

Chinese & Japanese

Tokyo Café

Spui 15 (489 7918/www.tokyocafe.nl). Tram 1, 2, 4, 5, 9, 14, 16, 24, 25. **Open** 11am-11pm daily. **Main courses** €10-€23. **Set menu** *Lunch* €12-€14. *Dinner* €19-€50. **Credit** AmEx, DC, MC, V. **Map** p330 D4 ⓰

Thought to be haunted, this Jugendstil monument now hosts its upteenth eatery in the form of a Japanese café, complete with lovely terrace, teppanyaki pyrotechnics and sushi and sashimi bar. Their high quality, all-you-can-eat sushi (€18.90 basic selection Mon-Wed, €24 deluxe selection Thur) will most likely keep the ghosts at bay.

Dutch & Belgian

Brasserie De Roode Leeuw

Damrak 93-94 (555 0666/www.restaurantderoodeleeuw.com). Tram 4, 9, 14, 16, 24, 25. **Open** 7am-11.30pm daily. *Kitchen* noon-10pm. **Main courses** *Lunch* €6-€29.50. *Dinner* €18-€32. **Credit** AmEx, DC, MC, V. **Map** p326 D3 ⓱

This brasserie is housed in the oldest covered terrace in Amsterdam. As you might guess, it harks back to classier times, but what's more surprising is its embrace of the digital age as a Wi-Fi point. It specialises in rather expensive Dutch fare and wine.

Keuken van 1870

Spuistraat 4 (620 4018/www.keukenvan1870.nl). Tram 1, 2, 5. **Open** 4-10pm Mon-Sat. **Main courses** €6.50-€12. **Set menu** 3 courses €7.50. **No credit cards. Map** p326 C2 ⓲

This former soup kitchen has been renovated and re-invented but retains a menu of authentic Dutch standards and, in a homage to its roots, the promise to continue serving a set three-course menu for €7.50. Diners often end up sharing tables, so get ready to rub shoulders with the Dutch.

D'Vijff Vlieghen

Spuistraat 294-302 (530 4060/www.d-vijffvlieghen.com). Tram 1, 2, 5, 13, 17. **Open** 6-10pm daily. **Main courses** €27-€32. **Set menu** 4-6 courses €41-€52. **Credit** AmEx, MC, V. **Map** p326 C3/D3 ⓳

'The Five Flies' achieves a rich Golden Age vibe – it even has a Rembrandt room, with etchings – but also works as a purveyor of over-the-top kitsch. The food is best described as poshed-up Dutch. Unique.

Global

Supperclub

Jonge Roelensteeg 21 (344 6400/www.supperclub.nl). Tram 1, 2, 5, 13, 17. **Open** 7.30pm-1am Mon-Thur, Sun; 7.30pm-3am Fri, Sat. **Set menu** 5 courses €65. **Credit** AmEx, DC, MC, V. **Map** p326 D3 ⓴

With its white decor, beds for seating, irreverent food combos that change weekly and wacky acts, this arty and utterly unique joint is casual to the point of being narcoleptic. They also have a cruise ship that trawls the local waters and outposts in Rome, Istanbul and San Francisco.

Vegetarian

Green Planet

Spuistraat 122 (625 8280/www.greenplanet.nl). Tram 1, 2, 5, 13, 17. **Open** 5.30pm-midnight Mon-Sat; 5.30-10.30pm Sun. *Kitchen* 5.30-10.30pm daily. **Main courses** €11-€17. **No credit cards. Map** p326 C3 ㉑

The best veggie in town builds organic ingredients into soups, lasagnes and stir fries. Finish with the house cognac and a slice of chocolate heaven.

Western Canal Belt

Cafés & snack stops

Foodism

Oude Leliestraat 8 (427 5103). Tram 1, 2, 5, 13, 17. **Open** noon-10pm daily. **Main courses** €9-€13. **No credit cards. Map** p326 C3 ㉒

English and Serbo-Croat are the languages of choice in this comfortable café-restaurant, perfect for post-joint munchies. Choose from sandwiches, salads, pastas and hearty shakes; it's also good for takeaway.

Greenwoods

Singel 103 (623 7071). Tram 1, 2, 5. **Open** 9am-6pm Mon-Thur; 9am-7pm Fri-Sun. **Light meals** €4.50-€13. **No credit cards. Map** p326 C2 ㉓

Service at this teashop is friendly but can tend to be on the slow side. Everything is freshly made, though, so forgive them: cakes, scones and muffins are baked daily on the premises. In summer, take your purchase and sit on the terrace by the canal for the ultimate al fresco eating experience.

't Kuyltje

Gasthuismolensteeg 9 (620 1045). Tram 1, 2, 9, 24, 25. **Open** 7am-4pm Mon-Fri. **Sandwich** €1.90-€3.95. **No credit cards. Map** p326 C3 ㉔

The wonderful and deeply filling world of Dutch *broodjes* (sandwiches) has its greatest champion in this takeaway, one of very few that still features proper homemade meat (roast beef!) and fish salads in their buns, as opposed to the hugely unappealing factory-prepared product that's taken over the sandwich market. An awesome lunch every time.

Loekie

Prinsengracht 705A (624 4230/www.loekie.net). Tram 1, 2, 5, 6, 7, 10. **Open** 9am-5pm Mon-Fri; 10am-6pm Sat; 11am-5pm Sun. **Sandwich** €2-€10. **No credit cards. Map** p330 D4 ㉕

Loekie isn't cheap, and you'll have to queue, but a French stick with Italian fillings makes for a meal. Fine quiche, cheesecake and tapenade, too.

Other locations Utrechtsestraat 57 (624 3740).

Dutch & Belgian

Lieve

Herengracht 88 (624 9635/www.restaurantlieve.nl). Tram 1, 2, 5, 13, 17. **Open** 5.30-10.30pm daily. **Main courses** €14-€18. **Set menu** 3 courses €23.50-€28.50. **Credit** V. **Map** p326 C2 ㉖

Caters to those with an abiding love for Belgium's crowning glory, its beers, by recommending the best choice of beverage to accompany each dish. Menus are available in three degrees: hearty living room fare, more formal Belgian Baroque and a gut-busting gastronomical lineup for serious eaters.

Indonesian & Thai

Blue Pepper

Nassaukade 366 (489 7039/www.restaurantblue pepper.com). Tram 7, 10. **Open** *Dinner* 6pm-midnight daily. *Kitchen* 6-10pm. **Main courses** €18-€23. **Set menu** €45-€55. **Credit** AmEx, DC, MC, V. **Map** p330 C5 ㉗

An Indonesian restaurant near Leidseplein that combines tongue-tantalising food with designer decor. Add a decent bottle of wine and it's the perfect date, fashionable without being fussy and always impressive both in terms of atmosphere and eats.

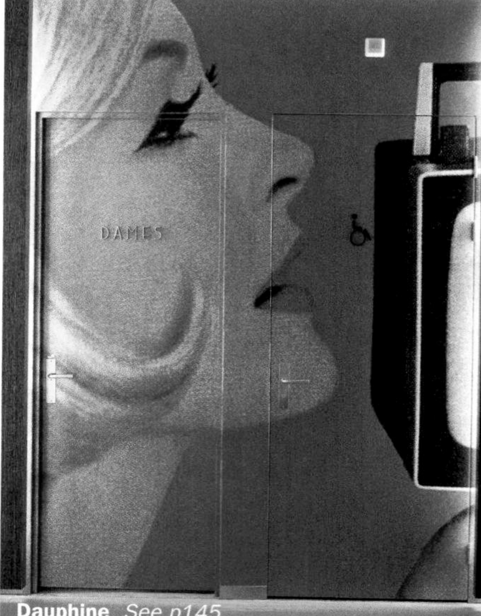

Dauphine. *See p145.*

Eat, Drink, Shop

Italian

Envy

Prinsengracht 381 (344 6407/www.envy.nl). Tram 13, 14, 17. **Open** 6pm-1am Mon, Tue; noon-4pm, 6pm-1am Wed, Thur, Sun; noon-4pm, 6pm-3am Fri, Sat. *Kitchen* till 11.30pm daily. **Set menu** 5 courses €50. **Credit** AmEx, MC, V. **Map** p326 C3 ㉘

A poshed-up designer deli-cum-restaurant serving an arsenal of delicacies from the streamlined refrigerators that line the walls, and from their able kitchen. The perfect place for those times when you want to try a bit of everything.

Southern Canal Belt

Chinese & Japanese

An

Weteringschans 76 (624 4672/www.japans restaurantan.nl). Tram 6, 7, 10. **Open** 6-10pm Tue-Sat. **Main courses** €19-€24. **No credit cards**. **Map** p331 E5 ㉙

An serves some of the city's best Japanese cuisine – sushi as well as starters and grilled dishes. Staff are friendly and the place is comfortable.

Japan Inn

Leidsekruisstraat 4 (620 4989). Tram 1, 2, 5, 6, 7, 10. **Open** 5.30-11.30pm daily. **Main courses** €10-€35. **Credit** AmEx, DC, MC, V. **Map** p330 D5 ㉚

Japan Inn offers quality and quantity. The fresh sushi and sashimi are served from the open kitchen and are hits with students (who dig the quantity) and Japanese tourists (who come for the quality). Either way, you'll be happy you found it.

Wagamama

Max Euweplein 10 (528 7778/www.wagamama.com). Tram 1, 2, 5, 6, 7, 10. **Open** noon-10pm Mon-Wed, Sun; noon-11pm Thur-Sat. **Main courses** €9-€15. **Credit** AmEx, MC, V. **Map** p330 D5 ㉛

Amsterdam's branch of the popular London franchise of quick 'n' cheap noodle bars. You may not fancy lingering in the minimalist canteen setting, but you certainly can't fault the speedy service or the tasty noodle dishes and soups.

Other locations Zuidplein 12 (620 3032).

Dutch & Belgian

Hap Hmm

1e Helmerstraat 33 (618 1884/www.hap-hmm.nl). Tram 1, 6, 7, 10. **Open** 4.30-8pm Mon-Fri. **Main courses** €6-€10. **No credit cards**. **Map** p330 C5 ㉜

Hungry but hard up? You need some of the Dutch grandma cooking served up in this canteen with a living-room feel. 'Yummy Bite', near Leidseplein, will happily pack your empty insides with meat and potatoes for not much more than €6. *Photo p137.*

Koffiehuis de Hoek

Prinsengracht 341 (625 3872). Tram 1, 6, 7, 10. **Open** 7.30am-4.30pm Tue-Fri; 9am-3pm Sat. **Main courses** from €2.50. **No credit cards**. **Map** p326 C3 ㉝

A traditional Dutch sandwich and lunch shop where all walks of life collide – from construction workers to the ad folks of KesselsKramer (*see p56*)

Fish

Le Pêcheur

Reguliersdwarsstraat 32 (624 3121/www.lepecheur.nl). Tram 1, 2, 5. **Open** *Lunch* noon-3pm Mon-Fri. *Dinner* 5.30-11pm Mon-Sat. **Main courses** €21.50-€40. **Credit** AmEx, MC, V. **Map** p330 D4 ㉞

Multilingual menus let you choose from à la carte or the menu of the day with minimal effort at this popular temple to all things oceanic and edible. The service is friendly but formal; the mussels and oysters are particularly excellent, as is the Golden Age patio.

French & Mediterranean

Gala

Reguliersdwarsstraat 38 (623 6303). Tram 16, 24, 25. **Open** 6-11pm Wed-Sun. *Kitchen* 6-10pm. **Main courses** €5-€18. **Credit** AmEx, MC, V. **Map** p330 D4 ㉟

New Catalan tapas hotspot that is in peaceful contrast to the hectic Mexican noise-fest Rose's Cantina, which it joins on to. Simple and pure.

Puri Mas

Indonesian ´Rijsttafels´
you will never forget!

La Rive

Amstel Hotel, Prof Tulpplein 1 (520 3264/www.restaurantlarive.com). Tram 6, 7, 10/Metro Weesperplein. **Open** *Lunch* noon-2pm Mon-Fri. *Dinner* 6.30-10.30pm Mon-Sat. Closed first two weeks in Aug. **Main courses** €22.50-€45. **Set menu** €95-€110. **Credit** AmEx, DC, MC, V. **Map** p331 F4 36

While Hôtel de l'Europe (*see p59*) has the Excelsior, it's actually La Rive at the Intercontinental Amstel Amsterdam (*see p67*) that overshadows the hotel competition, and it does so by serving chef Edwin Kats' superb regional French cuisine without the excessive formality that can too often mar such a place. For the perfect meal when money is no object.

Segugio

Utrechtsestraat 96A (330 1503/www.segugio.nl). Tram 4, 6, 7, 10. **Open** 6-11pm Mon-Sat. **Main courses** €23-€36. **Set menu** 5 courses €54.50. **Credit** AmEx, MC, V. **Map** p331 E4 37

Best. Risotto. Ever. In fact, this Italian has all the elements to make the perfect lingering meal for foodies and romantics alike. A wide variety of fresh ingredients and flavour combinations embellish and embolden this most luxurious of dishes. Bellissima!

Global

Beddington's

Utrechtsedwarsstraat 141 (620 7393/www.beddington.nl). Tram 4. **Open** 5.30-10.30pm Tue-Sat. **Set menu** 3 courses €42; 4 courses €48. **Credit** AmEx, MC, V. **Map** p331 E4 38

Proprietor and chef Jean Beddington is doing what she does best: cooking up creations in which one single dish can hint at French haute cuisine, Japanese macrobiotic and English country cooking all at the same time. The restaurant's peaceful interior allows you to concentrate on the delicate flavours.

Eat at Jo's

Marnixstraat 409 (638 3336). Tram 1, 2, 5, 6, 7, 10. **Open** noon-9pm Wed-Sun. **Main courses** €11-€13. **No credit cards**. **Map** p330 C5 39

Each day brings a different fish, meat and vegetarian dish to the menu of this cheap and tasty international kitchen. Star spotters take note: whichever act is booked to play at the Melkweg (*see p233* and *p243*) may very well chow down here beforehand, so keep eyes peeled and autograph books to hand.

Janvier Proeflokaal

Amstelveld 12 (626 1199/www.proeflokaaljanvier.nl). Tram 16, 24, 25. **Open** 4pm-midnight Tue-Thur, Sun; 4pm-1am Fri, Sat. *Kitchen* 4-10pm. **Main courses** €16.50-€27.50. **Set menu** 3 courses €39.50; 4 courses €44.50; 6 courses €57.50. **Credit** AmEx, DC, MC, V. **Map** p331 E4 40

A bit of a lost opp, truth be told. While its modern French 'with a twist' cuisine is reasonable, it remains more about the location than anything else: a wooden church – once the stable for Napoleon's horses – with easily one of the city's greatest terraces.

Indonesian & Thai

Bojo

Lange Leidsedwarsstraat 51 (622 7434/www.bojo.nl). Tram 1, 2, 5. **Open** 4pm-2am Mon-Thur; 4pm-4am Fri; noon-4am Sat; noon-2am Sun. **Main courses** €6-€13.50. **Credit** AmEx, MC, V. **Map** p330 C5 41

Bojo is a fine Indo-eaterie, and one of the few places that stays open into the small hours. The price is right and the portions are large enough to glue your insides together before or after an evening of excess. Its sister operation at No.49 compensates for its earlier closing time by serving alcohol.

Tempo Doeloe

Utrechtsestraat 75 (625 6718/www.tempodoeloerestaurant.nl). Tram 4, 6, 7, 10. **Open** 6-11.30pm daily. **Main courses** €19.50-€25. *Rice table* €26.50-€38. **Credit** AmEx, DC, MC, V. **Map** p331 E4 42

Tails of herring-do

You must, yes, you really must try raw herring. We simply don't want to hear any excuses. The best time is between May and July when the *nieuw* (new) catch hits the stands, as this doesn't need any extra garnish like onions and pickles, since their flesh is at its sweetest – thanks largely to the high fat content that the herring was planning to burn off in the arduous business of breeding. There's a quality fish stall or store around most corners, but here are some of the best purveyors of not only herring but also smoked eel and other – perhaps less controversial – fish for the sandwich. And they're as cheap as chips (or at least a hell of a lot cheaper than sushi). All told, this is one authentic Dutch eating experience you'd be mad to miss.

Altena

Stall at Stadhouderskade/Jan Luijkenstraat, Museum Quarter. Tram 2, 5, 6, 7, 10.

Huijsman

Zeedijk 129, Old Centre: New Side (624 2070). Tram 4, 9, 14, 24, 25/Metro Nieuwmarkt.

Kromhout

Stall at Singel/Raadhuisstraat, Old Centre: New Side. Tram 13, 14, 17.

Volendammer Viswinkel

1e Van der Helststraat 60, the Pijp (676 0394). Tram 6, 7, 10.

Hotel de Goudfazant.

This cosy and rather classy Indonesian restaurant (heck, it even has white linen) is widely thought of as one of the city's best and spiciest purveyors of rice table, and not without good reason. Book ahead or, if you turn up on the off-chance and find the place full, use neighbour Tujuh Maret (Utrechtsestraat 73, 427 9865, www.tujuh-maret.nl) as a tasty Plan B – or the Tibetan next door to that as Plan C.

South American

Los Pilones

Kerkstraat 63 (320 4651/www.lospilones.com). Tram 1, 2, 5, 11. **Open** 4pm-midnight Tue-Thur, Sun; 4pm-1am Fri, Sat. **Main courses** €11-€13. **Credit** AmEx, DC, MC, V. **Map** p330 D4 43

A splendid Mexican cantina with an anarchic bent, Los Pilones is run by two young and friendly Mexican brothers; one of them does the cooking, so expect authentic grub rather than standard Tex-Mex fare. There are 35 – yes, 35 – tequilas on offer, so don't be surprised if the evening ends in a blur.

Jodenbuurt, the Plantage & the Oost

Global

De Kas

Kamerlingh Onneslaan 3 (462 4562/www.restaurantdekas.nl). Tram 9/bus 59, 69. **Open** noon-2pm, 6.30-10pm Mon-Fri; 6.30-10pm Sat. **Set menu** *Lunch* 4 courses €35. *Dinner* 5 courses €47.50. **Credit** AmEx, DC, MC, V.

In Frankendael Park, way out east, is a renovated 1926 greenhouse. It's now a posh and peaceful restaurant that inspires much fevered talk among local foodies. Its international menu changes daily, based on whatever goodies they harvested that day.

Dauphine

Prins Bernardplein 175 (462 1646/www.caferestaurantdauphine.nl). Tram 9/bus 59, 69. **Open** 10am-midnight Mon-Thur, Sun; 10am-1am Fri, Sat. **Main courses** €9.75-€27.50. **Credit** AmEx, MC, V.

This newcomer is located in a former Renault showroom and oozes old-school modernism. Indulge in French bistro classics – from burgers to lobster – for breakfast, lunch or dinner. *Photos p140.*

The Waterfront

French & Mediterranean

Wilhelmina-Dok

Noordwal 1 (632 3701/www.wilhelmina-dok.nl). Ferry from Centraal Station to IJplein-Meeuwenlaan. **Open** 11am-midnight daily. *Kitchen* 6-10pm. **Main courses** *Lunch* €3.75-€13. *Dinner* €15.50-€19.50. **Credit** AmEx, MC, V. **Map** p326 D1 44

Through the large windows of this cubic building you get great views of the eastern docklands. Come for soup and sandwiches by day and a daily menu of Mediterranean dishes by night. DJs, terrace and an open-air cinema spice it up in summer.

Global

11

Oosterdokskade 3-5, 11th Floor (625 5999/www.ilove11.com). Walk from Centraal Station. **Open** 11am-midnight Mon-Wed, Sun; 11am-4am Thur-Sat. *Kitchen* 11am-10pm daily. **Main courses** *Lunch* €5-€12. *Dinner* 3 courses €29.50. **No credit cards. Map** p327 E1 45

This vertical wonder at the top of Post CS (*see p114*) is very un-Amsterdam. While acting as the Stedelijk café by day with soups, salads and sandwiches, its celeb chefs offer a fixed globe-hopping three-course dinner in the evening before the whole place evolves into a club by night (*see p245*). Book ahead and do it before 2009, when the whole place is closing down.

Blijburg

Bert Haanstrakade 2004, IJburg (160 0330/www.blijburg.nl). Tram 26/bus 326. **Open** *Summer* 10am-10pm daily. *Winter* 2-10pm Thur, Fri; noon-10pm Sat; 10am-10pm Sun. **Main courses** €8-€22. **No credit cards.**

Being 25 kilometres (15 miles) from the sea, Amsterdam was hardly anyone's choice for a beach holiday until sand was tipped on the artificial islands of IJburg, where 45,000 people will come to live. While construction continues, the vast expanse of sand and surrounding fresh-water lake are being exploited for their surreal beach-like properties. The restaurant/bar Blijburg – with barbecues, bands and DJs – is on hand to cater to eating and drinking whims. *See also p159* **United we sand.**

Fifteen

Jollemanhof 9 (0900 343 8336/www.fifteen.nl). Tram 16, 26. **Open** noon-1am daily. *Kitchen* noon-11pm. **Set menu** €46. **No credit cards. Map** p327 F1 46

While Jamie Oliver has only found one gap in his hectic TV and cooking schedule to visit the Amsterdam outpost of his culinary empire, this franchise of sorts – complete with TV show that documented the transformation of challenged street kids into a well-oiled kitchen brigade – is inspired by his love for dishes honest and fresh. The beautiful and massive waterfront location is marred by the bogus graffiti and the fact that there's only one set menu.

Hotel de Goudfazant

Aambeeldstraat 10H (636 5170/www.hoteldegoudfazant.nl). Ferry from Centraal Station. **Open** 6pm-1am Tue-Sun. **Main courses** €12.50-€15. **Set menu** €24.50. **Credit** MC, V.

Deep in the north and deeper within a warehouse, this is post-industrial dining at its best. Yes, it's about location, but there's also some excellent and affordable cookery from French to delicate pizza.

Kilimanjaro

Rapenburgerplein 6 (622 3485). Bus 22, 43. **Open** 5-10pm Tue-Sun. **Main courses** €10-€19.50. **Credit** AmEx, MC, DC, V. **Map** p327 F2 47
This relaxed and friendly pan-African eaterie offers an assortment of traditional recipes from Senegal across to the Ivory Coast, Tanzania and Ethiopia. Refreshment comes in the cooling form of the fruitiest of cocktails and the strongest of beers.

Odessa

Veemkade 259 (419 3010/www.de-odessa.nl). Tram 10, 26/bus 26. **Open** 4pm-1am Wed, Thur, Sun; 4pm-3am Fri, Sat. *Kitchen* 4-10.30pm daily. **Main courses** €17.50-€22.50. **Set menu** 3 courses €32. **Credit** AmEx, MC, V.
Hipsters make the trek to the unlikely environs of a Ukrainian fishing boat for the fusion food and the revamped interior. The vibe is 1970s James Bond filtered through a modern lounge sensibility. On warmer nights, dine on the funkily lit deck, while DJs spin from 10pm at weekends.

Pont 13

Stravangerweg 891 (770 2722/www.pont13.nl). Bus 22. **Open** 5-10pm Tue-Sat; 1-10pm Sun. **Main courses** €14.50-€19. **Credit** AmEx, MC, V.
This transformed old ferry in the Western havens – amidst a neighbourhood of students living in revamped shipping containers – is all-round intriguing, if a bit out of the way. *Photo p148.*

The Jordaan

Cafés & snack stops

Small World Catering

Binnen Oranjestraat 14 (420 2774/www.smallworld catering.nl). Bus 18, 22. **Open** 10.30am-8pm Tue-Sat; noon-8pm Sun. **Main courses** €6-€10. **No credit cards**. **Map** p325 B1 48
The home base for this catering company is a tiny deli, which feels like the kitchen of the lovely proprietor. Besides superlative coffee and fresh juices, enjoy salads, lasagnes and sublime sandwiches.

Foodware

Looiersgracht 12 (620 8898/www.foodware.nl). Tram 13, 14, 17. **Open** noon-9pm Mon-Fri; noon-7pm Sat. **Main courses** €4-€10.50. **No credit cards**. **Map** p330 C4 49
A takeaway – with a few chairs – with superlative soups, sandwiches, salads and meals. Ask for a fork and hit a canalside bench.

Dutch & Belgian

Amsterdam

Watertorenplein 6 (682 2666/www.cradam.nl). Tram 10. **Open** 10.30am-midnight Mon-Thur, Sun; 10.30am-1am Fri, Sat. *Kitchen* 10.30am-10.30pm Mon-Thur, Sun; 10.30am-11.30pm Fri, Sat. **Main courses** €10.50-€17.60. **Credit** AmEx, DC, MC, V.
This spacious monument to industry just west of the Jordaan pumped water from the coast's dunes for around a century. Now it pumps out honest Dutch and French dishes – from krokets to caviar – under a mammoth ceiling and floodlighting rescued from the old Ajax stadium. It's a truly unique – and child-friendly – experience.

Moeder's Pot

Vinkenstraat 119 (623 7643). Tram 3, 10. **Open** 5-9.30pm Mon-Sat. **Main courses** €4-€11. **No credit cards**. **Map** p325 B1 50
Mother's Pot serves up – you guessed it – the sort of simple and honest fare a Dutchman would expect to get from his mum. The decor is woody farmer's kitsch, and the grub's not bad at all.

French & Mediterranean

Balthazar's Keuken

Elandsgracht 108 (420 2114/www.balthazars keuken.nl). Tram 7, 10. **Open** 6-11pm Wed-Fri. **Set menu** €24.50. **Credit** AmEx, DC, MC, V. **Map** p330 C4 51
This tiny restaurant is always packed tight, so you really need to book ahead to make sure of enjoying its excellent set menu of meat or fish dishes.

Bordewijk

Noordermarkt 7 (624 3899/www.bordewijk.nl). Tram 3. **Open** 6.30-10.30pm Tue-Sun. **Main courses** €22-€29. **Set menu** €39-€54. **Credit** AmEx, DC, MC, V. **Map** p325 B2 52
Ideal for sampling some of the city's finest original food and palate-tingling wines in a decent designer interior. The service and atmosphere are both relaxed, and Bordewijk has a very reliable kitchen.

Duende

Lindengracht 62 (420 6692/www.cafeduende.nl). Tram 3, 10. **Open** 4pm-1am Mon-Thur, Sun; 4pm-3am Fri, Sat. *Kitchen* 4-11.30pm daily. **Tapas** €2.50-€15.50. **Credit** AmEx, MC, V. **Map** p325 B2 53
Get a taste of Andalusia with the fine tapas at Duende. Place your order at the bar and prepare to share your table with an amorous couple or a flamenco dancer who might offer you free lessons before getting up to stamp and strut. There are performances every Saturday night (11pm).

Toscanini

Lindengracht 75 (623 2813/www.toscanini.nu). Tram 3, 10. **Open** 6-10.30pm Mon-Sat. **Main courses** €15-€19. **Set menu** 6 courses €40. **Credit** AmEx, DC, MC, V. **Map** p325 B2 54
The authentic and invariably excellent Italian food at this bustling spot is prepared in an open kitchen. Don't go expecting pizza, but do make sure that you book early (from 3pm) if you want to get a table.

Yam-Yam

Frederik Hendrikstraat 90 (681 5097/www.yamyam.nl). Tram 3. **Open** 6-10.30pm Tue-Sun. **Main courses** €8.50-€18. **No credit cards**. **Map** p325 A3 55

Ferry fine dining at **Pont 13**. *See p147.*

Unparalleled and inexpensive pastas and pizzas (from wood oven!) in a hip and casual atmosphere: no wonder Yam-Yam is a favourite of clubbers and locals alike. Well worth the trip west of the Jordaan, but be sure to book in advance.

Global

De Aardige Pers

2e Hugo de Grootstraat 13 (400 3107). Tram 10. **Open** 1-11pm daily. **Main courses** €11-€18. **No credit cards**. **Map** p329 B4 56

'The Nice Persian' sums it up. Iranian cuisine served up family style and with family grace. Lovely lamb with *sabzi* greens, plus chicken in walnut and pomegranate sauce. A surprising experience for anyone not yet versed in this rich culinary culture.

Semhar

Marnixstraat 259-261 (638 1634/www.semhar.nl). Tram 10. **Open** 4-10pm daily. **Main courses** €11.50-€14.50. **Credit** MC, V. **Map** p325 B3 57

A great spot to sample the *injera* (a type of sourdough pancake) and veggie-friendly food of Ethiopia (best washed down with a calabash of beer) after an afternoon spent wandering the Jordaan.

Indian

Balraj

Haarlemmerdijk 28 (625 1428/www.balraj.nl). Tram 3. **Open** 4.30-11.30pm daily. **Main courses** €9.75-€17.50. **No credit cards**. **Map** p325 B1 58

A small, cosy eating house with several decades of experience. The food is reasonably priced and well done, with vegetarians generously catered for, but if you want it hot, you need to ask for it.

Vegetarian

De Vliegende Schotel

Nieuwe Leliestraat 162 (625 2041/www.vliegende schotel.com). Tram 13, 14, 17. **Open** 5-11.30pm daily. *Kitchen* 5.30-10.15pm. **Main courses** €7.80-€14.50. **Credit** AmEx, MC, V. **Map** p325 B3 59

The venerable 'Flying Saucer' serves up a splendid array of dishes, buffet style, for meat-avoiders with meaty appetites. If it's booked up, the nearby De Bolhoed (Prinsengracht 60-62, 626 1803) also offers hearty vegan dishes as a consolation prize.

The Museum Quarter, Vondelpark & the South

Cafés & snack stops

Bagels & Beans

Van Baerlestraat 40 (675 7050/www.bagelsbeans.nl). Tram 3, 5, 12. **Open** 8am-6pm Mon-Fri; 9.30am-6pm Sat, Sun. **Main courses** €3-€6.95. **Credit** AmEx, DC, MC, V. **Map** p330 D6 60

An Amsterdam success story, this branch of B&B has a wonderfully peaceful back patio. Perfect for an economical breakfast, lunch or snack; sun-dried tomatoes are employed with particular skill, elevating the humble sandwich to the status of something far more sublime and satisfying.

Other locations Ferdinand Bolstraat 70 (672 1610); Keizersgracht 504 (330 5508).

Fish

Vis aan de Schelde

Scheldeplein 4 (675 1583/www.visaandeschelde.nl). Tram 5, 25. **Open** *Lunch* noon-2.30pm Mon-Fri. *Dinner* 5.30-11pm daily. **Main courses** €25.50-€39.50. **Credit** AmEx, DC, MC, V.

This eaterie out near the RAI convention centre has become a fish temple for the connoisseur. French favourites collide with Thai fish fondue in a menu that travels the waters of the world.

French & Mediterranean

Eetcafé I Kriti

Balthasar Floriszstraat 3 (664 1445/www.ikriti.nl). Tram 3, 5, 12, 16. **Open** 4pm-1am daily. *Kitchen* 4-11pm daily. **Main courses** €12.50-€17.95. **Credit** DC, V. **Map** p331 E6 61

Eat and party Greek style in this evocation of Crete, where a standard choice of dishes is lovingly prepared. Bouzouki-picking legends drop in on occasion and pump up the frenzied atmosphere, further boosted by plate-lobbing antics. Nearby, De Greikse Taverna (Hobbemakade 64-65, 671 7923, www.de grieksetaverna.nl, 6pm-midnight daily) may lack plate-smashing atmosphere but competes on taste.

The dark past of Dutch dining

The British historian Simon Schama wrote of 17th-century Holland that it was 'not a dietary democracy, much less a culinary utopia'. It is safe to say that, four whole centuries later, the Netherlands is still more famous for its sex, drugs and rock 'n' roll than for its food. This is a sad state of affairs, as traditional Dutch food was once great. But a strange twist of history led to its virtual disappearance.

No one knows this better than Johannes van Dam. The Netherlands' pre-eminent restaurant critic and author of numerous books, including *Delicious Amsterdam* – an English-language guide to the best places to eat in the capital – Van Dam has been dishing out his strict but fair judgment of Dutch food for over 25 years.

'A common misconception that most visitors to Amsterdam have is that there are many restaurants that serve real Dutch food,' says Van Dam. 'It's a culinary fact that many Dutch dishes are now very much associated with America: coleslaw, doughnuts, cookies. It's also a fact that Dutch cuisine was as rich as French until the end of the 19th century.'

It was around this same time that the first *huishoudscholen* appeared. Set up with the noble intention of teaching the local poor to make easy, affordable meals, these food schools unintentionally ended up stripping Dutch cuisine of its richness and making the simplified versions of the dishes standard fare among the populace.

Van Dam says a Dutch home is still best for trying Dutch food. However, if you are unable to secure a dinner invitation, he suggests trying **Brasserie De Roode Leeuw** (*see p139*) and **Moeder's Pot** (*see p147*). Also, the relatively new **Greetje** (Peperstraat 23, 779 7450, www.restaurantgreetje.nl) is doing a great job of reintroducing old favourites such as eel soup, black pudding, sugar bread and liquorice ice-cream to 21st century diners across the capital.

The Netherlands' location and climate have also resulted in some tasty additions to Dutch cuisine. Shrimps from the North Sea have found their way into the ubiquitous *bitterbal* (a smaller version of the croquette, a ragout covered in breadcrumbs and deep fried, which can be filled with almost anything), while herring is a popular snack (*see p143* **Tails of herring-do**). A healthy fish in its own right due to its oils, the famous herring is also reportedly good for curing hangovers.

However, Van Dam says there is a little-known 'rule' when it comes to eating it. 'Chopped onion is seen as a gourmet condiment, and if you don't watch out you will undoubtedly be served it with your fish. It is unnecessary and even harmful. Good herring is in fact ruined by onion.' The famous fish can be found at numerous stalls across the city (*pictured*).

And yet, the food most associated with the Netherlands is cheese. The low-lying land and wet weather make it much easier to raise cows than grow corn. The Dutch consume their dairy products with gusto – one of the reasons given for why they are so tall. The most famous cheese is Gouda, but 'avoid factory-made versions,' cautions Van Dam. 'Look instead for more palatable *boeren* or farmers' Gouda.' This can be found at the numerous markets around Amsterdam and in speciality cheese shops. For something really different, try some of the lesser-known cheeses that are flavoured with cloves or cumin seeds.

While Dutch cuisine may never have fully recovered from the misguided intentions of the *huishoudscholen*, Amsterdam is doing its level best to prove what Van Dam has always believed – that it is indeed 'delicious'.

Holy kitsch! North African cooking in **Bazar**'s vividly refurbished church. *See p152.*

Le Garage

Ruysdaelstraat 54-56 (679 7176/www.restaurantlegarage.nl). Tram 3, 5, 6, 12, 16. **Open** *Lunch* noon-2pm Mon-Fri. *Dinner* 6-11pm daily. **Set menu** *Lunch* €29.50. *Dinner* 2 courses €39.50; 3 courses €49.50. **Credit** AmEx, DC, MC, V. **Map** p330 D6 62

Don your glad rags to blend in at this fashionable brasserie, which is great for emptying your wallet while watching a selection of Dutch glitterati do exactly the same. The authentic French regional cuisine – and 'worldly' versions thereof – is pretty good. They also have a more loungey sister establishment, En Pluche (Ruysdaelstraat 48, 471 4695), next door.

Global

De Peperwortel

Overtoom 140 (685 1053/www.peperwortel.nl). Tram 1, 6, 7, 10. **Open** 4-9pm daily. **Main courses** €8.50-€15.50. **No credit cards. Map** 330 C5 63

One could survive for weeks eating nothing but takeaways from Riaz (*see below*) and the fabulous 'Pepper Root'. After all, indulging in a wide range of dishes that embraces Dutch, Mexican, Indian and Spanish cuisines is always a pleasure, never a chore.

Vakzuid

Olympisch Stadion 35 (570 8400/www.vakzuid.nl). Tram 16, 24/bus 15, 23. **Open** 10am-1am Mon-Thur; 10am-3am Fri; 4pm-3am Sat; 3-10pm Sun. *Kitchen* noon-3pm, 6-10.30pm Mon-Fri. **Main courses** *Lunch* €15-€24. *Dinner* €16-€24. **Credit** AmEx, DC, MC, V.

Head chef Andy Tan mixes French and Asian flavours at Vakzuid, with its view over the Olympic Stadium and modish cons, making it popular with working trendies. Thursday to Saturday nights it transforms into a club, with Sundays child-friendly.

Indonesian & Thai

Djago

Scheldeplein 18 (664 2013). Tram 4. **Open** 5-9.30pm Mon-Fri, Sun. **Main courses** €11-€23. **Credit** AmEx, DC, MC, V.

Djago's West Javanese eats are praised to the hilt by Indo-obsessives. Set near the RAI convention centre, it's a bit out of the way, but worth the trip south.

Middle Eastern

Paloma Blanca

JP Heyestraat 145 (612 6485/www.palomablanca.nl). Tram 7. **Open** 6-11.30pm daily. **Main courses** €13-€19. **No credit cards. Map** p329 B6 64

This is the place for consumers of couscous. The surroundings are simple and there's no alcohol.

South American

Riaz

Bilderdijkstraat 193 (683 6453/www.riaz.nl). Tram 3, 7, 12, 17. **Open** 11.30am-9pm Mon-Fri; 2-9pm Sun. **Main courses** €5-€14. **No credit cards. Map** p329 B5 65

Amsterdam's finest Surinamese restaurant is where Ruud Gullit scores his rotis when he's in town.

Vegetarian

De Peper

Overtoom 301 (779 4913/www.depeper.org). Tram 1, 6. **Open** 6pm-1am Tue, Thur-Sat. *Kitchen* 6pm-9pm. **Set menu** 2 courses €6; 3 courses €7.50. **No credit cards. Map** p329 B6 66

The purveyor of the cheapest and best vegan food in town is located in the 'breeding ground' OT301 (*see p213*). De Peper is a collectively organised, non-profit project combining culture with kitchen and there's usually a DJ to aid digestion. But do reserve: call 412 2954 after 4pm on the day of your visit.

The Pijp

Cafés & snack stops

De Taart van m'n Tante

Ferdinand Bolstraat 10 (776 4600/www.detaart.nl). Tram 16, 24, 25. **Open** 10am-6pm daily. **Light meals** €2.75-€5. **No credit cards. Map** p331 E5 ⓱67

'My Aunt's Cake' started life as a purveyor of over-the-top cakes (which they still make) before becoming the campest tea-room in town. In a glowing pink space filled with mismatched furniture, it's particularly gay-friendly (note the Tom of Finland cake). A genuine local gem with bags full of character.

Chinese & Japanese

Albine

Albert Cuypstraat 69 (675 5135). Tram 16, 24, 25. **Open** 10.30am-10pm Tue-Sun. **Main courses** €4.80-€14.50. **No credit cards. Map** p331 E6 68

One in a whole row of cheap Suri-Chin-Indo spots, Albine – where a Chinese influence predominates – gets top marks for its lightning service and solid vegetarian or meat meals of roti, rice or noodles.

Yamazato

Okura Hotel, Ferdinand Bolstraat 333 (678 8351/www.okura.nl). Tram 12, 25. **Open** 7.30-9.30am, noon-2pm, 6-9.30pm daily. **Main courses** €25-€48. **Set menu** €55-€70. **Credit** AmEx, DC, MC, V.

If you want class, head out here and surrender to the charming kimono-clad staff, the too-neat-to-eat presentation and the restful views over a fishpond.

French & Mediterranean

District V

Van der Helstplein 17 (770 0884/www.district5.nl). Tram 12, 25. **Open** 6pm-1am daily. *Kitchen* 6-10.30pm. **Set menu** 3 courses €29.50. **Credit** AmEx, MC, V. **Map** p331 F6 69

District V not only offers a good and economical French-inspired daily menu, but sells the locally designed plates, cutlery and tables it is served on. The patio is a lovely spot to sit in summer.

Renato's Trattoria

Van der Helstplein 31 (673 2300). Tram 12, 25. **Open** 5.30-11pm daily. **No credit cards. Map** p331 F6 70

It's like stepping into Italy with hospitality and kitchen action to match. Pizza – heavily loaded but with crispy crust – is their speciality, great for sharing between friends or on a romantic date.

Global

Aleksandar

Ceintuurbaan 196 (676 6384). Tram 3. **Open** 5-10pm Tue-Sun. **Main courses** €16-€31. **Credit** MC, V. **Map** p331 E6 71

Balkan food comes in huge heaps, as does the hospitality. Surrender to the grilled selections and the slivovic, a plummy and poetic hard liquor that will have you hymning the frogs' legs and snails.

Bazar

Albert Cuypstraat 182 (675 0544/www.bazaramsterdam.nl). Tram 16, 24, 25. **Open** 9am-1am Mon-Thur; 9am-2am Fri, Sat; 9am-midnight Sun. **Main courses** *Breakfast/lunch* €4-€10. *Dinner* €8-€15. **Credit** AmEx, DC, MC, V. **Map** p331 E6/F6 72

This former church, now an Arabic-kitsch café, is one of the glories of Albert Cuypmarkt. Sticking to the winning formula set by its Rotterdam mothership, its menu lingers in North Africa. *Photos p151.*

Burger Meester

Albert Cuypstraat 48 (670 9339/www.burgermeester.eu). Tram 16, 24, 25. **Open** noon-11pm daily. **Main courses** €5.50-€8.50. **No credit cards. Map** p331 E6 73

This new designer burger specialist can compete with the Getto (*see p228*). Fancy a beef, lamb, tuna or falafel burger? With toppings like wild mushrooms, wasabi, grilled peppers or pancetta? Look no further than the Burger Meester.

Mamouche

Quellijnstraat 104 (673 6361/www.restaurantmamouche.nl). Tram 3, 12, 24, 25. **Open** 6-11pm daily. **Main courses** €14.50-€21.50. **Credit** AmEx, DC, MC, V. **Map** p331 E5 74

In the heart of the multicultural Pijp is a new Moroccan restaurant with a difference: it's posh, stylish (in a sexy, minimalist sort of way) and provides groovy background music that can only be described as 'North African lounge'.

Indonesian & Thai

Siriphon

1e Jacob van Campenstraat 47 (676 8072). Tram 6, 7, 10. **Open** 3-10.30pm daily. **Main courses** €10.50-€14. **Credit** MC, V. **Map** p331 E5 75

A small comfy Thai with a green kaeng khiaw curry that's positively to die for, and many other dishes that are worthy of at least a culinary coma.

Warung Spang-Makandra

Gerard Doustraat 39 (670 5081/www.spangmakandra.nl). Tram 6, 7, 10, 16. **Open** 11am-10pm Tue-Sat; 1-10pm Sun. **Main courses** €4.50-€10. **No credit cards. Map** p331 E6 76

An Indonesian-Surinamese restaurant where the Indo influence always comes up trumps with their addictive Javanese rames. A relaxed vibe and beautiful dishes encourage lingering over meals.

Bars

Blowing the froth off one of Europe's most quaffable drinking cultures.

Café Brandon, an intimate time capsule of Amsterdam drinking days gone by. *See p157.*

With a few exceptions, it's nigh on impossible to find yourself drinking in a duff boozer in this city. Bars come in all shapes and sizes, from grand cafés to hole-in-the-wall *proeverijen* or 'tasting houses'. They are, it is fair to say, ubiquitous. Note, however, that coffeeshops can no longer sell alcohol.

The café bar is central to Dutch life. It's home from home, off-site office, canteen, debating society and sometimes even nightclub all rolled into one. It's possible to breakfast, lunch, eat supper and have a post-prandial piss-up into the wee hours – with attendant greasy snacks – without budging so much as an inch. Every now and then an old-fashioned bar closes to be replaced by something more á la mode, but the *bruin café* (read: no-frills, nicotine-stained boozer) is – hurrah! – here to stay.

WHAT TO ORDER

Beer is served in two sizes: small (a *vaasje*) and miniscule (a *fluitje*, regarded as a lady's beer and no more than a couple of gulps). Some places keep a few pint pots, but generally only if they are Irish-themed or in touristy areas. Local brews Heineken or Amstel (owned by the same company) are standard in most places, though you'll sometimes find Palm, Brand and

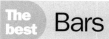

> ❶ Pink numbers in this chapter correspond to the locations of individual bars as marked on the street maps. *See pp325-332.*

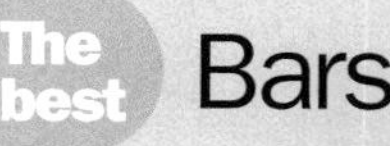

The best Bars

't Arendsnest
Drink your way around the Netherlands from the comfort of your bar stool. *See p157.*

De Jaren
A grand café in modern clothes. *See p157.*

Onder de Ooievaar
Sweet, simple pleasures: strong beer, great views and a pool table. *See p160.*

't Smalle
A stunning waterside terrace on a jaw-droppingly beautiful canal. *See p162.*

Wijnbar Boelen & Boelen
A genuine adventure playground for more serious wine buffs. *See p163.*

Something brewing

If you'd mentioned in-house beer breweries to a citizen of 17th-century Amsterdam, he or she would have guffawed in your face. Back then chunks of the city itself were dedicated to the suds. Brouwersgracht isn't called the 'Brewer's Canal' for nothing: in the 17th and 18th centuries the whole area was perfumed by mulching hops and bubbling booze.

Zoom to 1864, and a big name is building a brewhouse on Nieuwezijds Voorburgwal (now Die Poort van Cleve). Six years later, Gerard Heineken moved his successful enterprise to Stadhouderskade. Rumour had it that a secret pipe ran from there to Koekenbier, a café round the corner – perhaps that's why production shifted to Zoetewoude and Den Bosch, reducing the number of Amsterdam breweries to just a handful. The good news is that those remaining create ales of truly exceptional quality – and, sometimes, also strength. A good place to start sampling is the **Bekeerde Suster** (*see p155*), situated in a place with a long history of beer-making. The 'Reformed Sister' of the name is one of the original nuns of the Maria Magdalena van Bethaniën convent, which stood here in the Middle Ages; still, the veiled ladies wouldn't be shocked by contemporary intemperance, since they brewed beer themselves. The inside of this brewpub by the Amsterdamse Stoombierbrouwerij (Amsterdam Steam Beer Brewery) is lined with shining copper vats and sparkling tubes, part of a system that can create up to a thousand litres of beer at a time under the guidance of master-brewer Harry Vermeer. The truly keen can go for a guided tour to see what all the knobs and levers do (minimum ten people, reserve on 423 0112), while dilettantes sit back among the beer-related ephemera and sample the house tipples. Witte Ros ('White Rose') goes down a treat with a slice of lemon on hot days, the self-explanatory Blonde Ros gives Leffe a run for its money and seasonal specialities include summer and October Bock Ros.

Best known is **Brouwerij 't IJ** (*see p160; pictured*). Tours run for both individuals and small groups every Friday afternoon at 4pm, a chance to learn how the 12 different specialities are made in their enormous capacity microbrewery. Back in the tasting room, try the hoppy Plzen, the rich double-style Natte or tripel Zatte. Treat the fruity Struis with respect: it's 9% ABV.

The latest addition to the beer scene is brewery-with-a-conscience **De Prael** (408 4470, www.deprael.nl), whose dedicated workforce is made up entirely of people with mental disabilities. The beers themselves, in boldly designed bottles, are named after local singers: Mary, a tripel, kicks like a mule at 9.6%; lighter is Kölsch-style blond Johnny and May bock André. Tipples can also be tried in specially arranged tours and tastings, and you can even spend a day making your own beer. Other places in town to pick up De Prael are **'t Arendsnest** (*see p157*) and the excellent off-licence **De Bierkoning** (*see p187*).

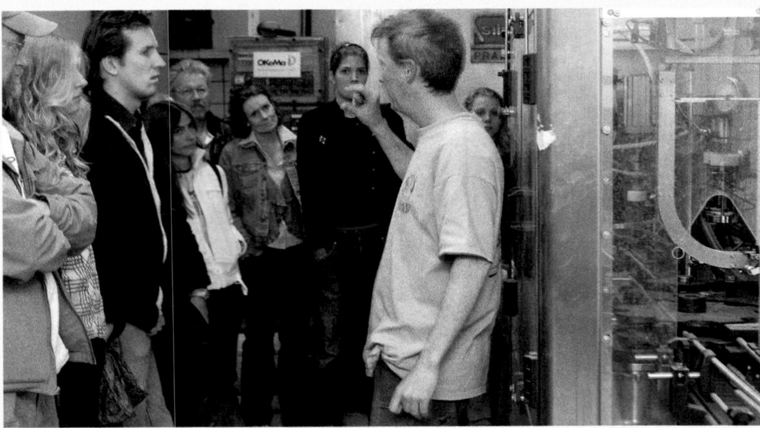

(Belgian) Jupiler. Many bars have an excellent range of Belgian beers, mainly bottled, but sometimes on draught: Affligem and La Chouffe are very popular at the moment. These pack such a punch that the logic behind those measly measures makes sense. In spring and autumn there are *bokbiers*, which have a kick like a stag.

Jenever is the spirit of choice: *jong* is like a lighter, more refreshing gin, and *oud* is darker and fuller favoured. It also comes in fruity forms such as lemon and blackberry. If wine's your tipple, you'll usually just get unspecified red or white in a Duralex beaker, though some places are cottoning on and offering more specialised choices. In summer, rosé is ubiquitous on canalside terraces.

Bar snacks range from the usual nachos and nuts to a wide selection of really rather delicious deep-fried nibbles based around meat, potato and grease (*bitterballen*); meat, spice and grease (*vlammetjes*); or more vegetarian-friendly cheese and grease (*kaasstangels*). Proost!

The Old Centre

The Old Side

De Bekeerde Suster

Kloveniersburgwal 6-8 (423 0112/www.beiaard groep.nl). Tram 4, 9, 14, 16, 24, 25. **Open** 4pm-1am Mon; noon-1am Tue-Thur; 11am-2am Fri, Sat; noon-midnight Sun. **Credit** AmEx, DC, MC, V. **Map** p326 D2 ❶

The Amsterdam Steambrewery Company has been making beer onsite for five years (though the building's history stretches back to the Middle Ages, when it was a house for fallen women). Part of a national chain, other branches include De Beiaard at Spui 30 (622 5110) and Marie Heinekenplein 5 (379 0888). *See also p154* **Something brewing**.

Bubbles & Wines

Nes 37 (422 3318/www.bubblesandwines.com). Tram 4, 9, 14, 16, 24, 25. **Open** 3.30pm-1am Mon-Sat. **Credit** AmEx, MC, V. **Map** p326 D3 ❷

This long, low-ceilinged room has the feel of a wine cellar, albeit one with mood lighting and banquettes. There are more than 50 wines available by the glass and 180 by the bottle, and accompanying posh nosh (Asetra caviar, truffle cheese, foie gras). Wine flights are served, assembling the products of particular regions in several samples.

De Diepte

St Pieterspoortsteeg 3-5 (no phone). Tram 4, 9, 14, 16, 24, 25. **Open** 10pm-3am Mon-Thur, Sun; 10pm-4am Fri, Sat. **No credit cards. Map** p326 D3 ❸

Whatever time it is, it always feels like the middle of the night down in 'The Depths'. This den of hard-drinking, cheap rock 'n' roll punkiness is a favourite of many bands. One of the few bars in town with a late license (which it regularly loses for staying open after hours), at time of press it was up and running.

De Doelen

Kloveniersburgwal 125 (624 9023). Tram 9, 14/Metro Waterlooplein. **Open** 9am-1am daily. **No credit cards. Map** p327 E3 ❹

An old-fashioned drinking hole – complete with gritted floors – on one of the main tourist drags. Rough edges are smoothed out by sophisticated breakfasts (fruitshakes, muesli), international snacks (houmous, tapenade) and jugs of sangria in summer.

De Jaren

Nieuwe Doelenstraat 20-22 (625 5771/www.cafe-de-jaren.nl). Tram 4, 9, 14, 16, 24, 25. **Open** 10am-1am Mon-Thur, Sun; 10am-2am Fri, Sat. **Credit** V. **Map** p326 D3 ❺

All of Amsterdam – students, tourists, lesbigays, cinema-goers, the fashion pack – come here for lunch, coffee or something stronger all day long, making it sometimes difficult to bag a seat. Upstairs becomes a restaurant after 5.30pm. Be prepared to fight for a spot on the Amstel-side terrace in summer, with its sweeping views beloved of tourists.

Kapitein Zeppos

Gebed Zonder End 5 (624 2057/www.zeppos.nl). Tram 4, 9, 14, 16, 24, 25. **Open** 11am-1am Mon-Thur, Sun; 11am-3am Fri, Sat. **Credit** AmEx, MC, V. **Map** p326 D3 ❻

A hidey-hole down a poetically named alleyway: 'Prayer Without End', from the Santa Clara convent that stood here in the 17th century. Now it's a light-drenched, multi-roomed café-cum-restaurant with an undertstated Belgian theme: it's named after a '60s Flemish TV detective, there's Belgian beer and the soundtrack of choice is chanson.

Katoen

Oude Turfmarkt 153 (626 2635/www.goodfood group.nl). Tram 4, 9, 14, 16, 24, 25. **Open** 10am-1am Mon-Thur, Sun; 11am-3am Fri, Sat. **No credit cards. Map** p326 D3 ❼

If shopping on Kalverstraat gets too much, run screaming across Rokin to this oasis of calm on the edge of the Old Centre. It has the stripped-down looks of the 1950s (formica tables, polished wood) and a decent lunch menu of salads, rolls and wraps.

Van Kerkwijk

Nes 41 (620 3316). Tram 4, 9, 14, 16, 24, 25. **Open** 11am-1am Mon-Thur, Sun; 11am-3am Fri, Sat. **No credit cards. Map** p326 D3 ❽

Far from the bustle of Dam Square, though really just a few strides away, on one of Amsterdam's most charming streets. Airy by day, romantic and candle-lit by night, it's equally good for group chats or tête-a-têtes. Lunch brings sandwiches and the evening more substantial food, though the emphasis is as much on genteel drinking. (Beware the near-vertical stairs leading down to the bar toilets, which have claimed more than their share of drunk tourists.)

XTRACOLD
AMSTERDAM
SMIRNOFF

Tara

Rokin 85-89 (421 2654/www.thetara.com). Tram 4, 9, 14, 24, 25. **Open** 10am-1am Mon-Thur, Sun; 10am-3am Fri, Sat. **Credit** AmEx, MC, V. **Map** p326 D3 ⑨
Never overdoing the Irish theme, this multi-roomed bar has many faces: the Nes side is loungey; the Rokin side is full of rowdy, football-watching Brits; and the middle is a snug conversation pit with sofas, an open fire and even a pulpit. There's the black stuff, Caffrey's, Murphy's and cider. Food is good and – hallelujah! – snacks include Walkers crisps.

Wynand Fockink

Pijlsteeg 31 (639 2695/www.wynand-fockink.nl). Tram 4, 9, 14, 16, 24, 25. **Open** 3-9pm daily. **No credit cards**. **Map** p326 D3 ⑩
It's standing room only at this historic tasting-house. Hidden behind the Krasnapolsky, unchanged since 1679, this has been a meeting place for Freemasons since the beginning; past visitors include Churchill and Chagall. The menu of liqueurs and jenevers (many available in take-out bottles) reads like a list of unwritten novels: Parrot Soup; The Longer the Better; Rose Without Thorns.

The New Side

Belgique

Gravenstraat 2 (625 1974). Tram 1, 2, 5, 16, 24, 25. **Open** noon-1am Mon-Thur; noon-3am Fri, Sat; 2pm-1am Sun. **No credit cards**. **Map** p329 C2/3 ⑪
A goblin's cave hiding behind the palace, there's barely room for 20 customers in here, but the atmosphere – enhanced by dripping candles – is intimate rather than cramped and always cheerful.

Café Luxembourg

Spui 24 (620 6264/www.luxembourg.nl). Tram 1, 2, 5, 16, 24. **Open** 9am-1am Mon-Thur, Sun; 9am-2am Fri, Sat. **Credit** AmEx, DC, MC, V. **Map** p330 D4 ⑫
A slice of Paris on the Spui, waiters in long white aprons glide among tables, serving a huge range of drinks, (reasonably good) Dutch brasserie food and cigars (from PGC Hajenuis, *see p193*). Customers range from business diners taking advantage of the Wi-Fi to football managers and tourists.

Café de Dokter

Rozenboomsteeg 4 (626 4427/www.cafe-de-dokter.nl). Tram 1, 2, 4, 5, 9, 13, 14, 16, 17, 24, 25. **Open** 4pm-1am Tue-Sat. **No credit cards**. **Map** p326 D3 ⑬
Definitely the smallest bar in Amsterdam at just a handful of square metres, the Doctor is also one of the oldest, dishing out the cure for whatever ails you since 1798. Centuries of character and all kinds of gewgaws are packed into the highly compact space. Whisky figures large (there's a monthly special) and snacks include smoked *osseworst* with gherkins.

Franken & Kok

Torensteeg 2 (427 4079). Tram 2, 5, 13, 14, 17. **Open** 11am-1am Mon-Thur; 11am-3am Fri, Sat; noon-1am Sun. **No credit cards**. **Map** p326 C3 ⑭
Small, stylish and handy for relaxing after retail therapy in Magna Plaza, a night of chat, or sinking a few before hitting the local nightclubs.

Getaway

Nieuwezijds Voorburgwal 250 (627 1427). Tram 1, 2, 5, 13, 14, 17. **Open** 5pm-1am Mon-Thur, Sun; 5pm-3am Fri, Sat. **No credit cards**. **Map** p326 C3 ⑮
No longer the nightlife supremo it once was, the Getaway is still a reliable destination for a drink and maybe a dance among relatively young, hip and arty locals. Diep (Nieuwezijds Voorburgwal 256, 420 2020) and Bep (Nieuwezijds Voorburgwal 260, 626 5649), both a boogie away, complete the troika of chandeliered, disc-jockeyed design bars.

Harry's Bar

Spuistraat 285 (624 4384). Tram 1, 2, 5, 13, 14, 17. **Open** 5pm-1am Mon-Thur, Sun; 3pm-3am Fri, Sat. **Credit** MC, V. **Map** p326 D3 ⑯
Small, dark and intimate, this is the perfect place to lounge on a leather sofa for a long night of cheerful mixology. There is everything here to suit all kinds of movers and shakers, from Cristal champagne to monumental Montecristo cigars.

Vaaghuyzen

Nieuwe Nieuwstraat 17 (420 1751/www.vaaghuyzen.net). Tram 1, 2, 5, 13, 14, 17. **Open** 5pm-1am Mon-Thur, Sun; 5pm-3am Fri, Sat. **No credit cards**. **Map** p326 C2 ⑰
This dinky DJ bar is a great place to pick up flyers and find out what's happening. There are also plenty of reasons to stay, like top-notch turntablists and interactive evenings like Singles Night, where punters bring and play their own tunes.

The Canals

Western Canal Belt

't Arendsnest

Herengracht 90 (421 2057/www.arendsnest.nl). Tram 1, 2, 5, 13, 14. **Open** 4pm-midnight Mon-Thur, Sun; 4pm-2am Fri, Sat. **Credit** MC, V. **Map** p326 C2 ⑱
A temple to the humble hop, the 'Eagle's Nest', in a lovely canal house, sells only Dutch beer. Many of the customers are real-ale types, but even amateurs will enjoy the 350 standard brews and 250 seasonal, from cheeky house ale Herengracht 90 to Texelse Skuumkoppe. *See also p154* **Something brewing**.

Café Brandon

Keizersgracht 157 (626 4191). Tram 1, 2, 5, 13, 14, 17. **Open** 11am-1am Mon-Thur, Sun; 11am-3am Fri, Sat. **No credit cards**. **Map** p326 C2 ⑲
When the previous owners hung up their pinnies in the '80s after 40 years behind the bar, they sealed up their café, retired upstairs and eventually passed away. Twenty years later, the new owners reopened this ghost bar just as they found it; furniture, photos, billiard room and all. The old-fashioned atmosphere is enhanced by background jazz. *Photo p153.*

Kobalt

Singel 2 (320 1559/www.cafekobalt.nl). Tram 1, 2, 5, 9, 13, 17, 24, 25. **Open** 8am-1am Mon-Thur, Sun; 8am-3am Fri, Sat. **No credit cards. Map** p326 C2 ⑳

This rather sophisticated bar near Centraal Station is a great way of beating train delay blues. There's free Wi-Fi, round-the-clock food from breakfast to tapas to dinner, and any drink you like from ristretto to bottles of champagne. DJs spin Friday nights, while Sunday afternoons are for slinky live jazz.

De Pels

Huidenstraat 25 (622 9037). Tram 1, 2, 5. **Open** 10am-1am Mon-Thur, Sun; 10am-3am Fri, Sat. **No credit cards. Map** p330 C4 ㉑

The Nine Streets are littered with characterful bars, and this one is a lovely, old-style, tobacco-stained example with an intellectual bent. Once a Provo hangout, now writers, journalists and political groups regularly meet to chew the fat, and it's a nice spot even if you aren't feeling cerebral. On Sunday mornings, it's one of the few places to get breakfast, which makes it popular with the hangover crowd.

Twee Zwaantjes

Prinsengracht 114 (625 2729/www.detweezwaantjes.nl). Tram 1, 2, 5, 13, 14, 17. **Open** 11am-11pm Mon, Thur, Sun; 7pm-11pm Tue; 11am-3am Fri, Sat. **No credit cards. Map** p326 C2 ㉒

Oom-pah-pah, oom-pah-pah: that's how it goes at this salt-of-the-earth bar. It's relatively quiet during the week, but weekends are real swinging singalong affairs, with revellers booming out tear-jerkers about love, sweat and the Westerkerk. All together now: '*Op de Amster-dam-se grachten…*'

Southern Canal Belt

Café Kale

Weteringschans 267 (622 6363/www.cafekale.nl). Tram 6, 7, 10, 16, 25. **Open** 10am-1am Mon-Thur; 10am-2am Fri; 11am-2am Sat; 11am-1am Sun. **Credit** AmEx, DC, MC, V. **Map** p331 E5 ㉓

If you're burnt out by the Museum District, you can do far worse than recover at this smart locals' café set back from the main road. Although it calls itself a 'real brown bar', styling is sleek, colourful and modern. Food is far from old fashioned, with griddled veg and chorizo putting in regular appearances. If you don't make a night of it here, Rembrandt- and Leidseplein are both within walking distance.

Het Land van Walem

Keizersgracht 449 (625 3544/www.cafewalem.nl). Tram 1, 2, 5. **Open** 10am-1am Mon-Thur, Sun; 10am-2am Fri, Sat. **Credit** AmEx, DC, MC, V. **Map** p330 D4 ㉔

One of the city's first designer bars still cuts it after nearly 25 years, from the Rietveld-designed exterior to the great international menu. The clean lines and flavours attract fashionistas and designer types – plus a good chunk of gays and lesbians – who scope each other on the patio and admire the views.

Twstd

Weteringschans 157 (320 7030/www.twstd.nl). Tram 6, 7, 10, 16, 24, 25. **Open** 6pm-1am Mon-Thur, Sun; 6pm-3am Fri, Sat. **No credit cards. Map** p331 E5 ㉕

A mecca for serious clubbers, there is someone behind the decks here seven days a week. One day it could be the next big thing, another the flavour of the month. Dave Clark, Marshall Jefferson and Ken Ishii have all spun here, if proof were needed.

Vyne

Prinsengracht 411 (344 6408/www.vyne.nl). Tram 1, 2, 5, 7, 10, 13, 14, 17. **Open** 5pm-1am Mon-Thur, Sat; 4pm-1am Fri; 3pm-midnight Sun. **Credit** AmEx, DC, MC, V. **Map** p330 C4 ㉖

A tasteful – in every sense of the word – addition to the city's drinking scene. The gorgeous, slimline interior is dominated by an amazing wall of wine, and emphasis is put on pairing drink with nibbles; for example, Weissburgunder with fine sausage, or smoked eel and Sancerre. It's a streamlined version of sister-restaurant Envy (*see p141*).

Around Leidseplein

Café Eijlders

Korte Leidsedwarsstraat 47 (624 2704/www.eijlders.nl). Tram 1, 2, 5, 6, 7. **Open** noon-1am Mon-Thur, Sun; noon-2am Fri, Sat. **No credit cards. Map** p330 C5 ㉗

Neon tat to one side, trendy Wendys to the other; Eijlders is a cerebral alternative to both. A meeting place for the resistance during the war, it now has a boho feel, with exhibitions, poetry nights and live music – sometimes jazz, sometimes classical. Décor is handsome, with stained glass and dark wood.

Kamer 401

Marnixstraat 401 (620 0614/www.kamer401.nl). Tram 1, 2, 5, 6, 7. **Open** 6pm-1am Wed, Thur; 6pm-3am Fri, Sat. **No credit cards. Map** p330 C5 ㉘

Art students and the terminally hip gather at this red-lacquered temple to pleasure, where there is no food or frippery, just booze and DJ-spun music with a party mood. Nearby Lux (Marnixstraat 403, 422 1412) and Weber (Marnixstraat 397, 622 9910) offer a similar formula and ensure that the party people wear a wavering track between the three.

Around Rembrandtplein

Café de Nachtwacht

Thorbeckeplein 2 (622 4794/www.de-nachtwacht.nl). Tram 4, 9, 14. **Open** 4pm-noon Mon-Thur, Sun; 4pm-2am Fri, Sat. **Credit** AmEx, MC, V. **Map** p331 E4 ㉙

Totally touristy and thus thoroughly uncool, this deserves a mention for its utterly unreconstructed 1970s interior. Forget ironic retro reinventions. This is what the decade that taste forgot *really* looked like: heavy wood, studded leather, coloured glass and nets – even the food is authentically served on wood platters. That said, it's a decent enough spot for a drink right in the thick of it, and service is good.

United we sand

In this city of water, with sounds of gently lapping eddies and cawing gulls constantly in the air, a need for the seaside comes often. But sometimes you have neither the time nor inclination to head to the coast, which is when the urban beach bars, with which Amsterdam is richly served, save the day.

There is more sand here than in any other capital city – or any other city that's not on the coast, at least – and canny entrepreneurs have capitalised on the urbanite need for a quick bucket-and-spade fix with gusto.

The true trailblazer was **Blijburg aan Zee** (Bert Haanstrakade 2004, 416 0330, www.blijburg.nl; *pictured*), which opened a bar and restaurant on an artificial beach in the middle of the IJburg construction site in summer 2003. The city's best-loved beach has been going strong ever since, and proves itself both stoic (weekend winter openings provide a ray of sunshine) and adaptable (in 2006 it shifted half a kilometre down the dunes due to building works). As well as being one of few beaches where swimming is permitted, it's home to a happening bar and a good restaurant serving global dishes (*see p145*).

Another year-round option is **Strand West** (Stavangerweg 900, 682 6310, www.strand-west.nl), in the industrial sprawl of the western docklands. The loungey bar-restaurant has big outdoor decks for summer, and is popular with students who occupy nearby sea-container accommodation. It's also host to a monthly lesbian night (*see p230*).

Open Easter until September, **Buitenland** (Oude Haagseweg 51, www.buitenland.org), on the shores of the Nieuwe Meer close to the Amsterdamse Bos, is the artiest of the beach bunch, with cultural outpourings of workshops, poetry readings, live music and, most popular, the Drijf In ('Float In') Cinema, where viewers bob in boats of all kinds while watching movies from the lake.

Amsterdam Plage sets up sun brollies in June on a spit of sand on Westerdokseiland. No swimming over here, alas (there's too much water traffic), but that's compensated for with a carousel, a lively programme of bands and DJs, and excellent eats ranging from tapas to full dinners at the Cantina Mobilé – a 100-seater restaurant that unpacks from a Mercedes-Benz truck.

If an urge to slap on sunscreen and slob by the water grabs you in the vicinity of Centraal Station, then hit Renzo Piano's roof for **NEMO Summertime** (www.nemosummertime.nl). Running from the end of June to the start of September, it's kid-friendly, plus there's catering and a great view, but it's the only beach with an entrance fee (€2.50).

At the other end of town (and handy for the RAI railway station) is **Strand Zuid** (between RAI and Beatrixpark, 544 5970, www.strand-zuid.nl), open throughout the summer. The loungey surroundings, with plenty of beds and beanbags on the sand, attract a glam pack who leave their boats in special moorings while they dance at the regular club nights.

Keeping cheeky afternoon beers on lock at **Café de Sluyswacht**.

Café Krom

Utrechtsestraat 76 (624 5343). Tram 4, 6, 7, 10. **Open** 9am-1am Mon-Thur; 10am-2am Fri, Sat; 10am-1am Sun. **No credit cards**. **Map** p331 E4 ㉚

A glass cabinet of trophies and trinkets and a jukebox give this bar an easygoing 1950s feel. It's an Amsterdam classic, by night full of bar-room philosophers and locals mixed with younger night-owls working their way up to Rembrandtplein. By day it's a more genteel spot for a coffee.

Onder de Ooievaar

Utrechtsestraat 119 (624 6836/www.onderde ooievaar.nl). Tram 4. **Open** 10am-1am Mon-Thur; 10am-3am Fri, Sat; 10.30am-1am Sun. **No credit cards**. **Map** p331 E4 ㉛

This place achieves much by not trying too hard. What you get is an uncomplicated venue for an evening's carousing among a mixed bunch of trendies, locals and the odd visitor. Highlights include 't IJ beer on tap, the downstairs pool table (a genuine rarity in Amsterdam bars) and the lovely Prinsengracht-side terrace for al fresco tipples.

Vooges

Utrechtsestraat 51 (330 5670/www.vooges.nl). Tram 4, 6, 7, 10. **Open** 4pm-midnight Mon-Thur, Sun; 4pm-3am Fri, Sat. **Credit** Amex, MC, V. **Map** p331 E4 ㉜

A big bow window lets light in to every nook and cranny of this classy, split-level bar. Inside, décor is simple yet self-conciously styish – a '50s Juliette Greco poster, '70s chairs, '20s chandeliers – rather like Vooges' patrons. The slightly older, moneyed crowd come for post-work or pre-theatre drinks, food from the mod-European menu, or to while away an evening drinking from the compact, well-priced wine list. There is also a sophisticated seaside version, Vooges Strand, on the beach in Zandvoort.

Jodenbuurt, the Plantage & the Oost

Amstelhaven

Mauritskade 1 (665 2672/www.amstelhaven.nl). Tram 3/Metro Weesperplein. **Open** 4pm-1am Mon-Thur, Sun; 4pm-3am Fri, Sat. **Credit** Amex, MC, V. **Map** p332 F4 ㉝

Occupying a prime spot on a side-canal of the Amstel, this bar's cavernous insides are filled with yuppies chowing down posh Dutch food and grooving to weekend DJs. But that's not the point. Amstelhaven's raison d'etre is summer days spent plopped on the vast deck's sofas and beanbags, watching boats bob as staff serve salty dogs in situ.

Brouwerij 't IJ

Funenkade 7 (320 1786/www.brouwerijhetij.nl). Tram 6, 10. **Open** 3-8pm Wed-Sun. **No credit cards**.

The famous tasting house at the base of the Gooyer windmill, where wares from award-winning local brewery 't IJ can be sampled. Inside is bare (still retaining the look of the municipal baths it once was) and seating minimal, so if weather permits, grab a beer and park on the pavement outside. Their standard range includes pale Plzen and darker, stronger Colombus. *See also p154* **Something brewing**.

Café de Sluyswacht

Jodenbreestraat 1 (625 7611/www.sluyswacht.nl). Tram 9, 14/Metro Waterlooplein. **Open** 11.30am-1am Mon-Thur; 11.30am-3am Fri, Sat; 11.30am-7pm Sun. **Credit** MC, V. **Map** p327 E3 ㉞

Listing crazily, this wooden-framed bar has been pleasing drinkers for decades, though the building itself has been around since 1695, when it began life as a lock-keeper's cottage. Suited to balmy and inclement boozing, inside is snuggly and warm, while outside commands great views of Oude Schans. A great place for a sneaky sundowner.

Dantzig

Zwanenburgwal 15 (620 9039) Tram 9, 14/Metro Waterlooplein. **Open** 9am-10pm Mon-Thur; 9am-1am Fri, Sat; 10am-10pm Sun. **Credit** Amex, DC, MC, V. **Map** p327 E3 ㉟

The grandness of this vast café on the corner of the Stopera complex belies the fact that it's modern: velvet drapes, Chesterfields and faux oil paintings give the feel of a gentleman's club. The outside terrace has unmatched views of the river, and it's a handy pit-stop after the Waterlooplein fleamarket or before a concert at the Muziektheater. (Note that the opening hours sometimes vary, depending on whether there's a concert being performed or not.)

Hesp

Weesperzijde 130-131(665 1202/www.cafehesp.nl). Tram 12. **Open** 10am-1am Mon-Thur; 10am-2am Fri, Sat; 11am-1am Sun. **Credit** Amex, DC, MC, V. **Map** p332 H5 ㊱

In a nutshell, this is a brown café with knobs on. It's occupied a lovely site on the river near Amstel station for 110 years, and offers all the joys of an old-fashioned boozer, but has moved with the times. The wine list is longer than most bars', the snacks classy and classic (wasabi sits alongside mustard) and entertainment ranges from big bands to latin to lindyhop. In summer, the huge terrace on the water is illuminated by life-size electric palm trees.

De Hogesluis

Sarphatistraat 23 (624 1521/www.hogesluis.nl). Tram 3/Metro Weesperplein. **Open** 11am-1am daily. **Credit** Amex, MC, V. **Map** p331 F4 ㊲

From the Taittinger poster to the glowing fittings to the midnight-blue leather seats, this place oozes understated class, though it's not in the slightest bit snooty. Half of the large space overlooking the river is given over to a (pricey) restaurant, but it's best used as the perfect spot for a sundowner. Patrons range from moneyed guests popping in from the nearby Amstel Hotel to locals sinking a few after walking the dog. Service is that rare double whammy of cheerfully chatty and highly efficient.

The Waterfront

Bickers aan de Werf

Bickerswerf 2 (320 2951/www.bickersaandewerf.nl). Tram 3. **Open** noon-1am Wed-Sun. **Credit** V. **Map** p325 B1 ㊳

The western islands feel like a secluded retreat from the city's bustle, and this modern glass cube is great for a break after aimless exploring. Food caters to all pockets, from a slice of spongecake to caviar, while coffee here becomes an indulgence with a side order of truffles from Jordino. The drinks menu is outstanding: Japanese Iki beer, specialist whiskies and loads of wine by the glass, bottle or half-litre carafe.

Onassis

Westerdoksdijk 40 (330 0456/www.onassisamsterdam.nl). Tram 3. **Open** noon-1am Mon-Thur, Sun; noon-3am Fri, Sat. **Credit** MC, V. **Map** p326 C1 ㊴

Sleek lines, burnished mahogany, banquettes and voluptuous lounge decks: all create the mood of a yacht fit for a Greek shipping magnate. You'll need the wealth of one, too, to properly enjoy this place, with lunchtime sandwiches averaging in at €8.50. A rich experience in every respect. *Photo p163.*

Ot en Sien

Buiksloterweg 27 (636 8233/www.otensien.nl). Ferry from Centraal Station. **Open** noon-1am Mon-Thur, Sun; noon-3am Fri, Sat. **No credit cards.**

Just a short ferry hop from Centraal Station, this little bar feels like it's miles away in the heart of the countryside. There are no pretentions here, just friendly service and a fantastic range of Dutch and Belgian beer, including a truly mighty La Trappe Quadrupel and Bourgogne des Flandres. There's a small patio for summer, but it's particularly cosy in winter when decked out in fairy lights.

Wilhelmina-dok

Noordwal 1 (632 3701/www.wilhelmina-dok.nl). Ferry from Centraal Station. **Open** 11am-midnight daily. **Credit** AmEx, DC, MC, V.

The terrace of this café-restaurant in a former dry dock juts right into the IJ opposite Centraal Station, affording great views of passing river traffic. Unfortunately, a couple of years ago one cruiseliner got a bit too close, smashing right into – and destroying – the patio. Oops. It's all ship-shape again now though, and the perfect spot for summer drinking. The usual *borrelhapjes* are bolstered with posh snacks like quail's leg confit and oysters.

The Jordaan

Café Chris

Bloemstraat 42 (624 5942/www.cafechris.nl). Tram 13, 14, 17. **Open** 3pm-1am Mon-Thur; 3pm-2am Fri, Sat; 3pm-9pm Sun. **No credit cards. Map** p325 B3 ㊵

Not much has changed since 1624 at the oldest bar in town, where builders from the Westerkerk would come to receive their pay after a hard day's graft. Now local workers still come to unwind in unpretentious surroundings, adorned with darts trophies and other bric-a-brac from the bar's long history as a mainstay of the Jordaneese drinking scene, something it remains to this day.

Café de Laurierboom

Laurierstraat 76 (623 3015/www.laurierboom.nl). Tram 10. **Open** 3pm-1am Mon-Thur; 3pm-3am Fri; 1pm-3am Sat; 1pm-1am Sun. **No credit cards. Map** p325 B3 ㊶

If you want to exercise your brain as well as your elbow, head for this chess, bridge and darts café. Willing playmates are always to hand and there are regular contests and tournaments. Strong brews – including potent Belgians like Chimay – help to cheer up sore losers after games.

Café Soundgarden

Marnixstraat 164-166 (620 2853). Tram 10, 13, 17. **Open** 1pm-1am Mon-Thur; 1pm-3am Fri; 3pm-3am Sat; 3pm-1am Sun. **No credit cards**. **Map** p329 B4 42

A dirty old rockers bar where musos, journos and everyone else who refuses to grow up gets smashed in one big, sloppy melée. The soundtrack is the entire back-catalogue of classic alternative pop, often from DJs and bands, and sometimes accompanied by (inexpert) dancing. Bliss. At the back is a surprisingly restful terrace where boats can moor when it's time for a break from the canal touring. There's also pool, pinball and a good range of beer.

Harlem

Haarlemmerstraat 77 (330 1498). Tram 3/bus 18, 22. **Open** 10am-1am Mon-Thur; 10am-3am Fri, Sat; 11am-1am Sun. **No credit cards**. **Map** p326 C2 43

Good-looking, very hip bar with friendly staff and a funky soundtrack. The advertised 'soul food' is hit and miss (though it's always filling and reasonable) but drinking is as important here as eating.

Hegeraad

Noordermarkt 34 (624 5565). Tram 1, 2, 5, 13, 17, 20. **Open** 8am-1am Mon-Thur; 8am-3am Fri, Sat; 9am-1am Sun. **No credit cards**. **Map** p325 B2 44

The polar opposite – geographically and figuratively – of Finch and Proust (*see below*), this gabled building has been a café for as long as the church it looks onto has been standing.

De Nieuwe Lelie

Nieuwe Leliestraat 83 (622 5493). Tram 3, 13, 14, 17. **Open** 2pm-1am Mon-Thur, Sun; 2pm-3am Fri, Sat. **No credit cards**. **Map** p325 B3 45

Old and new Jordaan meet in this split-level bar in a gorgeous 17th-century building on a quiet residential corner. Brown café credentials are pumped up with art exhibitions and a pool table.

Papeneiland

Prinsengracht 2 (624 1989). Tram 3. **Open** 11am-1am Mon-Thur, Sun; 11am-2am Fri, Sat. **No credit cards**. **Map** p325 B2 46

A wonderful spot for a drink and a chinwag in a beautiful Delft-tiled bar. A definite talking-point is the café's fascinating history: apparently, there's a tunnel that runs under the canal that, when Catholicism was outlawed in the 17th century, secretly delivered worshippers to their church opposite, which explains the name: Pope's Island.

Proust

Noordermarkt 4 (623 9145/www.goodfoodgroup.nl). Tram 1, 2, 5, 13, 17, 20. **Open** 9am-1am Mon; 5pm-1am Tue-Thur; noon-3am Fri; 9.30am-3am Sat; 11am-1am Sun. **Credit** AmEx, MC, V. **Map** p325 B2 47

Still trendy after all these years, and great for a market pit-stop or bar crawl kick-start. Inside is sleek and pared down in style – like the punters. If full, try Finch next door; on warm days, both bars' terraces merge into one convivial whole to lend an atmosphere than is pure Amsterdam.

't Smalle

Egelantiersgracht 12 (623 9617). Tram 13, 14, 17, 20. **Open** 10am-1am Mon-Thur, Sun; 10am-2am Fri, Sat. **No credit cards**. **Map** p325 B2/3 48

One of the most scenic terraces on one of the prettiest canals, it's no surprise that waterside seats are snared early in the day, so patience – or an alarm clock in good working order – are essential. Inside it's extremely cute, too, with gleaming brass fixtures harking back to the heady drinking days of the 18th century, when it was the Hoppe distillery.

The Museum Quarter, Vondelpark & the South

't Blauwe Theehuis

Vondelpark 5 (662 0254/www.blauwetheehuis.nl). Tram 1, 2, 6. **Open** 9am-11pm Mon-Thur, Sun; 9am-1am Fri, Sat. **No credit cards**. **Map** p330 C6 49

One of the few landmarks which you can nestle down inside with a beer, HJAB Baanders' extraordinary 1930s teahouse – a sort of UFO-hat hybrid that manages to confuse as many people as it charms – is the choice spot for fair-weather drinking. In summer there are DJs and barbecues.

Caffe Oslo

Sloterkade 1A (669 9663/www.caffeoslo.nl). Tram 1. **Open** 9am-1am Mon-Thur, Sun; 9am-3am Fri, Sat. **Credit** AmEx, MC, V.

So slick a bar comes as a surprise plonked canalside in an unremarkable residential area not far from the Vondelpark. Inside it's all blonde wood, cool, creamy colours and a beautiful crazy-paving floor. Punters are slightly older, style-hungry locals who come for breakfast and stay late for the fashionable menu and inimitable laid-back atmosphere.

Wildschut

Roelof Hartplein 1-3 (676 8220/www.goodfood group.nl). Tram 3, 5, 12, 24. **Open** 9am-1am Mon-Thur; 9am-3am Fri; 10.30am-2am Sat; 9.30am-1am Sun. **Credit** AmEx, DC, MC, V. **Map** p330 D6 50

A stunning example of Amsterdam School architecture, this elegant semi-circular place puts the 'grand' into grand café and drips with nouveau detail. Drink and food choices mirror the upmarket surroundings, as does the clientele, which include flush locals, loud yuppies and art-weary tourists in desperate need of refuelling.

The Pijp

Bloemers

Hemonystraat 70 (400 4024). Tram 3, 4, 25. **Open** 10am-1am Mon-Thur, Sun; 10am-3am Fri, Sat. **Credit** MC, V. **Map** p331 F5 51

A justifiably popular neighbourhood bar on the eastern fringes of the Pijp, the dark wood interior is enlivened with old posters and chandeliers. A kitchen pumps out well-priced international classics and there's a charming summer terrace.

Buna Bet

Van Woustraat 74 (673 9449/www.bunabet.nl). Tram 3, 4, 25. **Open** 8am-5pm Mon-Sat. **No credit cards. Map** p331 F5 52

No booze here, but coffee with a conscience on Amsterdam's up-and-coming foodie street. Choose from an extensive range of Fairtrade coffees (and a few cakes), or get a group together for a traditional Ethiopian coffee ceremony in an interior that's equal parts African- and space age-inspired. A cultural drinking experience that won't leave you with a hangover or feeling out of pocket the next day.

Café de Pijp

Ferdinand Bolstraat 17-19 (670 4161/www.goodfood group.nl). Tram 16, 24, 25. **Open** 3.30pm-1am Mon-Thur; 3.30pm-3am Fri; noon-2am Sat; noon-1am Sun. **No credit cards. Map** p331 E6 53

Popular with the neighbourhood's more affluent young people, there's a mod-retro feel here – lacquered walls, 1970s lamps, school chairs – and weekends are livened up with DJs spinning tunes to separate the party animals from the meek and mild. There's a full menu, plus upmarket snacks like mini pizzas and merguez for those hankering for more than just a beer buzz. A trendy place for sure, but one that welcomes newcomers as well as old hands.

Café Krull

Sarphatipark 2 (662 0214) Tram 3, 4, 16, 24, 25. **Open** 3.30pm-1am Mon-Thur; 2pm-3am Fri, noon-2am Sat; noon-1am Sun. **No credit cards. Map** p331 E6/F6 54

Light from the enormous windows floods this delightful locals' café that's busy at all hours with students taking advantage of Wi-Fi, parents treating offspring to (excellent) hot chocolate and, later, evening imbibers of every stripe. The barman's music choice is exquisite (disco, Motown, easy listening, rockabilly), and the pavement picnic tables looking onto the park are a drinker's dream.

Onassis. *See p161.*

Gollem

Daniel Stalpertstraat 74 (676 7117/www.cafe gollem.nl). Tram 16, 24, 25. **Open** 4pm-1am Mon-Thur, Sun; 2pm-2am Fri, Sat. **No credit cards. Map** p331 E6 55

A simply outstanding place to get sozzled, this dark and cosy Belgian beer specialist offers more than 150 bottled brews – including 42 abbey beers and 14 trappist – and 14 on tap, from easy drinkers to demonic head-splitters like Delirium Tremens. The helpful menu lists the strengths of the suds for those erring on the side of caution. There's also a branch at Raamsteeg 4, on the New Side.

Kingfisher

Ferdinand Bolstraat 24 (671 2395). Tram 16, 24, 25. **Open** 11pm-1am Mon-Thur; 11pm-3am Fri, Sat; 1pm-1am Sun. **No credit cards. Map** p331 E6 56

The bar that began the gentrification of the Pijp is now one of the old guard, but its sleek-with-a-twist-of-kitsch chic (glossy red walls, American fridges) still sets the agenda for other young pretenders in the area, as does its loungey feel, cocktails and world-fusion snacks menu. The hip clientele have aged gracefully along with their watering-hole, but make room for a dash of new blood.

Quinto

Frans Halstraat 42 (679 6848/www.cafequinto.nl). Tram 16, 24, 25. **Open** noon-1am Mon-Thur, Sun; noon-2am Fri, Sat. **Credit** DC, MC, V. **Map** p331 E6 57

Pre-war-style furnishings and booths add up to a *Brief Encounter* aesthetic, and the charming service makes you feel special in an old-fashioned way – though hair is let down on weekends with DJs after midnight spinning laidback grooves to keep punters interested. As well as the standard roster of drinks and lunchtime sandwiches there's an evening, meat-heavy menu. If it's full – and it often is – there are plenty of other excellent choices on the street.

Wijnbar Boelen & Boelen

1e van der Helststraat 50 (671 2242/www.wijn bar.nl). Tram 3, 4, 16, 24, 25. **Open** 6pm-midnight Tue-Sun. **Credit** MC, V. **Map** p331 E5/6 58

Many people come here for the Frenchified food, but, as the name implies, the wine is the star at this compact yet airy boozer on the edge of the Pijp's main nightlife strip. Dozens are available by the glass, more by the bottle, and prices range from pocket-friendly to splurge. The emphasis is on old world, but there are good selections from the antipodes and the Americas and the friendly owners – who have a shop at nearby Rustenbergerstraat 387 – can offer suggestions and samples.

Coffeeshops

Built to get your brain buds tingling.

Abraxas. *See p166.*

If every drug were removed from the planet, humans would probably grab the nearest hard object and bang themselves on the head to escape reality. Drug wars are seldom won, something the Dutch acknowledged in 1976 when they decriminalised marijuana and hash.

Since then, the laws on cannabis have always been fuzzy, and it has never technically been legal. But two numbers remain clear: five and 30. You can purchase up to five grams per shop, and you may carry up to 30 grams. However, if you walk outside with 30 grams rolled into one smouldering joint hanging from your lips, the police could hand out a fine – but this is uncommon. Generally, it's simply considered polite not to toke outside a coffeeshop (some pubs and clubs will allow it, but always ask before lighting up).

As for over-the-counter sales, coffeeshops weren't legalised until 1980. Many were around before, but arguments abound on which was the first. The **Melkweg** (*see p233*) originally sold soft drugs to hippies in 1970, but it was never a coffeeshop. **Mellow Yellow** (Vijzelgracht 33) opened in 1972, but now resides in a different building on another side of town. And if signs on the **Bulldog** (Oudezijds Voorburgwal 90, www.bulldog.nl) say it was the first, ask why its registration number reads 002. To truly experience the first ever, you must leave Amsterdam and go to Utrecht where **Sarasani** (Oudegracht 327, www.sarasani.nl) still inhabits the same dimly lit basement in which it began its work in 1968.

Surviving that long isn't easy: coffeeshops are under continual watch and must regularly dance with the law. They can legally sell to you, but cannot buy from growers – legislators assume ganja magically appears in the store-room. A public smoking ban was almost passed a couple of years back, potentially eradicating all coffeeshops; it was pushed back to 2009, and it's likely that coffeeshops will be exempt.

Since 1 April 2007, alcohol has been prohibited in coffeeshops. To survive, some will convert to pubs, others will offer additional quaff and victuals. But fret not: Mary Jane has had a rough ride since the beginning, yet she still enjoys more freedom here than anywhere else. For a broader survey of the role played by drugs in modern Dutch culture, *see pp50-54*.

DOORS OF PERCEPTION

For many, stepping into their first coffeeshop is a moment of lost virginity: the initial encounter might be awkward, but it feels great just to get inside. Whether you're new to the smoke or an old-time pro, arriving well-versed in coffeeshop etiquette can certainly smooth things out.

When you first walk in, ask to see a menu: it will list the available drugs and their prices, and staff can explain the effects of each. You're welcome to see and smell everything before you buy. Prices vary: expect to pay around €5 to €6 for a gram of decent bud or a chunk of hash. For better quality, bring more currency.

Hash is typically named after its country of origin (Moroccan, Afghan, Lebanese), whereas cannabis usually bears invented names loosely referring to an element of the strain (White Widow, Super Skunk, Silver Haze). These are mostly genetic hybrids developed over the years for supreme effect.

Previously, the big rage was for extremely potent weed grown hydroponically under indoor lights. This is still available, but lately many people prefer remaining conscious while getting high. Thus, organic herb is surging in popularity. Various coffeeshops carry a good bio selection; some sell nothing but.

To save your lungs, opt for eating spacecake. It's generally strong and delicious – just make sure you're free for the next five hours. Many coffeeshops also offer bongs, pipes and even vaporisers for use. But if you want to blend in with the locals, roll a joint. All shops provide free rolling papers and tips. If you lack the skills, pre-rolled joints are always available, but usually contain low-grade ingredients (though a few shops pride themselves on excellent pre-rolls). If you've already got grass and need a place to smoke, no shop will deny you having a seat, but you should at least buy a drink.

In terms of ambience, every establishment is different. Some serve amazing food, others offer brilliant couches. Some have a terrible atmosphere but the best hash in town. Others have it all. The following list is by no means complete, but let it serve as a guideline for what a great coffeeshop can be. With roughly 300 in town, you could easily stumble onto your own personal favourite just around the next corner.

Coffeeshops

One of very few decent lesbian bars in town, **Saarein II** (*see p230*), organises a popular homegrown contest every November.

The Old Centre: Old Side

Greenhouse

Oudezijds Voorburgwal 191 (627 1739/www.greenhouse.org). Tram 4, 9, 14, 16, 24, 25. **Open** 9am-1am Mon-Thur, Sun; 9am-3am Fri, Sat. **No credit cards. Map** p326 D3.

This legendary coffeeshop tenders highly potent weed with prices to match. They've won the Cannabis Cup over 30 times and, with the Grand Hotel next door, occasional celebrities stop by to get hammered. The vibe inside has grown a bit commercial, but it's still worth a peek, if only to see the beautifully handmade interior with sunken floors, mosaic stones and blown-glass lamps.

Other locations Waterlooplein 345 (no phone); Tolstraat 91 (members only; 673 7430).

Greenhouse Effect

Warmoesstraat 53 (624 4974/www.greenhouse-effect.nl). Tram 4, 9, 16, 24, 25. **Open** 9am-1am Mon-Thur, Sun; 9am-3am Fri, Sat. **No credit cards. Map** p326 D2.

This snug shop is shaped like a long, sleek train carriage with a polished interior and high-quality ganja. It tends to fill up fast, but they have a separate space operating a similar policy under the same name next door. There you'll find a full bar, regular DJs and, if the drink and dope combination renders you immobile, a good variety of hotel rooms upstairs (*see p62*). Across the street is Getto (*see p228*), arguably the single best gay/straight-friendly bar in town, where the green smoke is also allowed.

Hill Street Blues

Nieuwmarkt 14 (no phone/www.hill-street-blues.nl). Tram 4, 9, 14, 16, 24, 25/Metro Nieuwmarkt. **Open** 9am-1am daily. **No credit cards. Map** p326 D2.

With comfy couches and natural lighting via some well-placed windows, this cosy corner on the Nieuwmarkt is ideal for a mellow high. Delectable milkshakes, smoothies, space cookies and space truffles are also worth indulging in. But if harder and louder is more to your liking, head to the sister shop on Warmoesstraat 52, where the walls and furniture are covered in barely decipherable graffiti. The basement has pool tables and arcade games, and with a police station next door, you can savour a legal toke near the law. A favourite of Irvine Welsh.

Other locations Warmoesstraat 52 (no phone).

The best Coffeeshops

Abraxas
A goblin's cannabis cave. *See p166.*

Barney's
Bangers and hash for high fryers. *See p169.*

Hill Street Blues
Cop your cannabis here. *See p165.*

De Rokerij
Open sesame and make a wish. *See p169.*

La Tertulia
Greenly serene pastures. *See p169.*

Eat, Drink, Shop

Rusland

Rusland 16 (627 9468). Tram 4, 9, 14, 16, 24, 25/ Metro Nieuwmarkt/Waterlooplein. **Open** 10am-midnight Mon-Thur, Sun; 10am-1am Fri, Sat. **No credit cards. Map** p326 D3.

Known as the longest-running coffeeshop in all Amsterdam, this 'Russian' den has hardwood floors and colourful cushions that complement an efficient multi-level design. The top floor has a bar with forty different loose teas, down below is a decent pipe display, and a dealer's booth up front provides the main attraction. It's also off the tourist path, meaning cheaper prices and smaller crowds.

The Old Centre: New Side

Abraxas

Jonge Roelensteeg 12-14 (625 5763/www.abraxas.tv). Tram 4, 9, 16, 24, 25. **Open** 10am-1am daily. **No credit cards. Map** p326 D3.

Tucked away down a narrow alley, this lively shop is a tourist hot-spot. The staff are friendly, internet is free and chess boards are plentiful – as are the separate rooms connected by spiral staircases. They also have a healthy-sized drug menu, including half a dozen bio weeds and spacecakes. *Photo p164.*

Anti-smoke signals

On 1 February 2007, for the first time in history, a 'no toking' traffic sign was installed in Amsterdam. Though most countries prohibit cannabis in general, no one ever bothered putting up a traffic sign as a reminder. That night, soon after the blowverbod sign was put in place, it was stolen for posterity. Not to be deterred, the council put up a second sign the following day, also immediately pilfered.

Hoping to curb the thievery, which would likely never end, the authorities opted to sell the signs commercially. Hundreds of orders came in, most from the US, and many websites popped up offering replicas, along with T-shirts and stickers (although, with an official price of €90, some locals still prefer the initial method of acquiring the sign). The original design has a joint expelling black smoke with white ganja leaves enclosed within a bright red circle (*pictured*).

The ban is intended as a one-year experiment in De Baarsjes, a poor neighbourhood where there were many complaints about youthful misbehaviour (*see p120* **Blowing minds in De Baarsjes**). Critics of the ban say the signs – which warn of €50 fines for anyone caught toking in public – are a mere distraction from the actual problems. Even with the ban in force, residents claim many walls are still being urinated on, only now it's mostly by 'older gentlemen'. At a nearby old people's home, where many complaints originated, workers claim that geriatrics always find something to grumble about, and the signs have certainly not stopped that. Political party GroenLinks (Green Left), which was against the signs from the beginning, made a parody displaying an exhaust pipe blowing deadly fumes, a hint that they'd prefer a ban on cars in the city.

What does all this mean for you, the largely innocent tourist? In reality, not much at all. Wandering around the centre, you'll probably never see the sign outside of a local souvenir shop. As for toking outdoors, the laws have never been clear. And though technically you can be fined for blowing anywhere outside a coffeeshop, this is very uncommon. If you see a *blowverbod* sign, however, it would be wise to put out your fire and find a more 'tolerant' area in which to smoke yourself silly.

High and mighty: toking gestures at the legendary **Dampkring**.

Dampkring

Handboogstraat 29 (638 0705/www.dedampkring.nl). Tram 1, 2, 5. **Open** 10am-1am Mon-Thur; 10am-2am Fri, Sat; 11am-1am Sun. **No credit cards. Map** p330 D4.

Known for its unforgettable (even by stoner standards) interior, the visual experience acquired from Dampkring's decor could make a mushroom trip look grey. Moulded walls and sculpted ceilings are covered in deep auburns laced with caramel-coloured wooden panelling, making a perfect location for the movie *Ocean's 12*. In case you missed it, in-house monitors loop the same scene all day long.

Dutch Flowers

Singel 387 (624 7624). Tram 1, 2, 5. **Open** 11am-11pm Mon; 10am-11pm Tue-Thur, Sun; 10am-2pm Fri, Sat. **No credit cards. Map** p325 B2.

Squeezed on a little corner near the copious book and art sales on the Spui, this small shop has all its decor slightly askew – even the CD rack. It's known for exceptional, high-grade hash, including pre-rolled joints. The large window up front boasts a truly beautiful view of city life on an old sloping street.

Homegrown Fantasy

Nieuwezijds Voorburgwal 87A (627 5683/www.homegrownfantasy.com). Tram 1, 2, 5, 13, 17. **Open** 10am-midnight Mon-Thur, Sun; 10am-1am Fri, Sat. **No credit cards. Map** p326 C2.

This brightly lit shop bears an ever-changing line-up of artwork, tables with chess boards and a UV light in the toilet that makes your pee a trippy colour. The ganja's all organic and Dutch-grown, including their famous Cheese weed, and the (non-alcoholic) drink selection is vast. Glass bongs and a vaporiser are available. For those who like to get mashed before joining a cult (it helps, apparently) across the street is a large Scientology building.

Tweede Kamer

Heisteeg 6 (422 2236). Tram 1, 2, 5. **Open** 10am-1am Mon-Thur, Sun; 10am-2am Fri, Sat. **No credit cards. Map** p326 D3.

Small and intimate, this shop embodies the refined look and feel of old jazz sophistication. Aided by a bakery around the corner, their spacecakes are sweet and lovely. The hash is highly regarded, but seating is extremely limited (it's really rather tiny inside), and the place is notorious for getting very crowded at peak times. If there's no room, walk twelve steps to Dutch Flowers (*see left*).

Western Canal Belt

Amnesia

Herengracht 133 (no phone). Tram 13, 14, 17. **Open** 9.30am-1am daily. **No credit cards. Map** p326 C2.

eat, sleep and drink
in the center of Amsterdam

Grey Area. See p170.

A shop with swank decor, comfortable cushions and deep red walls. Located off the main tourist routes, it's often cool and quiet – though it occasionally fills up with locals. Their pre-rolled joints are strong and smokeable. Summertime brings outdoor seating on their large, quiet canal street.

Barney's

Haarlemmerstraat 102 (625 9761/www.barneys.biz). Tram 13, 14, 17. **Open** 7am-8pm daily. **No credit cards. Map** p326 C2.

By far the biggest and best kitchen any coffeeshop has to offer. The hearty menu includes daily lunch specials, vegetarian options and, to balance a wake 'n' bake session, a tremendous Irish breakfast. Their organic buds complement the food perfectly. But if you're still hungry, head a few doors down to Barney's Brasserie at number 98. Alcohol is sold there, and you're welcome to bring your ganja.

Siberië

Brouwersgracht 11 (623 5909/www.siberie.nl). Tram 1, 2, 4, 5, 13, 17. **Open** 11am-11pm Mon-Thur, Sun; 11am-midnight Fri, Sat. **No credit cards. Map** p326 C2.

Friendly and mellow, Siberië has regular free horoscope readings, open mic nights, exhibitions, and DJs at weekends. There's also internet access and plenty of board games, making it a cool place to while away any rainy day with great coffee or one of their forty different loose teas (no nasty bags on a string here). The same owners run De Supermarkt (Frederik Hendrikstraat 69, 486 2479, www.desupermarkt.net) and well-established neighbourhood coffeeshop De Republiek (2e Nassaustraat 1A, 682 8431, www.republiek.nl), both west of the Jordaan.

La Tertulia

Prinsengracht 312 (no phone/www.coffeeshopamsterdam.com). Tram 7, 10, 13, 14, 17. **Open** 11am-7pm Tue-Sat. **No credit cards. Map** p330 C4.

This mellow mother-and-daughter-run joint is decorated with plenty of plants, a little waterfall and lots of sunlight, which balances harmoniously with their all-bio buds and scrumptious weed brownies. Two floors provide space for relaxation, quiet reading or gazing at the canal. Look for the seriously stoned Van Gogh painted outside.

Southern Canal Belt

De Rokerij

Lange Leidsedwarsstraat 41 (622 9442/www.rokerij.net). Tram 1, 2, 5, 6, 7, 10. **Open** 10am-1am Mon-Thur, Sun; 10am-3am Fri, Sat. **No credit cards. Map** p330 D5.

A marvellous discovery on an otherwise hideous touristy street by Leidseplein, De Rokerij is an Aladdin's cave. Lit by wall-mounted candles and beautiful metal lanterns, it's decorated with colourful Indian art and a variety of seating (ranging from mats on the floor to decorative 'thrones') – all of which is highly appealing to those feeling the effects. It gets very busy in the evening and on weekends. **Other locations** Amstel 8 (620 0484); Singel 8 (422 6643); Elandsgracht 53 (626 3060).

The Jordaan

Grey Area

Oude Leliestraat 2 (420 4301/www.greyarea.nl). Tram 1, 2, 5, 13, 14, 17. **Open** noon-8pm daily. **No credit cards. Map** p326 C3.

Run by two blokes living the modern American dream: get the f*@k out of America. They did so by opening this stellar coffeeshop, which offers some of the best weed and hash on the planet (try the Bubble Gum or Grey Mist Crystals). Also on offer are large glass bongs, a vaporiser and free refills of organic coffee. The owners are highly affable and often more baked than the patrons: sometimes they stay in bed and miss the noon opening. *Photos p169.*

Paradox

1e Bloemdwarsstraat 2 (623 5639/www.paradox amsterdam.demon.nl). Tram 10, 13, 14, 17. **Open** 10am-8pm daily. **No credit cards. Map** p325 B3.

One of the most easygoing coffeeshops around. This down-to-earth joint, with its understated decor and bare wooden tables, feels like a friendly corner café – with the kitchen to match. Substantial foodstuffs include sandwiches, soups, burgers and shakes. A note to late risers: the kitchen closes at 3pm.

Samenentereng

2e Laurierdwarsstraat 44 (624 1907). Tram 10, 13, 14, 17. **Open** 11am-1am daily. **No credit cards. Map** p329 B4.

The only coffeeshop that looks like it's run by a hippie stoner (which it is). It's jammed full of knick-knacks and antiques, all for sale: old kitchenware, funky lamps, little tables, a hookah, even a saw. Sit among the bric-a-brac and smoke the modest weed. Simply a must-see for its uniqueness, the building remains standing thanks to four large tree trunks leaning against the facade.

The Museum Quarter, Vondelpark & the South

Kashmir Lounge

Jan Pieter Heijestraat 85-87 (683 2268). Tram 1, 6, 7, 11, 17. **Open** 10am-1am Mon-Thur; 10am-3am Fri, Sat; 11am-1am Sun. **No credit cards. Map** p329 B6.

Lit with little beyond candlelight, Kashmir may seem too dark at first, but once your eyes adjust, it's an opulent cavern of Indian tapestries, ornate tiles, hand-carved walls and cushions swathed in zebra and cheetah prints. With a multitude of obscure corners and enclosed tables, you can feel VIP at no extra charge. Kashmir is also located outside the centre, so prices remain unusually low.

The Pijp

Yo-Yo

2e Jan van der Heijdenstraat 79 (664 7173). Tram 3, 4. **Open** noon-7pm Mon-Sat. **No credit cards. Map** p331 F5.

Located on a leafy street near Sarphatipark and the Albert Cuypmarkt (*see p190*), this chill spot lacks the commercialism and crowds found in more central shops. The herb is all-organic and it's run by a pleasant woman who bakes hot apple pie every day.

Events

For the **High Times Cannabis Cup**, *see p201.*

Highlife Hemp Fair

Highlife, Discover Publisher BV, Postbus 362, 5460 AJ, Veghel (073 549 8112/www.highlife.nl).

Organised by *Highlife* magazine, this huge international event celebrates the cannabis plant, with an emphasis on the industrial value of hemp. The exhibition holds displays detailing the many uses for the plant, and there are around 100 stands selling smart drugs, weed tea and coffee, and all sorts of soft drug paraphernalia. A highlight is the presentation of the Highlife Cup for the best Dutch weed and hash. The event takes place in the Jaarbeurs (Utrecht) every January and usually attracts around 13,000 people.

Legalize! Street Rave

Stichting Legalize!, Postbus 59723, 1040 LE, Amsterdam (427 5065/www.legalize.net).

In an attempt to raise awareness on drug issues, this voluntary group organises a street rave through the city every first Saturday in June – attracting both party and political animals to the festivities. They also stage a rally in May and organise a number of international actions and benefit parties.

Information

For **Hash Marihuana Hemp Museum**, *see p93.*

Cannabis College

Oudezijds Achterburgwal 124, Old Centre: Old Side (423 4420/www.cannabiscollege.com). Tram 4, 9, 14, 16, 24, 25/Metro Nieuwmarkt. **Open** 11am-7pm daily. **Admission** free. **Map** p326 D3.

The college, occupying two floors in a 17th-century listed monument in the Red Light District, provides the public with an impressive array of information about the cannabis plant (including its medicinal uses). Admission is free; however, staff request a €2.50 donation for a look at the indoor garden.

Drugs Information Line

0900 1995. **Open** 1-9pm Mon-Fri; Dutch recorded message at other times. 10 cents per minute.

A national advice and information line for the Trimbos Institute (Netherlands Institute of Mental Health and Addiction). To the relief of drug-addled tourists, the operators speak excellent English.

Shops & Services

From cutting-edge fashion houses to flea markets: buy in haste, repent at leisure.

Let's cut to the chase – your mates may have come to get high, get cultured or sample some of the city's superb cuisine. You, on the other hand, came to Amsterdam to shop.

The beauty of this burg is that, with many of the neighbourhoods bursting with unique boutiques, eateries of every kind, coffeeshops and, yes, galleries for the culture vultures, there's no need for any ugly scenes, hair pulling or shaking of tiny fists over how the day gets spent. They can do what they need to do. You, meanwhile, can get out the shopping bags and start waving the plastic about.

Ramble through the 'Nine Streets', stuffed to the gills with upmarket boutiques of the stealth wealth variety; delve into the Jordaan's many dinky and quirky merchants; or tackle the ritzy glam that is the PC Hooftstraat, the place you are most likely to rub shoulder pads with a native celebrity in the process of re-wardrobing. Wherever you set foot, you are assured retail treasures of every stripe. The rest of your posse will have a field day as well – but you'll have far more to carry. Ah, Amsterdam: shoppers' delights, canals lined with treasures, lashings of bargains and plenty of distractions to keep non-shoppers happy. For more on shopping areas, *see p177* **Where to spend it**.

Shops

Spoiled
For a fashionable new you. *See p175.*

Marlies Dekkers
For slinky Dutch smalls. *See p180.*

Wegewijs
For cheesy pleasers. *See p183.*

Puccini Bomboni
For cutting-edge chocolates. *See p185.*

De Bierkoning
Around the world in 80 beers. *See p187.*

Kitsch Kitchen
For neon plastic overload. *See p190.*

Noordermarkt
For a good rummage. *See p191.*

Concerto
For a one-stop record shop. *See p192.*

Nic Nic
For retro design classics. *See p188.*

Antiques & auctions

Visit Spiegelgracht, Nieuwe Spiegelstraat or the markets (*see p190*). For a more rarefied air, try **Sotheby's** (De Boelenlaan 30, 550 2200, www.sothebys.com) and **Christie's** (Cornelis Schuytstraat 57, 575 5255, www.christies.com).

Art & art supplies

Check museum shops for prints and postcards.

Art Multiples

Keizersgracht 510, Southern Canal Belt (624 8419). Tram 1, 2, 5. **Open** 1-6pm Mon; 10am-6pm Tue, Wed, Fri, Sat; 10am-7pm Thur; noon-5pm Sun. **Credit** AmEx, DC, MC, V. **Map** p330 C4.
The most comprehensive collection of international photographs and posters in the Netherlands, and the largest collection of postcards in Western Europe, good for tourists seeking token gifts with gusto.

J Vlieger

Amstel 34, Southern Canal Belt (623 5834). Tram 4, 9, 14, 16, 24, 25. **Open** noon-6pm Mon; 9am-6pm Tue-Fri; 11am-5.30pm Sat. **Credit** AmEx, DC, MC, V. **Map** p327 E3.
Papers and cards of every description monopolise the ground floor; upstairs are paints, pens and inks, as well as small easels and hobby materials.

Peter van Ginkel

Bilderdijkstraat 99, Oud West (618 9827/www.petervanginkel.nl). Tram 3, 7, 12, 17. **Open** 10am-5.30pm Mon-Fri; 10am-4pm Sat. **Credit** MC, V. **Map** p329 B5.
Heaven for creative types. The shelves at Peter van Ginkel groan with paints and pigments, canvases and many types of paper for artists in residence.

Bookshops

The best of Dutch literature is celebrated in the third week of March, while the second week of October sees the focus turn to children's books. For more on Amsterdam's book markets, *see p190. See also p172* **A life in books**.

A life in books

Unsurprisingly for a city that adores books (there's a dedicated book week each year in March) and speaks English with such élan, Amsterdam's shelves are awash with English tomes. And, while buying new literature in the language is usually an eye-wateringly expensive affair, savvy second-hand shoppers will, with a little rooting around, be able to find the best for their bookshelves at pleasing prices.

Big events to look out for are the **Boeken Op De...** fairs, which take place monthly from spring to autumn on Dam Square, Marie Heinekenplein or along the Amstel in front of the Stopera; look out for posters around town for dates. These huge affairs are usually well organised around a single theme – travel books, for example, or photography – and always have a good range of works in English alongside plenty of cheapo soft-covers and real rarities for more dedicated collectors.

Little sister to these bumper bonanzas is the popular weekly **book market** on the Spui (www.deboekenmarktophetspui.nl); chock-full of specialist dealers who come from around the country, it's a rummager's delight, and some real paper- and hardback bargains can be found here, from Penguin Classics to old art volumes.

Most neighbourhoods in the city have their own unobtrusive little second-hand stores where the best bargains and esoteric finds are to be had; one of the finest is in the Pijp. The seriously great **Sporadisch Antiquarisch** (Sarphatipark 127, 675 4209), as its name – the Sporadic Antiquarian – suggests, keeps unusually irregular hours, but even if it's shut it's worth dropping by, as the windowsill outside is usually filled with books that sell at 50 cents a pop; when you've made your choice, squat down and put your money through the letterbox. Gems unearthed here in the past have ranged from an entire collection of American gay pulp fiction spanning nearly four decades to a book of the 1970s HTV Wales series *Paint Along With Nancy*. You truly do not know what you will find. A few minutes' walk away is **Antiquariaat Streppel** (Hemonystraat 48, 676 7610), which is most particularly strong on English-language quality fiction and kitsch cook and travel books.

Understandably enough, the Old Centre, filled as it is with University of Amsterdam buildings, is studded with excellent used book opportunities. Most charismatic are the stalls in **Oudemanhuispoort**, a quaint covered alleyway running in between Kloveniersburgwal and Oudezijds Voorburgwal. This Monday to Saturday market has been providing bibliophiles with a fix since 1787. Subjects tend towards the academic and conditions are high. Just round the corner is the **Book Exchange** (Kloveniersburgwal 58, 626 6266; *see p173*), where you could while away whole days among the stacks. British and American volumes are the speciality of this sprawling, multi-roomed shop, which buys, sells and swaps. Also worth checking out are more mainstream retailers like the **Athenaeum Nieuwscentrum** (*pictured*; *see p172*).

General

American Book Center
Spui 12, Old Centre: New Side (625 5537/www.abc.nl). Tram 1, 2, 4, 5, 9, 14, 16, 24, 25. **Open** 10am-8pm Mon-Wed, Fri, Sat; 10am-9pm Thur; 11am-6.30pm Sun. **Credit** AmEx, DC, MC, V. **Map** p326 D3.
Now located in a fancier location a mere two blocks from the old shop and an Amsterdam institution since 1972, the American Book Center stocks English-language books and magazines from the US and UK, mostly to bilingual Dutch customers.

Athenaeum Nieuwscentrum
Spui 14-16, Old Centre: New Side (bookshop 514 1460/news centre 514 1470/www.athenaeum.nl). Tram 1, 2, 5. **Open** *Bookshop* 11am-6pm Mon; 9.30am-6pm Tue, Wed, Fri, Sat; 9.30am-9pm Thur; noon-5.30pm Sun. *News centre* 8am-8pm Mon-Wed, Fri, Sat; 8am-9pm Thur; 10am-6pm Sun. **Credit** AmEx, MC, V. **Map** p330 D4.
This is where Amsterdam's most highbrow literary browsers choose to hang around. The Athenaeum Nieuwscentrum, as its name might suggest, also stocks newspapers from all over the world, as well as a wide choice of magazines, periodicals and, the bookworm's staple, tomes in many languages.

Book Exchange
Kloveniersburgwal 58, Old Centre: Old Side (626 6266). Tram 4, 9, 14/Metro Nieuwmarkt. **Open** 10am-6pm Mon-Fri; 10am-6pm Sat; 11.30am-4pm Sun. **No credit cards**. **Map** p326 D3.
The owner of this bibliophiles' treasure trove is a shrewd buyer who's willing to do trade deals. Choose from a plethora of second-hand English and American titles (mainly paperbacks).

Waterstone's
Kalverstraat 152, Old Centre: New Side (638 3821/www.waterstones.co.uk). Tram 1, 2, 4, 5, 9, 14, 16, 24, 25. **Open** 10am-6pm Mon; 9.30am-7pm Tue, Wed, Fri; 9.30am-9pm Thur; 10am-6.30pm Sat; 11am-6pm Sun. **Credit** AmEx, MC, V. **Map** p326 D3.
Thousands of books – mainstream and literary – plus magazines and videos, all in English. The large children's section is delightful.

Specialist

Architectura & Natura
Leliegracht 22, Western Canal Belt (623 6186/www.architectura.nl). Tram 13, 14, 17. **Open** noon-6pm Mon; 9am-6pm Tue, Sat; 9am-6.30pm Wed-Fri. **Credit** AmEx, MC, V. **Map** p326 C3.
The stock at 'Architecture and Nature', which includes many works in English for monoglots, is exactly what you'd expect from its name: books on architectural history, plant life, gardens and animal studies. Leliegracht 22 is also home to Antiquariaat Opbouw, which deals in antiquarian books covering architecture and associated topics.

Lambiek
Kerkstraat 132, Southern Canal Belt (626 7543/www.lambiek.nl). Tram 1, 2, 5. **Open** 11am-6pm Mon-Fri; 11am-5pm Sat; 1-5pm Sun. **Credit** AmEx, MC, V. **Map** p330 D4.
Lambiek, founded in 1968, claims to be the world's oldest comic shop and has thousands of books from around the world; its on-site cartoonists' gallery hosts exhibitions every two months.

Pied-à-Terre
Overtoom 135-137, Museum Quarter (627 4455/www.piedaterre.nl). Tram 1, 2, 5. **Open** 10am-6pm Mon-Wed, Fri; 10am-9pm Thur; 10am-5pm Sat. **No credit cards**. **Map** p330 D4.
Travel books, international guides and a huge range of maps for active holidays. Adventurous walkers should talk to the helpful staff before embarking on a trip out of town (*see also pp272-294*).

Department stores

De Bijenkorf
Dam 1, Old Centre: New Side (0900 0919 (0.20/min)/www.bijenkorf.nl). Tram 1, 2, 4, 5, 9, 13, 14, 16, 17, 24, 25. **Open** 11am-7pm Mon; 9.30am-7pm Tue, Wed; 9.30am-9pm Thur, Fri; 9.30am-6pm Sat; noon-6pm Sun. **Credit** AmEx, DC, MC, V. **Map** p326 D3.
Amsterdam's most notable department store has a great household goods department and a decent mix of clothing (designer and own-label), kids' wear, jewellery, cosmetics, shoes and accessories. The top floor Chill Out department caters to funky youngsters in need of streetwear, clubwear, wacky foodstuffs and kitsch accessories, while the store's restaurant, La Ruche, is a good lunch spot. The Christmas displays are always hugely popular.

Metz & Co
Leidsestraat 34-36, Southern Canal Belt (520 7020/www.metzenco.nl). Tram 1, 2, 5. **Open** 11am-6pm Mon; 9.30am-6pm Tue-Sat; noon-5pm Sun. **Credit** AmEx, DC, MC, V. **Map** p330 D4.
Metz is wonderful for upmarket gifts: designer furniture, glass and opulent accessories are all available. For lunch with a view, make for the top-floor restaurant designed by Gerrit Rietveld. At Yuletide their Christmas shop will put the holiday spirit back into the even Scroogiest customer.

Vroom & Dreesmann
Kalverstraat 203, Old Centre: New Side (0900 235 8363/www.vroomendreesmann.nl). Tram 4, 9, 14, 16, 24, 25. **Open** 11am-6.30pm Mon; 10am-6.30pm Tue, Wed, Fri; 10am-9pm Thur; 10am-6.30pm Sat; noon-6pm Sun. **Credit** AmEx, MC, V. **Map** p326 D3.
V&D means good quality at prices just a step up from HEMA (*see p191* **Back to basics**). There's a staggering array of toiletries, cosmetics, leather goods and watches, clothing and underwear for the whole family, kitchen items, suitcases, CDs and videos. There's also a decent in-house bakery, Le Marché, plus self-service restaurant La Place, which is a great spot for a healthy lunch.

Drugs

Conscious Dreams Dreamlounge

Kerkstraat 119, Southern Canal Belt (626 6907/ www.consciousdreams.nl). Tram 1, 2, 5. **Open** *Apr-Oct* noon-10pm daily; *Oct-Apr* noon-10pm Wed-Sat. **Credit** AmEx, DC, MC, V. **Map** p330 D4.

Conscious Dreams was the original proponent of the smart drugs wave in Amsterdam. The staff here really know their stuff – the owner worked as a drugs adviser for five years – and you're more or less guaranteed to find whatever you're after. Now a few doors down from its original location, it boasts a bigger, brighter space and internet café.

Other locations Kokopelli Warmoesstraat 12 (421 7000).

Hemp Works

Niewendijk 13, Old Centre: New Side (421 1762/ www.hempworks.nl). Tram 1, 2, 5, 13, 17. **Open** 11am-7pm Mon-Wed, Sun; 11am-9pm Thur-Sat. **Credit** AmEx, DC, MC, V. **Map** p326 C2.

One of the first shops in Amsterdam to sell hemp clothes and products, and now one of the last, Hemp Works has had to diversify into seed sales and fresh mushrooms, and it's also been a Cannabis Cup-winner for its strain of the stinky weed.

Dampkring

Prins Hendrikkade 10-11, Old Centre: Old Side (422 2137/www.dampkringshop.com). Tram 1, 2, 4, 5, 9, 16, 17, 24, 25/Metro Centraal Station. **Open** 9am-6pm Mon-Fri; 9am-5pm Sat. **Credit** MC, V. **Map** p326 D2.

A new member of the legendary Dampkring family, this delightful emporium has everything needed to set up a grow centre at home: from hydroponics and organic equipment to bio-growth books and videos.

Fabrics & trimmings

Capsicum

Oude Hoogstraat 1, Old Centre: Old Side (623 1016/ www.capsicumtextiles.com). Tram 4, 9, 14, 16, 24, 25. **Open** 11am-6pm Mon; 10am-6pm Tue, Wed, Fri, Sat; 10am-9pm Thur. **Credit** AmEx, DC, MC, V. **Map** p326 D3.

All the fabrics here are made from natural fibres, such as cotton woven in India. Staff spin the provenance of each fabric into the sale. A gem.

H J van de Kerkhof

Wolvenstraat 9, Western Canal Belt (623 4666). Tram 1, 2, 5. **Open** 11am-6pm Mon; 10am-6pm Tue-Thur. **Credit** MC, V. **Map** p330 C4.

Tassel maniacs go wild. A sea of shakeable frilly things, lace and rhinestone banding.

Stoffen & Fourituren Winkel a Boeken

Nieuwe Hoogstraat 31, Old Centre: Old Side (626 7205). Tram 4, 9, 16, 24, 25. **Open** noon-6pm Mon; 10am-6pm Tue, Wed, Fri; 10am-8pm Thur; 10am-5pm Sat. **Credit** MC, V. **Map** p327 E3.

The Boeken family has been in the rag trade, hawking fabrics since 1920. Just try to find somewhere else with the kind of variety on offer here: latex, Lycra, fake fur and sequins abound.

Fashion

Children

Funky vintage clothes for kids can be found at **Noordermarkt** (*see p191*); for budget garments, try **Albert Cuypmarkt** (*see p190*).

Broer & Zus

Rozengracht 104, the Jordaan (422 9002/www. broerenzus.nl). Tram 13, 14, 17. **Open** noon-6pm Mon; 10.30am-6pm Tue-Fri; 10am-6pm Sat. **Credit** AmEx, MC, V. **Map** p325 B3.

For the baby or toddler who has it all, Broer & Zus makes gift-giving a cinch with its handmade toys, adorable T-shirts with goofy slogans and a selection of some seriously stylish kit.

Geboortewinkel Amsterdam

Bosboom Toussaintstraat 22-24, Museum Quarter (683 1806/ www.geboortewinkel.nl). Tram 3, 7, 10, 12. **Open** 1-6pm Mon; 10am-6pm Tue-Fri; 10am-5pm Sat. **Credit** MC, V. **Map** p330 C5.

A beautiful range of maternity and baby clothes (including premature sizes) in cotton, wool and linen. You'll also find cotton nappies, plus various childbirth videos for those still antipating the big event.

't Klompenhuisje

Nieuwe Hoogstraat 9A, Old Centre: Old Side (622 8100/www.klompenhuisje.nl). Tram 4, 9, 14/Metro Nieuwmarkt. **Open** 10am-6pm Mon-Sat. **Credit** AmEx, DC, MC, V. **Map** p327 E3.

Delightfully crafted and reasonably priced shoes, traditional clogs and handmade leather and woollen slippers from baby sizes up to size 35, perfect for turning kids into pint-sized Dutchies for the day.

Designer

American Apparel

Westerstraat 59-61, the Jordaan (330 2391/www. americanapparel.net). Tram 10, 13, 14, 17. **Open** 9am-7pm Mon; 10am-7pm Tue-Sat; 10am-9pm Thur; noon-5pm Sun. **Credit** AmEx, MC, V. **Map** p325 B2.

Dov Charney picked Amsterdam for his newest American Apparel outlet, perhaps because the town has a casual attitude perfect for the sweatshop-free, relaxed style of his cotton T-shirts and other pieces. (Or perhaps he just needed new fresh meat for his pervy magazine ads. Only time will tell.)

Azzurro Due

Pieter Cornelisz Hooftstraat 138, Museum Quarter (671 9708). Tram 2, 3, 5, 12. **Open** 1-6pm Mon; 10am-6pm Tue, Wed, Fri; 10am-9pm Thur; 10am-5.30pm Sat; noon-5pm Sun. **Credit** AmEx, DC, MC, V. **Map** p330 C6.

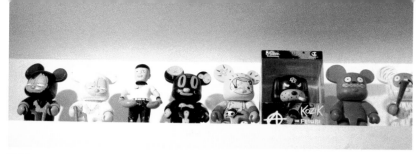

Spoiled.

If you've got to splurge, this is as good a spot as any. Saucy picks from Anna Sui, Blue Blood, Chloé and Stella McCartney attract the usual mediacrities.

Bits and Pieces

Cornelis Schuytstraat 22, Museum Quarter (618 1939). Tram 16. **Open** noon-6pm Mon; 10am-6pm Tue-Fri; 10am-5pm Sat. **Credit** AmEx, DC, MC, V. **Map** p330 C5.

Mixes new designers with established names such as Martine Sitbon, Clements Ribeiro and Earl Jean, and often featured in the papers next to an A-lister's 'what is she wearing/where did she get it' tagline.

For Our Friends

Pieter Cornelisz Hooftstraat 142, Museum Quarter (676 6220/www.bluebloodbrand.com). Tram 2, 5. **Open** 10am-6pm Mon-Wed, Fri; 10am-9pm Thur; 10am-5.30pm Sat; noon-5pm Sun. **Map** p330 C6.

The new concept home of local denim label Blue Blood Jeans has all the lovely aspirational gear any upwardly mobile trendster could ever want, all under one perfectly curated roof. From denim to scooters, sneakers to toys, gold-embossed Smythson journals and treats beyond one's imagining.

Spoiled

Wolvenstraat 19, Western Canal Belt (626 3818/ www.spoiled.nl). Tram 1, 2, 5. **Open** 1-6pm Mon, Sun; 10am-6pm Tue, Wed, Fri, Sat; 10am-9pm Thur. **Credit** AmEx, MC, V. **Map** p330 D4.

Spoiled ups the ante at its fancy-pants new location on the Nine Streets with loads of fashion, art, weird gadgets, designer toys, a hair salon and a new jeans concept called DENIMBAR, where one can throw back a drink while the staff relate all the news on the latest denim styles and fashion. Labels include Tiger of Sweden, Cycle, Nudie, Freitag and Evisu, plus limited collections from Nike and Levis.

SPRMRKT

Rozengracht 191-193, the Jordaan (330 5601/www. sprmrkt.nl). Tram 13, 14, 17. **Open** By appt Mon; 10am-6pm Tue-Sat. **Credit** MC, V. **Map** p325 B3.

A whopping 450sq m (4,850sq ft) store (that's big for Amsterdam) of exceptionally cool duds. The prize is the shop-within-the-shop, SPR+, featuring picks from Margiela, Rick Owens, the Acne Jeans collection, Wendy & Jim and more. *Photo p180.*

2πR

Oude Hoogstraat 10-12, Old Centre: Old Side (421 6329). Tram 4, 9, 14, 16, 24, 25. **Open** noon-7pm Mon; 10am-7pm Tue, Wed, Fri, Sat; 10am-9pm Thur; noon-6pm Sun. **Credit** AmEx, DC, MC, V. **Map** p326 D3.

This funky little number's just for the boys (the Gasthuismolensteeg branch does womenswear). Two shops side by side on Oude Hoogstraat offer urban streetwear threads from the likes of Helmut Lang, Psycho Cowboy, D-Squared and Anglomania.

Other locations Gasthuismolensteeg 12 (528 5682).

Van Ravenstein

Keizersgracht 359, Western Canal Belt (639 0067). Tram 13, 14, 17. **Open** 1-6pm Mon; 11am-6pm Tue-Fri; 11am-7pm Thur; 10.30am-5.30pm Sat. **Credit** AmEx, MC, V. **Map** p330 C4.

Superb boutique with the best from the Belgian designers: Martin Margiela, Dirk Bikkembergs, AF Vandervorst and Bernhard Willhelm, among others. Victor & Rolf form the Dutch contingent. Don't miss the itsy-bitsy bargain basement for similarly stylish endeavours with less serious price tags.

Glasses & contact lenses

Brilmuseum/Brillenwinkel

Gasthuismolensteeg 7, Western Canal Belt (421 2414/ www.brilmuseumamsterdam.nl). Tram 1, 2, 5. **Open** noon-5.30pm Wed-Fri; noon-5pm Sat. **No credit cards. Map** p326 C3.

Officially this 'shop' is an opticians' museum, but don't let that put you off. The fascinating exhibits are of glasses through the ages, and most of the pairs you see are also for sale to customers.

Donald E Jongejans

Noorderkerkstraat 18, the Jordaan (624 6888). Tram 3, 10. **Open** 11am-6pm Mon, Sat. **No credit cards. Map** p325 B2.

Where to spend it

Here's a cheat sheet detailing the general characteristics of Amsterdam's main shopping districts to help make your spree a breeze.

Damstraat

A street at war with its former self, Damstraat is fighting to jettison the sleaze and change into a boutique-lined oasis. Alas, its proximity to the Red Light District means that the countless laddish types out on the town can impinge on this otherwise lovely area.

Magna Plaza

Right behind Dam Square, this architectural treat was once a post office. Its subsequent reincarnation as a five-floor mall is beloved by tourists, although the locals are less keen.

Kalverstraat and Nieuwendijk

Kalverstraat and its more scruffy extension Nieuwendijk are where the locals come for their consumer kicks. Shops here are largely unexciting, yet they still get insanely busy on Sundays. Still, it's pedestrian-only, so you can forget the dreaded bikes and focus on the tills.

Leidsestraat

Connecting Koningsplein and Leidseplein, Leidsestraat is peppered with fine shoe shops and boutiques, but you'll still have to dodge trams to shop there. Cyclists: note that bikes aren't allowed in this part of town.

Nine Streets

The small streets connecting Prinsengracht, Keizersgracht and Herengracht in between Raadhuisstraat and Leidsegracht offer a very diverse mix of boutiques, antiques and a good range of quirky speciality stores.

The Jordaan

Tiny backstreets laced with twisting canals, cosy boutiques, lush markets, bakeries, galleries, restful and old-fashioned cafés and bars. The Jordaan captures the spirit of Amsterdam like nowhere else in the city.

PC Hoofstraat

Amsterdam's elite shopping strip has had a rocky ride in the last few years, but with a new infusion of designer shops embracing both established and up-and-coming names, things are looking better all the time.

Spiegelkwartier

Across from the Rijksmuseum and centred on Spiegelgracht, this area is packed with antiques shops selling real treasures at accordingly high prices. Dress for success and keep your nose in the air if you want to fit in with the legions of big-spending locals.

The Pijp

This bustling district is notable mainly for the Albert Cuypmarkt and its ethnic food shops.

This vintage frame specialist sells unused frames dating from the mid 1800s to the present day. Most frames are at fabulously low prices and built to last – and the staff are friendly, too.

Hats & handbags

Many markets have huge selections of hats and bags; try the **Albert Cuypmarkt** (*see p190*).

Accessorize

Leidsestraat 68, Southern Canal Belt (627 1693/ www.accessorize.nl). Tram 1, 2, 5. **Open** 10am-6pm Mon-Wed, Fri, Sat; 10am-9pm Thur; noon-6pm Sun. **Credit** MC, V. **Map** p330 D4.

Owned by the people behind Monsoon, this branch of the popular British chain is home to scores of cheap jewellery, scarves and bags to complement even the most challenged of wardrobes.

Bag habits die hard

Had enough of bikes and bordellos? How about taking a bag break? A must-see for both curious and fetishist alike is **Tassenmuseum Hendrikje Museum of Bags and Purses**, the world's single largest collection of its kind, clocking in at a gaga-baga total of 3,500 bags and still counting.

Once just the innocent hobby of an antique-collecting couple, Tassenmuseum Hendrikje spent over a decade of its quirky-yet-quiet museumhood in a private home in sleepy Amstelveen. But after one bag stored under their bed too many, Hendrikje and Heinz Ivo decided to pack their bags – all of 'em. Flash forward to June 2007, and the museum has reopened in a city-centre canalside mansion, a listed rijksmonument with 17th- and 18th-century ceiling paintings and marble floors.

Besides ogling celebrity clutches, such as Madonna's Versace from the *Evita* premiere, or a Lieber rhinestone collectible named 'Socks' for Hillary Clinton's cat, you can get a good overview of the history of the handbag. Starting back in the 1500s, the fourth floor displays half a millennium's worth of precious purses, including the chatelaine 'body necklaces' onto which wearers suspended everything from spoons to small Bibles, coin purses made of human hair and tortoise-shell reticules. One flight down dawns the 20th century and the handbag as fashion statement, with every fad from 1920s imitation ivory and 1950s funky plastics to more timeless leather. Alongside the classic Kelly and Lady Dior, you observe how technology goes trendy (a telephone bag that can be plugged in and used for calls) and how the industry went ecologically conscious with a bag using skin of environmental terror the Nile perch, responsible for the extinction of several fresh-water species.

After a snack in the café, a stroll through the Robert Broekema-designed historical garden or fetching the kids from bag-making lessons in the children's atelier, return to the ground floor. Exhibitions showcase up-and-coming designers from home and abroad, with a bag-happy museum shop to boot.

Not only was the museum's new home inhabited by Amsterdam mayor Cornelis de Graeff in the 1660s, but two centuries later by Jeltje de Bosch Kemper, famous for having founded one of the city's early housekeeping schools as a means to liberate women from their domiciles. You wonder if she would have agreed with this 19th-century French dictum cited by the museum: 'The lady can leave her husband but not her bag.'

Tassenmuseum Hendrikje

Hendrikje Herengracht 573 (524 6452/www. tassenmuseum.nl). Tram 4, 9. **Open** 10am-5pm daily. **Admission** €6.50; €5 groups of 10 or more, students, over-65s; €2.50 13s-18s; free under-13s. **Map** p331 E4.

Cellarrich Connexion

Haarlemmerdijk 98, the Jordaan (626 5526/www.cellarrich.nl). Tram 1, 2, 4, 5, 13, 14, 16, 17, 24, 25. **Open** 1-6pm Mon; 11am-6pm Tue-Fri; 11am-5pm Sat. **Credit** AmEx, MC, V. **Map** p325 B2.

Nab a sophisticated Dutch handbag in materials from leather to plastic. Many (but not all) of the creations are produced by four local designers.

De Hoed van Tijn

Nieuwe Hoogstraat 15, Old Centre: Old Side (623 2759/www.dehoedvantijn.nl). Tram 4, 9, 14, 16, 24, 25. **Open** noon-6pm Mon; 11am-6pm Tue-Fri; 11am-5.30pm Sat. **Credit** AmEx, DC, MC, V. **Map** p327 E3.

Mad hatters will delight in this vast array of bonnets, Homburgs, bowlers, sombreros and caps, plus second-hand and handmade items.

High street

Be sure to cruise the Kalverstraat, as it's high street heaven. Below are the usual suspects.

Diesel

Heiligeweg 11-17, Old Centre: New Side (638 4082/www.diesel.com). Tram 1, 2, 4, 5, 9, 14, 16, 24, 25. **Open** noon-6pm Mon, Sun; 10am-6pm Tue, Wed, Fri, Sat; 10am-9pm Thur. **Credit** AmEx, MC, V. **Map** p330 D4.

Three storeys filled with Diesel and Diesel alone.

Hennes & Mauritz

Kalverstraat 125-129, Old Centre: New Side (524 0440/www.hm.com). Tram 1, 2, 4, 5, 9, 14, 16, 24, 25. **Open** noon-6.30pm Mon; 10am-6.30pm Tue, Wed, Fri, Sat; 10am-9pm Thur; 10am-6pm Sun. **Credit** AmEx, DC, MC, V. **Map** p326 D3.

Prices range from reasonable to ultra-low; quality varies too. Clothes for men, women, teens and kids. **Other locations** throughout the city.

Lucky Brand Jeans

Heiligeweg 34-36, Old Centre: New Side (422 0502/www.luckybrand.com). Tram 1, 2, 4, 5, 9, 14, 16, 24, 25. **Open** noon-6pm Mon; 10am-6pm Tue-Fri; 10am-9pm Thur; 10am-5.30pm Sat; noon-5pm Sun. **Credit** p326 D2. **Map** p330 D4.

A recent addition to the Amsterdam high street, Lucky sits kitty corner from Diesel just off the Kalverstraat, making it denim central.

Zara

Kalverstraat 72, Old Centre: New Side (530 4050/www.zara.com). Tram 1, 2, 4, 5, 9, 14, 16, 24, 25. **Open** noon-6pm Mon, Sun; 10am-6pm Tue, Wed, Fri, Sat; 10am-9pm Thur. **Credit** AmEx, MC, V. **Map** p326 D3.

Imagine you have a lean, mean fashion machine that can almost instantaneously churn out decent approximations of the latest catwalk creations at a fraction of the price you'd pay at the outlet shops of the designers. Now imagine how much money you'd make doing it. Oops! Too late, Zara beat you to it. The styles are hot, the quality sometimes not.

Jewellery

For diamonds, *see p110* **Amsterdam: rock city**.

Grimm Sieraden

Grimburgwal 9, Old Centre: Old Side (622 0501/www.grimmsieraden.nl). Tram 16, 24, 25. **Open** 11am-6pm Tue-Fri; 11am-5pm Sat. **Credit** AmEx, DC, MC, V. **Map** p326 D3.

While Elize Lutz's shop features the most avant garde of Dutch jewellery designers, she has the decency – not to mention the sound commercial sense – to concentrate her stock on the most wearable pieces from their various ranges.

Jorge Cohen Edelsmid

Singel 414, Southern Canal Belt (623 8646/www.jorgecohen.nl/). Tram 1, 2, 5. **Open** 10am-6pm Mon-Fri; 11am-6pm Sat. **Credit** AmEx, DC, MC, V. **Map** p330 D4.

The kind of art deco-inspired jewellery you'd be proud to pass off as the real thing. Pieces use salvaged jewellery, silver, plus antique and new stones.

MK Jewelry

Reestraat 9, Southern Canal Belt (427 0727/www.mk-jewelry.com). Tram 13, 14, 17. **Open** 11am-6pm Tue-Sat. **Credit** AmEx, DC, MC, V. **Map** p326 C3.

Pressing your nose to the immaculate windows you might be afraid of intruding, but you'll be glad you did. Once inside, all is calm and relaxed, allowing the glitter of a million reflected, refracted rays of light to work their mesmeric magic. Prices start low.

Large sizes

High and Mighty

Singel 465, Southern Canal Belt (622 1436/www.highandmighty.co.uk). Tram 1, 2, 5. **Open** 1-6pm Mon; 9am-6pm Tue, Wed, Fri; 9am-9pm Thur; 9am-5pm Sat; noon-5pm 1st Sun of mth. **Credit** AmEx, DC, MC, V. **Map** p330 D4.

Big and tall men are going to love the selection: now they can have the same brands as their buddies. From Ben Sherman through to Yves Saint Laurent, if you wear a 58 or larger, you're in luck.

Mateloos

Kwakarsplein 1-7, Oud West (683 2384/www.mateloos.nl). Tram 3, 12, 13, 14, 17. **Open** 10am-6pm Mon-Fri; 10am-5pm Sat. **Credit** AmEx, DC, MC, V. **Map** p329 B5.

Mateloos cares for curves. Clothes from sizes 44 to 60: evening wear, sportswear, lingerie – the works.

Lingerie

Hunkemöller

Kalverstraat 162, Old Centre: New Side (623 6032/www.hunkemoller.com). Tram 1, 2, 5, 9, 14, 16, 24, 25. **Open** 11am-6pm Mon; 9.30am-6pm Tue, Wed, Fri, Sat; 9.30am-9pm Thur; noon-6pm Sun. **Credit** AmEx, MC, V. **Map** p326 D3.

Female fancy pants fanciers should check out this chain (you can call 035 646 5413 for details of other branches). The undies manage to be feminine and attractive, simply designed and more reasonably priced than at similar enterprises.

Marlies Dekkers

Cornelis Schuytstraat 13, Museum Quarter (471 4146/www.marliesdekkers.nl). Tram 16. **Open** noon-6pm Mon; 10am-6pm Tue-Fri; 10am-5pm Sat. **Credit** Amex, DC, MC, V. **Map** p330 C5.

Local lingerie designer Marlies Dekkers is already a legend for having given women the world over such stylish, understated underwear, and her wildly wonderful flagship store doesn't disappoint. Besides the lingerie and swimwear lines, there's a variety of treats to help set the mood: scented candles, locally handmade bonbons, and beautifully boxed sets of champagne for slipping lingerie into. Truly dazzling gifts to stir the senses. *Photo p182.*

Paars

Spuistraat 242, Old Centre: New Side (618 2828/ www.paarslingerie.nl) Tram 1, 2, 5, 13, 17. **Open** 1-7pm Mon; 11am-7pm Tue-Fri; 11am-9pm Thur; 10am-6pm Sat; 1-6pm Sun. **Credit** MC, V. **Map** p326 C2.

Easily the most sophisticated lingerie shop in Amsterdam right now, Paars' collections are high end and vary regularly, making it interesting to true lingerie lovers. Galliano, Argentovivo, Ravage, Lise Charmel, Chantal Thomass, Marlies Dekkers, Pin Up, D&G, Malizia, Black Label, Pain de Sucre and Roberto Cavalli are all on sale.

Repairs & cleaning

Luk's Schoenservice

Prinsengracht 500, Southern Canal Belt (623 1937). Tram 1, 2, 5, 6, 7, 10. **Open** 9am-5.30pm Tue-Fri; 9am-5pm Sat. **No credit cards**. **Map** p330 D5.

Reliable and speedy shoe repairs.

Powders

Kerkstraat 56, Southern Canal Belt (0646 27243). Tram 16, 24, 25. **Open** 7am-11pm daily. **No credit cards**. **Map** p331 E4.

Washing and dry-cleaning at a central location.

Shoes

For new shoes try Leidsestraat or Kalverstraat; for second-hand wares there's **Waterlooplein** or **Noordermarkt** (for both, *see p191*).

Big Shoe

Leliegracht 12, Western Canal Belt (622 6645/www. bigshoe.nl). Tram 13, 14, 17. **Open** 10am-6pm Wed, Fri; 10am-9pm Thur; 10am-5pm Sat. **Credit** AmEx, DC, MC, V. **Map** p326 C3.

Fashionable footwear for men and women in large sizes only: men's from 47 to 50; women's 42 to 46.

Betsy Palmer

Rokin 9-15, Old Centre: Old Side (422 1040/www. betsypalmer.com). Tram 4, 9, 14, 16, 24, 25. **Open** 10am-6.30pm Mon-Wed, Fri; 10am-9pm Thur; 10am-6pm Sat; 1-6pm Sun. **Credit** MC, V. **Map** p326 D3.

SPRMRKT. *See p175.*

Tired of seeing the same shoes in every store, Dutch fashion buyer Gertie Gerards put her money where her mouth was and set up shop. Betsy Palmer is her in-house label, which sits alongside a huge variety of other labels that change as they sell out.
Other locations Van Woustraat 46 (470 9795).

Onitsuka Tiger

Herengracht 356 Western Canal Belt (528 6183/ www.onitsukatiger.com). **Open** 1-6pm Mon; 10am-6pm Tue-Sat. **Credit** AmEx, MC, V. **Map** p330 C4.
Small but perfectly formed outlet for the iconic Japanese trainer brand Onitsuka Tiger, which is making waves the world over. Should your fave pair not be on the shelves, staff will happily order it.

Paul Warmer

Leidsestraat 41, Southern Canal Belt (427 8011). Tram 1, 2, 5. **Open** 1-6pm Mon, Sun; 10am-6pm Tue, Wed, Fri, Sat; 10am-9pm Thur. **Credit** AmEx, DC, MC, V. **Map** p330 D4.
Fashionista heaven: refined footwear for men and women. Gucci, Roberto Cavalli and Emillio Pucci are among the upmarket designers represented.

Seventy Five

Nieuwe Hoogstraat 24, Old Centre: Old Side (626 4611/www.seventyfive.com). Tram 4, 9, 14/Metro Nieuwmarkt. **Open** noon-6pm Mon; 10am-6pm Tue-Sat; noon-5pm Sun. **Credit** MC, V. **Map** p327 E3.
Trainers for folk who have no intention of ever having to insert a pair of Odor Eaters: high fashion styles from Nike, Puma, Converse and Diesel.

Shoe Baloo

Koningsplein 7, Southern Canal Belt (626 7993/www. shoebaloo.nl). Tram 2, 3, 5, 12. **Open** noon-6pm Mon; 10am-6pm Tue, Wed, Fri, Sat; 10am-9pm Thur; 1-6pm Sun. **Credit** AmEx, MC, V. **Map** p330 C6.
A space age men's and women's shoe shop with a glowing Barbarella-pod interior. Über cool, but, for all that, still worth taking the time to cruise for Miu Miu, Costume Nationale and Patrick Cox.
Other locations Leidsestraat 10 (330 9147); PC Hooftstraat 80 (671 2210).

Street

To look good for less, hunt down streetwear from the market at **Waterlooplein** (*see p191*).

8cht

Vijzelstraat 105, Southern Canal Belt (320 7007/ www.8-sneakers.nl). Tram 16, 24, 25. **Open** 12.30-6pm Mon; 10.30am-6pm Tue-Fri; 1.30-9pm Thur; 10.30am-5pm Sat; noon-5pm Sun. **Credit** AmEx, MC, V. **Map** p330 D4.
Pronounced 'acht' (Dutch for eight), this is the latest streetwear haunt with maximum cred thanks to its super-exclusive kicks, toys and T-shirts.

America Today

Magna Plaza, Nieuwezijds Voorburgwal 182 (ground floor), Old Centre: New Side (638 8447/www.america today.nl). Tram 1, 2, 5, 13, 14, 17. **Open** 11am-7pm Mon; 10am-7pm Tue, Wed, Fri, Sat; 10am-9pm Thur; noon-7pm Sun. **Credit** AmEx, MC, V. **Map** p326 C2.

Money can't buy love, but **Marlies Dekkers**' lingerie comes a close second. *See p180.*

This giant started as the tiniest of ventures; today it sells street classics from Converse, Ben Sherman, Timberland and the like. It also holds the accolade of being the only place in town to get Gap.
Other locations Kalvertoren Singel 457 (638 8812); Sarphatistraat 48 (638 9847).

Independent Outlet

Vijzelstraat 77, Southern Canal Belt (421 2096/www.outlet.nl). Tram 16, 24, 25. **Open** 1-6pm Mon; 11am-6pm Tue, Wed, Fri, Sat; 11am-9pm Thur; 1-6pm Sun. **Credit** AmEx, MC, V. **Map** p330 D4.
Customised boards, Vans shoes and labels like Fred Perry, plus a great selection of punk imports.

Tom's Skate Shop

Oude Hoogstraat 35-37, Old Centre: Old Side (625 4922/www.tomsskateshop.nl). Tram 4, 9, 14/Metro Nieuwmarkt. **Open** noon-6pm Mon; 10am-6pm Tue-Sat; noon-6pm Sun. **Credit** AmEx, MC, V. **Map** p326 D3.
Dual-gender gear from the likes of Nike SB, Zoo York and London label Addict. Also stocks limited edition trainers, shades by Electric and skateboards.

Vintage & second-hand

Loads of vintage clothes and accessories can be found (often cheaply) at **Noordermarkt** and also at **Waterlooplein** (for both, *see p191*).

Episode

Berenstraat 1, Western Canal Belt (626 4679/www.episode.eu). Tram 13, 14, 17. **Open** 1-6pm Mon; 11am-6pm Tue, Wed; 11am-8pm Thu; 11am-7pm Fri; 10am-7pm Sat; 1-6pm Sun. **Map** p330 C4.
The spacious downstairs canalside location makes this new vintage clothing shop a must-see in the Nine Streets area. An instant magnet to stylists, with pieces from prom dresses to dolphin shorts showing up in all the local magazines.
Other locations Waterlooplein 1 (320 3000).

Lady Day

Hartenstraat 9, Western Canal Belt (623 5820/www.ladydayvintage.com). Tram 1, 2, 5. **Open** 11am-6pm Mon-Wed, Fri, Sat; 11am-9pm Thur; 1-6pm Sun. **Credit** AmEx, MC, V. **Map** p326 C3.
Beautifully tailored second-hand and period suits, plus sportswear classics for those rocking the retro aesthetic. Vintage wedge shoes, pumps and accessories complete the stylish ensemble.

Laura Dols

Wolvenstraat 6-7, Western Canal Belt (624 9066/www.lauradols.nl). Tram 1, 2, 5. **Open** 11am-6pm Mon-Wed, Fri, Sat; 11am-9pm Thur; 1-6pm Sun. **Credit** MC, V. **Map** p330 C4.
A treasure trove of period clothing, mainly from the '40s and '50s, Laura Dols has many of the sumptuous dresses of the time, as well as some menswear.

Ree-member

Reestraat 26, Western Canal Belt (622 1329). Tram 1, 2, 5. **Open** 1-6pm Mon; 11am-6pm Tue-Sat; 1-6pm Sun. **Credit** AmEx, MC, V. **Map** p326 C3.
Ree-member stocks a terrific collection of vintage clothes and '60s standards. The shoes are the best in town and priced to match. If you're strapped for cash, then you'll be pleased to learn that they sell their less-than-perfect pieces on Noordermarkt by the kilo and at seriously discounted prices.

Zipper

Huidenstraat 7, Western Canal Belt (623 7302). Tram 1, 2, 5. **Open** 11am-6pm Mon-Sat; 1-5pm Sun. **Credit** AmEx, MC, V. **Map** p330 C4.

It's not cheap, but the jeans, cowboy shirts, '80s gear and '70s hipsters are worth a gander; there's real treasure to be found on them there rails.

Other locations Nieuwe Hoogstraat 8 (627 0353).

Flowers

It's tempting to bring home a selection of bulbs from Amsterdam. However, although travellers to the UK and Ireland will be fine, some other countries' import regulations either prohibit the entry of bulbs or, in the case of the US, require them to have a phytosanitary certificate. You'll find that some of the packaging is marked with flags indicating the countries into which the bulbs can be safely carried, but most Dutch wholesalers know the regulations and can ship bulbs all the way to your home. In terms of cut flowers, travellers to the UK and Ireland can take an unlimited quantity, as long as they're not chrysanthemums or gladioli, while US regulations vary from state to state.

Bloemenmarkt (Flower Market)

Singel, between Muntplein and Koningsplein, Southern Canal Belt. Tram 1, 2, 4, 5, 9, 14, 16, 24, 25. **Open** 9am-6pm Mon-Sat; 11am-5.30pm Sun. **No credit cards**. **Map** p330 D4.

This fascinating collage of colour is the world's only floating flower market, with 15 florists and garden shops (although many also hawk cheesy souvenirs these days) permanently ensconced on barges along the southern side of Singel. The plants and flowers usually last well and are good value.

Plantenmarkt (Plant Market)

Amstelveld, Southern Canal Belt. Tram 4, 6, 7, 10. **Open** 9.30am-6pm Mon. **No credit cards**. **Map** p331 E4.

Despite a general emphasis on plants, pots and vases, the Plantenmarkt also has cut flowers for sale. Each spring sees the house plants go on sale, while the later months of the year burst into colour with the transient glory of garden annuals.

Florists Gerda's

Runstraat 16, Western Canal Belt (624 2912). Tram 1, 2, 5. **Open** 9am-6pm Mon-Fri; 9am-5pm Sat. **Credit** DC, MC, V. **Map** p330 C4.

Amsterdam's most inspired florist, Gerda's diminutive shop is full of fantastic blooms and sports legendary window displays. If you're lucky, you'll spy sculptural bouquets on their way out the door. Local deliveries from anywhere in the world.

Jemi

Warmoesstraat 83A, Old Centre: Old Side (625 6034/ www.jemi.nl). Tram 4, 9, 16, 24, 25. **Open** 9am-6pm Mon-Fri. **No credit cards**. **Map** p326 D2.

Amsterdam's first stone-built house is now occupied by a delightfully colourful florist. Jemi arranges splendid bouquets, provides tuition in the art of flower-arranging and stocks tons of pots and plants.

Food & drink

Bakeries

For bread, rolls and packaged biscuits, go to a *warmebakker*; for pastries and delicious cream cakes, you need a *banketbakker*.

Vlaamsch Broodhuis

Haarlemmerstraat 108, the Jordaan (528 6430/ www.vlaamschbroodhuys.nl). Tram 3/bus 18, 22. **Open** 11am-6.30pm Mon; 8.30am-6.30pm Tue-Fri; 9am-5pm Sat. **No credit cards**. **Map** p326 C2.

The name may be a mouthful, but it's worth a visit to wrap your gums round their tasty sour-dough breads, fine French pastries and fresh salad greens from restaurant De Kas, among other treats.

Other locations Vijzelstraat 109 (626 0654); Cornelis Schuytstraat 26 (397 5195).

Runneboom

1e Van der Helststraat 49, the Pijp (673 5941). Tram 16, 24, 25. **Open** 7am-5pm Mon-Sat. **No credit cards**. **Map** p331 E5.

This Pijp bakery is a staunch favourite with locals, who queue into the street in all weathers. A huge selection of French, Russian, Greek and Turkish loaves is offered, with rye bread the house speciality.

Cheese

The younger (*jong*) the cheese, the creamier and milder it will be; riper (*belegen*) examples will be drier and sharper, especially the old (*oud*) cheese. Most popular are Goudse (from Gouda), Leidse (flavoured with cumin seeds) and Edammer (aka Edam, with a red crust). Don't miss Leerdammer, Maaslander (both mild with holes) or the rather enigmatic Kernhem (a dessert cheese).

De Kaaskamer

Runstraat 7, Western Canal Belt (623 3483). Tram 1, 2, 5. **Open** noon-6pm Mon; 9am-6pm Tue-Fri; 9am-5pm Sat; noon-5pm Sun. **No credit cards**. **Map** p330 C4.

De Kaaskamer offers over 200 varieties of domestic and imported cheeses, plus pâtés, olives, pastas and wines. Have fun quizzing the staff on the different cheese types and related trivia. *Photos p185.*

Wegewijs

Rozengracht 32, the Jordaan (624 4093/www. wegewijs.nl). Tram 13, 14, 17. **Open** 8.30am-6pm Mon-Fri; 9am-5pm Sat. **No credit cards**. **Map** p325 B3.

The Wegewijs family started running this shop more than a century ago. On offer are around 50 foreign cheeses and over 100 different domestic varieties of caseus, including *graskaas*, a grassy-tasting

cheese that is available in summer. For those nervous about buying a strange cheese, Wegewijs allows you to try Dutch varieties beforehand.

Chocolate

Australian

Leidsestraat 101, Southern Canal Belt (622 0897/ www.australianhomemade.com). Tram 1, 2, 5. **Open** 11am-11pm Mon-Fri, Sun; 11am-noon Sat. **No credit cards**. **Map** p330 D4.

Check out the delicious selection of bonbons, ice-creams and coffees with all natural ingredients as you ponder how the Amsterdam branch of a Belgian chain ended up with this name.

Other locations throughout the city.

Pâtisserie Pompadour

Huidenstraat 12, Western Canal Belt (623 9554/ www.patisseriepompadour.com). Tram 1, 2, 5, 7. **Open** 10am-6pm Mon-Fri; 10am-5pm Sat. **Credit** MC, V. **Map** p330 C4.

This fabulous bonbonnerie and tearoom – with an 18th-century interior imported from Antwerp – is likely to bring out the little old lady in anyone. A relatively new branch (Kerkstraat 148, Southern Canal Belt, 9am-6pm daily) also sports a decent tearoom serving sublime designer sandwiches. *Photo p186.*

Puccini Bomboni

Staalstraat 17, Old Centre: Old Side (626 5474/ www.puccinibomboni.com). Tram 9, 14/Metro Waterlooplein. **Open** noon-6pm Mon; 9am-6pm Tue-Sat; noon-6pm Sun. **Credit** MC, V. **Map** p327 E3.

Tamarind, thyme, lemongrass, pepper and gin are just some of the flavours of these delicious hanmade chocolates, completely without artificial ingredients.

Other locations Singel 184 (427 8341).

Unlimited Delicious

Haarlemmerstraat 122, the Jordaan (622 4829/ www.unlimiteddelicious.nl). Tram 3/bus 18, 22. **Open** 9am-6pm Mon-Sat. **Credit** AmEx, V. **Map** p326 C2.

Known for such twisted treats as balsamic vinegar and tomato bonbons and a caramel balsamic chocolate pie with a brownie bottom, Unlimited Delicious also offers individual or group courses in bonbon-making so you can devise your own mad combos for dinner parties or simply for stuffing at home.

Delicatessens

Raïnaraï

Prinsengracht 252, Western Canal Belt (624 9791/ www.rainarai.nl). Tram 13, 14, 17. **Open** 10am-10pm daily. **No credit cards**. **Map** p326 C4.

Mouth-watering North African fodder, from take-away to an assortment of items no pantry should be without. A self-proclaimed 'nomadic kitchen', they will come and cater wherever you please, although most people can't resist eating right on the premises as the food is so damn tasty.

De Kaaskamer. *See p183.*

Eat, Drink, Shop

Oh, to live on Sugar Mountain. Life is sweet at **Pâtisserie Pompadour**. *See p185*.

Uliveto

Weteringschans 118, Southern Canal Belt (423 0099). Tram 6, 7, 10. **Open** 11am-8pm Mon-Fri; noon-6pm Sat. **No credit cards**. **Map** p331 E5.

Uliveto is a superb Italian deli that – along with the usual wines, pastas and fruity olive oils for dipping bread – has an irresistible takeaway selection of tender roasted seasonal vegetables, grilled fish, rack of lamb and polenta, plus ricotta cheesecake.

Ethnic & speciality

Eichholtz

Leidsestraat 48, Southern Canal Belt (622 0305). Tram 1, 2, 5. **Open** 10am-6.30pm Mon-Sat; 9am-6.30pm Tue, Wed, Fri; 9am-9pm Thur; 9am-6.30pm Sat; noon-6pm Sun. **Credit** (over €23) AmEx, MC, V. **Map** p330 D4.

Beloved by expats, this is the place where Yanks can get their hands on chocolate chips and homesick Brits can source Christmas puddings.

Oriental Commodities

Nieuwmarkt 27, Old Centre: Old Side (626 2797/ www.orientalgroup.nl). Tram 4, 9, 14, 16, 24, 25/ Metro Nieuwmarkt. **Open** 9am-6pm Mon-Sat; 10.30am-5pm Sun. **No credit cards**. **Map** p326 D2.

Visit Amsterdam's largest Chinese food emporium for the full spectrum of Asian foods and ingredients, from shrimp- and scallop-flavoured egg noodles to fried tofu balls and fresh veg. There's also a fine range of Chinese cooking appliances and utensils.

Waterwinkel

Roelof Hartstraat 10, Museum Quarter (675 5932/ www.springwater.nl). Tram 3, 24. **Open** 1-6pm Mon; 10am-6pm Tue-Fri; 10am-5pm Sat. **Credit** AmEx, DC, V. **Map** p330 C5.

Mineral water, water everywhere, and every drop to drink. The variety of native and imported versions may induce emergencies in the weaker of bladder.

Health food

See also p190 Markets.

Delicious Food

Westerstraat 24, the Jordaan (320 3070). Tram 3. **Open** 10am-7pm Mon, Wed-Fri; 9am-6pm Sat; 11am-3pm Sun. **No credit cards**. **Map** p325 B2.

Organic produce has reached the self-contradictory pinnacle of urban rustic chic at what can only be described as a bulk food boutique. Come here for the most enticing displays of pastas, nuts, exotic spices, plus upmarket oils and vinegars.

BioMarkt

Weteringschans 133, Southern Canal Belt (638 4083/www.biomarkt.nl). Tram 6, 7, 10. **Open** 8am-8pm Mon-Sat; 11am-7pm Sun. **Credit** MC, V. **Map** p331 E5.

The largest health food supermarket that there is in all of Amsterdam. You'll find everything here, from organic meat, fruit and vegetables (delivered fresh daily) to really quite surprisingly tasty sugar-free chocolates and organic wine and beer.

Other locations throughout the city.

Organic© Food For You

Cornelis Schuytstraat 26-28, Museum Quarter (379 5195/www.organicfoodforyou.nl). Tram 16. **Open** 9am-7pm Mon-Fri; 9am-6pm Sat. **No credit cards**. **Map** p330 C5.

Top-end organic supermarket with daily staples like sugar and flour and more exotic fare like 30-year-old balsamic vinegar, caviar and wild salmon for those with less ordinary shopping lists.

Night shops

It's 11pm and you're in dire need of ice-cream/condoms/cigarettes/toilet roll/beer/chocolate (delete as applicable). This is where the city's night shops come into their own. But since the customers are desperate and the staff costs higher, the prices are generally steeper than in their diurnal competitors.

Avondmarkt

De Wittenkade 94-96, West (686 4919/www.deavondmarkt.nl). Tram 10. **Open** 4pm-midnight Mon-Fri; 3pm-midnight Sat; 2pm-midnight Sun. **No credit cards. Map** p325 A2.

The biggest and best of all night shops, this is basically a supermarket, albeit a late-opening one, though it must be said that the selection of wine and beer here puts most standard supermarkets to shame. Worth the trek way out to just west of the Jordaan for the wow factor alone.

Big Bananas

Leidsestraat 73, Southern Canal Belt (627 7040/www.bigbananas.nl). Tram 1, 2, 5. **Open** 9am-1am daily. **No credit cards. Map** p331 D4.

A passable selection of wine, some odd-looking canned cocktails and a variety of sandwiches are stocked here. Expensive, even for a night shop.

Sterk

Waterlooplein 241, Jodenbuurt (626 5097). Tram 9, 14/Metro Waterlooplein. **Open** 8am-2am daily. **Credit** MC, V. **Map** p327 E3.

Less of a night shop and more of a deli: quiches, pastries and salads are made onsite, and there's also fruit and veg. Be prepared to ask for what you want here – there's no self-service. Its branch is known as 'Champagne Corner', which hints at what's on offer. **Other locations** De Clercqstraat 1-7 (618 1727).

Off-licences (Slijterijen)

De Bierkoning

Paleisstraat 125, Old Centre: New Side (625 2336/www.bierkoning.nl). Tram 1, 2, 5, 13, 14, 16, 17, 24, 25. **Open** 1-7pm Mon; 11am-7pm Tue, Wed, Fri; 11am-9pm Thur; 11am-6pm Sat; 1-6pm Sun. **Credit** AmEx, DC, MC, V. **Map** p326 C3.

Named in honour of its location behind the Royal Palace, the 'Beer King' stocks a head-spinning 850 brands of beer from around the world, and a range of fine glasses for supping from.

Cadenhead's Whisky

Rozengracht 232, Western Canal Belt (330 6287/www.cadenhead.nl). Tram 1, 2, 5, 7. **Open** 11am-6pm Tue-Sat; 11am-6pm every 2nd and 4th Sun in mth. **Credit** AmEx, MC, V. **Map** p330 C4.

This Shangri-la for whisky (and whiskey) lovers has a great selection of elixirs from Scotland, Ireland and America, and a range of Scottish mineral waters should you wish to pollute the true water of life.

Supermarkets

A few tips for shopping in Dutch supermarkets. Unless a per piece (*per stuk*) price is given, fruit and vegetables usually have to be weighed by the customers. Put your produce on the scale, press the picture of the item and press the 'BON' button to get the receipt. You must pack your groceries yourself, too – and if you want a plastic bag, you'll have to ask (and pay) for it. For **Albert Heijn**, *see p191* **Back to basics**.

Dirk van den Broek

Marie Heinekenplein 25, the Pijp (673 9393/www.lekkerdoen.nl). Tram 16, 24, 25. **Open** 9am-9pm Mon-Fri; 9am-8pm Sat. **No credit cards. Map** p331 E5.

Suddenly fashionable – its red bags are now must-haves for the town's designer lemmings and have even been spotted on the arms of the fashion ratpack overseas – Dirk remains cheaper than Albert Heijn, while choice has improved, but it's not the most glam of supermarkets. *See also p191* **Back to basics**. **Other locations** throughout the city.

Tea & coffee

Geels & Co

Warmoesstraat 67, Old Centre: Old Side (624 0683/www.geels.nl). Tram 4, 9, 14, 16, 24, 25. **Open** *Shop* 9.30am-6pm Mon-Sat. **Credit** MC, V. **Map** p326 D2.

Coffee beans and loose teas, plus a large range of coffee-making contraptions and serving utensils. Upstairs is a small museum of brewing equipment, which is open only on Saturday afternoons.

Simon Levelt

Prinsengracht 180, Western Canal Belt (624 0823/www.simonlevelt.com). Tram 13, 14, 17. **Open** 10am-6pm Mon-Fri; 10am-5pm Sat. **Credit** AmEx, DC, MC, V. **Map** p325 B3.

Anything and everything to do with brewing and drinking, stocked in a remarkable old shop. The premises date from 1839 and the place still has much of the original tiled decor in situ. **Other locations** throughout the city.

Furniture

For intensive browsing of the finest in designer furnishings, don't miss **Overtoom** (*map p330 C5-C6*), reinvented as a furniture boulevard.

De Kasstoor

Rozengracht 202-210, the Jordaan (521 8112/www.dekasstoor.nl). Tram 13, 14, 17. **Open** 10am-6pm Tue-Sat. **Credit** AmEx, MC, V. **Map** p325 B3.

De Kasstoor is not your average modern Dutch interior design shop; it also has hand-picked collectors' pieces from the likes of Le Corbusier, Eames and Citterio, and a very extensive upholstery and fabrics library. Plan on excess luggage for the return trip.

Pols Potten

KNSM-laan 39, The Waterfront (419 3541/www.polspotten.nl). Tram 10, 26. **Open** 10am-6pm Tue-Fri; 10am-5pm Sat; noon-5pm Sun. **Credit** MC, V. **Map** p116.
'Pol's Pots'. Quite why a shop stocking innovative furnishings and home accessories should wish to associate itself with a genocidal mass-murderer remains a mystery, but it does have lots of pots, and a design team to help you pull off the latest trends.

Vintage

Nic Nic

Gasthuismolensteeg 5, Western Canal Belt (622 8523/www.nicnicdesign.com). Tram 1, 2, 5, 13, 17. **Open** noon-6pm Mon-Fri; 10am-5pm Sat. **Credit** AmEx, MC, V. **Map** p326 C3.
We consider this the single best shop of its kind in Amsterdam, selling '50s and '60s furniture, lamps, ashtrays and kitchenware, mostly in mint condition.

Games, models & toys

Joe's Vliegerwinkel

Nieuwe Hoogstraat 19, Old Centre: Old Side (625 0139/www.joesvliegerwinkel.nl). Tram 4, 9, 16, 24, 25/Metro Nieuwmarkt. **Open** noon-6pm Mon; 11am-6pm Tue-Fri; 11am-5pm Sat. **Credit** DC, MC, V. **Map** p327 E3.
Kites, kites and yet more kites – well, you've got to do something with all the Dutch wind. Also a quirky array of boomerangs, yo-yos and kaleidoscopes can be found at this wonderfully colourful shop.

Kramer/Pontifex

Reestraat 18-20, Western Canal Belt (626 5274/www.pontifex.fiberworld.nl). Tram 13, 14, 17. **Open** 10am-6pm Mon-Fri; 10am-5pm Sat. **No credit cards**. **Map** p326 C3.
Broken Barbies and battered bears are restored to health by Mr Kramer, a doctor for old-fashioned dolls and teddies who has practised here for 25 years. In the same shop, Pontifex is a traditional Dutch candle seller oozing old world atmosphere.

Schaak en Go het Paard

Haarlemmerdijk 173, the Jordaan (624 1171/www.schaakengo.nl). Tram 3/bus 18, 22. **Open** 1-5.30pm Mon; 10am-5.30pm Tue, Wed, Fri, Sat; 10am-8pm Thur. **Credit** AmEx MC, V. **Map** p325 B1.
Budding Kasparovs take note: this is the place to come to for a glorious selection of chess sets, from African to ultra-modern examples.

Schaal Treinen Huis

Bilderdijkstraat 94, Oud West (612 2670/www.schaaltreinenhuis.nl). Tram 3, 7, 12, 13, 14, 17. **Open** 1-5pm Mon; 9.30am-5.30pm Tue-Fri; 9.30am-5pm Sat. **Credit** AmEx, DC, MC, V. **Map** p329 B5.
DIY kits and a ready-made parade that includes electric trains, modern and vintage vehicles and some truly adorable and intimate dolls' houses.

Gifts & souvenirs

Delftshop

Spiegelgracht 13, Southern Canal Belt (421 8360/www.delftshop.com). Tram 4, 9, 16, 24, 25. **Open** 9.30am-6pm Mon-Sat; 11am-6pm Sun. **Credit** AmEx, DC, MC, V. **Map** p330 D5.
Souvenirs with provenance. Delftshop are the official dealers of Royal Delft and Makkum pottery, the bread and butter of the Dutch antique trade. The stock here includes antiques too, with some pieces dating from the 17th century – for a price, of course.
Other locations: Prinsengracht 440 (627 8299); Muntplein 12 (623 2271).

Tesselschade: Arbeid Adelt

Leidseplein 33, Southern Canal Belt (623 6665/www.tesselschade-arbeidadelt.nl). Tram 1, 2, 5, 6, 7, 10. **Open** 11am-6pm Tue-Fri; 10am-5pm Sat. **Credit** AmEx, MC, V. **Map** p330 D5.
Everything here is sold on a non-profit basis by Arbeid Adelt ('Work Ennobles'), an association of Dutch women. There are plenty of toys and decorations, as well as more utilitarian household items such as tea cosies and decorated clothes hangers.

Health & beauty

Douglas

Kalverstraat 71, Southern Canal Belt (627 6663/www.douglas.nl). Tram 1, 2, 4, 5, 9, 14, 16, 24, 25. **Open** noon-6pm Mon; 10am-6pm Tue, Wed, Fri, Sat; 10am-9pm Thur; noon-6pm Sun. **Credit** AmEx, MC, V. **Map** p326 D3.
The scents and labels you'd expect, plus rarer brands like La Prairie, Urban Decay and Versace. This new two-storey superstore also features hair products not normally found outside salons.
Other locations throughout the city.

Jacob Hooy & Co

Kloveniersburgwal 12, Old Centre: Old Side (624 3041/www.jacobhooy.nl). Tram 4, 9, 14, 16, 24, 25/Metro Nieuwmarkt. **Open** 1-6pm Mon; 10am-6pm Tue-Fri; 10am-5pm Sat. **Credit** V. **Map** p326 C3.
Established in 1743, this chemist sells medicinal herbs, teas, homeopathic remedies and cosmetics, many under their own brand. The untouched 18th-century interior is worth a visit in itself.

Lavendula

Westerstraat 45, the Jordaan (420 9140/www.lavendula.nl). Tram 1, 2, 5, 13, 17. **Open** noon-5pm Mon; noon-6pm Tue; 10am-6pm Wed-Fri; 10am-5.30pm Sat. **Credit** AmEx. **Map** p325 B2.
Browse the fancy supplements in this tiny store or just melt in to one of owner Simone's facials.

Rituals

Kalverstraat 73, Old Centre: New Side (344 9220/www.rituals.com). Tram 4, 9, 14, 16, 24, 25. **Open** noon-6pm Mon; 10am-6pm Tue, Wed, Fri; 10am-9pm Thur; 10am-5pm Sat; noon-5pm Sun. **Credit** AmEx, MC, V. **Map** p326 D3.

Design driven

The history of Dutch design has always fluttered between intrinsic orderliness (reinforced by Calvinism and De Stijl; *see p48*) and a desire for personal expression (perhaps an echo of the stubbornness required to battle the sea). And the added fact that this design is often both ingeniously functional and downright witty has resulted in a rash of worldwide acclaim – so much so that even the tourist board has jumped on the design bandwagon at www.coolcapitals.com. In fact, design has now infiltrated every level of Dutch life and death, as witnessed by designer coffin outfit **De Ode** (Levantkade 51, 419 0882, www.uitvaart.nl/ode) in the docklands area (*see p116* **Architectural reflections**).

Droog Design

Staalstraat 7A/B, The Old Centre: Old Side (523 5050/www.droogdesign.nl). Tram 4, 9, 14, 16, 24, 25. **Open** noon-6pm Tue-Sat. **Credit** MC, V. **Map** p327 E3.

This internationally acclaimed Dutch design collective has its own shop (*pictured*) with the wittiest of selections: Marcel Wanders, Hella Jongerius, Richard Hutten and Jurgen Bey.

Frozen Fountain

Prinsengracht 645, Western Canal Belt (622 9375/www.frozenfountain.nl). Tram 1, 2, 5. **Open** 1-6pm Mon; 10am-6pm Tue-Fri; 10am-5pm Sat. **Credit** AmEx, V. **Map** p329 C4.

While staying abreast of innovative young Dutch designers such as furniture god Piet Hein Eek, the 'Froz' also exhibits and sells stuff by internationals like of Marc Newsom, plus modern classics and photography.

Galerie Binnen

Keizersgracht 82, Western Canal Belt (625 9603). Tram 1, 2, 5, 13, 17. **Open** noon-6pm Wed-Sat or by appointment. **No credit cards**. **Map** p326 C2.

These noted industrial and interior design specialists have plenty of room in which to show work by unusual names (Sottsass, Kukkapuro, Studio Atika) and to host bizarre exhibits of things like toilet brushes, Benno Primsela vases or subversive Dutch art (www.dutch-souvenirs.org).

Pakhuis Amsterdam

Oosterdokkade 3-5, Waterfront (421 1033/ www.postamsterdam.nl). Tram 1, 2, 4, 5, 6, 9, 13, 16, 17, 24, 25, 26. **Open** 11am-5pm Mon-Sat; noon-5pm Sun. **Map** p327 E1.

In 2004, this showroom for 30 of Europe's top design companies settled into this former post office building alongside Centraal Station with the Stedelijk Museum (*see p125*).

SML.X

Donker Curtiusstraat 11, Westerpark (681 2837/www.sml-x.com). Tram 10/bus 18. **Open** noon-6pm Fri; noon-5pm Sat. **No credit cards**. **Map** p325 A3.

A T-shirt shop with a difference, offering an open podium for Dutch graphic/contemporary designers and graffiti artists to design and silkscreen their own shirts, then sold on site.

WonderWood

Rusland 3, Old Center: Old Side (625 3738/ www.wonderwood.nl). Tram 6, 7, 10. **Open** noon-6pm Wed-Sat. **Credit** AmEx, MC, V. **Map** p326 D5.

The name says it all: wonderfully sculpted wood in the form of shop-made originals, re-editions of global classics and plywood creations from the '40s and '50s. Wonderful.

Also...

Rozengracht and Haarlemmerstraat streets and the 'Nine Streets' are good for general design. Department store **HEMA** (*see p191* **Back to basics**) often has savvy knock-offs. **Athenaeum Nieuwscentrum** (*see p173*) is the place for design books and mags. And, of course, the **Condomerie het Gulden Vlies** (*see p193*) is a veritable Valhalla for designer peniswear. Don't knock it until you've tried it.

Kitsch Kitchen.

A store integrating products for body and home. We all have to brush our teeth and do the dishes, so the shop is full of products to ritualise such daily grinds.

Skins Cosmetics Lounge

Runstraat 9, Western Canal Belt (528 6922/www.skins.nl). Tram 1, 2, 5, 13, 14, 17. **Open** 1-7pm Mon; 11am-7pm Tue, Wed, Fri; 11am-9pm Thur; 10am-6pm Sat; noon-5pm Sun. **Credit** AmEx, DC, MC, V. **Map** p330 C4.
Sleek, sexy and full of top-of-the-range products you'll have trouble finding anywhere else in town: REN, Benefit, Creed and so on.

De Witte Tandenwinkel

Runstraat 5, Western Canal Belt (623 3443/www.dewittetandenwinkel.nl). Tram 1, 2, 5, 13, 14, 17. **Open** 1-5.30pm Mon; 10am-5.30pm Tue-Fri; 10am-5pm Sat. **Credit** AmEx, MC, V. **Map** p330 C4.
The store that's armed to the teeth with brushes and pastes to ensure that your gnashers are pearly white when you most need them to shine.

Home accessories

Kitsch Kitchen

Rozengracht 8, the Jordaan (622 8261/www.kitschkitchen.nl). Tram 13, 14, 17. **Open** 10am-6pm Mon-Sat. **Credit** AmEx, DC, MC, V. **Map** p325 B3.
Mexican Mercado with a twist. Even the hardiest resistors of tat will love the colourful culinary and household objects (including wacky wallpapers).

Outras Coisas

Herenstraat 31, Western Canal Belt (625 7281). Tram 1, 2, 5. **Open** noon-5pm Mon, Sun; 10am-6pm Tue-Sat. **Credit** AmEx, DC, MC, V. **Map** p326 C2.
All the pieces to round off your dream house: Missoni tea towels and throws, bone spoons for sampling caviar – all of life's little necessities.

Santa Jet

Prinsenstraat 7, Western Canal Belt (427 2070/www.santajet.com). Tram 1, 2, 5. **Open** 11am-6pm Mon-Fri; 10am-5pm Sat; noon-5pm Sun. **Credit** AmEx, DC, MC, V. **Map** p326 C2.
Live la vida loca with Mexican housewares. Olé!

What's Cooking

Reestraat 16, Western Canal Belt (427 0630/www.whatscooking.nl). Tram 13, 14, 17. **Open** 11am-6pm Tue-Sat. **Credit** AmEx, MC, V. **Map** p326 C3.
Pink salad bowls, green sauces, orange peppermills: culinary gifts don't come any more retina-searing.

Markets

Albert Cuypmarkt

Albert Cuypstraat, the Pijp. Tram 4, 16, 24, 25. **Open** 9.30am-5pm Mon-Sat. **No credit cards**. **Map** p331 E5.
Amsterdam's largest general market sells everything from pillows to prawns at great prices. The clothes on sale tend to be run-of-the-mill cheapies.

Boerenmarkt

Westerstraat/Noorderkerkstraat, the Jordaan. Tram 3, 10. **Open** 9am-3pm Sat. **No credit cards**. **Map** p326 B2.
Every Saturday, the Noordermarkt turns into an organic farmers' market. Groups of singers or medieval musicians sometimes perform al fresco, making the whole experience feel more like a cultural day trip than a grocery run.

Dappermarkt

Dapperstraat, Oost. Tram 3, 6, 10, 14. **Open** 9am-4pm Mon-Sat. **No credit cards**. **Map** p332 H3.
Dappermarkt is a locals' market: prices don't rise to match the number of visitors. It sells all the usual market fodder, and plenty of cheap clothes.

Looier Art & Antique Centre

Elandsgracht 109, the Jordaan (624 9038/www.looier.nl). Tram 7, 10, 17. **Open** 11am-5pm Mon-Thur, Sat, Sun. **Credit** AmEx, DC, MC, V. **Map** p330 C4.

Mainly antiques, with plenty of collectors' items. It's easy to get lost in the quiet premises and find yourself standing alone by a stall crammed with antiquated clocks ticking eerily away.

Noordermarkt

Noordermarkt, the Jordaan. Tram 3, 10. **Open** 7.30am-1pm Mon. **No credit cards**. **Map** p326 B2.

North of Westermarkt, Noordermarkt is frequented by the serious shopper. The huge stacks of (mainly second-hand) clothes, shoes, jewellery and hats need to be sorted with a grim determination, but there are real bargains to be had. Arrive early or the best stuff will probably have been nabbed. They also have an organic farmers' market on Saturdays.

Oudemanhuis Book Market

Oudemanhuispoort, Old Centre: Old Side. Tram 4, 9, 14, 16, 24, 25. **Open** 11am-4pm Mon-Fri. **No credit cards**. **Map** p326 D3.

People have been buying and selling books, prints and sheet music here since the 18th century.

Postzegelmarkt

Nieuwezijds Voorburgwal, by No.276, Old Centre: New Side. Tram 1, 2, 5, 13, 17, 20. **Open** 11am-4pm Wed, Sun. **No credit cards**. **Map** p326 D3.

A specialist market for collectors of stamps, coins, postcards and commemorative medals.

Rommelmarkt

Looiersgracht 38, the Jordaan. Tram 7, 10, 17. **Open** 11am-5pm daily. **No credit cards**. **Map** p330 C4.

A flea market where, nestled among the junk, you're likely to stumble across bargains such as a boxed set of Demis Roussos records. Tempting, no?

Waterlooplein

Waterlooplein, Jodenbuurt. Tram 9, 14, 20/Metro Waterlooplein. **Open** 9am-5.30pm Mon-Fri; 8.30am-5.30pm Sat. **No credit cards**. **Map** p327 E3.

Amsterdam's top tourist market is basically a huge flea market with the added attraction of loads of new clothes stalls (though gear can be a bit pricey and, at many stalls, a bit naff). Bargains can be found, but they may be hidden under piles of cheap 'n' nasty toasters and down-at-heel (literally) shoes.

Westermarkt

Westerstraat, the Jordaan. Tram 3, 10. **Open** 9am-1pm Mon. **No credit cards**. **Map** p326 B2.

Back to basics

The Dutch have a uniquely close relationship with their biggest of supermarket superbrands, the ubiquitous **Albert Heijn**. As a photocopy is a 'Xerox', so Dutchies call supermarkets 'Albert Heijns'. The chain was founded in 1887 in Oostzaan as a cornershop, a replica of which can be visited at the open-air museum **De Zaanse Schans** (*see p277*). And today you can rest assured that you're always within rock-throwing range of an Albie: it may be a regular AH, an 'AH XL' or a small 'AH To Go'.

You may also want to know that **Dirk van den Broek** (*see p187*) has increased selection while keeping its prices low; certainly its red 'Dirk' branded shopping bags are a bona fide hype with the fashion- and design-conscious crowd. And another tip: if you want to buy *really* cheap stuff – 39 cent beer, anyone? – keep your eyes peeled for ultra-cheap chains like **Aldi**, **Lidl** and **C1000**.

Meanwhile, in the world of department stores, **HEMA** is the undisputed heavyweight champ. A quarter of the Dutch population wakes to the ring of a HEMA alarm clock, one in three men wears HEMA underwear and one in four women wears HEMA bras. Yes, the department store chain has come a long way since 1926, when it started as a 'one price business' selling products for ten, 25 and 50 cents. It was 1969 before it stocked a product that cost more than *f*100 – an electric drill – which wreaked total havoc on the two-digit cash registers. While HEMA remains an economic place to shop for basics, it's also made a name for itself as a source of genuinely affordable design objects – even its sale flyers are graphics classics. If you like to shop, you'll love HEMA.

Albert Heijn

Nieuwezijds Voorburgwal 226, Old Centre: New Side (421 8344/www.ah.nl). Tram 1, 2, 4, 5, 9, 13, 14, 16, 17, 24, 25. **Open** 8am-10pm daily. **No credit cards**. **Map** p326 D3. **Other locations** throughout the city.

HEMA

Kalvertoren, Kalverstraat 212, Southern Canal Belt (422 8988/www.hema.nl). Tram 1, 2, 4, 5, 9, 14, 16, 24, 25. **Open** 11am-6.30pm Mon; 9.30am-6.30pm Tue, Wed, Fri; 9.30am-9pm Thur; 9.30am-6pm Sat; noon-6pm Sun. **Credit** MC, V. **Map** p326 D3. **Other locations** Ferdinand Bolstraat 93A (676 3222); Kinkerstraat 313 (683 4511); Nieuwendijk 174-176 (623 4176).

A market selling all sorts of stuff. The people packing the pavement are proof of the reasonable prices and range of goods, including new watches, pretty (and not so pretty) fabrics and cheap clothes.

Music

Vintage vinyl collectors should also head to the **Noordermarkt** and **Waterlooplein** (for both, *see p191*). The contemporary dance music vinyl junkie/DJ will find a plethora of small independent shops on both Nieuwe Nieuwstraat and its narrower parallel, Sint Nicolaasstraat.

Blue Note from Ear & Eye

Gravenstraat 12, Old Centre: New Side (428 1029). Tram 1, 2, 4, 5, 9, 13, 16, 24, 25. **Open** 11am-6pm Tue-Sat; noon-5pm Sun. **Credit** AmEx, DC, MC, V. **Map** p326 C3.

This conveniently central shop stocks a full spectrum of jazz, from '30s stompers to mainstream, avant-garde and Afro jazz. Effortlessly ool.

Charles Klassiek en Folklore

Weteringschans 193, Southern Canal Belt (626 5538). Tram 6, 7, 10, 16, 24, 25. **Open** 1-6.30pm Mon; 10am-6.30pm Tue, Wed, Fri; 10am-9pm Thur; 10am-5.30pm Sat. **Credit** AmEx, DC, MC, V. **Map** p331 E5.

Distortion Records.

Literally, 'classical and ethnic'. A good place for some of the smaller German and French labels and, bucking trends, for good, old-fashioned vinyl.

Concerto

Utrechtsestraat 52-60, Southern Canal Belt (623 5228/www.concerto.nu). Tram 4. **Open** 10am-6pm Mon-Wed, Fri, Sat; 10am-9pm Thur; noon-6pm Sun. **Credit** AmEx, DC, MC, V. **Map** p331 E4.

Head here for classic Bach recordings, obscure Beatles items, or that fave Diana Ross album that got nicked from your party. There are also second-hand 45s and new releases at decent prices.

Distortion Records

Westerstraat 244, the Jordaan (627 0004/www.distortion.nl). Tram 10. **Open** 11am-6pm Tue, Wed, Fri; 11am-9pm Thur; 10am-6pm Sat. **No credit cards**. **Map** p325 B2.

Vinyl from '70s punk rock, jazz, funk, soul, Latin, and soundtracks, through lo-fi, indie, noise, garage and industrial, to '80s and '90s indie, electro, hip hop and reggae, ending up in break beats and house for those with more dancefloor-oriented interests.

Fame

Kalverstraat 2-4, Old Centre: New Side (638 2525/www.fame.nl). Tram 1, 2, 5, 13, 14, 17. **Open** 10am-7pm Mon-Wed, Fri-Sun; 10am-9pm Thur. **Credit** AmEx, MC, V. **Map** p326 D3.

The biggest record store in Amsterdam sits bang on its busiest shopping thoroughfare. Fame offers a vast array of stock in a variety of genres.

Fat Beats

Singel 10, Western Canal Belt (423 0886/www.fatbeats.com). Tram 1, 2, 5. **Open** 1pm-7pm Mon-Wed, Fri-Sun; 1pm-9pm Thur. **Credit** AmEx, MC, V. **Map** p326 C2.

Amsterdam's one-stop hip hop shop and distributor. With its roots in NYC, Fat Beats has all the vinyl and CDs that any DJ (or aspiring upstart) could dream of. Staff are seriously informed and have all the dirt on the local party and music scene.

Get Records

Utrechtsestraat 105, Southern Canal Belt (622 3441/www.getrecords.nl). Tram 4. **Open** noon-6pm Mon, Sun; 10am-6pm Tue, Wed, Sat; 10am-7pm Thur, Fri. **Credit** AmEx, DC, MC, V. **Map** p331 E4.

A popular store propped up by a dedicated pack of regulars. Much of the vinyl has been cleared away to make room for a savvy pick of alternative and independent CDs; it's also good for roots, Americana and dance. Don't miss the 'cheapies' corner at the front.

Palm Guitars

's Gravelandseveer 5, Old Center: Old Side (422 0445/www.palmguitars.nl). Tram 4, 9, 16, 24, 25. **Open** noon-6pm Wed-Sat. **Credit** AmEx, DC, MC, V. **Map** p327 E3.

Palm Guitars stocks new, antique, used and rare musical instruments (and their parts). The excellent website features a calendar of upcoming local gigs, all of a worldly and rootsy nature.

Holy smoke! **PGC Hajenius** does the stogie boogie.

Pharmacies

Dam Apotheek

Damstraat 2, Old Centre: Old Side (624 4331/www.dam-apotheek.nl). Tram 4, 9, 14, 16, 24, 25. **Open** 8.30am-5.30pm Mon-Fri; 10am-5pm Sat. **No credit cards. Map** p326 D3.

This central pharmacy has extended opening hours. Should you need a late pharmacy, *see p305.*

Lairesse Apotheek

Lairessestraat 40, Museum Quarter (662 1022/www.delairesseapotheek.nl). Tram 3, 5, 12, 16. **Open** 8.30am-6pm Mon-Fri; 10am-4pm Sat. **Credit** MC, V. **Map** p330 D6.

One of the largest suppliers of alternative medicines in the country, chemist Marjan Terpstra wanted her shop to reflect her speciality. Designed by Concrete, the shop is out of the way if you're just popping in for haemorrhoid cream, but the interior is so inspiring it should be on any design junkie's must-see list.

Sex shops

Absolute Danny

Oudezijds Achterburgwal 78, Old Centre: Old Side (421 0915/www.absolutedanny.com). Tram 4, 9, 16, 24. **Open** 11am-9pm Mon-Thur, Sun; 11am-10pm Fri, Sat. **Credit** AmEx, DC, MC, V. **Map** p326 D2.

A stalwart of the sex scene in a city known for doing the deed, Absolute Danny stocks everything from rubber clothes to erotic toothbrushes.

Condomerie het Gulden Vlies

Warmoesstraat 141, Old Centre: Old Side (627 4174/www.condomerie.com). Tram 4, 9, 14, 16, 24, 25. **Open** 11am-6pm Mon-Sat. **Credit** AmEx, DC, MC, V. **Map** p326 D2.

A variety of rubbers of the non-erasing kind to wrap up trouser snakes of all shapes and sizes in a store that's equal parts amusing and inspiring.

Female & Partners

Spuistraat 100, Old Centre: New Side (620 9152/www.femaleandpartners.nl). Tram 1, 2, 5, 13, 17. **Open** 1-6pm Mon, Sun; 11am-6pm Tue, Wed, Fri, Sat; 11am-9pm Thur. **Credit** AmEx, DC, MC, V. **Map** p326 C2.

It's fair to say that, in terms of the sex industry at least, Amsterdam is a man's world. The opposite of most enterprises here, Female & Partners bucks the trend by welcoming women (and, yes, their partners) with an array of clothes, videos and toys.

Mail & Female

Nieuwe Vijzelstraat 2, Southern Canal Belt (623 3916/www.mailfemale.com). Tram 7, 10, 16, 24, 25. **Open** 11am-7pm Mon-Sat. **Map** p331 E5.

The Netherlands' oldest mail-order shop for saucy toys and clothes now has a friendly walk-in outlet.

Stout

Berenstraat 9, Western Canal Belt (620 1676/www.stoutinternational.com). Tram 13, 14, 17. **Open** noon-7pm Mon-Fri; 11am-6pm Sat; 1-5pm Sun. **Credit** AmEx, DC, MC, V. **Map** p330 C4.

Naughty and nice lingerie and sex toys for the thinking gal: La Fille D'O, Marvel & Malizia, Dolce & Gabbana, John Galliano, Eres and more.

Tobacconists

PGC Hajenius

Rokin 92-96, Old Centre: New Side (623 7494/www.hajenius.com). Tram 4, 9, 14, 16, 24, 25. **Open** noon-6pm Mon; 9.30am-6pm Tue, Wed, Fri; 9.30am-9pm Thur; noon-5pm Sat, Sun. **Credit** AmEx, DC, MC, V. **Map** p326 D3.

A smoker's paradise (tobacco, not dope) for over 250 years, Hajenius offers cigarabilia from traditional Dutch pipes to own-brand cigars. With its art deco interior and inimitable old world aesthetics, even anti-smokers should pop in for a whiff.

lean water. It's the most basic human necessity. Yet one third of all poverty related deaths
re caused by drinking dirty water. Saying *I'm in* means you're part of a growing movement
hat's fighting the injustice of poverty. Your £8 a month can help bring safe water to some
f the world's poorest people. We can do this. We *can* end poverty. Are you in?
shouldn't everyone get clean water? I don't think that's too much to ask for
et's end poverty together.
ext 'WATER' and your name to 87099 to give £8 a month.
tandard text rates apply. Registered charity No.202918
oxfam.org.uk
i'm in
Oxfam
Sarite Morales, Greenwich

Arts & Entertainment

Features

Festivals & Events

Come rain or shine, Amsterdam has a whole host of dates for your diary.

Although they're generally reserved, the Dutch do often shed their inhibitions and dive into a fun-seeking frenzy. On the likes of **Oudejaarsavond** (New Year's Eve; *see p202*) and **Koninginnedag** (Queen's Day; *see p197* and *p202* **Orange for all**), and whenever Ajax win a big game, the city falls into an orange-tinted psychosis of song, drink and dance. Not every event is so booze-dependent: check out the **Dam tot Damloop**, **Museum Night** or **Open Monument Days**. That said, could the **High Times Cannabis Cup** really be held anywhere else?

The **AUB** (0900 0191, www.aub.nl) and the **Amsterdam Tourist Board** (0900 400 4040; *see p312*) list many upcoming events, as does the free-around-town *Amsterdam Weekly* (www.amsterdamweekly.nl). For a list of public holidays, *see p312*. Unless otherwise stated, all events are free.

Frequent events

Arts & crafts markets

Spui *Old Centre: New Side (www.artplein-spui.nl). Tram 1, 2, 4, 5, 9, 14, 16, 24, 25.* **Map** p330 D4. **Date** 10am-6pm Sun.
Thorbeckeplein *Southern Canal Belt (www.modern-art-market.nl). Tram 4, 9, 14.* **Map** p331 E4. **Date** *Mar-Oct* 10am-6pm Sun.

Festivals

Amsterdam Dance Event
Clubbing without limits. *See p201.*

Amsterdam Gay Pride
Sheer bloody madness. *See p200.*

Koninginnedag
A right royal knees-up. *See p197.*

Kunstvlaai
Art in the coolest of parks. *See p198.*

Museum Night
Culture in the dark. *See p201.*

Uitmarkt
A taste of the cultural season. *See p200.*

Oil paintings, acrylics, watercolours, graphic arts, sculpture, ceramics and jewellery are all offered at these two small weather-dependent open-air Sunday arts and crafts markets. The one on Spui has a rotating system for the 60 or so artists, and both have buskers to help the browsing crowds choose. It's not the most original art in the world, but it makes for a nice Sunday afternoon stroll.

Antiques market

Nieuwmarkt, Old Centre: Old Side. Tram 9, 14/Metro Nieuwmarkt. **Map** p326 D2. **Date** *Apr-Aug* 9am-5pm Sun.
A few streets away from the ladies in the windows, this antiques and bric-a-brac market attracts browsers looking for other kinds of pleasures. There are plenty to be found, too, such as books, furniture and objets d'art.

Rowing contests

Amsterdamse Bos, Bosbaan 6 (646 2740/www.knrb.nl). Bus 170, 171, 172. **Date** Apr-Dec.
In this huge man-made forest in the south of the city, rowing contests take place almost all year-round. Check local press or the tourist board for details.

Book markets

Various locations (627 5794). **Date** varies.
Head for the year-round book stalls on Spui (9am-6pm Fri) and Oudemanhuispoort (noon-6pm Mon-Sat; *see p191*), but don't miss out on the four temporary markets in summer. Two of them sit along the Amstel, behind Waterlooplein (art book market, mid June; religion, mid Aug) and two emerge on Dam (children's, mid May; mysteries, mid July). Also, once a year – in summer or autumn and on a non-fixed date – there's a small bookmarket on Marie Heinekenplein in the Pijp.

Spring

Spring is awaited with anticipation. After the long, grey and chilly winter, the tulips and crocuses come alive and push through the earth, and the locals follow them. As soon as the sun shows its face, terraces are hastily erected and punters move outside en masse. After a season with little going on, spring is also the start of a new buzzing cultural year.

Amsterdam Restaurant Week

Various locations (www.restaurantweek.nl). **Date** Mar.
A three-course gourmet meal in a top restaurant for only €25? Only in Amsterdam Restaurant Week. Just like in New York, where the idea originated,

local restaurant owners think this is a great way to promote their businesses, especially since January and February are slow months in food-land. The food isn't fast, but your reservation should be: tables get booked up very quickly.

Stille Omgang (Silent Procession)

Starts at Spui, Begijnhof (www.stille-omgang.nl).
Date weekend after 10 Mar.

This singular annual event commemorates the 1345 'Miracle of Amsterdam'. A sick man, thought to be dying, was being administered the last rites, at which point which he vomited. Since he had already been given the viaticum, what was thrown up was put into the fire. But the Blessed Sacrament was discovered the next day, undamaged by fire or digestion, and the man miraculously recovered. Every year since, local Catholics make a silent nocturnal walk that begins and ends at Spui. The candlelit procession through the Red Light District at night is both a surreal and extremely moving experience.

World Press Photo

Oude Kerk, Oudekerksplein 23, Old Centre: Old Side (625 8284/www.worldpressphoto.nl). Tram 4, 9, 16, 24, 25. **Admission** €5. **Map** p326 D2. **Date** mid Apr.

Running since 1955, this is the world's largest photography competition, and includes exhibits from thousands of photojournalists. The exhibition is held in the Oude Kerk (*see p93*); after kicking off in Amsterdam, it goes on tour to another 70 locations around the world. A book containing the prize-winning entries is published each year.

National Museum Weekend

Around the Netherlands (www.museumweekend.nl).
Admission mostly free. **Date** early-mid Apr.

Around a million visitors flock to one or more of the 500 state-funded museums, which offer free or discounted admission and special activities during National Museum Weekend. To find out where to go, simply pick up the NMW newspaper at any of the major museums.

Koninginnedag (Queen's Day)

Around the city. **Date** 30 Apr.

The most popular event in the city actually kicks off the night before, with street parties and late-night drinking sessions in cafés. The date in question was the late Queen Juliana's birthday and not that of Beatrix, but it doesn't matter: locals and tourists still crowd the streets in search of a bargain (there's a huge open-air market where people are allowed to sell their attic junk), and to sing and dance. The best areas to experience the festivities are the Jordaan, Rembrandtplein and the centre; Vondelpark is for the kids. *See also p202* **Orange for all**.

Painting the town orange on **Koninginnedag (Queens Day)**.

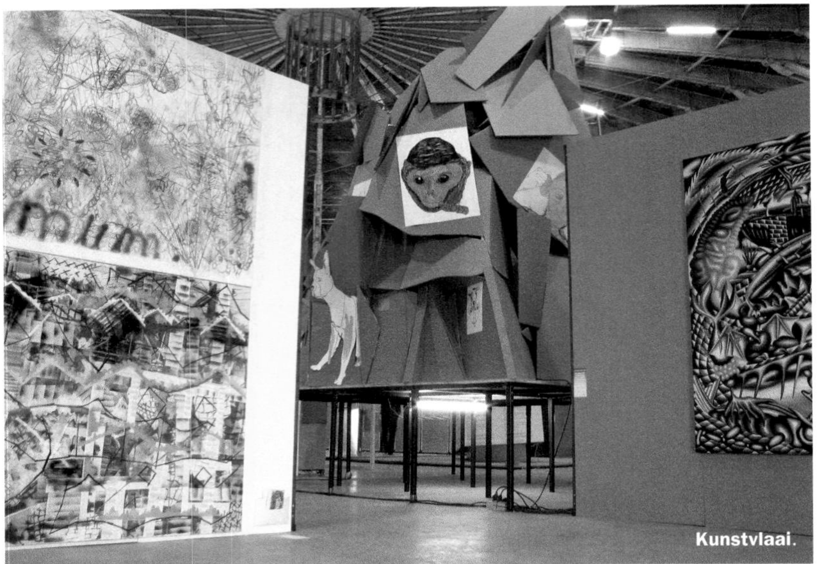
Kunstvlaai.

Herdenkingsdag & Bevrijdingsdag (Remembrance Day & Liberation Day)

Remembrance Day *National Monument, Dam, Old Centre: Old Side. Tram 1, 2, 4, 5, 9, 13, 14, 16, 17, 24, 25.* **Map** p326 D3. **Date** 4 May.
Liberation Day *Vondelpark, Museum Quarter. Tram 1, 2, 3, 5, 6, 12.* **Map** p330 C6. **Date** 5 May.
Ooosterpark Festival *Oosterpark Oost (www. oosterparkfestival.nl). Tram 3, 6, 9, 14.* **Map** p332 H3. **Date** 5 May.
In the presence of the Queen and many dignitaries, those who lost their lives during World War II are remembered at the National Monument on Dam Square on 4 May at 7.30pm. After the laying of wreaths, there's a two-minute silence at 8pm. Gays and lesbians have their own ceremony at a remembrance service at the Homomonument (*see p221*) and there are also other ceremonies in various quarters around the city.

Liberation Day is celebrated on 5 May with music and speeches. There's also a market where you can sell the unwanted junk you bought while drunk on Queen's Day a week earlier. The best areas for visitors are Museumplein, Leidseplein and Westermarkt, the focal point of the gay commemorations. In Oosterpark, in the culturally varied east of Amsterdam, the Oosterparkfestival is all about emphasising community between different nationalities through the shared mediums of music, cultural customs, sports and food.

National Windmill Day

Around the Netherlands (0900 400 4040/ www.visitamsterdam.nl). **Date** 2nd Sat in May.
Got a windmill on your mind? On this day, about 600 state-subsidised windmills spin their sails and open to the public. Most of them have demonstrations and activities; you can even buy products such as flour and mill bread made the traditional way.

National Cycling Day

Around the Netherlands (0900 400 4040/ www.visitamsterdam.nl). **Date** late May.
On your marks, get set, go! Roughly 200,000 cyclists spin their wheels around 200 special cycle routes of varying lengths and difficulty, making this a day for both *fiets* fanatics and families.

Art Amsterdam

RAI Congresgebouw, Europaplein, Zuid (549 1212/www.kunstrai.nl). Tram 4, 25/NS rail RAI station. **Admission** €10-€15. **No credit cards**. **Date** mid May-early June.
A hundred or so galleries, both national and international, present their artists' work at this huge commercial five-day exhibition (formerly known as KunstRAI). Expect everything from ceramics and jewellery to paintings and sculptures.

Kunstvlaai

Westergasfabriek, Haarlemmerweg 8-10, Westerpark (588 2400/www.sandberg.nl/www.kunstvlaai.nl). Tram 10. **Map** p325 A1. **Date** biannual: May 2008.
This edgy art market was the answer to the more commercial KunstRAI, now Art Amsterdam (*see above*), but now works in collaboration with its erstwhile rival. It focuses on new and more original artists, groups and galleries.

Open Ateliers (Open Studios): Kunstroute de Westelijke Eilanden

Prinseneiland, Bickerseiland & Realeneiland (627 1238/www.oawe.nl). **Date** mid May.
Neighbourhoods with populations of artists and artists' studio complexes, among them the Jordaan and the Pijp, hold open days in spring and autumn, when dozens of artists (both starving and successful) open their doors to the public over the course of a weekend. The annual Westelijke Eilanden is the most popular: situated on the picturesque and peaceful islands around Prinseneiland, the streets are all connected by traditional 'skinny bridges'.

Europerve

Information: Demask, Zeedijk 64, Old Centre: Old Side (620 5603/www.demask.com). **Admission** prices vary. **Date** May.
The reputation of this wicked evening attracts an international crowd for whom nothing is too bizarre or too kinky. What started out as an opening party for the shop Demask in 1990 has gone big and gone global, and now includes DJs, performances, fashion shows, dancing, naughty games and friction fun. There's a large play area for the publicly inclined. Leather, latex, PVC and/or adult-sized nappies are required dress. A bizarre experience that will baffle the uninitiated.

Summer

Summertime, and the living is easy. Locals love the sun, and drop everything to move outdoors. Hot spots for sunbathing include the nearby beaches at Bloemendaal, Zandfoort and Wijk aan Zee, along with the city's urban beaches (*see p159* **United we sand**); IJburg, a short tram ride from Central Station, is the favourite, as it allows swimming. Vondelpark, the city's green lung, gets jammed with skaters, joggers, sun-worshippers, bongo players and artists during the season at Vondelpark Openluchttheater (*see below*).

Vondelpark Openluchttheather

Vondelpark (www.vondelpark.nl). Tram 1, 2, 5, 3, 12. **Date** early June-mid Aug.
Each year in the summer months, the big open-air stage in the popular park is used to the max. Tuesday is classical music, Friday is dancing, Saturday afternoon is for kids, Saturday evenings are for stand-up and Sunday is for pop music. It's great to watch and dance, or just to chill and relax: few places capture the laid-back vibe of Amsterdam in the summer with quite such conviction. To find out who's playing when, check out the posters at the gates or look online.

Holland Festival

Stadsschouwburg, Leidseplein, Southern Canal Belt (530 7110/www.holndfstvl.nl). Tram 1, 2, 5, 6, 7, 10. **Admission** €10-€40. **Credit** AmEx, MC, V. **Map** p330 C5. **Date** early-mid June.
In 2007, this hugely popular festival of the arts celebrated its 60th anniversary. On the menu are art, dance, opera, theatre, literature and a whole lot more. The programme includes both mainstream and oddball works, and is held in the Stadsschouwburg (*see p240*) and other venues such as Westergasfabriek and Het Muziektheater. Tickets go on sale months before the event: in 2007, they were offered as early as March, so do check the online reservation service or head to the venue in plenty of time.

Canal Gardens in Bloom

Around Amsterdam (www.amsterdamsegrachtentuin.nl). **Date** mid June. **Admission**: €12.
This event sees owners of the beautiful, hidden gardens behind posh canal houses open their doors, giving the public a chance to have a peek at these stunning secret gems. Dogs and prams are sadly not allowed and wheelchair access is almost impossible.

Kwak addicts

There are not a lot of reasons for visitors to go to Bijlmermeer, in the south-east of Amsterdam. Sure, there's the ArenA football stadium (*see p251*), the Heineken Music Hall (*see p232*) and even an 'Office of the Future' (www.livtom.nl) for those interested in exploring the doubtless fascinating future of corporate sponsorship. But the area is still most famous as the site of a devastating Boeing 747 crash in 1992, in which countless people were killed (the precise number is unknown because many residents were unregistered illegal residents).

Money has been pumped into the area over the last decade, and the preponderance of barbecued Surinamese eateries remains a definite plus for the culturally curious, but Bijlmermeer remains truly desperate for more positive marketing. Still, there is one definite high spot: **Kwakoe**, a free, family-orientated festival that takes place over six weekends during the height of summer.

If it's a sunny weekend, Kwakoe becomes the ultimate multicultural festival in this most multicultural of towns. Drop in on the event and you might find excellent music, out-there theatre, alternative film, exciting sports and a large range of exotic food stalls, all drawn from outside the usual orbit of most Amsterdammers. If you squint a bit and settle into one of the 'beach tents' in the woods beyond the football field, it's even possible to imagine that you're in a tropical paradise.

De Parade

Martin Luther Kingpark, Zuid (033 465 4555/www.deparade.nl). Tram 25/Metro Amstel. **Admission** free-€10. **No credit cards. Date** 1st 2wks in Aug (3pm-1am Mon-Thur, Sun; 3pm-2am Fri, Sat).

When this travelling show (Rotterdam, the Hague and Utrecht are also on their route) lands in the city, locals flock en masse to sip litres of rosé, hang out in a beer garden and catch an act (cabaret, music, comedy, drama) in one of the many kitschly decorated tents that gives the whole thing a vibe of ancient carnivals. Afternoons are child-friendly.

Amsterdam Gay Pride

Prinsengracht, Canal Belt (620 8807/www.amsterdampride.nl). Tram 13, 14, 17. **Map** p326 C1. **Date** 1st Sat in Aug 2-5pm.

Though Gay Pride is always surrounded by drama and controversy, whether around money, politics or big egos, the atmosphere is just fabulouslytastic *dahlink* during the spectacular boat parade. Around 250,000 spectators line the Prinsengracht to watch the 80 boats, all with garish decorations and loud sound systems crewed by bare-chested sailors. It's the climax to a whole weekend of activities; check the website for the full array of what's on offer.

Appelsap

Oosterpark, Oost (www.appelsap.net). Tram 3, 6, 9, 14. **Map** p332 H3. **Date** mid Aug.

This free outdoor hip hop festival is organised by Appelsap, who also run club nights and parties. No matter the unpredictable weather, the atmosphere is always hot, with a programme of up-and-coming artists and some local favourites.

Hartjesdag

Zeedijk, Old Centre: Old Side (625 8467/www.hartjesdagen.nl). Tram 4, 9, 14, 16, 24, 25. **Map** p326 D2. **Date** mid Aug.

An ancient Amsterdam celebration from the Middle Ages, 'Hearts Day' was held on the last Monday of August and involved much drinking, cross-dressing and firecrackers. It was in abeyance for decades after the Germans banned it in 1943 but was resurrected in 1997 on the initiative of local shopkeepers, once the formerly seedy street had been cleaned up and rid of druggies, and now focuses primarily on the boozing and dressing-up side of things. Though not a drag queen festival, it's predictably popular with the city's transvestite population, as are its associated theatrical and music events.

SAIL

Around Amsterdam (681 1804/www.sail-amsterdam.nl). **Date** 19-23 Aug 2010.

An event that started in 1975 to celebrate the city's 700th birthday has turned into the largest nautical gathering in Europe. An extraordinary 2.5 million visitors stroll along Oostelijke Handelskade every five years (it's next due in 2010), admiring dozens of tall ships and thousands of more modern boats. The flotilla of related events includes music, food, extreme sports and art.

Open Haven Podium

On and around Java-eiland (423 5615/www.openhavenpodium.nl). **Date** mid Aug.

Whether or not you go by boat, the western tip of Java-eiland is the place to head in August for an array of harbour-themed art, music, theatre and children's activities. Delightfully, it's all organised by the bars, theatres and galleries in the immediate neighbourhood.

Uitmarkt

Various locations. 2007: Oostelijke Handelskade (www.uitmarkt.nl). **Date** last weekend in Aug.

From Friday to Sunday, the chaotic Uitmarkt previews the coming cultural season with foretastes of theatre, opera, dance and music events. It's all free, and as such it gets very crowded.

Autumn

It's raining, it's pouring… but the city certainly isn't boring. Weather-wise, autumn might not the best season for outdoor activities (notwithstanding the occasional Indian summer), but don't let that put you off. Come September, the droves of tourists and backpackers slowly disappear, and the city starts to breathe again. At the same time, touring bands once again return to the Melkweg, the Paradiso and the Heineken Music Hall, and the true spirit of the city comes bubbling back to the surface. Just be sure to bring a brolly and be prepared to duck into a bar to avoid the elements. Hardly a hardship.

Open Monument Days

Around Amsterdam (552 4888/www.openmonumentendag.nl). **Date** 2nd weekend in Sept.

'Heritage Days', as it's officially called, gives you the chance to visit buildings that are normally closed to the public. Some are breathtaking historic buildings from the Golden Age; others, though, are schools, industrial buildings (old factories, say) or even farms. The event is defined by a different theme each year. Look out for the Monumenten flag, check the website or pick up a brochure at the VVV. Don't worry if you happen to be out of town: roughly 85 per cent of Dutch municipalities participate.

Dam tot Damloop

Prins Hendrikkade in Amsterdam, to Peperstraat in Zaandam (72 533 8136/www.damloop.nl). **Entry fee** €3-€13.50. **Date** 3rd Sun in Sept.

The annual 'Dam to Dam Run' stretches 16.1km (ten miles) from Amsterdam to Zaandam, including running through the IJ tunnel and then back again. Up to 200,000 people gather to watch the 30,000 participants trying to finish in the two-hour limit. If you're not a world-class athlete, you can participate in the recreational four-mile mini-marathon. Bands line the route along the way and there's a circus in Zaandam to keep the little ones amused.

High Times Cannabis Cup

Melkweg, Lijnbaansgracht 234A (531 8181/www.cannabiscup.com). Tram 1, 2, 5, 6, 7, 10. **Entry fee** varies. **No credit cards. Map** p330 C5. **Date** Nov.

In the past few years, the city council has become less easygoing when it comes to coffeeshops and other soft drugs. However, no restrictions are made for the annual High Times contest, where all things related to wastedness are celebrated over five days. There are banquets, bands, cultivation seminars and a competition where hundreds of judges (including you, if you wish) ascertain which of the hundreds of weeds are the wickedest, dude. The event is scattered all over town (as, frankly, are the minds of the participants), but it's invariably focused on the Melkweg at night.

Crossing Border

Various locations in the Hague (70 346 2355/www.crossingborder.nl). Den Haag CS. **Admission** *Day* €5. *Evening* €25-€28. **Date** Oct/Nov.

This festival is a crossover between writers, poets and musicians. It's held in the Hague city centre, only a 45-minute train trip away; past participants have include Razorlight, David Byrne, David Sedaris, Henry Rollins, Robert Crumb, Norman Mailer, Dave Eggers, Jill Scott and Irvine Welsh.

Amsterdam Dance Event

Around Amsterdam (035 621 8748/www.amsterdam-dance-event.nl). **Admission** varies. **Date** mid Oct.

The organisers claim that this festival, which draws 30,000 each year, is the world's biggest festival of clubbing. It combines business with pleasure: during the day, there are conferences and workshops, while at night, roughly international 400 acts and DJs make sure your feet don't stay still.

Bock Beer Festival

Beurs van Berlage, Damrak, Old Centre 277 (530 4141/www.beursvanberlage.nl/www.pint.nl). Tram 4, 9, 14, 16, 24, 25. **Date** late Oct.

The former stock exchange (*see p84*) is the site of this annual, three-day celebration of seasonal beer. Though there are performances, the real reason to visit is to taste some of the 50 or so different varieties of this full-bodied, slightly sweet and usually dark beer of German origin. Boozehounds should also check the PINT website above for details of other local beer festivals.

Museum Night

Around Amsterdam (621 1311/www.n8.nl). **Date** Nov.

The success of this night (tickets sell fast) shows that the locals like to mix art with entertainment. Almost every museum and gallery in town opens late and organises something special to complement the regular exhibits. You might watch Kirk Douglas as Vincent in *Lust for Life* at the Van Gogh Museum, or dance the night away in the shadow of Rembrandt's *Night Watch*.

Sinterklaas Intocht

Route via Barbizon Palace on Prins Hendrikkade, Damrak, Dam, Raadhuisstraat, Rozengracht, Marnixstraat, Leidseplein. **Date** mid Nov.

Anticipated for weeks by every kid, Sinterklaas (St Nicholas) marks the beginning of the Christmas season by stepping ashore from a steamboat at Centraal Station. In his white beard, red robe and mitre, St Nick parades around the centre of town on his horse. His staff, dozens of blacked-up Zwarte Piet (Black Peter) helpers, hand out sweets. Some believe that Black Peter was originally the devil; the colour and appetite

Uitmarkt.

for mischief are the only leftovers of an evil vanquished by Sinterklaas; others say he got his dark skin from climbing down chimneys to deliver sweets.

Winter

Winter is relatively quiet in Amsterdam, and people generally stay in and prepare for the family festivals: St Nicholas's Day, as important to the Dutch as Christmas, and New Year's Eve. The days when the main canals regularly froze solid enough for skating are sadly long gone. Still, you might be lucky to catch a cold snap, and find many locals skating along the Amstel and smaller waterways nearby.

Sinterklaas

Around Amsterdam. **Date** 5, 6 Dec.

While St Nicholas, aka Sinterklaas, is directing his Black Peter helpers down chimneys on the eve of his feast day (6 December), families celebrate by exchanging small gifts and poems. The tradition started when the Church decided to tame the riot and disorder that had always accompanied the end of the slaughter season. It began by ruling that the traditional celebration should be based around the birthday of St Nicholas, the patron saint of children (and, for that matter, of prostitutes, of thieves and of Amsterdam itself); a once-violent tradition was reborn as a Christian family feast. Sinterklaas eventually emigrated to the States, changed his name to Santa Claus and gave out presents on 25 December.

Oudejaarsavond (New Year's Eve)

Around Amsterdam. **Date** 31 Dec.

No, you haven't got off the wrong train or plane, and you're not in a war zone: New Year's Eve is a riot of champagne, *oliebollen* (greasy deep-fried blobs of dough, apple and raisins), and tons and tons of scary fireworks that officially only go on sale the day before. Come midnight, people take to the streets (and bars, many of which only open at midnight) to celebrate. The best areas to visit are Nieuwmarkt and Dam Square; the latter often stages a big council-sponsored concert, with Dutch acts and DJs to help keep things moving.

Chinese New Year

Nieuwmarkt, Old Centre: Old Side (06 2476 0060/ www.zeedijk.nl). **Map** p326 D2. **Date** late Jan/ early Feb.

The Nieuwmarkt is a focal point for Amsterdam's Chinatown, complete with restaurants, a temple and a fantastic supermarket selling all things Asian. Chinese New Year is welcomed during the daytime with lion dances, firecrackers, and Chinese drums and gongs.

Amsterdam International Fashion Week

Westergasfabriek (www.aifw.nl). **Date** Jan, July.

Twice a year, in summer and winter, aspiring designers and those who've already made it show their new collections at the Westergasfabriek. Sip cocktails and marvel at the models on show.

Orange for all

First-time visitors to Amsterdam arriving on 30 April often get confused. 'I heard it was a happening town,' you'll hear them exclaim, 'but I didn't know it was like *this*.' It isn't, of course; indeed, it's pretty lucky for everyone that the chaotic, incomparable **Queen's Day**, (Koninginnedag, in the local lingo) occurs only once a year. Lovers of parties, collectors of crap and students of the surreal should ensure that their visit coincides with April 30, when up to one million extra people pour into the city. Making any grand plans for May 1 isn't really advisable.

In theory, Queen's Day is a celebration of Beatrix's birthday. As it happens, her birthday falls in winter, but the ever-pragmatic Dutch choose to celebrate it on her mother's birthday, when the climatic conditions are more clement. Still, Her Highness is soon forgotten amid all the revelry. You might discover a leather-boy disco party on one side street, boogie through to hear an old-school Jordaan crooner on another, before a boat bellows by with a heavy metal band on deck, whose amps get short-circuited at the next bridge when a gang of boys dressed in head-to-toe orange urinate on them. If nothing else, you'll come away with a few unhinged stories of debauched derring-do to tell your grandchildren. (If you have your own offspring in tow, head straight to Vondelpark, which is dedicated to children.)

The gay and lesbian festivities spread like ripples from the Homomonument (*see p221*) and the Reguliersdwaarsstraat, while Dam Square becomes a fairground. Minds get clogged with an overdose of sensations, and pockets slowly empty as punters get tricked into buying just what they always (read: never) wanted. How are you going to explain that pair of orange clogs when you get back home? No matter: with all the performances, the markets, the crowds and, of course, the alcohol, the streets of Amsterdam have all you ever dreamed of finding... and plenty that was far beyond your imagination.

Children

Sticking up for the little guy.

To be a kid in Amsterdam is to be pretty damn lucky – so lucky, in fact, that a 2007 UNICEF report deemed the Netherlands the best place in the world to grow up. The huge amount of activities on offer – culturally, educationally and just for fun – is staggering, both for those passing through and those in it for the long haul.

Trendy parents have come to the right place: Amsterdammers do love to hang out with their kids without compromising their style. Some of the hippest shops, cinemas, cafés and cultural hotspots welcome the younger customer. On Wednesday afternoons, when all schools finish at midday, there's particularly plenty going on. Check out the 'Jeugd' or 'Kind' sections in one of several free mags like *NL20*, *Zone 020* or the newcomer especially for kids, *Yeah Baby!*.

Unlike most major cities, Amsterdam's small scale and intrinsic attractiveness make it a real pleasure to walk around, even for those with smaller legs and stamina. The old wonky houses, the canals and wacky bikes can keep boredom at bay for a decent amount of time, and when a break is needed there's always a café close at hand for a mug of *warme chocolademelk* and a *tosti kaas*. Changing facilities, on the other hand, are few and far between: the best bets are department stores or the public library. Hire bikes if you want to do as the Dutch do; mini *bakfiets* (bikes with containers at the front, often divided into seats) are great for loading in your pre-pedalling offspring. If you're bringing kids in a pushchair, trams may be a necessity, but can be a bit of a nightmare – especially older ones. You'll find yourself in competition with other buggy-wielding parents determined to nab the best spot – it's each family unit for itself. Without a pushchair, trams make an excellent and cheap way of viewing the city at leisure.

A trip on the canals is a must for all ages: either take one of the numerous tourist cruises or rent canal bikes. Kids get a huge kick out of pedalling themselves around (although you might feel a bit of a prat). For a free ride, catch the IJ ferry linking Noord to the rest of the city; boats leave from behind Centraal Station every ten minutes or so. If you're lucky enough to be visiting when the canals freeze over, you'll be able to join in a unique event, when hundreds of families take to the ice for skating fun. For more information about transport, *see p296*.

The best Kids' stuff

TunFun
Great balls of fun! *See p207*.

Klankspeeltuin
Come on feel the noise. *See p207*.

Nemo
Recreational science for Frankenstein's little monsters. *See p205*.

Vondelpark
Fresh air, exercise and ice cream. A real pleasure for young and old alike. *See p205*.

Cinekid
For miniature movie buffs. *See p205*.

Amsterdam

Creative arts

Akooka Works

Witte de Withstraat 22, Oud West (778 6655/www.akookaworks.nl). Tram 7, 17. **Open** 2-3.30pm, 3.30-5pm Sat and by appointment. **Cost** €12.50 per session. **Map** p329 A5.

The whole family is welcome at this brightly coloured studio workshop where children (and adults) can explore their artistic fantasies under the guidance of owner/artist Anouk. All paints, pastels and inks used are professional standard, and the price includes a canvas that you get to keep. There are special activities over the school holidays and themed birthday parties are available.

Keramiekstudio Color Me Mine

Roelof Hartstraat 22, Museum Quarter (675 2987/www.amsterdam.colormemine.nl). Trams 3, 5, 12, 24. **Open** 11am-7pm Tue, Wed; 11am-10pm Thur-Sat; noon-6pm Sun (family day). **Cost** painting time €14.50 over-12s; €10 under-12s, plus cost of ceramic item. **Credit** MC, V.

Children choose a ceramic from a selection of 400 – ranging from tiny buttons to giant vases – and then decorate them, or they can design and make their own mosaic. All the materials are non-toxic, and staff are happy to advise little ones suffering an early onset of artist's block. Tots under six need to be accompanied by an adult.

CriCri

Overtoom 303, Oud West (616 2886/www.cricri.nl). Tram 1. **Open** varies. **Cost** €10-€15 per session. **Map** p329 B5.

A creative enterprise unlike any other. The owner of CriCri has developed her own personal style derived from traditional Florentine decorative arts such as marbling, antiquing and colour washing, which she combines with crafts such as felt-work and candle-making. This unique style using natural materials gives her shop-cum-studio a magical fairy-tale feel, with great child appeal. The kids' workshops include candle-making, felt-crafting, collage and bead work, but are individually tailored according to each child's particular interests.

Films

Most films are dubbed, but you can often catch the same movies being shown in their original language at off-peak times (look for 'OV' in the listings). A number of independent cinemas have regular international children's programmes, usually on Wednesday and Sunday afternoons. Check the **Kriterion** (*see p210*), the **Rialto** (*see p212*) and the **Nederlands Filmmuseum** (*see p213*). Also, the good children's bookshop **Helden en Boeven** (De Waag, Nieuwmarkt, 427 4407, www.heldenboeven.nl) has regular screenings in the impressive old Waag (*see p88*), opposite their shop on the Nieuwmarkt.

Nemo.

The *filmladder* (hung in most cafés) has times and other information on all but the smallest of cinemas. During the autumn holidays, the excellent **Cinekid** film festival (531 7890, www.cinekid.nl) takes place in Amsterdam, offering quality films from around the globe, including many in English.

Museums

Dry and dull they ain't: the Dutch take huge pride in their innovative approach. Museums are either highly interactive, extraordinarily life-like or sometimes even the real thing, like the **Woonbootmuseum** (*see p104*), where you can experience life on a houseboat. Or catch a ride on the **Electrische Museumtramlijn** (*see p126* **Museums for the mildly obsessed**), an antique tram taking a scenic route through the Amsterdamse Bos. The popular **Van Gogh Museum** hosts children's sessions every Saturday and Sunday at 11.30am-1.15pm and 2-3.45pm. They begin with a full tour of the museum and end in the kids' studio where the children make their own paintings. Great value at €4 a time; children can also take the audio tour (in Dutch) for €2.50. Likewise the **CoBrA Museum** (*see p128*), over in Amstelveen, which also stimulates kids' interests with the colours of the CoBrA artists. Every Sunday from 11am to 2pm it hosts the *kinder atelier*, where children can paint, draw and discuss art under the guidance of a teacher. For a genuine *Pirates of the Caribbean* experience, check out the **Scheepvaartmuseum** (*see p115*). Skip the museum itself (a bit boring for kids) and head straight for the reconstructed ship peopled with 'real' sailors. Other museums with kid-appeal are the **Anne Frank Huis** (*see p103*), **Nemo** (*see p115*) and the **Tropenmuseum** (*see p113*).

Parks

Vondelpark (*see p125*) remains the most popular – in particular for its playgrounds, splash pools and free Wednesday afternoon summer performances on the outdoor stage – but you'll find at least one park per district, as well as smaller play areas and city farms. The revamped **Westerpark** (*see p122*) has been transformed into an innovative terrain featuring nature reserves, a children's farm, play parks, a paddling pool and several cafés. At **Amstelpark** (*see p127*), kids can catch the miniature train that runs around the park, get lost in the maze or take a pony ride. For a wilder experience take the whole day to explore the **Amsterdamse Bos** (*see p128*); particularily great for kids are the working organic goat farm and the pancake house.

Restaurants

The city is dotted with eateries and brown cafés where children are welcome. We recommend **De Taart van m'n Tante** (*see p152*) to wow the kids with extraordinary cakes; **De Jaren** (*see p155*) for a centrally located nappy change; **Latei** (*see p135*) for crazy retro décor and the yummiest Dutch apple pie; and **Vakzuid** (*see p127*), where parents and children alike can kick back while a DJ spins at the Sunday afternoon lounge party. At the funky **Kinderkookkafe Kattenlaan**, situated in Vondelpark (625 3257, www.kinderkookkafe.nl), kids help themselves to biscuit dough, roll out and cut cookies that are then baked in the oven while you wait. Self-squeezed juices and healthy sandwiches are also on offer. Those seeking more alternative dining will love **De Peper** (*see p151*). Housed in an ex-squat, it serves up organic vegan meals for a super-cheap price. They offer baby seats, plenty of toys and have a high child tolerance.

Swimming, sports & saunas

Good for children are **De Mirandabad** (a sub-tropical pool with a wave machine, toddler pool and slide), the **Zuiderbad** indoor pool, and the **Brediusbad** and **Flevoparkbad** outdoor pools. One of the city's more child-friendly saunas is **Fenomeen** (*see p229*). For saunas, *see p256*; for swimming pools, *see p258*.

Snowplanet

Recreatieschap Spaarnwoude, Heuvelweg 6-8, Velsen-Zuid (0255 545848/www.snowplanet.nl). Bus 82. **Open** *Sept-Apr* 9am-11pm daily. *Apr-Sept* 3-11pm Mon-Fri; 11am-11pm Sat, Sun. **Admission** from €16 1hr; from €13.50 1hr 6s-12s. *Equipment hire* €6.

Winter sport thrills are available here all year round. With two pistes – for beginners and the more advanced – and real snow, it's almost like the real thing. Even sprogs can sample the snow during introductory sessions for three to four year olds.

Klimhal Amsterdam

Naritaweg 48 (681 0121/www.klimhalamsterdam.nl). NS Station Sloterdijk. **Open** 5-10.30pm Mon, Tue, Thur; 2-10.30pm Wed; 4-10.30pm Fri; 11am-10.30pm Sat; 9.30am-10.30pm Sun. **Admission** €10.75 adults; €7.25 under-17s. **Rental** set €5.50. **No credit cards**.

A massive hall houses the biggest indoor climbing centre in the Netherlands, featuring different walls and 'mountains' to suit kids from six years up.

Theatre & circus

The Dutch love of all things cultural readily extends to children, with a wide selection of shows for all ages: check with **Uitlijn** (0900 0191) for details of children's shows or look under 'Jeugd' in *Uitkrant*.

Circustheater Elleboog

Passeerdersgracht 32, Western Canal Belt (626 9370/www.elleboog.nl). Tram 1, 2, 5, 7, 10. **Open** 9am-5pm Mon-Fri. *Bookings* 10am-2pm Mon-Fri. **Activities & shows** times vary, call for more info. **Admission** €8.50 adults; €6 under-15s. **No credit cards. Map** p330 C4.

Performances for all the family. Regular workshops for children between four and 17 teach circus and clowning tricks, juggling, stilts, tightrope and ball-walking, culminating in performances.

De Krakeling

Nieuwe Passeerdersstraat 1, Western Canal Belt (625 3284/reservations 624 5123/www.krakeling.nl). Tram 7, 10. **Shows** 2.30pm Wed, Sun; 7.30pm Thur-Sat. **Admission** €10.50 adults; €8.50 adults with child; €7.50 4s-17s. **No credit cards. Map** p330 C4.

De Krakeling is the only Dutch theatre that programmes exclusively for children. There are separate productions for over-12s and under-12s. For non-Dutchies, there are puppet and mime shows.

Toy libraries

A visit to the local *speel-o-theek* (toy library) could be the move that saves the day. There's space for the young and toys, all free. To find one, look up 'Speel-o-theek' in the *Gouden Gids*. The **Centraal Bibliotheek** (*see p307*) has English-language books, a play area, changing rooms and storytelling in English on Friday mornings.

Urban farms

Free entertainment for small animal lovers is to be found at any of the 17 or so children's farms dotted around the city. Admission is usually free; check the *Gouden Gids* under 'Kinderboerderijen'. There's also **Artis** (*see p111*), the zoo.

Outside Amsterdam

These attractions are easy to reach by train or car. Check with the local **Amsterdam Tourist Board**, **ANWB** shops or the Dutch railways (**NS**) for ideas on day trips. For details of other out-of-town attractions, *see pp272-294*.

Archeon

Archeonlaan 1, Alphen aan den Rijn (0172 447744/www.archeon.nl). 50km (31 miles) from Amsterdam; A4 to Leiden, then N11 to Alphen aan den Rijn. **Open** *Apr-July* 10am-5pm Tue-Sun. *Aug, Sept* 10am-5pm daily. Some winter events from Nov to opening. **Admission** €14.90; €13.90 65+; €12.90 4s-10s; free under-4s (€1.50 mid July-mid Aug). **Credit** MC, V.

Archeon plunges visitors into life as it was in the Netherlands during three different periods: the prehistoric, the Roman Empire and the Middle Ages. You can walk through authentically constructed streets and talk to 'residents' about life back then, ideal for more historically-minded kids.

Efteling

Europalaan 1, Kaatsheuvel, Noord Brabant (0900 0161/UK agent 01242 528877/www.efteling.nl). 110km (68 miles) from Amsterdam; take A27 to Kaatsheuvel exit, then N261. **Open** *July, Aug* 10am-6pm Mon-Fri, Sun; 10am-midnight Sat. *Apr-Oct* 10am-6pm daily. **Admission** €26-€28; €24-€26 60+, disabled (2 caregivers permitted at same price); free under-4s. **Credit** AmEx, MC, V.

If your children insist on the big Disney experience (with prices to match), this is the next best thing. An enormous fairytale forest peopled with dwarves and witches, characters from Grimm stories and the *Arabian Nights*, enchanted and haunted castles, and even talking rubbish bins. Even the most cynical kids will be sucked in. This massive (and massively popular) amusement park is packed with state-of-the-art thrills, as well as more traditional fairground rides for the really tiny. Busy in summer.

Apenheul

JC Wilslaan 21, Apeldoorn (055 3575757/www.apenheul.com). 90km (58 miles) from Amsterdam. **Open** *Aug-July* 9.30am-5pm daily. *July-Aug* 9.30am-6pm daily. **Admission** €16; €12 65+, 3s-9s, disabled; free under-3s. **Credit** AmEx, MC, V.

Set in the beautiful nature reserve of Berg en Bos, this expansive primate park is home to all manner of monkeys, bonobos, apes, macaques, gorillas and orang-utans. The animals are all free to roam the grounds at their leisure, and visitors can do likewise. Apenheul works together with conservation groups worldwide to protect threatened species. A playground, Fairtrade shop, Amazonian carousel and rainforest exhibition are also on hand.

Madurodam

George Maduroplein 1, The Hague (070 355 3900/070 416 2400/www.madurodam.nl). 57km (35 miles) from Amsterdam; take A4 to The Hague. **Open** *Mar 15-June 30* 9am-8pm daily. *July 1-Aug 31* 9am-11pm daily. *Sept 1-Mar 14* 9am-6pm daily. **Admission** €13; €12 65+; €9.25 3s-11s; free under-2s. **Credit** AmEx, DC, MC, V.

Over 700 scale models of the Netherlands' most famous sights built on a 1:25 ratio, and boasting the largest minature railway in the world. Go on a summer evening, when the models are lit from the inside by over 50,000 tiny lamps.

Childminders

Check the *Gouden Gids* under 'Oppascentrales'.

Oppascentrale Kriterion

624 5848/www.kriterionoppas.org. **Bookings** 9-11am, 4.30-8pm daily; 24hrs per day online. **Rates** from €5-€6/hr; additional charge Fri, Sat. *Administration charge* €3 per booking. *Annual membership fee* €13. **No credit cards.**

This service uses male and female students aged over 18, all of whom are carefully vetted both before and during service. Advance booking advised, register first online or by phone.

State of play

There's no shortage of public playgrounds of the swings, slide and sandpit variety. Located in each of the city parks – and with at least one serving every neighbourhood, too – you'll find them well maintained and equipped.

But there are also some special playgrounds that are worth checking out. **Speeltuin de Waag** (Oudeschans 14, 638 6463) is a well-kept secret. Half-hidden in the old part of town, opposite the landmark Schreierstoren, it's open all year round (11am-7pm). Apart from a good selection of equipment, mobile toys such as cars and bikes are also brought out to play by the resident caretaker. There's nothing unusual about the **Melkhuis** (Vondelpark 2, 612 9674, www.groot-melkhuis.nl), but it's a very popular playground due to the fact that it's situated inside the café grounds, so adults can relax with a drink while offspring happily romp within eyesight. The selection of kids' equipment, sandpit included, will be good for a coffee at least. **De Blauwepoort** (Recreatiegebied Het Twiske, Oostzaan, 075 684 4338, www.recreatienoordholland.nl) is a free, water-themed playpark open from April to October. Kids up to 12 years can make a splash playing on the pirate ship, a complex of self-operating locks or the big 'water-curtain'. For younger ones, there are also water slides and paddling pools for all the splashing about kids could want.

The place to go if it's raining and you have nippers in tow is **TunFun** (Mr Visserplein 7, 689 4300, www.tunfun.nl; *pictured*). An urban recycling success, this cavernous indoor playground used to be an underpass. Three huge soft-play constructions, plus numerous other entertaining activities provide endless joy for ages one to 12. Take that book you've been meaning to read – believe me, they'll hardly know you're there! Children should most definitely be seen and heard over at the **Klankspeeltuin** (Piet Heinkade 1, 788 2010, www.klankspeeltuin.nl), literally translated as 'noise playground'. Kids from seven to 11 play with sound on specially constructed music machines, installations and computers, ending the hour-and-a-half sessions with an informal performance of their compositions.

Also well worth a day trip out of town is the highly popular and always packed **Linnaeushof** (Rijksstraatweg 4, Bennebroek, 023 584 362, www.linnaeushof.nl). The single largest playground in Europe, it offers an amazing 350 separate attractions, which include just about every concievable ride you can possibly imagine: high in the air, down on the ground and in the water, plus rope walkways, mini-golf, trampolines, water play areas and go-karts, and with a separate play area for the under-fives. Plus they'll be so drained from the drama that they'll sleep all the way home.

Film

Lights, cameras, satisfaction.

After a couple of shocked years following the murder of controversial filmmaker Theo van Gogh (*see p27*), 2006 seemed to mark a return to some stability in Dutch cinema. The biggest event was the homecoming of Paul Verhoeven, who returned from his Hollywood hideout with *Black Book*, the most expensive film ever to be shot in the Netherlands, and filled to the brim with banging explosions, ravishing beauties, noble Nazis and traitorous resistance fighters. One more recent cinematic style that still continues to flourish is the multicultural comedy genre, whose biggest exponent is Martin Koolhoven. His films, like *'N Beetje Verliefd*, tend to draw large, young crowds attracted to the irreverent sense of humour and playful stereotypes, though critics argue that they view the problems of integration through rose-coloured glasses. That's something that can't really be said of Eddy Terstall, perhaps the most relevant Dutch director working today. Terstall's films usually take place in his own neighbourhood of the Jordaan – like *Simon*, his acclaimed story of the friendship between a gruff pot dealer with a big heart and a gay dentist – and promote the best of tolerant Dutch values. With *Sextet* and *Vox Populi* – the two remaining parts of his ideological trilogy – on the horizon, he's someone to keep an eye out for. Some other noteworthy directors are David Lammers, who set *Langer Licht*, his genuinely touching, poetic film about the aftermath of a family tragedy, in folksy Amsterdam Noord, and Pieter Kuijpers, whose *Van God Los* is one of the few genuinely badass Dutch crime flicks. Kuijpers is back with a vengeance with *Dennis P*, a madcap crime comedy once again based on real-life events. Chances are you won't get the best out of Dutch film, at least in Amsterdam, without first mastering the language (look out for the subtitled versions at home) but then again, you'll probably recognise Dutch household names like Famke Janssen from the *X-Men* films, Yorick van Wageningen from *The New World*, or his spiritual predecessor Rutger Hauer from *Blade Runner* and *Sin City*. And don't forget that Amsterdam itself has starred as a big-screen belle in movies of

Pathé Tuschinski. *See p210.*

varying quality, from huge blockbuster *Ocean's 12*, which caused major city-centre stargazing, to *Deuce Bigalow: European Gigolo*, which managed to cause much gnashing of teeth.

THE CINEMAS

The city has a large and growing quantity of cinemas, which fall roughly into the multiplex or arthouse (*filmhuis*) categories. In the more-bangs-for-more-bucks camp are the Pathé multiplexes showing standard Hollywood fare, spiced up with the occasional European blockbuster, while the arthouses cater to more refined tastes by showing foreign films, documentaries, classics and retrospectives. All cinemas bar the Uitkijk offer refreshments and snacks (it's advisable – but against house rules – to sneak your own into pricey Pathés), while most art cinemas also have a cosy café, which is a crowd-puller in its own right.

TICKETS & INFORMATION

Films open on Thursdays, but special, early screenings and sneak previews are becoming increasingly common. The 'Filmladder' listings, in the Wednesday editions of major newspapers or online at www.filmfocus.nl, will tell you what's on when and where; the paper version is also on display in many bars, cafés and cinemas. The listings are in Dutch only, but it's not too difficult to work out what's playing. English-language listings and reviews, independent and mainstream, can be found in the free listings newspaper *Amsterdam Weekly* (*see p306* **Word on the street**).

It's best to reserve tickets between Thursday and Sunday. You can go to the booking office, book online using www.belbios.nl or phone to make a reservation. But beware: Pathé cinemas run a computerised phone line which is in Dutch only, some cinemas charge a small booking fee and none at all accept payment by credit card. Pick up your ticket(s) at least 30 minutes before the film, otherwise they will be sold on.

Multiplexes always show about 15 minutes of adverts and previews before each film, while arthouse theatres usually limit themselves to previews. Most films are shown in their original language, with Dutch subtitles, though kids' films are shown in dubbed and also subtitled versions. To avoid getting stuck in a screening of *Cars* that's been dubbed in Dutch, look for the letters O(riginal) V(ersion) after the title. Some cinemas offer discounts for students or on weekday mornings, and some arthouses (the Cinecenter, for example) still stick a 15-minute interval in the middle of every film, though this is increasingly rare. Only a few cinemas hold late or midnight screenings: The Movies and Pathé de Munt are the most consistent in this.

Cinemas

First run

City

Kleine-Gartmanplantsoen 15-19, Southern Canal Belt. Tram 1, 2, 5, 6, 7, 10. **Tickets** €4-€8. **Screens** 7. **No credit cards. Map** p330 D5.

Once the cinematic equivalent of a used-car salesman, this former multiplex is finally receiving a long-overdue restyle and is due to reopen mid-2008 as an arthouse cinema (with, bizarrely, a casino in the basement), with the emphasis firmly on quality programming. Part of the plan is also to restore the façade (by Jan Wils, noted architect of the Olympic Stadium) to its full 1935 art deco glory.

Pathé ArenA

ArenA Boulevard 600, Bijlmermeer (0900 1458 premium rate/www.pathe.nl). Metro Bijlmer. **Tickets** €5-€9. **Screens** 14. **No credit cards.**

This multi-screened complex is one of the best places to enjoy those guilty-pleasure blockbusters with little or no chance of bumping into someone you know, because of its peripheral location way out by the Ajax stadium. Styled with all the finesse of a big brick house, it nonetheless has comfortable seating and boasts the only IMAX screen in Amsterdam.

Pathé de Munt

Vijzelstraat 15, Southern Canal Belt (0900 1458 premium rate/www.pathe.nl). Tram 4, 9, 14, 16, 24, 25. **Tickets** €4.75-€9. **Screens** 7. **No credit cards. Map** p330 D4.

Another monster-sized multiplex, this is the town centre's only decent mainstream alternative to the shabby City. In its favour are huge screens and comfortable, spacious seating, and when the City goes upmarket, this will be the place to visit for the more big budget Hollywood fare.

Cinemas

Cinecenter
Lounge, drink, watch an art flick. *See p210.*

Kriterion
Run by volunteers, enjoyed by absolutely everyone. *See p210.*

The Movies
For fine food and a fab film. *See p210.*

Pathé Tuschinski
Grand, gracious and gloriously over the top. *See p210.*

De Uitkijk
No thrills or frills, just quality. *See p212.*

Het Ketelhuis.

Pathé Tuschinski

Reguliersbreestraat 26-34, Southern Canal Belt (0900 1458 premium rate/www.pathe.nl). Tram 4, 9, 14, 16, 24, 25. **Tickets** €4.75-€10. **Screens** 4. **No credit cards. Map** p331 E4.

This extraordinary cinema is named after Abraham Tuschinski, Amsterdam's single most illustrious cinematic entrepreneur. Built in 1921 as a 'world theatre palace', the decoration is an arresting clash of rococo, art deco and Jugendstil, which can make it difficult to keep your eyes on the silver screen. This is where glittering premieres usually take place to road-blocking effect. *Photos p208.*

Pathé Tuschinski Arthouse

Reguliersbreestraat 34, Southern Canal Belt (0900 1458 premium rate/www.pathe.nl). Tram 4, 9, 14, 16, 24, 25. **Tickets** €4.75-€10. **Screens** 3. **No credit cards. Map** p330 D4.

The Tuschinski's plain little sister next door shows artier fare than her scene-stealing sibling.

Arthouses

Cinecenter

Lijnbaansgracht 236, the Jordaan (623 6615/www.cinecenter.nl). Tram 1, 2, 5, 6, 7, 10. **Tickets** €5-€8. **Screens** 4. **No credit cards. Map** p330 C4.

A snug, arty cinema that features a cosmopolitan array of films. One of the few places that still has intervals during the film, which gives you opportunity to eye up the stylish clientele and make a dash for the swanky bar to stock up on alcoholic drinks.

Filmhuis Cavia

Van Hallstraat 51-52, West (681 1419/www.filmhuiscavia.nl). Tram 3, 10. **Tickets** €4. **Screens** 1. **No credit cards. Map** p325 A3.

Housed in a once-squatted school above a gym, the left-of-mainstream Cavia specialises in obscure, queer and/or political pictures. You can also rent it for film parties of your own.

Het Ketelhuis

Haarlemmerweg 8-10, the Jordaan (684 0090/www.ketelhuis.nl). Tram 10/bus 18, 22. **Tickets** €7-€8. **Screens** 3. **No credit cards. Map** p325 A1.

The old Ketelhuis used to be of little interest to non-Dutch-speaking film fans (it once specialised in unsubtitled homegrown movies), but this new and improved version now screens interesting international art films alongside Holland's finest flicks. The revival of the Westergas area and new blood in the form of regular festivals hasn't hurt its popularity among cinematically-minded Amsterdammers.

Kriterion

Roetersstraat 170, Oost (623 1708/www.kriterion.nl). Tram 6, 7, 10/Metro Weesperplein. **Tickets** €5.50-€8; €5.50 children's matinées, previews. **Screens** 2. **No credit cards. Map** p332 G3.

Founded in 1945 by resistance-fighter undergraduates, the cinema continues to be run by a bunch of students – to great success. Their unbeatable formula is to show quality films, first run as well as contemporary classics, and to host some great festivals, while the CinemaDiscutabel programme of films plus debate guarantees thought-provoking discussions. The Kriterion's sneak previews are always sold out, while the convivial bar facilitates after-film analysis. The concept is so popular that another venue is being set up on Borneostraat in the Indische Buurt, slated to open in 2007.

The Movies

Haarlemmerdijk 161, the Jordaan (624 5790/www.themovies.nl). Tram 3. **Tickets** €8; €6.50 children; €7 students, 65+; €65 10-visit card. **Screens** 4. **Credit** *Restaurant* MC, V. **Map** p325 B1.

The oldest cinema in Amsterdam to remain in regular use, The Movies has been circulating celluloid since way back in 1912, and it still exudes a genteel atmosphere of sophisticated elegance to this day. The excellent adjoining Wild Kitchen restaurant serves decent set dinners, and the cost – between €26 and €37 – includes a ticket. *Photo p213.*

Kriterion for success

The fashionably clad students sipping drinks in the spacious bar and the state-of-the-art digital projection systems suggest that arty picture-house **Kriterion** (*pictured*; *see also p210*) is a brand new city cinema. However, this particular building has housed a cinema for more than 60 years, and has been run by students for the same time. In the 1940s, then 25-year-old law undergraduate Piet Meerburg, one of the guiding lights in the Resistance, came up with a plan to help students ensure the financial security needed to complete their studies without the meddling of parents or government. With the support of several prominent businessmen, the Student Mutual Support Foundation was started and its first outlet was the film theatre on the Roetersstraat. Six decades on, Kriterion is still one of the most vibrant cinemas in town, which can be attributed to its workforce of cine-mad students, whose clash with the foundation in 1982 led to an occupation of the cinema and its subsequent independence.

Kriterion's well-stocked, well-priced bar is a refreshing change from the stale popcorn and overpriced soda peddled by multiplexes, and also allows great post-viewing discussions. Though the crowd is mostly students, many mature connoisseurs are also regulars.

The two current screens will be joined by a third in the near future, while a new branch will blossom in September 2007 in the form of Studio K at Timorplein 21, in the Indische Buurt. It will show not only arthouse fare, but films aimed at its ethnically diverse neighbourhood. Besides two screens, there'll also be a café-restaurant, in-house theatre and forward-thinking 'digital playground'.

Current initiatives may be as diverse as a petrol station, babysitting agency and the recently opened diner with a cultural twist 'Skek, but Kriterion has consistently been the breeding ground of several national and international cinematic institutions. The internationally acclaimed CINESTUD festival, where such illustrious directors as Polanski, Jarmusch and Scorsese were first discovered by Dutch audiences, started in Kriterion. The leading national film journal *De Filmkrant* started out as the *Kriterion Filmkrant*, and Hubert Bals, founder of the International Film Festival Rotterdam (*see p213*), headed the cinema in the '80s. Kriterion was also the first place to introduce the sneak preview to the Netherlands, and still draws big crowds every Tuesday night. Besides the tri-annual CINESTUD, other festivals calling the cinema home are the Unheard festival (*see p212* **If you screen it, they will come**), and the computer-orientated Machinima Bits. Most of the festivals turn into spontaneous parties as DJs transform the foyer into a club.

The regular cinema billing always includes a modern classic every Monday evening, and a selection of popular arthouse fare. On Sunday afternoons, Kriterion plays host to a socially, ecologically or otherwise eye-opening film under the CinemaDiscutabel label, following up screenings with a debate among a panel of experts to bring the subject to life.

With plans afoot for the export of the Kriterion formula to Sarajevo and beyond, the Kriterion way of life could be on your street before you know it. But don't let that stop you from sampling the original product in situ during your stay in Amsterdam.

Rialto

Ceintuurbaan 338, the Pijp (676 8700/www.rialto film.nl). Tram 3, 12, 24, 25. **Tickets** €5.50-€8.50; €30 5-visit card; €55 10-visit card. **Screens** 3. **No credit cards. Map** p331 F6.

The neighbourhood cinema of Oud-Zuid and the Pijp, the Rialto offers up an eclectic mix of arty features, documentaries, classics, festivals and kids' fare. They broaden the mix with frequent avant film premières, as well as regularly holding introductory talks to films chosen by guest speakers. The Rialto also has good disabled access.

De Uitkijk

Prinsengracht 452, Southern Canal Belt (623 7460/ www.uitkijk.nl). Tram 1, 2, 5, 6, 7, 10. **Tickets** €6.50-€7.50. **Screens** 1. **No credit cards. Map** p330 D5.

This charming little hole-in-the-wall place shows select arthouse flicks for a discerning audience.

If you screen it, they will come

Discover Amsterdam's cornucopia of film festivals and a plethora of exotic alternatives to the regular fare suddenly appear. Whether you want to submerge yourself in the film experience or just take a little dip in the celluloid pool, here is a selection of festivals well worth checking out.

The festival season kicks into gear at the end of January an hour-long train ride away with the annual **International Film Festival Rotterdam** (www.filmfestivalrotterdam.com), which is the largest film festival as well as one of the largest cultural events in the country. The 2007 edition lasted twelve days and was visited by almost 370,000 people. The city-wide IFFR specialises in arthouse fare and exotic films from all over, with a traditionally strong helping of esoteric Asian flicks, and large numbers of directors show up for Q&As and talk shows. Befriend a volunteer for access to the best after-parties.

The **Amnesty Film Festival** (www.amnesty filmfestival.nl; *see also p213*) takes place at venues in the middle of March and is the perfect opportunity to see quality films that will either depress you about the state of the world or encourage you to go out and change it. You'll also get plenty of opportunities in the post-film discussions and presentations to speak your mind on the subjects portrayed.

The **Unheard Film Festival** (www.unheard film.nl), at Kriterion (*see p210*), is a smaller festival focused on the use of sound in films, filling up four days at the end of March. Some films get a soundtrack makeover by a famous Benelux band, some are selected for their exceptional soundtracks, while clips from others are given wholly new audio.

The end of April heralds the **Amsterdam Fantastic Film Festival** (www.afff.nl; *see also p213*), which caters to gore-hounds and kids alike. The former go mad for the infamous Night of Terror, while the latter get to terrorise the stately Filmmuseum with dress-up parties, films and a range of movie frights. That said, ghoulish appearances notwithstanding, the crowds and crew are a good-natured bunch and the festival has grown large enough to offer up intriguing flicks while maintaining a cosy atmosphere for all-comers.

The start of July might not seem like a good date for a film festival, but **Cinedans** (www.cinedans.nl) solves that with outdoor performances at the Vondelpark open-air theatre. If the mention of a dance film brings back scary memories of *Dirty Dancing*, this international dance film festival should have a good chance of changing your mind.

Even Amsterdam nights can get sultry in August, so get comfortable in front of one of the many open-air screens that litter the city, with the one at the Amsterdam Plage even devoting several nights to screening the unreleased gems of that year at the free festival **Pluk de Nacht** (www.plukdenacht.nl).

September's **Africa in the Picture** festival (www.africainthepicture.nl) focuses on the many overlooked films coming from the continent, giving the emerging African Nouvelle Vague a much-needed platform by organising a host of outdoor screenings, discussions and parties.

The kids are alright during October's autumn break when **Cinekid** (www.cinekid.nl), the largest kid-orientated film festival on the planet, has its annual play date, with animation-happy adults often just as giddy as the tots at the centre of proceedings.

The biggest documentary festival in the world touches down in Amsterdam at the end of November in the form of the **IDFA** (www.idfa.nl; *see also p210*), which spawned the appropriately named **Shadow Festival** (www.shadowfestival.nl). Where the IDFA's massive quantity of titles is geared towards neophyte and die-hard alike, Shadow is more experimental in nature, with both positive and negative results. Both festivals have the usual Q&As and cinematic workshops, but Shadow has better parties.

Picture perfection at **The Movies**. *See p210.*

Multimedia centres

OT301

Overtoom 301, Oud West (779 4913/www.squat.net/overtoom301). Tram 1, 6. **Tickets** from €4. **Screens** 1. **No credit cards**. **Map** p329 B6.

A former Dutch film academy transformed by squatters into a cultural 'breeding ground', OT301 has a radio station, a vegan restaurant and an art-house cinema showing off-the-beaten-track films.

De Balie

Kleine-Gartmanplantsoen 10, Southern Canal Belt (553 5100/www.debalie.nl). Tram 1, 2, 5, 6, 7, 10, 20. **Tickets** €5-€7. **Screens** 2. **No credit cards**. **Map** p330 D5.

A temple to high culture, De Balie is also a bar, a theatre, a debating ground and host to several festivals, ranging from the IDFA (*see below*) to the ResFest.

Melkweg

Lijnbaansgracht 234A, Southern Canal Belt (531 8181/www.melkweg.nl). Tram 1, 2, 5, 6, 7, 10, 20. **Tickets** €6; €5 students (incl membership). **Screens** 1. **No credit cards**. **Map** p330 C5.

The Melkweg (*see p233* and *p234*) shows great films, although the racket that comes through the floor when there's a band playing elsewhere in the building might distract you from your flick.

Tropeninstituut

Kleine Zaal Linnaeusstraat 2, Oost; Grote Zaal Mauritskade 63, Oost (568 8500/www.kit.nl/tropentheater). Tram 9, 10, 14. **Tickets** €6-€7. **Screens** 2. **Credit** MC, V. **Map** p332 H3.

Next to the Tropenmuseum (*see p113*), this highly cultural venue sporadically shows documentaries from developing countries.

De Nieuwe Anita

Frederik Hendrikstraat 111, West (no phone/www.denieuweanita.nl). Tram 3, 10, 14. **Tickets** €2. **Screens** 1. **No credit cards**.

This former squat is a buzzing hive of activity, with live performances and laid-back lounging nights attracting a creative crowd. Mondays feature staggeringly obscure but highly enjoyable films.

Filmhuis Griffioen

Uilenstede 106, Amstelveen (598 5100/www.filmhuisgriffioen.nl). Tram 5. **Tickets** €4.50-€6. **Screens** 1. **No credit cards**.

A small student-run cinema on the campus of the Free University, the Filmhuis Griffioen is a cheap and eminently enjoyable way to check out the films you missed in their first run.

Nederlands Filmmuseum (NFM)

Vondelpark 3, (Library: Vondelstraat 69-71), Museum Quarter (589 1400/library 589 1435/www.filmmuseum.nl). Tram 1, 2, 3, 5, 6, 12. **Open** *Library* 1-5pm Tue-Fri (closed for a month every summer). **Tickets** €8; €6.50 students, 65+; €4.50 members. *Membership* €20/yr. **Screens** 3. **No credit cards**. **Map** p330 C6.

The most important centre of cinematography in the Netherlands, the NFM specialises in major retrospectives and edgier contemporary fare. In the summer, be sure to take in a terrace screening at Café Vertigo for a unique al fresco cinema experience.

Film festivals

For more on film festivals, *see p212* **If you screen it, they will come**.

Amnesty International Film Festival

773 3621/www.amnesty.nl/filmfestival. **Date** Mar-Apr.

This five-day biennial event on human rights features films, lectures, discussions and a workshop.

Amsterdam Fantastic Film Festival

679 4875/www.afff.nl. **Date** Apr.

The AFFF is a must for lovers of fantastic cinema, with generous amounts of gore playing alongside child-friendly fantasy and lots more besides.

International Documentary Filmfestival Amsterdam (IDFA)

627 3329/www.idfa.nl. **Date** last wk in Nov.

The biggest documentary film festival in the world, the IDFA enjoys friendly competition with the more edgy Shadow Festival (www.shadowfestival.nl).

International Film Festival Rotterdam

Information 010 890 9090/reservations 010 890 9000/www.filmfestivalrotterdam.nl. **Date** late Jan/early Feb.

Although it doesn't take place in Amsterdam, the Netherlands' biggest film festival is just an hour's train journey away, and attracts around 360,000 visitors to its programme of 250-odd films.

Galleries

Turning the monsters of modern art into the Old Masters of tomorrow.

Just why is Amsterdam so notoriously arty? Certainly, 'there's money' remains one of the more compelling explanations. Ever since the Golden Age, major artists like Rembrandt and Vermeer have been able to make a living from a middle-class rabid to invest in their quest for status. And in Amsterdam, little has changed: the locals still remain enthusiastic for original artworks and there are plenty of galleries to meet demand. (Despite this, both Rembrandt and Vermeer managed to go bankrupt.)

Another theory is based on how the Dutch have evolved innate organisational skills, from the order required to keep the sea at bay, to the almost constant spring-cleaning required to maintain a sense of space in this modestly proportioned land. A dedication to arrangement is certainly on display as one descends onto Schiphol and sees the Mondrian-like grid pattern of the landscape. Some even see it in the balletic elegance of Dutch football players, who open space to score and close space to defend.

But where there's order, there's chaos. And there's been a strong Dionysian strand that has sought to rebel against the rules, both overt and hidden, required in keeping the sea at bay and living with such a density of people. As such, the major developments of modern Dutch art can be seen as a battle between order and chaos.

The best Galleries

ARCAM

Architecture in a silver snail. *See p218.*

Chiellerie

The ultimate artists' hang-out. *See p216.*

Oude Kerk

New in the old. *See p217.*

Platform 21

Mixing it all up. *See p219.*

Smart Project Space

Pathologically cutting-edge. *See p219.*

W139

Renewed location and vision. *See p217.*

Representing that part of the Dutch psyche that aspires to order, the abstractionists of De Stijl (the Style), founded in 1917 and involving the likes of Theo van Doesburg, Piet Mondrian and Gerrit Rietveld, sought rules of equilibrium that are as useful in everyday design as in art. You just have to surf the internet, leaf through *Wallpaper**, visit IKEA or purchase a White Stripes album to see their influence. However, some later painters chose to become disciples of chaos, embracing an antidotal muse. Under the moniker of CoBrA, such artists as Karel Appel and Eugene Brands interpreted the Liberation that ended World War II as a signal for a new spontaneity and the expression of immediate urges. Where their Surrealist forebears had embraced Freud, they preferred Jung, wiring themselves into the unconscious of primitives, children and the mentally ill (for the **CoBrA Museum of Modern Art**, *see p128*). CoBrA can take a lot of credit for bringing 'outsider art' into the world's galleries.

Money and rebellion were also to define the heady 1980s. While subsidies and a general global boom in the modern art market supported some artists and made yet others rich – like Rob Scholte – the decade was marked by the punk attitude of 'do-it-yourself', and squats became more cultural than political as artists sought settings for making and exhibiting new work.

THE FUTURE'S BRIGHT

The reaction against the anti-functionalism of conceptual art continues unabated – a trend that would have pleased adherents of De Stijl, who hoped the future would bring a frenzy of cross-disciplinary action. Not only can photographers (Anton Corbijn, Rineke Dijkstra), cartoonists (Joost Swarte), and architects (Rem Koolhaas) easily pass themselves off as 'artists', but the inspired work of John Körmeling and Atelier van Lieshout, equal parts artistry and oddball carpentry, embodies a perfect fusion of function, whimsy and good old-fashioned aesthetics. On the other hand, many people who would have called themselves artists in the past now proudly call themselves designers (*see p189* **Design driven**). Even graffiti kids are being recast as street artists (*see p216* **Let us spray**).

Besides straddling a fine line between order and chaos, Dutch graphic/multimedia designers are now also surfing between the pure and purely commercial. Having achieved global acclaim for formulating a universal visual language where stylistic simplicity (De Stijl) doesn't rule out personal expression (CoBrA), many are now being employed by 'guerrilla' or 'viral' ad agencies, who have been set up to take advantage of this talent pool for international campaigns. The nation's many art, design and architecture colleges have helped this process by making artists and designers study together and by welcoming foreign students.

Compared with the art factories of Paris, New York and London, Amsterdam's galleries remain adventurous and welcome up-and-comers. But you will also note a backlash against all this cutting-edge stuff, with many artists returning to good, old-fashioned painting, drawing and sculpting.

With **Westergasfabriek** (*see p263*) and **NDSM** (*see p262*) coming of age (the latter home to a number of studios), there's a brand new slew of exhibition spaces. Between this culture park and the Jordaan is Stadsliedenbuurt, host of **Art Walk** (www.artwalkamsterdam.nl), which seeks to fill unused spaces and display windows with art in various forms.

Another new trend that is hard to miss is the generating of new alternative exhibition spaces such as the **PSWAR** (www.pswar.org) atop the roof of **OT301** (*see p213*), **De Kattenbak** (www.kattenbak.org), who like to take their art to the street, and the **Horse Move Project Space** (www.horsemove.nl), hidden under a road by Stedelijk CS. And, most recently, the neighbourhood of De Pijp (*see pp129-130*) seems to be the place where alternative galleries are setting up shop – especially around Gerard Douplein. Happy exploring!

SHOWING OUT

Besides the **Stedelijk Museum of Modern Art** (*see p124*), now in **Post CS** (*see p114*), there are several other world-famous museums of modern art: the **Haags Gemeentemuseum** in The Hague (Stadhouderslaan 41, 070 338 1111, www.gemeentemuseum.nl; *see p286*); outdoor **Rijksmuseum Kröller-Müller** (near the Otterloo entrance to Hoge Veluwe, 0318 591 241, www.kmm.nl), the **Groninger Museum** in Groningen (*see p284* **Going for Groningen**), and the renewed **Stedelijk van Abbemuseum** (Bilderdijklaan 10, 040 238 1000, www.vanabbemuseum.nl), the latter situated in Eindhoven.

Photography buffs would do well to visit **Huis Marseille** (*see p101*) and **Foam** (*see p107*). For the more antique/collectible side of art try Spiegelgracht/Nieuw Spiegelstraat.

Art spaces in Amsterdam appear and vanish all the time. For the most up-to-date list, buy the monthly *Alert* (available at **Athenaeum Nieuwscentrum**; *see p173*); written in Dutch, but with galleries all sorted into areas and marked on maps. Also, scan flyers at art and design book store **Artbook** (Van Baerlestraat 126, Museum District, 664 0925, 1-6pm Mon, 10am-6pm Tue-Sat); check gallery shows in free papers *Amsterdam Weekly*, *Uitkrant* (www.uitkrant.nl), or the art listings pamphlet published every two months by **AKKA**, whose website (www.akka.nl) links to the various galleries across Amsterdam.

Many galleries close during July or August and have a relaxed attitude to opening hours the rest of the time, so call ahead. For the **Art Amsterdam** art fair, **Kunstvlaai**, its edgier equivalent, and open studios, *see pp198-199*.

Chiellerie. *See p216.*

Galleries

The Old Centre: Old Side

Amsterdam Centrum voor Fotografie

Bethaniënstraat 9-13 (622 4899/www.acf-web.nl). Tram 16, 24, 25. **Open** 1-5pm Thur-Sat. Closed July, Aug. **No credit cards. Map** p326 D3.

This may be a city more famous for its paintings than its prints, but photo buffs love this sprawling space within flashing distance of the Red Light District. Besides exhibitions (also at No.39), it has workshops and a black-and-white darkroom for hire.

Chiellerie

Raamgracht 58 (320 9448/www.chiellerie.nl). Metro Nieuwmarkt. **Open** 2-6pm Wed-Sun; openings Fri 5-10pm. **No credit cards. Map** p327 E3.

As home to 'Night Mayor' Chiel van Zelst (*see p242* **Night Mayor on Fun Street**), and with a new exhibition of local art every week or two, this is more hang-out than mere art hanger. *Photo p215.*

Let us spray

You don't need to head indoors in order to get your fix of art and culture: Amsterdam has a very active street art scene, which means you can peruse it on every corner of town, in many shapes and sizes, from freehand graffiti to stencils, sculptures, tags and even stickers.

One of the more prolific practitioners is **Laser 3.14**. Dubbed Amsterdam's very own 'guerrilla poet', his words of wisdom are dotted all over town. No building site is safe from his aerosol and postmodern one-liners. 'Swallowed by your own introspective vortex' is one such example; 'She fears the ghouls that reside in her shadow' is another. But whereas Laser 3.14 prefers the old-school spray can, sticker artist **DHM** has a different approach, carefully glueing tribal tattoo-style animals all over the urban jungle.

Further familiar sights throughout the inner city – particularly the Pijp – are the spray-painted stereos and crazed electricity poles courtesy of **Morcky**, who, with partner **Boghe**, is also making a name for himself outside the street scene. Together they've created websites for the likes of The Wu Tang Clan and their art has been featured in Dutch rock diva Anouk's videos.

Arguably the most prolific and well-known group of artists from the street scene are the **London Police (TLP)**. The collective, started by three British men, put their own stamp across the Dutch capital with their 'lads': deceptively simplistic black-and-white blob characters that tended to pop up on electricity boxes in town, but later found their way into galleries.

Like many urban galleries around the world, those in Amsterdam have seized upon street art. **Studio Apart** (Prinsengracht 715, 422 2748, www.studioapart.com) represents a number of designers and artists with a graffiti background, and holds changing exhibitions by people like Ottograph, Juice and KMDG, a collective made up of different disciplines and working together on various projects.

Clothing shops like **Hanazuki** (Vijzelstraat 87, 422 9563, www.hanzuki.com), trendy **Wolf & Pack** (232 Spuistraat, 427 0786, www.wolfandpack.com) and also **Henxs** (St Antoniebreestraat 136, 638 9478, www.henx.com) host their own exhibitions of street art. At Henxs, you even run the risk of coming face to face with the street artists themselves, since it's here that they stock up on spray cans and markers. The store itself is hard to miss: the sticker-covered front porch is a kind of who's who of the Amsterdam street scene. The same goes for the corridor and lifts at **11** (*see p145* and *p245*); in an unofficial wall of fame, the club's halls are all covered with work from Amsterdam and beyond; a real spray-painted sight to behold.

Oude Kerk

Oudekerksplein 23 (625 8284/www.oudekerk.nl). Tram 4, 9, 14, 16, 24, 25. **Open** 11am-5pm Mon-Sat; 1-5pm Sun. During World Press Photo 10am-6pm Mon-Sat; 1-6pm Sun. **Admission** €5, €4 students, seniors; free under-12s. **No credit cards. Map** p326 D2.

The 'Old Church', home of World Press Photo (*see p197*), exhibits everything from contemporary aboriginal art to photographs documenting the life of albinos in Africa. *See also p93.*

W139

Warmoesstraat 139 (622 9434/www.w139.nl). Tram 4, 9, 14, 16, 24, 25. **Open** 11am-7pm Tue-Sun, varies with exhibitions. **No credit cards. Map** p326 D2.

In its two decades of existence, W139 has never lost its squat aesthetic, nor its occasionally overly conceptual edge. A new renovation has just brought more light and fresh inspiration. Legendary openings.

The Old Centre: New Side

Arti et Amicitiae

Rokin 112 (623 3508/www.arti.nl). Tram 4, 9, 14, 16, 24, 25. **Open** 1-6pm Tue-Sun. **No credit cards. Map** p326 D3.

This marvellous building houses a private artists' society, whose members gather in the first-floor bar, while members of the public can climb a Berlage-designed staircase to its large exhibition space.

Western Canal Belt

Montevideo/TBA

Keizersgracht 264 (623 7101/www.montevideo.nl). Tram 13, 14, 17. **Open** 1-6pm Tue-Sat. **No credit cards. Map** p326 C3.

Montevideo is dedicated to applying new techniques to visual arts, alongside photography and installations. Admire tech in an old world space, or read up on an assortment of topics in the reference room. There's usually a token entry fee for exhibitions.

Southern Canal Belt

De Appel

Nieuwe Spiegelstraat 10 (625 5651/www.deappel.nl). Tram 16, 24, 25. **Open** 11am-6pm Tue-Sun. **Admission** €4; free under-18s. Free 1st Sun of mth. **No credit cards. Map** p330 D4.

An Amsterdam institution that showed its mettle by being one of the first galleries in the country to embrace video art. It still has a nose for things modern, and gives international and rookie guest curators freedom to follow their muse.

Galerie Akinci

Lijnbaansgracht 317 (638 0480/www.akinci.nl). Tram 6, 7, 10, 16, 24, 25. **Open** 1-6pm Tue-Sat. **No credit cards. Map** p331 E5.

From squatting to seating at **W139**.

Part of a nine-gallery complex that includes Lumen Traven, Art Affair, Oele and Meti, Akinci thrives on surprise, with shows that employ every contemporary art medium: from the dark heart of Esther Tielemans to the mutant puppets of Gerben Mulder.

Gallery Lemaire

Reguliersgracht 80 (623 7027/www.gallery-lemaire.com). Tram 4, 16, 24, 25. **Open** 11am-5pm Thurs-Sat. **Credit** AmEx, MC, V. **Map** p331 E4.

In the same family for three generations, this maze-like gallery fills a huge canal house with tribal art from around the world – in short: a heaven for collectors. Phone ahead to confirm opening times.

Melkweg

Marnixstraat 409 (531 8181/www.melkweg.nl). Tram 1, 2, 5, 6, 7, 10. **Open** 1-8pm Wed-Sun. **No credit cards. Map** p330 D5.

The Melkweg reflects the broad interests of director Suzanne Dechart, with quality shows of contemporary photography. Expect anything from portraits of the descendents of runaway slaves to quirky pop photography. *See also p233* and *p243.*

Reflex Modern Art Gallery

Weteringschans 79A (627 2832/www.reflex-art.nl). Tram 6, 7, 10. **Open** 11am-6pm Tue-Sat. **Credit** AmEx, MC, V. **Map** p330 D5.

You can almost smell the Big Apple in Reflex. The New York flavour extends to its international names, like Araki and Christo, as well as celebrity

ARCAM.

locals such as Dadara and Erin Olaf. This is where to come for that inflatable *Scream* doll. They also have a exhibition space across the street.

Walls

Prinsengracht 737 (616 9597/www.walls.nl). Tram 1, 2, 5. **Open** noon-5pm Wed-Sun. **Credit** AmEx, MC, V. **Map** p330 D5.
Walls filled with everything and anything painterly, most of it well priced, local and unpretentious.

Jodenbuurt, the Plantage & the Oost

ARCAM

Prins Hendrikkade 600 (620 4878/www.arcam.nl). Tram 9, 14/Metro Waterlooplein/bus 42, 43. **Open** 1-5pm Tue-Sat. **No credit cards**. **Map** p327 E3.
Architecture Centrum Amsterdam is obsessed with the promotion of Dutch contemporary architecture, and organises tours, forums, lectures and exhibits.

The Waterfront

Many more galleries are likely to follow the Stedelijk – now temporarily housed in Post CS (*see p114*) – to the eastern docklands. Besides **Lloyd Hotel** (*see p72*), the former warehouse **Loods6** (KNSM-Laan 143, www.loods6.nl) puts on occasional exhibitions of an art/design nature, as does the hip street accessory shop **90 Square Meters** (Levantplein 52, KNSM-Eiland, 419 2525, www.90sqm.com).

Mediamatic

Post CS building, 5th floor, Oosterdokskade 5 (638 9901/www.mediamatic.net). 10min walk from Centraal Station. **Open** varies. **No credit cards**. **Map** p327 E1.
This bleeding-edge organisation dedicated to the outer reaches of technology and multimedia is now housed in the happening Post CS and has an exhibition space on the ground floor. Also check out near-neighbours Horse Move Project Space (www.horsemove.nl, 2-8pm Fri-Sun), where each exhibiting artist picks the next one to show.

Pakt

Zeeburgerpad 53 (06 5427 0879 mobile/www.pakt.nu). Tram 7, 10. **Open** 2-6pm Thur-Sun. **No credit cards**.
This new, slightly out-of-the-way address is worth a visit for sheer inspired quirkiness. Expect the 'pure image and sound' of Park 4DTV (www.park.nl) or the mobile art/hotdog kiosks of aptly named Ki-osk.

Galerie Paul Andriesse

Withoedenveem 8 (623 6237/www.galeries.nl/andriesse). Tram 13, 14, 17. **Open** 11am-6pm Tue-Fri; 2-6pm Sat; 2-5pm 1st Sun of mth. **No credit cards**.
While perhaps no longer all that innovative, there's still a selective savvy at work that embraces both older and wiser artists (Marlene Dumas often shows new works here) and up-and-coming names such as Rineke Dijkstra, Hellen van Meene, Thomas Struth and Jan van de Pavert.

The Jordaan

Annet Gelink Gallery

Laurierstraat 187-189 (330 2066/www.annetgelink.com). Tram 13, 14, 17. **Open** 11am-6pm Tue-Fri; 1-6pm Sat. **No credit cards**. **Map** p329 B4.
Annet Gelink has plenty of space and light to lavish on notable names in Dutch and international art: Ed van der Elsken (the famed photographer of 1960s Amsterdam), Alicia Frames, Barbara Visser, Ryan Gander and Virgil Marti, who achieved fame with a wallpaper patterned by the rather skewed web of a marijuana-addled spider.

Galerie Diana Stigter

Hazenstraat 17 (624 2361/www.dianastigter.nl). Tram 7, 10, 13, 14, 17. **Open** noon-6pm Wed-Sat; 2-5pm 1st Sun of mth. **No credit cards**. **Map** p330 C4.
Curator Diana Stigter finds a home for the odd animation of Martha Colburn, the videos of Saskia Olde Wolbers and strange paintings by Maaike Schoorel.

Galerie Fons Welters

Bloemstraat 140 (423 3046/www.fonswelters.nl). Tram 13, 14, 17. **Open** 1-6pm Tue-Sat. **No credit cards**. **Map** p325 B3.
Fons Welters likes to 'discover' the latest new (and often local) talent, and has shown remarkable taste in both sculpture and installation, having provided a home to Merijn Bolink, Rob Birza and Jennifer Tee.

Galerie Buuf

Eerste Anjeliersdwarsstraat 36 (616 2400/www.galeriebuuf.nl). Tram 7, 10, 13, 14, 17. **Open** 11am-6pm Wed-Sat; 1-6pm Sun. **Map** p325 B2.

This relatively new gallery shows all manner of modern art, but its claim to fame is its enjoining gallery featuring the work of legendary forger Geert Jan Jansen, who has gone straight: he now signs his own name to 'tributes' to Henry Matisse, Pablo Picasso, Karel Appel and Andy Warhol.

GO Gallery

Prinsengracht 64 (422 9580/www.gogallery.nl). Tram 13, 14, 17. **Open** noon-6pm Wed-Sat; 1-5pm Sun. **Credit** AmEx, DC, MC, V. **Map** p325 B2.

Owner Oscar van den Voorn is an energetic supporter of art who manages to display a sense of humour. Visitors can expect stained-glass, graffiti, LSD-inspired art and sporadic themed dinners (check the website for details).

Gallery KochxBos

1e Anjeliersdwarsstraat 3-5 (681 4567/www.kochxbos.nl). Tram 13, 14, 17. **Open** 1-6pm Wed-Sat, 1st Sun of mth. **No credit cards. Map** p325 B3.

Luminary 'lowbrow' artists like Ray Caesar, Mark Ryden, Tim Biskup, Joe Sorren and Glenn Barr. Art for those who like their hot rods ablaze, their punk snotty and their films in the Lynchian tradition.

De Praktijk

Lauriergracht 96 (422 1727/www.depraktijk.nl). Tram 7, 10. **Open** 1-6pm Wed-Sat, 2-5pm 1st Sun of month. **No credit cards. Map** 329 D4.

'The Practice', appropriatedly founded by a former dentist, is a real drill when it comes to finding mostly Dutch contemporary painters with a career ahead of them, such as Nick Goulis and Rinke Nijburg.

Stedelijk Museum Bureau Amsterdam

Rozenstraat 59 (422 0471/www.smba.nl). Tram 13, 14, 17. **Open** 11am-5pm Tue-Sun. **Map** p329 B4.

The Stedelijk's Rozenstraat outpost is often hipper than its mothership, with shows including the subversive female figures of Lucy Stein, the Ed Wood-inspired spacecraft of Guido van der Werve and the sperm paintings of Arnoud Holleman.

Torch

Lauriergracht 94 (626 0284/www.torchgallery.com). Tram 7, 10. **Open** 2-6pm Thur-Sat. **Credit** AmEx, DC, MC, V. **Map** p329 D4.

If you like your art edgy you'll love Torch, which brings Richard Kern, Jake & Dino Chapman, Micha Klein and Anton Corbijn to Amsterdam.

Vassie

Eerste Tuindwarsstraat 16 (489 4042/www.hughug.info). Tram 13, 14, 17. **Open** Wed-Sat 1-6pm. **No credit cards. Map** p325 B3.

Excellent photography exhibiters who embrace range, from American masters like Lee Miller to the archly subversive Brits Antoni + Alison.

Platform 21.

The Museum Quarter, Vondelpark & the South

Serieuze Zaken Studioos

Bilderdijkstraat 66 (427 5770/http://serieuzezaken.photonet.nl). Tram 3, 12. **Open** noon-6pm Tue-Sat; noon-5pm 1st Sun of mth. **No credit cards. Map** p329 B5.

Rob Malasch was already known as a quirky theatre type and journalist before opening this gallery in the Jordaan. Shows here might feature Brit Art, or works by contemporary Chinese painters.

Platform 21

Prinses Irenestraat 19 (301 8000/www.platform21.com). Tram 5. **Open** noon-6pm Wed-Sun. **No credit cards.**

Organizing a variety of activities and exhibitions, Platform 21 is indeed a platform where the effects of art, design, fashion and business in shaping our world are explored. Its location in a round modernist chapel is worth the visit alone – as will be their brand new nature-themed café and restaurant, opening at time of going to press.

Smart Project Space

Arie Biemondstraat 101-111 (427 5951/www.smartprojectspace.net). Tram 1, 3, 6, 12. **Open** noon-5pm Tue-Sat. **No credit cards. Map** p329 B6.

Relocated in a former pathology laboratory and reopening at time of going to press, Smart will no doubt remain loyal to 'hardcore art' in its huge new exhibition space, which also has two cinemas, a media lab, lecture hall and a café-restaurant.

Gay & Lesbian

From harmless fun to happy hardcore, Amsterdam wears its sexuality with Pride.

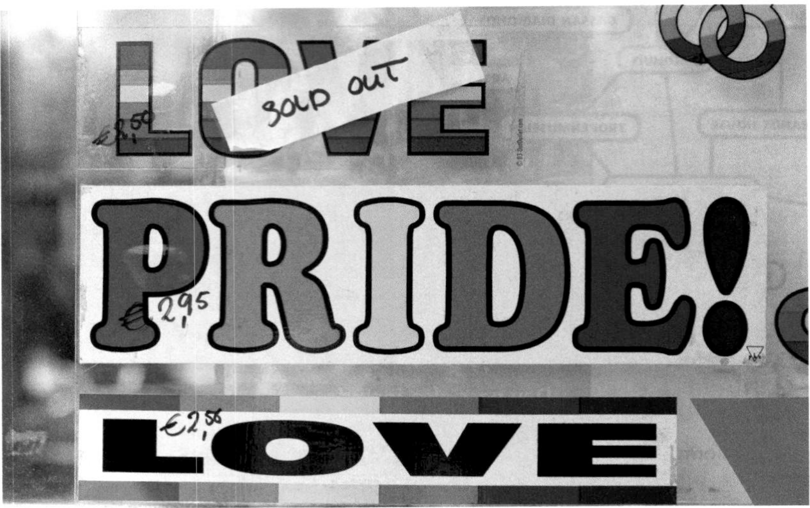

Queer questions answered at **Pink Point**.

After some homophobic incidents that left Amsterdam wondering whether or not it still deserved the title of Gay Capital, the city now seems to be getting back on track. Local political parties made a real effort to make Amsterdam gay-friendly for residents and visitors alike, and even the council promotes the pinkness of the city abroad on www.amsterdam4gays.nl. On top of this, Amsterdam Gay Pride has gone corporate with major companies and banks having their own float to make sure spectators get the message on employee diversity.

The scenes for gay men and lesbians are still quite separate. Each tends to keep to their own favourite places and only get together on special occasions like Queen's Day and Pride, and at one-off parties like Love Dance.

That said, there's plenty to amuse, whether it's shopping for books or toys, watching a film in a gay audience or simply having a night on the tiles. One different and energetic way to discover the city is with the world's only lesbian and gay cycle tour. Available from Mac Bike (*see p300*), the self-guided tour costs €1.50 and takes you through historic parts of the city by day and the nightlife after dark.

ESSENTIAL INFORMATION

So the Dutch capital is still a happy homo haven? Well, not everything is rose tinted. The COC, a long-standing meeting place for all kinds of lesbians and gays (*see p304*), lost its bar and club facilities due to lack of funding. It now only exists as a campaigning centre. Cruising areas, most notably the hugely popular Nieuwe Meer – good for sunbathing, swimming and round-the-clock man action, have been made less attractive by pruned bushes, police patrols and the introduction of Highland cattle to scare off the fun-seekers. Homophobia, whether religious or individual, is still something to watch out for. In 2005, and ironically on Queen's Day – very much a gay day in Amsterdam – the American gay-activist Chris Crain was assaulted in the busy Leidsestraat by some youths, simply because he was walking hand-in-hand with his boyfriend, and no bystander gave a helping hand. In 2006 a gay man was beaten up at Nieuwe Meer by a group of well-off students out for a laugh. That year there was also debate about a Dutch Christian school which forbade its gay staff from entering gay relationships. Also highly controversial is the directive issued by the new government which allows civil servants to refuse to officiate at gay marriage ceremonies on personal religous grounds. On the other hand, the government said yes to a new law which gives the children of lesbian couples the same legal rights as those of straight couples. The council also subsidised Pink Grey, ensuring this club night for elderly gays and lesbians can continue. Also on the upside, clubland has been reinvigorated: new bars have opened and several new one-off parties are going strong.

A word of warning when you party: free condoms aren't universal on the scene and STDs – including HIV – are always on the up; barebacking is as popular and controversial here as anywhere else in the world.

For information about HIV and other gay and lesbian matters, *see p304*.

Homomonument

Westermarkt, Western Canal Belt. Tram 13, 14, 17. **Map** p326 C3.

Unveiled 20 years ago, Karin Daan's three-sectioned pink triangle – symbolising past, present and future – was a world first. It's also a place to celebrate and to be proud: on Queen's Day and Pride it gets annexed to the open-air disco and market.

Pink Point

Westermarkt, Western Canal Belt (428 1070/ www.pinkpoint.org). Tram 13, 14, 17. **Open** *Dec-March* 10am-6pm daily. *April-Dec* 10am-9pm daily. **Map** p326 C3.

Queer queries? Need to know which party to go to? Looking for political pamphlets? Or just a gay post-card or a street map? Head to this year-round information kiosk near the Homomonument with friendly and chatty staff. Pink Point also publishes the *Bent Guide To Amsterdam* (€9.95).

PUBLICATIONS

Naturally, most of the lesbigay printed matter available is in Dutch, but it's good to know that a fair chunk is bilingual or in English. Falling into the latter camp are *Gay & Night* and *Gay News* (www.gay-news.com) – they also have a useful website and publish a gay map of the city – which are published monthly and available free in many bars, as is the map.

Butt looks like a low-rent porn mag (and there are plenty of sexy pictures) but pulls off some of the most interesting interviews of any gay publication, anywhere; Edmund White, Rufus Wainwright and Mark Jacobs are just three of the names to appear between its pink sheets. From the same stable comes *Fantastic Man*, a 'gentleman's style journal' that, if not strictly gay, is at the very least doused in homosexual sensibility.

The English-language cultural newspaper *Amsterdam Weekly* (www.amsterdamweekly.nl) has comprehensive lesbian and gay listings. Two useful online-only publications (both in English) are *GAY.NL* (www.gay.nl), which offers news and chatrooms, and *Night Tours* (www.nighttours.nl) which has easily the most complete nightlife listings for both Amsterdam and the rest of the country.

If you can read some Dutch, *PS*, *Het Parool*'s glossy Saturday supplement also has pink listings, while the lifestyle/news digest *De Gay Krant*, in print since 1980, has some English-language articles on its website (www.gk.nl) and even some lesbian content.

Lesbians are less well served, but they do get the excellent, style-driven *Girls Like Us* (*see p226* **Girls like Girls Like Us**), which is also in English. In Dutch, and at the other end of the spectrum, is *Zij aan Zij*, a general lesbian glossy covering the usual celebrity interviews, L Word articles, emotional issues and the like. Back copies of the mag are available online (www.zijaanzij.nl). Online-only *La Vita* (www.la-vita.nl) offers a similarly bland diet, and both have national listings, although these are in Dutch only.

RADIO & TV

The gay community gets two regular broadcast outlets on Dutch TV (one hour a week on Saturdays) and radio (every night).

MVS Radio

106.8 FM or 88.1 or 103.3 on cable (638 6386/ www.mvs.nl). **Times** 7-8pm Mon-Sat; 6-8pm Sun.

Daily news, features, interviews and music with a gay twist. In Dutch, Sunday programme in English.

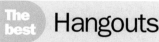

Hangouts

F*cking POP Queers
Fashionable punters and great music in a seriously funky venue. *See p227.*

GLU parties
Gorgeous girls, chunky electro, performance art. *See p226.*

Pink Grey
Clubby atmosphere for senior gays and lesbians. *See p227.*

Prik
Cute guys and sexy sounds. *See p227.*

Web
Leather, cheap beer and cheese. *See p223.*

Queer year

Spring

While most of the town turns bright orange during **Koninginnedag** (30 April), pockets of Amsterdam are shocking pink as queers and dykes celebrate the late Queen Juliana's birthday – festivities focus on the memorial Homomonument and the Amstel.

The Homomonument itself is at the centre of a more sombre commemoration on **Remembrance Day** (4 May), when victims of Nazi persecution are remembered with flowers and speeches. The following day is **Liberation Day**, a huge party with plenty of dancing at the monument.

AIDS Memorial Day in late May remembers victims around the world with songs, music, candles and speeches. It takes place at the Dominicus Church in Spuistraat.

Every second May is the **Transgender Film Festival** (www.transgenderfilmfestival.com).

Summer

The biggest event of the summer is, of course, **Amsterdam Gay Pride**, the largest visitor attraction after Queen's Day. Taking place over four days in the first week of August, this all-encompassing event includes cultural and sports activities, but is really just a big party. The main attraction is the Canal Parade on Saturday with around 70 floats, boats and thousands of spectators. *See also p200.*

Autumn

In October, a more dark and intimate party takes place. **Leather Pride** is celebrated with FF, rubber and other men-only parties in the main leather bars. To top it off, there's a huge Playground party where, as the name suggests, guys come to have all kinds of unfeasibly pervy fun behind closed doors.

Winter

World Aids Day on 1 December is marked with a conference at the RAI Exhibition Centre. It attracts doctors, journalists and other HIV-AIDS professionals from around the world. The same day Paradiso hosts **Love Dance**, a massive and hugely popular AIDS-benefit party with DJs, performances and fashion shows.

The year ends on an upbeat note with **Roze Filmdagen**, a week-long celebration of LGBT film, both international and home-grown. The opening and closing night parties are popular.

MVS TV

A1 (Salto): channels 39+/616MHz (638 6386/ www.mvs.nl). **Times** 8-9pm Sat.

The lesbian and gay community media company broadcasts shows on all aspects of gay life, from visiting porn stars to retired hairdressers to lesbian movers and shakers, and all points in between. Usually in Dutch but with occasional English-language items, some programmes are also online.

Where to stay

The hotels listed below are specifically gay-run. The **Gay & Lesbian Switchboard** (*see p304*) has more details of gay- and lesbian-friendly hotels. For more hotels, *see p58*.

Amistad

Kerkstraat 42, Southern Canal Belt, 1017 GM (624 8074/www.amistad.nl). Tram 1, 2, 5. **Rates** €65-€115 single; €80-€150 double; €95-€170 triple. **Credit** AmEx, DC, MC, V. **Map** p330 D4.

Run by owners – and hubbies – Johan and Joost, this hip hotel shines like the pages of a trendy glossy magazine. The rooms are cosy, and the breakfast area on the ground floor doubles as a gay internet lounge every day after 1pm. The lounge is also open to non-residents.

Black Tulip Hotel

Geldersekade 16, Old Centre: Old Side, 1012 BH (427 0933/www.blacktulip.nl). Tram 1, 2, 4, 5, 9, 13, 16, 17, 24, 25. **Rates** €115 single; €125-€195 double. **Credit** AmEx, DC, MC, V. **Map** p326 D2.

Housed in a 16th-century building, this leather hotel mixes luxury with lust. Perfect for those who don't need much sleep; seven of the nine rooms come with TV, VCR and S&M facilities.

ITC Hotel

Prinsengracht 1051, Southern Canal Belt, 1017 JE (6230 230/www.itc-hotel.com). Tram 4. **Rates** €70-€95 single; € 90-€135 double; €109-€165 triple. **Credit** AmEx, MC, V. **Map** p331 E4.

Situated in a listed building on a quiet stretch of Prinsengracht convenient for the gay hot spots, the ITC Hotel has 20 charming rooms. The free internet and e-mail access, and 24hr free gay TV channels all go towards ensuring a pleasant stay.

Golden Bear

Kerkstraat 37, Southern Canal Belt, 1017 GB (624 4785/www.goldenbear.nl). Tram 1, 2, 5. **Rates** €71-€132 single; €62-€132 double. **Credit** AmEx, MC, V. **Map** p330 D4.

The first gay hotel in town, the Golden Bear's rooms are spacious and comfortable, though not all have private bathrooms. Single rooms have double beds.

Bars & nightclubs

The gay scene is concentrated around four areas in the centre. Getting between them is easy and quick, though each has its own identity. Clubs and bars are listed by area below, with specialist establishments – restaurants, cafés, coffeeshops and lesbian bars – and the pick of one-off club nights and sex parties listed separately. Entry to bars and clubs listed here is free unless stated otherwise.

Warmoesstraat

The long and narrow Warmoesstraat is the oldest street in town. Although nothing to do with 'warm', it is just around the corner from the red-lit HQ of the oldest profession. Packed in the tourist season, it's full of cheap hostels and eateries, coffeeshops, bars and sex shops aimed at the – backpacking – visitor. **Getto** (*see p228*) provides a warm haven to rest and eat. It's also the street with leather/sex bars, a gay porn cinema/shop and a gay hotel. Be aware that junkies and drug sellers think tourists are easy prey, so act streetwise.

Argos

Warmoesstraat 95 (622 6595/www.argosbar.com). Tram 4, 9, 16, 24, 25. **Open** 10pm-3am Mon-Thur, Sun; 10pm-4am Fri, Sat. **No credit cards. Map** p330 D2.

'No perfume' it says at the door. Argos, the most venerable and most famous leather bar in town, likes men to smell like men. Friendly staff, porn on a big screen, and hot clientele of all ages, some of whom just come for the basement darkroom with cabins and a sling for less sedate entertainment.

Cockring

Warmoesstraat 96 (623 9604/www.clubcockring.com). Tram 4, 9, 16, 24, 25. **Open** 11pm-4am Mon-Thur, Sun; 11pm-5am Fri, Sat. **Admission** free Mon-Fri, Sun; €5 and up on Sat & special events. **No credit cards. Map** p326 D2.

The big sign of this men-only club gets photographed daily. Inside, on the small dancefloor, shirtless muscle marys throb to the hard house from female (!) DJ Debra. It's cruisey and touristy, and expect to queue at weekends, particularly after 1am. Twice a month it hosts steamy Sunday sex parties and every third Sunday of the month it's home to a sweltering Asian Disco Night.

Eagle

Warmoesstraat 90 (627 8634). Tram 4, 9, 16, 24, 25. **Open** 10pm-4am Mon-Thur, Sun; 10pm-5am Fri, Sat. **No credit cards. Map** p326 D2.

Known for its reputation – sexy and friendly punters, but dirty toilets and unfriendly staff – this men-only cruise bar can get absolutely packed. The downstairs darkroom is always action-filled and so is the upstairs area late at night; it has some cosy benches should you want to get intimate and a pool table complete with adjustable sling above it. Eagle is also home to SOS (aka Sex on Sunday), FF parties and also co-hosts regular Rubber Only parties with fetish shop Black Body (*see p229*).

Behind the mask at **Black Body**. *See p229.*

Web

Sint Jacobsstraat 6 (623 6758). Tram 1, 2, 3, 5. **Open** 2pm-1am Mon-Thur, Sun; 2pm-2am Fri, Sat. **No credit cards. Map** p326 D2.

The cheap booze, the sexiest bartender in town, the cheesy/classic dance tracks, the sex shop-vouchers lottery on Wednesdays, the Sunday 5pm snack afternoon; these ingredients make this men-only leather/cruise bar heave with a crowd from all ages. The upstairs darkroom is hygienic and the numerous cubicles almost resemble those at a gym/swimming pool: great to act out that locker room porn fantasy that you've always dreamed of.

Zeedijk

Once full of junkies, this notorious street just off Nieuwmarkt and running all the way to Central Station has been cleaned up, and is full of Asian eateries, bars and restaurants. Still, stay on guard, as it's not a country lane.

De Barderij

Zeedijk 14 (420 5132). Tram 4, 9, 16, 24, 25/Metro Centraal Station. **Open** 4pm-1am Mon-Thur; 4pm-3am Fri; noon-3am Sat; noon-1am Sun. **No credit cards**. **Map** p326 D2.

This no-frills bar attracts older gays and straight locals who all enjoy the living room-like atmosphere. Before you know it you're chatting and boozing with the unpretentious guys until the early hours.

Queen's Head

Zeedijk 20 (420 2475/www.queenshead.nl). Tram 4, 9, 16, 24, 25/Metro Centraal Station. **Open** 4pm-1am Mon-Thur; 4pm-3am Fri, Sat; noon-1am Sun. **No credit cards**. **Map** p326 D2

Fun, attitude-free bar and clientele, with a great view over a canal at the back. Tuesdays is Show Night with drag acts and Thursdays is ArtLaunch café. It also hosts special parties on – not surprisingly – Queen's Day, plus skin-nights, football-nights (most usually during the World Cup season), Eurovision Songcontest-night and so on.

Rembrandtplein

Not just the main drag for commercial nightlife and tourist hotspots, Rembrandtplein is also home to many of Amsterdam's gay and lesbian bars. Although just a few minutes' stroll from the Reguliersdwarsstraat, the scene here is much more light-hearted and a lot camper. There's also a couple of reasons for lesbians to visit: the bar **Vive La Vie** (*see p230*) and dance club **You II** (Amstel 178, 421 0900, www.youii.nl), which is a funny old mix of dykes and off-duty rent boys, though it can be a laugh if you're in the right frame of mind.

Halvemaansteeg is a short lane of brash, loud bars full of male punters of all ages (with the odd lesbian and straight girl to leaven the mix). They're attitude-free, and will burst into a Eurovision singalong at the drop of a feather boa. Round the corner on the Amstel are a few more bars that blast out cheesy hits.

Amstel Taveerne

Amstel 54 (623 4254). Tram 4, 9, 14, 24, 25. **Open** 5pm-1am Mon-Thur, Sun; 5pm-3am Fri-Sat. **No credit cards**. **Map** p331 E4.

A bunch of generally older guys come here to drink, chat and sing along to the Dutch hits blasting from speakers and on video screens, and things go even further every second Sunday in the month with a dedicated karaoke night. At time of going to press the bar was about to undergo a major renovation.

Entre Nous

Halvemaansteeg 14 (623 1700). Tram 1, 2, 4, 5, 9, 14, 16, 24, 25. **Open** 9pm-3am Mon-Thur; 9pm-4am Fri-Sun. **No credit cards**. **Map** p331 E4.

Although it looks slightly terrifying from the outside – put that down to the blacked-out windows– on the inside Entre Nous is actually pretty fluffy, full of younger gay guys with a thirst for cheap music and good fun. Many local gay folk flit between this place and the Montmartre, opposite.

Lellebel

Utrechtsestraat 4 (427 5139/www.lellebel.nl). Tram 4, 9, 14, 20. **Open** 9pm-3am Mon-Thur; 8pm-4am Fri, Sat; 3pm-3am Sun. **No credit cards**. **Map** p331 E4.

Lellebel is a tiny drag bar where the cross-dressing clientele provide all the entertainment themselves . Though most people will be found in drag, admirers and friends are welcome and the atmosphere is friendly. Entertainment runs all week: Tuesday is karaoke night, Thursday is salsa and Monday is Whatever You Want, You Get, when the punters themselves are responsible for providing the music.

Mix Café

Amstel 50 (420 3388/www.mixcafe.nl). Tram 4, 9, 14, 20. **Open** 8pm-3am Sun-Thur; 6pm-4am Fri; 8pm-4am Sat. **No credit cards**. **Map** p331 E4.

A total cheesefest of a bar that attracts attitude-free lesbian and gay customers, who get down and dance to the music of Kylie and the like. The alarmingly strong house drink is a 'heugemeug', a B52-style booze bomb that should be downed in one. Nearby bars Hotspot (Amstel 102) and Rouge (Amstel 60) are similarly jaunty joints if you're out for a night on the razzle with your gang.

Prik. See p227.

Reguliersdwarsstraat

It's the gayest stretch of street in the city; practically every other bar on the miniature strip between Koningsplein and Vijzelstraat is gay, and all the other businesses in between have been broadly tarred with the pink brush, absorbing overspill from the bars or aiming for gay euros, whether it be stylish shirts or state-of-the-art kitchenware. It's also the most style-conscious of the city's gay scenes, though never intimidatingly so, and parading around in the latest styles remains optional. As with most of the scene, the men predominate, but women won't feel out of place. In summer the largest part of this street turns pedestrian to make it even more of a catwalk.

ARC

Reguliersdwarsstraat 44 (689 7070/www.bararc.com). Tram 1, 2, 4, 5, 9, 16, 24, 25. **Open** 4pm-1am Mon-Thur, Sun; 4pm-3am Fri, Sat. **Credit** AmEx, MC, V. **Map** p329 D4.

Still looking sleek and space age, ARC is well and truly established these days and continues to attract a stylish, moneyed, polysexual crowd who come to primp and pose. The cocktails and 'finger food' are tasty (and pricey) but service can be slow and ditsy.

Café April

Reguliersdwarsstraat 37 (625 9572/www.cafeapril.eu). Tram 1, 2, 4, 5, 9, 16, 24, 25. **Open** 2pm-1am Mon-Thur, Sun; 2pm-2am Fri, Sat. **No credit cards. Map** p329 D4.

Although there's an odd ski-chalet theme (complete with cable car cabin), the April is at its best when the sun shines and the sexy crowd spills out onto the terrace. Sunday's Shuffle Bubble happy hour (actually two hours: 6pm-8pm) gets rammed with punters taking advantage of the cheap booze.

Exit

Reguliersdwarsstraat 42 (625 8788/www.clubexit.eu). Tram 1, 2, 4, 5, 9, 16, 24, 25. **Open** 11pm-4am Thur-Sun; 11pm-5am Fri, Sat. **Admission** €5 Fri; €7 Sat. **No credit cards. Map** p329 E4

Multi-levelled club with each floor dedicated to a different musical genre; choices when we visited included pop, R&B and bouncy house. There's also a popular darkroom. Women have their own night once a month (*see p230*), but will also have a good time on regular nights. On Thursday, clubbing is generally free of charge.

't Leeuwtje

Reguliersdwarsstraat 105 (639 3012/www.realitybar.nl). Tram 1, 2, 4, 5, 9, 16, 24, 25. **Open** 3pm-1am Sun-Thur; 3pm-3am Fri, Sat. **No credit cards. Map** p329 E4.

In contrast to the more image-concious bars surrounding it, the newest café on the block is a regular ol' boozer that aims for a nice, comfortable feel: on Tuesdays there is free soup to warm the cockles of the coldest hearts, while Sundays provide a free cup of coffee with any booze order.

Reality

Reguliersdwarsstraat 129 (639 3012/www.realitybar.nl). Tram 1, 2, 4, 5, 9, 16, 24, 25. **Open** 8pm-3am Mon-Thur, Sun; 8pm-4am Fri, Sat. **No credit cards. Map** p329 E4.

One of the few bars in town where black and white gay guys regularly meet and mingle, this place is always popular during the happy hour, which runs from 8.30pm to 10pm. Things really get going later on though, when ferociously uptempo Latin music pumps from the speakers to get the crowd moving.

Soho

Reguliersdwarsstraat 36 (422 3312/www.pubsoho.eu). Tram 1, 2, 4, 5, 9, 16, 24, 25. **Open** 6pm-2am Mon-Thur, Sun; 6pm-4am Fri, Sat. **No credit cards. Map** p329 E4.

Looking like a cross between a British boozer and an English country house – complete with leather chesterfields and roaring fires – Soho attracts a young, fashionable and good-looking bunch of men who fill every nook and cranny of this sprawling bar. There's a nightly happy hour (10-11pm) and on weekends, downstairs gets dancing to house spun by DJs into the early hours. Sunday evening is a much quieter live jazz affair, if you need relax and kick back at the end of the weekend.

Girls like Girls Like Us

Cool. Sexy. Cutting edge. Lesbian. It's not often you get to say those words in a row, let alone append 'and in Amsterdam'. Thank God, then, for Jessica Gysel and Kathrin Hero (pictured), the girls from **Girls Like Us (GLU)**, a magazine with a side order of excellent parties that has injected hope into the city's dowdy dyke scene. Gysel was responsible for *Kutt*, *Butt*'s short-lived sister (*see p221*), a magazine that went down in lesbian lore for the interview with Chloe Sevigny in which she revealed she dabbled in girl-on-girl action.

GLU was launched at the end of 2005, says Gysel, 'out of frustration with existing lesbian magazines'. Hero adds that 'we needed a fun lesbian mag that we could really identify with, one neither totally mainstream – and therefore boring – nor underground, small and therefore too marginal'.

Published quarterly, *GLU* is a mixture of chatty interviews, fashion-driven art shoots and random ephemera dug from dusty old archives. This is a magazine totally at ease with the many facets of sexuality: never forgetting dyke history (previous issues have included repros of sheet music for *Tipping the Velvet*-style male impersonators), never afraid of cranking up the lesbian semiotics (Peaches dressed as Gia Carangi on the first cover) and not shy of subverting stereotypes (issue three's photo-feature on straight girls who look lez). They haven't – yet – snared their dream interviewees (Jil Sander and Jodie Foster – 'I really want to know all about her relationships' – for Gysel; Deneuve for Hero). Subjects so far have ranged from hip-as-hell, like Beth Ditto, to more highbrow, like Judith Halberstam. But in one respect, *GLU* is unique among dyke rags: cool people want a piece of it. Wolfgang Tillmans and Richard Kern have both contributed, and its reader profiles are pretty diverse, because, as Hero clearly states, 'I think it's also a style magazine; not all of our readers are lesbians.'

And, as much of an oxymoron as it might seem, a 'lesbian style magazine' is what *GLU* is – surely a world first. It's international in outlook and availability (it's Amsterdam-made, NY-published and available in fashion capitals: Magma in London is a stockist) and also in its launch and 'pop up' parties. Taking place in Paris, LA, NYC, and, on home turf, in Studio 80 (*see p245*), these electro-heavy nights – self-styled '3D versions of the magazine' – have featured Peaches on the decks, always include someone who's in the magazine and are full of the coolest dykes that you'll ever see in the city of Amsterdam.

But what do they themselves make of the scene that they've revitalised? Hero herself is quite despondent. 'I really hope other people will come up with nice and strong ideas, it's so boring,' she laments. Her colleague is more upbeat: 'I quite like it. There are some good places to hang out. And I tend to go out outside of the lesbian scene, which can be very inspiring at times, and healthy too.'

In 20 years' time, gender studies students will be writing theses on this phenomenon. But in the meantime, go sniff some *GLU*.

Kerkstraat

Home to the **Thermos Night Sauna** (*see p230*) and the **Bronx** sexshop (*see p229*), this quiet street off the busy Leidsestraat sure is gay. It even has a few gay hotels. Yet it is less posing pink than other areas. Nearby you'll find Holland's only Arabian gay bar, **Habibi Ana** (Lange Leidsedwarsstraat 4-6, no phone), with a strict Arabian-music-only policy, but a mixed, young and handsome international crowd.

De Spijker

Kerkstraat 4 (620 5919/ wwwspijkerbar.nl). Tram 1, 2, 5. **Open** 3pm-1am Mon-Thur; 1pm-3am Fri, Sat; 1pm-1am Sun. **No credit cards. Map** p330 C4.

This small boozer used to be a theatre in its previous life. Punters still liven things up and it can become rather crowded, rowdy and smokey. Its diverse clientele covers the waterfront from cute young guys to older muscle men and a few women, and all mingle happily. On the downside, the pool table always seems to be occupied. Every Tuesday is Beer Bust (cheap beer) and XXXLeather nights are once a month on Sundays.

Other areas

Mankind

Weteringstraat 60, Southern Canal Belt (638 4755/ www.mankind.nl). Tram 6, 7, 10, 16, 24, 25. **Open** noon-10pm Mon-Sat. **No credit cards. Map** p329 D5.

Mankind is quiet locals' place tucked down a side-street near the Rijksmuseum and the antique shops and art galleries of Spiegelstraat. Not just an excellent stop for culture cruisers, this bar also provides delicious sandwiches and a cheap dish of the day. In summer the canal-side patio is perfect to catch some sun, read the international magazines or simply to watch the world go by.

Prik

Spuistraat 109 (320 0002/www.prikamsterdam.nl). Tram 1, 2, 5, 13, 17. **Open** 4pm-1am Tue-Thur, Sun; 4pm-3am Fri, Sat. **No credit cards.**

Queer or not – Prik is hot. Indeed, true to the bar's slogan this recent addition to the scene succeeds in attracting a diverse crowd who enjoy its movie nights, delicious snacks and groovy sounds. Hairy fairies meet here every third Sunday of the month, when it hosts Furball (*see below*). *Photo p225.*

One-off club nights

For one-off lesbian club nights, *see p230.*

Art Launch

www.artlaunch.nl

Art Launch provides top-notch entertainment. The lads at Studio 80 (*see p285*) combine sets from up-and-coming DJs, underground performance and arty themes for 'Black Box' or 'Amsterdam Meets' nights.

Asian Disco Night

East meets west at this club night. Held at Cockring (*see p223*) every third Sunday of the month from 8pm to midnight.

Danserette

Early Sunday one-nighter at Akhnaton (www.akhnaton.nl) for those who need to get up early the following Monday. On the decks are classic disco hits and recent dance tunes.

De Trut

Bilderdijkstraat 165, Oud West (612 3524). Tram 3, 7, 12, 17. **Open** 11pm-4am Sun. **Admission** €1.50. **No credit cards. Map** p329 B5.

If you don't want the weekend to end, head to this alternative dance night in a former squat on Sundays. It's cheap, it's crowded, it's fun and it's been going on for about 20 years. Arrive early, before 11pm, or you might find you have to queue for a long time.

F*cking POP Queers

Trendy and underground Studio 80 (*see p245*) has a roster of remarkably queer-friendly nights like Black Box and Fashion Radio, but this Wednesday outing is its only specifically lesbian and gay night. The music policy is pop – from Madonna to electro.

Fresh

www.clubrapido.com

Little brother to Rapido (*see p228*), this more intimate club night attracts the same body beautifuls. It touches down every first Friday of the month at Escape (*see p243*) from 11pm-5am.

Furball

www.furball.nl

This hirsute heaven for hairy men and their smooth admirers is held at various venues around town. It's great dance night, sometimes with a theme. There's no dress code, no darkroom, just plenty of sweaty hairy guys, in all shapes, sizes and all ages, having a furry old time.

Hi Victory

A club night for HIV positive party people and their friends and supporters, Hi Victory takes place every couple of months at the Queen's Head (*see p224*), and is the brainchild of Amsterdam scene DJ Jarb.

Pink Grey/Art Launch

A dinner cabaret is held every first Wednesday of the month at the bijou Paleis van de Weemoed theatre-restaurant (Oudezijds Voorburgwal 15-17, www.paleis-van-de-weemoed.nl). Expect music from the 1930s to the '70s, drag acts and Dutch artists, and an older audience.

Rapido

www.clubrapido.com

Superpopular – but irregular – club night, that sells out quickly at Paradiso (*see p245*) where shirtless muscle marys dance and flirt to pumping house.

Reflexx

A glam new night from the crew behind Rapido and Fresh, this irregular event at Escape (*see p243*) aims to put that joyful feeling back into clubbing. DJs from around the world pump out happy vocal house.

Spellbound Productions

www.spellbound-amsterdam.nl
Held at OCCII (*see p234*), this is a cheap and alternative club night, which is popular with a non-scene crowd. Whether 'Disco Hospital' or 'Queer Underground', its success is easily explained by the heavy beats, performances and the snug bar.

Unk

An alternative mixed gay-straight night of bouncy electro from DJ Lupe, hosted every fourth Saturday of the month at the very cool, graffiti-sprayed Club 8 (Club 8, www.club-8.nl, Admiraal de Ruiterweg 56), on top of a pool hall, and a short cycle ride out west.

Cafés

Coffeeshop Downtown

Reguliersdwarsstraat 31, Southern Canal Belt (622 9958/www.coffeeshopdowntown.nl). Tram 4, 9, 16, 24, 25. **Open** 11am-8pm daily. **No credit cards. Map** p330 D4.
No cannabis in this coffeshop, but sandwiches, cakes, drinks and international mags. You might need the latter – as service can be slow when busy. Ah well, there's always the hunky, dressed-to-a-T guys to look at in this tiny multi-level hangout. In summer the lovely and popular terrace sometimes attracts straight couples from the nearby Flowermarket, who suddenly realise their mistake.

Le Monde

Rembrandtplein 6, Southern Canal Belt (626 9922). Tram 4, 9, 14. **Open** 8am-1am daily. **Credit** V. **Map** p331 E4.
Breakfast, lunch or supper, the long opening hours make this cosy eaterie on the bustling central square a very handy spot for a bite.

Film & theatre

Most of the independent cinemas in Amsterdam screen gay and lesbian flicks when released, and even the mainstream Pathé chain has caught on. The first Wednesday in the month at **Pathé de Munt** (*see p209*) is Gay Classics night, where you get a drink – pink champagne – at the cinema thrown in with your ticket, and another at the popular **Café April** (*see p225*) after the show. Though films shown here can often stretch the definition of what constitutes a 'classic', it's a fun night out. Tuesday night is film night at **Prik** (*see p227*); it's free and the choice of movies is sound. **De Balie** (*see p213*) and **Filmhuis Cavia** (*see p210*) are host to December's queer film festival **Roze Filmdagen** (Pink Film Days, www.rozefilmdagen.nl), a five- to ten-day event of features, shorts and international documentaries, while De Balie plays host to the biennial **Nederlands Transgender Film Festival** (www.transgenderfilmfestival.com) during May. Yet another two-yearly festival, spring's **Cinemasia** (www.cinemasia.nl), first started as the Queer & Asian Film Festival, and remains lesbian-run to this day.

The Queen's English Theatre Company (www.qetc.nl) gives the queer eye to classic English-language plays a couple of times a year. The Gay & Lesbian Switchboard (*see p304*) can tell you which cinemas and theatres are running gay and lesbian programmes.

Restaurants

Plenty of restaurants in Amsterdam have more than their fair share of gay diners, even if they are not specifically gay. A good rule of thumb: if a place is brand spanking new or has rather spectacular decor it's sure to attract the homo herds. The eateries listed below are gay run, or have significant numbers of gay diners.

Garlic Queen

Reguliersdwarsstraat 27, Southern Canal Belt (422 6426/www.garlicqueen.nl). Tram 1, 2, 4, 5, 9, 16, 24, 25. **Open** 6pm-1am Wed-Sun. *Kitchen* 6-11pm Wed-Sun. **Main courses** €17-€22. **Credit** AmEx DC, MC, V. **Map** p330 D4.
Portraits of the real queen, Beatrix, smile onto the metaphorical queens – as well as a wide range of other diners – chowing down in this campy temple to the stinking rose. Every dish contains at least one clove of the stuff – one contains 60 – though spoilsports can order any dish garlic-free.

Getto

Warmoesstraat 51, Old Centre: Old Side (421 5151/www.getto.nl). Tram 4, 9, 16, 24, 25. **Open** 4pm-1am Tue-Thur; 4pm-2am Fri, Sat; 4pm-midnight Sun. *Kitchen* 6-11pm Tue-Sun. **Main courses** €10-€15. **Credit** AmEx, DC, MC, V. **Map** p326 D2.
Cheap, cheerful, tasty, filling. That's what the food is like at this sparkly diner at the back of the thoroughly mixed lesbian and gay lounge. On Wednesday night all burger dinners (a house speciality) cost just €10. Combined with the weekday, two-for-the-price-of-one cocktail happy hour, this is the ideal place to take a cheap date.

Kitsch

Utrechtsestraat 42, Southern Canal Belt (625 9251/www.restaurant-kitsch.nl). Tram 4, 9, 14. **Open** 6pm-2am Mon-Sun. *Kitchen* 6-11pm. **Main courses** €15-€32. **Credit** AmEx, DC, MC, V. **Map** p331 E4.
There's Abba on the stereo, there's sassy service, and its all set off with glitterballs and faux fur. The wine list honours Betty Ford (she of celebrity rehab clinic fame), and dishes also carry cheeky names.

Despite Kitsch's playful nature, food is taken seriously here (foie gras, caviar) and there's plenty to satisfy the most discerning palette, albeit with a similarly impressive price tag.

Sex parties

Apart from the lesbian leather and S&M group **Wild Side** (www.wildside.dds.nl) who organise events, parties and workshops in different venues, there are no women-only sex parties in Amsterdam; just occasional, mixed fetish parties. But gay visitors will have no difficulty finding relief. Just remember to play it safe.

The popular **XXXLeather** parties have recently moved to the basement of Club More (Rozengracht 133, www.xxxleather.nl) but not to everyone's joy as it's a small venue. The future of **Club Trash** – another leather/sex party – looks a bit uncertain, so check gay press or www.nighttours.nl. The **Stable Master Hotel** (Warmoesstraat 23, 625 0148, www.stablemaster.nl) has been hosting jack-off parties for ages – open to non-guests too – at 9pm Thursdays through Mondays. **SOS** (Sex on Sunday) is held every second and last Sunday of the month between 4-8pm (doors close 5pm) at **Eagle** (*see p223*). If you fit the **Cockring** (*see p223*) – you get in for free if you peak at 18cm (7.2in) or more – it hosts a 'shoes-only' **Nude Club** every first Sunday of the month and its 'nude or underwear-only' **Horsemen & Knights** is on every third Sunday of the month. **Spijker** now hosts XXXLeather nights once a month on a Sunday, though it's more of a 'cruise & grab' atmosphere than a real sex party. Meanwhile 'erotic café' **Same Place** (Nassaukade 12, 475 1981, www.sameplace.nl), goes gay every Monday night between 9pm and 1am and on the last Sunday of the month between 3pm and 7pm.

Shops & services

Bookshops

The stores below all have dedicated gay stock, though you'll find gay books and magazines on sale in most of Amsterdam's bookshops. The **American Book Center** has a well-stocked gay section, and while **Waterstone's** (for both, *see p173*) doesn't have a dedicated gay section, it does carry the major British gay titles.

Intermale

Spuistraat 251, Old Centre: New Side (625 0009/ www.intermale.nl). Tram 1, 2, 5, 13, 14, 17. **Open** 11am-6pm Mon; 10am-6pm Tue, Wed, Fri, Sat; 10am-9pm Thur; noon-5pm Sun. **Credit** AmEx, MC, V. **Map** p326 C3.

Apart from a wide selection of new and recently published gay men's books, this shop also has some rare and out-of-print books, plus books in Spanish.

Vrolijk

Paleisstraat 135, Old Centre: New Side (623 5142/ www.vrolijk.nu). Tram 1, 2, 5, 13, 14, 17. **Open** 11am-6pm Mon; 10am-6pm Tue-Thur; 10am-5pm Sat; 1-5pm Sun. **Credit** AmEx, DC, MC, V. **Map** p326 C3.

The best international selection of rose-tinted reading, whether fiction or fact – plus CDs, DVDs, guides and the best gifts you'll find in town. It also has a second-hand section and sells a good range of gay T-shirts, condoms and cheeky gifts.

Hairdressers

Cuts 'n' Curls

Korte Leidsedwarsstraat 74, Southern Canal Belt (624 6881/www.cutsandcurls.nl). Tram 1, 2, 5, 6, 7, 10. **Open** 10am-8pm Tue-Thur; 10am-7pm Fri; 10am-4pm Sat. **Credit** AmEx, DC, MC, V. **Map** p330 D5.

Butch and basic haircuts with a sensitive side: all their shampoos and conditioners are vegan-friendly.

Leather/rubber/sex

Whether just in need of a tattoo, a piercing, some kinky toys or a complete leather outfit, Amsterdam's Leather Lane is where to find it all. **Mr B** (Warmoesstraat 89, 420 8548, www.mrb.nl) sells anything from a simple and cheap cockring to expensive chaps. It also does tattoos and piercings (there's a female piercer too), plus DVDs and tickets for all the big gay events. The street's **RoB of Amsterdam** branch is more for accessories; here you can pick up a wristband before hitting the bars (Warmoesstraat 89, 422 003, www.rob.nl); the Weteringschans branch (No.253, 428 3000) has the full complement of leather/rubber gear. If rubber is more your thing, you can make your fantasies come true at **Black Body** (Lijnbaansgracht 292, 626 2553, www.blackbody.nl; *photo p223*). Two sex shops with porn cinemas are **Bronx** (Kerkstraat 53-5, 623 1548, www.thebronx.nl) and **Drakes** (Damrak 61, 627 9544). Women with a dirty mind should head to **Female & Partners** or **Stout** (for both, *see p193*). **Demask** (Zeedijk 64, 620 5603, www.demask.com) is fun for all. For erotic and fetish shops, *see p193*.

Saunas

Fenomeen

1e Schinkelstraat 14, Zuid (671 6780/http://sauna fenomeen.nl). Tram 1, 2. **Open** 1-11pm daily. Women only Mon; closed Aug. **Admission** €8 before 6pm, €3 after 10pm. **No credit cards**.

A relaxed, legalised squat sauna, housed in old horses' stalls, that's popular with lesbians on women-only Mondays. It houses a sauna, steam bath, cold bath, chill-out room with mattresses and showers in the courtyard. Massages are also available. The café is ecologically-minded, with vegetarian dishes and vegan soup always on the menu.

Thermos Day

Raamstraat 33, Southern Canal Belt (623 9158/ www.thermos.nl). Tram 1, 2, 5, 7, 10. **Open** noon-11pm Mon-Fri; noon-10pm Sat; 11am-10pm Sun. **Admission** €18; €13.50 under-24s with ID. **Credit** AmEx, DC, MC, V. **Map** p330 C4.

Quite busy during the week and absolutely packed at weekends, this four-level sauna offers it all: a tiny steam room, large dry-heat room, darkroom, porn cinema, private cubicles, bar, hairdresser, masseur, gym and small roof terrace. For those who want to heat, meet and eat, there's a restaurant, too.

Thermos Night

Kerkstraat 58-60, Southern Canal Belt (623 4936/ www.thermos.nl). Tram 1, 2, 5. **Open** 11pm-8am Mon-Sun. **Admission** €18; €13.50 under-24s & over-65s with ID. **Credit** AmEx, DC, MC, V. **Map** p330 D4.

Thermos's night-time sessions are even more popular than their day operation, especially after the bars and clubs close. On Friday and Saturday nights it gets extremely busy and hot.

Lesbian

The lesbian scene isn't brilliant, but it's not as bad as it has been in the past, and at the moment there's a fair variety of bars and one-off club nights to satisfy most tastes. That said, there's not even a smidgeon of the variety of the men's scene and, given the lack of any genuinely mixed bars (apart from Getto, see p228), that's reason enough reason for lesbians to gird their loins and go to the men's bars. Apart from a few strictly men-only places (generally sex clubs), women are welcome everywhere around the city – though they will, of course, be in the minority.

Garbo in Exit

www.garboinexit.nl

Every fourth Sunday in the month, Exit (*see p225*) becomes a women-only space. This relaxing and fun afternoon session (from 4-10pm) attracts women of all ages and types who do their thing on the (no smoking) dancefloor to 1970s and '80s hits. There's even a tasty Indonesian rijstafel buffet if you're feeling peckish.

Garbo for Women

www.garboforwomen.nl

Run by friends of the club above, Garbo for Women has a similar formula and takes place every first Saturday in the month at Strand West (*see p159* **United we sand**) from 5pm to midnight.

GLU Parties

One-off club nights for cool girls. *See also p226* **Girls like Girls Like Us**.

Flirtation

www.letsbeopen.nl

As the biggest lesbian night in the country – currently housed in Panama (*see p245*) – this extravaganza claims to attract more than a thousand women a pop. The secret of its success? Themed parties – angels & devils or cowgirls & showgirls – where dressing up is encouraged, a playlist of house and a keep-'em-hungry-for-more policy.

Saarein II

Elandstraat 119, the Jordaan (623 4901/www. saarein.nl). Tram 7, 10. **Open** noon-1am Tue-Thur, Sun; noon-2am Fri, Sat; *Lunch* noon-4pm. **No credit cards**. **Map** p330 C4.

Never in fashion, so never out of it, this hardy perennial of the lesbian scene is particularly popular at weekends. The women it attracts tend to be slightly older, but young bucks certainly make an appearance. The only lesbian pool table in town resides in the basement.

Sappho

Vijzelstraat 103, Southern Canal Belt (06 1714 0296/www.sappho.nl). Tram 16, 24, 25. **Open** noon-1am Tue-Thur, Sun; noon-3am Fri, Sat. **No credit cards**.

Women-friendly during the week, Sappho turns totally lez on Friday nights, as a couple of hundred gay girlies and their friends of every gender and sexuality cram in to dance to DJ-spun house and retro hits. After a recent facelift split this once good-looking bar into two (there's now a miniscule lounge), the jury's still out on whether it's an improvement on the original.

Sugar

Hazenstraat 19, the Jordaan (06 1401 3143/www. les-bi-friends.com). Tram 7, 10. **Open** 6pm-1am Sun, Mon, Wed, Thur; 6pm-3am Fri, Sat. **No credit cards**. **Map** p330 C4.

A minute's walk away from Saarein (*see above*) this neat lesbian bar opened its doors in 2005. Small and loungey, it attracts a slightly younger, cooler crowd than its big sister along the street, but there's much cheerful to-ing and fro-ing between the two, especially during the summer months.

Vive la Vie

Amstelstraat 7, Southern Canal Belt (624 0114/ www.vivelavie.net). Tram 4, 9, 14. **Open** noon-1am Mon-Thur, Sun; noon-3am Fri, Sat. **No credit cards**. **Map** p330 E4.

The walls of this small and basic bar just off Rembrandtplein are lined with pictures of female Hollywood icons. Under the watchful gaze of Elizabeth Taylor, a varied bunch of lesbians (and their friends) drink and dance to mainstream and Dutch hits. It gets packed late on Saturday night, so arrive early if you want a seat.

Music

A city built on marsh but founded on rock.

Café Pakhuis Wilhelmina. See p232.

Rock, Roots & Jazz

We'll grant you this much: a list of Dutch musical icons fails to trip easily off the tongues of many visitors. But that's not to say that they don't exist. From the electronically generated beats delivered by Tiësto and Junkie XL to the globally renowned Royal Concertgebouw Orchestra via the classy, jazzy movies of stars such as Misha Mengelberg, not to mention the array of underground talent working in everything from heavy metal to Frisian fado, Amsterdam's native music scene shouldn't be underestimated.

But that's just the local perspective. In addition to all the acts emanating from the city, Amsterdam has long been established as one of the world's most important ports of call for international musicians, and major acts in virtually every imaginable genre are constantly passing through town. Whatever you're seeking, it'll be readily available within close proximity to the canal ring: keep your eyes and ears peeled and you may discover that a performance by your favourite band or DJ is but a tram ride away.

TICKETS AND INFORMATION

For full event listings, head to the **AUB Ticketshop** (0900 0191, www.aub.nl), or check Ticketmaster (www.ticketmaster.nl), free Dutch-language monthly *Uitkrant*, or national music magazine *Oor* (www.oor.nl). For alternative listings, check the English-language *Amsterdam Weekly*. Book in advance.

Rock & roots

Where rock music is concerned, bigger isn't always better. Away from the clubs and venues listed below, there's a thriving underground scene of squat happenings and concerts. See *Amsterdam Weekly*, www.squat.net and www.underwateramsterdam.com for details. In particular, check out **OT301** (*see p213*), Zaal 100 and independent show promoter Subbacultcha (www.subbacultcha.nl). For **Bitterzoet**, a multi-purpose venue that stages a programme of frequent gigs and great hip hop nights throughout the year, *see p243*.

ArenA

ArenA Boulevard 1, Bijlmermeer (311 1333/ www.amsterdamarena.nl). Metro Bijlmer.
Open hours vary. **Admission** from €40.

When the football season ends, Ajax's stadium is reborn as a musical amphitheatre hosting tours by the likes of U2, Madonna and the Rolling Stones, outdoor raves, and even a few Dutch stars. Bring your lighter, and don't forget binoculars if you're trapped in those garishly coloured cheap seats.

Badcuyp

1e Sweelinckstraat 10, the Pijp (675 9669/www.badcuyp.nl). Tram 4, 16, 24, 25. **Open** 11am-1am Tue-Thur, Sun; 11am-3am Fri, Sat. **Admission** free-€9. **Credit** MC, V. **Map** p331 F5.

The focus at this small and friendly venue is on world and jazz. Besides the intriguing range of international talents that play the main hall, the cute café plays host to regular salsa, African, jazz and open jam sessions that draw a hugely diverse crowd.

Café Pakhuis Wilhelmina

Veemkade 576, Docklands (419 3368/www.cafepakhuiswilhelmina.nl). Tram 26/bus 42. **Open** hours vary Wed-Sun. **Admission** €5-€8. **Credit** MC, V.

Part of the Pakhuis Wilhelmina breeding ground for underground young artists in the docklands, this café aims to host challenging dance nights and interesting live acts. That said, regular events such as Hardrock Karaoke and themed tribute nights are also great fun if you're looking for more familiar sounds or fancy getting out the leather trousers and treading the boards. *Photo p231.*

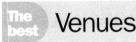

Venues

Bimhuis
Intimate, clean and jazz-tastic. *See p235.*

Concertgebouw
A genuinely timeless venue. *See p238.*

Cruise Inn
Rockin' and rollin' through time. *See p232.*

Maloe Melo
Amsterdam's longstanding house of the blues. *See p232.*

Melkweg
A song and dance to the stars. *See p233.*

Muziekgebouw
The future sounds fantastic. *See p239.*

Paradiso
A pop temple from all angles. *See p235.*

'Skek
Live in your living room – almost. *See p235.*

Tropentheater
International perspective for all. *See p235.*

Carré

Amstel 115-25, Southern Canal Belt (0900 252 5255/www.theatercarre.nl). Tram 4, 6, 7, 10. **Open** *Box office* 4-8pm daily. *Telephone reservations* 9am-8pm daily. **Admission** €15-€80. **Credit** AmEx, DC, MC, V. **Map** p330 F4.

This beautiful circus theatre opened in the late 19th century and boasts a rich history. Refurbished in recent years, it's still a top-notch venue. However, the bookers do shy away from risks, resulting in a programme of family-friendly musicals, cabarets, operas and pop concerts. For two weeks during winter, it hosts the World Christmas Circus.

Club 3VOOR12

Studio Desmet, Plantage Middenlaan 4A, the Plantage (035 671 2222/studio Desmet 521 7100/www.3voor12.nl). Tram 9, 14. **Open** 9pm-1am Wed. **Admission** free. **Map** p327 F3.

This old film theatre bursts into life on Wednesday nights for a live national radio and TV show. Each broadcast throws up a diverse line-up – one week it's three little-known local acts, the next it's international stars in town for a sold-out gig. Entry is free, but there's limited capacity: reserve a spot by emailing club3VOOR12@vpro.nl, though you won't know who you'll be seeing when you apply.

Cruise Inn

Zuiderzeeweg 29, Zeeburg (692 7188/www.cruise-inn.com). Tram 14/bus 22, 37. **Open** 9pm-1am Sat (until 3am on concert nights). **Admission** free-€11; jam sessions free. **No credit cards**.

Amsterdam's home of rockabilly and swing has had a rough time since the city confiscated its land and moved the club into temporary accommodation. Despite its troubles, it has the most loyal audience of any venue in town: while it's stuck firmly in the past, it puts on a mighty fine retro party. And if you dress for the occasion, it'll be even better.

Heineken Music Hall

ArenA Boulevard 590, Bijlmermeer (0900 300 1250/www.heinekenmusichall.nl). Metro Bijlmer. **Open** *Box office* from 6.30pm, concert days only. **Admission** from €27.50. **Credit** AmEx, MC, V.

A surprisingly cosy musical arena in the ArenA complex, the Heineken Music Hall regularly plays host to pop, rock and dance acts who are too big for the more central venues. Its modern design lacks character but makes up for it in acoustics. It isn't hard to get up close to your musical heroes.

Maloe Melo

Lijnbaansgracht 163, Western Canal Belt (420 4592/www.maloemelo.com). Tram 7, 10, 13, 14, 17. **Open** 9pm-3am Mon-Thur, Sun; 9pm-4am Fri, Sat. **Admission** free-€5. **No credit cards**. **Map** p331 E5.

Well, I woke up this morning, feeling Maloe Melowed... This small, fun little juke joint on Lijnbaansgracht is Amsterdam's native house of the blues. Quality rockabilly and roots acts also play here on a regular basis, so shed your gloom and enjoy the boogie.

Meervaart

Meer en Vaart 300, West (410 7777/www.meervaart.nl). Tram 1, 17/bus 23, 192. **Open** *Box office* 10am-4pm Mon-Fri; 11am-4pm Sat. **Admission** €15-€35. **Credit** MC, V.

Its modern architecture and peripheral location do nothing for its ambience, but the Meervaart does offer an interesting mix of cabaret and theatre shows, along with a mish-mash of musical styles.

Melkweg

Lijnbaansgracht 234A, Southern Canal Belt (531 8181/www.melkweg.nl). Tram 1, 2, 5, 6, 7, 10, 20. **Open** *Box office* from 4.30pm daily; 4.30pm-3am Fri, Sat. *Club* hours vary; usually 8.30pm-4am daily. **Admission** €5-€32. *Membership* (compulsory) €3/mth; €15/yr. **No credit cards. Map** p330 D5.

A former dairy (the name translates as 'Milky Way'), the Melkweg acts as a home away from home for music of all styles, and thus draws a suitably eclectic crowd. Its two decent-sized concert halls offer a full programme year-round; after a refit in 2007, which brought the capacity of the Max room up to 1,500, you've got an even better chance of getting tickets for the big shows. Music isn't the sole remit for this diverse venue: the complex is also home to a theatre, a cinema, an art gallery and a café, and stages weekend club nights to boot. All in all, it's a key cultural beacon in the centre of the city; music fans would be mad to miss it.

Mulligans

Amstel 100, Southern Canal Belt (622 1330/www.mulligans.nl). Tram 4, 9, 14, 16, 24, 25. **Open** *Bar* 4pm-1am Mon-Thur; 4pm-2am Fri; 2pm-3am Sat; 2pm-1am Sun. Music starts at 10pm, sessions at 7pm. **Admission** free. **No credit cards. Map** p327 E3.

You'll find Irish pubs in every major European town, but only a handful are as much fun as Mulligans. The formula will be familiar to anyone who has frequented similar places in the past: the music on offer ranges from traditional Celtic acts to modern-day rock and pop singers and songwriters. There's even an open session on Sundays, great fun for onlookers and musicians alike.

Nationaal Pop Instituut

Prins Hendrikkade 142, Old Centre: New Side (428 4288, media centre 618 9217/www.popinstituut.nl). Bus 22, 23. **Open** 10am-5pm Mon-Fri. **Admission** varies. **Credit** MC, V. **Map** p326 D2.

The NPI exists to support Dutch music across the country and throughout the world, be it good, bad or excruciating. Its lack of bias is heroic, and anyone can ask for help or access their impressive media libraries stored inside. Most jawdropping of all, however, is its online history of Dutch music, available in English at www.hollandrocks.com). In addition, the NPI's online national Concertagenda (a gig guide, basically) is ideal if you want to plan ahead for performances during your stay.

Music of the sphere

So, what do Youssou N'Dour, Goran Bregovic, Souad Massi, Zap Mama, Ozomatli, Femi Kuti and Ravi Shankar have in common? There are probably many possible answers to that teaser. But for the purposes of this book, the main one is that they've all played at **Amsterdam Roots** (www.amsterdamroots.nl): staged every June, it's an annual celebration of culture and music from around the world.

It's a big event: the 50 or so concerts are held across most of the city's major venues, among them the Concertgebouw, the Melkweg, the Tropentheater and the Paradiso. The climax of the event is Roots Open Air, a Sunday afternoon event that sees Oosterpark transformed into a collection of 'villages' that host an array of free performances. More than 50,000 locals come together to see 50-plus acts over six stages, soaking up the good vibes at this awesome event.

World music enthusiasts should also consider taking the train to Park Brakkenstein in Nijmegen during the first weekend of June for **Music Meeting** (www.musicmeeting.nl), a cutting-edge festival that prides itself on bringing together future stars from around the world. Besides catching such major players as Toumani Diabaté's Symmetric Orchestra, Béla Fleck, Manu Dibango, Trio Mocoto and Balkan Beat Box, visitors have witnessed Maori songs mixed with wild electro beats (Wai), or an accordion quintet that features a blind Austrian who knows his stuff when it comes to Mongolian throat singing (the inimitable Accordion Tribe).

Other world music festivals often raise hackles about how a potentially useful definition like 'crossover' has been appropriated to describe dreadlocked white kids jumping up and down. But volunteer-driven festivals such as Amsterdam Roots and Music Meeting, both of which have been fighting the good fight for two decades, act as a reminder that when different good things are put together, it often results in... well, even better things. Thanks to these initiatives, the term 'globalisation' may eventually be defined not by economic and political irregularities, but by the potential positives of embracing other cultures.

De Nieuwe Anita

Frederik Hendrikstraat 111, West (no phone/www.boulderdash.nl/dna/dna.html). Tram 3, 12. **Open** hours vary. **Admission** varies. **No credit cards. Map** p329 A4

A new fixture in Amsterdam's subculture, DNA has become a sparkling promoter of fresh talents in the world of independent rock and electronica. It may keep itself to itself, but for those in the know it's the place to be. Programming is sporadic and based on good relations with understanding neighbours; check the website first before heading out.

OCCII

Amstelveenseweg 134, Museum Quarter (671 7778/www.occii.org). Tram 1, 2. **Open** 9pm-2am Mon-Thur, Sun; 10pm-3am Fri, Sat. **Admission** €3-€7. **No credit cards.**

Formerly a squat, this friendly bar and concert hall is tucked away at one end of Vondelpark. While its squat-scene days may be over, their legacy remain: the roster offers touring underground rock, experimental and reggae acts plus adventurous local bands, and there's a good chance of witnessing something special if you turn up with an open mind.

Moving music

Many local jazzbos were worried when the legendary **Bimhuis** (*pictured*; *see p235*), which had hosted everyone from smooth jazz legends to squawking avant-gardists over the course of three decades, left its old and wonderfully grubby digs in 2005 for the high-tech **Muziekgebouw** (*see p239*). Conceived as a replacement for the equally venerable Het IJsbreker, the Muziekgebouw (literally, 'music building') was designed to provide a new home for a whole slew of the nation's foremost contemporary music ensembles, among them the Asko Ensemble, the Schönberg Ensemble, the Nieuw Ensemble, the Ives Ensemble, the Orkest de Volharding and the Amsterdam Sinfonietta.

No expense was spared in the construction of the Muziekgebouw: €52 million was spent building its wildly jutting transparent cubes and kitting it out with all the latest technical and acoustical mod cons. Greeted with architectural awards, critical raves and public acclaim, it's been a resounding success. Indeed, the opening of the Muziekgebouw seemed to jump-start the cultural flowering of this long up-and-coming area along the eastern docks, envisioned by city planners as a cultural boulevard linking the streets of the old city (Centraal Station is but a short walk away) with those of the new.

A few years after opening, the halls have hosted almost every imaginable combination of sound and rhythm; in 2006, the venue even hosted a festival devoted to the Jew's harp. To clear your head afterwards (or even for some pre-show sustenance), head to the grand café-restaurant overlooking the scenic wateriness of the Ij. The complex is also home to studios, rehearsal rooms, convention facilities, an exhibition space and the Klankspeeltuin (*see p207* **State of play**), a unique 'sound playground' where kids get to make music of their own. Needless to say, the jazzbos aren't worrying any more.

Panama

Oostelijke Handelskade 4, the Waterfront (311 8686/ www.panama.nl). Bus 28, 43, 39. **Open** *Telephone* 11am-6pm daily. *Theatre/club* hours vary. **Admission** from €10. **Credit** AmEx, MC, V. **Map** p327 F1.

The Panama, a music venue, restaurant and night-club under one roof, offers concerts, dance nights, comedy shows and occasional theatre events.

Paradiso

Weteringschans 6-8, Southern Canal Belt (626 4521/ www.paradiso.nl). Tram 1, 2, 5, 7, 10. **Open** hours vary. **Admission** from €5. *Membership* €3/mth; €18/yr. **No credit cards. Map** p330 D5.

A cornerstone of the Amsterdam scene, this former church is in such high demand that it often hosts several events in one day. The main hall has a rare sense of grandeur, with multiple balconies and stained-glass windows peering down upon the performers. The smaller hall upstairs is a great place to catch new talent before the big time. Both are wonderfully intimate; bands feed off the surroundings, making for some special nights. What's more, the security is surprisingly relaxed: you can often even wander between halls to check out the differing vibes before settling in to watch the show that's best suited to your own tastes.

'Skek

Zeedijk 4-8 (427 0551/www.skek.nl). Tram 4, 9, 14, 16, 24, 25/Metro Nieuwmarkt. **Open** noon-1am Mon-Thur, Sun; noon-3am Fri, Sat. **Admission** free. **No credit cards. Map** p326 D2.

This cheap little joint is new to the scene but is already living up to its potential. Run by the same student organisation in charge of Filmtheater Kriterion, its focus is value and quality. While students lap up discounts, music lovers will appreciate regular singer/songwriter and jazz gigs, which are both entertaining and great for the wallet.

Tropentheater

Mauritskade 63, (568 8711/www.tropentheater.nl). Tram 7, 9, 10, 14/bus 22. **Open** *Box office* noon-6pm Mon-Fri; 2pm-6pm Sat. **Tickets** from €18. **Credit** MC, V. **Map** p332 H3.

Falling under the umbrella of the Royal Tropical Institute (KIT), an independent non-profit organisation that specialises in the areas of international and intercultural co-operation, the Tropentheater is the number one place to catch acts from every faraway corner of the world.

Vondelpark Openluchttheater

Vondelpark, Museum Quarter (673 1499/www. openluchttheater.nl). Tram 1, 2, 3, 5, 7, 10, 12. **Open** *June-Sept* dawn-dusk daily. **Admission** free. **No credit cards. Map** p330 C6.

On pleasant summer days, this famous Amsterdam park is packed; so from June to September, organisers put on music, dance, cabaret and children's activities throughout the week. Few places better capture the laid-back charm of the city in summer. Turn up early if you want a prime seating spot.

Winston Kingdom

Warmoesstraat 125-129, Old Centre: Old Side (623 1380/www.winston.nl). Tram 4, 9, 16, 24, 25. **Open** 9pm-3am Mon-Thur, Sun; 9pm-4am Fri, Sat. **Admission** €5-€10. **No credit cards. Map** p326 D3.

Part of a weird and wonderful hotel complex, the Winston is where artistic decadence collides with rock 'n' roll grime. Evenings offer new talent, both local and international, followed by a club (included in the entry price). After a long night of partying, collapse for a kip up in the hotel.

Jazz & blues

The best international acts tour Amsterdam regularly, but don't neglect the local talent. For **'Skek**, *see above*; in addition, **OT301** (*see p213*) stages underground jazz nights and weekly electro-acoustic experiments over at DNK-Amsterdam (www.dnk-amsterdam.com) every Monday. Since its arrival, **Nachttheater Sugar Factory** (*see p243*) has been one of the hippest clubs in town, offering a real alternative to the regular dance scene. But it also hosts frequent live shows, and it's perfect if you're looking for danceable grooves rather than chin-scratching mellowness: on Sundays, WickedJazzSounds provides a raw mix of old vinyl and some seriously expressive live sets.

Alto

Korte Leidsedwarsstraat 115, Southern Canal Belt (626 3249/www.jazz-cafe-alto.nl). Tram 1, 2, 5, 6, 7, 10. **Open** 9pm-3am Mon-Thur, Sun; 9pm-4am Fri, Sat. **Admission** free. **No credit cards. Map** p330 D5.

Small and often smoky, the widely renowned Alto is one of the city's older and better jazz venues. Renowned Dutch saxophonist Hans Dulfer (Candy's dad) has a long-running slot on Wednesday evenings, but the quality isn't generally much lower on the other six nights of the week.

Bimhuis

Piet Heinkade 3, Docklands (788 2188/www.bim huis.nl). Tram 16, 26. **Open** *Telephone reservations* noon-7pm Mon-Fri. *Box office* 7-11pm show nights, most shows 9pm. **Admission** from €14. **Credit** AmEx, DC, MC, V. **Map** p327 F1.

Jazz musicians from far and wide queue up for a chance to grace the stage at the Bimhuis, even after its relatively recent transplant to the Muziekgebouw aan 't IJ complex. The eye-catching building and familiar interior layout has more or less guaranteed the Bimhuis a healthy future; it's no longer a smoky jazz café, but the fantastic music remains. *See also p234* **Moving music**.

Bourbon Street

Leidsekruisstraat 6-8, Southern Canal Belt (623 3440/www.bourbonstreet.nl). Tram 1, 2, 5, 6, 7, 10. **Open** 10pm-4am Mon-Thur, Sun; 10pm-5am Fri, Sat. **Admission** usually free before 11pm, then €5-€8. **Credit** AmEx, DC, MC, VC. **Map** p330 D5.

Muziekgebouw aan 't IJ. *See p239.*

In the heart of the tourist area, this blues club has a spacious bar and a late liquor licence. Musicians are welcome at regular jam sessions; international acts drop in a couple of nights each week.

Festivals

The Dutch club scene slows in summer, but it's really more of a sideways step. Purpose-built beaches such as Blijburg, Strand West and Nemo Beach (on the roof of the science museum) spring up to host shows and mad parties all through the week, and one-off festivals crop up everywhere. Major musical events are scattered throughout the country from April to September, and many are completely free; check www.festivalinfo.nl for locations and line-ups. Tickets for larger festivals are available from the AUB Ticketshop (0900 0191) or through Ticketmaster (www.ticketmaster.nl).

Amsterdam Roots Festival

www.amsterdamroots.nl. **Date** June.
This festival brings some of the best world music acts to Amsterdam every year. *See p233* **Music of the sphere**.

A Camping Flight to Lowlands

www.lowlands.nl. **Date** late Aug.
The best place to bid farewell to summer is in the Lowlands. Holland's largest alternative music festival takes place over three days, attracting up to 60,000 young hipsters on each. The music, theatre acts and street performers create a lively atmosphere, and weather is largely unimportant – all the important stages are inside huge tents. Those seeking extra adventure can buy a ticket that includes entry to the Walibi World amusement park, which sits next to the festival site. All told, it's the closest thing Amsterdam has to a Glastonbury of its own. Long may it continue to thrive.

Crossing Border

www.crossingborder.nl. **Date** Nov.
Based in the Hague, this gathering puts words before melody. Crossing Border offers a stimulating mix of literature and music, with many well-known international authors and artists arriving in town for spoken-word and musical performances.

London Calling

www.londoncalling.nl. **Date** late Mar, mid Nov.
The twice-yearly London Calling concerts are often the first opportunity for Dutch audiences to catch the hottest new rock and pop talents from the UK. Thanks to its increasing popularity, additional specials have been creeping on to the calendar.

Motel Mozaique

www.motelmozaique.nl. **Date** mid Apr.
Rotterdam hosts this spectacular three-day festival blending music, theatre, art and hospitality. Expect an edgy line-up and hordes of hipsters wandering happily between venues. You can even stay on site: each year sees new weird and wonderful sleeping concepts, though places are limited.

Noorderslag Weekend

www.noorderslag.nl. **Date** mid Jan.
A rare midwinter fest stretched over three days in Groningen, Noorderslag Weekend is for those seriously into the rock and pop scenes. An international industry showcase, the first two days fall under the name Eurosonic and are all about acts expected to make an impact across Europe in the coming year. The final night, Noorderslag itself, celebrates homegrown artists both old and new.

North Sea Jazz

0900 300 1250/www.northseajazz.nl. **Date** mid July.
This three-day mega-event is a favourite among Dutch jazz fans and outsiders. Staging marvellous big-name line-ups (around 180 acts) and drawing 23,000 visitors per day, the festival has now settled into the Ahoy' complex in the south of Rotterdam. It's hardly the most attractive of locations, but it has allowed breathing space for further growth.

Parkpop

www.parkpop.nl. **Date** late June.
Loads of European cities claim to hold the largest free festival. Parkpop, in the Hague, is the Dutch contender: organisers usually expect 300,000 to 500,000 visitors for this family-type affair. Expect some surprisingly big international names, popular Dutch acts and upcoming urban outfits across the event's three side-by-side stages.

Pinkpop

www.pinkpop.nl. **Date** May/June.
Attracting a slightly younger and poppier crowd than A Camping Flight to the Lowlands, Pinkpop, staged down in the southern tip of the country, is somewhat less adventurous than its indie sister. Still, there are plenty of big names in the worlds of pop, rock, dance and metal at the three-day event. Just remember to wear something pink…

Classical & Opera

One of the most heartwarming aspects of the classical scene in Amsterdam is that the city promotes a classless adoration of beautiful music. Attending a concert is not a grand statement of one's arrival in society, but simply about a love of the music. The greatest orchestras in the world perform here, and there's easy access for all: tickets typically cost little more than the price of the biggest rock and pop concerts, and frequently go for less.

While orchestras elsewhere slip and slide towards financial doom, the arts in Amsterdam only seem to be improving. Funding is clearly in the right hands, and many organisations are

Battle of the bandwidths

From around the early 1980s, when radio broadcast equipment became smaller, cheaper and highly accessible, indie radio steadily grew in popularity all around the world, and the Netherlands was no exception. During this halcyon period, Dutch airwaves became filled with pirate stations, providing commercial-free, alternative programming in both news and music. Many of them came to be regarded as a valuable source of sound for anyone with curious ears (although with the commercial stations playing little beyond the top 40 and smooth jazz, this wasn't a particularly amazing feat). Stations such as Radio 100 became known for their wide roster of DJs; their limitless knowledge and record collections plugged a wild variety of themes, from African tribal music and modern classical to punk and the latest in underground news.

None of the stations was ever legal. Pirate radio simply fell fuzzily between the cracks of Dutch law; like soft drugs and prostitution, for example, which authorities chose to tolerate. But even Dutch forbearance has limits, especially when the profits of legal businesses are falling as a result. The executioner's axe began to cast a longer and longer shadow. And then, in February 2003, came the Dutch National Radio Policy, which caused a revolution on the airwaves.

The new diktat seemed designed to please commercial radio, which wanted to dominate the ether. The government claimed all unowned frequencies, selling them on to the highest corporate bidder; any stations unable to pay the exorbitant fees were ordered off air. Stations were raided, equipment was seized and hefty fines were handed out to remaining pirate broadcasters.

The laws scared away many stations, but a few escaped the crackdown. In the Hague, **Radio Tonka** survives at 92 FM. In Leiden, **Koekoeroe** lives on at 97.4 FM. And in Amsterdam, stations include the politically focused **Vrije Keiser** (96.3 FM), which broadcasts on Tuesdays from noon to 8pm, and **DFM** (formerly Radio 100), now online at www.dfm.nu. The newer **Radio Free Amsterdam** (www.radiofreeamsterdam.com) offers a brighter, more cheerful counterpoint to the squatter-dominated pirate scene.

The biggest survivor, though, is **Radio Patapoe** (88.3 FM and www.freeteam.nl/patapoe), which broadcasts 24 hours a day with an uncategorisable array of shows that lurch from Dr Doo Wop to Punk as Fuck, Psychadelicatessen to the child-oriented De Oktoscope. It's a brilliant representation of what free radio can be – long may it rule the airwaves.

planning for a bright future. As such, you'll not only hear the classics in the grand halls, but alongside canals, in parks and sometimes even on the streets themselves.

ENSEMBLES

The city is also home to some of the most renowned orchestras and soloists in Europe. Led by chief conductor Mariss Jansons, the **Royal Concertgebouw Orchestra** is one of the world's most prestigious large groups. The orchestra plays in the city during most weeks in the cultural season, and regularly welcomes guest conductors and soloists of the calibre of Carlos Kleiber, Kurt Sanderling and Christian Thielemann. In addition, the respected **Netherlands Philharmonic** and relative newcomers the **Holland Symfonia** frequently produce wonderful opera and ballet productions. And don't miss the **Rotterdam Philharmonic** if you head to Rotterdam during your stay.

A healthy music scene requires diversity, and Amsterdam delivers. On one side of the fence, the quest for fidelity to the composer's intentions has led to the foundation of many traditionalist ensembles, performing the classics on period instruments. **The Amsterdam Baroque Orchestra & Choir**, the **Amsterdam Bach Soloists**, and the **Orchestra of the 18th Century** have restored popular cantatas to their original state of crystalline clarity.

However, classical music cannot survive simply on its back catalogue, and there's also a thriving modern classical movement. Although they're not always a comfortable ride, these performances can nevertheless be an exciting auditory experience. Standout collectives include the **Schönberg Ensemble**, **Asko Ensemble** and the **Nieuw Ensemble**. In addition, keep an eye out for the experimental projects of the **Ensemble MAE** (formerly Maarten Altena Ensemble), which are always unpredictable and rewarding. Fans of modern works will also appreciate the Proms aan het IJ series, which runs over at the **Muziekgebouw aan 't IJ** (*see p239*) from October until May (www.promsaanhetij.nl).

TICKETS AND INFORMATION

Ticket prices in Amsterdam are very reasonable compared with other European cities. However, tickets for many of the larger venues are sold on a subscription system, and it can be difficult to get tickets on the fly. For big concerts and operas, try to book as far in advance as you can, but if you're just passing through, it's always worth checking for returns. If you're really lucky, you may find a bargain at the Last Minute Ticket Shop (www.lastminuteticketshop.nl).

For full listings information, pick up a copy of the free Dutch listings magazine *Uitkrant*, published by the AUB (0900 0191, www.aub.nl), or call in at the Amsterdam Tourist Board (0900 400 4040), which has information on upcoming shows. Discounts on tickets are often available for students and the over-65s on production of ID.

Concert halls

Bethaniënklooster

Barndesteeg 6b, Old Centre: Old Side (625 0078/ www.bethanienklooster.nl). Tram 4, 9, 14, 16, 24, 25/Metro Nieuwmarkt. **Open** hours vary. **Tickets** free-€15. **No credit cards**. **Map** p326 D2.

Hidden in a small alley between Damstraat and the Nieuwmarkt, this former monastery is a wonderful stage for promising new talent to cut their musical teeth. Amsterdam's top music students deliver regular free concerts, but you'll also find reputable professional ensembles and quartets.

Beurs van Berlage

Damrak 213, Old Centre: Old Side (521 7575/www.berlage.com). Tram 4, 9, 14, 16, 24, 25. **Open** *Box office* 2-5pm Tue-Fri; also from 2 hours before performance. Closed end June-mid Aug. **Tickets** from €12.50. **No credit cards**. **Map** p326 D2.

This former stock exchange, designed by Hendrik Berlage, is worth a visit in its own right as perhaps the most important piece of 20th-century architecture in Amsterdam. But the Beurs has now forgone its role as a temple to Mammon and become instead a cathedral of culture, comprising a large exhibition room, two concert halls and the offices of the building's three resident orchestras, the Netherlands Philharmonic, the Netherlands Chamber Orchestra, and the Amsterdam Symphony Orchestra. Its performance chambers are wonderful, though the music schedule can be surprisingly sparse.

Concertgebouw

Concertgebouwplein 2-6, Museum Quarter (671 8345/24hr information in Dutch and English 573 0511/www.concertgebouw.nl). Tram 2, 3, 5, 12, 16, 20. **Open** *Box office* 10am-7pm daily; until 8.15pm for that night's concert. By phone 10am-5pm daily. **Tickets** from €15. **Credit** MC, V. **Map** p330 D6.

With its beautiful architecture and clear acoustics, the Concertgebouw is a favourite venue of many of the world's top musicians, and is home to the world famous Royal Concertgebouw Orchestra. As you'd expect, the sound in the Grote Zaal (Great Hall) is excellent. The Kleine Zaal (Recital Hall) is perhaps less comfortable, but is the perfect size for chamber groups and soloists. Visiting stars push up the prices, but if you avoid the big names, the concerts are very affordable: the Robeco Summer Concerts (July, Aug) are a particular bargain. For a taster, pop into a free Wednesday-lunchtime concert: they often offer a trimmed-down recital from one of the week's key performances, and sometimes even feature the

Classical recitals at tranquil **Noorderkerk**.

Royal Concertgebouw Orchestra with a guest conductor. Visitors under 27 can arrive 45 minutes before the show to see if there are any remaining seats, which are then sold for €7.50; for information, call 573 0511).

For a full night of culture, precede your concert with a meal at the posh, pricey but wonderful Bodega de Keyzer (Van Baerlestraat 96, 675 1866) or Chinese fusion cuisine temple Chang-I (JW Brouwersstraat 7, 470 1700, www.chang-i.nl). Then, after the show, round things off at the unpretentious and convivial brown bar Café Welling (JW Brouwersstraat 32, 662 0155).

Muziekgebouw aan 't IJ

Piet Heinkade 1, Docklands (788 2010, tickets 788 2000/www.muziekgebouw.nl). Tram 16, 26. **Open** Telephone reservations noon-5pm Mon-Sat. **Admission** €8.50-€27.50. **Credit** MC, V. **Map** p327 E1.

Designed by Danish architects 3xNielsen, this is one of the most innovative musical complexes in Europe. Effectively a replacement for the IJsbreker, the Muziekgebouw retains its long-lasting favour for modern classical, jazz and world music. The programmers are pleasingly versatile: the weekly schedule typically bustles with all manner of musical delights, from cutting-edge multimedia works to music by composers from the last 150 years. The Grote Zaal (Main Hall) is completely adaptable; the rather smaller BAM Zaal and foyer host more intimate concerts. *See also p234* **Moving music**. *Photo p236.*

Churches

Much exquisite classical music was written not for performance in a concert hall but to serve within the liturgical confines of the mass. It's appropriate, then, that Amsterdam's beautiful churches should feature a rich array of concerts. Appropriate and also appealing: with acoustics that modern-day sound technicians can only dream of creating, it's easy to see why the town's churches draw such large crowds even when they're not staging services.

Few churches provide a box office, and some don't publish full schedules online. Details and tickets are available from the AUB (0900 0191) and online at www.amsterdamsuitburo.nl: search for 'kerk' (church).

Engelse Kerk

Begijnhof 48, Old Centre: New Side (624 9665/ www.ercadam.nl). Tram 1, 2, 4, 5, 9, 14, 16, 24, 25. **Open** hours vary. **Tickets** from ticket outlets or 30min prior to concert. **Admission** free-€20. **No credit cards. Map** p330 D4.

Nestled in an idyllic Old Centre courtyard, the English Reformed Church has been hosting weekly concerts of baroque and classical music since the 1970s. Its healthy evening schedule also raises funds to help secure its future as a venue.

Noorderkerk

Noordermarkt 48, the Jordaan (620 3119/www. noorderkerkconcerten.nl). Tram 3, 10. **Open** 11am-1pm Sat; concerts 2-3pm Sat. **Tickets** €10-€30; from ticket outlets or 45min prior to concert. **No credit cards. Map** p325 B2.

Sure, the wooden benches in this early 17th-century church are on the hard side, but the programme of music is great, attracting accomplished musicians. Reservations are recommended.

Oude Kerk

Oudekerksplein 23, Old Centre: Old Side (625 8284/ www.oudekerk.nl). Tram 4, 9, 14, 16, 24, 25. **Open** 11am-5pm Mon-Sat; 1-5pm Sun. **Tickets** €7.50-€15; reserve or 30min prior to concert. **No credit cards. Map** p326 D2.

Jan Sweelinck, the Netherlands' most famous 17th-century composer, was once the organist in this monumental church in what is now the Red Light District. Concerts include sublime organ and carillon recitals, plus choral and chamber music.

Westerkerk

Prinsengracht 281, Western Canal Belt (624 7766/ www.westerkerk.nl). Tram 13, 14, 17. **Open** *Office* 10am-3pm Mon-Fri. *Box office* 45min before concert. **Tickets** free-€35; €6-€8 concessions. **No credit cards. Map** p326 C3.

This landmark church features a wide range of lunch and evening concerts, many free of charge. Cantatas are performed during services, if you want to hear the music in its proper setting.

Opera

Here's a refuelling idea for hungry opera fans: staff at Pasta E Basta (Nieuwe Spiegelstraat 8, Southern Canal Belt, 422 2222, www.pastaebasta.nl) serve out fine Italian grub of the pasta variety while singing arias.

Muziektheater

Amstel 3, Old Centre: Old Side (625 5455/www.muziektheater.nl). Tram 9, 14/Metro Waterlooplein. **Open** *Box office* 10am-6pm Mon-Sat; 11.30am-2.30pm Sun; or until start of performance. **Tickets** from €15. **Credit** AmEx, DC, MC, V. **Map** p327 E3.

Home of the Dutch National Ballet, the Netherlands Opera and the more recently established Holland Symfonia (the combined forces of the Netherlands Ballet Orchestra and the North Holland Philharmonic Orchestra), the Muziektheater has a reputation for high-quality performances at good prices. Tickets go on sale three months in advance and often sell out, so it's advisable to book early.

Stadsschouwburg

Leidseplein 26, Southern Canal Belt (624 2311/www.ssba.nl). Tram 1, 2, 5, 6, 7, 10. **Open** *Box office* 10am-6pm or until start of performance Mon-Sat; from 2hrs before start of performance Sun. **Tickets** from €11.50. **Credit** AmEx, MC, V. **Map** p330 C5.

This resplendent venue on Leidseplein is known primarily for its theatre and opera productions, although contemporary music performances occasionally break into the schedule.

Out of town

Doelen

Kruisstraat 2, Rotterdam (010 217 1717/www.dedoelen.nl). NS rail Rotterdam Centraal Station. **Open** *Box office* noon-6pm Mon-Thur, Sat, Sun; noon-5pm Fri. *By phone* 10am-6pm Mon-Thur, Sat, Sun; 10am-5pm Fri; and one hour before concert. **Tickets** €12-€37. **Credit** AmEx, MC, V.

The Doelen appears cold, dreary and grey from the outside, but its interior is a scene of grandeur, promoting an electric atmosphere and offering beautiful acoustics. And to help the Doelen provide something for almost everyone, a smaller concert hall complements the main room, enabling the complex to host more than 600 events each year that run the gamut from opera to pop. It's home to the Rotterdam Philharmonic, another of the nation's great ensembles.

Vredenburg

Vredenburgpassage 77, Utrecht (box office 030 231 4544/www.vredenburg.nl). NS rail Utrecht. **Open** *Box office* noon-7pm Mon; 10am-7pm Tue-Sat; also from 45min before performance. **Tickets** from €12.50. **Credit** AmEx, MC, V.

Change is afoot in Utrecht. Previously located in the labyrinthine Utrecht train station complex, the Vredenburg is slowly being converted into perhaps the finest concert hall in the Netherlands. Renamed Het Muziekpaleis ('Music Palace'), it'll comprise five purpose-built halls for classical, pop, rock, roots and jazz. Until its unveiling in 2010, the venue's interesting mix of music will be split between two temporary locations: Vredenburg Leeuwenbergh, an intimate and elegant space in Utrecht's Museum Quarter, and Vredenburg Leidsche Rijn, an acoustically treated shed out in the city's green belt.

Festivals & events

Further details on all the events listed below can be obtained from the AUB (0900 0191; www.aub.nl) and the Amsterdam Tourist Board (0900 400 4040). In addition, the Uitmarkt (*see p200*) features a whole range of arts, including classical music.

Grachtenfestival

Various venues (421 4542/www.grachtenfestival.nl). **Date** mid Aug. **Tickets** free-€35. **Credit** varies.

What started out as a single free concert from an orchestra floating on a pontoon in front of the Hotel Pulitzer has grown into the 'Canal Festival'. Handel would be delighted to hear that this modern water music has expanded to more than 90 concerts, each set somewhere near or on the water.

Holland Festival

Various venues (788 2100/www.holndfstvl.nl). **Date** June. **Tickets** from €12. **Credit** AmEx, MC, V. **Map** p330 C5.

This month-long performing arts festival is the biggest in the country. It takes a refreshing approach to dance, literature, visual arts, theatre and film, but there's no doubting that music is its central theme, particularly in the realms of contemporary classical, experimental and electronic music. Attracting international stars and composers each year, you're guaranteed a series of groundbreaking premieres and reworkings that'll move on to make waves in other cultural capitals around the world.

Holland Festival Oude Muziek Utrecht

Various venues in Utrecht (030 232 9010/www.oudemuziek.nl). **Date** late Aug-early Sept. **Tickets** €10-€30. **No credit cards**.

Top baroque and classical artists converge on Utrecht each year. The festival is a staple of the season in the Netherlands because the use of period instruments allows aficionados to hear the music of Bach, Mozart or Handel as the composer intended.

International Gaudeamus Music Week

Various venues (519 1800/www.gaudeamus.nl). **Date** early Sept. **Tickets** free-€20. **Credit** varies.

An international competition for young composers organised by the Centre for Contemporary Music, the week includes intense discussion of the state of the art and performances of selected works.

Nightclubs

Reaching for the lasers with increasing conviction.

After years of so-so clubbing, in recent times Amsterdam has again become a great place for creatures of the night. There are more than enough excellent parties in summer, and – even in the off-season – Thursdays through Saturdays offer plenty of choice regardless of what kind of music floats your boat.

Clubbing in Amsterdam is no different from in any large city in the world. All venues have bouncers; few – if any – are susceptible to bribery. You're much better off showing up on time and in a mixed boy/girl group. For well-publicised events, always get a ticket in advance: many organisations offer e-tickets on their websites; flyers and tickets can also be picked up in stores listed under Tickets & Information (*see p249*). Storing your coat in a cloak room sets you back €1, but tipping is not mandatory. Toilets are €0.50-€1, but in many clubs outside the centre they're free. Dutchies are not great tippers at the bar, so don't feel bad for cheapskating: a 15 per cent tip is usually considered huge. Almost no one will actually be inside a club before midnight: people are either at home or in a bar somewhere else, and anyway, few venues offer discount prices if you show up before a certain time.

Taxis are viewed as expensive in a city where everyone rides a bike: most cycle to the venue. If you can spot hundreds of bikes in various states of decay outside, you can be sure you've found the place you were after. Once inside the club itself, don't be afraid to strike up a conversation with a fellow clubber – all the natives speak English well. One subject has been swept under the rug by a recent oppressive wave, though: drugs. While weed and hash are still fine, it is unwise to solicit for anything stronger, as undercover cops are appearing at the larger techno parties.

Club venues

Particular attention has been given to the most popular club nights held at each venue. For clubs and venues where the majority of nights are aimed at gays and lesbians (like hetero-friendly **Exit**, where straights are allowed in

Bitterzoet. *See p243.*

Night Mayor on Fun Street

Year after unexciting year, locals complained that Amsterdam's nightlife was dead in the water. Amsterdam's laws forced clubs and pubs to close early; underground parties were vigorously monitored and shut; even finding food in the wee hours proved difficult. It was generally agreed that if you sought bona fide nightlife, Rotterdam was the place to head. But not everyone was ready to give up and leave.

In 2003, an illustrious group of DJs and party organisers were chosen to collectively don the moniker of **Nachtburgemeester** – or 'Night Mayor' – for three years. Though not an official government post, they examined the many problems of Amsterdam's nightlife, proposed possible solutions, and worked to rebuild bridges of communication between the nocturnal souls and the politicians.

After a series of meetings, the group drafted the *Nachtnota* – a 15-page summary of what Amsterdam's nightlife was, is, and could be. Admittedly they had few achievements beyond words, but their main contribution was creating a positive atmosphere where the next Night Mayor could get things done. That's when Chiel van Zelst (*pictured*) stepped in.

In February 2006, Van Zelst was elected and few people could imagine a better man for the job. He goes out every night, talks to everybody who's still awake, and finds out what the locals really do (and do not) want from a night on the town. The general answer: most prefer a late-night scene that's low-key and eminently laid-back, not big and bold, or hip and trendy. And they want longer opening hours. 'By far,' says Van Zelst, 'the most common thing people say to me is: "Get later hours for nightlife!" That's what everybody wants.' He's relentlessly working to make that happen – so much so that, while English speakers confuse his title 'Night Mayor' with the word 'nightmare', many city council members joke that he truly is one when it comes to policy-making.

But this passion for night moves is nothing new to the native Amsterdammer. A self-titled 'Dutch Art Jockey', Van Zelst has spent much of his life in the underground art scene. He founded the legendary squat Vrieshuis Amerika, and for years helped to arrange openings for indie artists from all walks of life. His latest gallery, the Chiellerie (www.chiellerie.nl; *see p216*), boasts openings every Friday night, and serves as an ideal hangout for him and other hipsters from the scene (and you too, if you're around). Much of the city's emerging nightlife has its source at the Chiellerie, where new ideas are regularly concocted while drinking beer and taking in the latest art on the gallery walls.

'There are lots of small things bubbling away everywhere,' says Van Zelst. 'That's better than just having big events now and then. Lots of young people here are doing creative things. Of course, you can't begin to compare Amsterdam to New York or Barcelona or Berlin. But if you compare it to Rotterdam, then I'd say it's doing pretty well.'

To further spur nocturnal activities, Van Zelst arranges parties and awards, like the Prix de Nuit for the best new nighttime initiative. He was also essential in ensuring that the freight ship-turned-floating art haven, the mighty *MS Stubnitz*, has an annual home in the harbour. For an unofficial position with no real pay, it's quite a busy life. So when does the Night Mayor find time to sleep?

'Well, I try to get at least five hours of sleep a day. Last night I went to bed at 4am and rose at 9am. But,' he adds in hushed tones, 'I do go to bed early sometimes.'

Don't worry Chiel – your secret's safe with us.

most nights), *see p224*. For **Westergasfabriek**, *see p263*. For rock, pop and jazz venues whose concerts often run into club nights of some form or other, *see p231*. And don't forget the city's clutch of smaller, DJ-friendly bars like **Twstd** (*see p158*) and DJ café **Vaaghuyzen** (*see p157*).

The Old Centre

Bitterzoet

Spuistraat 2 (521 3001/www.bitterzoet.com). Tram 1, 2, 5. **Open** 8pm-3am Mon-Thur, Sun; 8pm-4am Fri, Sat. **Admission** €5 and up. **No credit cards**. **Map** p326 C2.

This busy, comfy and casual bar triples as a venue for theatre and music. Both bands and DJs tend to embrace the jazzy, world and urban side of sound, as demonstrated by once-a-monther Crime Jazz: words, poetry and beyond. DJ Maestro has set up camp, sampling Blue Note classics. *Photo p241.*

Dansen bij Jansen

Handboogstraat 11-13 (620 1779/www.dansen bijjansen.nl). Tram 1, 2, 4, 5, 9, 14, 16, 24, 25. **Open** 10pm-4am Mon-Thur, Sun; 10pm-5am Fri, Sat. **Admission** €2 Mon-Wed, Sun; €4 Thur-Sat. **No credit cards**. **Map** p330 D4.

It's a club Jim, but not as we know it: it says on the door you'll need valid student ID to get in. DJs spin cheerful chart tunes and drink prices are pleasantly affordable. But if you're over 25, you'll feel like Barbara Cartland at a booze-infused kindergarten.

Winston International

Warmoesstraat 125-129 (623 1380/www.winston.nl). Tram 1, 2, 5, 13, 14, 16, 17, 24, 25. **Open** 9pm-3am Mon-Thur, Sun; 9pm-4am Fri, Sat. **Admission** €5-€10. **No credit cards**. **Map** p326 D2.

An intimate venue that attracts a mixed crowd with its alternative rock and indie-tronica. Winston's yearly Popprijs gives hope to many student rock bands and entertainment to unsuspecting civilians. Cheeky Mondays bring relief to yet another working week with jungle and drum 'n' bass, while other nights see daily live music from garage and folk to funky hip hop and ska, followed by alternative DJs. When relieving yourself, look out for the enigmatic toilet art gallery. *See also p63.*

Southern Canal Belt

Escape

Rembrandtplein 11 (622 1111/www.escape.nl). Tram 4, 9, 14. **Open** 11pm-4am Thur; 11pm-5am Fri, Sat; 11pm-4:30am Sun. **Admission** €10-€20. **No credit cards**. **Map** p331 E4.

With a capacity of 2,000, this is about as big as clubbing gets in central Amsterdam – and in 2007 it will continue to expand with three new areas. Ever since club night Chemistry left, the place has disappeared from the national spotlight, resurfacing instead as a venue for a younger, more mainstream crowd. Queues still form on Saturday and Sunday evenings – the latter a succesful alternative to a lazy day spent on the couch. The bouncers are wary of groups of tourists, so squeeze into a slinky T-shirt, slap on some hair product and get in line early.

Jimmy Woo's

Korte Leidsedwarsstraat 18 (626 3150/www.jimmy woo.com). Tram 1, 2, 5, 6, 7, 10. **Open** 11pm-3am Wed, Thur, Sun; 11pm-4am Fri, Sat. **Admission** €7.50. **Credit** AmEx, MC, DC, V. **Map** p330 C5.

Amsterdam has never seen anything quite so luxuriously cosmopolitan as Jimmy Woo's. You, too, can marvel at the lounge area filled with a mixture of modern and antique furniture and then confirm for yourself the merits of its bootylicious light design and sound system. At times, the place looks just like a music video – and that includes musicians and actors. If you have problems getting in, cool off across the street at sister cocktail bar, Suzy Wong (Korte Leidsedwarsstraat 45, 626 6769).

Melkweg

Lijnbaansgracht 234A (531 8181/www.melkweg.nl). Tram 1, 2, 5, 6, 7, 10. **Open** varies. **Admission** €5-€32. *Membership* €3/mth (compulsory) or €15/year. **No credit cards**. **Map** p330 C5.

Former milk factory 'Milky Way' offers a galaxy of stellar programming and a newly rebuilt main hall. Often ridiculously crowded – but great value and down to earth – with a little bit of everything thrown into the mix. Watch out for Friday's Latin-flavoured ¿Que Pasa?, which has built up quite a following, plus techno parties Traffic and Mono, which consistently sell out. *See also p233.*

Ministry

Reguliersdwarsstraat 12 (623 3981/www.ministry.nl). Tram 16, 24, 25. **Open** 11pm-4am Mon, Sun; 11pm-5am Fri, Sat. **Admission** €10 and up. **No credit cards**. **Map** p330 D4.

Ministry is a small and stylish club with a music policy that tends towards funky and soulful urban sounds. Groove to the latest hip hop, R&B and dancehall tracks on Freaky Fridays. The door staff can be a bit picky, so dress up, be pretty and, most importantly of all, behave yourself.

Nachttheater Sugar Factory

Lijnbaansgracht 238 (626 5006/www.sugarfactory.nl). Tram 1, 2, 5, 7, 10. **Open** 9pm-4am Thur, Sun; 9pm-5am Fri, Sat. **Admission** €5-€17. **No credit cards**. **Map** p330 C5.

This 'night theatre' has found its niche as a place where performance meets clubbing. Every night brings a show of some kind, be it photos, classical dancers, MCs in various shapes and sizes, or actors mixing with the crowds. Monthly Vreemd ('Weird') nights see surprise acts, DJs stepping beyond the usual genre boundaries and classy decorations. WickedJazzSounds hosts a Sunday evening, and the cutting-edge Electronation brings top acts from the worlds of '80s synthesizer electro to current day minimal techno. Sweet it most certainly is. *Photo p246.*

Odeon

Singel 460 (521 8555/www.odeonamsterdam.nl). Tram 1, 2, 5. **Open** *Club* 11pm-5am Fri, Sat. *Lounges* from 6pm, DJ after 10pm, Thur-Sun. **Admission** free-€20. **Credit** AmEx, MC, V. **Map** p330 D4.

This three-storey, 1662-built venue comes complete with restaurant, cocktail bar, café (with great canal-side terrace), disco and cultural activities. It's hot with the students on Thursdays, and weekends see various local electro DJs. Don't be intimidated by the lush interior, and find a chair with a view during Friday's fabulous cocktail hour.

Paradiso

Weteringschans 6-8 (626 4521/www.paradiso.nl). Tram 1, 2, 5, 6, 7, 10. **Open** 7pm-4am Wed, Thur, Sun; 7pm-5am Fri, Sat. **Admission** from €5. *Membership* (compulsory) €3/mth; €18/yr. **No credit cards. Map** p330 D5.

As an Amsterdam institution, this large ex-church is a safe clubbing bet, with a trusty formula of following on from live shows with a DJ or club night from around 11pm. Saturday's Paradisco pulls in a youngish, up-for-it crowd, while Noodlanding ('Emergency Landing') on Wednesdays or Thursdays is particularly good for an alternative, indie feel. Bigger concerts (by the likes of international superstars such as Justin Timberlake or Gabriel Rios) sell out weeks in advance. *See also p235.*

Sinners

Wagenstraat 3-7 (620 1375/www.sinners.nl). Tram 4, 9, 14. **Open** 11pm-4am Thur; 11pm-5am Fri, Sat. **Admission** €10-€15. **No credit cards. Map** p327 E3.

The Sinners people are youthful, beautiful, well groomed and well funded – some of them are even famous, albeit in a 'big in Hollandwood' sort of way. Think *Sex and the City* meets the Fresh Prince. Think urban and groovy house classics. Saturday nights are reliably spirited and dirty.

Studio 80

Rembrandtplein 17 (521 8333/www.studio-80.nl). Tram 4, 9, 14. **Open** 10pm-4am Wed-Thur, Sun; 11pm-5am Fri, Sat. **Admission** free-€10. **No credit cards. Map** p331 E4.

In the middle of Rembrandtplein's neon glitz and ice cream-eating crowds lurks this ex-radio studio, a black pearl waiting to be discovered. Dirty disco, deep electronic acid and gritty hip hop are shown off at very reasonable fees. The city's most progressive techno and minimal crowds find their home here and have no trouble bringing disc-spinning or synthesizer-wielding friends from as far afield as Berlin or Barcelona. Wednesdays see nights held that are gay- and lesbian-friendly. *Photo p249.*

Zebra Lounge

Korte Leidsedwarsstraat 14 (612 6153/06 223 68 039 info and reservations/www.the-zebra.nl). Tram 1, 2, 5, 7, 10. **Open** 10pm-3am Thur, Sun; 10pm-4am Fri, Sat. **Admission** €5-€15. **Credit** Amex, MC, V. **Map** p330 C5.

Refused a 'sex permit' to operate as a pole-dancing club (as if Amsterdam needs another venue for men with gyroscope obsessions), the faux-sleazy Zebra Lounge took the path of lesser profit and is now a hip, respectable and pole-less venue. Buy your booze by the bottle in order to assure yourself a place in one of their glamorous booths.

The Waterfront, Eastern Islands and Oost

11

Oosterdokskade 3-5 (625 5999/www.ilove11.nl). Tram 16. **Open** 10pm-4am Fri, Sat. **Admission** €10-€15. **No credit cards. Map** p327 E1.

As is typical for this city, 'temporary' club 11 on the top floor of an old post office has proven to be not so temporary after all. Scheduled for demolition in 2008, the industrial building's demise is now being debated following the success of its club, office spaces and gallery basement. Home to Joost van Bellen and his rock 'n' rave evening Rauw, 11 also boasts the finest in techno, electro and minimal music, presenting top DJs and producers every week. During the day and evenings, 11 is a restaurant with a unique view; patrons get to stay while the place is converted into a club. *See also p145.*

Café Pakhuis Wilhelmina

Veemkade 576 (419 3368/www.cafepakhuiswilhelmina.nl). Tram 26. **Open** hours vary Wed-Sun. **Admission** €5-€8. **No credit cards.**

One of the most interesting venues in Amsterdam, Wilhelmina is often overlooked by casual clubbers. Is it the club's IJ-oriented location? The absence of bouncers? Or bottles of beer for only €2? In any case, don't miss it if your heart lies with today's leftfield music. Professor Nomad does weekly improv and theme nights, Ichi One features dubstep and drum 'n' bass and the unpolished eRRorKREW bring the underground's finest bubbling to the surface with raw basslines and broken beats.

Hotel Arena

's Gravesandestraat 51 (850 2420/www.hotelarena.nl). Tram 3, 6, 7, 10. **Open** 10pm-4am Fri-Sun. **Admission** €10-€20. **No credit cards. Map** p332 G3.

Another multi-purpose venue, these beautiful buildings were once an orphanage, before changing into a youth hostel. From there, it was only a short step to becoming a trendy hotel, bar and restaurant. Big city folk, used to long treks, will laugh at its accessibility, but Amsterdammers tend to forego the small detour eastwards, making it hard for the Arena to truly kick clubbing butt – monthlies like Salsa Lounge, with its sweltering Latin bias, and '80s Verantwoord are the exceptions.

Panama

Oostelijke Handelskade 4 (311 686/www.panama.nl). Tram 26. **Open** 9pm-3am Thur, Sun; 9pm-4am Fri, Sat. **Admission** €10-€20. **Credit** MC, V. **Map** p327 F1.

Nachttheater Sugar Factory. *See p243.*

A steady force in Amsterdam nightlife, restaurant/theatre/nightclub Panama overlooks the IJ in one of the city's most booming areas. A deserted strip back in 2000 when it opened, the neighbourhood has now been transformed with high-rise offices, steep rents and a shiny Muziekgebouw (*see p239*). Monthly Rush and Bold evenings bring the best in national DJs, while huge international artists such as Danny Howells and Sander Kleinenberg also find their way here. On Sunday, bring your kids to an intimate concert by the likes of Ellen ten Damme and let your cares wash away. *See also p235.*

The Jordaan and Westerpark

Flexbar

Pazzanistraat 1 (www.flexbar.nl). Tram 2, 5. **Open** 10pm-4am Thur, Sun; 10pm-5am Fri, Sat. **Admission** €5-€10. **No credit cards. Map** p325 A1.

Barely opened and already packed – it's unavoidable in a city that craves new impulses. Especially when electro music's own Eva Maria, house legend Wannabeastar and quintessential Damsko hip hoppers Rednose Distrikt have set up camp. Flexbar consists of two spaces, which often have different programming. Finger food is served in the evening.

Kingdom Marcanti

Jan van Galenstraat 6-10 (488 9888/www.kingdomvenue.com). Bus 21. **Open** hours vary. **Admission** free-€25. **No credit cards. Map** p329 A4.

Some venues pay designers pot-loads of money to try and buy their way to the seediness that the Kingdom manages without even trying. Weekly clubnight XL has cheesy DJs in all varieties and monthly Kinky Erotic Vibes delivers on the aforementioned seediness. The local in-crowd can't afford to be spotted here, but that doesn't stop the out-of-towners craving a hefty beat.

More

Rozengracht 133 (www.clubmore.nl) Tram 13, 14, 17. **Open** varies. **Admission** €10-€15. **No credit cards. Map** p329 B4.

Once hot, then despised, then reopened, then closed, More is now open once again. No weekly nights, but one-off events for local organisations such as Multigroove. Where once soap stars roamed its white interior, More now sees a more underground crowd, with even Mokum Hardcore not out of the question. Only time will tell what's next for this enigmatic club's ongoing evolution.

Strand West

Stavangerweg 900 (682 6310/www.strand-west.nl). Bus 22, 48. **Open** varies. **Admission** free-€15. **No credit cards.**

Following Blijburg's lead, *strandtenten* (beach hangouts) have popped up all over the city. This one promotes progressive house music at various one-off events approximately every month. The area is also well known for its strange student housing located in refurbished sea containers.

Museum Quarter & the South

The Mansion

Hobbemastraat 2 (616 6664/www.the-mansion.nl). Tram 2, 5. **Open** 6pm-1am Wed, Thur, Sun (restaurant only Sun); 6pm-3am Fri, Sat. **Admission** free-€15. **Credit** AmEx, DC, MC, V. **Map** p330 D5.

With the same owner as the Zebra Lounge, and design by Concrete (also responsible for Nomads and the Supperclub), this restaurant/bar/club has strong credentials: think less Hugh Hefner and more elegant gentleman's club (but with chicks allowed). The staff are decked in outfits designed by Europe's answer to Donna Karan, René Lezard, and the decor is plush chinoiserie. Expect live music, regular club DJs, loads of people keen to show off and, afterwards, a space in your wallet where your money used to be. You'll wonder how you lived without it.

Powerzone

Daniel Goedkoopstraat 1-3 (0900 769 379 663/www.thepowerzone.nl). Metro Spaklerweg. **Open** 11pm-5am Fri, Sat; occasional Sun 11pm-5am. **Admission** €12-€35. **Credit** AmEx, MC, V.

Packing in as many as 5,000 mainstream clubbers, the cavernous Powerzone is more like an outdoor dance party that has found its way indoors. The staff, however, are not particularly welcoming to gangs of tourists, so look pretty and feign a Swedish accent or you risk wasting the taxi fare out to this non-central venue. Most nights are oriented towards more urban music or offer house in its purest, most finger-snapping, body jacking form.

Outside Amsterdam

'What other place in the world could you find, where all of life's comforts, and all novelties that man could want, are so easy to obtain as here – and where you can enjoy such a feeling of freedom?' So wrote René Descartes about Amsterdam in 1628. The same is still true now, but that doesn't stop a good number of clubbers heading out of town, particularly for extra-late events or harder musical styles. If you are going further afield, check the website or flyer first and make sure you dress the part. For venues even further from Amsterdam, *see pp281-293.*

Bloemendaal Beach Cafés

Beach pavilions, Bloemendaal aan Zee (023 573 2152). NS rail to Haarlem or Zandvoort, then taxi (€12.50) or bus 81 to Bloemendaal aan Zee. **Open** *May-Oct* hours vary. **Admission** free-€5. **No credit cards.**

Once a wonderful secret, these beach bars now lure the clubbing thousands at weekends. Seven different cafés offer music, fashion and fabulous fixtures and fittings. There's a venue here to suit everyone, from kooky Woodstock to chic Bloomingdale to Ibiza-like Republiek. Beachbop (www.beachbop.info) sees them combine forces for a staggeringly big beach festival – 30,000 punters turned up in 2006.

Blijburg

Bert Haanstrakade 2004 (416 0330/www.blijburg.nl). Tram 26. **Open** *Summer* 10am-1am Mon-Thur, Sun; 10am-3am Fri, Sat. *Winter* 2pm-1am Thur, Fri; noon-1am Sat; 10am-midnight Sun. **Admission** free. **No credit cards**.

This beach place is great even when the weather sucks (thanks to the open fire, perhaps). It's not a club as such, more a restaurant/bar, but it does pull some top names and a very creative crowd. A brand new suburb of Amsterdam is still in the process of being constructed around your ears. *See also p145.*

De Hemkade

Hemkade 48, Zaandam (075 614 8154/www.hemkade.nl). NS rail Zaandam. **Open** 10pm-6am Fri, Sat. **Admission** €15-€35. **No credit cards**.

De Hemkade, north of Amsterdam, is a huge hall with adjoining rooms hosting music of the hard and heavy house/techno variety, plus there's the occasional fetish night thrown in.

Lexion

Overtoom 65, Westzaan (075 612 3999/www.lexion.nl). NS rail Zaandam. **Open** 10pm-6am Sat. **Admission** from €15. **Credit** AmEx, MC, V.

Freshly refurbished, Lexion expects you to be over 21, sans jeans or sports gear and, if you're male, accompanied by a lot of ladies, please. If you hate the hoi polloi, take advantage of Lexion's VIP room for four to 150 people. Worth checking out for the extra-late night events or for hard house and trance.

Patronaat

Zijlsingel 2, Haarlem (023 517 5858/www.patronaat.nl). **Open** 10pm-4am Thur-Sun. **Admission** €9-€20. **No credit cards**.

Like Paradiso in Amsterdam, Patronaat offers a blend of live concerts, '80s flashbacks and techno parties. Rocketfuel is a relaxed weekly night hosted by DJs from the Amsterdam region. Spektrum and Upstruct present top DJs from all over the globe, often for a few euros less compared to the equivalent you'll get in Amsterdam.

Underground scene

Try as they may to rid the city of alternative lifestylers, the powers-that-be haven't stopped underground culture from blossoming. And yet, the best thing about Amsterdam's underground scene is that it doesn't exclude ordinary folk: if you're up for it, they're up for you. Should you visit around a full moon, solstice or an equinox (the summer equinox is a better bet for outdoor shindigs than its winter complement), there'll almost certainly be some sort of mad party going on. Information on these events can be hard to come by: look for flyers in coffeeshops, eavesdrop on the conversations of dreadlocked locals, or see *Amsterdam Weekly* and www.underwateramsterdam.com. For more on squats, or 'breeding grounds', *see p35.*

Ruigoord

Ruigoord church, Ruigoord 15, Ruigoord (497 5702/ www.ruigoord.nl). Bus 82.

'Empower the Imagination', commands the website. If there's a crusty/shaman/fire-breather hidden deep down inside of you, this long-established artists' colony will bring him, her or it out. Their full-moon parties are hard to beat for fun of the appropriately lunatic variety. Ruigoord is about 15km from the centre of Amsterdam and it's home to the wacky Balloon Company crew (who also throw a not-to-be missed bash at Paradiso once a year in December). Utterly insane and thoroughly good fun.

Rokerij 1

Lange Leidsedwarsstraat 41 (622 9442). Tram 1, 2, 5, 7, 10.

Dreadlocks, spiral fluorescent designs, alternative lifestyles and plenty of cannabis. All four Rokerij outfits are central to the city's psychedelic trance and underground world music scene. Clan of Peace hosts Goa music events here, completed by musical accompaniment from flute and sitar.

Club night organisers

Look out for one-off events organised by the following outfits. The most extensive party listing is at www.gomagazine.nl: it's in Dutch, but decipherable. Local listings magazine *Amsterdam Weekly* and free bi-weekly mag *NL20* are also excellent guides to the club scene, with most club listings in English.

5 Days Off

www.5daysoff.nl

This festival is a must for fans of harder electronic music. Anyone who's anyone is present for five days of top-notch techno, bubbling drum 'n' bass, uplifting house and tearing electro.

ADHD Sessions

www.adhdsessions.com

Local DJs and live acts bring serious techno music to small venues all over town.

Amsterdam Dance Event

www.amsterdamdanceevent.nl

Every October, the city turns into one of Europe's largest electronic music conferences. Record deals are struck during the day, and at night, the clubs are packed with artists and visitors alike.

Amsterdamaged

www.amsterdamaged.org

Often hosted by word maestro MC Quest One, their nights are dedicated to next level drum 'n' bass.

Electronation

www.electronation.nl

These organisers have become quite a force in recent years, pulling in names such as Chicks On Speed and Peaches to all the major clubs in town.

De-frock and get ready to rock at **Studio 80**. *See p245.*

Eye on the Future

www.eyeonthefuture.nl
These bi-monthly events in Haarlem's Lichtfabriek offer innovative techno and progressive house.

eRRorKREW

www.errorkrew.nl
Winners of the Prix de Nuit award for the best nightlife initiative in 2006, eRRorKREW throw unpolished parties in various locations, where ragga-techno, breakbeat and disturbing noise are all on the menu The group originated in DJ-friendly café Vaaghuyzen, where they still can be found.

Extrema

www.extrema.nl
Active in the Southern part of the Netherlands, Extrema throw a fantastic summer festival near Eindhoven. Check the website for more information.

Housequake

www.housequake.nl
Drawing huge crowds, this concept-led outfit moves from city to city. Two Dutch DJs, Roog and Erick E, act silly on stage and play lashings of seriously funky house to seriously pleased punters.

ID&T

www.id-t.com
Think bigger: this organisation is responsible for dance mega-events such as Sensation, Innercity, Tiësto in concert and Trance Energy.

Kobyashi

www.kobyashi.nl
Small-scale and unexpected, Kobyashi is a friendly concept in various small venues such as Café Pakhuis Wilhelmina. Resident DJ Jeremy Norris brings the latest tunes to the tables.

Monumental

www.awakenings.nl
Monumental hosts the popular Awakenings hard techno parties in the Gashouder (Westergasfabriek). There's also a festival every July outside Amsterdam.

Salon USSR

www.salonussr.com
Purportedly an acronym of United Systems of Sentimental Realities, Amsterdam's very own Russian lads-about-town, Dima and Goldfinger, organise regular events that manage somehow to be both underground but utterly welcoming.

UDC

www.udc.nl/www.dancevalley.nl
UDC host the yearly Dance Valley festival and put on various dance-related events throughout the Netherlands. Check the website for information.

Voltt

www.voltt.com
Richie Hawtin and Sven Väth are just two of the regular DJs who spin at Voltt (and sister night Mono). Parties in Paradiso and Melkweg have become the stuff of legend; there's even a Voltt summer festival at the NDSM Wharf in Noord.

Tickets & information

Flyers and club tickets can be acquired at a variety of city venues. Try **Fat Beats** (*see p192*), **Conscious Dreams Dreamlounge** (*see p174*), **Episode** (Waterlooplein 1, 320 3000), **Zipper** (Huidenstraat 7, 623 7302) and also local record stores **Groove Connection** (Sint Nicolaasstraat 41, 624 7234) and **Rush Hour** (Spuistraat 98, 427 4505).

Sport & Fitness

Bums on bikes and balls on the brain. No changes there, then.

Theirs may be a relatively small landmass, but the Dutch people certainly take their sport seriously. Whatever the occasion, when the sons and daughters of the nation step out at competitions, home and abroad, the weight of the world rests expectantly on their fellow countrypeople's shoulders, reflected in the unmistakeable sea of orange cheering from the stands. Football remains the game most special to many, with fans still pining for the '70s and '80s glory days of Cruyff and Van Basten. While plenty of young starlets like Arjen Robben and Robin van Persie have made their names and riches internationally, the magic spark stays missing from the national team, and the country's heart is left battered and bruised after every failure. Yet that desire to be the best often pays off elsewhere, and in field hockey, ice skating, swimming, darts and cycling, Dutch stars consistently lap up medals, becoming national heroes in the process.

Away from the competition, Amsterdam is simply an active city, continually in motion. Every major sport is represented here, with numerous opportunities to get stuck in and keep in shape. For those taking their first steps on the fitness chain, walking and exploring is an ideal start. As well as pounding the city's streets, Noord-Holland's tourist information offices (www.noord-holland.com) can help you explore outlying areas, providing routes of various lengths and types. You might even be able to pass it off as sport with a couple of traditional Nordic walking poles.

For those seeking real physical exertion, contact the Municipal Sport and Recreation Department on 552 2490, or visit the website www.sport.amsterdam.nl (mostly in Dutch) for maps, schedules and links for almost every activity imaginable. The *Gouden Gids* ('Yellow Pages', again mostly in Dutch) can also help you find out what's on where.

The best Sports

Baseball
Beer, nuts, bats and balls: it's Americana in glorious mini. *See p251.*

Darts
A game? A sport? A religion? *See p251.*

Football
The beautiful game that both divides and conquers. *See p251.*

Road Skating
Pad up and glide, or just spectate: either way, the city buzzes with it. *See p256.*

TT Races
Glitz, glamour and seriously ear-splitting motoring machines. *See p252.*

Museums

Ajax Museum

ArenA Boulevard 29, Bijlmermeer (311 1336/www.amsterdamarena.nl). Metro Bijlmer. **Open** 10am-5pm daily. Opening hours on match days vary. **Admission** *Museum* €3.50; *stadium tour* from €8.50. **Credit** MC, V.

Great for football fans of all allegiances, this fine museum covers the rich history of the club, offering photographs, memorabilia, trophies and videos documenting their greatest players and triumphs.

Olympic Experience Amsterdam

Olympisch Stadion 2, Marathon Poort (671 1115/www.olympischstadion.nl). Tram 16, 24/bus 15, 23. **Open** 11am-5pm. **Admission** €5; €4 children.

A new addition to the stadium (built for the 1928 Olympiad), this multimedia centre attempts to document the complete Dutch Olympic experience, with the focus on the ten most popular sports.

Orange Football Museum

Kalverstraat 236, Old Centre: New Side (589 8989/www.supportersclub-oranje.nl). Tram 4, 9, 16, 24, 25. **Open** 11am-5pm Sat, Sun. **Admission** €7; €5 children. **No credit cards. Map** p330 D4.

This enthusiastic museum has four floors of photos, paintings, songs and videos relating to the 'Orange Experience' (namely, the national football team).

Spectator sports

American football

The Admirals are the pros; the Amsterdam Crusaders are the amateurs who can be reached on 617 7450 (www.amsterdam-crusaders.nl). Full details are available from the sport's governing body, AFBN (www.afbn.nl).

Amsterdam Admirals

Amsterdam ArenA, Arena Boulevard 1, Bijlmermeer (465 0550/tickets 465 4545/www.admirals.nl). Metro Strandvliet or Metro/NS rail Bijlmer. **Admission** €12-€48. **Season** Apr-June. **Credit** AmEx, DC, MC, V.
These Dutch representatives in the NFL Europa primarily play against German opposition, and pull in the punters for big fixtures. Successful in recent seasons, their reasonably priced Friday night home games draw crowds upwards of 20,000.

Baseball

The Netherlands is now one of the strongest baseball nations in Europe. Known locally as *honkbal*, international summer competitions such as the Haarlemse Honkbalweek (023 525 4545, www.honkbalweek.nl) and World Port Tournament in Rotterdam (010 880 8788, www.worldporttournament.nl) attract nations like Cuba, Japan and the USA. The season runs from April to October. For information contact the KNBSB (030 751 3651/www.knbsb.nl).

Cricket

At amateur level, cricket is played with fervour and dedication nationwide, with over 100 teams affiliated to the KNCB (030 751 3781, www.kncb.nl). Several are in Amsterdam; the biggest is the VRA (Volharding RAP Amstels, 641 8525, www.vra.nl). Most have junior, veteran and women's teams; newcomers are welcome.

Cycling

Not just a means of transport (or torture device for scaring tourists who stumble into bike lanes), cycling is also a serious sport. Fans turn out in huge numbers for stage, criterium (road circuit) and one-day road races, plus track, field, cyclo-cross and mountain biking varieties.

The biggest races are the Amstel Gold around Limburg in mid April (www.amstelgoldrace.nl); the Acht van Chaam, a 100km (62-mile) criterium held in Noord-Brabant on the first Wednesday after the Tour de France (late July/early August); and the ENECO Tour, a week-long tour of Holland and Belgium in August. Sometimes even the Tour de France crosses the Dutch border. For more details, contact the KNWU at Postbus 2661 3430 GB Nieuwegein (030 751 3300, www.knwu.nl).

If you have a racing bike, head for Sportpark Sloten. Two cycle clubs are based here: ASC Olympia (617 7510, secretary 617 3057, www.ascolympia.nl) and WV Amsterdam (secretary 690 1466, www.wvamsterdam.nl). There's also a 22km (12-mile) circuit round the park, and a modern indoor velodrome.

Those merely hoping to slip quietly into the countryside should go to Amsterdamse Bos' 50km (30 miles) of scenic lanes, or contact the NTFU (Postbus 326, 3900 AH Veenendaal, 0318 581 300, www.ntfu.nl) or the local tourist office for advice and information on routes.

Darts

Moves to have darts recognised as an Olympic sport would be supported en masse by the Dutch. Their king of kings, Raymond 'Barney' van Barneveld, has won the BDO world title four times, plus the PDC world championship. A host of other Dutch stars have followed in his wake, and fans turn up at national and international competitions, causing the decibel levels to soar. To check the Dutch tournament calendar contact the Nederlands Darts Bond on 070 36 67 206 (www.ndbdarts.nl).

Essentially still a café sport, Amsterdam has more than 300 teams affiliated to DORA (408 4184, www.dora.nl), which organises leagues from September to June, plus smaller summer competitions in and around the city. For a serious game of arrows, try De Vluchtheuvel (Van Woustraat 174, 662 5665, www.cafedevluchtheuvel.nl) in the Pijp.

Football

The Dutch turn out in huge numbers when it comes to football. From international matches played at ArenA, to amateur ones on wet winter afternoons, there's a real devotion that never diminishes through the ups and the downs. In terms of Dutch internationals, it's always a rollercoaster ride in the emotional stakes: just look at the agonising exits faced at every recent major tournament.

The home leagues don't demand the same level of foreign attention, as there's a huge gap between the big and smaller clubs. After Ajax, PSV, Feyenoord and AZ, it can be a long way down, but it doesn't necessarily mean games lack excitement. The season runs from late August until late May, with a short break from Christmas until early February.

As a deterrent to hooliganism, 'personal club cards' are needed for stadiums, so you can't just turn up without pre-planning. However, most clubs also offer temporary memberships for international visitors – contact your club of choice in advance. The ruling body KNVB (0900 8075, www.knvb.nl) has more information.

Ajax

Amsterdam ArenA, Arena Boulevard 29, Bijlmermeer (311 1444/www.ajax.nl). Metro Strandvliet or Metro/NS rail Bijlmer. **Tickets** €15-€41.50. **Credit** AmEx, DC, MC, V.

The country's most famous club is renowned worldwide for flair on the field and its excellent youth training programme. Although success isn't guaranteed, they're typically there (or thereabouts) and battles with main rivals Feyenoord and PSV are fought fiercely each season in the gladiatorial ArenA – and sometimes out of it (*see p254* **Turf wars**). In July, some of the world's biggest teams are invited to take part in the Amsterdam Tournament.

Feyenoord

De Kuip, Van Zandvlietplein 3, Rotterdam (010 292 6888/tickets 010 292 3888/www.feyenoord.nl). NS rail Rotterdam Centraal Station, then bus 46. **Tickets** €15-€35. **Credit** AmEx, DC, MC, V.

It's impossible to predict how Rotterdam's favourite sons will perform each year. One season they're invincible, the next they're dead and buried by Christmas. Rotterdammers remain loyal to everything Feyenoord, so be careful with your jibes.

PSV

Philips Stadium, Frederiklaan 10A, Eindhoven (040 250 5501/tickets 040 250 5505/www.psv.nl). NS rail Eindhoven, then bus 4, 13. **Tickets** €19-€48. **No credit cards**.

Founded in 1913 for employees of industrial giant Philips in Eindhoven, PSV have been consistently dominant in recent years, performing extremely well in the Champions League too.

Other teams

With their philosophy of 'attack, attack, attack!', games featuring AZ Alkmaar are worth the short train journey north. When Premier League games are sold out or too costly, try the First Division. Failing that, some of the top amateurs – Blauw Wit and Elinkwijk among them – play decent football. As in most footballing nations, the women's game is growing, but still at amateur level. To discover where to watch or play, visit online at www.vrouwenvoetbal.nl.

Hockey

The Dutch are especially passionate about field hockey and turn up in numbers that prove it. Although both men's and women's teams failed at the Athens Olympics, they'll head to Beijing in 2008 as favourites – the women are the most successful in the world, having won the World Cup six times; the men aren't bad either, with three wins to their name. Win or lose, a party spirit follows the national squads, and if you've never considered hockey a spectator sport, the Dutch may convert you.

With around 185,000 players nationwide, the country also boasts the largest number of affiliated teams of any equivalent association in the world, with the Wagener Stadium in Amstelveen the focus for club games and internationals. The season runs from September until May; details of local teams are available from the KNHB (030 751 3400, www.knhb.nl). For a quirky alternative, more outdoorsy players take to the beach for the summer tournaments (www.beachhockeynederland.nl).

If this all sounds a bit too sweaty, then check out hockey of the frozen variety – the Amstel Tijgers are the main local team. Seasons run from October to February. Contact the NIJB (079 330 5050, www.nijb.nl) for schedules.

Motor sport

Formula One may not actually take place in the Netherlands, but it remains popular. National drivers like Christijan Albers are heroes, and with the entry of the Dutch Spyker F1 team in 2007, popularity is surging (*see p253* **Driving ambition**). For those unable to travel to F1's locations, Bavaria City Racing (www.bavariacityracing.com) has established itself as a high-profile racing showcase each August, held in the streets of Rotterdam.

TT Races

TT Circuit Assen (0900 388 2488/www.tt-assen.com/advance tickets from TT Assen, Postbus 150, 9400 AD Assen, fax 0592 356 911). Exit Assen south off A28, then follow signs. **Tickets** €40-€87. **No credit cards**.

This circuit hosts sports cars, racing cars, trucks and other specials, but it's the motorcycles that are the biggest draw. The World Superbike Championship pulls up at the end of April, while the MotoGP's longest-serving race, the TT-Assen, attracts over 100,000 spectators on the last Saturday of June. Book Grand Prix tickets and accommodation early.

Zandvoort

Circuit Park Zandvoort, Burgermeester Van Alphenstraat 108, Zandvoort (023 574 0750/www.circuit-zandvoort.nl/for tickets www.ticketbox.nl). NS rail Zandvoort. **Tickets** €12-€150. **No credit cards**.

Only 24km (15 miles) outside Amsterdam, this former Formula One track hosts international races from February to November, the most high-profile of which is the A1GP – a competition for international race teams famous for featuring many ex-Formula One drivers on the tracks. Booking ahead is recommended, though tickets for small events can still be purchased on race days themselves.

Rugby

There are over 100 rugby clubs currently competing throughout the country. Unusually, women's rugby is as popular as men's, and there's also a wealth of youth teams. AAC (www.aacrugby.com) in Amsterdam caters for all of the above and welcomes visitors and new players alike. Seasons run from September to May and are interspersed with a selection of

Driving ambition

A new buzz has arisen throughout the nation with the formation of the **Spyker Formula One** team, which not only has key Dutch personnel, but has also resulted in those unmistakable orange cars whizzing around the world's top race tracks – with fans hoping that the Spyker *oranje* will one day be just as famous as Ferrari red.

The name Spyker goes back quite a long way. It first originated with a Dutch car manufacturer in the early 20th century, a company that folded before the end of the 1920s. The brand was brought back to life in 1999 by a new Dutch outfit specialising in exclusive hand-built sports cars; not content with the glamour of that business, the new Spyker took the opportunity to buy out the short-lived Midland F1 team in 2006, entering the most prestigious competition in the world.

Formula One is a seriously tough ride for smaller teams, but Spyker F1 certainly don't lack ambition. Their first full season in the limelight came in 2007, and while immediate success isn't guaranteed, the core Dutch team – including driver Christijan Albers, e-tycoon Michiel Mol in the role of director of Formula One and chief executive Victor Muller – hope to have gained valuable points in the 2008 season. Mol even announced in the build-up to their debut that they'd be ready to take their podium places and aim for the championship in five years' time.

With those sentiments in mind, F1 fans the world over were left with raised eyebrows, particularly because the Spyker driving team is relatively inexperienced. Eindhoven-born Albers only began Formula One in 2005, racing for the lowly Minardi team. Even so, the glam and glitz of the racing world has made him a household name for Dutch sports fans, and he's enjoyed a hero's welcome at the spectacular Bavaria City Racing meetings in the centre of Rotterdam. Maybe it's just the brash orange paint job at work, but for this fresh new team, the general consensus is that the only way is up.

tournaments ranging from 15-a-side to beach rugby sevens. Contact the National Rugby Board (480 8100, www.rugby.nl) for schedules. Gay rugby is also an international phenomenon: to play or watch contact NOP Amsterdam (www.nop-amsterdam.nl).

Volleyball

Thanks to the growing success of both men's and women's national teams, volleyball's popularity continues to rise. For details of events and local clubs, contact the national office of NeVoBo (030 751 3600, www.volleybal.nl) or its Amsterdam office (693 6458, www.holland.nevobo.nl).

Fitness & leisure

Athletics

The *Trimloopboekje* (Dutch Runners' Guide), published every August, lists all running events in the Netherlands. Amsterdam's major road events are the Vondelparkloop in January – part of the Rondje Mokum series (www.rondjemokum.nl), which includes seven separate 10km (15-mile) city races and also one 15km (9.3-mile) run – plus September's Dam tot Damloop from Amsterdam to Zaandam, and the Amsterdam Marathon in October. For club and training facilities, contact Phanos, based at the Olympic

Turf wars

To casual onlookers, the Netherlands appears to be a peaceful haven of tulips, bicycles and soft drugs. But when it comes to raw passion, little gets Dutch blood boiling like football. Unfortunately, fiery rivalries between teams mean that good-natured enthusiasm sometimes gives way to nasty violence.

The most notorious rivalry is that between Ajax and Feyenoord (effectively Amsterdam versus Rotterdam). When the two teams clash there's more at stake than goal-scoring. It starts with the insults – Amsterdammers refer to their arch rivals as 'Kakkerlakken' (cockroaches), while Ajax themselves are referred to as 'Joden' (Yids) or 'Neuzen' (Noses) because of the club's Jewish roots – but the deep-rooted hatred doesn't stop at racist name-calling. Over the years, many on-field clashes between the clubs have been marred by violent scenes off it. One of the most infamous in recent times was a running battle in the streets of Beverwijk in 1997, which resulted in the death of an Ajax fan. But there have been numerous instances of riots pre- and post-game since, and even evidence of trouble at youth matches: in 2004, Ajax hooligans attacked the Feyenoord under-21 players during a derby game.

It isn't limited to the two big teams, either. PSV Eindhoven, FC Utrecht, FC Den Bosch and also ADO Den Haag are others with hardcore elements among followers, and horrible incidents ensue nationwide. Yet it wasn't always this way. Hooliganism was only really introduced to the Dutch game in 1974, following Feyenoord's victory over Tottenham Hotspur in the final of the UEFA Cup. A large-scale riot marred the second leg, played in Rotterdam, which in turn ignited aggressive fans around the country.

The good news is that troublemakers are very much in the minority and the football fan is unlikely to run into problems. Compared to other European countries like Spain and Italy – where hooliganism is dealt with by shocking police brutality – the Netherlands prefers preventative measures, presided over by the all-seeing Centraal Informatiepunt Voetbalvandalisme (Dutch Central Information Unit for Hooliganism). Segregation is the key, and typically, from the moment travelling fans leave their home city to the point of sitting down to watch the game, their journey is controlled and carefully monitored.

Even local fans need to follow strict rules to watch their favourite team. To be eligible to buy a match ticket, you must first be a registered fan and own a club card – roughly equivalent to buying a personalised football passport for the stadium that you choose to visit – so clubs and the police not only have contact details for every person sitting there watching the game, but also photographs.

The downside is that such measures make it trickier for casual football fans, let alone tourists, to enjoy the sport in person. It takes some careful planning to arrange a trip to see your favourite team play, even if the stadium is empty. The smaller clubs are usually more helpful, and will arrange temporary entry. But a team like Ajax knows full well that it's held in high esteem, and prefers to welcome its guests with suitably expensive package deals.

For more on Dutch football, *see p251*.

The great indoors: pooling resources at **Het Marnix**. *See p258.*

Stadium (671 6086, www.phanos.org). Details on athletics in Holland are available from the KNAU (026 483 4800, www.knau.nl).

Badminton

Following international success from orange-shirted players like Mia Audina and Yao Jie, badminton players and sporting facilities are becoming all the more professional. Contact the Badminton Union Amsterdam (697 3758, www.bva-badminton.nl) and NBB (030 608 4150, www.badminton.nl) for further information on clubs and courts.

Basketball

Although public basketball courts are a rarity, several clubs in Amsterdam welcome players: contact the NBB Amsterdam office (0251 272 417, www.dunk.nl) for more details. Korfball, a mixed-sex sport sharing elements of basketball and netball, is popular: contact the Amsterdam KNKV (034 349 9600, www.noordwest.knkv.nl).

Climbing

The single highest point in the Netherlands, Vaalserberg, is no more than 321m (1,053ft) high. Fortunately, climbing walls are never far away. See 'Klimmen' in the *Gouden Gids*.

Klimhal Amsterdam

Naritaweg 48 (681 0121/www.klimhalamsterdam.nl). NS Station Sloterdijk. **Open** 5-10.30pm Mon, Tue, Thur; 2-10.30pm Wed; 4-10.30pm Fri; 11am-10.30pm Sat; 9.30am-10.30pm Sun. **Admission** €10.75 adults; €7.25 under-17s. **Rental** set €5.50. **No credit cards.**

One of the biggest climbing walls in all of the Netherlands, easily recognisable by its unusual exterior amongst a sea of office blocks, this offers great facilities catering for beginners and advanced climbers, plus supervised courses all year round.

Golf

While golf isn't a sport that the Dutch have made much of a mark in professionally, it continues to develop as a relaxing game for men, women and children of all backgrounds and levels. You can play at a private club if introduced by a member or if you belong to a British golf club. Public courses are open to all; many offer driving ranges and practice holes to tune up your game. For details, see the *Gouden Gids* or call the Amsterdam Golf Club (497 7866).

Golfbaan Sloten

Sloterweg 1045, Sloten (614 2402). Bus 145. **Open** *Mid June-mid Aug* 8.30am-dusk daily. *Mid Aug-mid June* 8.30am-6pm Mon-Fri. **Admission** €17-€20. **No credit cards.**

A nine-hole public course, with a driving range and practice green. Booking advisable on weekends.

De Hoge Dijk

Abcouderstraatweg 46, Zuid-Oost (0294 281 241/www.dehogedijk.nl). Metro Nieuw Gein; from Holendrecht stop, take bus 120, 126 to Abcoude. **Open** dawn-dusk daily. **Admission** *18-hole* €42; €47.50 weekend. *9-hole* €24; €28 weekend. *Short course* €20; €24 weekend. **Credit** AmEx, DC, MC, V.

A public, 18-hole polder course, with a par score of 71, plus four par five holes and five par threes to complete the usual glut of par fours. It's on the edge of Amsterdam and reservations are required.

Health & fitness

Amsterdam has a very interesting collection of health clubs thanks to proprietors' willingness to set up shop in the capital's quirky old houses and countless empty office blocks. Look under 'Fitnesscentra' in the *Gouden Gids* for the full listings. There are also international chains, so enquire with your home club about Amsterdam options before travelling. If you're coming for longer, check out the hip Shape All-In (2e Hugo de Grootstraat 2-6, 684 5857, www.shape-all-in.nl), which, sadly, only offers one-month minimum memberships. The University of Amsterdam's Sports Centre (De Boelelaan 46, 301 3535, www.usc.uva.nl), is open to the public as well as students and boasts an excellent range of cutting-edge equipment, treatments and advice. It's also the best value membership in town – the only catch being that subscriptions follow the university terms.

Barry's Fitness

Lijnbaansgracht 350, Southern Canal Belt (626 1036/www.barrysfitness.nl). Tram 16, 24, 25. **Open** 7am-11pm Mon-Fri; 8am-8pm Sat, Sun. **Admission** €15/day; €27.50/wk; €66/mth. **No credit cards.** **Map** p331 E5.

This popular health club has earned a solid reputation as one of the best body-building gyms in town. Free weights and machines, cardiovascular equipment, aerobics, massage and sauna are backed up by friendly, knowledgeable staff.

SportPlaza Mercator

Jan van Galenstraat 315, West (618 8911/www.sportplazamercator.nl). Tram 7, 13/bus 15. **Admission** €12.50/day; €190/qrt.

This brand-new fitness centre is aimed at young, old and fitness-mad alike. Housed in an impressive complex coated in greenery and glass, its cardio and weight facilities meet modern expectations alongside three swimming pools, a sauna and a day-care area. After a workout, chill in the roof garden.

Horse riding

While it's not particularly sensible to go trotting within the canal ring, riding is nevertheless fairly accessible. Two large riding centres, De Amsterdamse Manege (643 1342, www.amsterdamse-manege.com) and the Nieuw Amstelland Manege (643 2468, www.nieuwamstelland.nl), both offer rides daily in the sylvan expanses of Amsterdamse Bos for under €20 per hour; lessons are also available. For other options see 'Maneges' in the *Gouden Gids*.

Saunas

Leave your modesty in the changing room: covering up is frowned upon in most places. Unless stated otherwise, saunas are mixed, but most offer women-only sessions. For squat sauna Fenomeen, contact 671 6780 or www.saunafenomeen.nl. For more, look in the *Gouden Gids* under 'Saunas'.

Deco Sauna

Herengracht 115, Western Canal Belt (623 8215/www.saunadeco.nl). Tram 1, 2, 5, 13, 17. **Open** noon-11pm Mon, Wed-Sat; 3pm-11pm Tue; 1-7pm Sun. **Admission** from €15. **No credit cards.** **Map** p326 C2.

This beautiful art deco sauna offers Turkish bath, Finnish sauna, cold plunge bath and solarium. Massages, shiatsu, plus beauty and skincare are all available by appointment. Mixed bathing only.

Skateboarding, rollerblading & rollerskating

Amsterdam is an exciting place if you like spending your days dashing about on various types of tiny wheels. There are plenty of opportunities to wow onlookers with your skills on the half-pipe at Museumplein and other urban parks. Rollerblading is also hugely popular as both sport and transport method, with cycle lanes doubling as skating routes. Vondelpark is a rollerblader's paradise, but if it's dry, check out the popular city-wide tour that is the awesome Friday Night Skate (*see p124* **Skate of mind**). For an all-weather solution, head to Skatepark Amsterdam (www.skateparkamsterdam.nl) over at the NDSM yard, which caters for all wheeled adventures and hosts a monthly rollerdisco. Protective gear is, of course, strongly encouraged. Consult the *Gouden Gids* under 'Sport en Spelartikelen' for specialist shops and rental locations.

Vondeltuin/Rent A Skate

Vondelpark 7; entrance at Amstelveenseweg, Museum Quarter (664 5091/www.vondeltuin.nl). Tram 1, 2, 3, 5, 6, 12. **Open** 11am-10pm daily. **Rates** from €5 (€20 security deposit plus ID). **No credit cards. Map** p330 C6.

A skate rental outlet in the bustling Vondelpark. Vondeltuin is also integral to the regular Friday Night Skate sessions (*see above*).

Rowing on the Amstel. *See p258.*

Skating

As if the nation were afraid to move at walking pace, the Dutch are as fearless on ice as on bikes, strapping on a pair of blades as soon as temperature permits. Hugely competitive on the international speed-skating circuit, it's not uncommon to see skaters whooshing along narrow city canals; even park ponds become rinks when conditions are right.

Recent winters have been warmer, drastically reducing the amount of skating time: this is highlighted by the absence of the Elfstedentocht – a 200km (124-mile) race around the many towns of Friesland. This marathon-style event is hugely popular, with up to 16,000 skaters taking part. Unfortunately it depends on precise ice conditions and the race hasn't been held since 1997 – before that it was 1986. If you're tempted to compete, you'll need membership of the Elfstedenvereniging Association, great fitness, excellent skates and a lot of patience.

Though natural ice marathons are the most popular, normal skating races also take place frequently throughout the winter, both indoors and outdoors. The biggest arena is Thialf in Heerenveen (0900 202 0026, www.thialf.nl), hosting regular national, European and world championships for up to 10,000 fans.

If seeking something more casual, head to the outdoor Jaap Edenhal 400m (1,312ft) ice track at Radioweg 64 (694 9652, www.jaapeden.nl), open October to March. Contact the KNSB in Amersfoort (0334 892 000, www.knsb.nl) for details on conditions and events.

Skiing & snowboarding

There may be no hills in Amsterdam, but it's easy to spend time on the slopes. A quick train journey out of the city to the Snow Dome (Jaap Edenweg 10, 0900 3384 8463, www.deuithof.nl) in The Hague finds one of the biggest artificial skiing and snowboarding centres in the country. Equipment hire and lessons are available. In Amsterdam, there are indoor slopes at Ski Inn (W.G. Plein 281, 607 0148, www.ski-inn.nl).

Snooker & carambole

There are several halls in Amsterdam where you can play snooker or pool fairly cheaply. Carambole, with a pocket-free table, is a popular variation. Traditionally, billiards (*biljart*) has been associated with cafés: outside the centre there are many bars with billiards and pool tables. Check the *Gouden Gids* under 'Biljartzalen' or contact the KNBB (030 600 8400, www.knbb.nl).

Pool en Snookercentrum Amsterdam-Zuid

Van Ostadestraat 97, the Pijp (pool 676 7903/ snooker 676 4059/www.poolensnooker.com). Tram 3, 12, 24, 25. **Open** 2pm-1am Mon-Thur, Sun; 1pm-2am Fri. **Admission** €7.50/hr pool; €8/hr snooker. **No credit cards**. **Map** p331 F6.
Spread across four floors, this chilled joint has plenty to offer both casual and serious players. Its well-maintained tables – 27 pool, seven snooker and one billiards – are available to all.

Squash

For information on local clubs and competitions, contact the Dutch Squash Organisation (079 361 5400, www.squash.nl) or look in the *Gouden Gids* under the 'Squashbanen' section.

Squash City

Ketelmakerstraat 6, Westerpark (626 7883/www.squashcity.nl). Bus 18, 22. **Open** 7am-11pm Mon-Thur; 7am-10.30pm Fri; 8.45am-7pm Sat, Sun. **Admission** €7 before 5pm; €9.50 after 5pm. **Credit** MC, V.
An all-round fitness centre with a focus on squash. There are 13 courts, a sauna, a weights room and modern aerobics facilities.

Swimming

Most Amsterdam hotels barely have space for bedrooms, let alone a pool. Fortunately, the city is well-equipped with public baths, which operate strict regimes for babies, toddlers, women, families, nudes, gay and also lane swimmers. Look in the *Gouden Gids* under 'Zwembaden' and consider calling ahead to find the perfect time slot. For those seeking diving experiences contact the Dutch Underwater Sports Association (www.onderwatersport.org) for clubs and courses.

Sloterparkbad (indoor & outdoor)

President Allendelaan 3, West (506 3506/www.sloterparkbad.nl). Tram 14. **Open** 7am-10pm Mon-Fri; 9am-4pm Sat, Sun. **Admission** from €3.90. **No credit cards**.
The largest swimming complex in the city offers facilities for everyone. Alongside the main 50m (164ft) indoor pool that plays host to international meets, there is an outdoor water park, outdoor pool and indoor recreational areas simply for fun.

De Mirandabad (indoor & outdoor)

De Mirandalaan 9, Zuid (546 4444/www.mirandabad.nl). Tram 25/bus 15, 169. **Open** 7am-10pm Mon-Fri; 10am-5pm Sat, Sun. **Admission** from €3.40. **No credit cards**.
A sub-tropical pool, De Mirandabad is very clean, with a stone beach and a wave machine. It's not ideal for swimming lengths, but its waterslide, whirlpool and outdoor pool (opens from May through August) are plenty of fun. There are also squash courts, a fitness centre and a restaurant.

Het Marnix (indoor)

Marnixplein 1, (5246 000/www.hetmarnix.nl). Tram 3. **Open** 7am-10pm Mon-Thur; 7am-6pm Fri; 7am-8pm Sat, Sun. **Admission** from €3.50. **No credit cards**.
Newly renovated, this multi-purpose health centre features two pools that, thanks to an advanced filtration system, require very little chlorine. The Tuesday night naturist slot is popular. *Photo p255.*

Tennis

For details on competitions – including July's Dutch Open and the ABN AMRO World Tennis Tournament in February – and clubs, contact the KNLTB (033 454 2600, www.knltb.nl). For a full listing of tennis courts see the *Gouden Gids* under 'Tennisparken en hallen'.

Amstelpark

Koenenkade 8, Amsterdamse Bos (301 0700/www.amstelpark.nl). Bus 170, 171, 172 from Amsterdam Centraal Station; 169 from Amstel Station. **Open** *Apr 1-Oct 1* 8am-11pm Mon-Fri; 8am-9pm Sat, Sun. *Oct 1-Apr 1* 8am-midnight Mon-Fri; 8am-11pm Sat, Sun. **Admission** *Outdoor court* €20/hr; *indoor* €27.50/hr. **Credit** AmEx, DC, MC, V.
A total of 42 tennis courts (16 indoor and 26 outdoor), plus 12 squash courts, a Turkish bath, sauna, swimming pool, a shop and racket hire.

Watersports

Away from the canals and pedalos, there are plenty of recreational lakes within easy reach of Amsterdam where seadogs can take to the water. For sailing, visit coastal Loosdrecht (25km/ 15 miles south-east of Amsterdam) or go to IJsselmeer. Catamarans can be rented in Muiden (20km/12 miles east of Amsterdam).

Casual canoeists can take a Wetlands Safari tour (686 3445, www.wetlandssafari.nl). For details on other canoeing, phone the NKB (030 751 3750, www.nkb.nl). Most schools ask for a deposit and ID when you rent a boat.

There are rowing clubs on the Amstel and at the Bosbaan in Amsterdamse Bos, the latter holding the title of being the oldest man-made rowing course in the world. For info call the KNRB (646 2740, www.knrb.nl).

Gaasperplas Park

Gaasperplas Park, South-East. Metro Gaasperplas/ bus 59, 60, 174. **Open** 24hrs daily.
This park's large lake is a centre for watersports and windsurfing. There's also a campsite.

Theatre, Comedy & Dance

Powerful, progressive, provocative: the epitome of 21st-century performance.

Theatre

Welcome to the city in which you can see anything and everything you desire on stage. The flip side is that you may also witness anything and everything that you'd prefer *not* to see: this is a city in which artists are prepared to do whatever it takes to make an impression. No censors and no boundaries means that performers have plenty of room to shock – and they often do.

Experimentation happens across all forms and genres of stage performance, from staged readings to musicals, ballet to improv. Theatre and dance groups stage a wide variety of shows: original, multicultural, progressive and traditional. But even the straightest of paths may have a few unexpected twists.

If you're after progressive and cutting-edge performances, then the theatres along the Nes are good places to start. For mainstream performances, try **Theater Carré** (*see p261*) or the **Amsterdam RAI Theater** (*see p260*). If you're into staged readings, keep an eye out for **De Hollandse Nieuwe** (*see p265*), a multicultural festival run by Cosmic Theater that features well-known and unknown playwrights of many different backgrounds and races. And if commercial shows or musicals are more your thing, look out for big Joop van den Ende productions. Don't worry too much about the language barrier: many shows are visual enough that non-Dutch speaking visitors can get a good idea of what's going on. Whatever your tastes, there'll be something to satisfy your tastes.

Thanks to an array of festivals, summer is a wonderful time to dip your toes into the dramatic arts. The **Over het IJ** and **Parade** festivals are great, while the Vondelpark's **Openluchttheater** is a lovely place in which to while away a mellow summer's evening. If apocalyptic grandeur is your thing, try the **Robodock** festival. One recent addition is the prosaically named **Het Theaterfestival**, also incorporating the **Amsterdam Fringe Festival**. For all of the above, *see p265*).

Theatre

De Balie
International, interdisciplinary, intellectual, and a great café to boot. *See p260.*

Magpie Music Dance Company
Mixing texts, music and movement to make 21st-century happenings. *See p270.*

NDSM
Astonishing site-specific performances in a dark and moody warehouse. *See p262.*

Robodock
Quite simply the most insane multimedia event you'll ever witness. *See p265.*

Toomler
Superb English-language comedy. *See p267.*

TICKETS AND INFORMATION

For information about what's on, call or visit the **Uitburo** on Leidseplein, or contact the **Amsterdam Tourist Board** (*see p312*). The AUB's monthly *Uitkrant* has details of dance events in and around the city. If you prefer to play it by ear, visit the **Last Minute Ticket Shop** on Leidseplein; tickets for that night's shows are sold at half price.

The three theatres on Nes – **De Brakke Grond**, **De Engelenbak** and **Frascati** (*see pp260-261*) – all sell tickets through a central box office (Nes 45, 626 6866, www.indenes.nl, 1pm to 7.30pm Mon-Sat). The theatre's own box offices open only at 7.30pm on the night of performances.

Theatres

Amsterdam Marionetten Theater

Nieuwe Jonkerstraat 8, Old Centre: Old Side (620 8027/www.marionettentheater.nl). Tram 4, 9.
Box office *Phone* 10am-5pm Mon-Fri. *In person* from 2hrs before performance. **Tickets** €12-€15. **No credit cards**. **Map** p327 E2.

Arts & Entertainment

Opera as you've never seen it before: put together puppets in velvet costumes, puppeteers and operas by Mozart or Offenbach, and you've got a show by the Amsterdam Marionetten Theater. One of the last outposts of an old European tradition, the theatre also offers private lunches, dinners or high teas, consumed while puppets sing their wooden hearts out.

Amsterdam RAI Theater

Europaplein 8-22, Zuid (549 1212/www.raitheater.nl). NS Amsterdam RAI. **Box office** from 2hrs before performance. **Tickets** €20-€90. **Credit** MC V.

A huge convention and exhibition centre by day, the RAI is an enormous theatre by night and at weekends. Musicals, operas, comedy nights, ballets and spectacular shows can all be enjoyed in this sizeable hall. Not everyone loves the building, but it's what's inside that counts, after all.

De Balie

Kleine-Gartmanplantsoen 10, Southern Canal Belt (553 5100/www.debalie.nl). Tram 1, 2, 5, 6, 7, 10. **Box office** 5-9pm or until start of performance Mon-Fri; from 90min before performance Sat, Sun. **Tickets** €7-€15. **No credit cards. Map** p330 D5.

Theatre, new media, photography shows, cinema (*see p213*) and literary events sit alongside lectures, debates and discussions about cultural, social and political issues at this influential centre for the local intelligentsia. Throw in a visit to the café and you've got food for both mind and body. After all, what's culture without a little cake to go with it?

De Brakke Grond

Nes 45, Old Centre: Old Side (622 9014/www.brakkegrond.nl). Tram 4, 9, 14, 16, 24, 25. **Box office** *see p259.* **Tickets** €5-€12. **No credit cards. Map** p326 D3.

Belgian culture does stretch beyond beer, and De Brakke Grond is here to prove it. Mind you, some good Belgian beer will go down a treat after a fix of progressive Flemish theatre; if you're really lucky you might find an actor or two joining you at the bar of the adjoining café/restaurant.

Het Compagnietheater

Kloveniersburgwal 50, Old Centre: Old Side (520 5320/www.theatercompagnie.nl). Tram 4, 9, 14, 16, 24, 25. **Box office** 1-5.30pm Mon-Sat, or until 8pm on performance days. **Tickets** €12.50-€18. **No credit cards. Map** p326 D3.

This venue on Kloveniersburgwal is the home of De Theatercompagnie, a huge ensemble that emerged from the fusion of De Trust and Art & Pro. Under the astute direction of Theu Boermans, culturally and politically aware pieces (usually in Dutch) are the house speciality, so don't expect light-hearted fluff. The company also performs on a regular basis in the formidable Stadsschouwburg (*see p262*).

De Engelenbak

Nes 71, Old Centre: Old Side (information 626 3644/www.engelenbak.nl). Tram 4, 9, 14, 16, 24, 25. **Box office** *see p259.* **Tickets** €7.50-€11. **No credit cards. Map** p326 D3.

Amsterdam Marionetten Theater. *See p259.*

De Engelenbak offers an array of theatre productions by amateurs. The main draw is Open Bak, an open-stage event (10.30pm Tue) where anything goes: it's the longest-running theatre programme in the country, and everybody gets their shot. Arrive half an hour early to score a ticket (€7.50).

Frascati

Nes 63, Old Centre: Old Side (751 6400/tickets 626 6866/www.indenes.nl). Tram 4, 9, 14, 16, 24, 25. **Box office** *see p259.* **Tickets** €8.50-€14. **No credit cards. Map** p326 D3.

A cornerstone of progressive Dutch theatre since the 1960s, Frascati gives promising artists the chance to stage their productions on one of its three stages. Their mission? To challenge the bounds of traditional theatre by teaming up artists with trained backgrounds with those from the street, resulting in a varied selection of theatre and dance shows featuring MCs, DJs and VJs. Look out in particular for the youthful Breakin' Walls festival.

Gasthuis Werkplaats & Theater

Marius van Bouwdijk Bastiaansestraat 54, entrance opposite 1e Helmerstraat 115, Museum Quarter (616 8942/www.theatergasthuis.nl). Tram 1, 3, 6, 12. **Box office** *Phone* 10am-5pm Mon-Fri. *In person* from 1hr before performance. **Tickets** from €8. **No credit cards. Map** p325 B6.

The Gasthuis emerged from an influential group of squatters; even when their old home, a former hospital, was under threat, their activities contributed a great deal towards the building's eventual salvation. As you might expect, the programme is generally youthful and experimental. Some productions are performed in English.

De Kleine Komedie

Amstel 56-58, Southern Canal Belt (624 0534/www.dekleinekomedie.nl). Tram 4, 9, 14, 16, 24, 25. **Box office** noon-6pm Mon-Sat, or until start of performance. **Tickets** €9-€20. **No credit cards. Map** p327 E3.

Amsterdam's oldest theatre (built in 1786) and one of its most important, De Kleine Komedie is the nation's premier cabaret stage, though it also offers a wide range of musical acts. Extremely popular with locals, it's one of the more characterful theatrical venues in Amsterdam.

Koninklijk Theater Carré

Amstel 115-25, Southern Canal Belt (0900 252 5255 premium rate/www.theatercarre.nl). Tram 4, 6, 7, 10/Metro Weesperplein. **Box office** *Phone* 9am-9pm daily. *In person* 4-8pm daily. **Tickets** €15-€55. **Credit** AmEx, MC, V. **Map** p331 F4.

Many dream of performing in this glamorous space, formerly home to a circus and recently refurbished in grand style. The Carré hosts some of the best Dutch cabaret artists and touring operas, as well as the odd big music name. If mainstream theatre is more your thing, this is the place to come to see and hear Dutch versions of popular blockbusters such as *Grease* and *My Fair Lady* (*see p232*).

Water works at **Over het IJ**. *See p265.*

Het Rozentheater

Rozengracht 117, the Jordaan (620 7953/www.rozentheater.nl). Tram 13, 17. **Box office** *Phone* 1-5pm Mon-Sat, or until 8pm on performance days. *In person* from 5pm until start of performance. **Tickets** €7.50-€12.50. **No credit cards**. **Map** p325 B3.

After a big renovation, Het Rozentheater now hosts theatre by and for young people. The performers are professionals, theatre students or enthusiastic amateurs between aged 15 to 30, with most shows about issues facing young people in the here and now.

Stadsschouwburg

Leidseplein 26, Southern Canal Belt (624 2311/www.ssba.nl). Tram 1, 2, 5, 6, 7, 10. **Box office** 10am-6pm Mon-Sat, or until start of performance; from 2hrs before start of performance Sun. **Tickets** €10-€45. **Credit** AmEx, MC, V. **Map** p330 C5.

The Stadsschouwburg ('Municipal Theatre') is an impressive 19th-century building, constructed in traditional horseshoe shape and seating 950. It's currently being renovated, and will soon link up with the Melkweg. Nevertheless, in the meantime, productions by Toneelgroep Amsterdam continue to be staged here. The venue also stages contemporary music, dance and theatre. *Photos p266.*

Theater Bellevue

Leidsekade 90, Southern Canal Belt (530 5301/www.theaterbellevue.nl). Tram 1, 2, 5, 6, 7, 10. **Box office** 11am-start of performance daily. **Tickets** prices vary. **Credit** AmEx, DC, MC, V. **Map** p330 C5.

After the closure of partner Nieuwe de la Mar Theater in 2006, the Bellevue (which dates to 1840), has started on a solo journey. Shows are acted out on three podia: one for modern theatre, dance and music; one devoted to cabaret; and a third for literary events and short lunchtime performances (maximum one hour) by Dutch writers.

Theater de Cameleon

3e Kostverlorenkade 35, West (489 4656/www.decameleon.nl). Tram 1. **Box office** noon-6pm daily. **Tickets** €5-€15. **No credit cards**. **Map** p325 A3.

A relatively new theatre in the western part of town, De Cameleon offers a wide variety of theatre performances (often in English) along with acting and voice workshops for all ages.

Theater het Amsterdamse Bos

Amsterdamse Bos, Amstelveen (643 3286/www.bosttheater.nl). Bus 66, 170, 172, 176, 199. **Tickets** €12.50. **No credit cards**.

What better way to spend a dreamy midsummer night than picnicking beneath the stars in a sultry sylvan setting, while classic drama, Shakespeare included (translated into Dutch), is performed before you? No wonder the trees are talking. Get to the Bos early with your hamper, bag a place, settle back, open the wine and enjoy.

Theater Fabriek Amsterdam

Czaar Peterstraat 213 (522 5260/www.theaterfabriekamsterdam.nl). Tram 10, 26/bus 42, 43. **Box office** from 2hrs before performance. **Tickets** €25-€55. **No credit cards**.

Housed in an old factory that once built ship engines, Theater Fabriek organises big musical shows, popular operas and post-Cirque de Soleil performances for people who like a mixture of avant-garde and spectacle. Think Blue Man Group and Mayumana, and you're halfway there.

Cultural complexes

NDSM

TT Neveritaweg 15, Noord (330 5480/www.ndsm.nl). Ferry from Centraal Station/bus 35, 94.

A shipbuilding yard at the beginning of the last century, NDSM is now a cultural complex that's yet to be completed, a state of affairs that's rather in step with the constantly mutating needs of Amsterdam's vibrant artistic community. Despite being unfinished, it still manages to stage some of the most provocative dance, mime and theatre productions in Amsterdam. Apart from two stages, one of which is to be made completely of recycled materials, it serves as a breeding ground for artists (*see p56*); small-scale workshops and performances are held here almost daily in its labyrinth of studios and performance areas. Unfortunately, wrangling over the venue's fire and safety capabilities may threaten some of the large-scale activities held here, such as the mind-altering multimedia festival Robodock (*see p265* and *p263* **Oerol fixation**).

Westergasfabriek

Haarlemmerweg 8-10, West (586 0710/www.westergasfabriek.com). Tram 10/bus 18, 22.
On the sprawling terrain of the city's former gas works, the Westergasfabriek reopened in 2003 with much fanfare after years of renovation, asbestos removal and soil detoxification. With a wild variety of industrial buildings being re-invented as performance, event and exhibition spaces, the Westergasfabriek is quickly evolving into one of the city's premier cultural hubs; as it was through the 1990s, in fact, when it was a happening underground squat village. It's the new home for Cosmic (606 5050, www.cosmictheater.nl), a theatre troupe that has long been addressing the multicultural realities of the modern world, and Made in da Shade (606 5050, www.shade.nl), a group who make 'theatre for new times in old cities'. Now complete with acres of water and cypress-accented landscaping, the grounds are a lovely place for wandering; a wide range of cafés, including one belonging to the Ketelhuis cinema (*see p210*), provide welcome sustenance for the strolling visitor. All in all, it's well worth a visit, whether you're in the market for a theatre performance, a club night, an art exhibition or just a lengthy walk in the park. One of modern-day Amsterdam's most valued assets.

Theatre festivals

For Oerol, *see below* **Oerol fixation**.

Theaterfestival Boulevard

's Hertogenbosch (073 613 7671/www.festivalboulevard.nl). **Date** early Aug.
An effort to promote the arts in the province of Brabant, the Boulevard festival is an initiative that fills the medieval town of Den Bosch (short for 's Hertogenbosch) each summer with theatre, dance and children's activities. The main venues are tents erected in the square next to St Jan Cathedral, though performances are also staged in theatres and other less likely locations. Among the national and international companies that have taken part in recent years are Warner & Consorten, Hans Hof Ensemble and Australia's Snuff Puppets.

De Hollandse Nieuwe

Central Amsterdam (606 5050/www.cosmictheaters.nl). **Date** varies.
A chance for artists from all cultures to shine, the annual Hollandse Nieuwe festival focuses on texts written by established and up-and-coming playwrights from many different backgrounds. Every year, a selection of one-act plays are chosen and

Oerol fixation

The landscape of Terschelling, one of the five Frisian islands that sit off the north coast of Holland, is a unique mix of dunes, dykes and woodlands, shaped and shifted by the interaction of wind and man. A highly popular holiday destination for teenagers and twitchers (more than half the island is a bird sanctuary), it becomes a Bohemian haven during the ten-day **Oerol** theatre festival, which celebrated its 25th edition in 2006.

The whole island is transformed into stages on which around 200 acts perform: you might find international drama groups creating their own environments, world music acts drawing crowds to the beaches, theatre expeditions through the local woods, and shows taking place in old boathouses or disused barns. As wacky as this all sounds, Oerol reflects a long legacy in Dutch theatre, by which all things absurd, over the top and technologically cutting-edge are embraced, and the dividing lines between theatre, music, dance and circus are blurred.

The now venerable Dogtroep can be considered the spiritual forebears of this particular school of theatre. Seeing themselves as more laboratory than troupe, Dogtroep have compiled a huge resumé of sculpted dreamscape happenings rich in colour, wizardry, alien costuming and random exploding bits, each of which has evolved organically in response to the performance's site and context – be that Moscow's Red Square or a Belgian prison. Other Dutch groups such as Warner & Consorten and Vis a Vis, both Oerol favourites, have explored a similar muse, inspired by the setting in which they're performing.

The Dutch seem to be enamoured with a unique brand of what can only be called circus-opera, apparently all directed by a hallucinating cartoonist. You can also witness similar versions of this particular school of performance at festivals such as **Parade** and **Over het IJ**, and, in its extreme form, at **Robodock** (for all three, *see p265*), where the audience is confronted with battling robots, orchestral pyrotechnics, brain-melting video projections and frolicking mutants. But none of these festivals take place, as Oerol does, in such a natural setting that makes the public, the performers and the residents all feel at home. As always, it's a case of location, location, location. The event takes place every June; for details, call 0562 448448 or see www.oerol.nl.

Arts & Entertainment

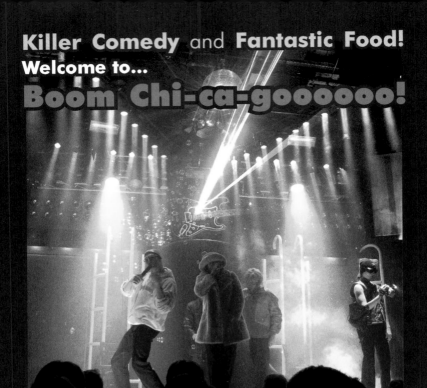

performed in staged readings. An awards show and a swinging party bring the festival to a close in typically raucous Amsterdam style.

ITs Festival

Around Amsterdam (530 5560/www.itsfestival.nl). **Date** June.

Something of a talent-spotter's dream, the International Theaterschool Festival is where students from all over the world show what they're made of. A mix of cabaret, dance, mime and drama takes place in the Theaterschool (*see p268*) and other venues in town. Each day ends with the talk show ITs Late, followed by a busy party. The ITs lounge in the Theaterschool building is usually bustling.

Noorderzon

Noorderplantsoen Groningen (050 314 02 78/ www.noorderzon.nl). **Date** Aug.

In a lovely park in faraway Groningen (*see p284* **Going for Groningen**), this crossover festival includes theatre, music, radio shows and cabaret, though there's also a DownTown programme that takes place in and outside the centre. Under the sterling leadership of Brit Mark Yeoman, a village fete has evolved into a true international meeting place.

Over het IJ

NDSM-werf Amsterdam Noord (492 2229/ www.overhetij.nl). **Date** July.

A summer feast of large theatrical projects and avant-garde mayhem, Over het IJ is usually interesting and frequently compelling. This festival of performance, set in the appropriately apocalyptic setting of NDSM (*see p262*), brings together international troupes united by a love of absurdity and the latest in multimedia. *Photo p262.*

Parade

Martin Luther Kingpark, Zuid (033 465 4555/ www.deparade.nl). Tram 25. **Date** Aug.

This unique event has captured the essence of the old circus/sideshow atmosphere that's usually so conspicuously absent at today's commercial fairgrounds. Parade offers a plentiful selection of bizarre shows, many in beautiful circus tents; spread between them are cafés, bars and restaurants, as well as the odd roving performer. Theatre, music, art, magic, oddities, spectacular shows and all kinds of attractions ring the audience, who are centre-stage instead of the other way around. The event has become very popular and many shows sell out quickly; it's best to go early, have dinner or a picnic, and book your tickets at the Parade Kiosk for the night, though note that some smaller shows sell their tickets separately. *See also p263* **Oerol fixation**.

Robodock

NDSM (www.robodock.org). **Date** late September.

The organisers have variously called Robodock a 'manifestival', and a 'free zone alternation'. But basically it's a temporary, post-apocalyptic village of open spaces, warehouses and haphazard structures that are all bursting with battling robots, orchestral pyrotechnics, brain-melting video projections, frolicking mutants and musical performances. Essentially, Robodock can simply be seen as radical recycling taken to the outer limits of guerrilla street theatre. It's indescribable and unmissable.

Het Theaterfestival

Around Amsterdam (624 2311/www.tf-1.nl). **Date** end Aug-beginning Sept.

Launched in 2006, the Theaterfestival is a showcase for Dutch and Belgian theatre. TF-1 presents a selection of shows, chosen by a jury, that were performed in the low countries over the past season. TF-2 is the Amsterdam Fringe, an uncurated, Edinburgh-style collection of smaller productions performed both indoors and outside. TF-3 consists of debates and readings on theatrical subjects, while TF-4, De Vlaamse Keuze, contains Belgian shows selected by the jury of Belgium's own Theaterfestival.

Vondelpark Openluchttheater

Vondelpark (673 1499/www.openluchttheater.nl). Tram 1, 2, 3. **Date** late June-Aug.

Theatrical events have been held in Vondelpark since 1865, and the tradition continues each summer with a variety of (free) shows. Wednesdays offer lunchtime concerts and mid-afternoon children's shows; Thursdays find the bandstand jumping to the sound of music; there's a dance and/or theatre show every Friday evening; various events (including workshops and theatre) take place on Saturdays; and yet more theatrical events and pop concerts are held every Sunday afternoon. Bring dancing shoes: if the genre of music demands it, the audience is positively encouraged to move.

Bookshop

International Theatre & Film Books

Leidseplein 26, in the Stadsschouwburg building, Southern Canal Belt (622 6489/www.theatreandfilmbooks.com). Tram 1, 2, 5, 7, 10. **Open** noon-6pm Mon; 10am-6pm Tue, Wed, Fri, Sat; 10am-7pm Thur. **Credit** (min €35) AmEx, DC, MC, V. **Map** p330 C5.

This shop caters to the theatre and film enthusiast, and how. It's the largest store of its kind in Europe, offering everything from books on circuses and musicals to production and technical manuals. There's plenty of stock in English.

Museum

For the **Theater Instituut**, *see p101.*

Comedy

While the Dutch have their own cultural history of hilarity, thanks in large part to their own very singular take on the art and practice of cabaret, stand-up is a fairly recent import to the Netherlands in general and Amsterdam

Stadsschouwburg. *See p262.*

in particular. However, it's become more popular in recent years, and shows usually feature a mix of international and local acts, often performing in English (although it's best to call ahead to check). Theatresport is also becoming popular: audiences throw roses on the stage to register their approval of acts and wet sponges at the jury when they disagree with the verdict. If that much interaction isn't for you, then there are always plain old improv shows, at which acts perform without the extra props to prop them up.

Boom Chicago

Leidseplein Theater, Leidseplein 12, Southern Canal Belt (423 0101/www.boomchicago.nl). Tram 1, 2, 5, 6, 7, 10. **Box office** 11am-8.30pm Mon-Thur, Sun; 11am-11pm Fri, Sat. **Shows** 8.15pm Mon-Fri, Sun; 7.30pm Sat; *Heineken Late Nite* 11.30pm Fri; 10.30pm Sat. **Tickets** €19.50-€39; *Heineken Late Nite* €13. **Credit** AmEx, MC, V. **Map** p330 C5.

The American improv troupe is one of Amsterdam's biggest success stories. With several different shows running seven nights a week (except Sundays in winter), all in English, the group offers a mix of audience-prompted improvisation and rehearsed sketches. Recent shows have included *Me, MySpace and iPod* and *Best of Boom: The Director's Choice*. Heineken Late Nite is particularly rewarding: if the improvisers like your suggestion, you get a free beer. The bar offers cocktails and DJs, and is something of an unofficial meeting point for countless wayward Americans; a restaurant serves lunch from noon until 4pm daily. They even publish a free magazine for visitors that are new to Amsterdam. All in all, a genuine cultural movement in an unexpected form.

Comedy Café Amsterdam

Max Euweplein 43-5, Southern Canal Belt (638 3971/www.comedycafe.nl). Tram 1, 2, 5, 6, 7, 10. **Shows** 9pm Mon-Sun; 9pm. **Tickets** €3-€15. **Credit** AmEx, MC, V. **Map** p330 C5.

The Comedy Café has been doing a decent job of bringing the art of stand-up to a wider audience. From Thursday to Saturday, there's a stand-up show in a mind-boggling blend of Dutch and English. Monday's shows vary between open-mic and theme nights (an evening of local comedy, for example). On Tuesdays and Wednesdays, comics try out new material at the venue's open-mic nights, while Sundays are reserved for the English-language improv show In Your Face!!. For those who want some grub before their laughs, there's also a restaurant for lunch and dinner; you can order a la carte or take up a dinner-and-show arrangement, thus ensuring fuller, more satisfying belly laughs.

Comedy Theatre

Nes 110 (422 2777/www.comedytheater.nl). Tram 4, 9, 14, 16, 24, 25. **Shows** 8.30pm daily. **Tickets** €10-€22. **Credit** Amex, MC, V. **Map** p326 D3.

Hyping itself as the 'club house' for comedians, the Comedy Theatre combines ascerbic, politically hard-hitting performers with those who do more straightforward stand-up. Expect local legends like Javier Guzman and international acts such as Tom Rhodes or Lewis Black. To make sure that at least some of the acts are English-speaking, it's best to call in advance before turning up.

Toomler

Breitnerstraat 2, Zuid (670 7400/www.toomler.nl). Tram 2, 5, 16, 24. **Box office** from 7pm (phone reservations 5.15-10pm) Wed-Sat. **Shows** 8.30pm. **Tickets** €5-€15. **No credit cards**.

Located next to the Hilton, this café hosts acts four nights a week. Most programming is stand-up in Dutch, but it's the English-language Comedy Train International, held in January, July and August, that has come to be most closely associated with the venue. On weekends, there's regular music (predominantly jazz) during Friday Night Live (11pm Fri) and Super Sundays Live (4pm). If you want to eat during the show, there's belly-laugh friendly tapas on offer to hungry punters.

Dance

Little more than half a century ago, the Dutch dance portfolio was as skinny as they come. But thanks to a number of forward-thinking pioneers and some generous government funding, the country has come along in leaps in bounds. The network of national stages, festivals, training centres, workshops and dance companies attracts key foreign choreographers and dancers, and keeps the Dutch dance landscape spicy and experimental. But traditional dance has retained a foothold here.

The country's two most bejewelled companies, Amsterdam-based **Dutch National Ballet** and **Netherlands Dance Theater** in the Hague, continue to mesmerise audiences, with pieces choreographed by the likes of Jirí Kylián, Lightfoot León, Hans van Manen and Ted Brandsen. Heavy hitters such as William Forsythe, Batsheva's Ohad Naharin and Wayne McGregor are also drawn here. And in addition to the companies listed below, choreographers such as Anouk van Dijk, Emio Greco, Hans Hof, Pieter de Ruiter, Nanine Linning and Beppie Blankert are also worth a look.

Hardcore dance lovers should ponder a visit in July, when the theatres around Leidseplein stage the **Julidans Festival**. The event's sheer diversity is usually a terrific reflection of the type of dance that's making waves in Europe and other regions of the world.

TICKETS AND INFORMATION

Tickets for the majority of performances can be bought at the venues themselves, or from any of the various phone, online or drop-in

Moving with the times

In July every year, the Stadsschouwburg (*see p262*) hosts **Julidans** (www.julidans.nl), a one-month showcase of world dance staged in theatres around the Leidseplein. The **International Concours for Choreographers** in Groningen, meanwhile, is a competition event at which prizes are given for ensemble choreographies. Details about the events' various competitions, performances, courses and workshops are available from the Theater Instituut Nederland (see *p101*).

For details of the **Holland Festival** and **Uitmarkt**, two major multicultural festivals that include a number of noteworthy dance performances from around the world in their pleasingly eclectic calendars, *see p199* and *p200* respectively.

Nederlandse Dansdagen & Dansweek

Nederlandse Dansdagen *various locations in Maastricht (www.nederlandsedansdagen.nl).* **Date** first week Oct.
Dansweek *various theatres in Holland (626 2062/www.dansweek.nl).* **Date** first week Oct.
During October, the Nederlandse Dansdagen in Maastricht form the official start of the national Dansweek, held in theatres all over the country to promote Dutch dance to a larger audience. During the festival, the best performances from the season are repeated and the main Dutch dance prizes are granted.

Holland Dance Festival

Nobelstraat 21, 2513 BC The Hague (070 361 6142/info 070 356 1176/ www.hollanddancefestival.com).
Date biennial: Oct, Nov 2007.
Held every two years in November, the Holland Dance Festival takes place at three venues (including the Hague's Lucent Danstheater; *see p269*), and is one of the biggest and most important festivals on the Dutch dance calendar. Many of the world's larger companies are attracted to the event thanks to its reputation, and the quality of the work is consistently high. Though a variety of Dutch acts usually perform at the event, Nederlands Dans Theater (*see p270*) is invariably the country's main representative.

Springdance

Postbus 111, 3500 AC Utrecht (030 230 2032/www.springdance.nl).
Date late Apr-early May.
Springdance, held annually in Utrecht in late April and early May, attempts to give a broad overview of recent developments in modern dance, film and music from around the world. A genuinely wide and open-minded approach to the medium sees everything from highly choreographed ballet to more spontaneous breakdance-influenced urban moves on show.

AUB operations. The AUB's free *Uitkrant* magazine lists local dance events; alternatively, check listings in *Amsterdam Weekly*.

Venues

Dance in all its forms is performed at a variety of venues in Amsterdam, the biggest of which are detailed below. Other local venues that stage occasional events include **Theater Bellevue**, the **Stadsschouwburg** (for both, *see p262*), the **Frascati**, **De Brakke Grond** (for both, *see p260*), **NDSM** (*see p262*), **OT301** (*see p213*) and **Het Rozentheater** (see p262). For festivals, *see above* **Moving with the times**.

DWA-Studio Theatre

Arie Biemondstraat 107b, Museum Quarter (689 1789/www.danswerkplaats.nl). Tram 1, 17. **Box office** *Phone* 10am-6pm Mon-Thur. *In person* 7.45pm until start of performance. **Tickets** free-€7.50. **No credit cards**.

Danswerkplaats is a podium for young, often recently graduated students to develop their choreographic talents. Performances have been staged at least once a month, both here and elsewhere in the city or country, since 1993.

hetveem Theater

Van Diemenstraat 410, Western Docklands (626 9291/www.hetveemtheater.nl). Tram 3/bus 18, 21, 22, 29. **Box office** *Phone* 10am-4pm performance days. *In person* from 1hr before performance. **Tickets** €8-€10; €3.50 theatre students. **No credit cards**.
A homophone for 'fame', hetveem Theater occupies the third floor of a renovated warehouse and hosts modern dance and multimedia productions from home and around the world. Performances usually take place at 8.30pm; between October and March, there's also a Sunday slot at 4pm.

KIT Tropentheater

Kleine Zaal Linnaeusstraat 2, Oost; Grote Zaal Mauritskade 63, Oost (568 8500/www.tropen theater.nl). Tram 7, 9, 10, 14/bus 22. **Box office** *Phone* 10am-6pm Mon-Fri; 2-6pm Sat. *In person* noon-

6pm, & from 1hr before start of performance Mon-Sat. **Tickets** €12-€20. **Credit** MC, V. **Map** p332 H3.
Right next to the Tropenmuseum (*see p113*), the Tropeninstituut organises performances in music and dance that are related to or drawn from various non-Western cultures. The dance programme varies from classical Indian styles all the way to South African, Indonesian to Argentinian.

Melkweg

Lijnbaansgracht 234a, Western Canal Belt (531 8181/www.melkweg.nl). Tram 1, 2, 5, 6, 7, 10. **Box office** from 4.30pm daily. **Performances** usually 8.30pm. **Tickets** €5-€45. *Membership* (compulsory) €3/mth. **No credit cards**. **Map** p330 C5.
This venerated multidisciplinary venue (*see also p233* and *p243*) opened its doors to national and international dance and theatre groups in 1973. For many years, the small stage hosted mainly dancers and choreographers at the start of their careers. Its renovated theatre lives up to tradition: many of the country's hottest new project groups perform between the higher-profile mainstays. As befits its reputation for one-stop eclecticism, the Melkweg places special focus on multimedia performances.

Muiderpoorttheater

2e Van Swindenstraat 26, Oost (668 1313/www.muiderpoorttheater.nl). Tram 3, 7, 9, 10, 14.
Box office from 1hr before performance. **Tickets** €8. **No credit cards**. **Map** p332 H2.
Renovated a few years ago, the Muiderpoorttheater is known primarily for performances by international acts. The popular fortnightly Mad Sunday programme combines music, dance and improvisation. There are plenty of other activities: check the theatre's website or call for details.

Muziektheater

Amstel 3, Old Centre: Old Side (625 5455/www.muziektheater.nl). Tram 9, 14/Metro Waterlooplein. **Box office** 10am-6pm or until start of performance Mon-Sat; 11.30am-6pm or until start of performance Sun. **Tickets** €20-€100. **Credit** AmEx, DC, MC, V. **Map** p327 E3.
The Muziektheater is Amsterdam at its most ambitious. This plush, crescent-shaped building, which opened in 1986, has room for 1,596 people and is home to both Dutch National Ballet (*see p270*) and De Nederlandse Opera, though the stage is also used by visiting companies such as Nederlands Dans Theater (see below), the Bill T Jones/Arnie Zane Dance Company and Batsheva. The lobby's panoramic glass walls offer impressive views out over the River Amstel.

Out of town venues

Lucent Danstheater

Spuiplein 152, The Hague (070 880 0333/www.ldt.nl). NS rail Den Haag Centraal Station. **Box office** *Phone* 10am-6pm Mon-Fri; noon-6pm Sat. *In person* noon-6pm Mon-Sat, & from 1hr before performance. **Tickets** €14-€35. **Credit** AmEx, DC, MC, V.
The Lucent Danstheater, located in the centre of the Hague, is the fabulous home of the world famous Nederlands Dans Theater (*see p270*), and boasts a stage facility built especially for dance. As well as mounting high-quality Dutch productions in both dance and opera, it's also become one of the country's foremost venues in which to see touring international dance companies.

Rotterdamse Schouwburg

Schouwburgplein 25, Rotterdam (010 411 8110/www.schouwburg.rotterdam.nl). NS rail Rotterdam Centraal Station. **Box office** noon-7pm Mon-Sat. Closed July-mid Aug. **Tickets** €12-€42.50. **Credit** AmEx, DC, MC, V.
This large, square theatre opened in 1988 and soon became known by the waggish nickname 'Kist van Quist' ('Quist's Coffin'; Wim Quist was the architect). The building hosts a generous variety of classical ballet and modern dance from both Dutch and international troupes in its two auditoria; one has 900 seats, while the other seats a mere 150.

De Theaterschool

Jodenbreestraat 3, Old Centre: Old Side (527 7700/www.the.ahk.nl). Tram 4, 9, 14, 16, 24, 25/Metro Waterlooplein. **Box office** times vary. **Tickets** free-€10. **No credit cards**. **Map** p327 E3.
This international theatre school brings together students and teachers from all over the world to learn and create in the fields of dance and theatre. Performances, some of which are announced in the *Uitkrant*, vary from studio shorts to evening-long events in the Philip Morris Danszaal. An annual showcase takes place in June.

Toneelschuur

Lange Begijnestraat 9, Haarlem (023 517 3910/www.toneelschuur.nl). NS rail Haarlem Centraal Station. **Box office** 2-9.45pm Mon-Fri; 1.30-9.45pm Sat-Sun. **Tickets** €13-€20. **No credit cards**.
With two stages and two cinemas housed within its hypermodern home designed by cartoonist Joost Swarte, Haarlem's Toneelschuur has every reason to be proud of its addition to the nation's cultural heritage. Its nationally renowned programme of theatre and modern dance has many Amsterdam culture vultures swooping in specially.

Companies

The following dance companies are all based in Amsterdam. Performances can be rather sporadic, and no one company is necessarily tied to a particular venue. For details on shows, call the numbers listed, check online or pick up a copy of *Uitkrant*.

Dansgroep Krisztina de Châtel

669 5755/www.dechatel.nl.
With more than 25 years' experience, 50 choreographies and even two films to her name, Hungarian Krisztina de Châtel's company has grown into an

internationally recognised dance group. Most productions last a whole evening, are often performed on location and combine dance, music, visual art and lay people, breaking down countless boundaries and garnering a good reputation in the process.

Het Internationaal Danstheater

Box office 623 5359/company 623 9112/ www.intdanstheater.nl.

This Amsterdam-based company has been performing since 1961. It aims to give traditional dance a theatrical form without compromising music, costumes or choreography. Their performers regularly work with guest choreographers who introduce authentic material from their country of origin and teach it to the dancers. The company prides itself on being the only professional dance company not bound by a particular culture, thus opening up endless performance potential.

Magpie Music Dance Company

616 4794/www.magpiemusicdance.com.

A collective of improvisers founded by the marvellously named dancer Katie Duck and her partner in music Michael Vatcher in 1994, Magpie uses improvisatory techniques to mix up a remarkable blend of dance, music and text into surprising night-long happenings. Although Magpie tours extensively, it still manages to maintain a season of performances at theatres across the capital.

Dutch National Ballet

Muziektheater box office 625 5455/ www.het-nationale-ballet.nl.

Amsterdam's premier dance company calls the Muziektheater its home and is one of the largest ensembles to be found on either side of the Atlantic. Toer van Schayk and Rudi van Dantzig were instrumental in developing the company's distinctive style, with many political and conceptual pieces using the strong personalities of the company's members. Since then, the company has become known for its excellent group of dancers and its proficiency in performing a wide repertoire range: from Graham and Cunningham to neoclassical dance (they have the largest Balanchine repertoire of any European company) via the traditional full-length classics with lush stagings as backdrops.

Out of town

The Amsterdam performances by the various companies detailed below are usually held in the Stadsschouwburg (*see p262*) or the Muziektheater (*see p269*).

Danceworks Rotterdam

010 436 4511/www.danceworksrotterdam.nl.

This ambitious and über-fit troupe, under the guidance of Ton Simons and an array of visiting choreographers, combines liveliness, purity and technique to make it a vigorous exponent of New York modern dance.

Netherlands Dance Theater

Lucent Danstheater box office 070 880 0333/ 070 880 0100/www.ndt.nl.

Founded in 1959, Netherlands Dance Theater is the country's most high-profile dance company; indeed, the exquisitely high level of choreography and dancers means that it's now considered one of the best dance troupes on the planet. Led by Anders Hellström, NDT tours the world extensively but does also perform regularly in the Netherlands; when in Amsterdam, it usually performs at the mighty Muziektheater (*see p269*). Aside from the main company, it's also worth looking out for NDT2: made up of spellbinding young novices and other up-and-coming Dutch dancers, it often delivers excellent performances.

Scapino Ballet Rotterdam

010 414 2414/www.scapinoballet.nl.

The oldest dance company in the country, Scapino used to be a little on the stuffy side. But in the 1990s, attention shifted from convention to innovation; once again, they're now a force to be reckoned with, under the tutelage of Ed Wubbe and his breathtaking group of professional dancers.

Conny Janssen Danst

010 452 9912/www.connyjanssendanst.nl.

Home-grown Conny Janssen's refreshing, recognisable and impressive choreographic style has led to a loyal following. Her dancers appear human and vulnerable yet iron-strong, and they're clearly very much into what they do. Since 1992, Janssen has embraced refined yet eclectic music, lighting and set choices, and whipped them on to the stage in a way that clicks perfectly.

NND/Galili Dance

050 579 9441/www.galilidance.nl.

Israeli Itzik Galili's company never fails to deliver tumultuous physical movement with some often magnetic theatrical elements. The dancers' delivery of Galili's wry-humoured works is dotted with quick wit, reeling limbs and dice-throwing acrobatics.

Courses & training

Henny Jurriëns Foundation

Bellamystraat 49, Oud West (412 1510/www.hjs.nl). Tram 7, 17. **Classes** 9.30am, 11am, 12.45pm Mon-Fri; 11am Sat. **Cost** €7.50 per class; €60 10 classes. **No credit cards. Map** p325 B3.

The Henny Jurriëns Foundation provides open training for professional dancers in both classical and modern dance techniques throughout the year. Their studio is at the top of the Olympia Building (an old cinema), has a New York loft-studio atmosphere, and overlooks the characterful Oud West neighbourhood. Instructors are a mixture of locals and visiting master teachers from abroad. The foundation also offers workshops, for which pre-registration is necessary. Give them a call to book your place, or to get more information about the programme.

Trips Out of Town

Features

Introduction

You ain't seen nothing yet.

Amsterdam is special. But before you can say you've truly visited the Netherlands, you must escape that city's suction and get to 'the real country'. Not that hard: it's a small place where most of the towns and cities worth visiting are under an hour away. Even the country's remote corners are accessible within a half-day drive or train ride. And be careful not to fall asleep: you might wake up in Belgium or Germany.

TRAVEL INFORMATION

The **Netherlands Board of Tourism** or VVV (Vlietweg 15, 2266 KA Leidschendam, 070 370 5705, www.visitholland.com) can help with information and accommodation, as can the **Netherlands Reserverings Centrum** (0299 689144, 8.30am-5.30pm). For transport listings (trains, buses and the Metro), contact the **OV Reisinformatie** information line (0900 9292 premium rate, also online at www.ov9292.nl), or you can get up-to-date train information at www.ns.nl, in Dutch but decipherable.

Getting around

Driving

The Netherlands' road system is extensive, well maintained and clearly signposted. For driving advice and detailed information on motoring organisation **ANWB**, *see p299.*

Buses & coaches

The national bus service is reasonably priced, but not as easy to negotiate as the railway. For information and timetables, phone **OV Reisinformatie** (*see above*).

Trips

For the future now

Rotterdam. *See p289.*

For a kinder, gentler Amsterdam

Haarlem. *See p283.*

For irritating Sancho Panza

Kinderdijk Windmills. *See p275.*

Cycling

The Netherlands is flat (though windy); little wonder the bike is the country's favourite mode of transport (*see p300*). Cycle paths are abundant and the ANWB and VVV offices sell cycle maps. Most major railway stations have bike hire depots and offer discounts to rail ticket holders. Road bikes cost around €7 per day and €25 per week; mountain bikes about twice that. Both are in short supply in summer; book at least a day ahead. You'll need proof of identity and a cash deposit (ranging from €50 to €200). For bike hire in Amsterdam, *see p300.*

Rail

Nederlandse Spoorwegen (aka NS, translatable as Netherlands Railway) offers an excellent service in terms of its cost, punctuality and cleanliness. Aside from singles and returns, you can also buy family and group passes, tickets that entitle you to unlimited travel on any given day (Dagkaarten), one that also entitles you to use buses, trams and the Metro (OV Dagkaarten) and, for selected places, NS Rail Idee tickets, all-in-one tickets that'll get you to a destination and also include the admission fee to one or more of the local sights. Services are frequent, and reservations are unnecessary.

As a rule, tickets are valid for one day only: if you make a return journey spanning more than one day you need two singles. A weekend return ticket is the exception to the rule: it's valid from Friday night until Sunday night.

With a rail ticket, you can avail yourself of **Treintaxi**, a special cab that takes you to any destination within a fixed distance of 110 stations for under €5.

DISABLED TRAVELLERS

NS produces a booklet in English called *Rail Travel for the Disabled*, available from all main stations or from the company direct. There is also disabled access to refreshment rooms and toilets at all stations. For special assistance, call 030 235 7822 at least a day in advance.

Centraal Station Information Desk

Stationsplein 15, Old Centre: New Side (0900 9292/ www.ns.nl). Tram 1, 2, 4, 5, 9, 13, 16, 17, 24, 25. **Open** *Information desk* 6.30am-10pm daily. *Bookings* 24hrs daily. **Credit** MC, V. **Map** p326 D1.

Excursions in Holland

Chasing idyllic Dutch dreams off the beaten track.

Petal to the metal: the enormous flower auction adding colour to **Aalsmeer**. *See p275.*

Stereotypes: you know you love 'em – especially when they are as charmingly presented as in the Netherlands. And happily, the majority of the most enduring sights are concentrated close to Amsterdam in Noord and Zuid Holland, and are also readily accessible by public transport. Besides the tourist boards listed below, there's an excellent new website, www.goudencirkel.nl, that covers the 'golden circle' of towns that surround the lake (and former sea) IJsselmeer to the north. Note that none of the establishments listed in this chapter take credit cards.

Charming Clichés

Cheese

Ah, yes. Cheese. It gives you strange dreams, or so they'll tell you. Not that the 'cheeseheads' – a nickname that actually dates from medieval times, when the Dutch sported wooden cheese moulds on their heads in battle – seem to mind. Indeed, few things are held higher in national affections. When they're not munching on it or exporting more than 400,000 tonnes of it every year, they're making a tourist industry of it.

One ritual for both tourists and members of the cheese porters' guild alike is the **Alkmaar Cheese Market** – the oldest and biggest cheese market in the world – which runs from 10am to noon every Friday between April and mid September. Pristine porters, wearing odd straw hats with coloured ribbons denoting their competing guilds, weigh the cheeses and then carry them on wooden trays hung from their shoulders. Then buyers test a core of cheese from each lot before the ceremony, which takes place at the Waag (Weigh House); here you can also find a variety of craft stalls and a **Cheese Museum**. But Alkmaar has more than cheese on offer and the VVV provides a walking tour of the medieval centre. Among the attractions at the **Biermuseum** is a cellar in which to taste various beers and the **Stedelijk Museum** has impressive art and toy collections.

The Netherlands' famous red-skinned cheese is sold at **Edam**'s cheese market, held every Wednesday in July and August from 10am until noon. Though the town, a prosperous

Welcome to cliché country

Despite efforts from the powers that be, who are keen to downplay them with the continual mantra 'there's more to Holland than this', the Dutch clichés – yep, that's windmills, tulips and clogs – continue to beguile visitors, no matter how cool they think they are. And rightly so: they're in the national DNA, and while you can stroll into a gallery anywhere and see a Van Gogh, there aren't many places you can sip beer under a windmill.

Clogs, sold in just about every tourist shop, make groovy wall decorations and are even seen on feet – mostly workmen's (they're EU-recognised safety shoes), then kids', and occasionally hicks from the sticks'. Just outside town is the surprisingly fascinating and fun **Klompenmakerij De Zaanse Schans** (Kraaienest 4, Zaandam, 075 617 7121, www.zaanseschans.nl), an enormous clog-making museum detailing the shoe's history and explaining its symbolism.

Tulips, meanwhile, are ubiquitous – flowers play a leading role in the Dutch economy. The most famous place to buy them is the floating **Bloemenmarkt** (Singel, between Koningsplein and Muntplein; *see p183*). Less dazzling than it sounds, it's still pretty. For the real action, you need to head out to **Aalsmeer's Flower Auction** (Legmeerdijk 313, 029 739 2185, www.vba-aalsmeer.nl), a vast complex shifting 19 million blooms daily in a nail-biting Dutch auction that never fails to delight tourists and adds real colour to the area.

Eight **windmills** remain in Amsterdam; most famous is **De Gooyer** (Funenkade 5), abutting award-winning brewery **'t IJ** (*see p160*). There are also photogenic examples on Haarlemmerweg: **De 1200 Roe** (No.701), built back in 1632, and **De Bloem** (No.465), a whippersnapper from 1878. Both were used until the 1950s. Grab a chance to see the improbably urban windmill **De Otter** (Gillisvan Ledenberchstraat 78) in Westerpark while you can. Its future is being wrangled over by the highest court in the land, no less, which is currently deciding if it should be allowed to move, brick by brick, to where some wind can actually reach the poor thing.

port during the Golden Age, tells many stories through its exquisite façades and bridges, they can't compete with the cheese. In 1840, Edams were used as cannon balls in Uruguay to repel seaborne attackers (imagine the humiliation of dying from a cheese injury). Then in 1956 a canned Edam, a relic from a 1912 expedition, was found at the South Pole – and when opened proved to be merely a trifle 'sharp'. The town itself added to this lore in 2003 by building a colossal cheese cathedral from 10,000 of the unholey orbs to raise repair funds for their ancient Grote Kerk (Big Church).

Meanwhile, over in **Gouda**, golden wheels of cheese go on sale at the market every Thursday from 10am in July and August. There are also many thatched-roof *kaasboerderijen* (cheese farms) near Gouda, several of which are on the picturesque River Vlist. See '*kaas te koop*' signs (cheese for sale) and you may be able to peer behind the scenes as well as buy fresh Gouda.

Still, Gouda does have other things going for it besides the yellow stuff. It's darn scenic and its candles are another classic: 20,000 of them light the square during the Christmas tree ceremony.

Alkmaar Biermuseum

Houttil 1, Alkmaar (072 511 3801/www.biermuseum.nl). **Open** 1-4pm Tue-Sat. **Admission** €3.50; €1.75 concessions.

Alkmaar Cheese Museum

De Waag, Waagplein 2, Alkmaar (072 511 4284/www.kaasmuseum.nl). **Open** *Apr-Nov* 10am-4pm Mon-Thur, Sat; 9am-4pm Fri. **Admission** €2.50; €1.50 under-11s.

Stedelijk Museum

Canadaplein 1, Alkmaar (072 548 9789/www.stedelijkmuseumalkmaar.nl). **Open** 10am-5pm Tue-Fri; 1-5pm Sat, Sun. **Admission** €4.50; €3 over-65s; free under-18s, MK.

Getting there

Alkmaar

By car 37km (22 miles) north-west. By train direct.

Edam

By car 10km (5 miles) north. By bus 110, 112, 114 from Amsterdam Centraal Station.

Gouda

By car 29km (18 miles) south-west. By train direct.

Tourist information

Alkmaar VVV

Waagplein 2, Alkmaar (072 511 4284/www.vvvweb.nl). **Open** *Apr-Oct* 1-5.30pm Mon; 9am-5.30pm Tue-Fri; 9.30am-5pm Sat. *Oct-Mar* 1-5.30pm Mon; 10am-5.30pm Tue-Fri; 10am-5pm Sat.

Edam VVV

Stadhuis, Damplein 1, Edam (0299 315125/www.vvv-edam.nl). **Open** *Apr-Nov* 10am-5pm Mon-Sat. *Nov-Apr* 10am-3pm Mon-Sat.

Gouda VVV

Markt 27, Gouda (0900 4683 2888 premium rate/www.vvvgouda.nl). **Open** 1-5.30pm Mon; 10.30am-5.30pm Tue-Fri; 10am-4pm Sat.

Flowers

Want a statistic that boggles the mind? Try this: the Netherlands produces a staggering 70 per cent of the world's commercial flower output, and still has enough left to fill up its own markets, botanical gardens, auctions and parades all year round.

The world's biggest flower auction is in the world's biggest trading building (120 football fields' worth) in Aalsmeer (*photo p273*). The **Verenigde Bloemenveilingen** handles more than 18 million cut flowers and two million pot plants each day, mostly for export. Its unusual sales method gave rise to the phrase 'Dutch auction'. Dealers bid by pushing a button to stop a 'clock' that counts from 100 down to one; thus, the price is lowered – rather than raised – until a buyer is found. Bidders risk either overpaying for the goods or not getting them if time runs out. The best action here is usually before 9am, except on Thursdays.

The 'countdown' bidding style was invented at **Broeker Veiling**, the oldest flower and vegetable auction in the world. It's a bit of a tourist trap, but nonetheless includes a museum of old farming artefacts, plus a boat trip.

There have been flowers everywhere at the **Keukenhof Bulb Gardens** since 1949. This former royal 'kitchen garden' dates from the 14th century, and contains 500 types of tulip and over six million bulbs in 1.25 square miles (over three square kilometres). The glass flower pavilion – all 6,500 square metres (70,480 square feet) – is just as interesting. Arrive early, as the gardens get packed.

For more on the district's history, including a look at the development of the flower bulb business, visit the **Museum de Zwarte Tulp**.

Broeker Veiling

Museumweg 2, Broek-op-Langerdijk (0226 313807/www.broekerveiling.nl). **Open** *1 Apr-1 Nov* 10am-5pm Mon-Fri; 11am-5pm Sat, Sun. **Admission** *Auction & museum* €6.50; €3.80 under-15s. *Auction, museum & boat trip* €10.35; €5.70 under-15s.

Keukenhof Bulb Gardens

Keukenhof, near Lisse (0252 465555/www.keukenhof.nl). **Open** *Mid Mar-mid May* 8am-7.30pm daily (ticket box closes 6pm). **Admission** €13; €12 over-65s; €6 4s-11s; free under-4s.

Museum de Zwarte Tulp

Grachtweg 2A, Lisse (0252 417900/www.museumdezwartetulp.nl). **Open** 1-5pm Tue-Sun. **Admission** €3; €2 under-12s.

Verenigde Bloemenveilingen

Legmeerdijk 313, Aalsmeer (0297 392185/www.vba.nl). **Open** *Apr-Sept* 6am-11am Mon-Fri. **Admission** €4.50; €2.50 under-12s.

Getting there

Aalsmeer

By car 15km (9 miles) south-west. By bus 172 from Amsterdam Centraal Station.

Broek-op-Langerdijk

By car 36km (22 miles) north. By train Amsterdam Centraal Station to Alkmaar, then bus 155.

Keukenhof/Lisse

By car 27km (17 miles) south-west. By train Amsterdam Centraal Station to Leiden, then bus 54.

Dutch Traditions

Small historic towns in the Netherlands – the ones that depend on tourism – are expert at capitalising on their traditions, right down to the lace caps, wooden shoes and windmills. Sure, authentic they ain't, but connoisseurs of kitsch should set course for them immediately.

Zuid-Holland & Utrecht

It's not catwalk glamour, but a sizeable minority of **Bunschoten-Spakenburg** residents still strut – or, rather, klog – their stuff in traditional dress on midsummer market Wednesdays between mid July and mid August; some older people actually wear it every day. Costumes are also worn at the summer markets in Hoorn (*see p279*), Medemblik (*see p278*) and Schagen, and on folkloric festival days in Middelburg.

In **Alblasserdam** a posse of 19 **Kinderdijk Windmills**, called a gang, can still be seen. Clustered to drain water from reclaimed land, they are now under sail for the benefit of tourists (from 1.30 to 5.30pm on Saturdays in July and August, and the first Saturday in May and June). During the second week in September they're illuminated; from April to September, a €3 boat trip gets you there.

Schoonhoven has been famous since the 17th century for its silversmiths. You can see antique pieces in the **Nederlands Goud-, Zilver- en Klokkenmuseum** and also at the former synagogue **Edelambachtshuis** (Museum of Antique Silverware). Olivier van Noort, the first Dutchman to sail around the world, and Claes Louwerenz Blom, who, locals

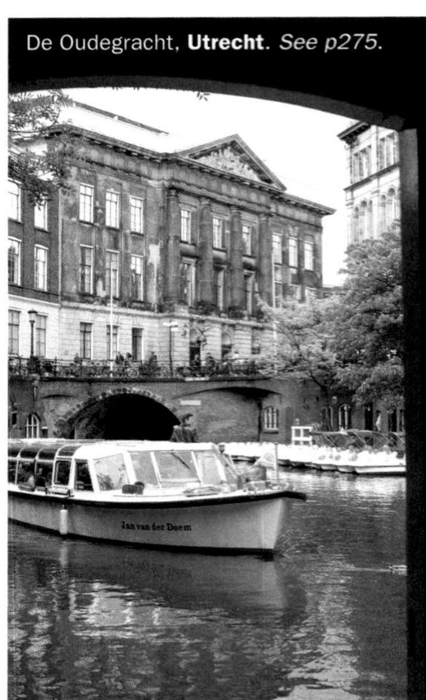
De Oudegracht, **Utrecht**. *See p275.*

believe, introduced the windmill to Spain in 1549, are in fact buried in the 14th-century **Bartholomeuskerk**, whose tower leans 1.6 metres (five feet). Not buried here is Marrigje Ariens, the last woman to be burned as a witch in the country – but a circle of coloured stones by the City Hall marks where she died in 1591.

Dating from the 11th century, **Oudewater** (north of Schoonhoven), once famed for its rope-making, also has a rich witch-hunting past. Reaching its peak in the 1480s, the fashion didn't die out until the beginning of the 17th century, and Oudewater achieved fame for its weighing of suspected witches and warlocks in the **Heksenwaag** (Witches' Weigh House); today, swarms of tourists step on the scales.

Edelambachtshuis

Haven 13, Schoonhoven (0182 382614/www.rikkoert.nl). **Open** 10am-5pm Tue-Sat. **Admission** €1.

Heksenwaag

Leeuweringerstraat 2, Oudewater (0348 563400/ www.heksenwaag.nl). **Open** *Apr-Nov* 10am-5pm Tue-Sun. **Admission** €4.25; €2 4s-12s, over-65s; free under-4s, MK.

Kinderdijk Windmills

Molenkade, Alblasserdam (078 692 1355/www. kinderdijk.nl). **Open** *Apr-Sept* 9.30am-5.30pm daily. **Admission** €3; €1.80 under-16s, over-65s.

Nederlands Goud-, Zilver- en Klokkenmuseum

Kazerneplein 4, Schoonhoven (0182 385612/www. ngzkm.nl). **Open** noon-5pm Tue-Sun. **Admission** €5; €4 students, 65+; free under-14s.

Getting there

Alblasserdam

By car 55km (34 miles) south-west. By train Centraal Station to Utrecht, then bus 154.

Bunschoten-Spakenburg

By car 35km (22 miles) south-east. By train Centraal Station to Amersfoort, then bus 116.

Oudewater

By car 40km (25 miles) south. By train Centraal Station to Utrecht, then bus 180.

Schoonhoven

By car 50km (31 miles) south. By train Centraal Station to Utrecht, then bus 195.

Tourist information

Alblasserdam VVV

Cortgene 2, inside City Hall, Alblasserdam (0786 921355). **Open** 9am-4pm Mon-Fri.

Bunschoten-Spakenburg VVV

Oude Schans 90, Spakenburg (0332 982156/www. vvvspakenburg.nl). **Open** *Apr-Sept* 1-5pm Mon; 10am-5pm Tue-Sat. *Oct-Mar* 1-5pm Mon-Fri; 10am-3pm Sat.

Oudewater VVV

Kapellestraat 2, Oudewater (0348 564636/www. vvvoudewater.nl). **Open** *Apr-Oct* 10am-4pm Tue-Sat; 11am-3pm Sun. *Oct-Apr* 10am-1pm Tue-Sat.

Schoonhoven VVV

Stadhuisstraat 1, Schoonhoven (0182 385009/ www.vvvschoonhoven.nl). **Open** *May-Oct* 1.30-4.30pm Mon; 9.30am-4.30pm Tue-Fri; 10am-3pm Sat. *Oct-May* 1.30-4.30pm Mon; 9.30am-4pm Tue-Fri; 10.30am-3pm Sat.

Waterland

Until the IJ Tunnel opened in 1956, the canal-laced peat meadows of Waterland north of Amsterdam were accessible mainly by ferry and steam railway. This isolation preserved much of the area's heritage; to see a prime example, look around the old wooden buildings at **Broek in Waterland** (*photo p278*). This area is best explored by bike before switching over to a canoe or electric motor boat, both of which can be rented from Zeilkamp Waterland (403 3209, www.kano-electroboot.nl).

Marken, reached via a causeway, was once full of fishermen (some of whom give excellent boat tours), but is now awash with tourists.

Visit off-season, however, and you'll likely find it quieter and more authentic than Volendam (*see below*). To protect against flooding, many houses are built on mounds or poles. **Marker Museum** offers a tour of the island's history.

The number of preserved ancient buildings, from Golden Age merchants' houses to the famous herring smokehouses, is what makes **Monnickendam** special. There's also a fine antique carillon on the bell-tower of the old town hall that's well worth hunting down.

Such was **Volendam**'s success as a fishing village that it's said the town flag was flown at half-mast when the Zuider Zee was enclosed in 1932, cutting off access to the sea. The village's enterprise was soon applied to devising a theme park from its fascinating historic features but, sadly, the cheerily garbed locals can barely be seen for the coachloads of tourists dumped there every day – and invariably pointed to the world's biggest collection of cigar bands (11 million in total), all of them on view to a seriously smoke-happy public at the popular **Volendams Museum** (Zeestraat 37, 0299 369258, www.volendams-museum.com).

De Zaanse Schans is not your typical museum village: people still live here. One of the world's first industrial zones, Zaan was once crowded with 800 windmills that powered the production of paint, flour and lumber. Today, amid the gabled green and white houses, attractions include an old-fashioned Albert Heijn store. Nearby in Zaandam, you can visit **Czaar Peterhuisje**, the tiny wooden house where Peter the Great stayed in 1697 while he was honing his new ship-building skills and preparing for the foundation of St Petersburg.

Czaar Peterhuisje

Het Krimp 23, Zaandam (075 616 0390/www.zaansescans.nl). **Open** *Apr-Oct* 1-5pm Tue-Sun. *Oct-Apr* 1-5pm Sat, Sun. **Admission** €2; €1 under-12s; free MK.

Marker Museum

Kerkbuurt 44-47, Marken (0299 601904/www.markermuseum.nl). **Open** *Apr-Nov* 10am-5pm Mon-Sat; noon-4pm Sun. **Admission** €2.50; €1.25 under-12s.

A year in flowers

For a complete list of the many flower-related parades and events in the country, there's a wealth of information online at the website http://corsoclubs.startpagina.nl, but bear in mind that it's entirely in Dutch.

SPRING

The year kicks off in mid to late February with the indoor **Holland Flowers Festival** (0228 511644, www.hollandflowersfestival.nl) in the town of Zwaagdijk-Oost. From late March to late May, the bulb district from Den Helder to Den Haag is carpeted with blooms of the principal crops: daffodils, crocuses, gladioli, hyacinths, narcissi and – of course – tulips. The **Noordwijk-Haarlem Flower Parade** (0252 428237, www.bloemencorso-bollenstreek.nl) takes place on the first Saturday after 19 April, departing from Noordwijk at 9.30am and arriving in Haarlem at 9pm. The floats are on show in Lisse and Hobahohallen for two days prior to the parade.

SUMMER

In The Hague, the lovely **Japanese garden** at Clingendael is in full flower from early May to mid June, while the **rose garden** in Westbroek Park, containing 350 varieties, bursts into colour during July and August. In late June, there's the **Floralia exhibition** at the Zuider Zee Museum in Enkhuizen. And on the third weekend in August, it's the **Rijnsburg Parade** (0714 094227, www.rijnsburgscorso.nl). The floats usually leave Rijnsburg on Saturday afternoon proceed through Katwijk aan de Rijn and onward up to Nordwijk, where they show at the Boulevard that evening and also throughout the following day.

AUTUMN

Heather purples the landscape – especially in Veluwe, in the province of Gelderland – during August and September, when the greenhouse flowers also emerge. The **Bloemencorso** (0297 325100, www.bloemencorsoaalsmeer.nl), Europe's single largest flower parade, winds from Aalsmeer to Amsterdam and back on the first Saturday in September, with float viewing the day before and after the parade in Aalsmeer. On the fourth Sunday in September, a wackier flower parade takes place in the miniature West Frisian town of Winkel, the **Bloemencorso Winkel** (0224 542533, www.bloemencorso.com/winkel), complete with street theatre.

WINTER

In November, the public and florists from all over the world view new varieties at the **Professional Flower Exhibition** at Aalsmeer Flower Auction. At Christmas, there's the **Kerstflora** show at Hillegom near Lisse.

De Zaanse Schans

Schansend 7, Information Center Pakhuis Vrede (0756 168218/www.zaanseschans.nl). **Open** *Apr-Sept* 9am-5pm daily. *Museums* 10am-5pm Tue-Sun. *Shops & windmills* 9am-5pm Tue-Sun. **Admission** free-€10; free-€4 under-13s.

Getting there

Broek in Waterland

By car 10km (6 miles) north-east. By bus 110, 111, 114 or 116 from Amsterdam Centraal Station.

Marken

By car 20km (12 miles) north-east. By bus 111 from Amsterdam Centraal Station to Marken, or 110, 114 or 116 to Monnickendam, then boat to Marken.

Monnickendam

By car 15km (9 miles) north-east. By bus 110, 114 or 116 from Amsterdam Centraal Station.

Volendam

By car 20km (12 miles) north-east. By bus 110 from Amsterdam Centraal Station.

De Zaanse Schans

By car 15km (9 miles) north-west. By train to Koog-Zaandijk. By bus 89 from Marnixstraat.

Tourist information

Volendam and Waterland VVV

Zeestraat 37, Volendam (0299 363747/www.vvv-volendam.nl). **Open** *Mid Mar-Oct* 10am-5pm Mon-Sat. *Nov-mid Mar* 10am-3pm Mon-Sat.

Zaandam VVV

Ebbehout 31, Zaandam (0900 400 4040/www.zaaninfo.com). **Open** 8.30am-4pm Mon-Wed; 8.30am-7pm Thur; 8.30am-noon Fri.

West Friesland

West Friesland faces Friesland across the northern IJsselmeer. Despite being a part of Noord Holland for centuries, it has its own customs, and far fewer visitors than its near-neighbour. One way to get there is to take a train to Enkhuizen, then a boat to Medemblik. From here, take the **Museumstoomtram** (Museum Steam Train) to Hoorn.

The once-powerful fishing and whaling port of **Enkhuizen** has many relics of its past, but most people today come here for the **Zuider Zee Museum**. Wander in either the indoor Binnenmuseum, which has exhibits on seven centuries of seafaring life around the IJsselmeer, or the open-air Buitenmuseum, a reconstructed village (complete with its own 'villagers') of 130 authentic late 19th- and early 20th-century buildings transplanted from nearby towns.

The Gothic Bonifaciuskerk and Kasteel Radboud dominate **Medemblik**, a port that dates from the early Middle Ages. The 13th-century castle is smaller than it was when it defended Floris V's realm, but retains its knights' hall and towers. Glassblowers and leatherworkers show off their skills at the Saturday market in July and August. Close nearby is the 'long village' of **Twisk**, with

Broek in Waterland. *See p276.*

its pyramid-roofed farm buildings, as well as the village of **Opperdoes**, built on a mound.

The pretty port of **Hoorn**, which dates from around 1310, grew rich on the Dutch East Indies trade; its success is reflected in its grand and ancient architecture. Local costumes and crafts can be seen at the weekly historic market, Hartje Hoorn (9am-5pm Wednesdays in July and August only). The local **Museum van de Twintigste Eeuw** (Museum of the 20th Century), while hardly living up to its name, does have plenty of interesting exhibits.

The **Westfries Museum**, which focuses on art, decor and the history of the region, was recently robbed of its major paintings, although, on the plus side, the renewed public penchant for 'disaster tourism' has led to a sharp increase in the number of visitors.

Museum van de Twintigste Eeuw

Bierkade 4, Hoorn (0229 214001/www.museum hoorn.nl). **Open** 10am-5pm Tue-Fri; noon-5pm Sat, Sun. **Admission** €4; €2 4s-16s, concessions.

Museumstoomtram Hoorn-Medemblik

Hoorn-Medemblik; tickets behind the station at Van Dedemstraat 8, Hoorn (0229 214862/www. museumstoomtram.nl), or Hoorn VVV. **Admission** (with boat trip) *Single* €10; €7.60 4s-11s. *Return* €18; €13.50 4s-11s.

Westfries Museum

Rode Steen 1, Hoorn (0229 280028/www.wfm.nl). **Open** 11am-5pm Mon-Fri; 2-5pm Sat, Sun. **Admission** €3.50; €1.50 6s-18s, 65+; free under-5s, MK.

Zuider Zee Museum

Wierdijk 12-22, Enkhuizen (0228 351111/www. zuiderzeemuseum.nl). **Open** *Apr-Nov* 10am-5pm daily. *Nov-Apr* 10am-5pm Tue-Sun. **Admission** €11.50; €11 65+; €10.35 students; €6.90 4s-12s; free under-4s.

Getting there

Enkhuizen

By car 55km (34 miles) north-east. By train direct from Amsterdam Centraal Station.

Hoorn

By car 35km (22 miles) north-east. By train direct from Amsterdam Centraal Station.

Medemblik

By car 50km (31 miles) north. By train direct from Amsterdam Centraal Station.

Tourist information

Enkhuizen VVV

Tussen Twee Havens 1, Enkhuizen (0228 313164/ www.vvvweb.nl). **Open** *Apr-Nov* 9am-5pm daily. *Nov-Apr* 9am-5pm Tue-Fri; 10am-3pm Sat.

Hoorn VVV

Veemarkt 4, Hoorn (072 511 4284/www.vvvweb.nl). **Open** *May-Sep* 1-6pm Mon; 9.30am-5pm Tue, Wed, Fri; 9.30am-9pm Thur; 9.30am-5pm Sat; 1-5pm Sun. *Sept-May* 1-5pm Mon; 9.30am-5pm Tue-Sat.

Medemblik VVV

Kaasmarkt 1, Medemblik (072 511 4284/www.vvv web.nl). **Open** *Apr-Oct* 11am-3pm Mon-Sat. *May, June, Sept* 11am-4pm Mon-Sat. *July, Aug* 10am-5pm Mon-Sat.

Ancient Castles

What Amsterdam lacks in palaces and castles, the rest of Holland more than makes up for. The country is studded with 400 castles and some of the best are in the province of **Utrecht**, within half an hour of Amsterdam. Almost 100 of the castles are open for tourists or for business conferences: the 15th-century Stayokay Heemskerk, between Haarlem and Alkmaar, is now a hostel (025 123 2288, www.stayokay.com), while the ultimate in power lunches can be had at Château Neercanne in Maastricht (043 325 1359, www.neercanne.nl) or Kasteel Erenstein in Kerkrade (045 546 1333, www.erenstein.com).

The fairy-tale splendour of **De Haar** is both appealing and oddly misleading. Though it looks the quintessential medieval castle, it's actually relatively recent. In 1892, the baron who inherited the ruins of De Haar (dating from 1391) re-created the original on a majestic scale, moving the entire village of Haarzuilens 850 metres (259 feet) to make room for Versailles-styled gardens. The lavish interior is visible only on one of the informative guided tours.

Many important events in Dutch history took place in the legendary stronghold **Muiderslot**. This moated castle, situated strategically at the mouth of the River Vecht, was originally built in 1280 for Count Floris V, who was murdered nearby in Muiderberg in 1296. Rebuilt in the 14th century, the fortress has been through many sieges and frequent renovations. The 17th-century furnishings originate from the period of another illustrious occupant, PC Hooft, who entertained in the castle's splendid halls. Between April and October you can take a boat from the dock here over to the charming medieval fort island of Pampus.

The star-shaped stronghold of **Naarden** is not only moated, but has arrowhead-shaped bastions and a very well-preserved fortified town; it was in active service as recently as 1926. All is explained in the **Vestingmuseum**. The fortifications date from 1675, after the inhabitants were massacred by the Duke of Alva's son in 1572; the slaughter is depicted above the door of the Spaanse Huis (Spanish House). Today, however, Naarden is the perfect setting for a leisurely Sunday stroll.

Meandering up the River Vecht into Utrecht, boat passengers can glimpse some of the homes built in the 17th and 18th centuries by rich Amsterdam merchants. Two of the trips afford close-up views of castles, the first stopping on the way back downriver for a one-hour tour of **Slot Zuylen**, a 16th-century castle that was renovated in 1752. The collections of furniture, tapestries and objets d'art displayed here give insight into the lives of the residents. Local tour boat company **Rondvaartbedrijf Rederij Schuttevaer** can arrange English guides with advance notice. Another boat drops passengers in the charming town of **Loenen**, which boasts the spectacular restored castle of Loenersloot; sadly, it's not open to the public.

De Haar

Kasteellaan 1, Haarzuilens, Utrecht (030 677 8515/ www.kasteeldehaar.nl). **Open** *End June-Sept* 11am-4pm Tue-Fri; noon-4pm Sat, Sun. *Sept-mid Nov* noon-3pm Tue-Fri; 1-3pm Sat, Sun. *Mid Feb-end June* noon-3pm Tue-Fri; 1-4pm Sat, Sun. *Dec* groups only. *Grounds* 10am-5pm daily. Sometimes closed for special events so best to call ahead. **Admission** *Castle & grounds* €8; €5 5s-12s (no under-5s); free MK. *Grounds only* €3; €2 5s-12s; free under-5s, MK.

Muiderslot

Herengracht 1, Muiden (0294 261325/www.muider slot.nl). **Open** *Apr-Oct* 10am-5pm Mon-Fri; noon-6pm Sat, Sun. *Nov-Apr* noon-5pm Sat, Sun. *Tours* on the hour, more frequent July-Sept. **Admission** €8.50; €6 4s-12s, over-65s; free MK.

Rondvaartbedrijf Rederij Schuttevaer

Oudegracht, opposite No.85, Utrecht (030 272 0111/ www.schuttevaer.com). **Times** *June-Sept* half-day trip to Slot Zuylen 10am Tue, Thur, returning 5.45pm. More day trip options listed on website. **Tickets** €7-€27; €5.50-€19.50 under-13s; reservations essential.

Vestingmuseum Turfpoortbastion

Westvalstraat 6, Naarden (035 694 5459/www. vestingmuseum.nl). **Open** *Mid Mar-Nov* 10.30am-5pm Tue-Fri; noon-5pm Sat, Sun. *Nov-mid Mar* noon-5pm Sun. **Admission** €5.50; €3-€4 concessions; free under-4s, MK.

Getting there

De Haar

By car 30km (19 miles) south. By train Amsterdam Centraal Station to Utrecht, then bus 127.

Muiderslot

By car 12km (7.5 miles) south-east. By bus 136 from Amstel Station.

Naarden

By car 20km (12 miles) south-east. By train direct from Amsterdam Centraal Station. By bus 136 from Amstel Station.

Tourist information

Naarden VVV

Adriaan Dortsmanplein 1B, Naarden (035 694 2836/ www.vvvnaarden.nl). **Open** *Jan-May* 10am-2pm Sat. *May-July* 11am-3pm Mon-Fri; 10am-2pm Sat. *July-Sept* 10am-3pm Mon-Fri; 10am-2pm Sat.

City Breaks

The art of urban expansion.

The Randstad – or 'Edge City', named for its coastal location on the Netherlands' western edge – is a loop bounded by Amsterdam, Delft, Haarlem, the Hague, Leiden, Rotterdam and Utrecht. In recent years, Gouda (*see p274*) and Dordrecht have come to be considered part of it. Though separately administered and fiercely independent, the individual towns actually work together for their common good. It's also one of the most densely populated areas in the world: no fewer than 40 per cent of the Dutch population inhabit this urban sprawl.

The road, rail and waterway networks are impressive, and the area's economy is strong. The Randstad's importance is based on several factors: Rotterdam's port; Schiphol Airport; Amsterdam's role as a financial and banking centre; the seats of government and royalty at The Hague; and a huge agricultural belt.

Regarded with a mix of awe, indifference and resentment by the outlying provinces, the Randstad is often accused of monopolising government attention and funds. However, it has no formally defined status and is prone to bitter rivalry between cities and municipalities – Amsterdam and Rotterdam in particular.

There's plenty beyond the Randstad – from the bogs of Drenthe to the frolicsome carnival celebrations of Limburg and the islands of Friesland (Texel and Terschelling can offer the perfect beach-and-dune escape weekend). You will find www.holland.com a handy resource. Hell, even the Belgian towns of Ghent, Bruges and Antwerp are within a two- to three-hour train trip away for beer-fuelled border-hopping.

Delft

Imagine a miniaturised Amsterdam – canals reduced to dinky proportions, bridges narrowed down, merchants' houses shrunken – and you have the essence of Delft. However, though it's small and scoffed at for its sleepiness, Delft is a student town with plenty going on.

Everything you're likely to want to see is in the old centre. As soon as you cross the road from the station towards the city centre, you encounter an introduction to Delft's past: a representation of Vermeer's *Milkmaid* in stone.

Delft, though, is of course most famous for its blue and white tiles and pottery, known as Delft Blue (or internationally as Royal Blue). There are still a few factories open to visitors – among them **De Delftse Pauw** and **De Porceleyne Fles** – but for a more historical overview of the industry, make for the **Museum Lambert van Meerten**. The enormous range of tiles, depicting everything from battling warships to randy rabbits, contrasts dramatically with today's mass-produced trinkets.

Delft was traditionally a centre for trade, producing and exporting butter, cloth, Delft beer – at one point in the past, almost 200 breweries could be found beside its canals – and, later, pottery. Its subsequent loss in trade has been Rotterdam's gain, but the aesthetic benefits can be seen in the city's centuries-old gables, hump-backed bridges and shady canals. To appreciate how little has changed, walk to the end of Oude Delft, the oldest canal in Delft (it narrowly escaped being drained in the 1920s to become a sunken tram-line), cross the busy road to the harbour, and compare the view to Vermeer's *View of Delft*, now on display in the **Mauritshuis** in the Hague (*see p286*).

Delft also has two spectacular churches. The first, the **Nieuwe Kerk** (New Church; *photo p282*) contains the tombs of philosopher Hugo de Groot and William of Orange (alongside his dog, who faithfully followed him to death by refusing food and water). It took almost 15 years to construct and was finally finished in 1396. Across the Markt is Hendrick de Keyser's 1620 **Stadhuis** (or City Hall); De Keyser also designed Prince William's black and white marble mausoleum. Not to be outdone, the town's other splendid house of worship, the Gothic **Oude Kerk** (c1200), is locally known as 'Leaning Jan' because its tower stands two metres (over six feet) off-kilter. Art-lovers note that it's the final resting place of Vermeer.

Delft's museums have the calming air of quiet private residences. **Het Prinsenhof Municipal Museum**, located in the former convent of St Agatha, holds ancient and modern art exhibitions along with displays about Prince William of Orange, who was assassinated here in 1584 by one of many keen to earn the price put on his head by Philip II of Spain during Holland's 80-year fight for independence. The bullet holes are still clearly visible on the stairs.

But though the museums are grand, it's also fun to simply stroll around town. The historic centre has more than 600 national monuments

Delft's **Nieuwe Kerk**, final resting place for both William of Orange and his dog. *See p281.*

in and around the preserved merchants' houses. Pick up a guide from the VVV and see what the town has to offer: the country's largest military collection over at the **Legermuseum** (Army Museum), for example, or western Europe's largest collection of poisonous snakes at the **Reptielenzoo Serpo**. One of the many places that may draw you in is the Oostpoort (East Gate), dating from 1394. And while at the VVV, ask if you can pay a visit to the **Windmill de Roos** and the grim torture chamber in **Het Steen**, the 13th-century tower of the historic city hall in the market square – they're both genuinely fascinating places.

De Delftse Pauw

Delftweg 133 (015 212 4920/www.delftsepauw.com). **Open** *Apr-Oct* 9am-4.30pm daily. *Nov-Mar* 9am-4.30pm Mon-Fri; 11am-1pm Sat, Sun. **Admission** free. **Credit** AmEx, DC, MC, V.

Legermuseum

Korte Geer 1 (015 215 0500/www.legermuseum.nl). **Open** 10am-5pm Tue-Fri; noon-5pm Sat, Sun. **Admission** €6; €3 seniors, 4s-17s; free under-4s, MK. **Credit** MC, V.

Museum Lambert van Meerten

Oude Delft 199 (015 260 2199). **Open** 10am-5pm Tue-Sat; 1-5pm Sun. **Admission** €6; free under-12s. **Credit** AmEx, MC, V.

De Porceleyne Fles

Rotterdamseweg 196 (015 251 2030/www.royal delft.com). **Open** *Apr-Oct* 9am-5pm daily. *Nov-Mar* 9am-5pm Mon-Sat. **Admission** €4.50 guided tour. **Credit** AmEx, DC, MC, V.

Het Prinsenhof Municipal Museum

Sint Agathaplein 1 (015 260 2358/www.prinsenhof-delft.nl). **Open** 10am-5pm Tue-Sat; 1-5pm Sun. **Admission** €5; €4 students, 65+, 12s-16s; free under-12s. **Credit** AmEx, MC, V.

Reptielenzoo Serpo

Stationsplein 8 (015 212 2184/www.serpo.nl). **Open** 10am-6pm Mon-Sat; 1-6pm Sun. **Admission** €7.50; €6.50 seniors; €5.50 4s-11s; free under-4s. **Credit** MC, V.

Where to eat & drink

Though many bars and cafés may appear to outsiders as survivors of a bygone era – white-aproned waiters and high-ceilinged interiors and all – it's the norm in Delft. Other cities offer hot chocolate finished with whipped cream; cafés here use real cream and accompany it with a fancier brand of biscuit, a real treat for visitors with an even vaguely sweet tooth.

Don't miss **Kleyweg's Stads Koffyhuis** (Oude Delft 133, 015 212 4625, www.stads-koffyhuis.nl), which has a terrace barge in the

summer and serves Knollaert beer, a local brew made to a medieval recipe. **De Wijnhaven** (Wijnhaven 22, 015 214 1460, www.wijnhaven.nl) and **Vlaanderen** (Beestenmarkt 16, 015 213 3311, www.vlaanderen.nl) provide delicious meals and excellent views at good prices.

Where to stay

De Ark (Koornmarkt 65, 015 215 7999, www.deark.nl) is upmarket, with rooms priced from €105 for a single and €132 for a double. **De Plataan** (Doelenplein 10, 015 212 6046, www.hoteldeplataan.nl) is more reasonable, costing €90 for a single, €100 for a double. Budget travellers should try the campsite at **Delftse Hout** (Korftlaan 5, 015 213 0040, www.delftsehout.nl), where a site for two costs €21.50-€25.50. During colder weather, try **De Kok** (Houttuinen 14, 015 212 2125, www.hoteldekok.nl). Singles cost from €66 to €110 and doubles go for €80 to €125.

Getting there

By car

60km (37 miles) south-west on A4, then A13.

By train

1hr from Amsterdam Centraal Station, changing at The Hague if necessary.

Tourist information

Toeristische Informatie Punt (Tourist Information Point)

Hippolytusbuurt 4 (0900 515 1555/www.delft.nl). **Open** *Apr-Oct* 10am-4pm Mon; 9am-6pm Tue-Fri; 10am-5pm Sat; 10am-4pm Sun. *Nov-Mar* 11am-4pm Mon; 10am-4pm Tue-Sat; 10am-3pm Sun.

Haarlem

Lying between Amsterdam and the beaches of Zandvoort and Bloemendaal, Haarlem – a gentler and older Amsterdam – is a mere stone's throw from the dunes and the sea, and attracts flocks of beach-going Amsterdammers and Germans every summer. All trace of Haarlem's origins as a tenth-century settlement on a choppy inland sea disappeared with the draining of the Haarlemmermeer in the mid 19th-century. But the town hasn't lost its appeal: the historic centre, with its lively main square, canals and charming almshouse courtyards, is beautiful.

To catch up with Haarlem's history, head to **St Bavo's Church**, which dominates the main square. It was built around 1313 but suffered fire damage in 1328; rebuilding and expansion lasted yet another 150 years. It's surprisingly bright inside: cavernous white transepts stand as high as the nave and are a stunning sight. The floor is made up of 1,350 graves, including one featuring only the word 'Me' and another long enough to hold a famed local giant, plus a dedication to a local midget who died of injuries from a game he himself invented: dwarf-tossing. Then there's the famous Müller organ (1738): boasting an amazing 5,068 pipes, it has been played by Handel and the young Mozart.

Haarlem's cosy but spacious Grote Markt is one of the loveliest squares in the Netherlands. Just a few blocks away is the former old men's almshouse and orphanage that currently houses the **Frans Halsmuseum**. Though it holds a magnificent collection of 16th- and 17th-century portraits, still lifes, various genre paintings and landscapes, the highlights are eight group portraits of militia companies and regents by Frans Hals (who's buried in St Bavo's). The museum also has collections of period furniture, Haarlem silver and ceramics and an 18th-century apothecary with Delftware pottery. Nearby is **De Hallen**, whose two buildings, the Verweyhal and the Vleeshal, house an extensive range of modern art between them, well worth tracking down if time permits.

Though it's rather in the shadow of the Frans Halsmuseum, the **Teylers Museum** is also excellent. Founded in 1784, it's the country's oldest museum; fossils and minerals sit beside antique scientific instruments, and there's a superb 16th- to 19th-century collection of 10,000 drawings by masters including Rembrandt, Michelangelo and Raphael. However, Haarlem is more than just a city of nostalgia: it's one of vision, with a truly creative vibe felt all over town. Local illustrator/cartoonist Joost Swarte designed the Toneelschuur theatre in the centre.

Frans Halsmuseum

Groot Heiligland 62 (023 511 5775/www.franshalsmuseum.nl). **Open** 11am-5pm Mon-Sat; noon-5pm Sun. **Admission** €7; free under-18s, MK. **No credit cards**.

De Hallen

Grote Markt 16 (023 5115775/www.dehallen.com). **Open** 11am-5pm Mon-Sat; noon-5pm Sun. **Admission** €5; free under-18s, MK. **No credit cards**.

Teylers Museum

Spaarne 16 (023 516 0960/www.teylersmuseum.nl). **Open** 10am-5pm Tue-Sat; noon-5pm Sun. **Admission** €7; €2 6s-18s; free under-5s, MK. **No credit cards**.

Where to eat & drink

There's plenty to choose from on Grote Markt, but cosier is the nearby **Jacobus Pieck Drink**

Going for Groningen

The northern capital city of Groningen is the furthest one can get from Amsterdam without actually leaving the country itself. Called the 'Amsterdam of the North', it packs a similarly contemporary punch while still retaining plenty of old world charm.

With half of its population of 178,000 under 35, and with over 36,000 students, Groningen is a city that rocks – especially at night. But it's not just another student town. It's been around since BC became AD, when it was quick to evolve into a bustling walled city with a major grain market and high stakes in sugar and shipbuilding. And its history as a natural gas reserve is reflected in the **Aardgas Headquarters** (Concourslaan 17), a classic example of organic architecture. In fact, you're greeted by several architectural classics as soon as you arrive. Not only is **Centraal Station** the most beautiful in the country, it is also across the street from the **Groninger Museum**, the funkiest art gallery on the planet – even Bilbao's Guggenheim looks prefabricated by comparison. Also nearby is an early work by superstar architect Rem Koolhaas: the **Urinoir**, featuring both stainless steel toilets and the homoerotic photography of Erwin Olaf. It's located on Kleine Der A in the scenic Westhaven district, also home to the brand new **Stripmuseum** (Comics Museum) that covers everything from Asterix to Zorro and beyond.

If you proceed up Folkingestraat you'll soon find yourself at Vismarkt and Grote Markt. The latter's image-defining church and tower are the **Martinikerk** and **Martinitoren**. Historians claim that they are named after St Martin rather than the cocktail, but suspicions rise, given that the surrounding square kilometre has the highest density of alcohol licences in the country. If all that isn't enough, the tower of nearby church **Jozefkerk** is nicknamed 'Drunken Man's Tower': each of its six faces has a clock and therefore at least two are always visible, creating a sense of double vision. Yep, it's a student town alright.

Groningen also provides the perfect base to explore nature. There's much within cycling distance – for instance, the moated manors of Menkemaborg or Fraeylemaborg – but you can also take a bus to the nearby port towns, whence ferries go to the Wadden islands of Schiermonnikoog and Ameland. (Incidentally, while both the islands are part of Friesland, Schiermonnikoog is due to enter Groningen province within the next ten to 20 years as the dunes that make up its surface are blown eastward.) The VVV can provide details of these and many other possibilities.

Groninger Museum

Museumeiland 1 (050 366 6555/www.groninger-museum.nl). **Open** 10am-5pm Tue-Sun. **Admission** €10; €9 over-65s; €6 12s-16s; €4 6s-11s; free under-6s, MK. **Credit** AmEx, DC, MC, V.

Nederlands Stripmuseum

Westerhaven 71 (050 317 8470/www.stripmuseumgroningen.nl). **Open** 10am-5pm Tue-Sun. **Admission** €7.50; €6.25 4s-11s; free under-4s. **No credit cards**.

Where to eat & drink

Welcome to the city that rocks! The always hip **Vera** (Oosterstraat 44, 050 313 4681, www.vera-groningen.nl) acts as ground zero during the Eurosonic/Noorderslag festival (www.noorderslag.nl) every January, when 150 happening bands and DJs come together in

& Eetlokaal (Warmoesstraat 18, 023 532 6144, www.jacobuspieck.nl), while the riverside **Eclectic Bar Restaurant Willendorf** (Bakenessergracht 109, 023 531 1970, www.willendorf.nl) is a hip space with regular DJs. At **Hotspot Lambermons** (Spaarne 96, 023 542 7804, www.lambermons.nl) you get a different French-inspired €9.50 course put in front of you every half hour from 6.30pm to 11pm; stay until you're full. For steak that you will remember for the rest of your life, go to **Wilma & Alberts** (Oude Groenmarkt 6, 532 1256, www.wilma-alberts.nl). For some of the best Indonesian in the country, head to **De Rijsttafel** (Kruisweg 70D, 023 534 3456, www.rest-de-rijsttafel.nl) and order the *rendang*.

If you're more into wooden panelling, leather wallpaper, chaotic conviviality and infinite beer choices, there's **In Den Uiver** (Riviervismarkt 13, 023 532 5399, www.indenuiver.nl). For bands and/or DJs, check out the recently renovated **Patronaat** (Zijlsingel 2, 023 517 5858, www.patronaat.nl), Haarlem's own equivalent of the mighty Melkweg. Nightclub **Stalker** (Kromme Elleeboogsteeg 20, 023 531 4652, www.clubstalker.nl) specialises in upfront dance.

an almighty sound clash. Even the 'high cultural' **De Oosterpoort** (Trompsingel 27, 050 368 0368, www.de-oosterpoort.nl) gets involved. Groningen also hosts an excellent theatre festival, the **Noorderzon** (*see p265*), drawing big crowds annually.

For drinking all year round, there are two main strips. Peperstraat is middle of the road but has a couple of stand-outs for live music: **Jazzcafe de Spieghel** (Peperstraat 11, 050 528 0588, www.jazzcafedespieghel.nl) features jazz of both the trad and acid varieties, while **De Kar** (Peperstraat 15, 050 312 6215, www.dekar.nl) offers everything from lounge to punk. But if you have to choose between them, Poelestraat is the trendier alternative. Meanwhile, the city's hipsters head over to popular arthouse **Filmtheater & Café Images** (Poelstraat 30, 312 0433, www.images.nu).

For unpretentious swilling, check out **Mulder** (Grote Kromme Elleboog 22, 050 314 1469), the classic and buzzing brown bar **De Drie Uiltjes** (Oude Ebbingestraat 47, 050 318 9147, www.3uiltjes.nl), or the equally cosy **'t Proeflokaal** (Gedempt Zuiderdiep 62, 050 313 6183), whose booze menu embraces locally brewed jenevers. For some all-night drinking in the city's own Red Light District, check out the sleazy area around **Benzinebar** (Hoekstraat 44, 050 312 8390), which is only open midnight Saturday until 10am Sunday (handy if you want to save on a hotel bill). A mellower proposition is coffeeshop favourite **Metamorfose** (Oude Boteringestraat 53, 050 314 4460), ever good for a smoke.

For eats,**'t Feithhuis** (Marinikerkhof 10, 050 313 5335, www.feithhuis.nl) is open all day, while **De Drie Gezusters** (Grote Markt 36, 050 312 7041) also offers reasonable food. Many consider the Italian-inspired **Groninger Museum Restaurant** (*see above*, book via 050 360 3665) to be the best place to eat in town. For a real treat, book a table far in advance at fancy, French-inspired **Onder de Linden** (Burgemeester van Barneveldweg 3, Aduard, 050 403 1406, www.slenema.nl), located in a 1733-built organic farm ten kilometres (six miles) outside town.

Check www.specialbite.com for the latest on the local culinary scene. And don't forget to order something with mustard: Groningen is famous for it. Bon appetit.

Where to stay

For a bit of class, try the revamped **Hotel de Ville** (Oude Boteringestraat 43-5, 050 318 1222, www.deville.nl), where doubles range from €110 to €190. Meanwhile, the central **Martini Budget Hotel** (Gedempte Zuiderdiep 8, 050 312 9199, www.martinihotel.nl) offers doubles from €77.50. On a budget, check **Simplon Youthhotel** (Boterdiep 72-73, 050 313 5221, www.simplonjongerenhotel.nl).

Getting there

By car

190 km (120 miles) on A7.

By train

2hr from Amsterdam Centraal Station, direct.

Tourist information

VVV

Grote Markt 25 (0900 202 3050/www.vvvgroningen.nl). **Open** *Sept-June* 9am-6pm Mon-Fri; 10am-5pm Sat. *July, Aug* 9am-6pm Mon-Fri; 10am-5pm Sat; 11am-3pm Sun.

Where to stay

Carlton Square Hotel (Baan 7, 023 531 9091, www.carlton.nl) is quite posh, with rooms for €99-€139. For a real splurge, book the €535 suite at **Park Tower Suite** (Florapark 13, 023 534 7773, www.parktowersuite.nl). The **Carillon** (Grote Markt 27, 023 531 0591, www.hotelcarillon.com) has doubles for €60-€65, while outside the centre, **Stayokay Haarlem** (Jan Gijzenpad 3, 023 537 3793, www.stayokay.com) has B&B for €21 to €36.

Getting there

By car

10km (6 miles) west on A5.

By train

15min, direct from Amsterdam Centraal Station.

Tourist information

VVV

Stationsplein 1 (0900 616 1600 premium rate/ www.vvvzk.nl). **Open** *Oct-Mar* 9.30am-5pm Mon-Fri; 10am-3pm Sat. *Apr-Sept* 9.30am-5pm Mon-Fri; 9.30am-3pm Sat.

The Hague

While never officially a city – in days of yore, the powers that be did not want to offend its more ancient neighbours, Leiden and Utrecht – The Hague (aka Den Haag) is the nation's power hub and centre for international justice. It began life as the hunting ground of the Counts of Holland before being officially founded in 1248, when William II built a castle on the site of the present parliament buildings, the **Binnenhof**. It was here that the De Witt brothers were lynched after being accused of conspiring to kill William of Orange; they were brutalised nearby in **Gevangenpoort**, now a grimly evocative torture museum.

Queen Beatrix arrives at the Binnenhof in a golden coach every Prinsjesdag (third Tuesday in September) for the annual state opening of parliament. Guided tours are organised daily to the Knights' Hall, where the ceremony takes place. The **Mauritshuis**, a former regal home, is open to the public with one of the most famous collections in the world: works by the likes of Rubens, Rembrandt and Vermeer.

The Hague's city centre is lively, with a good selection of shops lining the streets and squares around the palaces and along Denneweg. The city is also one of the greenest in Europe, and has a number of lovely parks. Clingendael has a Japanese garden; Meijendael, further out, is part of an ancient forest; and the Scheveningse Bosje is big enough to occupy an entire day. Between the Bosje and the city is Vredes Paleis (the Peace Palace), a gift from Andrew Carnegie that is now the UN's Court of International Justice. Meanwhile, over on Churchillplein, the grand International Criminal Tribunal was the setting for former dictator Slobodan Milosevic's sulky theatrics – and, later, his death.

Beyond Scheveningse Bosje is Scheveningen, a former fishing village and now a resort. The highlight is the **Steigenberger Kurhaus Hotel**: built in 1887, it's a legacy of Scheveningen's halcyon days as a bathing place for European high society. The town's history as a spa has been resurrected with the opening of **Kuur Thermen Vitalizee** (Strandweg 13F, 070 416 6500, www.vitalizee.nl), a spa bath that offers a range of treatments. Also here is the 'Sculptures by the Sea' exhibition, a multi-dimensional collection of statues at the **Museum Beelden aan Zee**. The renovated **Panorama Mesdag** houses not only the single largest painting in the country (120 metres, 400 feet, in circumference), from which it takes its name, but also works from The Hague (most of them seascapes) and Barbizon (landscapes and pastoral scenes from peasant life) schools.

None, though, is worth as much as *Victory Boogie Woogie*, Piet Mondrian's last work, which sold for a cool *f*80 million (€36 million) in 1998. It's now on display at the **Haags Gemeentemuseum**, which holds the world's largest collection of works by Mondrian as well as many works of paradoxical art by MC Escher in newly restored buildings. The Haags Gemeentemuseum is next door to the excellent **Museum of Photography** (Stadhouderslaan 43, 070 338 1144, www.fotomuseumdenhaag.nl) and linked to the **Museon**, an excellent science museum that induces wonder in both kids and adults, and the **Omniversum IMAX Theatre**, a state-of-the-art planetarium. The Gemeente's brand new sister museum, **Escher in het Paleis** on Lange Voorhout, is filled with yet further examples of the mind-melting art of MC Escher and supplemented with much interactive multimedia.

On the offchance that your stopover in the country consists of one afternoon only, one way of seeing everything is by visiting **Madurodam**, an insanely detailed miniature city that dishes up every Dutch cliché in the book. Windmills turn, ships sail and trains speed around on the world's largest model railway. But if you happen to visit on a balmy summer's evening, when the models are lit within by 50,000 miniature lamps, then Madurodam leaves behind any hint of ironic appreciation and becomes a place of wonder.

Binnenhof
Binnenhof 8A (070 364 6144/www.binnenhof bezoek.nl). **Open** 10am-4pm Mon-Sat. **Admission** €5-€7; €4-€6 under-13s. **No credit cards.**

Escher in Het Paleis
Lange Voorhout 74 (070 42 77730/www.escherin hetpaleis.nl). **Open** 11am-5pm Tue-Sun. **Admission** €7.50; €5 7s-15s; free under-7s, MK. **No credit cards.**

Gemeentemuseum
Stadhouderslaan 41 (070 338 1111/www.gemeente museum.nl). **Open** 11am-5pm Tue-Sun. **Admission** €8.50; free under-18s, MK. **Credit** AmEx, MC, V.

Gevangenpoort Museum
Buitenhof 33 (070 346 0861/www.gevangenpoort.nl). **Open** Tours hourly from 10am-4pm Tue-Fri; noon-4pm Sat, Sun. **Admission** €4; €3 under-13s. **No credit cards.**

Madurodam
George Maduroplein 1 (070 416 2400/www. madurodam.nl). **Open** *Mid Mar-June* 9am-8pm daily. *July, Aug* 9am-11pm daily. *Sept-mid Mar* 9am-6pm daily. **Admission** €13; €12 over-65s; €9.25 3s-11s; free under-3s. **No credit cards.**

Mauritshuis
Korte Vijverberg 8 (070 302 3456/www.mauritshuis.nl). **Open** *1 Apr-1 Sept* 10am-5pm Mon-Sat; 11am-5pm Sun. *2 Sept-31 Mar* 10am-5pm Tue-Sat; 11am-5pm Sun. **Admission** €9.50 incl. audio tour; €4.75 seniors; free under-18s, MK. **Credit** AmEx, MC, V.

Museum Beelden aan Zee
Harteveltstraat 1 (070 358 5857/www.beeldenaan zee.nl). **Open** 11am-5pm Tue-Sun. **Admission** €7; €3.50 5s-12s; free under-5s. **No credit cards.**

Panorama Mesdag
Zeestraat 65 (070 364 4544/www.mesdag.nl). **Open** 10am-5pm Mon-Sat; noon-5pm Sun. **Admission** €5; €4 over-65s; €2.50 3s-13s; free under-3s. **No credit cards.**

Where to eat & drink

Juliana's (Plaats 11, 070 365 0235, www. julianas.nl) is where the beautiful people dine, whereas **De Klap** (Koningin Emmakade 118A, 070 345 4060, www.klap.nl) is more down to earth. For inspired Indonesian, try **Dayang** (Prinsestraat 65, 070 364 9979), while for Indian food there's **Bogor** (Van Swietenstraat 2, 070 346 1628). Inside the catacombs of City Hall, **Catacomben** (Grote Halstraat 3, 070 302 3060, www.catacomben.nl) offers reasonably priced Caribbean, French, Asian and Middle Eastern eats, while chic **WOX** (Buitenhof 36, 070 365 3754) is a recent addition.

Alternative and dance music fans should check out the roster at **Paard van Troje** (Prinsegracht 12, 070 360 1838, www.paard.nl). Meanwhile, beer fans should try **De Paas** (Dunne Bierkade 16A, 070 360 0019, www. depaas.nl). The living-room feel at **Murphy's Law** (Dr Kuyperstraat 7, 070 427 2507, www. murphysjazz.nl) attracts a friendly if unlikely mix of alternative folk and drunk diplomats. Meanwhile, **Fab** (Spui 185, 363 0880, www. fab.nl) is, well, fab. **Silly Symphonies** (Grote Markt 25, 070 312 3610, www.sillysymphonies.nl) appeals to the clubber/drinker/eater, while for coffee artisans there's **Cremers** (Prinsestraat 84, 070 346 2346, www.cafecremers.nl).

Where to stay

Le Meridien Hotel Des Indes (Lange Voorhout 54-56, 070 361 2345, www.hague. lemeridien.com) is arguably the most luxurious hotel in town, with prices to match: superior single/doubles start at €375, or even cheaper if you want to risk still paying even if you cancel. However the new **Grand Winston Hotel** (Generaal Eisenhowerplein 1, Rijswijk, 070 414 1500, www.grandwinston.nl) may soon eclipse all competition; doubles start at €135 before escalating sharply. The hostel **Stayokay Den Haag** (Scheepmakersstraat 27, 070 315 7888, www.stayokay.com) charges around €25.25 for a bed and €67 to €74.50 for doubles.

Getting there

By car
50km (31 miles) south-west on A4, then A44.

By train
50min from Amsterdam Centraal Station to Den Haag Centraal Station; change at Leiden if necessary.

Tourist information

VVV
Hofweg 1, outside Centraal Station (0900 340 3505 premium rate/www.denhaag.com). **Open** 10am-6pm Mon-Fri; 10am-5pm Sat; noon-5pm Sun.

Leiden

Canal-laced Leiden derives a good deal of its charm from the Netherlands' oldest university, which was founded here in 1575 and which boasts such notable alumni as René Descartes, US president John Quincy Adams and many a Dutch royal. The old town teems with bikes and bars, boasts the most historic monuments per square metre in the country, and is thus a truly rewarding place to visit, ideal for a weekend away from comparatively frenetic Amsterdam.

In the Dutch Golden Age of the late 16th and 17th centuries, Leiden grew fat on textiles. It also spawned three great painters of that era:

Rembrandt van Rijn, Jan van Goyen and Jan Steen. Although few works by these three masters remain in the Leiden of today, the **Stedelijk Museum de Lakenhal** (Lakenhal Municipal Museum), where the Golden Age clothmakers met, does have a painting by Rembrandt, as well as works by other Old Masters and collections of pewter, tiles, silver and glass. Perhaps Leiden's most notable museum, though, is the **Rijksmuseum van Oudheden** (National Museum of Antiquities), which houses the largest archaeological collection in the Netherlands: in particular the display of Egyptian mummies should not be missed. The excellent **Rijksmuseum voor Volkenkunde** (National Museum of Ethnology) showcases the cultures of Africa, Oceania, Asia, the Americas and the Arctic.

The ten million fossils, minerals and stuffed animals exhibited at **Naturalis** (Natural History Museum) make it the country's largest museum collection, while the 6,000 species of flora at the **Hortus Botanicus**, one of the world's oldest botanical gardens, include descendants of the country's first tulips. If Dutch clichés are the things that you came here to see, head

Euromast, Rotterdam. *See p290.*

straight to the **Molenmuseum de Valk** (the Falcon Windmill Museum), a windmill-turned-museum where you can see living quarters, machinery and a picturesque view out over Leiden. But an even better panorama can be had from the top of the Burcht, a 12th-century fort on an artificial mound in the city centre.

Hortus Botanicus Leiden

Rapenburg 73 (071 527 7249/www.hortusleiden.nl). **Open** *Apr-Oct* 10am-6pm daily. *Nov-Mar* 10am-4pm Mon-Fri, Sun. **Admission** €5; €2.50 4-12s; free under 4s, MK. **Credit** AmEx, MC, V.

Molenmuseum de Valk

2e Binnenvestgracht 1 (071 516 5353/http://home.wanadoo.nl/molenmuseum/). **Open** 10am-5pm Tue-Sat; 1-5pm Sun. **Admission** €3; €1.70 6s-15s, concessions; free under-6s, MK. **No credit cards**.

Naturalis

Darwinweg (071 568 7600/www.naturalis.nl). **Open** 10am-5pm Tue-Fri; 10am-6pm Sat, Sun. **Admission** €9; €6 13s-17s; €5 4s-12s; free under-3s. **Credit** MC, V.

Rijksmuseum van Oudheden

Rapenburg 28 (0900 660 0600/www.rmo.nl). **Open** 10am-5pm Tue-Fri; noon-5pm Sat, Sun. **Admission** €8.50; €5.50 4s-17s; €7.50 over-65s; free under-4s, MK. **Credit** AmEx, DC, MC, V.

Rijksmuseum voor Volkenkunde

Steenstraat 1 (071 516 8800/www.rmv.nl). **Open** 10am-5pm Tue-Sun. **Admission** €7.50; €4 concessions; free MK. **No credit cards**.

Stedelijk Museum de Lakenhal

Oude Singel 28-32 (071 516 5360/www.lakenhal.nl). **Open** 10am-5pm Tue-Fri; noon-5pm Sat, Sun. **Admission** €4; €2.50 over-65s; free under-18s, MK. **No credit cards**.

Where to eat & drink

A traditional cosy atmosphere is to be had at **De Hooykist** (Hooigracht 49, 071 512 5809, www.dehooykist.nl) and **In Den Bierbengel** (Langebrug 71, 071 514 8056, www.indenbierbengel.nl), which specialise in meat, fish and wines. Bar-restaurant **Annie's Verjaardag** (Hoogstraat 1A, 071 512 5737, www.anniesverjaardag.nl) occupies eight candle-lit cellars underneath a bridge in the centre of town: its main selling point is the canal barge terrace.

Another unique location is **Restaurant City Hall** (Stadhuisplein 3, 071 514 4055, www.restaurantcityhall.nl), a budget hotspot in the city's ancient – yes, you guessed it – City Hall. For something ultra-cheap and cheerful, there's **La Bota** (Herensteeg 9, 071 514 6340, www.labota.nl) near the Pieterskerk, while excellent tapas and refreshing beers can be had from early to late at **Oloroso** (Breestraat 49, 071 514 6633, www.oloroso.nl).

For a walk on the grungy side, try **WW** (Wolsteeg 4-6, 071 512 5900, www.deww.nl), which has bands, dartboards and graffiti. **The Duke** (Oude Singel 2, 071 512 1972, www.jazzcafetheduke.com) offers live jazz, and **LVC** (Breestraat 66, 071 514 6449, www.lvc.nl) hosts smaller touring acts. A range of more traditional bars are dotted along Nieuwstraat, Breestraat and Nieuwe Beestenmarkt.

Where to stay

The **Golden Tulip** (Schipholweg 3, 071 522 1121, www.goldentulipleidencentre.nl) is the town's poshest hotel, with rooms between €144 and €210. Rather cheaper is the **Mayflower** (Beestenmarkt 2, 071 514 2641, www.hotelmayflower.nl), where rooms start at €65, while the **Pension De Witte Singel** (Witte Singel 80, 071 512 4592, www.pension-ws.demon.nl) is cheaper still at €43.50 to €85.

Getting there

By car

40km (24 miles) south-west on A4.

By train

35min from Amsterdam Centraal Station, direct.

Tourist information

VVV

Stationsweg 2d (0900 222 2333 premium rate/www.leidenpromotie.nl). **Open** 11am-5.30pm Mon; 9.30am-5.30pm Tue-Fri; 10am-4.30pm Sat.

Rotterdam

The antithesis of Amsterdam, both visually and in vibe, this port city brings an urban grit to the Dutch landscape. Almost completely flattened in World War II, it has blossomed as a concrete-and-glass jungle, and what it lacks in idyllic charm it makes up for in passion and creativity.

Culturally on top of its game, Rotterdam is a haven for artists, musicians, designers and cutting-edge architecture. Its citizens also love a good party – among its many festivals, multicultural celebration **Summer Carnival** (www.zomercarnaval.nl) draws no less than 900,000 spectators each July.

The city also remains in a continual state of regeneration; a fine example is **Rotterdam Centraal Station**, currently being rebuilt and transformed into another iconic structure. It may mean your entry point into the city is a building site, but the changes will almost certainly be breathtaking when it finally opens in 2010. In the meantime, it's a waiting game for all.

Other finished projects have already proved a huge success, resulting in a futuristic skyline along the banks of the River Maas. The **Oude Haven** (Old Harbour) is these days a work of imaginative modernism, the pinnacle of which is Piet Blom's witty bright yellow cubic houses. **Kijk-Kubus** remains a monument open to visitors, while other cubes are being converted into a hostel for 2008. Across the splendid white asymmetrical Erasmus Bridge, nicknamed 'the swan', don't miss activities in the **Las Palmas** (Willeminakade 66), a remnant of the 1950s cruise ship era that's been restored as a cultural beacon, housing the **Dutch Photography Museum**, among other institutions.

Across town, architectural wizard Rem Koolhaas designed his city's cultural heart, the Museumpark, where you'll find outdoor sculptures and five museums. The three best are the **Netherlands Architecture Institute**, which gives an overview of the history and development of architecture, especially in Rotterdam; the **Museum Boijmans Van Beuningen**, with a beautiful collection of traditional and contemporary art (including works by Bruegel, Van Eyck and Rembrandt), and the **Kunsthal**, which deals with art, design and photography, with regular travelling exhibitions. The adjoining street, Witte de Withstraat, offers contemporary art hub **TENT** (Witte de Withstraat 50, 010 413 5498, www.tentplaza.nl), many smaller galleries and a variety of excellent restaurants and bars, too. A bird's eye view of it all can be had from the nearby **Euromast** (*photos p288*), if you can handle the height (185 metres, or 607 feet).

The vastly sprawling **Historical Museum Rotterdam** includes the Dubbelde Palmboom (Double Palm Tree), housed in an old granary in Delfshaven and exploring life and work in the Meuse delta from 8000 BC to the present, and Het Schielandshuis, a palatial 17th-century mansion, another of the few buildings spared in the bombing. Old world charm also abounds at the neighbouring town of Schiedam (VVV, Buitenhavenweg 9, 010 473 3000), which houses the world's five tallest windmills and the planet's largest collection of Dutch gins and liqueurs in the tasting house of its distillery museum. For an 'out-of-Holland' experience, head over to **Motorschip Noordereiland** (www.noordereiland.org), an artistic island community on the River Maas, accessed from Willems Bridge.

Of the shopping areas, the Lijnbaan and Koopgoot cover more mainstream needs in pedestrianised comfort. Nieuwe Binnenweg, meanwhile, provides an escape from the shopping chains, offering trendy clothing, innovative furniture and design, and record shops especially popular with the younger crowd. Looking to go more upmarket? Make your way over to Van Oldenbarneveltstraat and Karel Doormanstraat.

If you're a backpacker, take advantage of **Use-it** (Schaatsbaan 41-45, 010 240 9158, www.use-it.nl), just moments from the exit of the station. Like a young person's VVV, it offers great tips for what to do in the city, as well as free lockers in which to ditch your bag.

Euromast

Parkhaven 20 (010 436 4811/www.euromast.nl). **Open** *Apr-Sept* 9.30am-11pm daily. *Oct-Mar* 10am-11pm daily. **Admission** €8.30; €5.40 4s-11s; free under-4s. **Credit** AmEx, DC, MC, V.

Historical Museum Rotterdam

Korte Hoogstraat 31 (010 217 6767/www.hmr.rotterdam.nl). **Open** 10am-5pm Tue-Sun. **Admission** €3; €1.50 4s-16s; free under-4s, MK. **No credit cards**.

Kijk-Kubus

Overblaak 70 (010 414 2285/www.cubehouse.nl). **Open** *Jan, Feb* 11am-5pm Sat, Sun. *Mar-Dec* 11am-5pm daily. **Admission** €2; €1.50 concessions; free under-4s. **No credit cards**.

Kunsthal

Westzeedijk 341 (010 440 0301/www.kunsthal.nl). **Open** 10am-5pm Tue-Sat; 11am-5pm Sun. **Admission** €8.50; €8 seniors; €5 students; €2 6s-18s; free under-6s. **No credit cards**.

Museum Boijmans Van Beuningen

Museumpark 18-20 (010 441 9400/www.boijmans.rotterdam.nl). **Open** 11am-5pm Tue-Sun. **Admission** €9; free under-18s, MK, Wed. **Credit** AmEx, MC, V.

Netherlands Architecture Institute

Museumpark 25 (010 440 1200/www.nai.nl). **Open** 10am-5pm Tue-Sat; 11am-5pm Sun. **Admission** €8; €5 seniors, students, 12s-18s; €1 4s-12s; free under-4s, MK. **Credit** AmEx, MC, V.

Where to eat & drink

Oude Haven, the Entrepot district and also Delfshaven all offer a wide choice of (grand) cafés and restaurants. For traditional thick pea soup while touring the town on a tram, check out the schedule of the **Snerttram** (010 414 8079, www.snerttram.nl). Less than a minute from Centraal Station, **De Engel** (Eendrachtsweg 19, 010 413 8256, www.engelgroep.com) offers a wide range of international cuisine. For veggies there's **Bla Bla** (Piet Heynsplein 35, 010 477 4448); **Foody's** (Nieuwe Binnenweg 151, 010 436 5163, www.engelgroep.com) looks stuck in the past, but its dining and wining menus are diverse and affordable; **El Faro Andaluz** (Leuvehaven 73-74, 010 414 6213, www.elfaroandaluz.nl) serves Spanish tapas; **La Pizza** (Scheepstimmermanslaan 21, 010 241 7797) produces trad and tasty wood-oven versions, while the best Chinese in town can be found at Rotterdam's Chinatown, Katendrecht. Check www.specialbite.com for regular offers.

Bars-wise, **De Schouw** (Witte de Withstraat 80, 010 412 4253) is a stylish brown café that now attracts artists and students. A lofty range of beers draws locals and tourists alike to **Locus Publicus** (Oostzeedijk 364, 010 433 1761, www.locus-publicus.com). Jazz fiends should try **Dizzy** ('s Gravendijkwal 129, 010 477 3014, www.dizzy.nl), one of the best jazz venues in the country, though many streets and cafés buzz with jazz when North Sea Jazz Festival hits in July. For bands and club nights, **Rotown** (Nieuwe Binnenweg 19, 010 436 2669, www.rotown.nl) focuses on indie and has a very fine bar/restaurant (11am-9.30pm). Mining a similar seam, with lots of hip hop and dancehall thrown in for good measure, is **Waterfront** (Boompjeskade 15, 010 201 0980, www.waterfront.nl). For a more experimental collection of music, parties and films in a vivid setting, head to **WORM** (Achterhaven 148, 010 476 7832, www.wormweb.nl).

Of the vast number of clubbing options, **Now&Wow** (www.now-wow.com), was long considered one of the best dance clubs in Benelux, but has now gone mobile and just organises parties in different locations; the excellent **Off Corso** (Kruiskade 22, 010 411 3897, www.off-corso.nl) has won the prestigious 'Golden Gnome' dance award; and **CLUBIMAX** (Leuvehaven 77, 010 213 0530, www.clubimax.nl) serves up commercial electro to a trendy crowd. For those about to rock, **Baroeg** (Spinozaweg 300, 010 432 5735, www.baroeg.nl) specialises in heavy metal and industrial.

Where to stay

Hotel New York is one of the most luxurious and historical places in town (Koninginnenhoofd 1, 010 439 0500, www.hotelnewyork.nl), but not unreasonably priced: doubles start at €105. Even if you don't stay here, pop in for a coffee or a plate of fruits de mer. **Hotel Bazar** (Witte de Withstraat 16, 010 206 5151, www.hotelbazar.nl) is also a little out of the ordinary: the rooms come decorated in a variety of Middle Eastern, African and South American styles, and it also hosts an excellent Middle Eastern restaurant. Doubles range from €75 to €120. For travellers on a budget, the **Sleep-In De Mafkees** (Schaatsbaan 41-45, 010 240 9158, www.sleep-in.nl) may only open during July, August and the International Film Festival Rotterdam in January, but is a bargain at €10 a night. For the rest of the year there's the hostel **Stayokay Rotterdam** (Rochussenstraat 107, 010 436 5763, www.stayokay.com); for about €20 to €32.60 you also get breakfast and the use of a communal kitchen.

Getting there

By car

73km (45 miles) south on A4, then A13.

By train

1hr from Amsterdam Centraal Station, direct.

Tourist information

VVV

Coolsingel 5 (0900 403 4065 premium rate/www.rotterdam.info). **Open** 9am-5.30pm Mon-Thur, Sat; 9am-9pm Fri; 10am-5pm Sun.

Utrecht

One of the oldest cities in the Netherlands, Utrecht was also, in the Middle Ages, the biggest, and was a religious and political centre for hundreds of years – at one point there were around 40 houses of worship in the city, all with towers and spires. From a great distance, it must have looked like a pincushion.

But there's more to Utrecht than mere history alone: the university is one of the largest in the Netherlands – still expanding and employing architects like Rem Koolhaas (who designed the Educatorium) – and the centre bustles with trendy shops and cafés. Happily, too, the Hoog Catharijne, the country's biggest shopping mall but not its prettiest, will soon be destroyed. For now, you'll have to wander its labyrinthine layout following signs to 'Centrum' in order to leave Central Station. Luxury-lovers should head for the boutiques and galleries in the vicinity of the classic-meets-postmodern city hall building, the **Stadhuisbrug**.

Linger a while on Oudkerkhof, where there's a concentration of designer shops, and visit the flower and plant markets along Janskerkhof and Oudegracht on Saturdays.

Bikes can be hired from **U-Stal** (Stationsplein 69, 030 231 7656, www.u-stal.nl), but the city is so compact that practically everything is within short walking distance. A starting place is the **Domtoren**, the cathedral tower. At over 112 metres (367 feet), it's the highest tower in the country and, with over 50 bells, the largest musical instrument in the Netherlands, too. The tower can be climbed, and the panorama is worth the 465 steps: vistas stretch 40 kilometres (25 miles) to Amsterdam on a clear day. Buy tickets across the square at **VVV** (Domplein 9; *see below*), where you can also get details on the rest of the city and the castles on its outskirts.

The space between the tower and the Domkerk was originally occupied by the nave of the huge church, which was destroyed by a freak tornado in 1674; the exhibition inside the Domkerk shows interesting 'before' and 'after' sketches.

Another fascinating place to explore is the Oudegracht, the canal that runs through the centre of the city, and its cafés and shops, excellent places for snacks and boat-watching.

Of the city museums, the **Catharijneconvent** (St Catharine Convent Museum) is situated in a beautiful late-medieval building. Mainly dedicated to Dutch religious history, it also has a great collection of paintings by Old Masters, including Rembrandt. The **Centraal Museum** has a varied collection, from paintings by Van Gogh to contemporary art and cutting-edge fashion. One wing is dedicated to illustrator Dick Bruna, who created that charming bunny, Miffy. Another Utrecht-born celebrity in the collection is De Stijl architect and designer Gerrit Rietveld, known for his rectangular chairs and houses: the **Rietveld-Schröderhuis,** just outside the city centre, can be reached on the Centraal Museum's tour bus. The world's single biggest collection of automated musical instruments can be found at the fun Nationaal Museum van Speelklok tot Pierement. The **Universiteitsmuseum** (University Museum) focuses on science education and also boasts a centuries-old botanical garden.

Utrecht is in an area rich with castles, forests and arboretums. **Slot Zuylen** (Zuylen Castle, Tournooiveld 1, Oud Zuilen, 030 244 0255, www.slotzuylen.com) presides over some exquisite waterfalls and gardens. Check the concerts and shows in **Kasteel Groeneveld**'s gorgeous gardens (Groeneveld Castle, Groeneveld 2, Baarn, 035 542 0446, www.kasteelgroeneveld.nl), north-east of Utrecht. Stroll in the **Arboretum von Gimborn** (Vossensteinsesteeg 8, 030 253 1826, www.bio.uu.nl/bottuinen) in Doorne, then to **Kasteel Huis Doorn** (Langbroekerweg 10, 034 342 1020, www.huisdoorn.nl), where Kaiser Wilhelm II lived in until his death in 1941.

Centraal Museum

Nicolaaskerkhof 10 (030 236 2362/www.centraalmuseum.nl). **Open** 11am-5pm Tue-Thur, Sat, Sun; noon-9pm Fri. **Admission** €8; €6 seniors, 13s-17s; €2 under 12s, MK. **Credit** MC, V.

Museum Catharijneconvent

Lange Nieuwstraat 38 (030 231 3835/www.catharijneconvent.nl). **Open** 10am-5pm Tue-Fri; 11am-5pm Sat, Sun. **Admission** €8.50; €7.50 over-65s; €4.50 6s-17s; free under-5s. **No credit cards**.

Nationaal Museum van Speelklok tot Pierement

Steenweg 6 (030 231 789/www.museumspeelklok.nl). **Open** 10am-5pm Tue-Sun. **Admission** €7; €4 4s-12s; €6 over-65s; free under-4s, MK. **Credit** MC, V.

Rietveld-Schröderhuis

Prins Hendriklaan 50 (030 236 2310/www.rietveld schroderhuis.nl). **Open** Hourly buses from Central Station Thur-Sun 11.45am-2.45pm. **Admission** €16; €13 12s-18s, over-65s; €8 under-12s. **Credit** MC, V.

Universiteitsmuseum

Lange Nieuwstraat 106 (030 253 8028/www.museum. uu.nl). **Open** 11am-5pm Tue-Sun. **Admission** €7; €3.50 seniors, students, 4s-17s; free under-4s, MK. **No credit cards**.

Where to eat & drink

De Winkel van Sinkel (Oudegracht 158, 030 230 3030, www.dewinkelvansinkel.nl) is a grand setting for coffee or food, especially at night, when its catacombs open for club nights and as a late-night restaurant. **Stadskasteel Oudaen** (Oudegracht 99, 030 231 1864, www. oudaen.nl), the only urban medieval castle left in the country, and **Goesting** (Veeartsenijpad, 030 273 3346, www.restaurantgoesting.nl), in a former kennels, are both rather posh, but those looking for dinner on the verge of a Michelin star ought to stop in on **Wilhelminapark** (Wilhelminapark 65, 030 251 0693, www. wilhelminapark.nl), at the centre of a beautiful green that makes an ideal summer hangout. **Mi Madre** (Oudkerkhof 44, 030 232 8648), meanwhile, serves excellent tapas, while superior sushi is munched at **Konnichi Wa** (Mariaplaats 9, 030 241 6388, www.konnichi wa.nl). If you want a local speciality, try the sweet and savouries at **Pancake Bakery de Oude Muntkelder** (Oudegracht aan de Werf, 030 231 6773, www.deoudemuntkelder.nl).

Most city centre bars heave with a gaggle of local students that one can't help feel should be hitting the books instead of the local beers. **ACU** (Voorstraat 71, 030 231 4590, www.acu.nl) has cheap eats and some of the city's edgier musical events; **België** (Oudegracht 196, 030 231 2666) serves over 300 types of beer, and **Het Hart** (Voorstraat 10, 030 231 9718, www. hethart.com) has the coolest crowd of all. **Tivoli** (Oudegracht 245, 0900 235 8486, www.tivoli.nl) is the best place to check for DJs and bands, while student favourite **Ekko** (Bemuurde Weerd Westzijde 3, 030 231 7457, www.ekko.nl) now focuses on indie and dance. Local muso hangout **dB's** (Cartesiusweg 90A, 030 293 8209, www. dbstudio.nl) regularly invites upbeat rock 'n' roll bands. Avant-garde music and truly daring theatre can be experienced at the ever innovative **Theater Kikker** (Ganzenmarkt 14, 030 231 9666, www.theaterkikker.nl).

Meanwhile, film fans congregate at **Louis Hartlooper Complex** (Tolsteegbrug 1, 030 232 0450, www.louishartloopercomplex.nl), run by famed local filmmaker Jos Stelling and located in a remarkable and charmingly refurbished 1928 police station.

Rietveld-Schröderhuis, Utrecht.

Where to stay

The four-star **Malie Hotel** (Maliestraat 2, 030 231 6424, www.maliehotel.nl) is a beautiful old merchant's house: a single costs from €95; a double costs from €105, including breakfast. Those on a tighter budget should try small hostel **Strowis** (Boothstraat 8, 030 238 0280, www.strowis.nl), with shared rooms for €14.50 to €17.50, or B&B **Utrecht** (Lucasbolwerk 4, 06 5043 4884, www.hostelutrecht.nl), with dormitory beds from €16.50.

Getting there

By car

40km (25 miles) south-east.

By rail

30min from Amsterdam Centraal Station, direct.

Tourist information

VVV

Domplein 9 (0900 128 8732 premium rate/ www.utrechtyourway.nl). **Open** noon-6pm Mon; 10am-6pm Tue-Wed, Fri; 10am-8pm Thur; 9.30am-5pm Sat; noon-5pm Sun.

Directory

Features

Directory

Getting Around

Getting around Amsterdam is easy. The city has efficient and cheap trams and buses, though if you're staying in the centre most places are reachable on foot. Locals tend to get around by bike: the streets are busy with cycles all day and most of the evening. There are also boats, barges and water taxis.

If you were thinking about bringing a car – don't. The roads simply aren't designed for them, and parking places are seriously elusive. Alas, public transport provision for those with disabilities is dire. Though there are lifts at all Metro stations, staff can't always help with wheelchairs.

Handy new service 9292ov (0900 9292, www.9292ov.nl) groups national bus, train, taxi, tram and ferry info; besides phoning, you can use their Dutch-language website for 'door-to-door' advice. Under *van* (from), type in the *straat* (street), *huisnummer* (house number) and *plaats* (town) you want to start from; then, under *naar* (to), the details for your destination; select the date and time, then select *aankomst* if that's your ideal arrival time or *vertrek* if that's your ideal departure time; then press *geef reisadvies* (give travel advice).

Arriving & leaving

By air

For general airport enquiries, ring Schiphol Airport on 0900 0141 (costs €0.10/min) or go to www.schiphol.nl.

British Airways
346 9559/www.britishairways.nl.

British Midland
346 9211/www.flybmi.com.

EasyJet
0900 265 8022 (costs €0.80/min) www.easyjet.co.uk.

KLM
474 7747/www.klm.com.

Connexxion Airport Hotel Shuttle

Connexxion counter, Section A7, Arrivals, Schiphol Airport (038 339 4741/www.airporthotel shuttle.nl). **Times** every 30min 6am-9pm. **Tickets** *Single* €12.50. *Return* €19.50. **No credit cards**.
This bus service from Schiphol Airport to Amsterdam is available to anyone prepared to pay, not just hotel guests. However, to get door-to-door service and the return pick-up, you'll have to be staying at one of the hundred-odd allied hotels (but with buses stopping at each of these, it's easy to get off very near your destination). Schedules and the expanding list of allied hotels are on the website (which also has a booking service).

Schiphol Airport Rail Service

Schiphol Airport/Centraal Station (information 0900 9292/www. 9292ov.nl). **Times** every 10min 4am-midnight, then every hr. **Tickets** *Single* €3.60; €2 4s-11s; free under-3s. *Return* €6.10; €2 4s-11s; free under-3s. **Credit** MC, V.
The journey to Centraal Station takes about 20 minutes. Make sure you buy your ticket before boarding, otherwise you'll incur a €35 fine. Note that return tickets are valid for that day only.

Taxis

There are always plenty of taxis at the main exit. They're pricey: a fixed fare from the airport to the south and west of the city is about €25, and to the centre is about €35.

Public transport

For information, tickets, maps and an English-language guide to all types of public transport tickets, visit the GVB, Amsterdam's municipal transport authority in person (an office is very conveniently located right opposite Centraal Station) or use their useful website. A basic map of the tram network is on p336.

See p272 for details of NS, the Netherlands' rail network.

GVB

Stationsplein CS, Old Centre: New Side (0900 8011/www.gvb.nl). Tram 1, 2, 4, 5, 9, 13, 16, 17, 24, 25. **Open** *Telephone enquiries* 8am-10pm daily. *In person* 7am-9pm Mon-Fri; 8am-9pm Sat, Sun. **Map** p326 D1.
The GVB runs Amsterdam's Metro, bus and tram services, and provides information on all.
Other locations *Head Office*: Arlandaweg 100 (lost articles); Bijlmer station; Metro stations; Rembrandtplein; Leidseplein (night buses only, midnight-6am Fri, Sat).

Fares & tickets

Don't travel on a bus or tram without a ticket. Uniformed inspectors make regular checks and passengers lacking a valid ticket will be fined €35 on the spot. Playing the ignorant foreigner won't work.

Strippenkaarten

A 'strip ticket' system operates on trams, buses and the Metro. It's initially confusing, but ultimately good value for money. Prices begin at €1.60 for a strip of two units or €6.40 for 8 units; these you can buy from any bus or tram driver. But you only really start saving if you spend €6.80 for a 15-unit card or €20.10 for 45 units; these can only be bought at GVB offices, post offices, train stations, major supermarkets and many tobacconists and souvenir shops. Children under 3 travel free, and older children (4s-18s) and seniors (+65) pay reduced fares (€4.50 for a 15-strip card).

Tickets must be stamped on boarding a tram or bus and on entering a Metro station. The city is divided into five zones: Noord (north), West, Centrum, Oost (east) and Zuid (south); most of central Amsterdam falls within Centrum. Strip tickets are also valid on trains that stop at Amsterdam stations, with the exception of Schiphol.

For travel within a single zone, two units must be stamped, while three are stamped for two zones, four for three zones and so on. On trams, if a conductor is not there, you can stamp your own tickets in the yellow box-like contraption near the doors: fold the ticket so that the unit you need to stamp is at the end. On buses, drivers stamp the tickets, and on the Metro there are stamping machines located at the entrance to stations.

More than one person can travel on one 'strip ticket', but the correct number of units must be stamped for each person. Stamps are valid for one hour; during this time you can transfer to other buses and trams without having to stamp your card again. If your journey takes more than an hour, you have to stamp more units, but no single tram journey in the centre should take that long. *Strippenkaarten* remain valid for one year from the date of the first stamp.

Dagkaarten

A cheap option for unlimited travel in Amsterdam, a 'day ticket' costs €6.50. All pensioners aged over 65 (with Dutch ID or valid passport), students with ID and children (4s-11s) pay €4.50. Child day tickets are valid on night buses. A day ticket is valid on trams, buses and the Metro on the day it is stamped until the last bus or tram runs. You need to buy a new ticket for night buses (€3). Only the one-day ticket can be bought from drivers on trams and buses. After you've stamped the day ticket on your first journey, you don't need to stamp it again. You can also buy tickets for two days (€10.50) and three days (€13.50). The I Amsterdam Pass is an extended day ticket (*see p82*) valid for one, two or three days (€33-€53), from GVB or the Amsterdam Tourist Board (*see p312*).

Travel advice

For current information on travelling to a specific country – including the latest news on health issues, safety and security, local laws and customs – contact your home country's government department of foreign affairs. Most have websites with plenty of useful advice for would-be travellers.

Australia
www.smartraveller.gov.au

Canada
www.voyage.gc.ca

New Zealand
www.safetravel.govt.nz

Republic of Ireland
http://foreignaffairs.gov.ie

UK
www.fco.gov.uk/travel

USA
http://travel.state.gov

Sterabonnement

'Season tickets' can be bought at GVB offices, tobacconists and post offices, and are valid for a week, a month or a year. A weekly pass for the central zone (Centrum) costs €10.80, monthly €35.80 and yearly €358. Children (4s-18s) and seniors get cheaper season tickets: €7.15/day, €23.60/month and €236/year. You'll need a passport photo to get yourself a season ticket.

OV-Chipcard

Train, bus, tram and bus travellers are also able to pay using an 'OV-chipkaart', a sort of credit card, available from GVB ticket and information offices. The card itself (valid for five years) costs €7.50, and different ticket types can be uploaded; weekly, monthly and annual season tickets can only be bought at GVB offices, while other jouneys can be added at ticket machines. There are also 'disposable' OV cards. See www.gvb.nl for a full explanation of OV-Chipcard rates and fares.

Trams & buses

Buses and trams are a good way to get around. Tram services run from 6am from Monday to Friday, 6.30am on Saturday and 7.30am on Sunday, with a special night bus service that takes over late in the evening. Night buses are numbered from 351 to 363; all go to Centraal Station. Night bus stops are indicated by a black square at the stop with the bus number printed on it. Night buses run from 1am to 5.30am daily from Monday to Friday, and until 6.30am on weekends.

During off-peak hours and at quieter stops, stick out your arm to let the driver know that you want to get on.

Yellow signs at tram and bus stops indicate the name of the stop and further stops. There are usually maps of the entire network in the shelters and route maps on the trams and buses. The city's bus and tram drivers and conductors are generally courteous and will give directions if asked; most can do so in English.

Other road users should be warned that trams will only stop if absolutely necessary. Cyclists should listen for tram warning bells and be careful to cross tramlines at an angle that avoids the front wheel getting stuck; motorists should avoid blocking tramlines: cars are allowed to venture on them only if they're turning right.

To get on or off a tram, wait until it has halted at a stop and press the button by the doors, which will then open. On some

Weather report

	Temp	Rainfall	Sun (hrs/dy)
Jan	4°C/39°F	68mm/2.7in	1.8
Feb	6°C/43°F	48mm/1.9in	2.8
Mar	9°C/48°F	66mm/2.6in	3.7
Apr	13°C/55°F	53mm/2.1in	5.5
May	17°C/63°F	61mm/2.4in	7.2
June	20°C/68°F	71mm/2.8in	6.6
July	22°C/72°F	76mm/3.0in	6.9
Aug	22°C/72°F	71mm/2.8in	6.7
Sept	19°C/66°F	66mm/2.6in	4.4
Oct	14°C/57°F	73mm/2.9in	3.3
Nov	9°C/48°F	81mm/3.2in	1.9
Dec	6°C/43°F	84mm/3.3in	1.5

trams you can buy a ticket from the driver at the front; on others from either a machine in the middle, or a conductor at the back; on new trams, conductors sit in a booth in the middle.

Note that Metro 51, 53 and 54 are, confusingly, fast trams that run on Metro lines. This is not the same as the number 5 tram, which is actually called a *sneltram* (fast tram).

Despite being continually threatened with termination, the Opstapper, an eight-seater white minibus, continues to plough along Prinsengracht between Centraal Station and Waterlooplein (30min trip, 9am-5.30pm Mon-Sat) picking up mostly the elderly along the way. That said, absolutely anyone can use it as long as they pay with *strippenkaarten* or €1.60 cash. Just wave one down when you see it.

Metro

The Metro uses the same ticket system as trams and buses (*see p296*), and serves suburbs to the south and east. There are three lines, 51, 52 and 53, which terminate at Centraal Station (sometimes abbreviated to CS). Trains run from 6am Monday to Friday (6.30am Sat, 7.30am Sun) to around 12.15am daily.

Taxis

You can order a cab by calling 677 7777. The line is often busy Friday and Saturday nights: expect a phone queue.

Check that the meter starts at the minimum charge (€3.40). Always ask the driver to tell you the cost of the journey before setting out. Even short journeys are expensive: on top of €3.40, you will be expected to pay €1.94 per kilometre for the first 25 kilometres, then €1.45 per kilometre thereafter.

If you feel that you've been ripped off, ask for a receipt, which you are entitled to see before handing over cash. If the charge is extortionate, phone the TCA, the central taxi office (650 6506, 9am-5pm Mon-Fri) or contact the police. Rip-offs are relatively rare but it's always a good idea to check that the cab you are getting into has the 'TCA' sign.

Sometimes it's very hard to hail a taxi in the street, but ranks are dotted around the city. The best central ones are found outside Centraal Station, alongside the bus station at the junction of Kinkerstraat and Marnixstraat, Rembrandtplein and Leidseplein.

Wheelchairs will only fit in taxis if they're folded. If you're in a wheelchair, phone the car transport service for wheelchair users (633 3943, 7am-5pm daily). You'll need to book your journey one or two days in advance and it costs around €2 per kilometre.

Happily, there are now taxi companies out to help break the monopoly of TCA. Tulip Taxi (636 3000) begins with a minimum charge of €2.55 before adding 85 eurocents/ minute for the initial 15 kilometres. After that they charge €1.50/kilometre. This can save you up to 50% on inner-city rides. Unfortunately, they do not have a large fleet and you are often left waiting.

Driving

If you absolutely must bring a car to the Netherlands, join a national motoring organisation beforehand. This should issue you with booklets that explain what to do in the event of a breakdown in Europe. To drive in the Netherlands you'll need a valid national driving licence, although ANWB (*see below*) and many car hire firms favour photocard licences (Brits need the paper version as well for this to be legal; the photocard takes a couple of weeks to come through if you're applying from scratch). You'll need proof that the vehicle has passed a road safety test in its country of origin, an international identification disk, a registration certificate and insurance documents.

Driving in Amsterdam, as already mentioned, is far more of a hassle than it's worth, but major roads are usually all well maintained and clearly signposted. Motorways are labelled 'A'; major roads 'N'; and European routes 'E'. Brits in particular should note that the Dutch drive on the right. Both drivers and front-seat passengers must always wear seatbelts. Speed limits are 50kmph (31mph) within cities,

70kmph (43mph) outside them, and 100kmph (62mph) when on motorways. If you're driving in Amsterdam, always look out for cyclists. Many streets in Amsterdam are now one-way.

Royal Dutch Automobile Club (ANWB)

Museumplein 5, Museum Quarter (673 0844/customer services 0800 0503/24hr emergency line 088 269 2888/www.anwb.nl). Tram 2, 3, 5, 12, 16. **Open** *Customer services* 9.30am-6pm Mon-Fri; 9.30am-5pm Sat. **Credit** MC, V. **Map** p330 D6.
If you haven't joined a motoring organisation, enrol here for a yearly €49.50-€69.50 (the Wegenwacht Service), which covers the cost of assistance if your vehicle breaks down. Members of a foreign motoring organisation may be entitled to free help. Remember that crews may not accept credit cards at the accident scene.

Car hire

Dutch car hire (*autoverhuur*) firms generally expect at least one year's driving experience and will want to see a valid national driving licence (with photo) and passport before they lend vehicles. All will require you to pay a deposit by credit card, and you generally need to be over 21. Prices given below are for one day's hire of the cheapest car available excluding insurance and VAT.

Adam's Rent-a-Car

Nassaukade 344-346, Oud West (685 0111/www.adamsrentacar.nl). Tram 7, 10, 17. **Open** 8am-6pm Mon-Fri; 8am-8pm Sat. **Credit** AmEx, MC, V. **Map** p330 C5.
One-day hire costs from €32; the first 100km (62 miles) are free, and after that the charge is €0.14/km. Branch at Middenweg 51.

Dik's Autoverhuur

Van Ostadestraat 278-280, the Pijp (662 3366/www.diks.net). Tram 3, 4. **Open** 8am-7.30pm Mon-Sat; 9am-12.30pm, 8-10.30pm Sun. **Credit** AmEx, DC, MC, V. **Map** p331 F6.
Prices from €34 per day. The first 100km are free, then it's €0.14/km.

Hertz

Overtoom 333, Oud West (612 2441/www.hertz.nl). Tram 1, 6. **Open** 8am-6pm Mon-Fri; 8am-2pm Sat; 9am-2pm Sun, public holidays. **Credit** AmEx, DC, MC, V. **Map** p329 B6.
Prices from €49 per day. The first 200km are free, then it's €0.22/km.

Clamping & fines

Wheel-clamp (*wielklem*) teams are swift and merciless. A sticker on your windscreen tells you to telephone 251 2222 (24-hour pay-and-go service). Someone will come to whom you can pay the fine by credit card (minimum €103.60) and have the clamp removed. To pay in cash after business hours you must go to Daniel Goedkoopstraat 7-9. During business hours go to any of the branches listed below and hand over your money. Once you've paid, return to the car and wait for the clamp to be removed. Thankfully, the declampers normally turn up fairly promptly, which is a small mercy in the grand scheme of misery incurred.

If you fail to pay the fine within 24 hours, your car will be towed away. It will cost around €150 or more, plus parking fine, plus a tariff per kilometre to reclaim it from the pound if you do so within 24 hours, and around €58 for every 12 hours thereafter. The pound is Daniel Goedkoopstraat 7-9. Take along your passport, licence number and cash, or a major credit card. If your car has been clamped or towed, go along to any of the following Stadstoezicht (parking service) offices to pay the fine.

All in all, it's just another reason to take public tranport.

Head office

Daniël Goedkoopstraat 7-9, Oost (553 0300/www.stadstoezicht.amsterdam.nl). Metro 51, 53, 54. **Open** 7am-11pm daily; 24/7 if your car has been towed. **Map** p327 F3.

Other locations *Beukenplein 50, Oost (553 0333). Tram 3, 9, 10, 14.* **Open** 9am-5.30pm Mon-Fri. **Map** p332 H4.
De Clercqstraat 42-44, Oud West (553 0333). Tram 3, 12, 13, 14. **Open** 8am-4.30pm Mon-Sat. **Map** p329 B4.

Parking

Parking in central Amsterdam is a nightmare: the whole area is metered from 9am up until at least 7pm – and in many places up to midnight – and meters are difficult to find. Meters will set you back up to €4.60 an hour. You can buy day passes for the centre (9am to 7pm: €27.60), evening passes (7pm to midnight: €18.40), or a week pass (€165.60 9am-7pm, €248.40 24 hours) – from the Stadstoezicht offices (*see above*). Car parks (*parkeren*) are indicated by a white 'P' on a blue square. After controlled hours, parking at meters is free. Below is a list of central car parks where you're more likely to find a space at peak times, although prices can be rather prohibitive.

When leaving your car anywhere across the city, be sure to empty it of valuables: cars with foreign plates are vulnerable to break-ins.

ANWB Parking Amsterdam Centraal

Prins Hendrikkade 20A, Old Centre: New Side (638 5330). **Open** 24hrs daily. **Rates** €3.50/hr; €45/24hrs. **Credit** AmEx, DC, MC, V. **Map** p326 D2.
Many nearby hotels offer a 10% discount on parking here.

Europarking

Marnixstraat 250, Oud West (0900 446 6880, €0.45/min). **Open** 6.30am-1am Mon-Thur; 6.30am-2am Fri, Sat; 7am-1am Sun. **Rates** €2.80/60min; €30/24hrs. **Credit** AmEx, MC, V. **Map** p329 B4.

De Kolk Parking

Nieuwezijds Kolk, Old Centre: New Side (427 1449). **Open** 24hrs daily. **Rates** €3.80/hr; €40/24hrs. **Credit** MC, V. **Map** p326 C2.

Petrol

There are 24-hour petrol stations (*tankstations*) at Gooiseweg 10, Sarphatistraat 225, Marnixstraat 250 and Spaarndammerdijk 218.

Water transport

Boats to rent

Amsterdam is best seen from the water. Sure, there are canal cruises (*see below*), but they don't offer the freedom to do your own exploring. To follow our canal tour (*see p106* **Canal Dreams**), you can try to bond with a boat owner; otherwise your options are limited to the pedal-powered canal bike or pedalo. Upon rental, don't ignore the introductory run-down of the rules of the water (put simply: stick to the right and beware canal cruisers).

Canal Bike

Weteringschans 24, Southern Canal Belt (626 5574/www.canal.nl). **Open** *Summer* 10am-6pm; in nice weather till 9.30pm daily. *Winter* 10am-5.30pm daily at Rijksmuseum; weekends also at Westerkerk & Leidseplein. **Moorings** Leidsekade at Leidseplein; Stadhouderskade, opposite Rijksmuseum; Prinsengracht, by Westerkerk; Keizersgracht, on corner of Leidsestraat. **Hire** four-person pedalo if 1 or 2 people, €8/person/hr; if 3 or 4 people, €7/person/hr. **Deposit** €50/canal bike. **Credit** AmEx, MC, DC, V. **Map** p330 D5.

Canal buses

Canal Bus

Weteringschans 27, Southern Canal Belt (623 9886/www.canal.nl). Tram 6, 10. **Open** 10am-7pm daily. **Tickets** 1 day €17; €11 under-12s. 1 day incl entrance to Rijksmuseum or Van Gogh Museum €26 (not available during special exhibitions). I Amsterdam Transport Pass €33. **Credit** AmEx, MC, V. **Map** p330 D5.

The I Amsterdam Transport Pass is valid for one day plus the morning of the following day.

Water taxis

Water Taxi Centrale

Stationsplein 8, Old Centre: New Side (535 6363/www.water-taxi.nl). Tram 1, 2, 4, 5, 9, 13, 16, 17, 24, 25. **Open** 8am-midnight daily. **Rates** 1-8 person boat €60 for first 30min, then €40/30min. 9-12 person boat €120 for first 30min, then €80/30min. 13-25 person boat €155 for first 30min, then €100/30min. 26-44 person boat €170 for first 30min, then €100/30min. **Credit** AmEx, DC, MC, V (accepted only prior to boarding). **Map** p325 D1.

They can pick you up and drop you anywhere in the city as long as they can get to the edge of the waterway. Try to book in advance.

Cycling

Cycling is the most convenient means of getting from A to B: there are bike lanes on most roads, marked by white lines and bike symbols. Cycling two abreast is illegal, as is going along without reflectors on the wheels. At night you should use bike lights; the police set up periodic check points. Your option if you are stopped is to pay a fine or buy lights from the police on the spot. Watch out for pedestrians stepping into your path.

Never leave a bike unlocked: it will get stolen. Attach the bike to something immovable, preferably using two locks: around the frame and through a wheel. If someone on the street offers you a bike for sale (*fiets te koop*), don't be tempted: it's almost certainly stolen, and there are plenty of good and cheap bike hire companies around, of which we list a selection below. Apart from these, check the *Gouden Gids* under the section 'Fietsen en Bromfietsen Verhuur'.

Note that almost all bikes in Amsterdam now use the reverse-pedal brake system rather than manual brakes attached to handlebars. Those used to the latter will find that this takes some getting used to, so be sure to practise before setting out on the streets.

You can also hail a 'bicycle cab' or order one with at least a day's notice (06 1859 5153 same day, 06 4158 5012 booking, www.wielertaxi.nl). If you're wondering, it's basically a high-tech rickshaw. Rates €1/3 minutes per person; pets and children under 2 free; children aged 2-12 half-price. A €2.50 fee is applied for phone orders plus normal rates. For more on the Dutch bike obsession, *see p32* **Two wheels good**.

Bike City

Bloemgracht 68-70, the Jordaan (626 3721/www.bikecity.nl). Tram 10, 13, 14, 17. **Open** 9am-6pm daily. **Rates** from €8.50/day 9am-5.30pm. **Deposit** €25. **Credit** AmEx, DC, MC, V. **Map** p325 B3.

Mac Bike

Centraal Station, Stationsplein 12, Old Centre: New Side (620 0985/www.macbike.nl). Tram 1, 2, 4, 5, 9, 13, 16, 17, 24, 25. **Open** 9am-5.45pm daily. **Rates** from €6 for 3hrs; from €8.50/day. **Deposit** €50 with a passport or credit card imprint. **Credit** AmEx, MC, V. **Map** p326 D1.

Other locations
Weteringschans 2 (620 0985); M. Visserplein (620 0985).

Mike's Bike Tours

Kerkstraat 134, Southern Canal Belt (622 7970/www.mikesbiketoursamsterdam.com). Tram 1, 2, 5. **Open** 9am-6pm daily. *Dec-Feb* 10am-6pm daily. **Rates** from €7/day. **No credit cards**. **Map** p330 D4.
Guided tours available.

Rent-A-Bike

Damstraat 20-22, Old Centre: Old Side (625 5029/www.bikes.nl). Tram 4, 9, 14, 16, 24, 25. **Open** 9am-6pm daily. **Rates** €7 til 6pm; from €9.50 24hrs; €25 deposit and passport/ID card or credit card imprint. **Credit** AmEx, DC, MC, V. **Map** p326 D3.
A 10% discount (excluding deposit) if you mention *Time Out* when you hire your bicycle.

Resources A-Z

Addresses

Amsterdam addresses take the form of street then house number, such as Damrak 1.

Age restrictions

In the Netherlands, only those over the age of 16 can purchase alcohol (over 18 for spirits), while you have to be 16 to buy cigarettes (18 to smoke dope). Driving is limited to over-18s.

Attitude & etiquette

Amsterdam's reputation as a relaxed city is well-founded, as anyone will find out after even the shortest of wanders around the famous Red Light District. However, not everything goes. Smoking dope is not accepted everywhere: spliffing up in restaurants is usually frowned upon. And while most of its restaurants don't have dress codes, many nightclubs ban sportswear and trainers.

Business

The construction of a new Metro line linking north and south Amsterdam is indicative of the city's status as a big business centre. The south of Amsterdam is where most of the action is, with corporate hotels rubbing shoulders with the World Trade Center and the RAI convention centre. www.amsterdampartners.nl is a mine of useful information.

Banking

The branches listed below are head offices. Most do not have general banking facilities, but staff will be able to provide a list of branches that do. For information about currency exchange, *see p308.*

ABN-Amro

Vijzelstraat 68-78, Southern Canal Belt (628 9393/0900 0024/www.abnamro.nl). Tram 6, 7, 10, 16, 24, 25. **Open** 9am-5pm Mon-Fri. **Map** p330 D4.
Locations all over Amsterdam.

Fortis Bank

Singel 548, Old Centre: New Side (624 9340/0900 8172/www.fortisbank.nl). Tram 4, 9, 14, 16, 24, 25. **Open** 1-5pm Mon; 9.30am-5pm Tue-Fri. **Map** p330 D4.
Full facilities in 50 banks.

ING Group

Bijlmerplein 888, de Amsterdamse Poort (563 9111/0800 7011/www.ing.com). Metro Bijlmer/bus 59, 60, 62, 137. **Open** 9am-4pm Mon-Fri.
Incorporates Postbank (*see below*).

Postbank

Postbus 94780, 1090 GT (591 8200/www.postbank.nl). **Open** *Enquiries* 8.30am-5pm Mon-Fri.
One in every local post office.

Rabobank

Dam 16, Old Centre: New Side (777 8899/www.rabobank.nl). Tram 1, 2, 5, 9, 13, 14, 16, 17, 24, 25. **Open** 9am-6pm Mon-Fri; 10am-6pm Sat; noon-5pm Sun. **Map** p326 D2.
Some 30 locations in Amsterdam.

Conventions & conferences

Congrex Convention Services

AJ Ernststraat 595, Southern Canal Belt (504 0200/www.congrex.nl). Tram 5/Metro 51. **Open** 9am-5.30pm Mon-Thur; 9am-5pm Fri. **Credit** AmEx, DC, MC, V. **Map** p331 E4.
Specialists in teleconferencing. Phone for information and prices.

RAI Congresgebouw

Europaplein 8-22, Zuid (549 1212/www.rai.nl). Tram 4, 25/NS rail RAI Station. **Open** *Office* 9am-5.30pm Mon-Fri.
A congress and trade fair centre in the south. The building contains 11 halls and 22 conference rooms that can seat up to 1,750 people.

Stichting de Beurs van Berlage

Damrak 277, Old Centre: Old Side (530 4141/www.beursvanberlage.nl). Tram 4, 9, 14, 16, 24, 25. **Open** 9am-5pm Mon-Fri. **Map** p326 D2.
Used for cultural events and for smaller trade fairs. Berlage Hall is a meeting and conference venue for between ten and 2,000 people.

Couriers & shippers

FedEx

0800 022 2333 freephone/500 5699/www.fedex.com/nl_english. **Open** *Customer services* 8am-6.30pm Mon-Fri. **Credit** AmEx, DC, MC, V.

TNT

0800 1234/www.tnt.com. **Open** 24hrs daily. **Credit** AmEx, DC, MC, V.

Office hire & business services

Many tobacconists and copy shops also have fax facilities.

Avisco

Stadhouderskade 156, the Pijp (671 9909/www.acsavcompany.com). Tram 3, 4, 16, 24, 25. **Open** 8am-5pm Mon-Fri. **Credit** AmEx, MC, V. **Map** p331 F5.
Slide projectors, video equipment, screens, cameras, plus overhead projectors, microphones and tape decks hired out or sold.

Euro Business Center

Keizersgracht 62, Western Canal Belt (520 7500/www.eurobc.nl/eu). Tram 1, 2, 5, 13, 14, 17. **Open** 8.30am-5pm Mon-Fri. **Credit** AmEx, DC, MC, V. **Map** p326 C2.
Office leases from one day to two years, virtual offices, meeting rooms and secretarial services.

World Trade Center

Strawinskylaan 1, Zuid (575 9111/www.wtcamsterdam.com). Tram 5/NS rail Amsterdam Zuid-WTC Station. **Open** *Office & enquiries* 9am-5pm Mon-Fri.
Offices let for long or short term and assorted business services available, including secretarial.

Translators & interpreters

Amstelveens Vertaalburo

Ouderkerkerlaan 50, Amstelveen (645 6610/www.avb.nl). Bus 65, 170, 172. **Open** 9am-5pm Mon-Fri. **No credit cards**.
Translation and interpreter service for most languages.

Mac Bay Consultants

PC Hooftstraat 15, Museum Quarter (24hr phoneline 662 0501/www.macbay.nl). Tram 2, 3, 5, 12. **Open** 9am-7pm Mon-Fri. **No credit cards**. **Map** p330 C6.
Specialists in financial and legal document services.

Useful organisations

For details of embassies and consulates, *see p304*.

American Chamber of Commerce

Schiphol Boulevard 171, 1118 BG Luchthaven Schiphol (795 1840/www.amcham.nl). **Open** 9am-5pm Mon-Fri.

British Embassy

Commercial Department, Lange Voorhout 10, 2514 ED, The Hague (070 427 0427/fax 070 427 0345/ www.britain.nl). **Open** 9am-5.30pm Mon-Fri. *Enquiries* 2-4pm Mon-Fri. For details of the Amsterdam consulate, *see p304*.

Commissariaat voor Buitenlandse Investeringen Nederland

Bezuidenhoutseweg 16A, 2594 AV, The Hague (070 379 8818/ fax 070 379 6322/www.nfia.nl). **Open** 8am-6pm Mon-Fri.
The Netherlands Foreign Trade Agency: the first port of call for businesses relocating to Holland.

Euronext (Stock Exchange)

Beursplein 5, Old Centre: New Side (550 5555/www.euronext.com). Tram 4, 9, 14, 16, 24, 25. **Open** free tours; email to book. **Map** p326 D2.
Stock for listed Dutch companies is traded here, plus Nederlandse Termijnhandel, the commodity exchange for trading futures, and Optiebeurs, the largest options exchange in Europe.

EVD: Economische Voorlichtingsdienst

Juliana van Stolberglaan 148, 2595 CL, The Hague (070 778 8888/www.hollandtrade.com). **Open** 8am-5pm Mon-Fri.
Dutch Agency for International Business and Cooperation which incorporates the Netherlands Council for Trade Promotion (NCH), both handy sources of information. You need to make an appointment in advance; don't turn up on spec.

Home Abroad

Weteringschans 28, Southern Canal Belt (625 5195/fax 624 7902/www.homeabroad.nl). Tram 6, 7, 10. **Open** 10am-5.30pm Mon-Fri. **Map** p331 E5.
Assistance with all aspects of life and business in the Netherlands.

Kamer van Koophandel (Chamber of Commerce)

De Ruyterkade 5, the Waterfront (531 4000/fax 531 4799/www.kvk.nl). Tram 1, 2, 4, 5, 9, 13, 16, 17, 24, 25. **Open** 8.30am-5pm Mon, Tue, Thur, Fri; 8.30am-8pm Wed. **Map** p326 C1.
Lists of import/export agencies, government trade representatives and companies by sector.

Ministerie van Buitenlandse Zaken

Bezuidenhoutseweg 67, Postbus 20061, 2500 EB, The Hague (070 348 4787/fax 070 348 4787/www.minbuza.nl). **Open** 9am-12.30pm Mon-Fri for the legalisation of documents.
The Ministry of Foreign Affairs. Detailed enquiries may be referred to the EVD (*see above*). You can also obtain public information from the Postbus 51 infoline, which is available via the free telephone number 0800 8051 on working days from 9am to 9pm. You can also send an email to buza@postbus51.nl.

Ministerie van Economische Zaken

Bezuidenhoutseweg 30, 2594 AV, The Hague (070 379 8911/ 0800 646 3951/fax 070 379 4081/www.minez.nl). **Open** 9am-5.30pm Mon-Fri.
The Ministry of Economic Affairs can provide answers to general queries concerning the Dutch economy. Detailed enquiries tend to be referred to the EVD (*see above*).

Netherlands-British Chamber of Commerce

Oxford House, Nieuwezijds Voorburgwal 328L, Old Centre: New Side (421 7040/fax 421 7003/www.nbcc.co.uk). Tram 1, 2, 5, 13, 14, 17. **Open** 9am-5pm Mon-Fri. **Map** p326 D3.

Consumer

If you have any complaints about the service you received from Dutch businesses that you were unable to resolve with them, call the National Consumentenbond on 070 445 4545/www.consumentenbond.nl (9am-9pm Mon-Thur; 9am-6pm Fri, Dutch only) to get one-off advice at cost.

Customs

EU nationals over the age of 17 may import limitless goods into the Netherlands for their own personal use. Other EU countries may still have limits on the quantity of goods they permit on entry. For citizens of non-EU countries, the old customs limits still apply when travelling. These are:

- 200 cigarettes or 50 cigars or 250g (8.82oz) tobacco;
- 2 litres of non-sparkling wine or one litre of spirits (over 22 per cent alcohol) or 2 litres of fortified wine (under 22 per cent alcohol);
- 60cc/ml of perfume;
- 500 grams coffee or 200 grams coffee extracts/essence;
- 100 grams tea or 40 grams tea extracts/essence;
- other goods to value of €175.

The import of meat or meat products, fruit, plants, flowers and protected animals to the Netherlands is illegal. Check www.holland.com (look under Practical Info) or call the toll-free Customs Information Line (0800 0143).

Disabled

The most obvious difficulty people with mobility problems face here is negotiating the winding cobbled streets of the older areas. Poorly maintained pavements are widespread, and steep canal house steps can present problems. But the pragmatic Dutch can generally solve any problems quickly.

Most large museums have facilities for disabled users but little for the partially sighted and hard of hearing. Most cinemas and theatres have an enlightened attitude and are accessible. However, it's advisable to check in advance.

The Metro is accessible to wheelchair users who 'have normal arm function'. There is a taxi service for wheelchair users (*see p298*). Most trams are inaccessible to wheelchair users due to their steps. The AUB (various outlets; www.aub.nl) and the Amsterdam Tourist Board (*see p312*) has brochures on accommodation, restaurants, museums, tourist attractions and boat excursions with facilities for the disabled.

Drugs

The locals have a relaxed attitude to soft drugs, but smoking isn't acceptable everywhere, so use discretion. Outside Amsterdam, public consumption of cannabis is largely unacceptable. For more information on drugs in Amsterdam, *see pp50-54*.

Foreigners found with harder drugs should expect to face prosecution from the authorities. Organisations offering advice can do little to help foreigners with drug-related problems, although the Jellinek Drugs Prevention Centre is happy to provide help in several languages, including English. Its helpline (408 7774, 3-5pm Mon-Thur) offers advice and information on drugs and alcohol abuse. There's also a 24-hour crisis/detox emergency number: 408 7777.

Electricity

The voltage here is 220, 50-cycle AC and compatible with British equipment, but because the Netherlands uses two-pin

Please leave

A cross that Amsterdammers sometimes have to bear is the rabid – and often stoned – ravings of visitors who are so bowled over by Amsterdam's mellow vibe that they want to move here. One word: don't. If you feel this urge overcoming you, read the Irvine Welsh novels *Filth* and *Porno*, or spare a thought for what happened to Theo van Gogh.

The housing situation in Amsterdam is so dire that students are actually living in revamped containers (*see p44*). That's right, people are literally living in boxes. So if you do manage to get your hands on one of those rare apartments, the only result will be to piss off long-suffering Amsterdammers. In short: we don't want you here.

However, stubborn expat-wannabes do have access to **Access** (Herengracht 472, 423 3217, www.access-nl.org), a new, volunteer-driven organisation founded to answer any of the countless questions you may have about life in the Netherlands. The website www.amsterdampartners.nl can also be very helpful when it comes to setting up a business. But to find a flat, you will also need friends, money and loads of luck.

There are two main price bands at work: below €450 per month and above €450 per month. Anything above €450 is considered free sector housing and can be found through agencies or in newspapers (in particular, the Wednesday, Thursday and Saturday editions of *De Telegraaf* and *De Volkskrant*), and every Tuesday and Thursday in the ads paper *Via Via*. Unfortunately, flatsharing is not common, and agency commissions are high.

If you're looking for properties under the €450 mark, you have two main choices; both require a residents' permit (*see p312*). If you're studying here, register with **Woning Net** (0900 202 3072, www.woningnet.nl), which charges a €60 one-off fee that allows you to react to any vacancies available via all the big housing co-ops. However, this method can take for ever given the huge shortage of properties and surfeit of clients. The other alternative is to register with one of the many non-profit agencies that hold their property lotteries among would-be tenants. This may seem bizarre, but they do at least give you a chance of eventually getting a room, which you might not get otherwise. Telephone **ASW Kamerbureau** (Nieuwezijds Voorburgwal 32, 523 0130, www.steunpuntwonen.nl). Holders of residents' permits can also apply for council (public) housing. Alternatively, register with the **Stedelijke Woning Dienst** (City Housing Service; Jodenbreestraat 25, 680 6806, www.wonen.amsterdam.nl).

Whatever you do, you can bank on a very long wait before moving into that quaint canalside apartment you'd set your heart on.

continental plugs you'll need an adaptor. American visitors may need a transformer.

Embassies

American Consulate General

Museumplein 19, 1071 DJ (575 5309/0900 872 8472 premium rate/www.usembassy.nl). Tram 3, 5, 12, 16. **Open** *US citizens services* 8.30-11.30am Mon-Fri. *Immigrant visas* 1.30-3pm. **Map** p330 D6.

Australian Embassy

Carnegielaan 4, 2517 KH, The Hague (070 310 8200/0800 0224 794 Australian citizen emergency phone/www.australian-embassy.nl). **Open** 8.30am-5pm Mon-Fri. *Visa and immigration info* 9am-noon Mon-Fri.

This embassy cannot issue you visas or accept visa applications. The nearest Department of Immigration and Multicultural Affairs outpost is over at the Australian Embassy in Berlin, Germany. Note that only general visa information is available via the Visa Information Officer.

British Consulate General

Koningslaan 44, 1075 AE (676 4343/www.britain.nl). Tram 2. **Open** *British citizens* 8.30am-1.30pm Mon-Fri. *Phone enquiries* 2-5pm Mon-Thur; 2-4.30pm Fri. *Visa enquiries* by appointment only 3-4.30pm Mon-Fri.

British Embassy

Lange Voorhout 10, 2514 ED, The Hague (070 427 0427/www.britain.nl). **Open** 9am-5.30pm Mon-Fri.

For visa and tourist information, contact the Consulate (*see above*).

Canadian Embassy

Sophialaan 7, 2514 JP, The Hague (070 311 1600/www.canada.nl). **Open** 9am-1pm, 2-5.30pm Mon-Fri. *Consular and passport section* 10am-1pm, 2-4.30pm Mon-Fri.

Irish Embassy

Dr Kuyperstraat 9, 2514 BA, The Hague (070 363 0993/www.irishembassy.nl). **Open** 10am-12.30pm, 2.30-5pm Mon-Fri. *Visa enquiries* 10am-12.30pm Mon-Fri.

New Zealand Embassy

Eisenhowerlaan 77N, 2517 KK The Hague (070 346 9324/visas 070 365 8037/www.immigration.govt.nz/Branch/TheHagueBranchHome). **Open** 9am-12.30pm, 1.30-5.30pm Mon-Fri.

Emergencies

In an emergency, call **112**, free from any phone (mobiles included), and specify police, ambulance or fire service. For helplines, *see p306*; for hospitals, *see p305*; for police stations, *see p309*.

Gay & lesbian

Help & information

COC Amsterdam

Rozenstraat 14, the Jordaan (626 3087/www.cocamsterdam.nl). Tram 13, 14, 17. **Open** *Phone enquiries* 10am-4pm Mon-Fri. **Map** p325 B3.

The Amsterdam branch of COC deals with the social side of gay life in and around the capital.

COC National

Rozenstraat 8, the Jordaan (623 4596/textphone 620 7541/www.coc.nl). Tram 13, 14, 17. **Open** 9.30am-5pm Mon, Tue, Thur, Fri; 9.30am-1pm Wed. **Map** p326 C3.

COC's head office deals with all matters gay and lesbian.

Gay & Lesbian Switchboard

Postbus 11573, 1001 GN (623 6565/www.switchboard.nl). **Open** noon-10pm Mon-Fri; 4-8pm Sat, Sun.

Whether it's general information or safe-sex advice you're after, the friendly English-speakers here are well informed.

Homodok-Lesbisch Archief Amsterdam (Gay and Lesbian Archives)

Nieuwpoortkade 2A, Westerpark (606 0712/fax 606 0713/www.ihlia.nl). Tram 10, 12, 14. **Open** 10am-4pm Mon-Fri.

A non-lending library of books, journals, articles and a large video collection. The collection is due to move to the city's brand new Centrale Bibliotheek (*see p307*).

IIAV

Obiplein 4, Oost (665 0820/www.iiav.nl). Tram 3, 7, 10, 14/bus 15, 22. **Open** noon-5pm Mon; 10am-5pm Tue-Fri.

This women's archive moved to Berlin during World War II, where it vanished. In 1992, it was found in Moscow, but the Russians are still refusing to return it. The current collection, started after the war, is officially an archive, but there are a lot of other resources, including several online databases.

Het Vrouwenhuis (The Women's House)

Nieuwe Herengracht 95, Southern Canal Belt (625 2066/fax 538 9185/www.akantes.nl). Tram 7, 9, 14/Metro Waterlooplein. **Open** *Office* 10am-5pm Mon-Fri. *Library, internet café* noon-5pm Wed, Thur. **Map** p327 F3.

There's a well-stocked library here (membership is €12.50 per year), free internet facilities (see hours above), courses (mostly in Dutch) and women's events (check website).

Other groups & organisations

Dikke Maatjes

Postbus 15456, 1001 ML (www.dikkemaatjes.nl).

'Dikke Maatjes' means 'close friends', although its literal translation is 'fat friends'. And that's what this gay club is for: chubbies and admirers.

Mama Cash

PO Box 15686, 1001 ND (689 3634/fax 683 4647/www.mamacash.nl). **Open** 9am-5pm Mon-Fri.

Helps to fund women's groups and women-run businesses, and has sponsored countless lesbian organisations and events.

Netherbears

Postbus 15495, 1001 ML (www.netherbears.nl).

A hairy men's club. Check website.

Sportclub Tijgertje

Postbus 10521, 1001 EM (06 1024 9026/www.tijgertje.nl).

Tijgertje organises a wide variety of sports activities, from yoga to wrestling, for gays and lesbians, plus an HIV swimming group.

Wild Side
c/o COC Amsterdam, Rozenstraat 14, the Jordaan (071 512 8632/ www.wildside.dds.nl).
Group for woman-to-woman S&M, which holds workshops, parties, and publishes its own bilingual newsletter. Check the website for information on getting involved.

Health

As with any trip abroad, it's of course advisable to take out medical insurance before you leave. If you're a UK citizen, you should also get hold of an E111 form (*see p307*) to facilitate reciprocal cover. For emergency services, medical or dental referral agencies and AIDS/HIV info, *see below*.

Afdeling Inlichtingen Apotheken
694 8709.
A 24-hour service that can direct you to your nearest chemist.

Centraal Doktorsdienst/Atacom
592 3333/www.atacom.nl.
A 24-hour English-speaking line for advice about symptoms.

Accident & emergency

In the case of minor accidents, try the outpatient departments at the following major hospitals (*ziekenhuis*), all open 24 hours a day year-round. The Dutch emergency number is 112; for more information, *see p304*.

Academisch Medisch Centrum
Meibergdreef 9, Zuid (566 9111/first aid 566 3333). Metro Holendreschp/bus 59, 60, 120, 126.

Boven IJ Ziekenhuis
Statenjachtstraat 1, Noord (634 6346/first aid 634 6200). Bus 34, 36, 37, 39, 171, 172.

Onze Lieve Vrouwe Gasthuis
's Gravesandeplein 16, Oost (599 9111/first aid 599 3016). Tram 3, 6, 10/Metro Weesperplein or Wibautstraat.

St Lucas Andreas Ziekenhuis
Jan Tooropstraat 164, West (510 8911/first aid 510 8161). Tram 13/bus 19, 47, 80, 82, 97.

VU Ziekenhuis
De Boelelaan 1117, Zuid (444 4444/first aid 444 3636). Metro Amstelveenseweg/bus 142, 147, 148, 149, 170, 171, 172.

Contraception & abortion

Note that morning-after pills are available over the counter at pharmacies (*see below*).

Amsterdams Centrum Voor Seksuele Gezondheid
Sarphatistraat 618-626, Plantage (624 5426/www.acsg.nl). Tram 6, 9, 10, 14/bus 22. **Open** 9am-4pm Mon-Fri; 6-9pm Tues. **Map** p332 G3.
An abortion clinic. Besides giving information on health, the staff at this family-planning centre can help visitors with prescriptions for contraceptive pills, condoms, IUD fitting and cervical smears. Prescription charges vary. You must make an appointment.

Polikliniek Oosterpark
Oosterpark 59, Oost (693 2151/ emergencies after hours 592 3809/www.oosterparkkliniek.nl). Tram 3, 6, 9. **Open** *Advice* 9am-5pm daily. **Map** p332 H4.
Advice on contraception and abortion. Non-residents will be charged for an abortion based on the term of the pregnancy. The website is comprehensive and also contains information in English.

Dentists

For a dentist (*tandarts*), call 0900 821 2230. Operators can put you in touch with your nearest dentist; lines are open 24 hours. Alternatively, make an appointment at one of the clinics listed below.

AOC
Wilhelmina Gasthuisplein 167, Oud West (616 1234). Tram 1, 2, 3, 5, 6, 12. **Open** 9am-noon, 1-4pm Mon-Fri. **Map** p329 B5.
Emergency dental treatment. They also have a Dutch-language recorded phone service on 686 1109 that tells you where a walk-in clinic will be open at 11.30am and 9.30pm that day. Ask staff at your hotel to call if you're not confident of understanding Dutch.

TBB
570 9595/0900 821 2230.
A 24-hour service that can refer callers to a dentist. Operators can also give details of chemists open outside normal hours.

Opticians

For details of opticians and optometrists in Amsterdam, *see p177* or have a look under 'Opticiens' in the *Gouden Gids*.

Pharmacies

For pharmacy hours, see below. For pharmacies, *see p193*.

Prescriptions

All chemists (*drogists*) sell toiletries and non-prescription drugs and are usually open between 9.30am and 5.30pm, Monday to Saturday. For prescription drugs, go to a pharmacy (*apotheek*), usually open from 9.30am to 5.30pm, Monday to Friday. Outside these hours, phone Afdeling Inlichtingen Apotheken (*see above*) or consult the daily *Het Parool*, which publishes details of which *apotheken* are open late that week. Details are posted at local *apotheken*.

STDs, HIV & AIDS

The Netherlands was one of the first countries to pour money into research once the HIV virus was recognised. But though the country was swift to take action and promote safe sex, condoms are still not distributed free in clubs and bars as they are in the UK.

As well as the groups listed below, all of which can provide assistance, the AIDS Helpline

Word on the street

You've just arrived in town and you want to plan a fun and memorable night out. What's it going to be? A comedy, film, play, gig, hip club or underground party? And where do you look for an up-to-date diary of what's going on for the rest of your stay?

Like most European cities, Amsterdam has lots of free listings magazines, a phenomenon that began a few years back with a sudden outburst of freebies including *nl20* and *Zone020*, both in full colour and in Dutch.

Neither makes for a particularly exciting read, even if you've mastered the language. Sure, they're handy for hints on what's on where, but it's all so blandly written to a tried-and-tested format. Then there's *PS*, the excellent Saturday cultural supplement to newspaper *Het Parool*. It's also full of listings, but again it's written entirely in Dutch.

Look out, then, for **Amsterdam Weekly**. As the name suggest, this is an English-language city paper, and every Wednesday you can pick up a fresh copy in cafés, shops, bars, cinemas and other cultural places – or simply download a PDF copy from its website (www.amsterdamweekly.nl). Although written in English, it's neither an expat paper nor aimed at tourists. Far from it: it just happens to be written in English – which is pretty handy for you. Apart from the extensive listings and previews, it carries articles, both lighthearted and serious, about people and politics in this city, plus a weekly restaurant review by the inimitable Undercover Glutton, so finding a decent restaurant (or knowing which ones to avoid) is easily sorted out.

The paper was modelled upon the *Chicago Reader*, a long-established and successful free city paper, and the *Weekly* has already won six European Newspaper Awards in its three-year existence.

Although some of them are Dutch, the writers for *Amsterdam Weekly* hail from all over the world, something adding real character to the paper. Different as they are, these people have one thing in common: they love to write about their town and to share ideas, opinions and stories with their readers. Many of them have contributed to this guide, as they know the city inside out.

Do yourself a favour and look for a copy as soon as you arrive, as it makes a perfect addition to this guide, not to mention a fun companion for your stay.

(689 2577, open 2-10pm Mon-Fri for personal assistance), part of HIV Vereniging (*see below*), offers advice and can put you in contact with every department you need. Also, the city's health department, the GGD, runs its own free STD clinics that are both completely anonymous and open to everyone.

GGD

Weesperplein 1 (555 5822/www.ggd.amsterdam.nl). Tram 9,14/ Metro Waterlooplein. **Open** 8.30-10.30am, 1.30-3.30pm Mon-Fri. **Map** p327 E3.

Examinations and treatment of STDs, including an HIV test, are free. Walk in or call to book an appointment.

HIV Vereniging

1e Helmersstraat 17 B3, Oud West (689 3915/www.hivnet.org, www.hivsite.nl). Tram 1, 2, 3, 5, 6, 12. **Open** 9am-5pm Mon-Fri. **Map** p330 C5.

The Netherlands HIV Association supports the interests of those who are HIV positive, including offering legal help, and produces a bi-monthly Dutch magazine, *HIV Nieuws* (€38 per year). There's an HIV café every Sun (4-8pm), a buffet on the first Sun of the month (5.30pm, call by Fri to reserve, cost €5),Tue dinners (from 6pm, cost €5); and Wed lunch (from 12.30pm, cost €2.50). Checkpoint is located here. You can get HIV test results in one hour. Call 689 2577 (2-6pm Mon-Fri) to make an appointment for the Friday evening clinic or walk in Fridays between 7pm and 9pm.

Schorer Gay and Lesbian Health

Sarphatistraat 35, Southern Canal Belt (573 9444/fax 664 6069/www.schorer.nl). Tram 7, 10. **Open** 9am-5pm Mon-Fri. **Map** p331 F4.

This state-funded agency offers psycho-social support, education and HIV prevention for gays and lesbians in Amsterdam. The staff are all very well informed and speak excellent English.

Stichting AIDS Fonds

Keizersgracht 390-392, Western Canal Belt (626 2669/fax 627 5221/www.aidsfonds.nl). Tram 1, 2, 5. **Open** 9am-5pm Mon-Fri. **Map** p330 C4.

This group runs fundraisers and channels money into research and safe sex promotion. It also runs a AIDS/STD info line for gay and lesbian-specific health questions (0900 204 2040, 2-10pm Mon-Fri) and runs workshops on anal sex. Parts of its website are in English.

Helplines

Alcoholics Anonymous

625 6057/www.aa-netherlands.org. **Open** 24hr answerphone.

A lengthy but highly informative message in English/Dutch details times and dates of meetings, and contact numbers for counsellors. The website is in English and you can locate meetings per day or per town. The 24-hour live service is a pilot program and may not extend beyond summer 2007.

Narcotics Anonymous

662 6307. **Open** 24hr answerphone in English/Dutch with contact numbers of counsellors.

SOS Telephone Helpline

675 7575. **Open** 24hrs daily.
A counselling service – similar to the Samaritans in the UK and Lifeline in the US – for anyone with emotional problems, run by volunteers. English isn't always understood at first, but keep trying and someone will help you.

ID

Everyone is required to carry some sort of identification, especially when opening accounts at banks or other financial institutions, job seeking, applying for benefits, if found on public transport without a ticket, when going to a professional football match or if caught riding a bicycle without a light. You have to register with the local council, which is in the same building as the Aliens' Police (*see p312*).

Insurance

EU countries have reciprocal medical arrangements with the Netherlands. British citizens will need form E111, which can be found in leaflet T6 at UK post offices or obtained by filling in the application form in leaflet SA30, available from the Dutch Post Office. Read the small print so you know how to get treatment at a reduced charge: you may have to explain this to the Dutch doctor or dentist who treats you. If you need treatment, photocopy your insurance form and leave it with the doctor or dentist concerned. Not all treatments are covered by the E111 form, so do take out private travel insurance covering both your health and personal belongings. Citizens of other EU countries should make sure they have obtained one of the forms E110, E111 or E112; citizens of all other countries should take out insurance before their visit.

Internet

Among Amsterdam's ISPs are Xs4all (www.xs4all.nl) and Chello (www.chello.nl). All global ISPs have a presence here (check websites for a local number). Local hotels are increasingly well equipped, whether with dataports in the rooms or a terminal in the lobby. For a selection of websites, *see p313*.

Internet cafés

Easy Internet Café

Damrak 33 Old Centre (no phone/www.easyeverything.com). Tram 16, 24, 25. **Open** 9am-10pm daily. **Rates** from €2.50/unit. **No credit cards**. **Map** p331 D4.
The amount of time one unit buys depends on how busy the place is: it can be as little as a half-hour or as much as six hours. Passes for one to 30 days are also available.

Freeworld

Nieuwendijk 30, Old Centre: New Side (620 0902/www.freeworld-internetcafe.nl). Tram 1, 2, 5, 13, 17, 20. **Open** 9am-1am Mon-Thur, Sun; 9am-3am Fri, Sat. **Rates** €1/30min. **No credit cards**. **Map** p326 D2.
You surf, you drink: refreshments are compulsory for customers.

Internet Café

Martelaarsgracht 11, Old Centre: New Side (no phone/www.internetcafe.nl). Tram 4, 9, 16, 20, 24, 25. **Open** 9am-1am Mon-Thur, Sun; 9am-3am Fri, Sat. **Rates** around €1/30min. **No credit cards**. **Map** p326 D2.
Compulsory drinks are offered frequently by the staff.

Left luggage

There is a staffed left-luggage counter at Schiphol Airport (601 2443, www.schiphol.nl) where you can store luggage for up to one month, open from 7am to 10.45pm daily, (€5/item/24hrs, €3.50/item/each 24hrs after). There are also lockers in the arrival and departure halls, while in Amsterdam there are lockers at Centraal Station with 24-hour access (from €4/24hrs).

Legal help

ACCESS

Herengracht 472 2nd flr (423 3217/www.access-nl.org). **Open** *Helpline* 10am-4pm Mon-Fri. *Visits* by appointment only.
The Administrative Committee to Coordinate English Speaking Services provides assistance in English through an information line, workshops and counselling.

Juridisch Loket

Vijzelgracht 21-25, Old Centre: New Side (0900 8020/www.hetjl.nl). Tram 1, 2, 5. **Open** 9am-5pm Mon-Fri; 9am-8pm Wed. **Map** p326 C3.
Qualified lawyers offering free or low-cost legal advice.

Libraries

You'll need to show proof of residence in Amsterdam and ID to join a library (*bibliotheek*) and borrow books. It costs €23 (23s-64s) or €13.50 (19s-22s, over-65s) per year and is free for under-18s. However, in public libraries (*openbare bibliotheek*) you can read books, papers and magazines without membership. For university libraries, *see p311*.

Centrale Bibliotheek

Oosterdokseiland 587, Old Center (523 0900/www.oba.nl). Tram 1, 2, 5. **Open** 1-9pm Mon; 10am-9pm Tue-Thur; 10am-7pm Fri; 10am-5pm Sat; *Oct-Mar* also 10am-5pm Sun. **Map** p327 E1.
Set to open its doors at time of going to press, this huge building will be the largest public library in Europe, complete with countless mod cons. Anyone can use the main public library for reference purposes. There's also a variety of English-language books.

Lost property

Report lost property to the police immediately; *see p309*. If you lose your passport, inform your embassy or consulate as well. For things lost at the Hoek van Holland ferry terminal or Schiphol Airport, contact the company you're travelling with. For lost credit cards, *see p309*.

Centraal Station

Stationsplein 15, Old Centre: Old Side (0900 321 2100/www.ns.nl). Tram 1, 2, 4, 5, 9, 13, 16, 17, 24, 25. **Open** 8am-6pm Mon-Fri; 7am-5pm Sat. **Map** p326 D1.

Items found on trains are kept here for three days (it's easiest to just go to any window where they sell tickets and ask) and then sent onwards to Centraal Bureau Gevonden Voorwerpen (Central Lost Property Office), 2e Daalsedijk 4, 3551 EJ Utrecht (030 235 3923, 8am-5pm Mon-Fri). Items are held for three months. To pick up costs €10, posting costs €15 and up.

GVB Lost Property

Arlandaweg 100, (0900 8011/ 460 6060). Tram 12. **Open** 9am-4pm Mon-Fri. **Map** p326 C1.

Wait at least a day or two before you call, describe what you lost on bus, metro or tram, and leave a number. They will call you back if it is found. Alternatively, there is an online form at www.gvb.nl (in Dutch) that a friend or hotel staff can help you fill in.

Police Lost Property

Stephensonstraat 18, Zuid (559 3005). Tram 12/Metro Amstel Station/bus 14. **Open** *In person* 9.30am-3.30pm Mon-Fri. *By phone* noon-3.30pm Mon-Fri.

Before contacting here, check the local police station.

Media

Newspapers & magazines

De Telegraaf is the country's biggest-selling paper, the nearest it has to a tabloid. *Het Parool* is a hip afternoon rag and rates as the Amsterdam paper (its own Saturday PS supplement also has easily decipherable entertainment listings). *De Volkskrant*'s readers are young liberals while *NRC Handelsblad* is the highbrow national.

For Anglophones, the Amsterdam Tourist Board publishes the monthly *Day by Day*, a basic listings guide available at VVV Tourist offices (€1.95), but the only local English-language paper is *Amsterdam Weekly* (*see p306* **Word on the street**).

Foreign magazines and papers are widely available, but pricey; British papers are around €2 for a daily, €4 for a Sunday. Athenaeum is a browser's dream; 100 metres away, Waterstone's stocks UK publications, and the American Book Center is nearby. For all, *see p173*.

Broadcast media

Besides the national basics (Ned 1, Ned 2 and Ned 3), Amsterdam also has its own 'city CNN' – the really quite cool AT5 (its site www.at5.nl has some English) – as well as Salto, which broadcasts typically local and low-budget culture/ cult stuff. There are also about a dozen national commercial stations; they include Yorin and Veronica (both painfully commercial); and NET5, RTL4 and RTL5 (mostly series and films from the US). There are now about 30 extra channels on cable, including stations in German, French, Italian and Belgian, various local channels, and multinationals such as BBC World, CNN and National Geographic. The basic deal includes BBC1 and BBC2, so no need to miss out on an episode of *EastEnders*. The wall-to-wall porn is largely an urban myth, so don't expect any late-night thrills unless your hotel has the 'extended service', which usually also features films, Discovery, Eurosport and other cable stalwarts. Dutch radio is generally as bland as the TV, but at least Radio Netherlands (www.rnw.nl) often has some interesting programming in English.

Money

Since January 2002 the Dutch currency has been the Euro.

ATMs

It's hard to believe, but so far cash machines are only found at banks here: as yet, no bank has been resourceful enough to set any up in shops or bars, as is increasingly the case in the UK and parts of the US. If your cashcard carries the Maestro or Cirrus symbols you should be able to withdraw cash from ATMs, though it's still worth checking with your bank a) that it's possible and b) what the charging structure is.

Banks

Amsterdam is a capital that clearly boasts more than its fair share of enormous banks. There's usually little difference between the rates of exchange offered by banks and bureaux de change, but banks tend to charge less commission. Most banks are open 9am to 5pm, Monday to Friday, with the Postbank opening on Saturday mornings as well. Dutch banks will buy/sell foreign currency and also exchange travellers' cheques, but few of them will give cash advances against credit cards. For a full list of banks, *see p301*, or check *Gouden Gids* under 'Banken'.

Bureaux de change

A number of bureaux de change can be found in the city centre. Those listed offer reasonable rates, though they usually charge more than banks. Hotel and tourist bureaux cost more.

GWK Travelex

Centraal Station, Old Centre: Old Side (0900 0566 €0.25/min/www.gwktravelex.nl). Tram 1, 2, 4, 5, 9, 13, 16, 17, 24, 25. **Open** 8am-10pm daily (Sun from 9am). *Telephone enquiries* 8am-11pm daily. **Map** p326 D1.
Other locations: Leidseplein 107-109 (8.30am-10pm daily); Schiphol Airport (7am-10pm daily); Damrak 86 (10am-10pm daily); Dam 23-25 (9.15am-7pm Mon-Sat, 10.15am-5.45pm Sun); Damrak 1-5 (9am-8pm daily); Leidseplein 31A (9.15am-5.45pm daily).

Credit cards

Credit cards are widely used. The majority of restaurants will take at least one type of card; they're less popular in bars and shops, so always carry some cash. Chip and pin is more and more prevalent. The most popular cards, in descending order, are Visa, Mastercard (aka Eurocard), American Express and Diners Club. If you lose your card, call the relevant 24-hour number immediately.
American Express 504 8666, freephone 0800 023 3405.
Diners Club 654 5511.
Mastercard/Eurocard 030 283 5555 if card was issued in the Netherlands; otherwise, freephone 0800 022 5821.
Visa 660 0611 if card was issued in the Netherlands; otherwise, freephone 0800 022 3110.

Tax

Sales tax (aka VAT) – 19 per cent on most items, six per cent on goods such as books and food, more on alcohol, tobacco and petrol – will be included in the prices quoted in shops. If you live outside the EU, you are entitled to a tax refund on purchases of up to €137 from one shop on any one day. At shops with the Global Refund Tax Free Shopping sign get the assistant to give you a Global Refund Cheque (export certificate), and then, as you leave the country, present it to a customs official who'll stamp it; you can then collect your cash at the ABN-AMRO bank at Schiphol Airport or via post at a later date (ask the official for information).

Opening hours

For all our listings in this guide we give full opening times, but as a general rule, shops are open from 1pm to 6pm on Monday (if they're open at all; many shops are closed Mondays); 10am to 6pm Tuesday to Friday, with some open until 9pm on Thursdays; and 9am to 5pm on Saturdays. Smaller shops are more erratic; if in doubt, phone. For shops that open late, *see p187*.

The city's bars tend to open at various times during the day and close at around 1am throughout the week, except for Fridays and Saturdays, when they stay open until 2am or 3am. Restaurants generally open in the evening from 5pm until 11pm (though some close as early as 9pm); many are closed on Sunday and Monday.

Police stations

Dutch police (www.politie-amsterdam-amstelland.nl, some English), are under no obligation to grant a phone call to those they detain – they can hold people for up to six hours for questioning if the alleged crime is not serious, 24 hours for major matters – but they'll phone the relevant consulate on behalf of a foreign detainee. If you are a victim of a crime, require practical or medical support, or have lost your documents – anything really that might go wrong as a tourist – the Police Station on Nieuwezijds Voorburgwal has a special Amsterdam Tourist Assistance Service (ATAS, see below). For emergencies, *see p304*. There is also a 24-hour police service line 0900 8844 for the Amsterdam area. You can also call 0800 7000 to report a crime anonymously.

Hoofdbureau van Politie (Police Headquarters)

Elandsgracht 117, the Jordaan (0900 8844). Tram 7, 10. **Open** 24hrs daily. **Map** p330 C4.

Amsterdam Tourist Assistance Service (ATAS)

Nieuwezijds Voorburgwal 104-108 (625 3246). Tram 1, 2, 5, 6, 13, 17. **Open** 10am-10pm daily. **Map** p326 C2.

Postal services

For post destined for outside Amsterdam, use the *overige bestemmingen* slot in regular letter boxes. The logo for the national postal service is TNT Post (orange letters on a white background). While orange is their main branding colour, many post boxes remain red. Most post offices (recognisable by their orange and blue signs) are open 9am to 5pm, Monday to Friday. The national postal information phone line is 058 233 3333. Housed in all post offices is a Postbank, a money-changing facility. It costs €0.67 to send a postcard to anywhere in Europe; €0.89 to send it to coutries outside of Europe. As well as in all post offices, stamps (*postzegels*) can also be bought from tobacconists and souvenir shops across Amsterdam.

Post offices

For all the post offices in the region, look in *Gouden Gids* under 'Postkantoren'. One of the handier central branches is Waterlooplein 10 (Jodenbuurt, 0900 767 8526, 9am-6pm Mon-Fri, 10am-2pm Sat).

Main Post Office

Singel 250, Old Centre: New Side (0900 767 8526). Tram 1, 2, 5, 13, 14, 17. **Open** 9am-6pm Mon-Fri; 10am-2pm Sat. **Map** p326 C3.

Post restante/ general delivery

Post Restante

Hoofdpostkantoor, Singel 250, 1016 AB Amsterdam. **Map** p326 C3.

If you're not sure where you're going to end up staying in the city – and some visitors remain unsure throughout their visit – people can send post to the above address. You'll be able to collect it from the main post office (*see p309*); take along some picture ID when you're collecting your mail.

Religion

Catholic

St John and St Ursula Begijnhof *30, Old Centre: New Side (622 1918/www.begijnhofamsterdam.nl). Tram 1, 2, 4, 5, 16, 24, 25.* **Open** *Chapel* 1-6.30pm Mon; 9am-6.30pm Tue-Fri; 9am-6pm Sat, Sun. *Adoration of the Eucharist* 4-5pm, 5.30-6.30pm Mon-Fri; 5-6pm Sat, Sun. *Services* 9am, 5pm Mon-Fri, 9am Sat; 10am (in Dutch), 11.15am (in French) Sun. Phone for details. **Map** p326 D3.

Check out the Begijnhof Shop tourist information and also religious books and souvenirs.

Dutch Reformed Church

Oude Kerk, Oudekerksplein, Old Centre: Old Side (625 8284/www.oudekerk.nl). Tram 4, 9, 16, 24, 25. **Open** 11am-5pm Mon-Sat; 1-5pm Sun. *Services in Dutch* 11am Sun. **Map** p326 D2.

Based at the stunning Oude Kerk (Old Church; *see p84*).

Jewish

Liberal Jewish Community Amsterdam *Jacob Soetendorpstraat 8, Zuid (540 0120/office rabbinate 540 0136/www.ljgamsterdam.nl). Tram 4.* **Open** *Rabbi's office* call for appointment. *Services* 8pm Fri; 10am Sat.

Orthodox Jewish Community Amsterdam *Van der Boechorststraat 26, Zuid (646 0046/www.nihs.nl). Bus 69, 169.* **Open** 9am-5pm Mon-Fri by appointment only. Information on orthodox synagogues and Jewish facilities. Website also has English content, including a list of places where you can buy and eat kosher.

Muslim

THAIBA Islamic Cultural Centre *Kraaiennest 125, Zuid (698 2526). Metro Gaasperplas.* Phone for details of mosques, prayer times and cultural activities.

Reformed Church

English Reformed Church *Begijnhof 48, Old Centre: New Side (624 9665/www.ercadam.nl). Tram 1, 2, 4, 5, 9, 16, 24, 25.* **Services** *in English* 10.30am Sun. **Map** p326 D3.

The main place of worship for the local English-speaking community.

Safety & security

Amsterdam is a relatively safe city, but that's not to say you shouldn't take care. The Red Light District is rather rife with undesirables who, if not violent, are expert pickpockets; do be vigilant, most especially on or around bridges, and try to avoid making eye contact with anyone who looks like they may be up to no good.

Take care on the train to Schiphol, where there's been a recent spate of thefts, and, if you cycle, lock your bike. Otherwise, just use common sense, keeping valuables in a safe place, not leaving bags unattended, and so on.

Smoking

Smoking is common, though an impending law (currently set for 2008) that aims to guarantee a smoke-free work environment for cafés, restaurants and bars may change that. Meanwhile, you'll have almost no problems sparking up. For information on dope laws, *see pp50-54*.

Study

Amsterdam's two major universities are the UvA (Universiteit van Amsterdam), which has around 27,000 students, and the VU (Vrije Universiteit), with 14,000. Many UvA buildings across town are historic and listed (recognise them by their red and black plaques), whereas the VU itself has just one big building at de Boelelaan, found in the south of Amsterdam.

Students are often entitled to discounts; presenting an ISIC card is usually enough.

Courses

A number of UvA departments offer both international courses and programmes at all levels. Details are available from the Office of Foreign Relations (Binnengasthuisstraat 9, 1012 ZA, 525 8080).

Amsterdam-Maastricht Summer University

Felix Meritis Building, Keizersgracht 324, Southern Canal Belt (620 0225/www.amsu.edu). Tram 1, 2, 5. **Courses** mid July-early Sept. **Map** p330 C4.

AMSU has a summer programme of courses, workshops and also seminars in the arts, economics, politics, sciences, European studies, plus classes in Maastricht.

Crea I

Turfdraagsterpad 17, Old Centre: Old Side (525 1400/www.crea.uva.nl). Tram 4, 9, 14, 16, 24, 25. **Open** *Office* 10am-5pm Mon-Thur. *Crea I* 10am-11pm Mon-Fri; 10am-5pm Sat; 11am-5pm Sun. **Map** p326 D3.

Inexpensive creative courses, lectures and also performances, covering theatre, radio, video, media, dance, music, photography and fine art. Courses are not in English. They've also got a new second branch to expand their offerings: Crea II, at Vendelstraat 2, (525 4889, open 10am-11pm Mon-Fri, 10am-5pm Sat).

UvA Service & Information Centre

Binnengasthuisstraat 9, Old Centre: Old Side (525 8080/www.english.uva.nl). Tram 4, 9, 16, 24, 25. **Open** *In person* 10am-5pm Mon-Fri. *Telephone enquiries* 9-10am Tue-Thur. *Free appointment* 11am-noon Tue-Thur. **Map** p326 D3.

Personal advice on studying and everything that goes with it.

VU Student Information

De Boelelaan 1105 (Office 598 7777/www.english.vu.nl). **Open** 9am-5pm Mon-Fri.
Courses and accommodation advice. Foreign students call the International Office (598 5035).

Student bookshop

VU Boekhandel

De Boelelaan 1105, Zuid (598 4000/www.vuboekhandel.nl). Tram 5/Metro 51. **Open** 9am-7pm Mon-Fri; 10am-3.30pm Sat. **Credit** AmEx, MC, V.

Students' unions

AEGEE

Vendelsstraat 2, Old Centre: Old Side (525 2496/www.aegee-amsterdam.nl). Tram 4, 6, 9, 24, 25. **Open** 2-5pm Mon-Fri. **Map** p326 D3.
The Association des Etats Généraux des Etudiants de l'Europe organises seminars, workshops, summer courses and sporting events.

SRVU

De Boelelaan 1083A, Zuid (598 9424/www.srvu.org). Tram 5/Metro 51. **Open** 1-4pm Mon-Fri.
SRVU is the union for VU students. It can help foreign students find a place to stay, and offers advice. Membership is €10 per year.

University libraries

Both libraries listed below hold many academic titles and also provide access to the internet. There is also an Adam Net-pas that allows you to use the UvA, VU libraries and public libraries (*openbare bibliotheek*), €35 a year with passport ID.

UvA Main Library

Singel 425, Old Centre: New Side (525 2055/www.uba.uva.nl). Tram 1, 2, 5. **Open** *Study* 8.30am-midnight Mon-Fri; 9.30am-5pm Sat; 11am-5pm Sun. *Borrowing* 9.30am-6pm Mon-Thur; 9.30am-5pm Fri; 9.30am-1pm Sat. **Map** p330 D4.
To borrow books you need a UB (*Universiteit Bibliotheek*, University Library) card (€22.50): foreign students can get one if they're in Amsterdam for three months or more. Cards can be issued for one day, one month or one year. Day (€20) and week (€7.50) cards will enable you to read books on the site but not withdraw them.

VU Main Library

De Boelelaan 1105, Zuid (598 5200/www.ubvu.vu.nl). Tram 5/Metro 51. **Open** *Study* 7am-11pm Mon-Fri; 8.15am-4pm Sat. *July, Aug* 8.15am-11pm Mon-Fri. *Borrowing* 9am-6pm Mon-Thur; 9am-5pm Fri.
Membership (€20/year) is open to foreign students.

Telephones

We list Amsterdam numbers without the city code, which is 020. To call within the city, you don't need the code: just dial the seven-digit number. To phone Amsterdam from elsewhere in the Netherlands, add 020 at the beginning of the listed number. Numbers in the Netherlands outside Amsterdam are listed with their code attached.

In addition to the standard city codes, three other types of numbers appear from time to time in this book. 0800 numbers are freephone numbers; those prefixed 0900 are charged at premium rates (€0.20 a minute or more); and 06 numbers are for mobile phones. If you're in doubt, call directory enquiries (0900 8008).

Dialling & codes

From the Netherlands

Dial the following code, then the number you're calling:
To Australia: 00 61
To Irish Republic: 00 353
To UK: 00 44, plus number (drop first '0' from area code)
To USA & Canada: 00 1

To the Netherlands

Dial the relevant international access code listed below, then the Dutch country code 31, then the number; drop the first '0' of the area code, so for Amsterdam use 20 rather than 020. To call 06 (mobile) numbers from abroad, there is no city code: just drop the first '0' from the 06 and dial the number as it appears after. However, 0800 (freephone) and 0900 (premium rate) numbers cannot be reached from abroad.
From Australia: 00 11
From Irish Republic: 00
From UK: 00
From USA: 011

Within the Netherlands

National directory enquiries: 0900 8008 (€1.15/call)
International directory enquiries: 0900 8418 (€1.15/call)
Local operator: 0800 0101
International operator: 0800 0410

Making a call

Listen for the dialling tone (a hum), insert a phonecard or money, dial the code (none for calls within Amsterdam), then the number. A digital display on public phones shows credit remaining, but only those coins that are wholly unused are returned. Phoning from a hotel is pricey.

International calls

International calls can be made from all phone boxes. For more information on rates, phone international directory enquiries (cost €1.15) on 0900 8418.

Telephone directories

Found in post offices (*see p309*). When phoning for information services, taxis or train stations you may hear this recorded message: '*Er zijn nog drie* [3]/*twee* [2]/*een* [1] *wachtende(n) voor u.*' This tells you how many people are ahead of you in the telephone queuing system.

Public phones

Public phone boxes are mainly glass with a green trim. There are also telephone 'poles', identifiable by the KPN logo. Most phones take cards rather than coins, available from the Amsterdam Tourist Board, stations, post offices and tobacconists. You can also use credit cards to make calls from many phones across the city.

Mobile phones

Amsterdam's mobile network is run on a mix of the 900 and 1800 GSM bands, which means all dual-band UK handsets should work here. However, it's always best to check with your service provider that it has an arrangement with a Dutch provider. US phone users should always contact their provider before departure to check of any compatability issues that may arise.

Time

Amsterdam is an hour ahead of Greenwich Mean Time (GMT). All clocks on Central European Time (CET) now go back and forward on the same dates as GMT.

Tipping

Though a service charge will be included in hotel, taxi, bar, café and restaurant bills, it's polite to round your payment up to the nearest Euro for small bills and to the nearest five Euros for larger sums – though a standard 10% is becoming more and more common – leaving the extra in change rather than filling in the blank on a credit card slip. In taxis, most people tend to tip ten per cent.

Toilets

For men there are the historic green metal urinals and some weekend conveniences over at places like Leidseplein. For the ladies, it's a sadder story: public loos are rare, and you may also be forced to buy something in a bar or café. Note that urinating into canals is now an offence (*see p94* **Water, water everywhere**).

Tourist information

Amsterdam Tourist Board (VVV)

Stationsplein 10, Old Centre: New Side (0900 400 4040/www.visit amsterdam.nl). Tram 1, 2, 4, 5, 9, 13, 16, 17, 24, 25. **Open** 9am-5pm daily. **Map** p326 D1.
The main office of the VVV is right outside Centraal Station. English-speaking staff can change money and provide details on transport, entertainment, exhibitions and day-trips in the Netherlands. They also arrange hotel bookings for a fee of €15 by phone (*see p58*) or €3.50 at a VVV office, and excursions or car hire for free. There is a good range of brochures for sale detailing walks and also cycling tours, as well as cassette tours, maps and, for €1.95, their monthly listings magazine *Day by Day*. The info line features an English-language information service (€0.40/min).
Other locations: Leidseplein 1 (9.15am-5pm Mon-Thur, Sun; 9.15am-7pm Fri, Sat); Centraal Station, platform 2B 15 (8am-8pm Mon-Sat; 9am-5pm Sun); Schiphol Airport, arrivals 2 (7am-10pm daily).

Visas & immigration

Citizens from the rest of the EU, the USA, Canada, Australia and New Zealand only need a valid passport for a stay up to three months. Citizens of other countries should apply in advance for a tourist visa. Confirm visa requirements well before you plan to travel with your local Dutch embassy, or consult www.ind.nl (which has a 'residency wizard' that walks you through all the info you need for your country).

For stays longer than three months, apply for a residents' permit (MVV visa), generally easier to get if you're from one of the countries listed above. (Technically, EU citizens don't need a residents' permit, but they will be required for all sorts of bureaucratic functions.)

When you have an address, take your birth certificate to Dienst Vreemdelingenpolitie (Aliens' Police Station; Johan Huizingalaan 757, Slotervaart; 559 6161/www.ind.nl), pick up or download a form and wait for an interview.

When to go

Climate

Amsterdam's climate is extremely changeable. January and February are cold, with summer humid. If you know Dutch, try the weather line on 0900 8003 (€0.60/min). *See also p298* **Weather report**.

Public holidays

Called *Nationale Feestdagen* in Dutch, they are as follows: New Year's Day; Good Friday; Easter Sunday and Monday; Koninginnedag (Queen's Day, 30 April); Remembrance Day (4 May); Liberation Day (5 May); Ascension Day; Whit (Pentecost) Sunday and Monday; Christmas Day, and Boxing Day.

Women

Aside from some pockets of the Red Light District late at night, central Amsterdam is fairly safe for women, as long as usual common-sense safety precautions are observed while wandering around alone.

De Eerstelijn and Meldpunt Vrouwenopvang

611 6022. **Open** 24hrs.
Call this number for support if you have been a victim of rape, assault, sexual harassment or threats. In cases of immediate threat or violence you will be referred to a safe house.

Working in Amsterdam

EU nationals with a residents' permit can work here; non-EU citizens will find it difficult to get a visa without a job in place. Jobs are hard to come by; more so with no visa. *See also p303* **Please leave**.

Further Reference

Books

Fiction

Baantjer *De Cock* series
This ex-Amsterdam cop used his experiences to write a series of crime novels set in town. Also a TV series.
Albert Camus *The Fall*
Man recalls his Parisian past while in Amsterdam's 'circles of hell'.
Arnon Grunberg *Blue Mondays*
Philip Roth's *Goodbye Columbus* goes Dutch in this 1994 bestseller.
Harry Mulisch *The Assault*
A boy's perspective on World War II. Also classic film.
Multatuli *Max Havelaar or the Coffee Auctions of the Dutch Trading Company*
The story of a colonial officer and his clash with the corrupt government.
Janwillem van der Wetering *The Japanese Corpse*
An off-the-wall police procedural set in Amsterdam.
Manfred Wolf (ed) *Amsterdam: A Traveller's Literary Companion*
The country's best writers tell tales of the city.

Non-fiction

Kathy Batista & Florian Migsch *A Guide to Recent Architecture: The Netherlands*
Part of the excellent pocket series, with great pictures.
Sean Condon *My 'Dam Life*
Offbeat insights by Australian wit.
Anne Frank *The Diary of Anne Frank*
The still-shocking wartime diary of the young Frank.
RH Fuchs *Dutch Painting*
A comprehensive guide.
Zbigniew Herbert *Still Life with a Bridle*
The Polish poet and essayist meditates on the Golden Age.
Etty Hillesum *An Interrupted Life: The Diaries and Letters 1941-1943*
The moving wartime experiences of a young Amsterdam Jewish woman who died in Auschwitz.
Geert Mak *Amsterdam: A Brief Life of the City*
The city's history told through the stories of its people.
Simon Schama *The Embarrassment of Riches*
A lively social and cultural history of the Netherlands.
David Winners *Brilliant Orange: the Neurotic Genius of Dutch Football*
Excellent delve into the Dutch psyche that takes in much more than just football.
Wim de Wit *The Amsterdam School: Dutch Expressionist Architecture*
Early 20th-century architecture.

Music

Albums

Arling & Cameron *Music for Imaginary Films* (2000)
Showered with acclaim, eclectic duo reinvent the history of film soundtracks.
Chet Baker *Live at Nick's* (1978)
Accompanied by his favourite rhythm section, Chet soars in one of his best live recordings.
The Beach Boys *Holland* (1973)
Californians hole up in Holland and start recording.
The Ex *Starters Alternators* (1998)
Anarcho squat punks/improv-jazzsters team up with Steve Albini.
Human Alert *Ego Ego* (2005)
Hysterically funny punk legends go orchestral.
Osdorp Posse *Origineel Amsterdams* (2000)
Nederhop maestros offer a primer in local street talk for *moederneukers*.

Films

Amsterdam Global Village
dir. Johan van der Keuken (1996)
A meditative and very long arty cruise through Amsterdam's streets and peoples.
Amsterdamned
dir. Dick Maas (1987)
Thriller with psychotic frogman and lots of canal chase scenes, made only slightly worse by continuity problems that result in characters turning an Amsterdam corner and ending up in Utrecht.
The Fourth Man
dir. Paul Verhoeven (1983)
Mr *Basic Instinct* films Gerard Reve novel with Jeroen Krabbe seething with homoerotic desire.
Hufters en Hofdames (Bastards and Bridesmaids)
dir. Eddy Terstall (1997)
Twentysomethings use Amsterdam as backdrop against which to have relationship trouble.
Karacter (Character)
dir. Mike van Diem (1997)
An impeccable father-son drama.
De Noorderlingen (The Northerners)
dir. Alex van Warmerdam (1992)
Absurdity and angst in a lonely Dutch subdivision.
Turks Fruit (Turkish Delight)
dir. Paul Verhoeven (1973)
Sculptor Rutger Hauer witnesses his babe's brain tumour.
Yes Nurse! No Nurse!
Dir. Pieter Kramer (2002)
Musical cult classic for connoisseurs of camp.
Zusje (Little Sister)
dir. Robert Jan Westdijk (1995)
A family affair with voyeuristic overtones.

Websites

www.amsterdam.nl
An accessible site with advice on living in and visiting Amsterdam. The searchable maps are terrific.
www.amsterdamhotspots.nl
An upbeat review-based site of, er, Amsterdam hotspots.
www.amsterdam-webcams.com
Some personal, some public, all in Amsterdam.
www.archined.nl
News and reviews of Dutch architecture, in both Dutch and English. Informative and interesting.
www.bmz.amsterdam.nl/adam
Fantastically detailed site devoted to Amsterdam's architectural heritage. Some pages in English.
www.channels.nl
Takes you, virtually, through Amsterdam's streets with reviews of their hotels, restaurants and clubs.
www.expatica.com
English news and reviews aimed at the expat in the Netherlands.
www.gayamsterdamlinks.com
What you'd expect.
www.panoramsterdam.nl
Over three hundred 360-degree shots of Amsterdam
gemeentearchief.amsterdam.nl
Dutch-only site of city archive.
www.nobodyhere.com
Winner of the 2003 Webby Award for best personal website. Weird and beautiful.
www.simplyamsterdam.nl
Aimed at the 'independent traveller'.
www.squat.net
The lowdown on the squat scene.
www.uitlijn.nl
Event listings for Amsterdam, in Dutch but fairly easy to navigate.
www.underwateramsterdam.com
An alternative listings e-mag in whose shallows several *Time Out* writers lurk.
www.urbanguide.nl
A guide to clubs, restaurants etc geared to the urban trendy hipster.
www.visitamsterdam.nl
The tourist board site which has gotten a tad hipper recently.
www.xs4all.nl/~4david
Drug techniques you never even knew existed.

Index

Numbers in **bold** indicate the key entry for the topic; numbers in *italics* indicate photos. Dutch personal names are indicated under their last element, eg Gogh, Vincent van.

b

j

m

n

Accommodation

Restaurants & cafés

Bars

Coffeeshops

Advertisers' Index

Please refer to the relevant pages for contact details

Selected House Number	*463*
Place of Interest and/or Entertainment	
Hospital or College	
Pedestrianised street	
Railway Station	
Metro Station	Ⓜ
Area Name	LEIDSEPLEIN

Maps

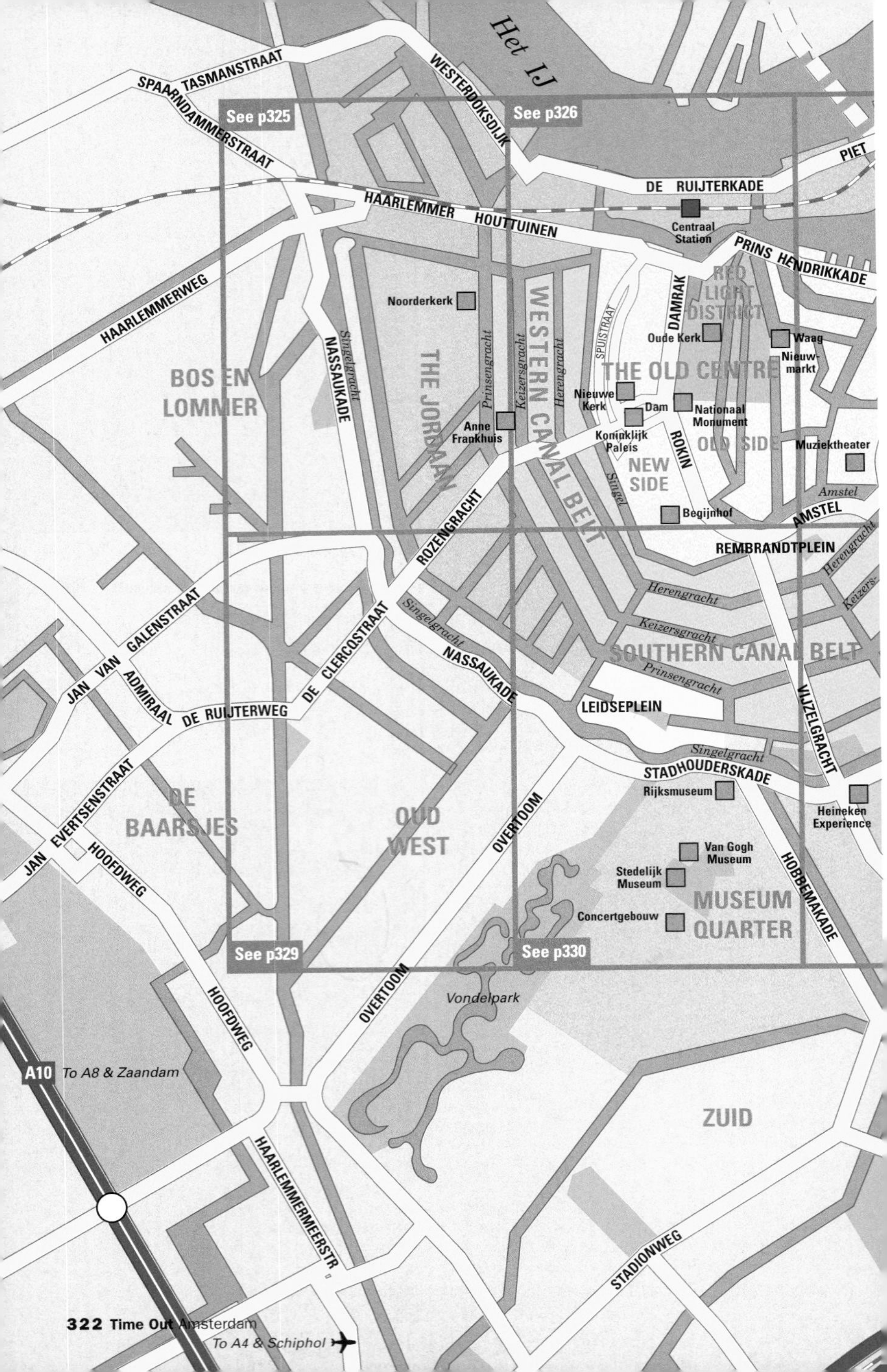
Het IJ
See p325
See p326
See p329
See p330
TASMANSTRAAT
SPAARNDAMMERSTRAAT
WESTERDOKSDIJK
DE RUIJTERKADE
PIET
HAARLEMMER HOUTTUINEN
Centraal Station
PRINS HENDRIKKADE
HAARLEMMERWEG
Noorderkerk
RED LIGHT DISTRICT
DAMRAK
Oude Kerk
Waag
Nieuwmarkt
SPUISTRAAT
THE OLD CENTRE
BOS EN LOMMER
NASSAUKADE
Singelgracht
THE JORDAAN
Prinsengracht
Keizersgracht
WESTERN CANAL BELT
Herengracht
Nieuwe Kerk
Dam
Nationaal Monument
Anne Frankhuis
Koninklijk Paleis
ROKIN
OLD SIDE
Muziektheater
NEW SIDE
Singel
Amstel
Begijnhof
AMSTEL
ROZENGRACHT
REMBRANDTPLEIN
Herengracht
Keizers-
Keizersgracht
JAN VAN GALENSTRAAT
DE CLERCQSTRAAT
NASSAUKADE
SOUTHERN CANAL BELT
Prinsengracht
ADMIRAAL DE RUIJTERWEG
LEIDSEPLEIN
VIJZELGRACHT
Singelgracht
STADHOUDERSKADE
Rijksmuseum
Heineken Experience
JAN EVERTSENSTRAAT
DE BAARSJES
OUD WEST
OVERTOOM
Van Gogh Museum
HOOFDWEG
Stedelijk Museum
HOBBEMAKADE
MUSEUM QUARTER
Concertgebouw
OVERTOOM
Vondelpark
HOOFDWEG
A10
To A8 & Zaandam
ZUID
HAARLEMMERMEERSTR.
STADIONWEG
To A4 & Schiphol

Amsterdam Overview

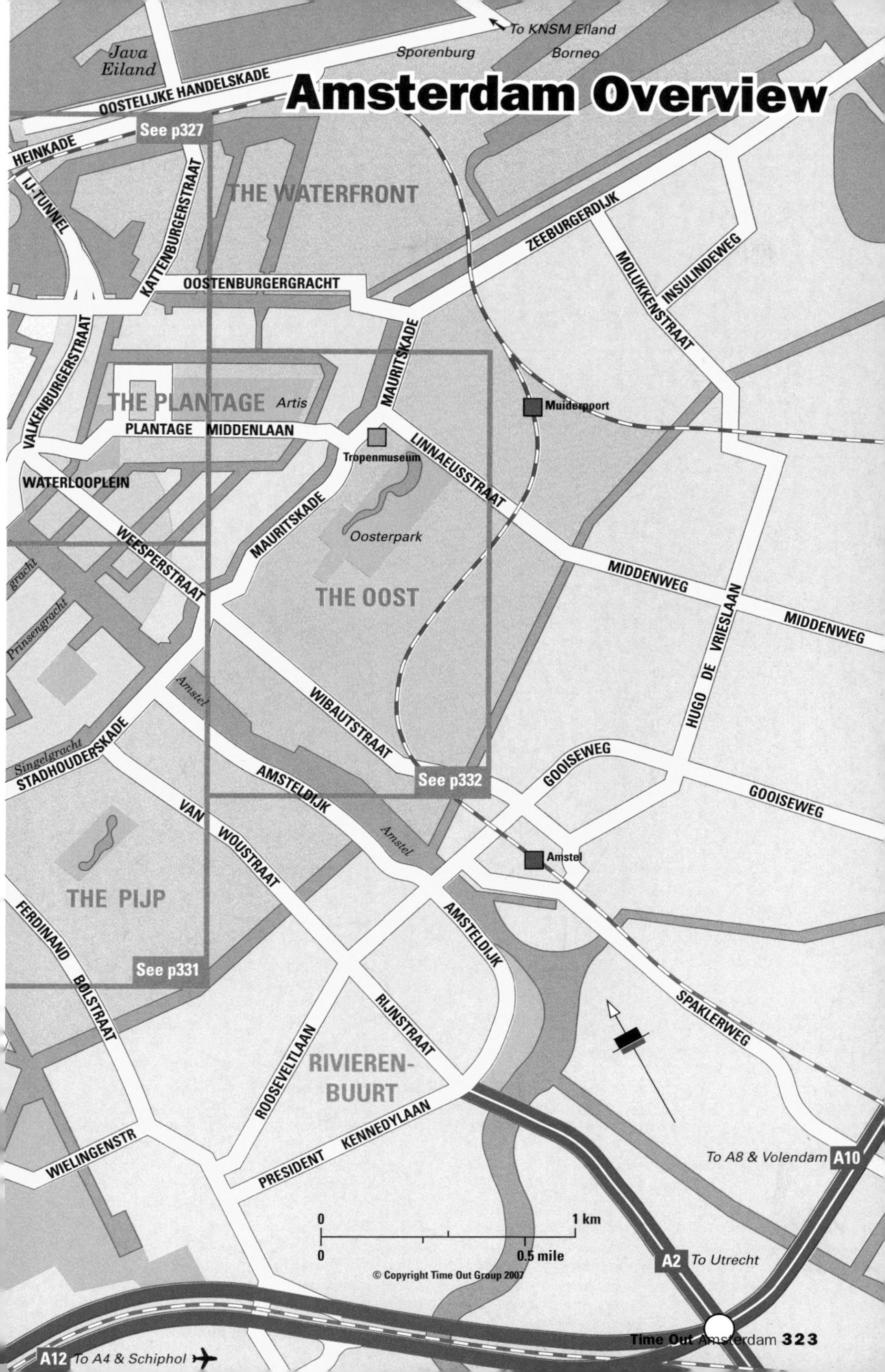

The Netherlands

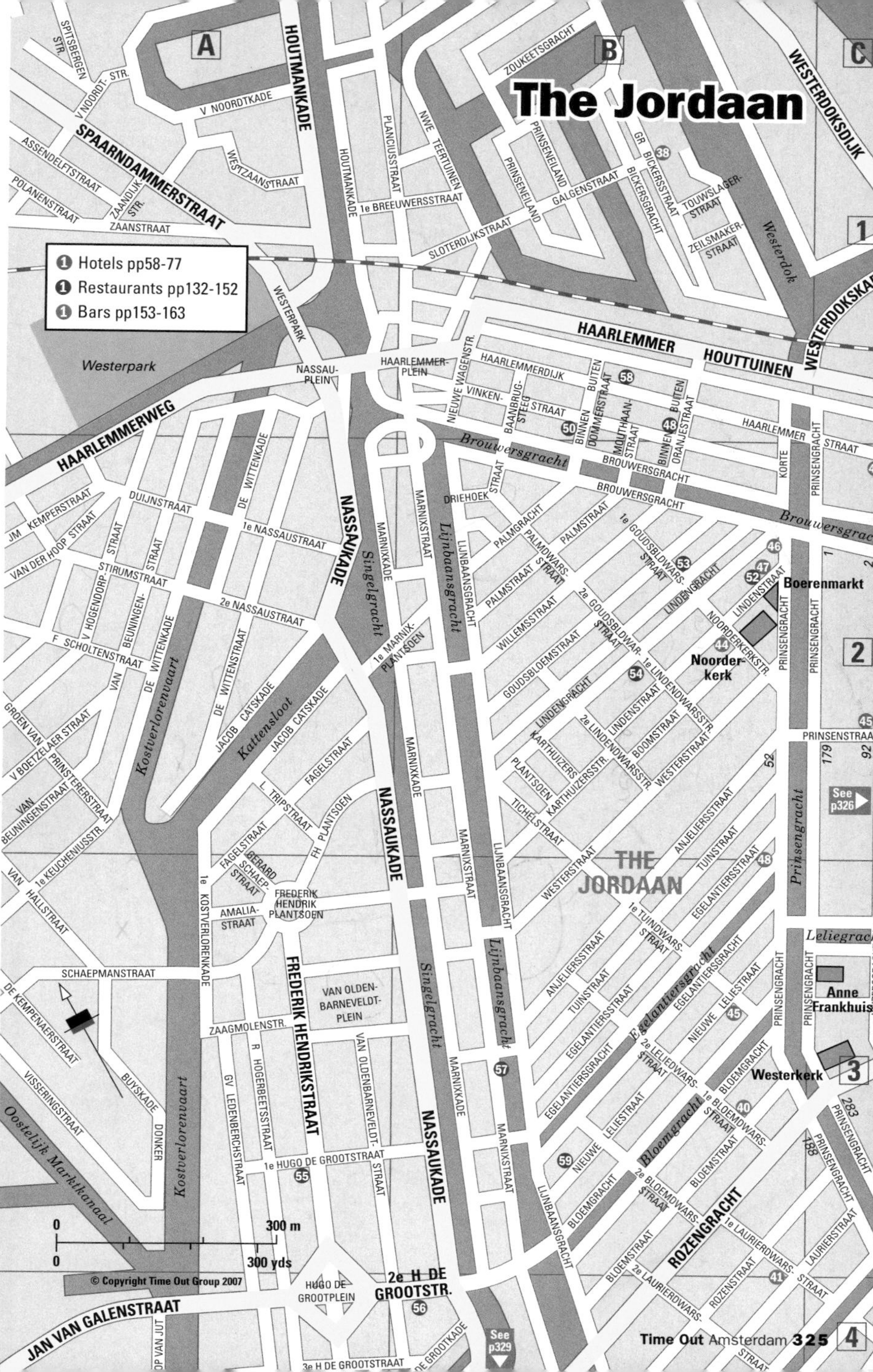
The Jordaan
A
B
C
1
2
3
4
❶ Hotels pp58-77
❶ Restaurants pp132-152
❶ Bars pp153-163
Westerpark
HAARLEMMERWEG
SPAARNDAMMERSTRAAT
HOUTMANKADE
V NOORDTKADE
V NOORDT- STR.
SPITSBERGEN STR.
ASSENDELFTSTRAAT
POLANENSTRAAT
ZAANDIJK. STR.
ZAANSTRAAT
WESTZAANSTRAAT
WESTERPARK
NASSAU-PLEIN
HAARLEMMER-PLEIN
PLANCIUSSTRAAT
NWE TEERTUINEN
1e BREEUWERSSTRAAT
SLOTERDIJKSTRAAT
ZOUKEETSGRACHT
PRINSENEILAND
GALGENSTRAAT
GR BICKERSSTRAAT
BICKERSGRACHT
TOUWSLAGER-STRAAT
ZEILSMAKER-STRAAT
Westerdok
WESTERDOKSDIJK
WESTERDOKSKADE
HAARLEMMER HOUTTUINEN
HAARLEMMERDIJK
NIEUWE WAGENSTR.
VINKEN-STRAAT
BAANBRUG-STEEG
BINNEN DOMMERSTRAAT
BUITEN DOMMERSTRAAT
MOUTHAAN-STRAAT
BINNEN ORANJESTRAAT
BUITEN ORANJESTRAAT
HAARLEMMER STRAAT
KORTE PRINSENGRACHT
Brouwersgracht
BROUWERSGRACHT
DRIEHOEK STRAAT
PALMGRACHT
PALMSTRAAT
PALMDWARS. STRAAT
1e GOUDSBLDWARS. STRAAT
2e GOUDSBLDWAR. STRAAT
LINDENGRACHT
LINDENSTRAAT
NOORDERKERKSTR.
Boerenmarkt
Noorderkerk
WILLEMSSTRAAT
GOUDSBLOEMSTRAAT
1e LINDENDWARSSTR.
2e LINDENDWARSSTR.
KARTHUIZERSSTR.
KARTHUIZERS PLANTSOEN
BOOMSTRAAT
WESTERSTRAAT
TICHELSTRAAT
ANJELIERSSTRAAT
TUINSTRAAT
EGELANTIERSSTRAAT
1e TUINDWARS. STRAAT
THE JORDAAN
Egelantiersgracht
EGELANTIERSGRACHT
NIEUWE LELIESTRAAT
2e LELIEDWARS. STRAAT
Leliegracht
Anne Frankhuis
Westerkerk
PRINSENSTRAAT
Prinsengracht
PRINSENGRACHT
KEIZERSGRACHT
See p326
BLOEMGRACHT
Bloemgracht
1e BLOEMDWARS. STRAAT
2e BLOEMDWARS. STRAAT
BLOEMSTRAAT
LELIESTRAAT
ROZENGRACHT
ROZENSTRAAT
1e LAURIERDWARS. STRAAT
2e LAURIERDWARS. STRAAT
LAURIERSTRAAT
LIJNBAANSGRACHT
Lijnbaansgracht
MARNIXSTRAAT
MARNIXKADE
1e MARNIX-PLANTSOEN
Singelgracht
NASSAUKADE
DE WITTENKADE
DUIJNSTRAAT
1e NASSAUSTRAAT
2e NASSAUSTRAAT
KEMPERSTRAAT
VAN DER HOOP STRAAT
V HOGENDORP-STRAAT
STIRUMSTRAAT
BEUNINGEN-STRAAT
F SCHOLTENSTRAAT
VAN DE WITTENKADE
DE WITTENSTRAAT
JACOB CATSKADE
Kattensloot
Kostverlorenvaart
GROEN VAN PRINSTERERSTRAAT
V BOETZELAER STRAAT
VAN BEUNINGENSTRAAT
1e KEUCHENIUSSTR.
VAN HALLSTRAAT
FAGELSTRAAT
L TRIPSTRAAT
FH PLANTSOEN
GERARD SCHAEP-STRAAT
FREDERIK HENDRIK PLANTSOEN
AMALIA-STRAAT
1e KOSTVERLORENKADE
SCHAEPMANSTRAAT
DE KEMPENAERSTRAAT
VISSERINGSTRAAT
BUYSKADE
DONKER
Oostelijk Marktkanaal
VAN OLDEN-BARNEVELDT-PLEIN
ZAAGMOLENSTR.
FREDERIK HENDRIKSTRAAT
R HOGERBEETSSTRAAT
GV LEDENBERCHSTRAAT
VAN OLDENBARNEVELDT-STRAAT
1e HUGO DE GROOTSTRAAT
HUGO DE GROOTPLEIN
2e H DE GROOTSTR.
3e H DE GROOTSTRAAT
DE GROOTKADE
JAN VAN GALENSTRAAT
VAN JUT
See p329
0 300 m
0 300 yds
© Copyright Time Out Group 2007
38
58
50
48
46
47
52
53
44
54
45
48
45
40
57
59
41
55
56
179
92
52
283
188

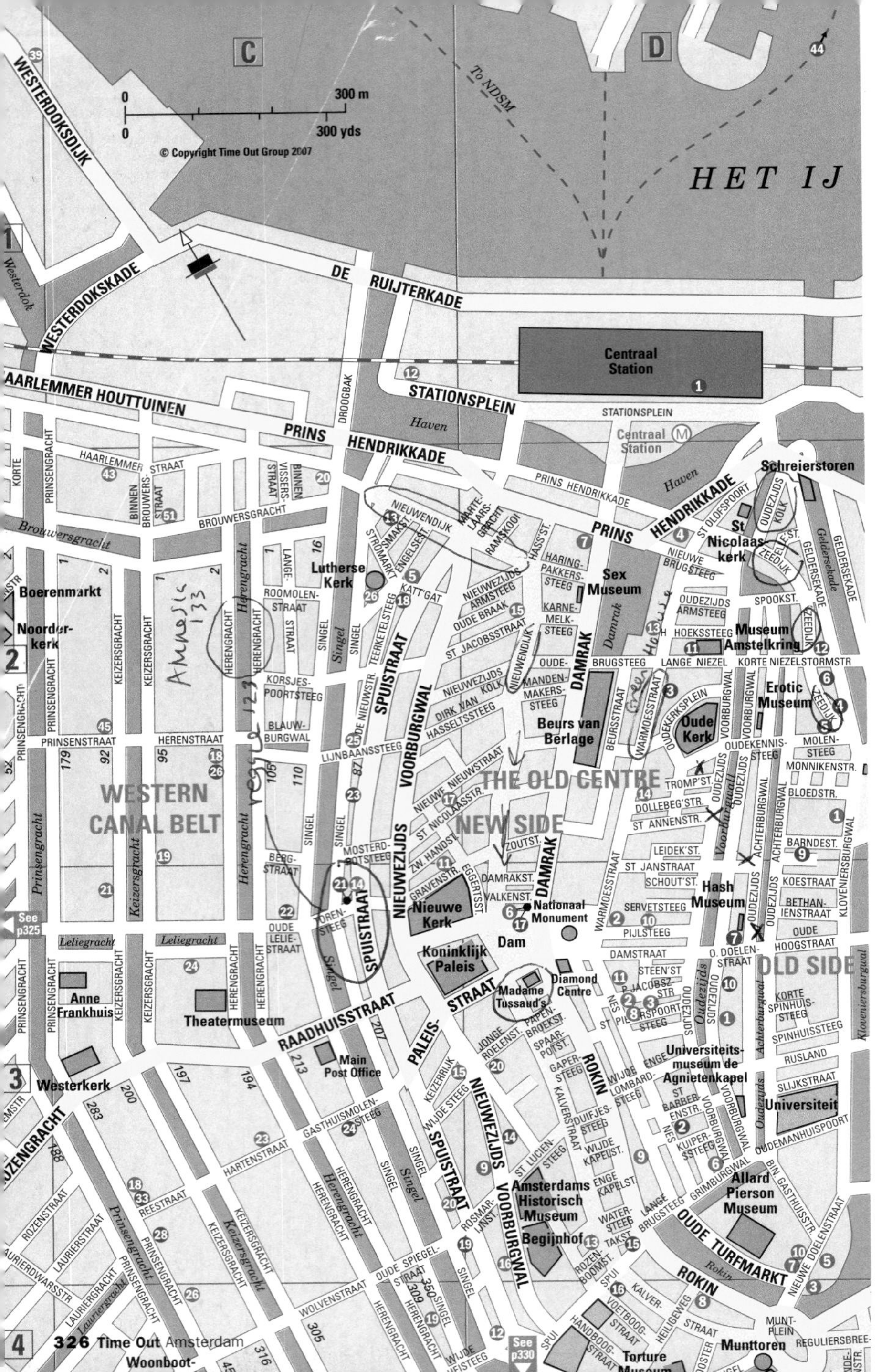
C
D
0
300 m
0
300 yds
© Copyright Time Out Group 2007
To NDSM
HET IJ
WESTERDOKSDIJK
Westerdok
WESTERDOKSKADE
DE RUIJTERKADE
Centraal Station
AARLEMMER HOUTTUINEN
STATIONSPLEIN
PRINS HENDRIKKADE
Haven
DROOGBAK
Centraal Station
HAARLEMMER STRAAT
BINNEN BROUWERS-STRAAT
VISSERS-STRAAT
BINNEN
BROUWERSGRACHT
Brouwersgracht
KORTE PRINSENGRACHT
Schreierstoren
PRINS HENDRIKKADE
St Nicolaas kerk
OUDEZIJDS KOLK
ZEEDIJK
GELDERSEKADE
Geldersekade
NIEUWENDIJK
SMAKST.
STROMARKT
ENGELSEST.
MARTELAARSGRACHT
RAMSKOOI
HASS'ST.
HARINGPAKKERSSTEEG
Lutherse Kerk
Sex Museum
Damrak
NIEUWE BRUGSTEEG
OUDEZIJDS ARMSTEEG
SPOOKST.
Boerenmarkt
Noorderkerk
LANGE-STRAAT
ROOMOLEN-STRAAT
KATT'GAT
NIEUWEZIJDS ARMSTEEG
OUDE BRAAK
KARNEMELKSTEEG
HOEKSSTEEG
Museum Amstelkring
Herengracht
HERENGRACHT
Singel
SINGEL
TEERKETELSTEEG
ST JACOBSSTRAAT
NIEUWENDIJK
OUDE-MANDENMAKERSSTEEG
DAMRAK
BRUGSTEEG
LANGE NIEZEL
KORTE NIEZEL
STORMSTR
KEIZERSGRACHT
PRINSENGRACHT
KORSJESPOORTSTEEG
BLAUWBURGWAL
DE NIEUWSTR.
SPUISTRAAT
NIEUWEZIJDS KOLK
DIRK VAN HASSELTSSTEEG
VOORBURGWAL
BEURSSTRAAT
WARMOESSTRAAT
OUDEKERKSPLEIN
Oude Kerk
Erotic Museum
Beurs van Berlage
PRINSENSTRAAT
HERENSTRAAT
LIJNBAANSSTEEG
OUDEKENNISSTEEG
MOLENSTEEG
MONNIKENSTR.
WESTERN CANAL BELT
THE OLD CENTRE
NEW SIDE
NIEUWE NIEUWSTRAAT
ST NICOLAASSTR.
TROMP'ST.
DOLLEBEG'STR.
ST ANNENSTR.
BLOEDSTR.
Voorburgwal
ACHTERBURGWAL
Prinsengracht
Keizersgracht
ZW. HANDST.
GRAVENSTR.
MOSTERDPOTSTEEG
BERGSTRAAT
ZOUTST.
LEIDEK'ST.
ST JANSTRAAT
BARNDEST.
KLOVENIERSBURGWAL
NIEUWEZIJDS
EGGERTSST.
DAMRAKST.
VALKENST.
SCHOUT'ST.
Hash Museum
KOESTRAAT
Nieuwe Kerk
National Monument
SERVETSTEEG
PIJLSTEEG
BETHANIENSTRAAT
TORENSTEEG
OUDE LELIESTRAAT
Dam
OUDE HOOGSTRAAT
Leliegracht
Koninklijk Paleis
DAMSTRAAT
O. DOELENSTRAAT
OLD SIDE
Anne Frankhuis
Theatermuseum
Madame Tussaud's
Diamond Centre
STEEN'ST
P.JACOBSZ. STR
NES
ST PIETERSPOORTSTEEG
Oudezijds
KORTE SPINHUISSTEEG
SPINHUISSTEEG
Kloveniersburgwal
RAADHUISSTRAAT
PALEISSTRAAT
JONGE ROELENST.
PAPENBROEKST.
SPAARPOTST.
Main Post Office
ROKIN
Universiteitsmuseum de Agnietenkapel
RUSLAND
Westerkerk
GAPERSTEEG
KALVERSTRAAT
LOMBARDSTEEG
WIJDE ENGE
SLIJKSTRAAT
ST BARBERENSTR.
Universiteit
KEIZERRIJK
WIJDE STEEG
GASTHUISMOLENSTEEG
HARTENSTRAAT
DUIFJESSTEEG
WIJDE KAPELST.
KUIPERSSTEEG
OUDEMANHUISPOORT
ZENGRACHT
ST LUCIENSTEEG
ENGE KAPELST.
GRIMBURGWAL
BIN. GASTHUISSTR.
Allard Pierson Museum
REESTRAAT
ROZENSTRAAT
LAURIERSTRAAT
LAURIERDWARSSTR
Lauriergracht
Amsterdams Historisch Museum
WATERSTEEG
LANGE BRUGSTEEG
OUDE TURFMARKT
Rokin
Begijnhof
ROSMARIJNST.
OUDE SPIEGELSTRAAT
TAKST.
ROZENBOOMST.
NIEUWE DOELENSTRAAT
WOLVENSTRAAT
SPUI
KALVERSTRAAT
HEILIGEWEG
VOETBOOGSTRAAT
HANDBOOGSTRAAT
MUNTPLEIN
REGULIERSBREE-
Munttoren
Torture Museum
Woonboot-
WIJDE HEISTEEG
See p325
See p330

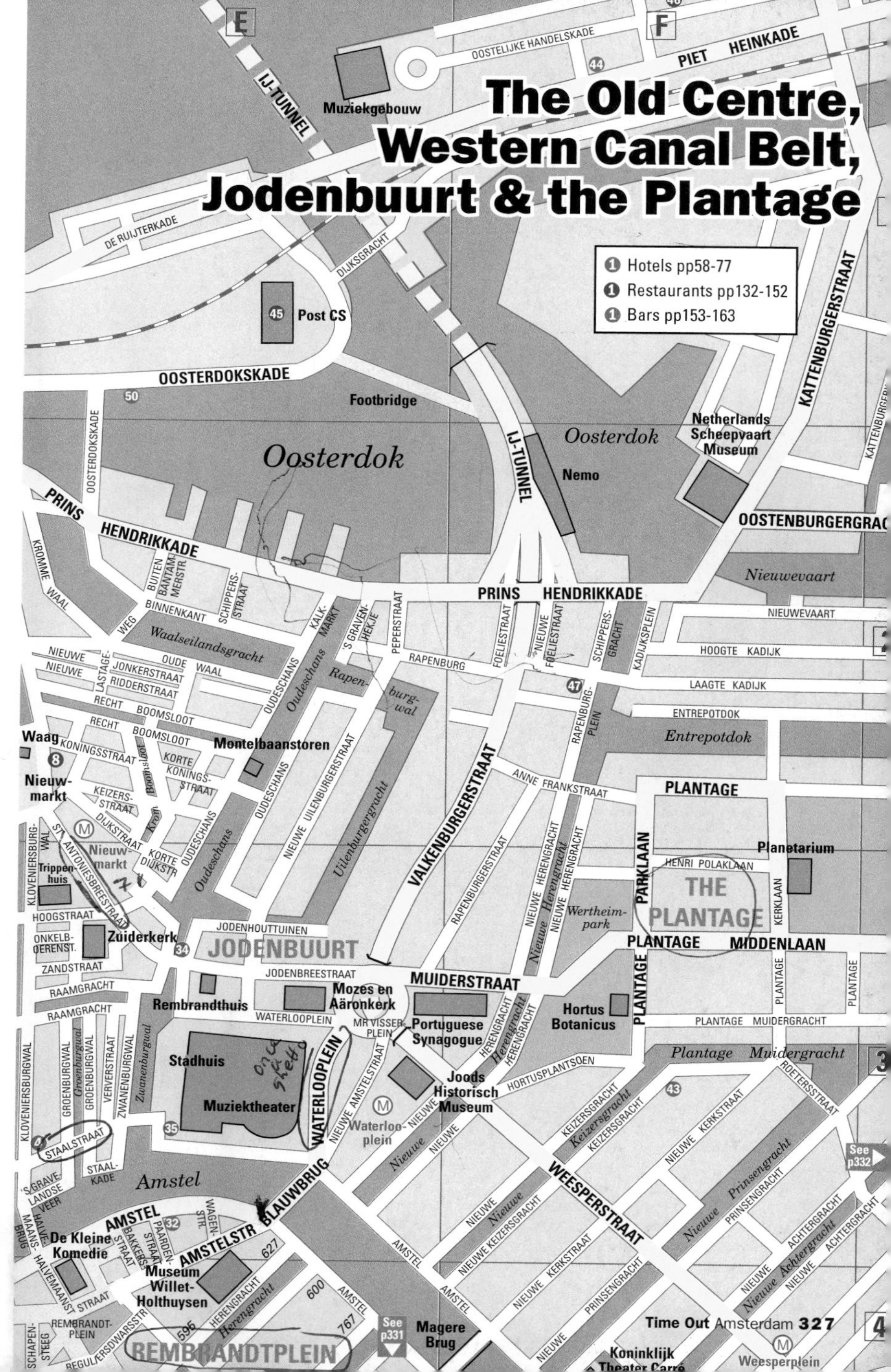
The Old Centre, Western Canal Belt, Jodenbuurt & the Plantage
Hotels pp58-77
Restaurants pp132-152
Bars pp153-163
Muziekgebouw
IJ-TUNNEL
PIET HEINKADE
OOSTELIJKE HANDELSKADE
DE RUIJTERKADE
DIJKSGRACHT
Post CS
OOSTERDOKSKADE
Footbridge
Oosterdok
Nemo
Netherlands Scheepvaart Museum
KATTENBURGERSTRAAT
OOSTENBURGERGRAC
Nieuwevaart
PRINS HENDRIKKADE
Waalseilandsgracht
Montelbaanstoren
Waag
Nieuwmarkt
Trippenhuis
Zuiderkerk
JODENBUURT
Rembrandthuis
Mozes en Aäronkerk
MUIDERSTRAAT
Portuguese Synagogue
Stadhuis
Muziektheater
WATERLOOPLEIN
Waterlooplein
Joods Historisch Museum
Hortus Botanicus
PLANTAGE
PARKLAAN
THE PLANTAGE
Wertheimpark
Planetarium
PLANTAGE MIDDENLAAN
VALKENBURGERSTRAAT
Entrepotdok
Plantage Muidergracht
WEESPERSTRAAT
BLAUWBRUG
Amstel
AMSTEL
AMSTELSTR
De Kleine Komedie
Museum Willet-Holthuysen
Magere Brug
REMBRANDTPLEIN
Koninklijk Theater Carré
Weesperplein
See p331
See p332

Oud West
Hotels pp58-77
Restaurants pp132-152
Bars pp153-163
A
B
C
4
5
6
See p325
See p330
JAN VAN GALENSTRAAT
HUGO DE GROOTPLEIN
2e H DE GROOTSTR.
3e H DE GROOTSTRAAT
V REIGERSBERGENSTRAAT
V HOUWENINGENSTRAAT
H DE GROOTKADE
FREDERIK HENDRIKSTRAAT
H de Grootgracht
BILDERDIJKPARK
DE CLERCQSTRAAT
ROZENGRACHT
Lijnbaansgracht
BLOEMSTRAAT
ROZENSTRAAT
LAURIERSTRAAT
LAURIERGRACHT
Lauriergracht
1e LAURIERDWARSSTRAAT
2e LAURIERDWARSSTRAAT
HAZENSTRAAT
ELANDSSTRAAT
3e LOOIERSDWARSSTRAAT
LIJNBAANSGRACHT
MARNIXSTRAAT
NASSAUKADE
Singelgracht
Politie
KINKERSTRAAT
DA COSTASTRAAT
DA COSTAKADE
Da Costagracht
POTGIETERSTRAAT
BILDERDIJKSTRAAT
BILDERDIJKKADE
Bilderdijkgracht
KWAKERSSTR.
BELLAMYPLEIN
BELLAMYSTRAAT
E WOLFFSTRAAT
A DEKENSTRAAT
TOLBURGSTRAAT
SCHIMMELSTRAAT
J HANZENSTRAAT
WENSLAUERSTRAAT
HASEBROEKSTRAAT
N BEETSSTRAAT
SCHOOLMEESTERSTR.
JACOB VAN LENNEPKADE
Jacob van Lennepkanaal
ARIE BIEMONDSTRAAT
JACOB VAN LENNEPSTRAAT
BORGERSTRAAT
JAN PIETER HEIJESTRAAT
LOOTSSTRAAT
KANAALSTRAAT
WILHELMINASTRAAT
WILHELMINA STR.
BREDERODESTRAAT
1e HELMERSSTRAAT
2e HELMERSSTRAAT
3e HELMERSSTRAAT
Polikliniek
2e C HUYGENSTRAAT
W GASTHUISPLEIN
WG PLEIN
A SPRENGLESTRAAT
OVERTOOM
BOSBOOM TOUSSAINTSTRAAT
VONDELSTRAAT
ANNA VAN DEN VONDELSTR.
G BRANDTSTR.
Vondelpark
0
300 m
300 yds
KOP VAN JUT
Westelijk Marktkanaal
Kostverlorenvaart
2e KOSTVERLORENKADE
GEUZENKADE
GEUZENSTRAAT
AV BERGENSTRAAT
DE ZWIJGERLAAN
WILLEM
ADMIRAAL
DE RUIJTERWEG
SLATUINENWEG
BAARSJESWEG
CHASSESTRAAT
V KINSBERGENSTR.
V SPEIJKSTRAAT
WITTE DE WITHSTRAAT
ADMIRALENGRACHT
STUYVESANTSTRAAT
POSTJESKADE

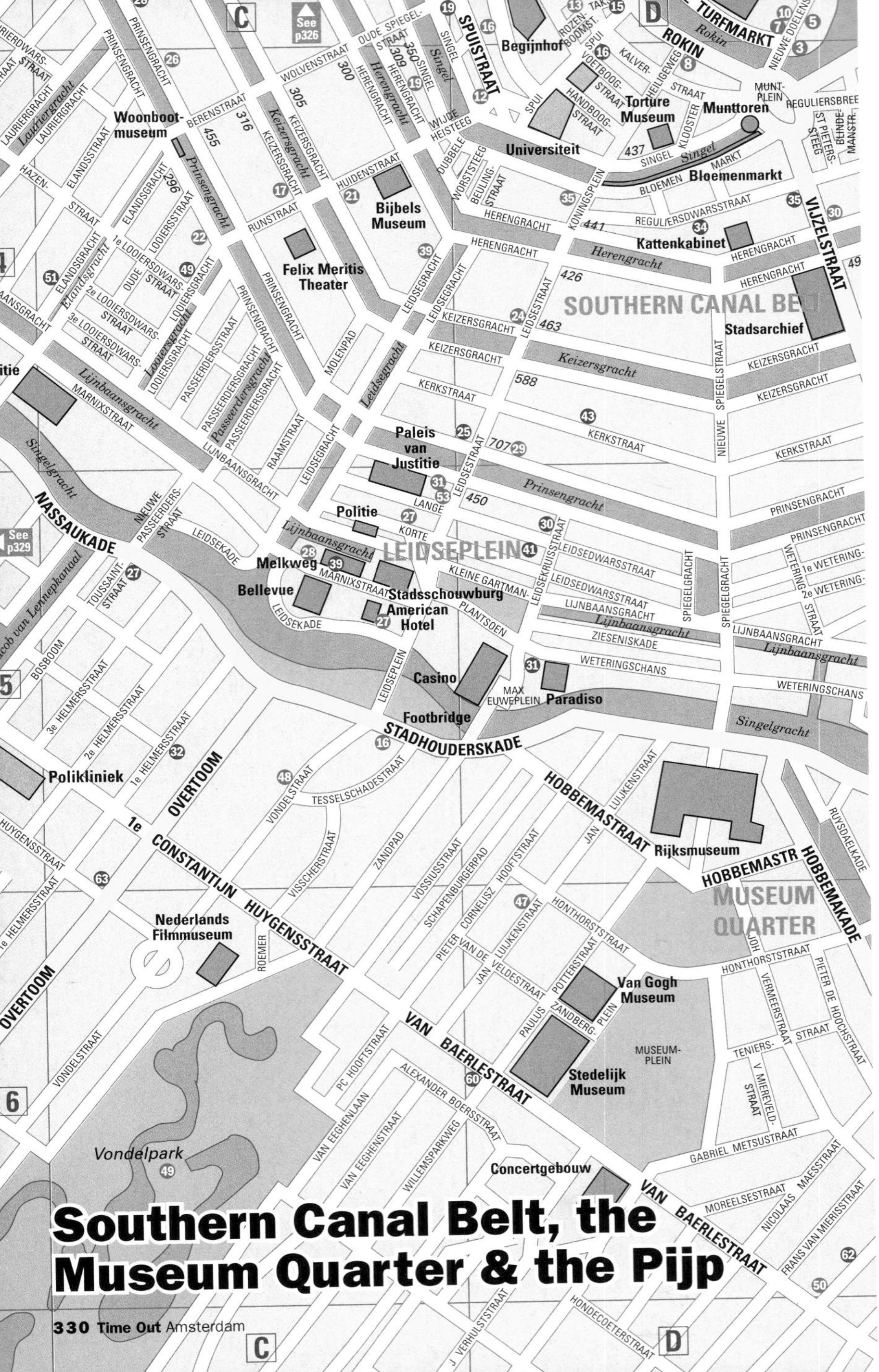
Southern Canal Belt, the Museum Quarter & the Pijp
SOUTHERN CANAL BELT
MUSEUM QUARTER
LEIDSEPLEIN
Begijnhof
Torture Museum
Munttoren
Universiteit
Bloemenmarkt
Woonboot-museum
Bijbels Museum
Felix Meritis Theater
Kattenkabinet
Stadsarchief
Paleis van Justitie
Politie
Melkweg
Bellevue
Stadsschouwburg
American Hotel
Casino
Footbridge
Paradiso
Polikliniek
Rijksmuseum
Nederlands Filmmuseum
Van Gogh Museum
Stedelijk Museum
Concertgebouw
Vondelpark
See p326
See p329
SPUISTRAAT
ROKIN
TURFMARKT
VIJZELSTRAAT
NASSAUKADE
STADHOUDERSKADE
HOBBEMASTRAAT
HOBBEMAKADE
OVERTOOM
1e CONSTANTIJN HUYGENSSTRAAT
VAN BAERLESTRAAT
Herengracht
Keizersgracht
Prinsengracht
Singel
Singelgracht
Lijnbaansgracht
Leidsegracht
Rokin